Paul and the Resurrection of Israel

The gospel promoted by Paul has for many generations stirred passionate debate. That gospel proclaimed equal salvific access to Jews and gentiles alike. But on what basis? In making sense of such a remarkable step forward in religious history, Jason Staples reexamines texts that have proven thoroughly resistant to easy comprehension. He traces Paul's inclusive theology to a hidden strand of thinking in the earlier story of Israel. Postexilic southern Judah, he argues, did not simply appropriate the identity of the fallen northern kingdom of Israel. Instead, Judah maintained a notion of 'Israel' as referring both to the north *and* the ongoing reality of a broad, pan-Israelite sensibility to which the descendants of both ancient kingdoms belonged. Paul's concomitant belief was that northern Israel's exile meant assimilation among the nations – effectively a people's death – and that its restoration paradoxically required gentile inclusion to resurrect a greater 'Israel' from the dead.

Jason A. Staples is an assistant teaching professor in the Department of Philosophy and Religious Studies at North Carolina State University. He is the author of *The Idea of Israel in Second Temple Judaism* (Cambridge University Press, 2021) and of numerous articles on the themes of ancient Judaism and early Christianity.

Paul and the Resurrection of Israel

Jews, Former Gentiles, Israelites

JASON A. STAPLES
North Carolina State University

Shaftesbury Road, Cambridge CB2 8EA, United Kingdom

One Liberty Plaza, 20th Floor, New York, NY 10006, USA

477 Williamstown Road, Port Melbourne, VIC 3207, Australia

314–321, 3rd Floor, Plot 3, Splendor Forum, Jasola District Centre,
New Delhi – 110025, India

103 Penang Road, #05–06/07, Visioncrest Commercial, Singapore 238467

Cambridge University Press is part of Cambridge University Press & Assessment,
a department of the University of Cambridge.

We share the University's mission to contribute to society through the pursuit of
education, learning and research at the highest international levels of excellence.

www.cambridge.org
Information on this title: www.cambridge.org/9781009376761

DOI: 10.1017/9781009376785

© Jason A. Staples 2024

This publication is in copyright. Subject to statutory exception and to the provisions
of relevant collective licensing agreements, no reproduction of any part may take
place without the written permission of Cambridge University Press & Assessment.

First published 2024

A catalogue record for this publication is available from the British Library.

A Cataloging-in-Publication data record for this book is available from the Library of Congress

ISBN 978-1-009-37676-1 Hardback

Cambridge University Press & Assessment has no responsibility for the persistence
or accuracy of URLs for external or third-party internet websites referred to in this
publication and does not guarantee that any content on such websites is, or will remain,
accurate or appropriate.

To my wife, Kari
And my mother, Brenda
תמכו בידיו מזה
אחד ומזה אחד
ויהי ידיו אמונה
They supported his hands
One on one side, one on the other
So his hands were faithful.
Exodus 17:12

Contents

List of Figures	page x
List of Tables	xi
Preface	xiii
Acknowledgments	xvii
Introduction: Jews, Former Gentiles, Israelites	1
Who Are Paul's (Former) Gentiles?	8
"All Israel Will Be Saved"	12
Empirical Ethnicity?	15
The Agenda of This Work	19
Excursus: The Audience of Paul's Letters	20
Excursus: Translating Key Terminology	28
Jews or Judaeans?	34
1 The God of Jews Only?	37
An Experiment in Criticism: Beyond the Insider/Outsider Paradigm	39
Two Nations under God: The Other Israelites	41
The Great Divorce: Israel and Judah	43
Great Expectations: The Restoration of Israel and Judah	45
Will the Real Israelites Please Come Back?	48
Revival in the Land and Israel's Ongoing Exile	52
There and Back Again: Israel and Restoration Eschatology	58
Return of the King: Jesus and the Gospel	63
2 Paul and the Israel Problem	68
Minister of a New Covenant	72
The New Covenant and Israel's Justification	75

The Spirit and the New Covenant	78
Spirits in Bondage: The Curse of the Torah and Israel's Infidelity	85
Smoke on the Mountain: The Letter and the Veil	91
The Curse of the Torah: Death (By Exile)	97
Deliverance from the Age of Wrath	101

3 The Israel Problem and the Gentiles — 107
- The Stumbling Block of Romans 1–2 — 112
- Paradise Lost: Judgment against Impiety and Immorality — 114
- The Discarded Image: Idolatry, Immorality, and the Knowledge of God — 117
- Pride and Prejudice: Israel and the Nations under Sin — 129
- The Abolition of Man: God's Impartial Justice — 132
- Justice and Mercy Have Kissed — 136
- Crime and Punishment: Impartial Judgment for Jews and Greeks Alike — 139

4 Salvation through Justification: Jews and Gentiles Alike — 145
- Jewish Identity and God's Impartiality — 150
- That Hideous Strength: The Three Traps of Belial — 154
- The Value of Circumcision — 162
- The Hidden Jew Belongs to God — 169
- Circumcised Jews, Uncircumcised Israelites — 172
- Doing Torah by the Spirit: Grace and Works — 174
- Restoration via the Spirit in Romans — 179

5 "Not My People": Israel's Infidelity and God's Fidelity — 182
- "Not All from Israel Are Israel" — 187
- God in the Dock: Potter, Clay, and Divine Pathos — 191
- God's Patience and Divine Pathos — 197
- Vessels of Wrath — 200
- "Not My People," Ethnic Mixture, and Vessels among the Nations — 201
- Notes from the Underground: Dishonored Vessels Redeemed — 209
- Have Gentiles Attained Righteousness? — 212
- The Business of Heaven: Redemptive Reversal — 219

6 God's Justice and the End of the Torah — 221
- Bringing the Messiah: Righteousness and Redemption — 225
- Righteousness and Restoration in the Torah and Prophets — 227

	The Yaḥad as Righteous Vanguard of Israel	230
	The Contingency of Israel's Restoration	233
	Repentance and Restoration in Rabbinic Traditions	234
	The Grand Miracle: Divinely Initiated Justness	236
	The One Who Lives: Messiah and the Justness of God	243
	Divine Deadlifting: The Resurrection of the Just One	247
	The Just One and Redemption from the Curse of the Torah	252
	The Logic of Galatians 3	255
	Reconsidering a So-called Antithesis	258
	He's the Messiah! Pledging Fealty to the Living Lord	265
7	**The Mystery of Israel's Salvation**	271
	Disobedience, Mercy, and Jealousy	274
	Jealous God, Jealous People	278
	Impartial Justice, Mercy to All	281
	Jealousy, Not-My-People, and a Non-Nation	285
	Consecrated by Incorporation	287
	The Olive Tree	289
	Broken Off and Grafted In	291
	Judgment and the Remnant	299
	Paul's Mystery Revealed	301
	A Mysterious Sequence?	303
	Paul's Mystery: The Fullness of the Nations	307
	"All Israel": Israel and Judah	312
	Surprised by Joy: Mercy to Israel, Mercy to All	317
8	**The End of the Matter**	323
	The Last Battle: Death, Resurrection, and the Vindication of YHWH	326
	Paul's Coherent Core: Israel's Resurrection	331
	Incorporation, Not Supersession	333
	Why Not Circumcision?	337
	Strengths of This Reading	341
	The Payoff: The Task Discharged	344

Bibliography 348
Primary Sources Index 403
Author Index 422
Subject Index 428

Figures

1.1 Jews as part of Israel *page* 52
1.2 Prophetic/sectarian view of Jews and Israel 62

Tables

1.1	Jews and Israelites in Josephus	*page* 50
5.1	Vessels of wrath in LXX Jeremiah 27:25 and Romans 9:22	195
6.1	Leviticus 18:5b and Paul's citations	245
6.2	God's justness, the Messiah, and fidelity	247
6.3	Parallelism in Galatians 3:11–12	259
7.1	Ephraim's seed: The fullness of the nations	308

Preface

I often imagine Pauline interpretation as akin to putting together a jigsaw puzzle to best represent the image sketched out by Paul's letters. As I see it, the dominant paradigms for Pauline interpretation have tended to start by putting the "easy" pieces (e.g., "justification by faith") together only to discover that several seemingly extraneous pieces don't seem to fit the reconstructed image at the end. Romans 2 and 9–11 have proven especially difficult to fit into common paradigms of Paul's theology, with some going so far as to suggest that these sections do not in fact represent the apostle's thought or that Paul was simply self-contradictory. But in my experience, when a few pieces remain on the table at the end, it usually means some part of the puzzle has been wrongly put together. I would be hesitant to board an airplane after learning that several pieces from the inside of the engine were still laying on the ground, regardless of reassurances from the airport's mechanic that they simply didn't fit when he was rebuilding the engine.[1] Instead, after discovering the pieces left out by the reconstruction, the only solution is to pull the whole thing apart and start anew beginning by figuring out where the problematic pieces fit and then building around them.

This book represents my attempt to do exactly that. Rather than beginning from consensus paradigms built on the seemingly easier passages and then trying to account for why certain passages fit so poorly, I have started from what are widely regarded as the most difficult and

---

[1] Will Timmins similarly compares the process to solving a Rubik's cube: "even a single piece which remains out of place betrays the need for a new solution" (*Romans 7 and Christian Identity* [2017], 9).

anomalous sections of the Pauline corpus. The idea is that by establishing the proper places for the most difficult pieces, the rest can more easily snap into place around them. Ultimately, if my argument here is correct, the reason these difficult chapters have fit so poorly with modern reconstructions of Paul's theology is that those modern reconstructions have built on faulty foundational assumptions, resulting in numerous loose ends. In other words, the primary problem in Pauline interpretation has not been what we don't know – it's that much of what we've thought we know isn't so.

If this is indeed the case, once those difficult pieces are properly placed, many other passages will need to be reexamined in light of what Paul is doing in the chapters addressed here. Thus, although this book focuses specifically on Paul's arguments about Israel, Torah, and the gospel in a series of specific passages, it represents an attempt to lay a foundation for a new and more robust paradigm for understanding Paul's letters and gospel proclamation in general. (Although my analysis is limited to the seven undisputed letters, in my judgment the framework proposed in this study applies equally well to the rest of the Pauline corpus.) By the end of the process, my hope is that by establishing a better foundation, a variety of specific insights from previous interpreters may be seen from a different and wider angle revealing more pieces at once, allowing the whole elephant to finally come into view.

Seeing from a wider angle also requires stepping outside the narrow world of Pauline studies, which too often treats the apostle in near isolation or only engages with outside sources as foils against which Paul, the unique and original thinker, is understood. But the Pauline letters involve highly compressed and allusive arguments that assume the readers share a great deal of foundational common knowledge – knowledge modern readers do not tend to share. Arriving late to a conversation makes it easy to misunderstand what is being said until others explain what was said earlier in the discussion, and when reading Paul's letters, we are hearing only one side of a conversation that builds on earlier discussions to which we have no access. Reading the Pauline corpus is therefore akin to trying to understand a meme-heavy exchange on the Internet, potentially inscrutable without shared knowledge of the movies, television, or other popular media reshaped and reapplied in new contexts. I am therefore persuaded that to understand Paul, one must first endeavor to reconstruct that common foundation as much as possible by immersing in the Hebrew Bible/LXX and other source materials from the Second Temple period, preparing to recognize the subtle, complex nuances embedded in seemingly straightforward statements, the simplicity in what may initially seem hopelessly complex or contradictory.

I endeavored to reconstruct some of that core foundation in *The Idea of Israel in Second Temple Judaism* (2021), of which this book serves as a sequel volume. As such, I am approaching Paul not as though he were a wholly original and unique individual disconnected from his temporal and cultural foundation but rather as a distinct representative of early Judaism – itself an exceedingly diverse phenomenon – in the context of the earliest Jesus movement. This book therefore aims to put Paul in conversation with other source material from the Second Temple period while simultaneously using that information to delve deeply into the exegesis of specific Pauline passages.

The result of this approach is that each individual chapter is both a specific, self-contained argument and an important foundation stone for the larger argument of the book. Nevertheless, no single chapter or specific argument is determinative for the larger argument as a whole – one might, for instance, disagree with much of my analysis of Rom 1 or 2 Cor 3 while still agreeing with the larger paradigm as a whole or vice-versa. Consequently, the reader most interested in the larger thesis will have to work through numerous detailed discussions of specific cases, since the larger paradigm I am proposing depends on a cumulative case about how the various pieces of the puzzle fit together. On the other hand, those more interested in my reading of a specific chapter or passage will need to consider the relationship of those specific parts to the comprehensive argument of the book (and in some cases foundational details found in the preceding volume), as the cumulative weight of other passages contributes to the plausibility of such specifics.[2]

In the interest of readability, I have not attempted to represent the full range of scholarship on the passages and subject matter covered in this volume, let alone Pauline studies as a whole, and have instead limited my engagement with previous scholarship to what seemed necessary to the discussion. At an editorial level, I have translated all substantive foreign-language quotes into English, providing the original quotations in corresponding footnotes when that seemed warranted. All translations of ancient materials are my own except where noted. I have also transliterated a few key terms frequently used in the body text (e.g., *Ioudaios*, *ekklēsia*) to make the book more accessible but have otherwise retained

---

[2] Cf. the similar caveats in Jason A. Staples, *The Idea of Israel in Second Temple Judaism* (2021), xiii; and E. P. Sanders, *Paul and Palestinian Judaism* (1977), xii.

Greek or Hebrew characters in parenthetical references or footnotes. All citations and abbreviations follow *The SBL Handbook of Style*, 2nd ed., though for economy I have eschewed the long first citation with full publication data in favor of abbreviated title and date, leaving other information to the bibliography, with a few exceptions where more information in context was deemed preferable. Abbreviations not included in the *SBLHS* follow the conventions of their respective fields. All references to the Hebrew Bible/Old Testament use the Hebrew versification ("ET" = English translation). Chapter 1, which summarizes the thesis of *The Idea of Israel in Second Temple Judaism*, borrows heavily from that book. Parts of Chapters 5 and 7 include material that has previously appeared in the *Journal of Biblical Literature* ("What Do the Gentiles Have to Do with 'All Israel'? A Fresh Look at Romans 11:25–27" [2011]) and *Harvard Theological Review* ("Vessels of Wrath and God's Pathos: Potter/Clay Imagery in Rom 9:20–23" [2022]).

Acknowledgments

This book began with ideas first formed and put forward in William L. Lyons' 2003 Hebrew Bible Prophets class, and I am profoundly thankful to Bill for all his encouragement and helpful feedback over the past two decades. I am also deeply indebted to my *Doktorvater*, Bart Ehrman, whose support, counsel, and generosity have been invaluable over the past fifteen years. I am also grateful to David Levenson for his training and mentorship when I was at Florida State – it turns out there was indeed work left to do on Paul after all! This book also may never have come to fruition without the early enthusiasm of the late Robert Jewett, who strongly advocated for the project from which this book grew. Bob went out of his way to vouch for the initial insights of a nascent project that departed so significantly from prior paradigms, volunteered to be an outside reader of my dissertation, and carved out time to discuss core concepts in the early stages of my research. He exemplified kindness, gentleness, generosity, and breadth of mind, and he demonstrated how to use senior status and influence to benefit those with less. May his memory be for a blessing.

I am deeply indebted to the generosity of those who read and provided valuable critiques and feedback of various parts of this book at different stages, especially Stephen Carlson, Paul Sloan, Sonya Cronin, David Schroder, Benjamin L. White, Logan Williams, and Isaac Soon. Paula Fredriksen's generous feedback and encouragement over the past decade – even when we have disagreed – have meant a great deal. I also owe gratitude to Eibert Tigchelaar, Joel Marcus, Jodi Magness, Douglas Campbell, Anathea Portier-Young, David Lambert, Zlatko Pleše, Jonathan Boyarin, and Ross Wagner for their critiques and support through early stages of this project. Richard Hays, James Crenshaw, and Fr. Ron Olszewski were generous teachers who also influenced this project in one way or another. I am deeply indebted to Svetla Slaveva-Griffin, Kathryn Stoddard, John Marincola, and Francis Cairns, who taught me to read Greek texts and do my own careful lexical work rather than merely trusting a lexicon and regurgitating glosses. In particular, Cairns' offhand comment in a 2005 Aeschylus seminar about the reciprocity inherent to the word χάρις – a small moment I will never forget – significantly impacted my understanding of Paul's gospel. Other long-suffering souls who have tolerated my obsession with this subject and proved especially valuable conversation partners during what must have seemed like an unending project include Jason Combs, T. J. Lang, Nathan Eubank, Isaac Oliver, Michael Barber, James Tabor, Mark Nanos, Scott Hahn, John Kincaid, Mark Goodacre, David Burnett, Matthew Grey, Jim Hayes, Fr. Gregory (Joshua) Edwards, and Tim Cupery.

This book grew out of my PhD dissertation at the University of North Carolina at Chapel Hill, where I was supported by a Jacob K. Javits Fellowship and a Thomas S. and Helen Borda Royster Dissertation Fellowship. Most of the book was written while in visiting faculty positions at Wake Forest, Duke, and NC State, and I am grateful to colleagues in those departments (Michael Pendlebury and William Adler in particular) and for the beneficence of the library staff at each institution. I am also grateful to my colleagues from Inside Carolina, especially Buck Sanders and Ben Sherman, who understood that this project was a priority and were patient when my output diminished at times in the offseason. Thanks also to the many who helped my wife and I stay afloat after our house fire in 2013 and to Michael G. Scott for help with the management of such a large project. Luis and Liz Marquez also supported this project in more ways than one, and for that I will always be grateful. Thanks also to the full Cambridge University Press team, especially for the patience and encouragement of Beatrice Rehl, whose vision of a two-volume project made this book possible. Two anonymous readers also provided helpful critiques that improved the final product. The deficiencies that remain in this work are of course my own responsibility.

This book is the product of many years of commitment, support, and sacrifice from family. In addition to producing music that helped fuel long hours of writing, my sister Stephanie and brother-in-law Erik have been supportive in a variety of ways. My father, Mark, laid the foundation of how I understand Paul's gospel and remains one of the finest teachers and brightest minds I have ever encountered. He planted and cultivated the seeds that have grown into this book, training me from the beginning to reexamine every tradition and question every interpretation, no matter how firmly established or widely believed, in the quest for truth. His readiness to recognize and admit his own errors and limitations also set a wonderful example of humility. His support has been unwavering over the years, and this book represents his toil as much as mine – it was possible only because I am standing on his shoulders.

Finally, this book is dedicated to the two women whose prodigious efforts and sacrifices made it possible. My mother, Brenda, has sacrificed more to ensure this book would come to fruition than I ever imagined possible. She has given beyond measure, and whatever good comes from this book should be credited to her account. Thank you, mom. My wife, Kari, has truly been my γνήσιος σύζυγος and has shared in the toil throughout the process; her support never wavered even when she knew following this path meant sacrificing luxuries like a consistent paycheck and retirement savings. The making of many books is endless and excessive study is exhausting, but she is more precious than life and her love is stronger than death. I hope one day to be worthy of it. May this book prove a lasting and valuable commemoration of that love.

Introduction

Jews, Former Gentiles, Israelites

There is neither Jew nor Greek, there is neither slave nor free, there is not male and female, for you are all one in Messiah Jesus.

Galatians 3:28

And thus all Israel will be saved.

Romans 11:26

Paul's thought contains one overarching difficulty, and he himself was aware of it: how does God's recent revelation in Christ relate to his former revelations to Israel?

E. P. Sanders[1]

A little over a century ago, Albert Schweitzer suggested that providing an explanation for how a small Jewish sect proclaiming a rabbi from the backwater town of Nazareth to be the messiah of Israel so quickly transitioned to a movement primarily involving non-Jews was "the great and still undischarged task which confronts those engaged in the historical study of primitive Christianity."[2] "The primary task," Schweitzer says, "is to define the position of Paul,"[3] the Jewish teacher who declared himself "apostle of nations/gentiles"[4] and insisted on the inclusion of

---

[1] E. P. Sanders, *Paul: A Very Short Introduction* (2001), 52.
[2] Albert Schweitzer, *Paul and His Interpreters* (1912), v. Further: "The system of the Apostle to the Gentiles stands over against the teaching of Jesus as something of an entirely different character, and does not create the impression of having arisen out of it. But how is such a new creation of Christian ideas – and that within a bare two or three decades after the death of Jesus – at all conceivable? ... This want of connection must have some explanation" (vii).
[3] Schweitzer, *Paul and His Interpreters*, x.
[4] Rom 11:13; cf. Gal 2:8–9; Rom 15:16, 18. See E. P. Sanders, "Patterns of Religion in Paul and Rabbinic Judaism" (1973).

non-Jews as equal members in the communities of Jesus-followers. Despite significant advances over the past century, the position of Paul has remained difficult to define and has been the subject of significant scholarly reappraisal in recent decades. Paul's distinctive insistence on the inclusion of uncircumcised "gentiles" (that is, non-Jews) as full members of communities devoted to following Jesus as the messiah of Israel served as a key pivot point in the transition from a small Jewish sect to the primarily gentile movement a generation later.[5] But the rationale for that inclusion – and how it fits with God's plan for Israel as Paul understands it – has continued to engender considerable inquiry and debate.[6]

That is not to say that no progress has been made, as much that could be taken for granted in Schweitzer's day has been weighed and found wanting. For example, even a generation ago, most scholarly work could presume a traditional (mostly Protestant) view in which Paul understood Jesus to have abolished the Torah, resulting in the universal "law-free" message of "justification by faith" as opposed to Jewish "legalism" or "works-righteousness" – that is, the idea that one must observe the Torah to achieve God's favor through one's righteous works, a task Paul allegedly found onerous and impossible before his "conversion" to "Christianity." In this model, the inclusion of gentiles in the new Christian community is therefore a natural outgrowth of Paul's realization that salvation could not be achieved through obedience to the Torah – which Christ abolished – but is instead freely available to anyone who believes in Christ without regard for works. Consequently, non-Jews now have the same access to salvation as Jews, whose "legalism" or "works-righteousness" provides the foil for Paul's universal message. In this model, Paul's new "Christian religion" has superseded "Judaism,"[7]

---

[5] See the excursus at the end of this chapter for discussion of the difficulties involved in the translation of the terms "Jews" and "gentiles."

[6] For summaries and assessments of some of the recent trends in this area, see Matthew Novenson, "Whither the Paul within Judaism *Schule?*" (2018); Magnus Zetterholm, "Paul within Judaism" (2015); N. T. Wright, *Paul and His Recent Interpreters* (2015); Wright, "Paul in Current Anglophone Scholarship" (2012); John M. G. Barclay, "Paul, Judaism, and the Jewish People" (2011); Christopher Zoccali, *Whom God Has Called* (2010); Christine Gerber, "Blicke auf Paulus" (2010); Gunther Wenz, "Old Perspectives on Paul" (2010); Magnus Zetterholm, *Approaches to Paul* (2009); Michael F. Bird and Preston M. Sprinkle, "Jewish Interpretation of Paul in the Last Thirty Years" (2008). For an older but still relevant summary of these issues, see Terence L. Donaldson, *Paul and the Gentiles* (1997), esp. 3–27.

[7] "Judaism" is another problematic term, in part because of centuries of baggage in which it has served to describe the (alleged) religious or cultural characteristics of Jews over and against Christianity. But the term is also difficult because it is an abstract category

and the church has become the "true Israel,"[8] effectively replacing the disobedient Jews who have refused the gospel.

Though this reading has by no means disappeared, it can no longer be taken for granted because of many faults found in its foundation – most notably in the alleged opposition between "Jewish legalism" and Paul's message of "grace" and "justification by faith." First, as Krister Stendahl famously pointed out in "Paul and the Introspective Conscience of the West," the apostle gives no indication of having had a guilty conscience or of having had any difficulty keeping the Torah – a view Stendahl identifies as having derived from Augustine rather than Paul. Instead, Paul had a "rather 'robust' conscience,"[9] declaring that he had been "blameless with respect to righteousness which is in the Torah" (Phil 3:6) and continuing to emphasize the importance of obedience throughout his letters, warning his hearers that all will reap what they have sown (Gal 6:7–8) and will be judged based on works (2:6–11). It is therefore unlikely that Paul arrived at the doctrine of justification by faith in opposition to obedience to Torah and then concluded that gentiles could be included on that basis.

Then, even more significantly, E. P. Sanders' landmark *Paul and Palestinian Judaism* (1977) demonstrated that Jewish belief and practice in Paul's day did not resemble the traditional legalistic image presumed by Pauline interpreters, making "works-righteousness" an implausible foil for Paul's gospel.[10] This more robust understanding of the Judaism of

---

describing the customs, culture, and boundaries of a particular social group (or set of groups) and because the characteristics of "Judaism" are variegated and encompass both what would typically be called "ethnic" and "religious" categories today. Where that term appears in this study, it refers to customs, practices, and theological perspectives common among those identified as *Ioudaioi* in the Second Temple period. On the difficulties inherent in the term "Judaism," see Michael L. Satlow, "Defining Judaism" (2006); Satlow, "A History of the Jews or Judaism?" (2005); Seth Schwartz, "How Many Judaisms Were There?" (2011); and the discussion in the excursus at the end of this chapter.

[8] See Marcel Simon, *Verus Israel* (1986), 65–97; Denise Kimber Buell, *Why This New Race?* (2005), 94–115.

[9] Krister Stendahl, "The Apostle Paul and the Introspective Conscience of the West" (1963), 200; a revised English version of Stendahl, "Paulus och Samvetet" (1960).

[10] Sanders was not the first to challenge the image of Judaism as a legalistic theology of merit but rather built on the work of earlier scholars such as C. G. Montefiore, *Judaism and St. Paul* (1914); George Foot Moore, "Christian Writers on Judaism" (1921); W. D. Davies, *Paul and Rabbinic Judaism* (1955); Solomon Schechter, *Aspects of Rabbinic Theology* (1961); and others. Markus Barth, *Ephesians* (1974), 244–48, also anticipates Sanders' more extended treatment in many respects. But whereas their protests had gone largely unheeded, Sanders synthesized a tour de force that could no longer be ignored, resulting

Paul's day led to a "New Perspective" on Paul's gospel.[11] Nevertheless, most proponents of the New Perspective have still operated from the assumption that Paul must have found *something* wrong with Judaism, following Sanders in understanding Paul and Judaism as representing two distinct "patterns of religion."[12] With "Jewish legalism" no longer an obvious foil, many have since relocated Paul's objection to Judaism from the supposed *rationale* for the inclusion of gentiles to the *fact* of the inclusion of gentiles itself. That is, Paul rejected Jewish insistence on ethnic identity as a necessary component of membership among God's people in favor of a racially inclusive Christianity exemplified in his declaration that "in Christ, there is neither Jew nor Greek" (Gal 3:28).[13] Essentially, rather than rejecting legalism, Paul's gospel is based on a rejection of racism, and the core of his gospel was, in N. T. Wright's words, "grace, not race."[14] James D. G. Dunn explains:

For the Judaism which focused its identity most fully in the Torah, and which found itself unable to separate ethnic identity from religious identity, Paul and the Gentile mission involved an irreparable breach.[15]

At its historic heart Christianity is a protest ... against any and every attempt to mark off some of God's people as more holy than others, as exclusive channels of divine grace.[16]

This model does have the advantage of not setting Paul against the imaginary and anachronistic bogeyman of legalism, but it lacks one strength of the traditional reading: a plausible explanation for Paul's objection to ethnocentrism. Instead, this approach simply presumes that

---

in a paradigm shift. See also Daniel R. Langton, "The Myth of the 'Traditional View of Paul'" (2005).

[11] James D. G. Dunn is usually credited with popularizing the term "New Perspective on Paul" in his 1982 Manson Memorial Lecture, published as "The New Perspective on Paul" (1983), though it would be more accurate to call it a new perspective on Judaism for Pauline studies. See the summary in Mark D. Nanos and Magnus Zetterholm, eds., *Paul within Judaism* (2015), 42–46.

[12] The phrase comes from the subtitle of Sanders, *PPJ*. Elsewhere, Sanders (*Paul, the Law, and the Jewish People* [1983], 207–8) concludes that "Paul's break [with Judaism] is clearly perceptible."

[13] E.g., James D. G. Dunn, *Jesus, Paul, and the Law* (1990), 194–203, 215–41; N. T. Wright, *The Climax of the Covenant* (1993), 240, 243, 247; Bruce W. Longenecker, *Eschatology and the Covenant* (2015), 278–80; Daniel Boyarin, *A Radical Jew* (1994).

[14] Wright, *Climax*, 238.

[15] James D. G. Dunn, *The Partings of the Ways between Christianity and Judaism* (1991), 230.

[16] Dunn, *The Partings of the Ways*, 258–59.

Paul's encounter with Jesus must have caused him to realize that openness and inclusiveness are prima facie superior to exclusivity and particularity, an unlikely conclusion for a Jew living in the first-century Roman Empire.

It is also hardly mere coincidence that a group of Western scholars from the late twentieth century discovered that Paul's gospel was really about inclusiveness and opposition to racism. "Inclusiveness" is, after all, arguably the highest virtue in postmodern Western culture. The New Perspective has therefore exchanged an antithesis more at home in the sixteenth century (merit/grace) for one better suited to the twenty-first century (racism/inclusiveness).[17] By interpreting Paul's message as the gospel of inclusiveness,[18] Paul's interpreters have once again looked down the deep well of history and seen their own faces reflected back at them.[19] Moreover, by trading "legalism" for "ethnocentrism," much New Perspective scholarship ironically and unfortunately represents a retreat to the anti-Jewish tendencies of pre-Schweitzer Pauline scholarship, effectively portraying Paul as the enlightened apostle of modern liberalism, embracing inclusive and progressive ideals over and against a regressive Jewish particularism.[20]

---

[17] David I. Starling, *Not My People: Gentiles as Exiles in Pauline Hermeneutics* (2011), 214.

[18] See, for example, the discussion in Jacob Neusner, "Was Rabbinic Judaism Really 'Ethnic'?" (1995), 283.

[19] This image is often associated with Schweitzer but in fact derives from George Tyrrell, *Christianity at the Cross-roads* (1909), 49.

[20] "Most scholarship takes as its starting point the position that Israel in the Judaism of that time is ethnic, but the Gospel, universal. Christianity improved on Judaism by bringing to all the peoples of the world what had originally been kept for one people alone .... The contrast between the ethnic Judaism and the universalist Christianity derives from the presentation of Israel by the apostle Paul" (Jacob Neusner, "The Premise of Paul's Ethnic Israel" [1995], 2). See also Mark D. Nanos, "Introduction" (2015), 6–7; Kathy Ehrensperger, *That We May Be Mutually Encouraged* (2004), 123–60. On the anti-Jewish perspectives of the pre-Schweitzer era, see Barclay, "Paul, Judaism, and the Jewish People," 190; for an example, see Ferdinand Christian Baur, *The Church History of the First Three Centuries* (1878), 1.47. Such an image of a progressive Paul at odds with regressive, racist Judaism is obviously coherent with the anti-Semitic zeitgeist leading up to the Holocaust, as the Jews were maligned for their unwillingness to leave behind their Jewish particularities and fully assimilate into their wider national societies, as was expected upon their emancipation. See Steven Beller, *Antisemitism* (2007), 32–33; David Jan Sorkin, *The Transformation of German Jewry, 1780–1840* (1987), 3–40; Jonathan M. Hess, "Jewish Emancipation and the Politics of Race" (2006); Hess, *Germans, Jews, and the Claims of Modernity* (2002); David Lee Brodbeck, *Defining Deutschtum* (2014), 43–52. For a closer look at how modern concerns have imposed on the interpretation of Rom 9–11, see Klaus Haacker, "Das Thema von Römer 9–11 als Problem der Auslegungsgeschichte" (2010).

That Paul's gospel amounts to a rejection of particularism is also difficult to square with the troublesome fact that Paul himself established groups set apart by and to the God of Israel.[21] Inasmuch as Paul's own groups had clear boundaries and expectations of insiders in distinction from outsiders, Paul does not reject particularity in principle. The dispute between Paul and his opponents does not pit "particularism" versus "inclusion" nor does it call into question whether there should be a particularist, exclusive people of God at all. Instead, the debate concerns the proper location of the boundaries for the exclusive community of God's people; and although many have assumed Paul found something wrong with Judaism leading to his conversion to Christianity, Paul presents his transition as a *revelation* and a *call* from Israel's God in continuity with the theological framework he had previously embraced.[22] Paul never presents himself as having departed from Israel or as having created something entirely new, instead declaring, "I too am an Israelite!" (Rom 11:1) and continuing to treat the Torah and Israelite prophets as authoritative scripture.[23]

Paul's own arguments are also strikingly ethnocentric, starting with his claim of Jewish priority in the gospel: the gospel is "first to the Jew and then to the Greek" (e.g., Rom 1:16). And contrary to Sanders' conclusion that Paul "denies two pillars common to all forms of Judaism: the election of Israel and faithfulness to the Mosaic law,"[24] Paul vigorously defends Israel's special status, concluding three full chapters defending God's fidelity to Israel (Rom 9–11) with the declaration "thus all Israel will be saved" (Rom 11:26). This ethnocentric dictum closely parallels the declaration of the Mishnah that "All Israel has a part in the world to come" (m. Sanh. 10:1) and would hardly be surprising from any other Jewish thinker of the period. But it would be an exceedingly strange sentiment coming from someone who denies the election of Israel.

Some modern interpreters have found Paul's declaration of Israel's salvation so foreign to Paul's thought as to suggest – despite the lack of any textual evidence – that it must be a later interpolation,[25] while others

---

[21] See Nanos, "Introduction," 7–8; Caroline Johnson Hodge, *If Sons, Then Heirs* (2007), 79–91.
[22] See Krister Stendahl, *Paul among Jews and Gentiles* (1976), 7–23.
[23] See Anders Runesson, "The Question of Terminology: The Architecture of Contemporary Discussions on Paul" (2015) and Mark D. Nanos, "Paul and Judaism: Why Not Paul's Judaism?" (2010), 129–31.
[24] Sanders, *PLJP*, 207–8.
[25] E.g., Christoph Plag, *Israels Wege zum Heil* (1969), 41. See also John C. O'Neill, *Paul's Letter to the Romans* (1975), 177.

have concluded that Paul here shows a "startling lack of logical consistency,"[26] backtracking on his prior claims about the equality of all before God.[27] Still others have suggested that Paul, aware his arguments could be taken too far, suddenly makes a defense for the very thing against which he has been arguing in order to prevent such abuse,[28] with Romans 9–11 and its conclusion (as Sanders declares) "a desperate expedient" to resolve "a problem of conflicting convictions."[29]

Recognizing this problem with the typical New Perspective approach, some scholars have proposed that rather than comparing "Paul and Judaism," it is better to think of "Paul within Judaism."[30] In this approach, Paul is understood as never having departed from Judaism at all. Instead, rather than Judaism serving as a "background" or a foil for the creation of something entirely new, Paul is understood as remaining part of a larger Jewish discourse, retaining his commitment to Israel's special election and the divine authority of the Torah, and continuing to practice Judaism as he understood it. Some taking this approach have suggested that Paul's gospel is ultimately focused on fixing the "gentile problem" – that is, the idolatrous and immoral nature shared by gentiles (but not Jews) that keeps gentiles from knowing God.[31] In this framework, both Jewish and gentile followers of Jesus must keep God's commands, but these commands differ for the two groups – Jews are "obligated to keep the whole Torah" (Gal 5:3), while gentiles are obligated to a smaller set of divine commands.[32] Paul therefore argues against

---

[26] Terence L. Donaldson, "Riches for the Gentiles" (1993), 88.
[27] E.g., Heikki Räisänen, "Paul, God, and Israel" (1988), 182, 192–96; Räisänen, *Paul and the Law* (1987), xxiii; Peter Richardson, *Israel in the Apostolic Church* (1969), 126–27; W. D. Davies, "Paul and the People of Israel" (1977), 33; Francis Watson, *Paul, Judaism, and the Gentiles* (2007), 334. William Campbell ("Divergent Images of Paul and His Mission" [2000], 189) argues that Paul should not be held to modern standards of consistency and logic. Nevertheless, although it is possible that Paul's arguments are contingent to the point of being contradictory or incoherent, this conclusion should only be a last resort.
[28] E.g., David Ravens, *Luke and the Restoration of Israel* (1995), 210.
[29] Sanders, *PLJP*, 198.
[30] See the recent collection of essays in Nanos and Zetterholm, *Paul Within Judaism*. On this group as "the Radicals," see Pamela Eisenbaum, "Paul, Polemics, and the Problem of Essentialism" (2005), 232–33. Cf. Zetterholm, *Approaches to Paul*, 127–63, under the subheading "Beyond the New Perspective." See also Nanos, "Why Not Paul's Judaism?"; William S. Campbell, "Perceptions of Compatibility between Christianity and Judaism in Pauline Interpretation" (2005); Bird and Sprinkle, "Jewish Interpretation of Paul"; Ehrensperger, *That We May Be Mutually Encouraged*, 177–202.
[31] See especially Matthew Thiessen, *Paul and the Gentile Problem* (2016).
[32] Thiessen, *Paul and the Gentile Problem*, 11.

gentile circumcision because the Torah does not command gentiles to be circumcised but only the descendants of Abraham, specifically those within Israel, the heir of Abraham's covenant.[33] Similarly, Paul's other arguments about the inefficacy of "works of Torah" apply only to non-Jews, while Jews remain responsible to keep the Torah of Moses in the same way they had been before Jesus' death and resurrection.

The "Paul within Judaism" perspective has much to commend it, and this book will similarly argue that Paul never abandoned the theological, eschatological, and ethnic framework he held before he came to identify Jesus as Israel's messiah. Nevertheless, it cannot be denied that Paul declares that "both Jews and Greeks are all under sin" (Rom 3:9), that "all who are from works of Torah are under a curse" (Gal 3:10), that Moses administered "the ministry of death" (2 Cor 3:7), that "messiah is the end/goal [*telos*] of Torah" (Rom 10:5), and that God has broken off "natural branches" from his people due to infidelity (11:19–23). These statements and many others like them are difficult to square with the idea that Paul understands his gospel and ministry as applying only to pagans while Jews are to continue as before.

WHO ARE PAUL'S (FORMER) GENTILES?

Whether considering Paul as operating within Judaism or otherwise, a persuasive explanation for how Paul understands the status of uncircumcised Jesus-followers has remained especially elusive. On the one hand, Paul continues to distinguish between these uncircumcised individuals and Jews (e.g., Rom 11:13; Gal 2:14) and vigorously argues that gentiles should not undergo circumcision or attempt to become Jews (e.g., Gal 5:1–6). On the other hand, Paul's gospel requires that these persons abandon their own gods and traditional norms and practices, pledging loyalty to Israel's messiah and worshiping only the God of Israel – commitments and practices otherwise associated with Jewish ethnicity. Even more significantly, Paul also regularly applies Israelite language and

---

[33] Pamela Eisenbaum, *Paul Was Not a Christian* (2009), 62–63. Others arguing along these lines (with some variation) include Lloyd Gaston, *Paul and the Torah* (1987); John G. Gager, *Reinventing Paul* (2000); Stanley K. Stowers, *A Rereading of Romans* (1994); Johnson Hodge, *If Sons, Then Heirs*; Runar M. Thorsteinsson, *Paul's Interlocutor in Romans 2* (2003); Rafael Rodríguez, *If You Call Yourself a Jew* (2014); Nanos and Zetterholm, *Paul within Judaism*; Thiessen, *Paul and the Gentile Problem*; and Paula Fredriksen, *Paul: The Pagans' Apostle* (2017).

ethnic markers – even prophecies specifically about Israel – to these uncircumcised individuals (e.g., Rom 2:14–15; 9:26) and goes so far as to call them *former* gentiles (1 Cor 12:2), include them among the seed of Abraham (Gal 3:29), and refer to them as descendants of biblical Israel (1 Cor 10:1).[34] These persons are therefore not Jews, but they are not exactly gentiles anymore,[35] and if they are descendants of biblical Israel, they cannot be "ex-pagan pagans," either.[36]

It should be noted that the idea that gentiles did not need to undergo circumcision or become Jews in order to worship the God of Israel or attain eschatological salvation was by no means unusual in early Judaism.[37] After all, there was a court of the nations at the temple to allow gentiles to worship YHWH, and the Prophets predicted that after Israel's restoration the nations would stream to Jerusalem and serve Israel's God. Consequently, the debate over whether gentiles should or must be circumcised only makes sense if it concerns gentiles becoming members of the covenant. Paul's opponents are advocating circumcision for adult gentiles as a means of incorporation in Israel's covenant, marking status transition from "gentile" to "Israelite."[38] Paul could have

---

[34] On Paul's portrayal of gentiles in quasi-Israelite terms, see Starling, *Not My People*; Cavan W. Concannon, *"When You Were Gentiles"* (2014). That Paul includes former gentiles as descendants of biblical Israel in 1 Cor 10:1 is a significant problem for the idea that he sees them as incorporated into Abraham but not Israel.

[35] As observed by Joshua D. Garroway, "The Circumcision of Christ: Romans 15.7–13" (2012), 7–8.

[36] Pace Fredriksen, *The Pagans' Apostle*, 73–77. Although elsewhere emphasizing the ethnic nature of ancient Mediterranean deities and theology, Fredriksen argues that Paul is an exception, such that the "sharp dichotomy [between Israel and the nations] is resolved *theologically* but not *ethnically*" (116, emphasis original), despite the fact that Paul explicitly uses ethnic terminology to refer to his ex-pagan converts. For a critique of Fredriksen's concept of "ex-pagan pagans" theologically but not ethnically included in the people of God, see Denys N. McDonald, "'Ex-Pagan Pagans'? Paul, Philo, and Gentile Ethnic Reconfiguration" (2022) and the response of Fredriksen, "Paul, Pagans and Eschatological Ethnicities: A Response to Denys McDonald" (2022).

[37] See Nanos, "Why Not Paul's Judaism?," 124–35; Eisenbaum, *Paul Was Not a Christian*, 99–115; Paula Fredriksen, "Judaism, the Circumcision of Gentiles, and Apocalyptic Hope" (1991); Donaldson, *Paul and the Gentiles*, 60–74; John M. G. Barclay, *Jews in the Mediterranean Diaspora* (1996), 438–39; Jerome Murphy-O'Connor, "Lots of God-Fearers?" (1992); Shaye J. D. Cohen, "Crossing the Boundary and Becoming a Jew" (1989), 20–26; John G. Gager, *The Origins of Anti-Semitism* (1983), 56–66; "Jews, Gentiles, and Synagogues in the Book of Acts" (1986).

[38] E.g., Jdt 14:10, which equates circumcision with being joined to Israel. On circumcision as the mechanism for full conversion, see Shaye J. D. Cohen, *The Beginnings of Jewishness* (1999), 137–38, 156–58, 218–20; Cohen, "Crossing the Boundary"; Thiessen, *Paul and the Gentile Problem*, 29–32. The frequency of conversions involving

responded by arguing that gentiles need not be incorporated into the covenant because they can and should be saved as gentiles outside Israel's covenant, but he does not. Nowhere does he suggest that these faithful gentiles are the fulfillment of the prophetic promises of the nations flocking to Jerusalem at the eschaton,[39] nor does he mention or cite the passages in which these promises occur.[40] He also nowhere argues that ethnic conversion is impossible, nor does he call attention to the timing of circumcisions or argue that circumcisions occurring after the eighth day are not efficacious for converting a gentile into a Jew.[41] Quite the contrary, he argues that such circumcision of gentiles does in fact bring them under the Torah (Gal 5:2–4), effectively putting them in the same position as Jews absent the redemption granted by Jesus and administered by the spirit (Gal 3:10–13).

Rather than objecting that conversion and circumcision cannot make gentiles into Jews, Paul says that the problem with the circumcision gospel

---

circumcision in this period is unknown, and there is considerable debate regarding the alacrity with which Jews proselytized in antiquity. See Louis H. Feldman, *Jew and Gentile in the Ancient World* (1996), 288–382; Bernard J. Bamberger, *Proselytism in the Talmudic period* (1968), 13–24; Scot McKnight, *A Light among the Gentiles* (1991), 49–77; Martin D. Goodman, *Mission and Conversion* (1994), 60–90.

[39] As suggested by Sanders, *PLJP*, 171–206; Fredriksen, "Apocalyptic Hope"; among others. See the discussion in Chapter 7.

[40] Donaldson, "Riches for the Gentiles," 92.

[41] As suggested by Thiessen, *Paul and the Gentile Problem*, 64–102. Thiessen (*Contesting Conversion* [2011], 67–86) argues that the book of Jubilees provides evidence that some Jews regarded any circumcision not performed on the eighth day as inadequate for Israelite membership, making it impossible for a gentile to become an Israelite via adult circumcision. But the primary texts on which Thiessen builds his argument do not have proselytes in view but only native-born Jews and Israelites. For example, when Jub 15:25 says, "there is no circumcision of the days, and no omission of one day out of the eight days," the dispute is with other Jews who might, for example, object to circumcising on the Sabbath, resulting in circumcision on the wrong day. Jubilees does state that those circumcised after the eighth day are "meant for destruction" (15:26), but the condemnation is because "he has broken the covenant of the Lord our God," which presumes an initial location within the covenant, casting doubt on whether such a condemnation could apply to a proselyte, especially since Jub 15:12–13 also commands the circumcision of adult slaves, who then appear to be included within the covenant ("my covenant will be in your flesh for an eternal ordinance" immediately follows this command). The application of Jubilees' statements about eighth-day circumcision to proselytes is therefore questionable at best. See the similar critiques in Genevive Dibley, "The Making and Unmaking of Jews in Second Century BCE Narratives" (2021), esp. 13–15, and Shaye Cohen's review of *Contesting Conversion* in *CBQ* (2013). In any case, the circumcision debate must have concerned the question of whether (and/or how) gentiles may attain full Israelite status. For more on Jubilees (a Hebrew work retelling the stories of Gen 1–Exod 24 generally dated to the second century BCE), see James C. VanderKam, "Recent Scholarship on the Book of Jubilees" (2008).

is that it implies that those who have the spirit but are not physically circumcised are not *already* Israelites of equal status. "They wish to exclude you," he protests, "so that you will seek them" (Gal 4:17). Paul, however, argues that these former gentiles must not be excluded because of their foreskins. Instead, these uncircumcised followers of Jesus have no need of fleshly circumcision because they have already been brought into Israel's covenant and are therefore already no longer gentiles. Rather than welcoming these non-Jews into the community as celebrated guests, he argues that they are "members in full standing."[42] They are already heirs of Abraham and descendants of Israel, having bypassed the need for fleshly circumcision or any other marker of identification with the written Torah or Jewish identity. For Paul, these faithful followers of Jesus are not saved "as gentiles" because they are no longer gentiles; instead, they have become equal members of Israel along with their Torah-observant Jewish siblings. It is this assertion that proved so unbearable for Paul's opponents. That gentiles could be saved as gentiles is little reason for concern or controversy, but the claim that uncircumcised gentiles are Israelites is a shocking claim that could easily be understood as representing a grave threat to traditional conceptions of Israelite identity. The debate in which Paul is engaged is therefore fundamentally over the status and identity of the people of Israel and what constitutes the proper boundaries of that ethnic group.

The centrality of the circumcision question is a strong indicator of the continued centrality of Israel and the covenantal promises to Israel in Paul's thought. Nowhere does the apostle suggest that God has established a new people independent of or parallel to Israel. Instead, as Joshua Garroway observes, "Paul sees but one people of God, which is Israel"[43] and consequently "insists upon the Abrahamic origins of baptized Gentiles because he believes that they have become a part of the genuine people of Israel."[44] But Garroway's own solution, that these former gentiles take on hybrid "mimic men" status, able "to become like Jews, but not quite Jews,"[45] still misses the essence of what Paul is claiming. The first problem is that such a solution situates these non-Jewish Jesus-followers in exactly the sort of secondary status within the people of God against which Paul objects. Second, while Garroway rightly emphasizes

---

[42] Nanos, "Why Not Paul's Judaism?," 145 cf. Sanders, *Paul*, 62.
[43] Joshua D. Garroway, *Paul's Gentile-Jews* (2012), 207 n. 50.
[44] Garroway, *Paul's Gentile-Jews*, 5.   [45] Garroway, *Paul's Gentile-Jews*, 156.

that Paul nowhere uses the term "Christian,"[46] Paul also nowhere refers to converted gentiles as "Jews."[47] Instead, although he frequently describes gentile converts in language associated with biblical Israel, he also regularly pairs "Jews and Greeks" or "Jews and gentiles" as separate groups brought together in the larger *ekklēsia* (e.g., Rom 9:24–26). And if these uncircumcised followers of Jesus are neither Jews nor gentiles, they can hardly be both.

But why should one presume that "Jew" and "gentile" are the only two options available for Paul? Although it is true that Paul does not operate within a "third race" paradigm like some later patristic writers,[48] these former gentiles seem to fit in neither of these two categories. These ex-pagans are definitely not Jews, but Paul insists they stand on equal footing with Jews as heirs to Abraham's promises and partakers in the heritage of Israel, and as Johnson Hodge rightly notes, he argues that "their separateness is necessary for God's plan for Israel, as God sees it."[49] The key to solving this problem, as this book will demonstrate, is better understanding how Paul and his early Jewish contemporaries understood "Israel."

"ALL ISRAEL WILL BE SAVED"

Understanding Paul's perspective on Israel has proven at least as difficult as following his logic about gentile inclusion. On the one hand, he insists that all, whether Jews or otherwise, stand on equal footing before God (e.g., Rom 2:2–11; 3:9, 22). On the other, he vigorously defends Israel's special election (Rom 9:4–5) and declares that "all Israel will be saved" (11:26). Remarkably, Paul puts these two elements together, asserting that "all Israel will be saved" only when the "fullness of the nations/gentiles has entered" (Rom 11:25). At least as pertains to how these two elements interface with one another, Schweitzer's judgment, that "present day criticism is far from having explained [Paul] ... all it has really done is to have gained some insight into the difficulties,"[50] seems even more

---

[46] Garroway, *Paul's Gentile-Jews*, 1–3.
[47] On Rom 2:28–29, which some have argued does refer to gentiles as Jews, see pp. 165–73.
[48] "The church is for him emphatically not a 'third race' that is *neither* Jewish nor gentile, nor even less an entity altogether void of ethnic ascription. Rather, the church is in one sense *entirely* 'Jewish,' and yet in another sense *both* Jewish and gentile" (Zoccali, *Whom God Has Called*, 7 n. 12). For more on the "third race" concept in early Christianity, see Buell, *Why This New Race*, 1–5, 35–62.
[49] Caroline Johnson Hodge, "The Question of Identity" (2015), 172.
[50] Schweitzer, *Paul and His Interpreters*, viii.

accurate today than it was then. What is more, because of the centrality of this question to Paul's thought, no paradigm for understanding Paul's gospel as a whole can succeed without satisfactorily addressing this question.

One traditional solution works hand in glove with the idea that Paul abandoned Judaism for a new, universal, ethnically inclusive Christianity. In this view, the Jews may well have been Israel at one time, but they have now been replaced by a new Israel mostly made up of gentiles. The old, ethnic entity (*vetus Israel*) has been superseded and replaced by the "true," "spiritual" Israel (*verus Israel*). An early version of this view appears as early as the second century, "eventually becoming patristic boilerplate."[51] The Epistle of Barnabas, for example, proclaims that the Israelite covenant "is ours [Christians'], but they [Jews] lost it forever" (Barn. 4:7), having been "perfected in their sins" just in time for "us" to swoop in and receive the covenant in their place (Barn. 14:5)[52] In this view, when Paul says "all Israel will be saved," he has radically redefined that term to mean something different from what it would mean to any other first-century Jew.

Recent decades have marked an increasing discomfort with this perspective, not least because of its anti-Jewish potential in a post-Holocaust world.[53] But even beyond such concerns, most modern interpreters have found such a radical redefinition of Israel implausible, pointing out the absence of any direct statement in Romans identifying gentiles as Israelites and observing that the term refers to historical Israel throughout these chapters.[54] Douglas Moo explains:

Paul has used the term "Israel" ten times so far in Rom. 9–11, and each refers to ethnic Israel ... a shift from the ethnic denotation [v. 25] to a purely religious one in v. 26a – despite the all – is unlikely.[55]

---

[51] Matthew Thiessen and Paula Fredriksen, "Paul and Israel" (2021), n.p. The classic study on this is Simon, *Verus Israel*.
[52] See Michael Kok, "The True Covenant People" (2010). Even earlier, 1 Clement and 1 Peter similarly suggest an association of the church with Israel (e.g., 1 Pet 2:9–12; 1 Clem 29:2–30:1). Zoccali (*Whom God Has Called*, 86) points to Rev 5:9–10 as another example. Justin Martyr similarly claims that Christians are Israel (e.g., *Dial.* 11.5), but he also explicitly rejects the idea that the Jews have therefore been rejected (*Dial.* 25.6–26.1). Thanks to Matthew J. Thomas for bringing the latter to my attention.
[53] Cf. Ehrensperger, *That We May Be Mutually Encouraged*, 16.
[54] E.g., Watson, *Paul, Judaism, and the Gentiles*, 311: "Nowhere in Romans 9–11 is 'Israel' said to include Gentiles."
[55] Douglas J. Moo, *Romans* (1996), 721. Those ten references are 9:6b (twice), 27 (twice), 31; 10:19, 21, 11:2, 7, 25. Similarly, Robert Jewett *Romans* (2006), 701: "in all the

Moreover, inasmuch as this very passage warns gentiles against arrogantly presuming their superiority against Jews currently situated outside the faithful community, any reading that concludes God has forsaken ethnic Israel "would be to fuel the fire of the gentiles' arrogance by giving them grounds to brag that 'we are the true Israel.'"[56] Rather than identifying Israel with the church, the current consensus is therefore that the church is a wholly "new entity of Jews and gentiles coming together in Christ equally."[57] As William Campbell explains, "However related to Israel, the church is not Israel; Israel's identity is unique and cannot be taken over by gentile Christ-followers, or even completely shared by them."[58]

In that light, "all Israel will be saved" is now generally understood as Paul's declaration that the Jews will ultimately be saved despite their present resistance to his gospel, though the meaning of " all" remains a seemingly intractable problem.[59] That is, does Paul mean to suggest a miraculous conversion of all Jews alive at the eschaton, or that all Jews throughout time will be saved through a separate path, or something else? Nevertheless, although the sense of "all" and the exact nature of the relationship between the church (*ekklēsia*) and Israel continues to be debated,[60] it is now widely agreed that when Paul says "all Israel," he means "ethnic" or "empirical" Israel.[61]

---

earlier references to 'Israel' in Romans, the ethnic Israel is in view." Cf. also James D. G. Dunn, *Romans* (1988), 681–82; Charles E. B. Cranfield, *Romans* (1979), 576–77.

[56] Moo, *Romans*, 721. Remarkably, Moo concedes that Paul is indeed willing to apply such terminology to the gentiles elsewhere but argues he would not do so here, where "the rhetorical situation is entirely different" (721).

[57] Mark D. Nanos, *The Mystery of Romans* (1996), 149.

[58] William S. Campbell, *Paul and the Creation of Christian Identity* (2006), 170.

[59] E.g., Cranfield, *Romans*, 446; Dunn, *Romans*, 681. For a detailed analysis of various prior scholarly proposals for how to understand the "all," see Zoccali, *Whom God Has Called*. These discussions typically include little to no analysis of what Paul means by "saved" here. Rather, most interpreters assume an effectively Protestant view of "salvation" – that is, that Paul's driving concern here is whether "all Israel" will go to heaven when they die. But this is more assumed than established, and there is reason to suspect it is anachronistic.

[60] Some interpreters, for example, have argued that Paul presents two Israels (or a bifurcated Israel), with the church having a claim to Israel's heritage not supplanting but rather parallel to historical Israel's continued status as the elect people of God. E.g., Dunn, *Romans*, 526–27; *The Theology of Paul the Apostle* (2006), 519–25; Donaldson, *Paul and the Gentiles*, 216–48. Wright (*Climax*, 238) also argues for a "two-Israel" position based on Rom 9:6, arguing that this verse establishes a "double 'Israel,'" one of flesh and the other a "true Israel," but unlike most contemporary interpreters, Wright does not argue that the fleshly Israel is included among the "all Israel" that will be saved according to Rom 11:26.

[61] E.g., Michael Bachmann, "Verus Israel" (2002), 510: "The term 'Israel' (and accordingly 'Israelite') ... is used by the apostle – at least beyond Gal 6.16 – exclusively for real Jews

EMPIRICAL ETHNICITY?

Unfortunately, despite its near-ubiquitous use, the language of "ethnic" or "empirical" Israel presents problems of its own. Functionally, both terms serve as a sort of shorthand to connect Paul's "Israel" terminology, the definition of which has historically been disputed, with the presumably less-disputed category of "Jews." But merely adding "ethnic" or "empirical" to "Israel" does not solve the problem or provide clarity but rather begs the question. First of all, this language implies a scientifically verifiable or self-evident category such that it is clear who counts as Israel and who does not. ("Empirical" is, of course, a way to say "ethnic" while sidestepping the potentially problematic racial connotations of the latter term.) But ethnicity is neither empirical nor self-evident even in the modern world, as attested by the controversies over the decisions of the Israeli government denying *aliyah* (immigration to Israel) to self-identified Jews, many of whom have been approved as Jews by other Jewish groups.[62] Empirically, what is the ethnic status of those received as Jews by Orthodox leaders in the diaspora but rejected as Jews by the nation of Israel?[63]

A second problem is that the language of "ethnic" Israel continues to frame the discussion by presuming an underlying contrast between Paul's Christian "religion" and Jewish "ethnicity" (recall the contrast in Moo's statement quoted above).[64] But such a distinction is anachronistic, as religion and ethnicity are modern categories not disentangled from one another in antiquity; to be a part of an *ethnos* meant (and still presumes!) observing cultural and cultic practices.[65] Dio Cassius, for example, explicitly states, "I do not know the origin of this name [*Ioudaios*], but it is

---

[wirkliche Juden] and never for non-Jews, never in the "figurative" sense"; Pablo T. Gadenz, *Called from the Jews and from the Gentiles* (2009), 277: "'All Israel' refers to ethnic Israel. Indeed, Paul has up to this point used the term 'Israel' to refer to ethnic Israel (or some part of it)"; Susan Grove Eastman, "Israel and the Mercy of God" (2010), 368–69: "In Romans, 'Israel' is widely understood to refer to empirical Israel"; Hans Hübner, *Gottes Ich und Israel* (1984), 20: "das empirische, das völkische Israel."

[62] See Gad Barzilai, "Who Is a Jew?" (2010); Tiffany Pransky, "Boundaries of Belonging" (2012); Roselle Tekiner, "Race and the Issue of National Identity in Israel" (1991); Benjamin Akzin, "Who Is a Jew – A Hard Case" (1970).

[63] E.g., Nathan Jeffay, "Israeli Government Rejects Orthodox Converts' Bids to Immigrate as Jews" (2011).

[64] See David G. Horrell, "Judaean Ethnicity and Christ-Following Voluntarism?" (2019); Horrell, *Ethnicity and Inclusion* (2020), esp. 21–94.

[65] See David G. Horrell, "Religion, Ethnicity, and Way of Life" (2021); *Ethnicity and Inclusion*, esp. 136–77, 217–48.

applied to all men, even foreigners, who follow their customs. This race is found even among Romans."⁶⁶ Similarly, Josephus reports that when the Roman proconsul Lucius Lentulus granted special privileges to Roman citizens in Ephesus who were *Ioudaioi*, he defined that group as "those who appear to me to have and do the sacred things of the Jews."⁶⁷ As Paula Fredriksen observes, in the ancient world, "gods really did run in the blood. Put differently: cult, as enacted and as imagined, defined ethnicity."⁶⁸ The evidence simply does not support any attempt to distinguish the ethnic and religious aspects of Israel or Jewishness in antiquity.⁶⁹

To make matters worse, although most Pauline interpreters treat ethnicity as self-evident and avoid defining the term at all, modern scholars often differ in their treatments and definitions (explicit or implied) of what constitutes ethnicity.⁷⁰ Shaye Cohen, for example, treats ethnicity as "closed, immutable, an ascribed characteristic based on birth."⁷¹ Others, however, have observed that ethnicity is not self-evident but is a socially constructed polythetic category with elastic boundaries that are always in the process of negotiation, highlighting evidence of the mutability of ethnicity and ethnic conversion in the ancient Mediterranean

---

⁶⁶ Dio Cassius 37.17.1. See Menahem Stern, ed., *Greek and Latin Authors on Jews and Judaism, Vol 2* (1980), #406. Thus Daniel and Jonathan Boyarin ("Diaspora" (1993), 694 n. 2) conclude: "We see from this quotation that race once had much suppler and more complex connections with genealogy, cultural praxis, and identity than it has in our parlance."

⁶⁷ *Ant.* 14.234; cf. 14.228, 237, 240. On these laws, see Miriam Pucci Ben Zeev, *Jewish Rights in the Roman World* (1998), 150–91. Christiane Saulnier, "Lois romaines sur les Juifs selon Flavius Josèphe" (1981), 168–69. Cf. also Shaye J. D. Cohen, "'Those Who Say They Are Jews and Are Not'" (1993), 31. Cf. also Sean Freyne, "Behind the Names: Samaritans, Ioudaioi, Galileans" (2000), 396.

⁶⁸ Paula Fredriksen, "Compassion Is to Purity as Fish Is to Bicycle" (2005), 57; cf. also Malcolm Lowe, "Who Were the ΙΟΥΔΑΙΟΙ?" (1976), 107, and the limitations noted by Schwartz, "How Many Judaisms," 234.

⁶⁹ Neusner, "Was Rabbinic Judaism Really 'Ethnic'?"; "Paul's Ethnic Israel," 4–5.

⁷⁰ For a demonstration of a variety of definitions of ethnicity and religion among scholars discussing Jewish and Christian identities in antiquity, see David M. Miller, "Ethnicity, Religion and the Meaning of Ioudaios in Ancient 'Judaism'" (2014), 234–42.

⁷¹ Cohen, *Beginnings of Jewishness*, 136, a baffling assertion since Cohen previously acknowledges that ethnicity "is imagined [and] can be willed into and out of existence" (5). Similarly, Neusner, "Was Rabbinic Judaism Really 'Ethnic'?"; "Paul's Ethnic Israel," 5–6. Miller observes that "ethnicity" has often functioned as a euphemism for the simplistic and discredited concept of "race" as a biological category, which is surely a factor in why it is often assumed to be a rigid or immutable category ("Ethnicity Comes of Age" [2012], 293–96). Buell embraces the term "race" despite its baggage in part to emphasize this point (*Why This New Race*, 12–20).

world.⁷² Most Pauline interpreters have tended to follow Cohen's approach by default, treating ethnicity as an immutable, monothetic category based on shared ancestry. This approach seems simple enough on the surface, but it is quickly complicated by adoption and more overtly fictive kinship, such as the Hasmonean "discovery" that "the Spartans and Jews are brothers and are of the family of Abraham" (1 Macc 12:21), let alone Jewish proselytes who become integrated in the people through the processes of conversion and intermarriage.⁷³ Those who have apostatized present additional complications – are those who have abandoned their ethnic culture and heritage to join other groups still to be considered part of their original ethnic group? What about their children, born and raised outside the group?

In practice, the messiness of embodied life means additional cultural criteria beyond physical descent are necessary even for groups ostensibly based on genealogy alone. With respect to "ethnic Israel," Matthew Thiessen observes:

> For Paul and his contemporaries, the question was how Israel's God reckoned descent. One could answer this in numerous ways: patrilineal descent (e.g., Genesis), matrilineal descent (e.g., later rabbis), bilateral descent (e.g., Ezra–Nehemiah), pneumatic descent (e.g., Paul), descent created by imitating Abraham in undergoing circumcision and adoption of the law (e.g., Paul's opponents), or something else altogether. All of these answers are constructions, but the first four seem to be more deeply (or at least straightforwardly) rooted in nature, because they each claim that there is a material connection – be that semen, blood, flesh, or *pneuma* – between ancestor and descendant.⁷⁴

It is therefore not the case that the boundaries of "ethnic Israel" can be easily defined along biological or genealogical grounds – other criteria, such as Torah observance, have always been involved in negotiating those

---

⁷² See Todd S. Berzon, "Ethnicity and Early Christianity" (2018); John M. G. Barclay, "Ἰουδαῖος: Ethnicity and Translation" (2018), 53–54; Buell, *Why This New Race*; Caroline Johnson Hodge, "Olive Trees and Ethnicities" (2004); *If Sons, Then Heirs*; Garroway, *Paul's Gentile-Jews*; Carmen Palmer, *Converts in the Dead Sea Scrolls* (2018). For the difference between "monothetic" and "polythetic" classification, see Jonathan Z. Smith, "Fences and Neighbors" (1982).

⁷³ Even highly exclusive groups like the sect associated with the Community Rule (1QS) and related Dead Sea scrolls allowed for the incorporation of gentile converts into the larger body of "Israel," as demonstrated by Palmer, *Converts in the Dead Sea Scrolls*, esp. 126–57, 185–96. Palmer distinguishes between the more open "mutable" approach of CD and the "D" tradition and the "S" tradition associated with 1QS and related scrolls, which she concludes does not grant full insider status to gentile converts.

⁷⁴ Matthew Thiessen, "Paul, Essentialism, and the Jewish Law" (2017), 82.

boundaries.[75] Even insiders starting from the premise of an innate, inborn ethnic nature that distinguishes members of one ethnicity from another ultimately derive their definitions of that nature and its origin from cultural resources such as Torah and tradition.[76] And as soon as traditional cultural elements like Torah interpretation or Torah observance come into play, the natural and immediate question is who or what defines proper Torah interpretation or observance.[77] Is Torah observance to be defined according to the standards of the Pharisees? Sadducees? Essenes? Orthodox? Reform? Conservative? Such appeals to "ethnic Israel" therefore run into precisely the question of status Paul and his interlocutors are debating: Who counts as "in," who counts as "out," and who gets to determine the "empirical" boundaries for the group?[78]

In this context, it is noteworthy that Paul asserts that he in no way opposes the Torah but instead establishes it (Rom 3:31), even arguing that one must receive the spirit in accordance with his gospel to properly fulfill the just requirements of the Torah (Rom 2:29; 8:4). Paul therefore claims that those who reject his gospel are on the outside not because the Torah has been abolished but rather because they are not properly fulfilling the Torah. There is little difference between this claim and what might have been said by any other sectarian Jew about others who did not keep the Torah in accordance with the specific halakhic interpretations held sacrosanct by the group in question (e.g., Matt 5:17–20; 4QMMT). Even the Mishnah's declaration about all Israel's participation in the

---

[75] "Gods, land, language, kinship, custom: this variable concept cluster expressed ... what we would designate as 'ethnicity'" (Paula Fredriksen, "What Does It Mean to See Paul 'within Judaism'?" [2022], 364).

[76] It is therefore imperative to distinguish between the rhetoric or reasoning of those debating the boundaries of the group and the functional work that rhetoric is doing. For example, "both Paul and his competitors reasoned in essentializing ways, even as they did the work of constructing ethnic identity" (Thiessen, "Paul, Essentialism, and the Jewish Law," 82).

[77] On "observance of Jewish practices" as key to Jewishness in antiquity and the difficulty of understanding exactly what this might entail given that "different Jews enacted Jewishness differently" (Fredriksen, "Paul 'within Judaism'?," 375), see Cohen, "Those Who Say," 31–35 and Karin Hedner Zetterholm, "The Question of Assumptions: Torah Observance in the First Century" (2015).

[78] "The debate is certainly not a dispute between two religious communities. Rather, the debate revolves around the question of what constitutes being a Jew or belonging to Israel" (Notger Slenczka, "Römer 9–11 und die Frage nach der Identität Israels" [2010], 475). See also the nuanced treatment of ethnicity and ethnic essentialism in Thiessen, "Paul, Essentialism, and the Jewish Law." Thiessen argues that Paul should be understood as an ethnic essentialist who believes the *pneuma* of Israel's messiah literally changes the ethnicity of those (former) gentiles who have received it.

world to come (m. Sanh. 10:1) is immediately followed by exceptions that set the boundaries of the people of Israel.[79] Similarly, the sectarian community behind the Dead Sea Scrolls looked forward to the ultimate redemption of Israel, but that redemption paradoxically included the disgrace and destruction of their opponents, both Jews and non-Jews.

Indeed, if there was one thing all the participants in these debates seem to have agreed upon, it's that being born an Israelite is not sufficient to retain membership in the covenant if one does not live according to the Torah.[80] But various groups disagreed (and still disagree) about what sufficiently constitutes living according to the Torah, and inasmuch as ethnic boundaries are not self-evident, those who might be considered part of Israel in the eyes of one group, sect, or person might be considered out in the eyes of another. Whose interpretation of the Torah should be followed to properly define the boundaries of Israel is always under debate – and again, that is precisely the subject of the debate reflected in the Pauline epistles. It is not enough to say that Paul's Israel is "ethnic" or "empirical." Since the boundaries of Israel have always been contested territory, one must still address how Paul defines ethnic Israel.

THE AGENDA OF THIS WORK

My previous book examined how the concept of "Israel" was constructed and understood by Paul's predecessors and contemporaries.[81] Building on that foundation, this book aims to show how Paul himself engages with and renegotiates the boundaries of Israel in his arguments about Israelite status, salvation, and gentile inclusion. Chapter 1 summarizes important foundational conclusions from other evidence from the Second Temple period and the earliest Jesus movement relevant to what Paul himself would likely have assumed about Israel as an apocalyptic Jew and participant in the early Jesus movement. In the remaining chapters, mostly through a close exegesis and analysis of key sections of 2 Corinthians 3 and Romans 1, 2, 9, 10, and 11 (all chapters interpreters have historically found especially difficult), I argue that Paul's assumptions about Israel are thoroughly rooted in the "restoration eschatology" familiar across much first-century Judaism and the early Jesus movement.

---

[79] See Sanders, *PPJ*, 147–50.
[80] Cf. Cohen, "Those Who Say," 31–35. See also Peter Enns, "Expansions of Scripture" (2001), 98.
[81] Jason A. Staples, *The Idea of Israel in Second Temple Judaism* (2021).

I argue that Paul believes that the eschatological restoration of Israel is already underway in the wake of the death and resurrection of Jesus and that his insistence on equal gentile incorporation is closely tied to his hopes for Israel's restoration. Specifically, since the full restoration of Israel must include all twelve tribes, Paul argues that the incorporation of gentiles into the eschatological assembly is the necessary means for the reconstitution and restoration of "all Israel," an entity not only including Jews but also non-Jewish Israelites restored from the nations among which northern Israel had assimilated. The destinies of both Israel and the nations are therefore interdependent, and the ethical transformation afforded by the spirit of Israel's Messiah paradoxically serves to redeem Israel through the redemption of all nations.

This book therefore demonstrates that Paul's gospel was by no means a rejection of supposed "Jewish ethnocentrism" – or Judaism in general – in favor of a different system.[82] Instead, Paul's emphasis on gentile ingathering was inextricably tied to his concern with Israel's restoration, which he equates with resurrection from the dead. For Paul, the equal incorporation of gentiles was not in tension with Israel's anticipated salvation but rather was the very means by which part of Israel was being restored. As a result, this study shows Paul's thinking to be much more in line with that of other first-century Jews expecting the restoration of Israel than previously appreciated; and although his insistence on the full inclusion of gentiles without conversion to Judaism marked a radical departure from his contemporaries, it is consistent with an eschatological framework evident through a broad swath of Jewish literature throughout the Second Temple period. The Paul revealed in this book is therefore most Jewish precisely where he most seems to depart from Judaism, and his uniqueness is paradoxically a reflection of his continuation within the mainstream of early Jewish eschatology.

EXCURSUS: THE AUDIENCE OF PAUL'S LETTERS

Before continuing any further, a brief word about the audience of Paul's letters is in order. Most interpreters have understood the audiences of Paul's letters as mixed groups of Jews and gentiles, but a small but growing number of scholars has argued that "in the letters we have from

---

[82] Cf. Thiessen, *Paul and the Gentile Problem*, 7.

him, Paul addresses gentiles and only gentiles,"[83] meaning Paul's arguments should therefore be understood as applying solely to gentiles and not to Jews.[84] This conclusion rests on two main premises: (1) Paul's limited sphere of authority as apostle (only) to gentiles and not Jews and (2) the letters themselves (Romans in particular) rhetorically encode the addressees/readers as gentiles and not Jews.

Taking the latter first, the idea that the "encoded explicit reader[s]" in Romans are exclusively gentiles rests largely on Rom 1:5–6,[85] where Paul presents his apostolic call "to bring about the obedience of fidelity in all the nations, among (ἐν) which you also are called of Jesus Messiah." Inasmuch as this falls in the letter's introduction, this would seem a strong case. The problem is that the very next verse – the "adscription" that formally identifies the letter's recipients – explicitly says the letter is addressed "to all who are in Rome, beloved of God, called saints" (1:7).[86] Surely this address should not be taken to mean that Paul imagines that only gentiles are beloved of God! Paul could easily have encoded an exclusively gentile audience by referring to "all *from the gentiles* (ἐξ [τῶν] ἐθνῶν) in Rome, beloved of God" or by leaving out the "all" in the adscription, but he did neither, instead explicitly addressing the letter to *everyone* in Rome who is beloved of God.

Recognizing this larger scope helps explain why Paul later (Rom 11:13) clarifies when he is explicitly addressing gentiles. Although some have argued that "11:13 makes it transparently clear that the letter

---

[83] Fredriksen, *The Pagans' Apostle*, 231 n. 52 (further 86, 131, 231–47). Cf. Rodríguez, *If You Call Yourself a Jew*, 7–8; A. Andrew Das, "The Gentile-Encoded Audience of Romans" (2012); *Solving the Romans Debate* (2007); Stowers, *A Rereading of Romans*, 21–41 (esp. 21–33).

[84] E.g., Thiessen, *Paul and the Gentile Problem*, 120: "Since his mission is to the gentiles, he spends very little time explicating what problem Jews face that requires this gospel of Christ."

[85] The phrase is from Stowers (*A Rereading of Romans*, 21), on whom subsequent arguments about a gentile-only encoded audience for Romans have depended.

[86] This verse is conveniently ignored by Stowers, *A Rereading of Romans* and Das, *Romans Debate*. Thorsteinsson, *Paul's Interlocutor*, 34–39, argues that the "all" of 1:7 is limited by 1:5–6, which "partly establish" the identity of the recipients "prior to the formal address in the adscription," namely "as being among those gentiles whose obedience of faith Paul was assigned to bring about" (38; cf. Runar M. Thorsteinsson, Matthew Thiessen, and Rafael Rodríguez, "Paul's Interlocutor in Romans" [2016], 11). But many Jews as well as gentiles were "among" the nations, and Thorsteinsson does not explain why Paul would use "all" in the formal adscription of 1:7 if it really were limited to gentiles only, especially since such a limitation could be understood to imply that Jews are not in fact "beloved of God."

addresses itself only to gentile believers,"[87] the verse is better understood as narrowing the scope of the immediately following verses to a specific subset of the audience, thereby implying that Jews are presumed to be in the audience.[88] Note that the preceding verses (11:11–12) refer to "gentiles" in the third person; having brought gentiles into the discussion, Paul now explicitly addresses them in 11:13. This reading is further confirmed by the specific content of the message that follows: "But to you gentiles I say:[89] indeed[90] inasmuch as I am an apostle of nations/gentiles, I magnify my ministry, if somehow I may provoke my fleshly kin to

---

[87] Stowers, *A Rereading of Romans*, 288; cf. Rodríguez, *If You Call Yourself a Jew*, 10. To make his case, Stowers asserts that the δέ "does not justify the idea, 'now at this point in the discourse'" but does not provide any evidence that precludes such a meaning, instead merely pointing out that δέ here could be understood as a coordinating particle connecting "three closely related thoughts" (288). But δέ regularly functions as a transitional particle introducing a new point, topic, or other aspect in the context of a larger discussion (Evert van Emde Boas et al., *The Cambridge Grammar of Classical Greek* [2019], 671 §59.16). A shift to address a subset in the audience is well within the range of δέ, and that sense cannot be ruled out in Rom 11:13. Ultimately, no definitive argument can be made based on the particle alone.

[88] See Robert B. Foster, *Renaming Abraham's Children* (2016), 109; cf. Anthony J. Guerra, *Romans and the Apologetic Tradition* (1995), 154; Anthony J. Guerra, "Romans: Paul's Purpose and Audience with Special Attention to Romans 9–11" (1990), 235; Cranfield, *Romans*, 559. Ross Wagner (*Heralds of the Good News* [2003], 268 n. 156) points to Rom 7:1 and 15:1 as examples of similar rhetorical moves in which Paul addresses a subgroup within the larger audience; Rom 2:17 is another.

[89] Most English translations render 11:13a as "I am speaking to you gentiles" (E.g., NRSV, NASB, ESV, NET; NIV: "I am talking"), as though this statement were a stand-alone comment about Paul's audience. But in every other case in the Pauline letters, ὑμῖν λέγω/λέγω ὑμῖν introduces a specific message to a specific group of people and is better rendered, "I say to you ..." (e.g., 1 Cor 6:5; 10:28; 11:22; 15:51; Gal 5:2; Phil 3:18; 1 Thess 4:15). Likewise, in Rom 11:13, ὑμῖν δὲ λέγω marks the beginning of a distinct message delivered to gentiles in the audience, the content of which comes in 11:13b–36. Stowers (*A Rereading of Romans*, 288) recognizes that 11:13a "relates closely to the rest of v. 13 and to v. 14" but fails to recognize that this suggests that 11:13a should not be understood as including the preceding text under the scope of its audience identification but instead as applying to what immediately follows, as in the other Pauline examples.

[90] The Greek particle combination μὲν οὖν here is best understood as an emphatic "pop" particle in which "the speaker vouches for the correctness or relevance of his/her utterance ... and indicates that it is presented in more relevant terms" (Boas, *Cambridge Grammar*, 699 §59.72). See also Rodríguez, *If You Call Yourself a Jew*, 220 n. 10 and Dunn, *Romans*, 555–56. Contra Cranfield, *Romans*, 559; Jewett, *Romans*, 678; and Stowers, *A Rereading of Romans*, 288, the last of whom peculiarly argues that 11:13 occurs "in the context of the paratactic diatribal style in which Paul asks and answers questions" and that μὲν οὖν therefore should be understood as "an adversative or corrective reply to something that has just been said," citing (and misrepresenting) J. D. Denniston, *The Greek Particles* (1954), 475–78. Denniston actually says such a μὲν οὖν can be "adversative or affirmative" (475) rather than just adversative as Stowers suggests.

Excursus: The Audience of Paul's Letters

jealousy and save some of them" (11:13–14). Paul here explains that that his ministry among gentiles is really aimed at the redemption of his "fleshly kin." That is, the apostle explicitly states that even when he *is* directly addressing gentiles, he does so with an eye toward an oblique audience.[91] In this light, even if Romans *were* to encode a solely gentile *direct* audience, Jews would nevertheless be included within the encoded *aspirational* audience – that is, the audience Paul *hopes* to influence.

The closing appeal in Rom 15:7–9 also implies a mixed audience, as Paul exhorts his hearers: "Accept one another, just as Messiah also accepted us for the glory of God. For I say that Messiah has become a servant to the circumcision for (ὑπὲρ) the truth of God to confirm the promises of the fathers, and for the gentiles to glorify God for (ὑπὲρ) his mercy." The parallel of "the circumcision" and "the gentiles" here strongly suggests that the "one another" Paul addresses here includes both Jews and gentiles, who he exhorts to be unified in Messiah in fulfillment of scripture.[92]

The idea that the letter encodes an exclusively gentile audience runs into even greater difficulty at Rom 2:17, where Paul explicitly addresses someone who is "called a Jew." Some have attempted to solve this problem by suggesting that the addressee of 2:17 is a proselyte whose adult circumcision Paul rejects as insufficient to truly become Jewish and is thus only someone who *calls himself* a Jew rather than being a "real" natural-born Jew.[93] The primary problem with this suggestion is that it rests on reading ἐπονομάζῃ as a reflexive ("call yourself") rather than a passive ("you are called"). Although the middle/passive form does allow for a reflexive meaning, a thorough survey of the lexical evidence demonstrates that the middle/passive of ἐπανομάζω is consistently used to denote a "customary passive," whereas the reflexive sense is denoted by the

---

[91] Foster, *Renaming Abraham's Children*, 107–9, observing, "There is [contemporary] precedent for authors writing to one audience with the aim of being overheard by another" (107), citing Polybius and Philo and pointing to modern Evangelical Christian apologetic literature as an analogous example (107 n. 60). See also Guerra, *Romans and the Apologetic Tradition*, 19.

[92] "The mention of 'the circumcision' [opposite "the nations"] in Rom 15:8–9 provides solid evidence that he implicates them into the epistolary conversation" (Foster, *Renaming Abraham's Children*, 109) Pace Stowers, *A Rereading of Romans*, 32–33; Das, *Romans Debate*, 105.

[93] See Thorsteinsson, *Paul's Interlocutor*; Matthew Thiessen, "Paul's Argument against Gentile Circumcision in Romans 2:17–29" (2014); Thiessen, *Paul and the Gentile Problem*; Rodríguez, *If You Call Yourself a Jew*; Garroway, *Paul's Gentile-Jews*. For more discussion, see pp. 150–54 below.

active form with a reflexive pronoun rather than the middle/passive form.⁹⁴ Consequently, it is far more likely that Paul's use of the middle/passive form reflects the customary passive rather than representing a singular example of an author using the middle/passive form of ἐπονομάζω for the reflexive sense.⁹⁵

A second problem is that even if Rom 2:17 did refer to a circumcised convert to Judaism, the presence of such a proselyte in the implied audience would still mean Romans is not addressed exclusively to an audience of gentiles, since, as Rafael Rodríguez concedes, "as a convert, he is now a Jew and no longer a gentile."⁹⁶ Put simply, even if one grants that Paul would not agree that such a person is authentically Jewish, it is unclear why he would imagine or imply that such a self-identified Jew would be present in an otherwise gentile-only gathering.⁹⁷ That Rom 3:9 then explicitly states that these early chapters "already charged that both Jews and Greeks are under sin" only reinforces this point, as 3:9 lacks the "if you are called" qualifier of 2:17, and the idea that by "Jews" Paul means "circumcised non-Jews" is implausible to say the least.

The other foundation of a "gentile-only" reading of Romans and the other Pauline letters is that Paul understood his authority as "apostle of nations/gentiles" (Rom 11:13; cf. 15:16) to be limited to gentiles alone. Andrew Das, for example, argues:

Paul claims that he had been called from the very beginning to preach the gospel to the nations/gentiles (ἔθνη, Gal 1:16). If Paul were called to go to the Jews too, it would be difficult to imagine why he would agree to the limitation of his work to the "gentiles" (ἔθνη), uncircumcised non-Jews, while Peter would go to the circumcised (Gal 2:7, 9). Paul's apostleship is therefore to the "gentile" peoples and

---

⁹⁴ See Lionel J. Windsor, "The Named Jew and the Name of God" (2021), 235–37.
⁹⁵ Windsor, "The Named Jew," 237, observing that "An extensive search yielded no reflexive renderings of ἐπονομάζῃ in Rom 2:17 prior to the twentieth century" (235 n. 30).
⁹⁶ Rodríguez, *If You Call Yourself a Jew*, 50 n. 12. Similarly, Fredriksen ("Apocalyptic Hope," 537) "the Gentile who converts is no longer a Gentile, but a Jew." Rodríguez nevertheless argues that "for our analytical purposes we need to retain a distinction between this proselyte to Judaism and a native-born Jew."
⁹⁷ It is telling that when in Galatians Paul refers to the agreement with the Jerusalem "pillars," he does not say, "we to the nations and they to the Jews" but rather "we to the nations and they to the circumcised," (2:9). A circumcised proselyte would be included in the latter group. As such, it is exceedingly unlikely that the address of Rom 2:17 is limited to circumcised proselytes on the basis that Paul would have identified them as gentiles and within his sphere of authority; there is no evidence that Paul viewed some of "the circumcised" under his sphere of influence but not others.

not to the "nations" as a geographical entity with no discrimination between Jew or gentile.[98]

Paul does say that he was specifically "entrusted with the gospel of the foreskin" (Gal 2:7) and testifies to an agreement with the Jerusalem pillars: "we [Barnabas and Paul] to the foreskinned and they [James, Cephas, and John] to the circumcised." Das takes these statements as evidence that Paul carefully restricted his ministry and authority to non-Jews alone and that Paul wrote to his Roman audience because they fell "within the sphere of Paul's apostolic authority because they too are gentiles."[99]

But the idea that Paul understood his authority as limited to gentiles while Jews fell under the authority of the Jerusalem pillars presumes precisely the sort of intra-*ekklēsia* division Paul categorically rejects at Corinth, where he objects to the idea that some follow him while others follow Cephas/Peter (1 Cor 1:11–13). There he explains that the gospel "*we* preach" is "a stumbling block (σκάνδαλον; cf. Rom 9:33; 11:9) to Jews and foolishness to gentiles, but to those called, both Jews and Greeks (cf. Rom 9:24), Messiah the power of God and the wisdom of God" – directly stating that he preaches not only to gentiles but to Jews. Paul's claim to have "five times received from Jews thirty-nine lashes" (2 Cor 11:24) – a specifically intra-Jewish punishment – is another strong indicator that he did not limit his efforts to gentiles and did in fact frequent synagogues as indicated by Acts.[100] Paul even explicitly asserts that in his proclamation of the gospel, he has made himself "a slave to all," including efforts directed toward Jews "so that I might gain Jews," acting as though under Torah "so that I might gain those who are under Torah" (1 Cor 9:19–20).[101]

---

[98] Das, *Romans Debate*, 65.
[99] Das, *Romans Debate*, 55; see also the discussions in A. Andrew Das, *Paul and the Jews* (2003), 63–69 and Thorsteinsson, *Paul's Interlocutor*, 87–122.
[100] E.g., Acts 9:20; 13:5; 13:14; 13:43; 14:1; 17:1, 10, 17; 18:4, 19; 19:8. Fredriksen, *The Pagans' Apostle*, 165: "clearly he witnessed to Jews as well as to gentiles—at the very least, the disciplinary lashings he received presuppose synagogue settings" (further 82–83, 218 n. 48). See also Sanders, *PLJP*, 186–92; Martin D. Goodman, "The Persecution of Paul by Diaspora Jews" (2005). Contra Markus Oehler, "The Punishment of Thirty-Nine Lashes (2 Corinthians 11:24) and the Place of Paul in Judaism" (2021).
[101] Paul's statement that he "became like one under Torah" (1 Cor 9:20) suggests that he understood himself as having remained Torah-observant in a traditional fashion. See Paula Fredriksen, "Why Should a 'Law-Free' Mission Mean a 'Law-Free' Apostle?" (2015); Mark D. Nanos, "The Myth of the 'Law-Free' Paul Standing between Christians

In this light, although Paul agreed to go "to the foreskinned,"[102] he seems not to regard this as limiting the scope of his apostolic authority or the reach of his gospel solely to non-Jews. Indeed, contrary to Das' statement quoted above, Paul does not say in Gal 1:16 that he was called to preach "*to* the nations/gentiles" but "*in/among* (ἐν) the nations," the same phrase often similarly misrendered in Rom 1:5.[103] This is an important distinction, as such a call would not exclude Jews or Samaritans living among (ἐν) the nations. The "gentile-only" reading also requires that ἔθνη be understood as specifically referring to "gentiles" rather than "nations," such that when Paul identifies himself as "apostle of ἔθνη" (Rom 11:13) or refers to his ministry "among the ἔθνη" (Gal 1:16; cf. Rom 1:5), he is identifying himself as an apostle exclusively to non-Jews, who are obviously not gentiles. But in much the same way that Jeremiah's call to be a "prophet to the nations" (προφήτην εἰς ἔθνη; Jer 1:5) included a significant prophetic career in Judah, Paul seems to construe "Jews" as one subgroup among the nations and therefore as falling under his ministry purview as well.[104]

It should also be recalled that Romans is not a missionary treatise in which Paul is trying to persuade outsiders to become followers of Jesus or to come under his authority as their patron apostle. It is instead a letter to insiders who have already received the gospel as preached by others. In this context, rather than asserting his authority over his Roman audience, Paul delicately explains that he has "written boldly in part as a reminder" (Rom 15:15) and explains his practice of preaching where others have not yet gone, which is why he has not yet visited Rome, to which the gospel had previously spread (15:20–22). He writes the letter not to bring them under his authority as "apostle of gentiles" but in the hopes of their support, "as I go to Spain, for I hope to see you in passing and to be sent there by you, if first I may be in part satisfied by you" (15:24; cf. 1:11–15). In addition to clarifying what he is preaching among the nations, the letter therefore serves as his gift sent in advance to them in the hopes of material return on his arrival, establishing a relationship of mutual encouragement and reciprocity (1:11–12). Even if it were true that Paul preached solely to gentiles, such a framing by no means requires an exclusively gentile

---

and Jews" (2009). Whether Paul's contemporaries and opponents agreed with his assessment is another matter altogether.

[102] Gal 2:9; cf. Acts 13:46–47 (Isa 42:6 LXX); 18:6; 22:21.

[103] E.g., Thorsteinsson refers to "Paul's introductory account of his mission to 'all the gentiles'" in Rom 1:5 (*Paul's Interlocutor*, 87).

[104] E.g., Rom 11:13–14; 1 Cor 9:20–22. See Theodor Zahn, *Der Brief des Paulus an die Römer* (1910), 47.

audience for Romans – indeed, Paul would surely have found it even more advantageous to receive support from Jews in addition to gentiles.

The reference to Paul's mission "among (ἐν) all the nations" (Rom 1:5; cf. Gal 1:16) should therefore be understood as denoting *place* or *position*,[105] including both gentiles and Jews in the diaspora – a reading that has the strength of numerous prophetic passages proclaiming the scattering of Israel and Judah "among (ἐν) the nations" and then restoration from that situation.[106] Ultimately, as will become clearer through the remainder of this book, Romans cannot be regarded as exclusively applicable to a gentile audience. Instead, Paul's argument applies to "all the nations" (1:5) – Israel included.[107] Paul's proclamation of good news "in all the nations" (1:5) should therefore be understood exactly as he frames it: "to the Jew first and then to the Greek" (1:16; 2:9–10), not solely to the Greek.

One final question regarding Paul's audience pertains to his expectations of their capacity to follow his often sophisticated, subtle, and highly condensed arguments and to recognize the scriptural backgrounds to which he appeals.[108] Here it is important to remember that the Pauline letters were not merely personal letters to be read once and then discarded. They were instead sent to communities with the expectation that they would stimulate extended discussion and meditation, and all but Romans were sent to communities Paul himself had founded, where he could assume that some in the audience knew the foundational elements of his teaching.[109] They were also hand-delivered by Paul's own coworkers, who could answer questions and clarify specific points.[110] Paul did not merely slip Romans into a postbox – he sent it with Phoebe.[111]

---

[105] See Cranfield, *Romans*, 67–68.   [106] E.g., Jer 9:15; Ezek 12:15; 36:20–23; Hos 8:8.
[107] For the universal scope of Paul's rhetoric in Rom 1:5 and 1:16, see Stephen L. Young, "Romans 1.1–5 and Paul's Christological Use of Hab. 2.4 in Rom. 1.17" (2012), 281.
[108] The actual capabilities of Paul's audience (as opposed to his perception of such) are of less relevance for this study, which is focused on the letters themselves rather than their reception. For why this distinction is important, see Christopher D. Stanley, *Arguing with Scripture* (2004), 38–61; "Paul's 'Use' of Scripture" (2008).
[109] Wagner, *Heralds of the Good News*, 39: "The Corinthian assembly discussed Paul's 'prior letter' at some length; when they could not agree on the meaning of Paul's instructions or desired further clarification of some things he had said, they sent him a letter of their own (1 Cor 7:1; cf. 5:9–11)."
[110] On the letter-carrier as supplementary interpreter, see Peter M Head, "Named Letter-Carriers among the Oxyrhynchus Papyri" (2009), 288–89; Wagner, *Heralds of the Good News*, 28; Richard F. Ward, "Pauline Voice and Presence as Strategic Communication" (1994).
[111] On Phoebe's role and importance, see Allan Chapple, "Getting *Romans* to the Right Romans: Phoebe and the Delivery of Paul's Letter" (2011); Alan H. Cadwallader, "Paul

One would expect such a letter to be carefully crafted to reward deeper inquiry and discussion, including subtle allusions and references for the more knowledgeable readers – the letter-carrying readers in particular – to bring out through close examination and discussion. Nevertheless, Paul did have a reputation for overshooting the capabilities of his readers, as attested by 2 Pet 3:15–16, and it is difficult to disagree with Robert Foster's conclusion that "Paul writes ... out of his own expertise and not on the basis of his readers' competency."[112] That being the case, one must be careful not to limit the potential meaning of any passage to what one might reasonably expect an audience to have comprehended on first exposure to a given letter.[113] Finally, the sophistication of second-generation works like Luke–Acts and 1 Clement is evidence of at least some readers surely capable of handling Paul's rhetoric and use of scripture.

EXCURSUS: TRANSLATING KEY TERMINOLOGY

Writing about Paul inevitably brings up the difficult matter of translation, as many key Pauline terms and phrases express ideas not easily rendered in English. Moreover, even trained biblical scholars typically knew these texts in translation long before learning Greek and consequently tend to see specific Greek words as equivalents of their traditional English glosses even as they look at the Greek texts. But those familiar English terms often have nebulous, imprecise, and often flatly wrong definitions based on later theological paradigms that are often unknowingly read back into Pauline texts. Familiarity and reverence therefore often produce a sort of sacred stupor, a deafness to the words themselves in which it becomes difficult to bridge the gap between modern conceptions and the meaning of those words in their original context.[114]

Speaks Like a Girl: When Phoebe Reads Romans" (2015). Note, however, that Phoebe need not have been the lector despite her likely explanatory role (see Head, "Letter-Carriers," 297–98).

[112] Foster, *Renaming Abraham's Children*, 25.
[113] See the arguments to this effect made by Foster, *Renaming Abraham's Children*, 22–25; Wagner, *Heralds of the Good News*, 36–39; Brian J. Abasciano, "Diamonds in the Rough" (2007).
[114] Aldous Huxley, *The Perennial Philosophy* (1947), 4: "Familiarity with traditionally hallowed writings tends to breed, not indeed contempt, but something which, for practical purposes, is almost as bad – namely a kind of reverential insensibility, a stupor of the spirit, an inward deafness to the meaning of the sacred words."

I have therefore chosen to render many important terms and phrases with different language both to express the concepts with greater precision and to jolt readers out of comfortable and frequently false familiarity. Since I expect that many readers of this book will not have facility in Greek and/or Hebrew, I have also chosen to transliterate a few frequently used key terms to emphasize their importance without obscuring them with inadequate English glosses. To help orient readers to specific decisions I have made on especially important terms, the following discussion provides a guide to which the reader may easily return whenever it might be helpful.

(1) "Messiah": I will default to rendering the Greek word Χριστός (*Christos*) as "messiah" rather than "Christ" because most modern readers treat "Christ" as simply a synonym (or surname) for "Jesus." For Paul, however, this word is an honorific title derived from Jewish eschatology designating the "anointed one," the rightful heir to the throne of David and king of the eschatologically renewed and restored Israel.[115] Recognizing this especially impacts the interpretation of Romans 10, as will be discussed in Chapter 6. "Messiah" also has the additional benefit of emphasizing the fundamental *Jewishness* of Paul's perspective and arguments as represented in his letters, reminding the reader that Paul was an apocalyptic Jew proclaiming Israel's messiah. The more we remember this – and the more it forces us to grapple with our distance from Paul, whose foreignness is too often insufficiently appreciated by modern readers – the better. That said, when discussing previous scholarship in which "Christ" is used in ways that tacitly presume its identification with Jesus, I will use that terminology and then shift back to "messiah" terminology when putting forward my own case. "Messiah" will be capitalized when it appears without the article and when it serves as a shorthand way of referring to Jesus by title (e.g., "Jesus Messiah"), but more general references to "the messiah" that do not refer explicitly to Jesus of Nazareth will be left in lowercase.

(2) "Fidelity" and "Trust": I will also default to translating the Greek word πίστις (*pistis*) as "fidelity" rather than "faith" and the verbal form πιστεύω (*pisteuō*) as "trust" rather than "believe" or "have faith." Each

---

[115] On "Christ" as a title akin to "Caesar" rather than a name, see Matthew V. Novenson, *Christ among the Messiahs* (2012), esp. 64–178; "The Jewish Messiahs, the Pauline Christ, and the Gentile Question" (2009). See also Joshua W. Jipp, *Christ Is King* (2015), esp. 1–11, 139–210; Adela Yarbro Collins and John J. Collins, *King and Messiah as Son of God* (2008), esp. 122.

of these options better approximates the relational nuances of Paul's language than the more traditional English "faith" and "believe," which over time have come to be read as little more than cognitive assent by modern English readers. That "fidelity" derives from the Latin *fides*, a chief virtue familiar to Paul's Roman audience is an additional benefit, as it nods to layers of nuance likely implicit in Paul's use of *pist-* language as he attempts to represent covenantally based Jewish concepts for a Greek-speaking audience in the Roman Empire.[116]

(3) Justice language is central throughout Romans, and many passages involve wordplay using multiple forms of the *dik-* stem (e.g., δικαιόω, δίκαιος, δικαίωμα, δικαιοσύνη, ἄδικος) that is difficult or impossible to reproduce in English translations, which tend to render the verb with "justify" and the nouns with cognates of "righteous."[117] Others have tried to rectify this problem in various ways, perhaps most notably E. P. Sanders' neologism "to righteous" as a verbal form in place of the traditional "to justify."[118] I have chosen to go the opposite direction, as I suspect modern English readers are more likely to interpret "righteous" as a term of religious piety rather than ethics, while I am persuaded that Paul's *dik-* language is rooted in ethical and relational/covenantal contexts better represented by the English concept of "justice," which involves doing what is right and performing one's social, relational, or customary obligations.[119] The Yiddish word "mensch" also gets fairly close to the idea of a δίκαιος person as used by Paul, and I must confess to being tempted to translate Paul's *dik-* language with cognates of mensch, resulting in "menschify," "menschification," and "menschness." But since these would be just as foreign to most English readers as the

---

[116] On πίστις and πιστεύω, see Teresa Morgan, *Roman Faith and Christian Faith* (2015); Matthew W. Bates, *Salvation by Allegiance Alone* (2017); Nijay K. Gupta, *Paul and the Language of Faith* (2020); Douglas A. Campbell, *The Quest for Paul's Gospel* (2005), 178–207; and Paula Fredriksen, "Judaizing the Nations" (2010), 235 n. 7.

[117] For more on the state of the debate with respect to these terms, see Michael F. Bird, *The Saving Righteousness of God* (2007).

[118] Sanders, *PLJP*, 13–14 n. 18, 46, 63 n. 140.

[119] In a Jewish context, those obligations are defined in the covenant, meaning such terms carry covenantal resonance, and justice necessarily involves fidelity to the covenant. See Richard B. Hays, "Justification" (1992), 1130–32; Mark A. Seifrid, "Righteousness Language in the Hebrew Scriptures and Early Judaism" (2001); N. T. Wright, *Paul and the Faithfulness of God* (2013), 795–815; Charles Lee Irons, *The Righteousness of God* (2015), 56–60. For a discussion of δικαιοσύνη (*dikaiosunē*) as the Greek word widely associated with the second tablet of the Torah and the command to love neighbor, see Fredriksen, "The Question of Worship" (2015), 188–91.

Greek terms themselves, I have resigned myself to using cognates of "justice" for words deriving from the *dik-* root in Greek.

I will therefore default to "justness" or "justice" rather than "righteousness" for the term δικαιοσύνη (*dikaiosunē*) and "just" for the noun δίκαιος (*dikaios*), though at times I will use the word pair "righteous/just." For the verb δικαιόω (*dikaioō*), I will default to "justify," which is like the Greek word in that it can represent being "made just," "declared just," or "vindicated." The neuter noun δικαίωμα (*dikaiōma*), a word meaning "just things" or "things of justice" deserves special attention since this word frequently appears in the Septuagint as a way of referring to the "statutes" or "ordinances" given to Israel by God, specifically the requirements of justice. Because of its specialized use and the distinctive way Paul uses this term to refer to the Torah's love command(s), my translations of this term will be contextually driven, though I will call attention to where this specific term underlies my translation in those places.

(4) "Sacred," "sanctity," and "sanctification": Paul's language of "holiness" or "sanctity" is another source of confusion for English readers, largely because much modern Christian theological discourse – even among trained biblical scholars – often treats sanctification (and the related terminology of "holiness") as a concept primarily in the moral or ethical domain, as though it referred to becoming obedient to God.[120] But the *hagi-* family of words (usually translated with English terms like "holiness" or "sanctity/sanctification") denotes a *cultic* rather than a *moral* category in the Greek Bible. Paul's ἁγιασμός (*hagiasmos*) and ἁγιάζω (*hagiazō*) are not about becoming better moral actors but are instead about separation from common domains and peoples and integration into the people and presence of God. As such, I will translate these concepts with "sacred" language (e.g., "consecrate," "consecration," "sanctity") that better represents a cultic, sacral domain closer to Paul's conception and more distant from the transfer of this language into moral

---

[120] This is largely the result of a shift in how "justification" (Paul's *dik-* language) came to be understood by many Protestants: "Until the sixteenth century, the western theological tradition understood justification primarily as a 'making righteous' through the impartation of an inherent righteousness to a believer. Although some early Protestant writers retain this understanding of 'justification,' Protestantism as a whole coalesced around the notion of justification as a forensic or judicial event in which the believer is 'reckoned as righteous' or 'accounted righteous,' tending to conceptualize the process of becoming righteous as 'regeneration' or 'sanctification.'" (Alister E. McGrath, *Iustitia Dei: A History of the Christian Doctrine of Justification* [2020], 8).

spheres in modern Christian theology (e.g., notions of "progressive sanctification").[121] This will likely be most jarring to readers in rendering πνεῦμα ἅγιος, typically translated "holy spirit," as "sacred spirit."[122]

(5) *Ekklēsia* (Greek ἐκκλησία): This word is typically translated "church" in most versions of the New Testament, misleadingly implying a specialized meaning distinct to Christian gatherings. But this word is widely used outside Christian contexts to mean "assembly," and in the Septuagint (LXX; the Greek translation of the Tanakh/Hebrew Bible),[123] it is the most common translation of the Hebrew קהל (*qāhāl*), referring to the assembled people of Israel.[124] In that context, membership in the "assembly of YHWH" (e.g., Deut 23:4, 9 [ET 3, 8]) amounts to something akin to citizenship within Israel.[125] I will therefore leave *ekklēsia* untranslated as a reminder that for Paul this term refers not to a separate "gentile church" but rather to elect eschatological Israel united by the *pneuma* of Israel's messiah and participating in the promised new covenant.

(6) *Pneuma/pneumatic* (Greek πνεῦμα/πνευματικός): These Greek words mean "wind," "breath," or "spirit" and are typically translated with the latter in the New Testament. Unlike the modern conception of "spirit," which tends to represent something disembodied and distinct from materiality, Paul's concept is something closer to "breath" – more akin to the older English meaning of "spirit" still evident in cognates such as

---

[121] On the modern Christian theological use of "sanctification" and "holiness" language and its distance from the ancient concepts from which that language derives, see Don J. Payne, *Already Sanctified* (2020).

[122] Here I agree with Isaac W. Oliver, "Torah Praxis After 70 CE" (2012), 360–62.

[123] In keeping with scholarly convention, I use "LXX" or "Septuagint" in a broad sense to refer not only to the Greek Torah but to the Old Greek Bible more generally. Unless otherwise marked, I will follow the text of Alfred Rahlfs, ed., *Septuaginta* (2006).

[124] See especially Jennifer Eyl, "Semantic Voids, New Testament Translation, and Anachronism: The Case of Paul's Use of *Ekklēsia*" (2014), who persuasively demonstrates that Paul's use of *ekklēsia* derives primarily from the Septuagint's translation of the Hebrew קהל. See also Ralph J. Korner, *The Origin and Meaning of Ekklēsia in the Early Jesus Movement* (2017); Young-Ho Park, *Paul's Ekklesia as a Civic Assembly* (2015); Boris Repschinski, "Ekklesia als Kultgemeinde oder Volksversammlung?" (2015); Paul Trebilco, "Why Did the Early Christians Call Themselves ἡ ἐκκλησία?" (2011); George H. Van Kooten, "'Ἐκκλησία τοῦ θεοῦ'" (2012).

[125] See Jeffrey H. Tigay, *Deuteronomy* (1996), 477–80, who notes that the question of entering "the assembly of YHWH" is connected in the text to questions about legitimate marriage and highlights evidence that many later interpreters construed the prohibitions against the inclusion of four nations in Deut 23 "as standing for all foreigners" (479). To enter "the assembly of YHWH" meant being received as a legitimate Israelite. See also Duane L. Christensen, *Deuteronomy 21:10–34:12* (2002), 537–38.

"respiration."[126] Although I will default to the more familiar translation of "spirit/spiritual" for these words, I will also employ transliterations to remind the reader of this distinction.

(7) "Gentiles," "nations," "pagans," and *ethnē*: The Greek word ἔθνος (plural ἔθνη) and Hebrew גוי (*goy*) typically refers to "nations" or what might today be called "ethnic" groups of people. But the plural (particularly the articular plural τὰ ἔθνη) often represents "the nations" other than Israel, the idea usually rendered in English as "the gentiles," and the singular can represent either an individual or a nation as a whole. Thus *ethnē* often denotes non-Israelite or non-Jewish individuals but can also mean the nations in a collective sense. In keeping with established scholarly discourse, this study will translate these terms with both "nation(s)" and "gentile(s)" depending on context and will occasionally use "pagan(s)" or transliteration.[127]

(8) "*Telos*": The Greek word τέλος is notoriously difficult to render in English, as it can represent the "end," "goal," or "culmination" of something, with the various senses sometimes simultaneously coexisting together. I have frequently transliterated this term to avoid narrowing its scope and reducing ambiguity.

(9) YHWH: the transliterated name of Israel's God when working from Hebrew or Aramaic texts.

(10) "Torah": When translating νόμος, I have preferred "Torah" rather than "law," since νόμος is the default Greek translation of the Hebrew word "Torah."

The result is sure to be jarring to some readers familiar with more traditional renderings of Paul's concepts. My hope is that such defamiliarization of these passages leads to more accurate and precise understanding, with the fresh tang of foreignness displacing the familiarity that can so easily obscure one's ignorance of the concepts in play.

---

[126] See the discussion in Thiessen, *Paul and the Gentile Problem*, 105–28 and the sources cited there.

[127] For a fuller discussion of ἔθνος and Paul's use of it, see James M. Scott, *Paul and the Nations* (1995), 57–134. For a comprehensive look at the development of the concept of "gentile" as a blanket category for individuals outside the covenantal people of God, see Adi Ophir and Ishay Rosen-Zvi, *Goy* (2018) and "Paul and the Invention of the Gentiles" (2015), though I am unpersuaded by their thesis that Paul himself was responsible for the final development of the category as denoting "non-Jews," partly because I agree with the conclusion of Arland J. Hultgren, *Paul's Gospel and Mission* (1985), 125–37, that Paul "did not think in terms of individual 'gentiles' so much as 'nations,' planting the church among the nations of the world known to him" (133).

JEWS OR JUDAEANS?

Readers will also have noticed that I have used the English term "Jews" rather than "Judaeans" or other options when referring to the ancient people group represented by the Greek term Ἰουδαῖος (*Ioudaios*). This choice runs counter to a recent scholarly trend to eschew the term "Jew" when referring to antiquity,[128] primarily on the grounds that the term "Judaean" better represents the "ethnic" ancient people without the anachronistic implications of the modern category of religion allegedly implied by the word "Jew."[129] But since ethnicity and religion were not distinct from one another in antiquity, the category of "ethnicity" is no less modern than the category of religion.[130] Consequently, any attempt to differentiate between these categories with respect to the Greek term *Ioudaios* and its ancient cognates by using separate terms for the "ethnic" or "religious" concepts is even more anachronistic than simply employing "Jew."

As such, I agree with Cynthia Baker's conclusion that "as a stand-in for 'ethnic group,' its [Judaean's] ability to clarify is matched only by its potential for obfuscation and misrepresentation."[131] It should also not be ignored that ancient *Ioudaioi* were distinctive as an *ethnos* in large part due to elements of culture that would be categorized as "religious" today.[132] The fact that proselytes to Judaism were also classified as

---

[128] This movement has been growing in influence; the new Brill translations of Josephus edited by Steve Mason, for example, consistently translate *Ioudaios* with "Judaean." On the other hand, Marc Zvi Brettler has suggested employing the word "Jew" when discussing the pre-exilic period, despite acknowledging the anachronism inherent to such use ("Judaism in the Hebrew Bible?" [1999]).

[129] E.g., Gary N. Knoppers, *Jews and Samaritans* (2013), 15; Steve Mason, "Jews, Judaeans, Judaizing, Judaism" (2007); Philip F. Esler, *Conflict and Identity in Romans* (2003), 68; BDAG, s.v. "Ἰουδαῖος," 478; John H. Elliot, "Jesus the Israelite Was Neither a 'Jew' Nor a 'Christian'" (2007).

[130] Michael L. Satlow, "Jew or Judaean?" (2014), 165–76; Miller, "Ethnicity, Religion," 239–40.

[131] Cynthia M. Baker, "A 'Jew' by Any Other Name" (2011), 178.

[132] Recall the judgment of Dio Cassius that being a *Ioudaios* amounts to following specific customs (37.17.1; see pp. 15–16 above). Other Roman authors regard *superstitio* to be the distinctive characteristic of the *Ioudaioi* (e.g., Cicero, *Pro Flacco* 28.67; Quintilian, *Ins. Or.* 3.7.21; Tacitus, *Hist.* 5.4.1, 5.7.2, 13.1). On ancient Jewish ethnicity as distinctly characterized by "religious" cultural forms, see Daniel Boyarin, "The IOUDAIOI in John and the Prehistory of Judaism" (2002), 221; Schwartz, "How Many Judaisms"; Daniel R. Schwartz, "Judeans, Jews, and Their Neighbors" (2013); Cohen, "Those Who Say," 32; Lawrence M. Wills, "Jew, Judean, Judaism in the Ancient Period" (2016), 175–76; Yuval Shahar, "Imperial Religious Unification Policy and Its Decisive Consequences" (2011), 110.

Ioudaioi (though some other *Ioudaioi* regarded their status as dubious) should also not be forgotten.[133] The Idumaeans, for example, became Jews after their territory was annexed by John Hyrcanus in the late second century BCE.[134] And whereas the term "Judaean" artificially and anachronistically limits the meaning of *Ioudaios* to a more geographical sense, which becomes especially problematic when describing the many *Ioudaioi* living in other regions (such as Galilee) throughout this period,[135] an ancient speaker or hearer had no simple way of conveying modern distinctions between the various ethnic, regional, cultural, or religious senses of *Ioudaios* when using that term.[136] Any efforts to distinguish between ancient "Jews" and "Judaeans" is thus doomed from the start, as the two English terms render the same word, making any such distinction untenable.

Fortunately, English does have an ambiguous term that applies to a comparable range of meanings as *Ioudaios*: the term "Jew," which applies with equal accuracy to members of the Chief Rabbinate in Israel and to "atheist, secularist, post-Zionist Jews of globalized postmodernity."[137] As such, the English word "Jew" is an ethnic term as much as it is a religious one,[138] and any attempt to limit its meaning to the latter ultimately derives from Christian polemical categorizations.[139]

---

[133] For the argument that some *Ioudaioi* did not regard proselytes as becoming Jewish, see Thiessen, *Contesting Conversion*.

[134] The fact that the Idumaean status remained a point of contention for many Jews, particularly as pertained to Herod the Great and his descendants, strengthens the case that some Jews were skeptical of or outright rejected such conversions. Cohen explains, "The Idumeans became [Jews], except that they also remained Idumeans" (*Beginnings of Jewishness*, 18). Foreigners being integrated into Judah or Israel was by no means a late development, however, as can be observed by the mention of the "mixed multitude" of the exodus (Exod 12:38), the prohibitions against the entrance of some (but not all) outsiders into the "assembly of YHWH" (Deut 23:3-8 [ET 4-9]), the numerous foreigners among David's inner circle (cf. 2 Sam 23:24-39), and the political marriages of the monarchs. But criticism of such integration of outsiders seems to have increased after the exile and is especially evident in Ezra-Nehemiah.

[135] Daniel R. Schwartz, "'Judaean' or 'Jew'" (2007), 3-6.

[136] John Ashton, "The Identity and Function of 'The Ἰουδαῖοι' in the Fourth Gospel" (1985), 55; cf. Wills, "Jew, Judean, Judaism," 171; Annette Yoshiko Reed, "*Ioudaios* Before and After 'Religion'" (2014).

[137] Baker, "A 'Jew' by Any Other Name," 174. The term does not, however, apply to O. J. Simpson, as observed by Adam Sandler, "The Chanukah Song" (1994).

[138] Schwartz, "'Judaean' or 'Jew,'" 8; Paula Fredriksen, "God Is Jewish, but Gentiles Don't Have to Be" (2019), 3. Cf. also Reed, "*Ioudaios*."

[139] Baker, "A 'Jew' by Any Other Name," 177.

Although many who have pushed for the "Judaean" rendering have done so in large part as an attempt to rescue ancient texts and modern readers from anti-Judaism in a post-Holocaust world,[140] Amy-Jill Levine has rightly pointed out that those good intentions produce a "*Judenrein* ('Jew free') text, a text purified of Jews," distancing Jesus, Paul, and other New Testament figures from Jews and Judaism.[141] I therefore find "Judaean" more problematic than "Jew" as a translation for *Ioudaios* in that it translates a richly polyvalent Greek word with a much more limited English word, leading to a loss of nuance and inevitably to misunderstanding. Where possible, ambiguity is best rendered with analogous ambiguity, so despite the potential problems inherent in using such a familiar modern term for an ancient one, "Jew" (or "Jewish person," given the adjectival form of *Ioudaios*) should be preferred over "Judaean" – though, as will be noted in Chapter 1, a more defensible case could be made for "Judahite" if an alternative for "Jew" is preferred. As such, I will default to "Jew" when translating *Ioudaios/Yehudi*, though I will also transliterate the relevant ancient terms where that seems more appropriate.

---

[140] For example, Sonya S. Cronin (*Raymond Brown, "The Jews," and the Gospel of John* (2015), 23–38, 154–86) has persuasively demonstrated how theological concerns influenced the work of Raymond Brown in this area.

[141] Amy-Jill Levine, *The Misunderstood Jew* (2006), 160, 165. The work of Bruce Malina has unfortunately validated Levine's concerns, arguing against the use of the term "Jew" in antiquity on the grounds of the Khazar theory, which claims that most modern-day Jews are biologically unrelated to ancient *Ioudaioi*. Malina consequently argues that the terms "Israel" and "Judaean" should be used of the first-century people, with the latter restricted to those geographically situated in Judaea (Bruce J. Malina and Richard L. Rohrbaugh, *Social-science Commentary on the Gospel of John* [1998], 44). The Khazar theory has been repeatedly discredited by genetic studies of various Jewish populations, and any scholarly model based on it is not only to be rejected but repudiated. See Gil Atzmon et al., "Abraham's Children in the Genome Era" (2010); Robert Myles and James G. Crossley, "Biblical Scholarship, Jews and Israel" (2012); James G. Crossley, "What a Difference a Translation Makes!" (2014).

I

The God of Jews Only?

> For the mistake happens in the beginning and the beginning is said to be half of the whole, so that even a minor mistake at the beginning is equal to those made at different stages.
>
> Aristotle, Politics 5, 1303b

> Empirical "Israel" may not have been simply identical to the "*Ioudaioi*" for some of the New Testament writers.
>
> Martina Böhm[1]

From Marduk in Babylon to Athena in Athens, ancient deities were characteristically regional, ethnic, and familial, serving as the patrons or matrons of their "families" – that is, specific people groups – who were expected to demonstrate loyal deference and respect to their gods through specific prescribed customs. In this respect, Paul's God was, as Paula Fredriksen observes, "much like his pagan colleagues,"[2] as illustrated by Paul's own characterization of God as "father" and those who have received the spirit as "children of God" (Rom 8:17). The God Paul proclaimed, Fredriksen explains,

> had his own people, Israel, with whom he shared a particular bond of love, and of whom he made specific ritual and ethical demands. He presented himself to them as their "father," and they were his "sons," as were, in a special way, the kings of David's line. ... According to Genesis 2:2–3, this god had observed that most Jewish of practices, the Sabbath; according to *Jubilees* 2:17–20, he observed it weekly, in the company of two orders of circumcised angels. This god might be "the god of the nations also" ... but he was first of all, and emphatically, "the god

---

[1] Martina Böhm, "Wer gehörte in hellenistisch-römischer Zeit zu 'Israel'?" (2012), 201–2.
[2] Paula Fredriksen, "God Is Jewish, but Gentiles Don't Have to Be" (2019), 5.

of the Jews" (Rom 3:29). In short, and like his people, according to these ancient criteria of ethnicity, God too was "Jewish."³

Ordinarily, inasmuch as ancient deities were ethnic and familial, incorporation into the family of a specific deity would involve an essentially ethnic conversion, as the individual in question becomes incorporated into the people group of that deity. Paul, however, distinctively argues for the integration of non-Jews within the family of his God without their becoming Jews, leading Fredriksen to conclude that for Paul, "God is Jewish, but Gentiles don't have to be."⁴ Although this pithy formulation rightly calls attention to the oft-ignored ethnic qualities of the God Paul preached, it does have one significant problem: YHWH is never actually *called* "Jewish" in extant ancient literature. Romans 3:29 provides the closest example, but even that passage does not declare that God is Jewish but rather asks a question implying a negative conclusion: "Is God [the God] of Jews only? Is he not also the God of gentiles/nations?" Aside from this single verse, phrases like "God of (the) Jews" or "Jewish God" are strikingly absent across early Jewish literature. Instead, another formulation is consistently preferred: YHWH is the "God of Israel."⁵

At first, this may seem like a pedantic distinction. After all, one might easily presume that "God of Israel" is simply an alternative way of saying "Jewish God." But a careful examination of the sources throughout the Second Temple period shows that these terms were not in fact treated as synonymous in this era, and understanding the distinction between them is critical to understanding Paul's presentation of his gospel – particularly his arguments about Jews, gentiles, and Israel.

---

³ Fredriksen, "God Is Jewish," 5; cf. Fredriksen, "How Jewish Is God? Divine Ethnicity in Paul's Theology" (2018); *The Pagans' Apostle* (2017), 115; N. T. Wright, "Paul and Empire" (2011), 287.
⁴ Fredriksen, "God Is Jewish," 3.
⁵ Observed by Saul Kaatz, *Die mündliche Lehre und ihr Dogma* (1923), 43. Cf. Solomon Zeitlin, "The Names Hebrew, Jew and Israel" (1953), 366–67; K. G. Kuhn, "Ἰσραήλ, Ἰουδαῖος, Ἑβραῖος in Jewish Literature after the OT," *TDNT* 3:360; James Richard Linville, *Israel in the Book of Kings* (1998), 28. The words τὸν θεὸν τῶν Ἰουδαίων do appear consecutively in Josephus, *Ant.* 18.286, but τῶν Ἰουδαίων does not modify θεὸν but is the object of the next word προμηθούμενον, which takes the genitive: "seeing that God provided for the Jews." The earliest example of "God of the Jews" is found in the late second-century CE apocryphal letter of Pilate to Claudius found in the *Acts of Peter and Paul* 19:3, in which "Pilate" says Jesus "came as the God of the Jews while I was governor over Judaea."

AN EXPERIMENT IN CRITICISM: BEYOND THE INSIDER/ OUTSIDER PARADIGM

It is a presumption nearly universally acknowledged that in Paul's day "Israel" meant "the Jews" and that "Jews" and "Israelites" were merely alternative appellations for the same group of people. Throughout scholarly literature, one frequently encounters casual assertions to this effect, such as, "'Israelites' is what Jews were called in earlier centuries,"[6] or "By Paul's day, 'Jew' had become a common designation of anyone who belonged to the people of Israel,"[7] or "my *presupposition* ... is straightforward: When Paul says 'Israel,' he means 'Jews.'"[8] Even detailed studies of the two terms have not questioned this assumption, instead treating it as foundational.[9] Countless scholars regularly alternate between these terms for stylistic reasons. But if the terms were truly interchangeable, one would expect them to be evenly distributed across the Pauline letters and other early Jewish sources. This is far from the case, however. Paul, for example, uses "Israel" and cognates thirteen times in Romans 9–11 but only six times in the rest of the seven undisputed letters.[10] *Ioudaios* and its cognates, on the other hand, appear twenty-nine times broadly scattered across the seven letters but only twice in 9–11.[11] This terminological shift – with over 70 percent of Paul's use of "Israel" terminology concentrated to three chapters – is by no means random and surely signals something

---

[6] John M. G. Barclay, "Ἰουδαῖος: Ethnicity and Translation" (2018), 55.
[7] Douglas J. Moo, *Romans* (1996), 159. Similarly, Carl R. Holladay, "Paul and His Predecessors in the Diaspora" (2003), 453: Paul "doubtless, although not explicitly, identifies [Israel] with the Jews of his own time." Cf. also Michael Bachmann, "Verus Israel" (2002), 510; Wilhelm Vischer, "Das Geheimnis Israels" (1950), 86.
[8] Paula Fredriksen, "'Circumcision Is Nothing': A Non-Reformation Reading of the Letters of Paul" (2022), 79, emphasis original. Cf. Fredriksen, "What Does It Mean to See Paul 'within Judaism'?" (2022), 376; Matthew V. Novenson, "*Ioudaios*, Pharisee, Zealot" (2022), 170.
[9] For example, Peter Tomson, "The Names Israel and Jew in Ancient Judaism and in the New Testament" (1986), 120, opens by referring to the two terms as "alternative appelations." Similarly, Graham Harvey states, "[*Hebraios*] was already an accepted gentilic synonymous with Ἰσραήλ or Ἰουδαῖος" (*The True Israel: Uses of the Names Jew, Hebrew, and Israel in Ancient Jewish and Early Christian Literature* [1996], 117, cf. 40), and Jennifer Eyl suggests that "Israelite" is coextensive with *Ioudaios* but with the nuance of "the revered air of the primordial past," meaning "a really, *really* ancient Judean" ("'I Myself Am an Israelite': Paul, Authenticity and Authority" [2017], 157, 154–55).
[10] "Israel" occurs once more in the disputed letters (Eph 2:12) and in the majority text of Rom 10:1.
[11] *Ioudaios* also occurs once in the disputed letters (Col 3:11).

important, especially given that similar patterns also emerge in Josephus, Philo, and other early Jewish literature.[12]

The most common explanation is that Paul shifts to "Israel" language to use the "insider" or "honorary" name preferred by Jews themselves in the chapters that explain how the gospel pertains to the Jews.[13] That is, as he turns to speak of his own people, he does so as an insider, employing "the honorary name 'Israelites.'"[14] This explanation derives from Karl Kuhn's 1938 *Theologische Wörtbuch zum Neuen Testament* article, in which Kuhn proposes that "Israel" is an "insider" term preferred by the people themselves while "Jew" is an "outsider" term, sometimes carrying a "derogatory or even contemptuous sense."[15] But this alleged derogatory nuance of "Jew" – for which Kuhn himself does not list an example but instead asserts as an established fact – is entirely unattested in pre-Christian antiquity.[16] This nuance was, however, unfortunately common in prewar Germany when Kuhn wrote his article, where *Jude* was frequently pejorative, while those wanting to be respectful preferred *Israelite*, the word associated with the biblical chosen people. German Jews understandably preferred the latter term, and German Jewish communities typically called themselves the *israelitische Gemeinde* (Israelite community) of a given area.[17]

Kuhn himself was clearly impacted by this environment, as he joined the Nazi party in 1932 and showed his enthusiasm for the cause by giving his lectures on Judaism at Tübingen while wearing a paramilitary Storm Detachment (*Sturmabteilung*) uniform complete with *Ehrendolch* (honorary dagger) with inscription of Nazi comradeship.[18] Kuhn was also one of fifteen members appointed to the Forschungsabteilung Judenfrage (Research

---

[12] For a detailed discussion, see Jason A. Staples, *The Idea of Israel in Second Temple Judaism* (2021).

[13] E.g., J. D. G. Dunn, *Romans* (1988), 526.

[14] Ulrich Wilckens, *Der Brief an der Römer* (1980), 187–88. Cf. (among many others) Joshua D. Garroway, "Ioudaios" (2017), 524; Robert Jewett, *Romans* (2006), 561–63; Otto Michel, *Der Brief an die Römer* (1978), 295; Tomson, "The Names Israel and Jew," 288; John H. Elliot, "Jesus the Israelite Was Neither a 'Jew' nor a 'Christian'" (2007), 144; Ulrich Luz, *Das Geschichtsverständnis des Paulus* (1968), 26–27, 269–70.

[15] K. G. Kuhn, "Ἰσραήλ, Ἰουδαῖος, Ἑβραῖος in Jewish Literature after the OT," *TDNT*, 3:360–68 (quote 368).

[16] As pointed out by Shaye Cohen, *Beginnings of Jewishness* (1999), 71 n. 5. Kuhn does anticipate this objection, protesting, "But it is plainly attested already in Jewish lit" (Kuhn, *TDNT* 3:368 n. 72), citing no examples.

[17] Daniel R. Schwartz, "'Judaean' or 'Jew'" (2007), 19–20; Maurice Casey, "Some Anti-Semitic Assumptions in the 'Theological Dictionary of the New Testament'" (1999), 283.

[18] M. A. Beek, review of *Achtzehngebet und Vaterunser und der Reim*, by Karl Georg Kuhn (1950), 21–22. The *Ehrendolch* with inscription was received due to Kuhn being one of the first thousand members of the *Sturmabteilung* (SA).

Department for the Jewish Problem) established by the Nazis in 1936, published multiple anti-Semitic works on *Weltjudentum* (World Judaism) and the so-called *Judenfrage* (Jewish Problem),[19] and delivered public addresses on these subjects.[20] Given this context, it is difficult to read Kuhn's statements about "the depreciatory element that clings so easily to [*Ioudaios*]" as anything but an indication of the assumptions Kuhn brought to the evidence due to the context in which he formulated his model.[21] Put bluntly, Kuhn's insider/outsider paradigm superimposes the anti-Semitic idiom of Nazi Germany upon the ancient evidence, resting on the assumption that the term *Ioudaios* shared the derogatory nuance *Jude* did in prewar Germany and therefore functioned as an "outsider" term as opposed to the more respectful "Israelite," providing a signal example of how modern ideologies can dramatically impact interpretation of the past.[22]

This insider/outsider paradigm has now been assumed by multiple generations of scholarship, with some scholars even ironically having marshaled it in the fight against anti-Jewish readings.[23] But again, the problem is that Kuhn's paradigm depends on an assumption entirely unsupported by the data; there is simply no evidence that *Ioudaios* ever carried a derogatory nuance in antiquity or that it was an outsider term while "Israel" was the preferred, "honorary" name for the same people. Instead, the evidence strongly indicates that the reason "Israelite" and "Jew" are used differently throughout the literature of the Second Temple period is that these terms were not synonymous or coextensive in the Second Temple period, nor can they justifiably be treated as such in Paul's letters.

TWO NATIONS UNDER GOD: THE OTHER ISRAELITES

The biggest obstacle to treating "Israel" as merely an alternative term for "the Jews" in this period is the fact that the Jews were not the only

---

[19] E.g., Karl Georg Kuhn, "Die Entstehung des talmudischen Denkens" (1937); "Weltjudentum in der Antike" (1937); "Ursprung und Wesen der talmudischen Einstellung zum Nichtjuden" (1938); *Die Judenfrage als weltgeschichtliches Problem* (1939); "Der Talmud, das Gesetzbuch der Juden: Einfuhrende Bemerkungen" (1941).

[20] For more on Kuhn's anti-Semitism and scholarly tendencies, see Staples, *The Idea of Israel*, 29–39.

[21] Contra Tomson, "The Names Israel and Jew," 121; David Goodblatt, "The Israelites Who Reside in Judah" (2009), 86–89; Beek, review of *Achtzehngebet und Vaterunser und der Reim*, by Kuhn, 22; J. S. Vos, "Antijudaismus/Antisemitismus im Theologischen Wörterbuch zum Neuen Testament" (1984), 94.

[22] See Casey, "Anti-Semitic Assumptions," 285–86.

[23] E.g., Elliot, "Jesus the Israelite"; Tomson, "The Names Israel and Jew."

Yahwistic ethnic group claiming the Israelite label in the Second Temple period.[24] Instead, there was a competing "Israel," the people best known as Samaritans, who preferred to call themselves *Shamerim* ("guardians" of the Torah) or simply "Israelites."[25] These claimants to Israelite status and heritage were decidedly not Jews, a fact most clearly illustrated by a famous passage in the Gospel of John, which informs the reader, "Jews [*Ioudaioi*] do not have common dealings with Samaritans" (4:9),[26] a statement that would be incoherent if Samaritans were considered Jews or a subset of *Ioudaioi*. Indeed, unlike the Idumaeans, who became *Ioudaioi* (though still, as Shaye Cohen notes, remaining Idumaeans) after the annexation of their territory under the Hasmoneans,[27] the Samaritans were never so identified.[28] Moreover, Lester Grabbe observes that, surprisingly,

> in the external references to peoples and kingdoms of Palestine, there is no evidence that "Israel" ever refers to Judah or the Judahites; rather "Judah," "Jews," and similar designations are always used, at least until the Christian era. The only group referred to as "Israelite" in Greco-Roman sources in the pre-Christian period is the Samaritan community associated with Mt Gerizim.[29]

Nevertheless, until recently, most modern scholars have treated the Samaritans not as a distinct people but rather as a sect of Judaism,[30]

---

[24] "The Jews were not the only strictly monotheistic, Torah-observant, and cultically active Yahwists in Palestine and the Diaspora. There was at the same time, both in the motherland of Palestine and in the diaspora, another large Torah-observant part of the population; and in the political-sociological sense, at least in Samaria, there is also an *ethnos* that likewise internally understood itself as 'Israel'" (Böhm, "Wer gehörte," 183).

[25] See Gary N. Knoppers, *Jews and Samaritans*, 15–16.

[26] Although a few early witnesses (most notably ℵ* D it) lack this explanation, it is unlikely to have been a secondary addition, and in any case the rest of the passage presumes the distinction. David Daube, "Jesus and the Samaritan Woman: The Meaning of συγχράομαι" (1950), 139–43; and Richard J. Coggins, *Samaritans and Jews* (1975), 139, render συγχράομαι "use together," meaning Jews and Samaritans do not share common vessels.

[27] Cf. *Ant.* 13.254, 257–58. See n. 134 on p. 35.

[28] See Cohen, *Beginnings of Jewishness*, 18.

[29] Lester L. Grabbe, "Israel's Historical Reality after the Exile" (1999), 13. Similarly, Zeitlin observes: "We never find the term Israel denoting the people of Judaea, in the entire tannaitic literature of the time of the Second Commonwealth. The term Israel was used only in contrast to the priests and Levites" ("Hebrew, Jew and Israel," 369).

[30] This view goes at least as far back as James Alan Montgomery, *The Samaritans, the Earliest Jewish Sect* (1907). Other important studies treating the Samaritans as a Jewish sect include Frank Moore Cross, "Samaria and Jerusalem in the Era of Restoration" (2000), 175; Stefan Schorch, "The Construction of Samari(t)an Identity from the Inside and from the Outside" (2013); Shaye J. D. Cohen, *From the Maccabees to the Mishnah* (1987); Lester L. Grabbe, *The Roman Period* (1992); Uriel Rappaport, "Reflections on the Origins of the Samaritans" (1999); Shemaryahu Talmon, "The Emergence of Jewish Sectarianism in the

largely due to the habit of treating Yahwism as equivalent to Judaism, an assumption itself owing to widespread scholarly acceptance of Jewish polemics dismissing Samaritan claims to distinct Israelite heritage.[31] More careful recent scholarship has called such treatment of the Samaritans into question,[32] and once it is recognized that the Samaritans were not Jews but instead called themselves – and were called by others – Israelites, the assumption of these terms' equivalence is no longer tenable. Certainly, many Jews rejected Samaritan claims of Israelite status, but that does not negate the fact that the Samaritans could not be ignored in the Second Temple period. The Samaritans therefore provide an important parallel to Paul's "former gentiles," another group that is neither Jewish nor gentile but something else.[33]

THE GREAT DIVORCE: ISRAEL AND JUDAH

The reason the Samaritans identified themselves as Israelites but not Jews is that they claimed descent from the northern Israelite tribes of Ephraim and Manasseh rather than from Judah.[34] Here we are reminded that in

---

Early Second Temple Period" (1987); Martina Böhm, *Samarien und die Samaritai bei Lukas* (1999), 63–64, 84; Alan D. Crown, "Another Look at Samaritan Origins" (1995); "Redating the Schism between the Judaeans and the Samaritans" (1991).

[31] See especially Böhm, "Wer gehörte," 181; Ingrid Hjelm, "What Do Samaritans and Jews Have in Common?" (2004), 25 (cf. also 46).

[32] Most notably Matthew Chalmers, "Representations of Samaritans in Late Antique Jewish and Christian Texts" (2019); "Rethinking Luke 10: The Parable of the Good Samaritan Israelite" (2020); Chalmers, review of *Judah and Samaria*, by Gary N. Knoppers (2021); Böhm, "Wer gehörte"; Ingrid Hjelm, "Changing Paradigms" (2005). For a survey of recent trends in Samaritan studies, see Matthew Chalmers, "Samaritans, Biblical Studies, and Ancient Judaism: Recent Trends" (2021).

[33] Knoppers, *Jews and Samaritans*, 220–21. Similarly, even after the Second Temple period, "most [Tannaitic] passages concerning the Samaritans mention non-Jews and *kutim* as separate categories" (Lawrence H. Schiffman, "The Samaritans in Tannaitic Halakhah" [1985], 325–26); it is not until sometime between the mid-second and fourth centuries that rabbinic materials more clearly distinguish Samaritans from Israelites and class them with foreigners or *goyim*. See also Adi Ophir and Ishay Rosen-Zvi, *Goy*, 185–92; Yuval Shahar, "Imperial Religious Unification Policy" (2011); Rocco Bernasconi, "Tannaitic 'Israel' and the Kutim" (2008); Yitzhak Magen, *The Samaritans and the Good Samaritan* (2008); Pieter W. van der Horst, "Anti-Samaritan Propaganda in Early Judaism" (2003); Yehudah Elitsur, "Samaritans in Tannaitic Texts" (2000); Reinhard Pummer, "Samaritanism in Caesarea Maritima" (2000).

[34] This claim by the Samaritans represents significant counterevidence to Michael Satlow's assertion that by the first century CE, tribal identity was "long defunct" (*How the Bible Became Holy* (2014), 301 n. 7).

the biblical narratives of the pre-exilic past, when the united kingdom of Israel ruled by David and Solomon splits into two, it is the northern kingdom that retains the moniker "Israel," while the southern kingdom based in Jerusalem is called Judah.[35] By the end of the Former Prophets, "Israel" is no longer in the picture, with Judah alone in view after the dissolution of the northern kingdom after a series of Assyrian invasions and deportations in the eighth century BCE.[36]

Remarkably, the kingdom of Judah nevertheless identified its patron deity as the "God of Israel," which Michael Stahl observes was "an act of religious appropriation that asserts, at least in ideal terms, a fundamental social-political and religious unity between Israel and Judah."[37] And yet it is striking that, although the political interests of the Hebrew Bible's primary authors and editors ... lay with Judah, not Israel,"[38] neither Kings nor Chronicles applies the name "Israel" to the southern kingdom or the Judahite exiles even after the Assyrian and Babylonian deportations.[39] This distinction is especially visible in the summary statements after the fall of Samaria:

> YHWH warned Israel and Judah ... but they did not listen and stiffened their neck like their ancestors, who did not trust in YHWH their God .... And they went after the empty things and became empty[40] – after the nations that surrounded them, which YHWH had commanded them not to do ....
>
> So YHWH was very angry with Israel, and he removed them from his sight. No one was left except the tribe of Judah. Judah also did not keep the commands of YHWH their God but followed the practices introduced by Israel. When he had torn Israel from the house of David, they made Jeroboam the son of Nebat king. Then Jeroboam drove Israel away from following YHWH and caused them to sin greatly. And the children of Israel walked in all the sins that Jeroboam committed and did not desist from them until YHWH removed them from his sight, just as he had spoken through all his servants the prophets. So Israel went into exile from their own land to Assyria to this day. (2 Kgs 17:13–15, 18–23)

Remarkably, the Assyrian invasions and deportations of Israel to which this passage refers are routinely ignored by scholars of Early Judaism and the New Testament, who typically begin any discussion of

---

[35] Gary N. Knoppers, "Did Jacob Become Judah?" (2011), 45.
[36] See Ingrid Hjelm, *Jerusalem's Rise to Sovereignty* (2004), 30–92, 117–18.
[37] Michael J. Stahl, *The "God of Israel" in History and Tradition* (2021), 2.
[38] Stahl, *The "God of Israel,"* 2. [39] Knoppers, "Did Jacob Become Judah," 45.
[40] LXX ἐματαιώθησαν, echoed in Rom 1:21 as the consequence for those who "despite knowing God refused to honor him as God or give thanks" (see pp. 124–25 below). MT: "went after the nothing (ההבל) and became nothing (ויהבלו)."

exile with the Babylonian Exile,[41] often mislabeled as the exile of Israel or "Israel's Babylonian captivity."[42] The result is that Israel and Judah and their respective exiles are regularly conflated, as though Israel as a nation had persisted until the fall of Jerusalem to the Babylonians.[43] The biblical authors, however, distinguished between the fall and captivity of *Israel* and that of *Judah* over a century later, long after Israel had ceased to exist as a nation.

GREAT EXPECTATIONS: THE RESTORATION OF ISRAEL AND JUDAH

The Hebrew prophets, however, declared that both Israel and Judah would ultimately be restored and focus on the fate of the northern Israelites to a surprising degree, though this fact has largely been ignored or overlooked due to the presumption that after the Babylonian exile the meaning of Israel narrowed to the remnant of Judah. But there is no evidence of such a shift within the prophetic corpus; instead, as Knoppers observes:

Jeremiah, Ezekiel, Zechariah, and other books hardly speak with one voice, but they assume the survival of Israelites and Judahites in a variety of territories and

---

[41] E.g., "The exile in Babylon had only been the first stage of a much longer process of God's people being enslaved to pagans" (N. T. Wright, *Paul and the Faithfulness of God*, 114). Timo Eskola, *A Narrative Theology of the New Testament* (2015), 16 begins his "short survey on Israel's exile" with the "Babylonian exile." The conflation is even assumed in the title of Rainer Albertz, *Israel in Exile: The History and Literature of the Sixth Century B.C.E.* (2003). See the critiques of Hjelm, "Changing Paradigms"; Brant Pitre, *Jesus, the Tribulation, and the End of the Exile* (2005), 31–40; Robert P. Carroll, "Exile! What Exile? Deportation and the Discourses of Diaspora" (1998), 69–79; Philip R. Davies, "Exile? What Exile? Whose Exile?" (1998), 132–38.

[42] E.g., John K. Goodrich, "Sold under Sin: Echoes of Exile in Romans 7.14-25" (2013), 477, 495; Richard N. Longenecker, *Romans* (2016), 505; Richard E. Averbeck, "Christian Interpretations of Isaiah 53" (2012), 53; G. K. Beale, *The Book of Revelation* (1999), 565. Similarly, Steven M. Bryan, "The Reception of Jeremiah's Prediction of a Seventy-Year Exile" (2018), 108, refers to "Jeremiah's prediction that Israel [sic] would serve the king of Babylon for seventy years (Jer 25:11–12)," but that prophecy is not about "Israel" but rather "all the people of Judah" (Jer 25:1). Bryan is therefore correct to point out that later readers understood Jeremiah's prophecy as having been fulfilled in the past, but this prophecy about the Babylonian captivity of *Judah* is irrelevant to the question of whether *Israel*'s exile was ongoing.

[43] E.g., "With the fall of Jerusalem to the Babylonians, the old 12-tribe association came to its effective end" (Stephen Westerholm, "Whence 'The Torah' of Second Temple Judaism" [1991], 31); "The political situation in Israel was unstable and quite soon after the death of Josiah (609), Syria and Palestine came under Babylonian rule" (Eskola, *A Narrative Theology*, 17).

prophesy their reconfiguration in some new political form within their ancestral land. But such prophetic passages are wishfully directed to the future; they do not refer in a past historical sense to something that has already occurred. According to the prophets, the deported northern groups never returned to the land of Israel.[44]

Nevertheless, the hope for a new era of YHWH's favor and Israel's obedience, the time when all Israel would return and be reunified, remains undiminished in the biblical prophetic books.[45] The situation in the Second Temple period, however, fell far short of the prophetic expectations of Israel's redemption. In particular, David Greenwood has called the numerous predictions regarding a restored northern kingdom "perhaps the most conspicuous example in the Tanak of patently false prophecy."[46] Consequently, as Jonathan Goldstein explains:

> Despite the joyous proclamations of the postexilic prophets, despite the return of many exiles to the Promised Land, despite the completion of the Second Temple, it was clear to believing [Jews] that they were still living in the "Age of [God's] Wrath."[47]

Nevertheless, as is often the case with unfulfilled prophecy, the long delay did not quench the hope of fulfillment.[48] Instead, as circumstances continually fell far short of prophetic expectations, those unfulfilled prophecies of restoration remained a source of hope to those still expecting their eventual fulfillment, shaping the perspectives of Jews

---

[44] Knoppers, *Jews and Samaritans*, 6.
[45] Stahl (*The "God of Israel,"* 372) argues that even "the use of the appellation 'God of Israel' to define the identity of the biblical deity – an identification that has persisted in religious and scholarly communities until the present day – must ultimately be seen as a post-biblical interpretive development, the roots of which can be traced back to the work of particular biblical authors and editors who sought, in their various ways, to define 'Israel' as the one people of God." That is, this emphasis on the whole people of Israel including but not limited to Judah is coded into the very description of the deity within these texts.
[46] David C. Greenwood, "On the Jewish Hope for a Restored Northern Kingdom" (1976), 384.
[47] Jonathan A. Goldstein, "How the Authors of 1 and 2 Maccabees Treated the 'Messianic' Promises" (1988), 70, citing CD 1:5.
[48] Cf. Leon Festinger, Henry W. Riecken, and Stanley Schachter, *When Prophecy Fails* (1956); Festinger, *A Theory of Cognitive Dissonance* (1962); Robert P. Carroll, "Ancient Israelite Prophecy and Dissonance Theory" (1977); J. Gordon Melton, "Spiritualization and Reaffirmation" (1985); Lorne L. Dawson, "When Prophecy Fails and Faith Persists" (1999); Chris Bader, "When Prophecy Passes Unnoticed" (1999); Simon Dein, "What Really Happens When Prophecy Fails: The Case of Lubavitch" (2001); Mathew N. Schmalz, "When Festinger Fails: Prophecy and the Watch Tower" (2011).

living both in the land and in the diaspora.⁴⁹ First-century Jews who looked to the prophets and the biblical narratives as their own authoritative history were therein consistently confronted with reminders of the present incompleteness of Israel and simultaneously instilled with hopes of a future restoration when YHWH would re-choose, reunify, and regather the people of Israel from the nations among which they had been scattered.⁵⁰ Nathan Thiel summarizes the situation as follows:

> That Jewish authors continued to have an active interest in an idealized Israel patterned after the biblical precedent should not surprise us.... The prevalence of "Israel" in prayer, liturgy, and more generally within texts like 1 Maccabees and in the early rabbinic corpus is influenced by speech situation but also by consciousness of the biblical narrative. Convergence between "Israel" and "Jews" as identity markers may have been taking place, but it was not yet complete.... For authors looking back to a golden age and looking forward to national restoration in the age to come, "Israel" expressed an idealized self-identity of which they were a part but not the only part.⁵¹

This distinction between northern Israel and southern Judah – maintained and even emphasized throughout the biblical tradition – is ultimately the source of the terminological distinctions between "Israelite" and "Jew" that continue to be made throughout the Second Temple period. The earliest extant examples of "Jew" (*Yehudi*) are found in later biblical texts and refer specifically to people from the kingdom of Judah,⁵² whereas "Israelite" in these sources typically represents those from the northern tribes – that is, those not from Judah. As such, "Israel" by

---

⁴⁹ See, e.g., Goldstein, "'Messianic' Promises," 69–70; Robert P. Carroll, "Deportation and Diasporic Discourses in the Prophetic Literature" (1997), 64. Cf. also Jon D. Levenson, *Resurrection and the Restoration of Israel* (2006). In contrast, Floyd, "Was Prophetic Hope Born of Disappointment" (2006), argues that such a view too closely resembles the early Christian *adversos Judaeos* interpretations of the prophets. Cf. also A. Thomas Kraabel, "Unity and Diversity among Diaspora Synagogues" (1992), 30; Robin Cohen, *Global Diasporas* (2008), 24–25; Jules Isaac, *The Teaching of Contempt* (1964). Although it is true that the exile/covenantal curse narratives were (and sadly still are) used in later anti-Jewish polemics, the interpretation that Israel remained under the covenantal curses with the restoration prophecies remaining unfulfilled is not a Christian innovation but was rather the dominant Jewish interpretation before the Common Era – one then easily leveraged by Christians for anti-Jewish purposes.

⁵⁰ Eskola, *A Narrative Theology*, 19–20. Cf. the continued preeminence of restoration eschatology in the Targumim, for example, as discussed in Bruce D. Chilton, "Messianic Redemption" (2011).

⁵¹ Nathan Thiel, "'Israel' and 'Jew' as Markers of Jewish Identity in Antiquity: The Problems of Insider/Outsider Classification" (2014), 99.

⁵² Jer 32:12; 34:9; 38:19; 40:11–12, 15; 41:3; 43:9; 44:1; 52:28, 30; 2 Kgs 16:6; 25:25; 1 Chr 4:18.

definition includes non-Jews. After the Babylonian deportations, "Jew" (*Yehudi/Ioudaios*) became the default term used to refer to Judahites, whether in the land or in the diaspora, and the returnees from Babylon established not a renewed Israel but rather a Persian province of *Yehud* (Judah) populated by *Yehudi* (Jews/Judahites).[53] Consequently, Thiel explains, the term "'Jews' could not replace 'Israel' because it was too narrow to carry the same meaning."[54] Whereas "Israel" could refer to any of its subsets by synecdoche, early Jewish literature consistently (and somewhat surprisingly) continues to represent Jews/Judah as only one – albeit the leading – part of the larger category of Israel.

WILL THE REAL ISRAELITES PLEASE COME BACK?

This background explains how the Samaritans could claim to be Israelites but not Jews: inasmuch as they claimed descent from northern stock, they were not "Judahites." For many Jews, however, Samaritan claims of Israelite status were illegitimate, as they regarded Samaritans as descended from the ethnic groups resettled in Israelite territory by the Assyrians in the eighth and early seventh centuries BCE according to 2 Kings 17:24–41. Such a view, for example, is evident in Ezra, when the "enemies of Judah and Benjamin" (note: not "enemies of Israel"), who are later identified as chiefly from Samaria (4:10),[55] initially offer to aid the returnees in building the temple (4:1–2) but are rebuffed by the Jewish elders who reject them as outsiders (4:3). Nevertheless, although Samaritan claims of Israelite status were rejected by many Jews, this did not imply that only Jews were Israelites but rather that the other *real* Israelites (the scattered northern tribes) remained in exile until the restoration and reunification with Judah promised by the prophets.

An especially clear example of this perspective can be seen in 4Q372 1, a fragmentary text found among the Dead Sea Scrolls.[56] This brief fragment laments the "fools" (=Samaritans) living in Joseph's land who provoke the

---

[53] For this as a surprising fact requiring explanation, see Goodblatt, "Israelites who Reside in Judah," 84–86; *Elements of Ancient Jewish Nationalism* (2006), 136–37; "Varieties of Identity in Late Second Temple Judah (200 B.C.E.–135 C.E.)" (2011), 17–18; "From Judeans to Israel: Names of Jewish States in Antiquity" (1998).

[54] Thiel, "'Israel' and 'Jew,'" 96.   [55] Cf. Josephus, *Ant.* 11.84–115.

[56] This fragment is generally regarded as pre-sectarian and dated to around the third century BCE, though it is by no means certain that it is pre-sectarian, particularly given its use of *yaḥad* (twice). For more on provenance and dating, see Eileen M. Schuller, "4Q372 1: A Text about Joseph" (1991), 371–76; Michael A. Knibb, "A Note on 4Q372 and

traditional southern tribes of "Judah, Levi, and Benjamin" to jealousy and anger (4Q372 1 10–11, 14), thereby fulfilling the role of the "foolish nation" of the Song of Moses (Deut 32:21), while the real Joseph and his brothers have been "given into the hands of foreigners devouring his strength and breaking all his bones until the time of the end" (4Q372 1 14–15). The fragment looks forward to the day when Joseph and his brothers will return and offer sacrifices and praise, when God will also "destroy [the foreigners] from the whole world" (22). Matthew Thiessen explains:

> The Samaritans function as a reminder to the southern tribes (Levi, Judah, and Benjamin) that, while they might be tempted to conclude that the exile is over, Israel (Joseph) still endures God's punishment. Restoration has not been achieved: Joseph is still in foreign lands .... While they remain in exile, full restoration is yet to come, even for those currently in the land. Through such means, the author attempts to convince his readers that the southern tribes' fate remains bound to the fate of the northern tribes.[57]

For Israel to be complete, Joseph and his brothers must return to their rightful land, joining "Judah, Benjamin, and Levi" at the restoration, accompanied by judgment on the "fools" and other nations. The fates of northern Israel and southern Judah (=the Jews) are therefore inextricably linked, as each awaits final restoration and reunification.[58]

Similarly, the War Scroll looks forward to an eschatological battle fought by all "twelve tribes of Israel" (1QM 3:14; 5:1–2), with the three southern tribes finally united with the eschatologically restored northern tribes, "the return of the exiles (*golat*) of the sons of light from "the wilderness of the peoples" (1:1–3). Remarkably, the Romans (Kittim) are identified with the *Assyrians* in this text, further highlighting that the current conditions are seen as continuous with the period of exile initiated by the Assyrian deportations of Israel. Despite living in the land, the Yaḥad sectarians consider Israel's exile as ongoing (e.g., 4QMMT^C 12b–14; CD 1:5–12) and present themselves as the righteous portion of the tribes of Levi, Judah, and Benjamin having departed to the wilderness to rejoin the rest of Israel in exile to await the coming eschatological restoration, which will include the destruction of the unjust nations and the wicked among Israel and Judah.[59]

4Q390" (1992), 166–70; Florentino García Martínez, "Nuevos textos no biblicos procedentes de Qumrán" (1991), 124–25.

[57] Matthew Thiessen, "4Q372 1 and the Continuation of Joseph's Exile" (2008), 395.

[58] Thiessen, "Joseph's Exile," 395.

[59] See Staples, *The Idea of Israel*, 259–89. Cf. Martin G. Abegg, "Exile and the Dead Sea Scrolls" (1997), 125; Noah Hacham, "Exile and Self-Identity in the Qumran Sect and in Hellenistic Judaism" (2010).

Josephus not only rejects Samaritan claims of Israelite heritage, calling them "Cutheans," a name derived from one of the groups mentioned in 2 Kings 17:24, and emphasizing that they are neither Jews nor legitimate heirs of Israel (*Ant.* 9.288–91; 11.340–47), he also consistently differentiates between the terms "Israelite" and "Jew" across his works. The distinction is striking: the terms "Israel" and "Israelite" appear 188 times in the first 11 books of the *Antiquities* but nowhere else in the Josephan corpus.[60] *Ioudaios*, on the other hand, appears approximately 1,188 times across Josephus' works but only 26 times in the first ten books of the *Antiquities* – the books in which he uses "Israel" (see Table 1.1).[61]

Table 1.1 *Jews and Israelites in Josephus*

	Israel/Israelite	Per 1,000	*Ioudaios*	Per 1,000
Ant. 1–10	174	1.12	27	0.17
11	14	1.02	90	6.55
12–20	0	0	530	3.85
War	0	0	468	3.73
Life	0	0	24	1.52
Ag. Ap.	0	0	51	2.48

Josephus explains that this transition from "Israelites" to "Jews" is not haphazard but occurs due to an important historical transition at a specific point in his narrative. While narrating the events of Ezra, he makes it clear that only a small portion of Israel returned to the land:

> when these Jews (*Ioudaioi*) learned of the king's piety towards God, and his kindness towards Ezra, they loved [him] most dearly, and many took up their possessions and went to Babylon, desiring to go down to Jerusalem. But all the people of Israel remained in that land. So it came about that only two tribes came to Asia and Europe and are subject to the Romans, but the ten tribes are beyond the Euphrates until now and are a countless multitude whose number is impossible to know. (*Ant.* 11.132–33)

Here Josephus clarifies that only two (southern) tribes, which he labels "Jews" (*Ioudaioi*), returned, while the remaining ten tribes of *Israel* did not return and remain beyond the Euphrates, outside Roman territory. In case the reader misses this distinction, Josephus explicitly calls attention to the shift in terminology a few paragraphs later:

---

[60] Of these, "Israel" occurs only twice, in the first and fourth books.
[61] This section summarizes Staples, *The Idea of Israel*, 43–53, 210–232.

From the time they went up from Babylon they were called by this name [*Ioudaios*] after the tribe of Judah. Since the tribe was the prominent one to come from those parts, both the people themselves and the country have taken their name from it.[62] (*Ant.* 11.173)

Josephus explains that he will henceforth use the term *Ioudaios* rather than Israelite or Hebrew because the narrative from this point forward will focus on a specific *subset* of Israel – specifically, the subset identified with the dominant southern tribe of Judah. The scope of his narrative narrows at this point from Israel as a whole to those derived from the southern kingdom of Judah, who are properly referred to as Jews (*Ioudaioi*), while "Israelites" includes the rest of Israel (i.e., the northern part), who Josephus has already stated did not return from exile, again drawing a distinction between the Jews and the rest of Israel.

Josephus therefore explains that although Jews are Israelites and Samaritans are (in his view) illegitimate impostors, Jews are not the *only* Israelites, and some Israelites cannot rightly be called Jews. Instead, "Jew" (*Ioudaios*) refers specifically to a person descended from the southern kingdom of Judah or otherwise incorporated into that ethno-religious group (e.g., proselytes or those incorporated by marriage). In its broader sense, the term includes not only those from the tribe of Judah but also Levites and Benjaminites, since persons from these tribes were included among the returnees from the southern kingdom of Judah to the Persian province of *Yehud* after the Babylonian exile and are thus among those now "subject to the Romans" (*Ant.* 11.133).

Consequently, when all twelve tribes are in play, Josephus prefers the more comprehensive term, "Israel," and during the divided kingdom Josephus uses it only for the northern tribes.[63] But once the northern tribes are off the stage in the so-called postexilic period, he avoids it entirely in favor of more precise terminology limited to those from the kingdom of Judah, the subset of Israel with which he identifies himself. Thus, rather than treating these terms as

---

[62] Contrary to Malcolm Lowe, "Who were the ΙΟΥΔΑΙΟΙ" (1976), 106, which reads "Judah was the first tribe to return from exile," and Ralph Marcus' Loeb translation (*Jewish Antiquities, Volume VI* [1937], 399), "the first to come to those parts," πρῶτος is best taken in the sense of "most important" here rather than "first" in a temporal sense. Neither the biblical accounts nor Josephus' account suggest that the tribe of Judah preceded the other tribes in returning to the land; rather, it was the dominant, prominent tribe of those that returned. Cf. Stephen C. Carlson, "Luke 2:2 and the Census" (2004).

[63] See Paul Spilsbury, *The Image of the Jew in Flavius Josephus' Paraphrase of the Bible* (1998), 40.

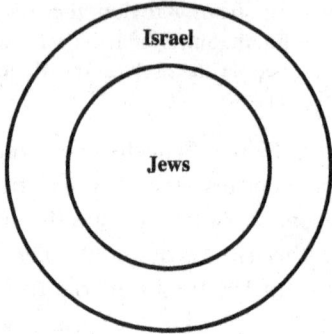

Figure 1.1 Jews as part of Israel

synonymous, Josephus carries forward the biblical distinction between these terms and explains that they have a *partitive* relationship, with Jews a subset of the larger category of Israel (see Figure 1.1).

This explanation of the distinction between "Israelite" and "Jew" accounts for the full pattern of Josephus' use of these terms as, even the few instances where the terms do appear to be interchangeable, the equivalence only works in one direction.[64] That is, before the divided kingdom (i.e., when the full people are in view), Josephus can be more flexible with his terminology, especially where he wishes to emphasize the connection between ancient Israel and contemporary *Ioudaioi*,[65] and in rare cases he does employ *Ioudaios* in place of "Israelites" – though always referring to activity in the southern territory. The reverse, however, never occurs. As for Israel's future, Josephus also reminds his audience that whereas many *Ioudaioi* are presently subject to the Romans, the "ten tribes" of *Israel* are not, obliquely hinting that this "innumerable multitude" will overwhelm the current Roman hegemony when God's promises are fulfilled, an expectation that also subtly emerges elsewhere in the Josephan corpus.[66]

REVIVAL IN THE LAND AND ISRAEL'S ONGOING EXILE

The examples discussed so far are by no means anomalous in their presentation of Israel's present plight and hope for the future. As has

[64] Cf. Spilsbury, *The Image of the Jew*, 38–40.
[65] Spilsbury, *The Image of the Jew*, 37–40, is right to point out that Josephus "regarded his description of these ancient people as fully relevant to the 'Jews' of his own day" (40).
[66] See Staples, *The Idea of Israel*, 216–32 and the sources cited there.

been widely recognized at least since the work of Peter Ackroyd and Odil H. Steck,[67] numerous early Jewish texts similarly presume that Israel's exile never ended and look forward to a future restoration.[68] Nevertheless, despite the prevalence of these themes in the literature of the Second Temple period, there has been significant pushback against the idea that Jews in this era actually considered exile to be ongoing. Erich Gruen, for example, concedes the pervasive presence of exile and redemption themes in early Jewish literature but argues that these texts are not reflective of the authors' views of their current situations:

A caveat has to be issued from the start. The majority of these grim pronouncements [about exile] refer to the biblical misfortunes of the Israelites, expulsion by the Assyrians, the destruction of the Temple, and the Babylonian Captivity. Were they all metaphors for the Hellenistic diaspora? The inference would be hasty, and it begs the question.[69]

Maurice Casey similarly objects:

At the time of Jesus, many Jews lived in Israel. Some lived permanently in Jerusalem. We would need stunningly strong arguments to convince us that these Jews really believed they were in exile when they were in Israel.[70]

By now, the problem with this critique should be evident: these first-century Jews did not live in *Israel* but rather in *Judah* (Judaea). By

---

[67] See Peter R. Ackroyd, *Exile and Restoration* (1968); Odil Hannes Steck, *Israel und das gewaltsame Geschick der Propheten* (1967); "Das Problem theologischer Strömungen in nachexilischer Zeit" (1968).

[68] James M. Scott has been especially influential in pushing the importance of these themes in the English-speaking world in recent decades. See "Paul's Use of Deuteronomic Tradition" (1993); "'For as Many as Are of Works of the Law Are under a Curse' (Galatians 3.10)" (1993); "Restoration of Israel" (1993); "The Use of Scripture in 2 Corinthians 6:16c–18 and Paul's Restoration Theology" (1994); *Paul and the Nations*; "Philo and the Restoration of Israel" (1996); "Exile and the Self-Understanding of Diaspora Jews in the Greco-Roman Period" (1997); *On Earth As in Heaven* (2005); "Exile and Restoration" (2013). Scott has built on Steck's idea of the pervasive influence of a "Deuteronomic worldview" (*Israel und das gewaltsame Geschick der Propheten*, 184–89, 274–78), though mostly dropping Steck's three-stage model for its development. For criticisms of Steck and Scott's paradigm, see Guy Prentiss Waters, *The End of Deuteronomy in the Epistles of Paul* (2006), 29–42, though Waters agrees that exile and restoration are important in early Judaism and for Paul's use of Deut 32 in Rom 9–11. For trenchant critiques of Waters' position, see David Lincicum, "Paul's Engagement with Deuteronomy" (2008), 50–53. See also the recent history of scholarship on restoration eschatological paradigms provided by Eskola, *A Narrative Theology*, 8–13 and the extensive discussion in Pitre, *Jesus*, 1–130.

[69] Erich S. Gruen, "Diaspora and Homeland" (2002), 20–21.

[70] Maurice Casey, "Where Wright Is Wrong" (1998), 99.

presuming that Israel had been reestablished – and the exile brought to an end – through the Persian-period returns and rebuilding of the temple narrated in Ezra–Nehemiah, such critiques conflate the restored "Israel" of prophetic expectation with the "Judah" of the Second Temple period.[71] In Gruen's words, "redemption came, the promise of a new Temple was kept. The lamentations do not apply to current conditions,"[72] meaning any connection between the historical misfortunes (and covenantal curse) of exile could only apply to the "Hellenistic diaspora" in a metaphorical sense. Interestingly, these assumptions also seem to be shared by N. T. Wright, with whom the concept of Israel's ongoing exile has become most closely associated in recent years, leading to his reinterpretation of the continuing "exile" in a more typological and metaphorical sense.[73]

But I am unaware of a single early Jewish text that treats the events of Ezra–Nehemiah as the restoration of Israel or the end of exile.[74] The book of Daniel, for example, brushes over the time when Jerusalem is rebuilt "with streets and moat and in times of oppression" (9:25), declaring that the *real* fulfillment of Israel's promised redemption would come centuries later, when an "anointed one, the prince" (Dan 9:25–26) would be "cut off" (cf. Isa 53:8),[75] setting in motion the final restoration and the "end of

---

[71] Similarly, Bryan ("Jeremiah's Prediction") conflates the end of *Judah's* Babylonian captivity in accordance with Jeremiah's prophecy of seventy years (Jer 25:11–12) with the end of *Israel's* exile despite the fact that Jer 25 is explicitly limited to Judah rather than pertaining to all Israel (25:1).

[72] Gruen, "Diaspora and Homeland," 24; cf. Ronald Charles, *Paul and the Politics of Diaspora* (2014), 6–7.

[73] E.g., N. T. Wright, *The New Testament and the People of God* (1992), 268–72; *Climax of the Covenant* (1993), 140–56; *Jesus and the Victory of God* (1996), xvii–xviii, 126–27, 203–4, 248–50; "In Grateful Dialogue: A Response" (1999). Similarly, Richard B. Hays, *Echoes of Scripture in the Letters of Paul* (1989), 46.

[74] "The 'restoration' of Judah under the Persians is really a scholarly rather than a biblical concept" (Philip R. Davies, "'Old' and 'New' Israel in the Bible and the Qumran Scrolls" [2007], 35).

[75] For the links between the Suffering Servant of Isa 52:13–53:12 and this anointed one who is "cut off," see William H. Brownlee, "The Servant of the Lord in the Qumran Scrolls I" (1953), 12–15; cf. Harold Louis Ginsberg, "The Oldest Interpretation of the Suffering Servant" (1953); John E. Goldingay, *Daniel* (1989), 300; Anathea E. Portier-Young, *Apocalypse against Empire* (2011), 272–76. The oft-repeated dictum that there is no evidence for the concept of a suffering and dying messiah or of a messianic interpretation of the Suffering Servant within pre-Christian Judaism is therefore mistaken. Dan 9:25–26 may refer to the murder of Onias III in 171 BCE (cf. Dan 11:22; see Louis Francis Hartman and Alexander A. Di Lella, *The Book of Daniel* [1978], 252), an event the author seems to regard as the beginning of the final period of trial immediately preceding the fulfillment of the prophetic promises of restoration, though the passage was obviously

the age of wrath" (Dan 8:19, 11:36).[76] Tobit similarly downplays the events of the Persian period,[77] looking forward to the time of the fuller restoration that will include Naphtalites like Tobit's family:

> God will again show mercy to them, and he will bring them back into the land, and they will build the house, not like the former one, until the appointed times of the age will be completed. Then, after this, they will return from their exiles,[78] and they will build Jerusalem honorably. And the house of God will be built in it as a glorious house for all generations of the age, just as the prophets said concerning it. Then all the nations will turn truly to fear the Lord God, and they will bury their idols, and all the nations will bless the Lord, and his people will acknowledge God, and the Lord will exalt his people. (Tob 14:5–7a)

Similar sentiments about the inadequacy of the events of the Persian Period and afterwards are expressed in Josephus,[79] Sirach,[80] Jubilees,[81] 1 Enoch 89,[82] 4Q390 1 2–10,[83] and the Damascus Document,[84] among others. Thus, although it is true that some Jews had indeed returned to the land and a new temple was operating in Jerusalem, these events are consistently understood in early Jewish sources as only an intermediate stage, with the restoration of *all Israel* – including the northern "house of Israel" – still to come. Remarkably, of this future era, the Damascus Document even declares, "When the number of years of this age are complete, there will no longer be joining with the house of Judah but rather each one standing on his watchtower" (4:11).

On this point, it is revealing that the Persian province, the Hasmonean kingdom, and the Roman province were all called "Judah" (*Yehud/*

---

interpreted differently by the first century CE. For more on Dan 9 and its interpretation in early Judaism, see Dean R. Ulrich, "How Early Judaism Read Daniel 9:24–27" (2014).

[76] John S. Bergsma, "The Persian Period as Penitential Era" (2009); Hartman and Di Lella, *Daniel*, 251–53.

[77] See Staples, *The Idea of Israel*, 292–302. See also Michael A. Knibb, "The Exile in the Literature of the Intertestamental Period" (1976), 268; Michael E. Fuller, *The Restoration of Israel* (2006), 30–31.

[78] The plural "exiles" (αἰχμαλωσιῶν) is significant, especially in a story about a Naphtalite family in exile. The NRSV (unfortunately quoted in Staples, *The Idea of Israel*, 300) obscures this detail with the singular "exile."

[79] Louis H. Feldman, "Restoration in Josephus" (2001), 231–41.

[80] Fuller, *The Restoration of Israel*, 39–40.

[81] Betsy Halpern-Amaru, "Exile and Return in Jubilees" (1997), 140.

[82] James C. VanderKam, "Exile in Jewish Apocalyptic Literature" (1997), 100.

[83] See Anja Klein, "New Material or Traditions Expanded?" (2016), 324–25.

[84] See Lawrence H. Schiffman, "The Concept of Restoration in the Dead Sea Scrolls" (2001), 220; see also John J. Collins, "The Construction of Israel in the Sectarian Rule Books" (2001), 28; Jonathan G. Campbell, "Essene-Qumran Origins in the Exile?" (1995), 148.

Judaea) rather than "Israel" – a marked contrast to the nomenclature chosen by the revolutionaries in both the first and second Jewish revolts against the Romans, each of which adopted "Israel" terminology in the expectation that the final restoration was imminent.[85] There is therefore no reason to imagine that the persistent focus on the Assyrian and Babylonian exiles in so many early Jewish texts was a metaphor for the Hellenistic diaspora because there is no evidence that Jews in this period regarded these things as distinct phenomena. That is, the Hellenistic diaspora is not something separate that happened after the other exiles had come to an end but is rather the continuation of the long "age of wrath" (CD 1:5) extending back (at least) to the eighth century BCE Assyrian invasions and continuing to the present day of the respective authors.[86]

Even Ezra–Nehemiah itself does not give a triumphant account of the promised restoration of Israel but instead presents a more ambivalent picture of "a little reviving" (Ezra 9:8) conspicuously limited to some from the southern tribes of "Judah and Benjamin and the priests and Levites" (cf. Ezra 1:5), while the rest of Israel remains jarringly absent.[87] The temple is built by "the elders of the Jews" (Ezra 6:14), while its dedication prominently features "a sin offering of twelve male goats, corresponding to the number of the tribes of Israel" (6:17). The juxtaposition here between the "elders of the Jews" and the twelve tribes of Israel underscores the absence of elders from the other tribes and calls attention to the continued hope for a fuller restoration including the tribal groups that had not yet returned.[88] The dedication of the temple also conspicuously lacks the glory of God that characterized the dedication of Solomon's temple and the tabernacle in the wilderness. Not

---

[85] See Staples, *The Idea of Israel*, 42–43, 169–73, 346.

[86] "The significance of the ongoing nature of the Assyrian exile is repeatedly ignored by most scholars, including Wright and both the defenders and critics of his exilic hypothesis" (Pitre, *Jesus*, 38).

[87] Pamela Barmash, "At the Nexus of History and Memory: The Ten Lost Tribes" (2005), 230, highlights a few passages that suggest some non-Judahite Israelites may have returned as well but concedes that the editor minimizes their presence, portraying the returns of Ezra–Nehemiah as insufficient to qualify as the restoration of all Israel. Ezra–Nehemiah also narrates not one but *three* returns to the land and restorations of Jerusalem occurring over about a century, those of Zerubbabel/Jeshua, Ezra, and Nehemiah, all of which share some overlapping features. See Lester L. Grabbe, "'Mind the Gaps'" (2001), esp. 84–85; "'They Shall Come Rejoicing to Zion' – or Did They?" (2009).

[88] *Pace* Joseph Blenkinsopp, *Ezra-Nehemiah* (1988), 130–31.

coincidentally, the returnees are repeatedly called "exiles" both in this passage and the remainder of the book as a whole.[89] The rebuilding of the temple is therefore a necessary and important step toward the fulfillment of the prophecies of restoration, but it is only a step.[90]

In case the reader misses these other indicators, the narrator punctuates the account of the temple's dedication with a remarkable anachronism, referring to the Persian ruler as "the king of Assyria" (Ezra 6:22) – surely no accident given the correct reference to the "king of Persia" only a few verses above (6:14).[91] The implication is clear: regardless of who is now ruling the empire, Israel has not yet been liberated from the oppression that began under Assyria, a freedom toward which the exiles look with hope as they observe the Passover – a festival that both celebrates the exodus from Egypt and looks forward to the future restoration.[92] The book also explicitly reminds the reader that the people remain "slaves" (Ezra 9:9). The captivity itself has not yet come to its end even for the returnees (Neh 1:3), a point further reinforced by the use of "province" (מדינה) rather than "land," reminding the reader that the land remains under the control of a foreign empire.[93]

The people's propensity for intermarriage is so disastrous from the perspective of Ezra–Nehemiah and its protagonists precisely because it illustrates the lack of repentance and purity among the returnees, without which the promised total restoration will never happen.[94] The book makes it clear that Nehemiah's victories – rebuilding the walls of Jerusalem, resettling Jerusalem via lottery, and fighting to keep the

---

[89] E.g., בני־גלותא ("children of exile"; Ezra 6:16); בני־הגולה ("children of the captivity"; Ezra 6:19, 20). Cf. Ezra 4:1; 8:35; 9:4.

[90] Wayne O. McCready, "The 'Day of Small Things' vs. the Latter Days" (1988), 230.

[91] Etienne Nodet, "Israelites, Samaritans, Temples, Jews" (2011), 125, misses the inference that the exile was still ongoing but correctly observes that "'Assyria' should not be viewed as a sloppy mistake, but as a coded message that now the Jerusalem temple is the only one for all of Israel, including any ancient returnees. In other words, the new temple is akin to Solomon's."

[92] Cf. Jer 6:14–21. See Barry Douglas Smith, *Jesus' Last Passover Meal* (1993), 40–50. Cf. Federico M. Colautti, *Passover in the Works of Josephus* (2002); Pitre, *Jesus*, 447.

[93] See especially Harm van Grol, "Indeed, Servants We Are" (1999), 219.

[94] E.g., Ezra 9:13–14; Neh 13:23–29; Neh 13:17–18. See J. Gordon McConville, "Ezra-Nehemiah and the Fulfillment of Prophecy" (1986), 216–17, 222–24. On the other hand, many people may have begun to intermarry with those within the land because they believed the new age had already begun – if Israel had already been restored, such precautions against intermarriage may no longer have been considered necessary. Either way, Ezra and Nehemiah are among those insisting that a greater future restoration contingent upon adequate repentance and purity awaits.

priesthood pure – are not insignificant. But they also serve as reminders that the prophets' promises remain unfulfilled. Each episode of Ezra–Nehemiah begins in hope and ends in disappointment, and the final chapter of Nehemiah emphasizes this disappointment by sequentially epitomizing the failure of all three reform movements reflected in the book: the Jerusalem temple is misused and forsaken (Neh 13:4–14), the people are violating the Sabbath and thus Ezra's instruction (13:15–22), and exogamy continues to be practiced (13:22–31).[95] Such behavior, Nehemiah declares, only "adds to the wrath on Israel" (13:18), a statement that strikingly assumes that Israel is presently under wrath. For Ezra–Nehemiah, Israel is not as it should be, and the return of some from Judah, Benjamin, and Levi to the land and the rebuilding of the temple by no means brought an end to the age of wrath.[96]

THERE AND BACK AGAIN: ISRAEL AND RESTORATION ESCHATOLOGY

The evidence therefore strongly indicates that the distinction between "Israel" and "the Jews" throughout the Second Temple period carries forward the distinction between Israel and Judah witnessed in the biblical texts, with *Yehudi/Ioudaios* ultimately meaning "Judahite," of which the English "Jew" is simply a shortened form. This pattern holds up with remarkable consistency across the extant evidence from the Second Temple period, wherein *Ioudaios* is consistently preferred (and Israel avoided) when referring to contemporary Jews, while that preference is reversed when (1) referring to the people of the biblical past, (2) in cultic or diachronic settings (e.g., "God of Israel" or in prayers), or (3) referring to eschatological Israel, including both Jews and northern Israelites.[97]

This last category is especially important. Rather than narrowing the concept of "Israel" to refer solely to Judahites after the Assyrian and Babylonian deportations, the Jewish literature of this period attests to a dominant theological paradigm looking backwards to biblical Israel and

---

[95] "Nehemiah's reforms were temporary, lasting only as long as he could maintain them by force. In the following century ... [we find] a community that took a rather different view from that of Nehemiah" (Lester L. Grabbe, "Triumph of the Pious or Failure of the Xenophobes?" [1998], 64; cf. Grabbe, "Mind the Gaps," 97).

[96] See McConville, "Ezra-Nehemiah," 211–12; Grabbe, "Mind the Gaps," 84, 97, 100–01.

[97] This conclusion depends on Staples, *The Idea of Israel*. Cf. also the observations of Böhm, "Wer gehörte," 182.

forwards to a future restoration of Israel far exceeding the small return of Judahites in the Persian period.[98] This paradigm, which I will call "Israelite restoration eschatology,"[99] reflects a narrative framework in which: (1) because of biblical Israel's covenantal infidelity and disobedience (2) Israel fell under the covenantal curses, most notably the dissolution, captivity/exile, and dispersion of Israel, sometimes characterized as the "death" of the people as a whole,[100] from which (3) God will redeem, reunify, and restore all twelve tribes of Israel to covenantal favor, including an inward ethical transformation of the people to ensure the restoration will be lasting, an eschatological miracle akin to resurrection from the dead (Ezek 37:1–14).[101] David Lambert observes that much of the prophetic corpus is framed within the dysfunctional second stage, in which "effective communication between the people and their God ceases ... God is now at war with his own people."[102] This is true not only of biblical prophetic literature but also of a sizable proportion of Jewish literature in general from the Second Temple period, which also portrays Israel as presently in stage two – the defining characteristic of a restoration eschatological perspective.

Once one recognizes that the distinction between Israel and Judah persists throughout the Second Temple period, a great deal of early Jewish discourse makes considerably more sense, and there is no need

---

[98] "In general terms it may be said that 'Jewish eschatology' and 'the restoration of Israel' are synonymous" (E. P. Sanders, *Jesus and Judaism* [1985], 97).

[99] I have followed Sanders' terminology of "restoration eschatology" (*Jesus and Judaism*, 90) rather than "apocalyptic" theology because the latter term is so variously used and defined that it lacks clarity (e.g., "prophetic" vs. "apocalyptic" theologies in studies on the Hebrew Bible, the "apocalyptic school" of New Testament interpretation). In this book, I will reserve the term "apocalyptic" and its cognates for references to revelatory material or mystical revelation in general. Note that "eschatology" in this context does not necessarily imply the end of the *world* but rather the end of the present *age* and the dawn of a new one.

[100] E.g., Ezek 37; Deut 30:17–20; 32:39; Hos 8:8; 13:1–16.

[101] Sanders, *Judaism: Practice and Belief 63 BCE–66 CE* (1992), 289–98, discusses four main themes of restoration eschatology: the restoration of the twelve tribes, the subjugation or conversion of the nations, the purification of the temple and Jerusalem, and the transformation of Israel into a pure and righteous people, noting that these themes were also often accompanied by messianic expectations. David E. Aune and Eric Clark Stewart, "From the Idealized Past to the Imaginary Future" (2001), discuss the same four plus the themes of the restoration of creation and paradise regained.

[102] David A. Lambert, *How Repentance Became Biblical* (2016), 96–97. In Lambert's model, the first stage involves "a reasonably functional relationship" and stage three involves "anticipated return to a normal relationship."

to redefine exile (as does Wright) in typological or metaphorical terms.[103] Instead, continued concern for northern (non-Jewish) Israel and the necessity of the regathering of all twelve tribes appears with striking frequency in early Jewish literature. The book of Tobit, for example, follows the progress of non-Jewish Israelites from the tribe of Naphtali, assuring the reader that God had preserved faithful Israelites even from the first northern tribe to be deported by Assyria.[104] The books of 4 Ezra, Baruch, and 2 Baruch all call special attention to the fate of northern tribes of Israel, looking forward to the eschatological day in which Israel will be reunited with Judah.[105] The Wisdom of Ben Sira shows surprising interest in and concern for the eschatological fate of Israel – and, tellingly, avoids using the term *Ioudaios*.[106] These discussions even persist well into the rabbinic era. Notably, the Mishnah records that the late first/early second century rabbis Aqiva and Eliezer took different positions on Israel's fate:

> The ten tribes are not destined to return (לחזור), since it says: "And he cast them into another land, as this day" [Deut 29:27 (ET: 29:28)]. As the day passes and does not return, so they have gone (הולכין) and will not return." These are the words of R. Aqiva.
> R. Eliezer says, "As this day is dark and then grows light, so for those in darkness it is destined to be light for them" [cf. Isa 9:2]. m. Sanh. 10:3 (cf. t. Sanh. 13:12)

The Mishnah gives R. Eliezer the last word without comment, suggesting the editor also favors his position.[107] Of this exchange, the Bavli reports the words of R. Yohanan that in this judgment, "R. Aqiva abandoned his love/piety," citing Jeremiah's proclamation of northern Israel's return (Jer 3:12), while Rabbi Judah ha-Nasi shared R. Eliezer's position against R. Aqiva on similar grounds (b. Sanh. 110b). Similar hopes for northern Israel also appear in Genesis Rabbah 98.

It is therefore not the case that, despite the return of Israel to the land, Jews continued to regard themselves as *metaphorically* in exile. On the contrary, Israel's *literal* exile had not ended because *Israel* – that is, the twelve-tribe totality but especially the ten northern (non-Jewish) tribes – had never been restored as promised. Here it is important to distinguish between individual Jews or Jewish groups believing *themselves* to be in exile versus understanding *Israel*, either as a whole or in part, to still be in

---

[103] Pitre, *Jesus*, 34.   [104] Staples, *The Idea of Israel*, 292–302.
[105] Staples, *The Idea of Israel*, 331–36.   [106] Staples, *The Idea of Israel*, 317–25.
[107] On the last word having favored status in the Mishnah, see Judith Hauptman, *Rereading the Mishnah* (2005), 138; Lisa Grushcow, *Writing the Wayward Wife* (2006), 199.

exile.[108] So long as the rest of Israel (the ten tribes) remained largely absent, the age of wrath had not ended and Israel as a whole – both those in the land and abroad – remained under the covenantal curses.[109]

In the minority of early Jewish texts that do apply the term "Israel" to the contemporary era, another pattern emerges: such usage consistently occurs in the context of groups that believe themselves to be a faithful remnant participating in the first stages of the promised restoration of Israel. Examples include the restoration attempts in Ezra–Nehemiah,[110] 1 Maccabees,[111] the Dead Sea Scroll sect,[112] the participants in the Bar Kokhba revolt, and the early Jesus movement. Notably, however, these groups still distinguish between Israel as a whole and Jews as a subset of that whole – and in most cases, these groups do not believe that all Jews will be included in the restored Israel but only those holding to a specific prophetic/sectarian perspective (see Figure 1.2), while the rest will be cut off as Israel is narrowed to those obedient to YHWH.[113]

Jacob Neusner is therefore correct to observe that the various "Judaisms" of this period and beyond are all tied together by a "formative Judaism" rooted in the generative myth of exile and return, the conception that Israel is currently in exile but still has hope of restoration.[114] This story of exile and restoration, he explains, became

---

[108] Along these lines, Sean Freyne, "Studying the Jewish Diaspora in Antiquity" (2002), 4, wonders whether living in Galilee "was a form of Diaspora existence for a Jew," while Tessa Rajak, *Translation and Survival* (2009), 95, notes that "the Jews were in fact always a minority in much of Palestine, subject to the same circumstances and the same rulers as Jews further afield."

[109] On exile as the most prominent (but by no means the only one) of the covenantal curses, see Steven M. Bryan, *Jesus and Israel's Traditions of Judgement and Restoration* (2002), 12–20; Thomas Richard Wood, "The Regathering of the People of God" (2006), 55, 172–73; Pablo T. Gadenz, *Called from the Jews and from the Gentiles* (2009), 49–50; Jeffrey Wisdom, *Blessing for the Nations and the Curse of the Law* (2001), 43–64. As will be discussed below, Paul understands the ultimate curse of the Torah to be death itself, with Israel's redemption involving not only restoration from the situation of exile but the gift of (eternal) life, which he understands as promised in the Torah.

[110] Staples, *The Idea of Israel*, 143–61.   [111] Staples, *The Idea of Israel*, 166–73.

[112] Staples, *The Idea of Israel*, 259–89.

[113] In Lambert's words, the transition from the age of wrath to a renewal of covenantal relationship "usually entails the violent removal of whatever cuts Israel off from [God] ... often through the elimination of a portion of the people" (*How Repentance Became Biblical*, 97).

[114] See Jacob Neusner, *The Way of Torah* (1993), 9–15; "Exile and Return as the History of Judaism" (1997); and especially the explanations in Neusner, "What Is 'a Judaism'?" (2001), 6, and *Judaism When Christianity Began* (2002), 55–66. For the diaspora as formative and central to Jewish identity, see Daniel Boyarin and Jonathan Boyarin, "Diaspora: Generation and Ground of Jewish Identity" (1993).

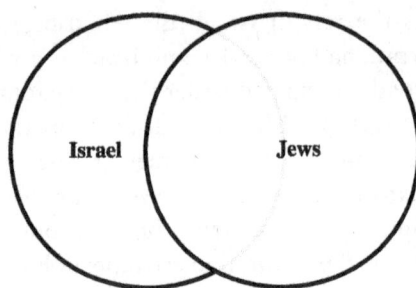

Figure 1.2 Prophetic/Sectarian View of Jews and Israel

"the paradigmatic statement in which every Judaism, from then to now, found its structure and deep syntax of social existence, the grammar of its intelligible message."[115] That is, despite the tremendous diversity across the various forms of Judaism (or, if one prefers, "Judaisms") throughout the Second Temple period, this perspective of Israelite restoration eschatology, together with the related concept of covenant, seems to have functioned as a shared grammar assumed within the discourse, mediated through the reading of authoritative texts in synagogues, the Torah in particular.[116] In this restoration eschatological framework, Israel is presently in the "age of wrath" (CD 1:5; cf. Dan 8:19, 11:36), awaiting the time when all Israel will be restored, reunited, and exalted above the other nations as promised in the Torah and Prophets.[117]

In this light, "Israel" cannot be treated as merely an alternative appellation for "the Jews" in the Second Temple period, regardless of whether one puts "ethnic" or "empirical" before the term. Whereas "Jew" consistently denotes a person from a specific (Judahite) subset of Israel, there was persistent debate about and competition over who properly comprised (or would comprise) Israel, particularly in light of other claimants to Israelite identity such as the Samaritans, and there is no evidence to suggest that Jews believed Israel had been narrowed down to Judah alone. Instead, throughout the Second Temple period, "Israel" is a category that includes both Jews and non-Jewish Israelites from other tribes of Israel.

---

[115] Neusner, *Judaism When Christianity Began*, 61.

[116] On such a shared discourse mediated through Torah and synagogue practices, see Michael L. Satlow, "Defining Judaism" (2006), 845; Scott, "Self-Understanding," 181–82.

[117] It should be noted that it is not necessary (or likely) that all Jews maintained a restoration eschatological perspective. What matters is that restoration eschatology was a prominent, foundational part of the wider Jewish theological discourse in this period.

Jews are Israelites, but they do not comprise all Israel, nor are all Israelites Jews (see Figures 1.1 and 1.2).[118] Consequently, when the term "Israel" is used in this period outside the context of ritual or prayer, we should always be aware of its larger scope, and our ears should be primed for eschatological, messianic, and restorationist connotations.

RETURN OF THE KING: JESUS AND THE GOSPEL

The same patterns are also evident in the New Testament itself. It is now widely accepted that the earliest Jesus movement was focused on the impending restoration of Israel, which the Gospels call the coming of the "kingdom of God."[119] Indications of restoration eschatology are so consistently present on nearly every page of the Gospels that even a brief survey of Gospel traditions easily illustrates just how central the full restoration of all Israel was to Jesus' proclamation and that of his earliest followers:[120]

(1) The very term "gospel" (εὐαγγέλιον) echoes key restoration promises in the prophets (esp. Isa 40:9; 52:7; 61:1; cf. also Joel 3:5 LXX [ET 2:32]; Nah 2:1 [ET 1:15]; Ps 67:12 LXX [68:11 MT]).[121]

(2) Jesus appoints twelve disciples (Mark 3:13–19 // Matt 10:1–4; Luke 6:12–16), "which either symbolizes, foreshadows, or inaugurates the reconstitution of the tribes."[122]

---

[118] It bears emphasizing at this point in the study that I am *not* suggesting that "Israel" refers exclusively or even primarily to the so-called lost tribes"(as some slanderously report – their condemnation is just) but rather that the term Israel is not limited to Jews and is preferred when the whole people, including the non-Jewish northern tribes, is in view.

[119] E.g., Sanders, *Jesus and Judaism*, 95–105; John P. Meier, "Jesus, the Twelve, and the Restoration of Israel" (2001); Dale C. Allison, *Constructing Jesus* (2010), 42–43, 71–76; Michael F. Bird, *Jesus and the Origins of the Gentile Mission* (2007); Fuller, *The Restoration of Israel*; John A. Dennis, *Jesus' Death and the Gathering of True Israel* (2006); Bryan, *Jesus and Israel's Traditions*; Craig A. Evans, "Jesus & the Continuing Exile of Israel" (1999); Scot McKnight, *A New Vision for Israel* (1999); Joel Willitts, *Matthew's Messianic Shepherd-King*" (2007); Pitre, *Jesus*. This scholarly trajectory ultimately builds on Albert Schweitzer, *Von Reimarus zu Wrede* (1906) (ET: Albert Schweitzer, *The Quest of the Historical Jesus* [2001]) through Ben F. Meyer, *The Aims of Jesus* (1979) and eventually Sanders.

[120] Much but not all of the following list derives from the one found in Tucker S. Ferda, "John the Baptist, Isaiah 40, and the Ingathering of the Exiles" (2012), 156.

[121] Pitre, *Jesus*, 256–61; Evans, "Continuing Exile," 100; cf. Wagner, *Heralds of the Good News*, 29–33; Daniel J. Harrington, *The Gospel of Matthew* (1991), 72.

[122] Ferda, "Ingathering of the Exiles," 156; cf. Gerhard Lohfink, *Jesus and Community* (1984); Sanders, *Jesus and Judaism*, 98, 106; Wright, *Victory of God*, 430–31; Evans,

(3) Even more plainly, Jesus promises his disciples that they will "sit on twelve thrones judging the twelve tribes of Israel" (Matt 19:27–30 // Luke 22:28–30).[123] Inasmuch as there were not twelve tribes in Jesus' day, this is a very clear declaration that Jesus was initiating the long-awaited restoration of those twelve tribes.

(4) Jesus says he was sent (and sends his disciples) "to the lost sheep of the house of Israel" (Matt 10:6; 15:24).[124]

(5) Jesus calls himself the "good shepherd" (John 10:11–14), tying himself to prophecies that God would restore Israel and Judah and "appoint over them one shepherd, my servant David" (Ezek 34:23), replacing the bad shepherds who had abused the flock (cf. Isa 40:10–11; Ezek 34:10–23; 37:24).[125]

(6) The Lord's Prayer (Matt 6:9–13; Luke 11:2–4) is replete with restoration motifs and pleas for Israel's restoration, such as "hallowed be your name" (cf. Ezek 36:23; 39:7, 25), "your kingdom come," and the plea to be spared from trial (πειρασμός).[126]

(7) The significance of the Samaritans in Luke–Acts and John (e.g., Luke 9:52; 10:33; 17:16; John 4:1–42; 8:48) suggests a connection with the northern tribes and expectations for the restoration of both northern and southern portions of Israel.[127]

"Continuing Exile," 91–93; "The Twelve Thrones of Israel" (2001); Meier, "Jesus, the Twelve"; Scot McKnight, "Jesus and the Twelve" (2001).

[123] See Meier, "Jesus, the Twelve," 386–87; McKnight, "Jesus and the Twelve," 208–09; Evans, "Continuing Exile," 91–93.

[124] See Willitts, *Matthew's Messianic Shepherd-King* and the abbreviated version in "Matthew's Messianic Shepherd-King" (2008). Willitts highlights the territorial aspects of Jesus' ministry, arguing that "the phrase refers to the oppressed and marginalized remnant of the former Northern Kingdom to whom Jesus sends his disciples" ("Matthew's Messianic Shepherd-King, 379"). See also Young S. Chae, *Jesus as the Eschatological Davidic Shepherd* (2006).

[125] Mary Katharine Deeley, "Ezekiel's Shepherd and John's Jesus" (1997); Gary T. Manning, *Echoes of a Prophet* (2004), 100–35.

[126] See Pitre, *Jesus*, 132–59 and the numerous references found there. See also N. T. Wright, "The Lord's Prayer as a Paradigm of Christian Prayer" (2001); Raymond E. Brown, "The Pater Noster as an Eschatological Prayer" (1968). *Pace* Jeffrey B. Gibson, "Matthew 6:9–13//Luke 11:2–4: An Eschatological Prayer?" (2001), though Gibson's analysis of the prayer as a petition to avoid apostasy is not (as he suggests) necessarily at odds with a restoration eschatological perspective underlying the prayer.

[127] On Samaritans and Israel in Luke–Acts, see Isaac W. Oliver, *Luke's Jewish Eschatology* (2021), 122–25; Chalmers, "Rethinking Luke 10"; Jeannine K. Brown and Kazuhiko Yamazaki-Ransom, "The Parable of the Good Samaritan and the Narrative Portrayal of

(8) Jesus' promise that he would make his disciples "fishers of humans" (Mark 1:17 // Matt 4:19 // Luke 5:10; cf. Matt 13:41–42) echoes Jer 16:14–16, which promises that God would appoint "many fishers" to search out and restore Israel in a new exodus.[128]

(9) Many will come "from east and west" (Matt 8:11–12 // Luke 13:29; cf. Ps 107:2–3; Isa 43:5) and eat with the patriarchs in the kingdom (cf. Isa 25:6–9).[129]

(10) Numerous gathering/scattering passages allude to the exile and restoration,[130] most notably the allusion to Zech 2:6 (MT 2:10) that the Son of Man will send his angels to "gather the elect from the four winds" (Mark 13:27 // Matt 24:31).[131]

(11) The last supper narrative is full of Israelite restoration themes, presenting Jesus as inaugurating the new exodus (cf. Jer 16:14–18; 23:7–8) through his symbolic and prophetic actions.[132]

Samaritans in Luke-Acts" (2021); Vanmelitharayil John Samkutty, *The Samaritan Mission in Acts* (2006); Ravens, *Luke and the Restoration of Israel*, 72–106; Richard J. Coggins, "The Samaritans and Acts" (1982); Jacob Jervell, "The Lost Sheep of the House of Israel" (1972). On the same in John, see Albert S. Geyser, "Israel in the Fourth Gospel" (1986); Jürgen Zangenberg, *Frühes Christentum in Samarien* (1998); Charles H. H. Scobie, "Johannine Geography" (1982); Margaret Pamment, "Is There Convincing Evidence of Samaritan Influence on the Fourth Gospel?" (1982); John Bowman, "Samaritan Studies" (1958). See also Charles H. H. Scobie, "The Origins and Development of Samaritan Christianity" (1973); "Israel and the Nations" (1992), 294.

[128] Ferda, "Ingathering of the Exiles," 156; William L. Lane, *The Gospel according to Mark* (1974), 67; M. Eugene Boring, *Mark* (2006), 59; Harrington, *Matthew*, 72; pace Jack J. Gibson, *Peter between Jerusalem and Antioch* (2013), 22 n. 9. Note that this reading seems to cut against the grain of the Jeremiah passage itself, which seems to regard the "fishers" as agents of judgment. See William L. Holladay, *Jeremiah 1* (1986), 477–79; D. Rudman, "The Significance of the Phrase 'Fishers of Men' in the Synoptic Gospels" (2005); Wilhelm H. Wuellner, *The Meaning of "Fishers of Men"* (1967).

[129] Ferda, "Ingathering of the Exiles," 156; cf. Dale C. Allison, *The Jesus Tradition in Q* (1997), 176–91.

[130] E.g., Matt 3:12 // Luke 3:17; Matt 12:30 // Luke 11:23; Mark 4:29; Matt 13:24–30; Matt 22:9–10; Luke 14:21–23; Matt 25:32.

[131] Cf. also Deut 30:3–4; Isa 11:12; 54:7; 27:13; 60:4; Jer 23:3; 29:14; 31:8; 31:10; 32:37; Ezek 11:17. See Evans, "Continuing Exile," 97–98; Sanders, *Jesus and Judaism*, 98; Wright, *Victory of God*, 430–31.

[132] See Pitre, *Jesus*, 439–51; Wright, *Victory of God*, 554–63; Morna D. Hooker, *The Signs of a Prophet* (1997), 48–54; W. David Stacey, "Appendix: The Lord's Supper as Prophetic Drama" (1997), 80–95; John P. Meier, *A Marginal Jew* (1991), 3.153.

In this light, it is evident that the "kingdom of God" Jesus proclaimed was the restored Israel promised by the prophets, through which God himself would bring justice to all the nations. This was the radical message Jesus went to the cross proclaiming and expecting to initiate. Not coincidentally, it is also exactly the sort of revolutionary message that would get an apocalyptic Jew executed by the Romans.

Restoration eschatological themes are by no means limited to the Gospels and appear throughout the rest of the New Testament. The epistle of James, for example, is addressed "to the twelve tribes in the dispersion" (Jas 1:1), an especially remarkable statement in light of the fact that there were not twelve tribes of Israel in this period.[133] Similarly, Revelation depicts the "sealing" of 12,000 members from each of the twelve tribes of Israel (7:1–8),[134] not just the three southern tribes, and appears to identify this group with the multitude from every nation that praises God and the Lamb in 7:9–12.[135] And although the book does not explicitly mention "Israel" or the twelve tribes, 1 Pet 1:1 is addressed to "the elect strangers of the diaspora," again hinting at the restorationist identification of the book's addressees.[136]

Tellingly, whether in the Gospels or elsewhere, these restoration eschatological passages consistently employ Israel language. But when referring to contemporary Jews outside the context of eschatological renewal, the books of the New Testament, like other early Jewish evidence, employ the term *Ioudaios*, a category that also includes Jesus and his disciples. This pattern is especially noticeable in John and Acts, where *Ioudaios* appears 71 and 79 times, respectively, always referring to contemporary Jews. In contrast, whereas contemporary Jews could, as part of a subset of Israel, be referred to as "Israelites" (particularly in the vocative address, "men, Israelites"),[137]

---

[133] Cf. Joel Marcus, "'The Twelve Tribes in the Diaspora' (James 1.1)" (2014). For more on restoration eschatology in James, see Eskola, *A Narrative Theology*, 394–97.

[134] The "sealing" here is reminiscent of 2 Cor 1:22. On the twelve tribes in this passage, see Richard J. Bauckham, "The List of the Tribes in Revelation 7 Again" (1991); Christopher R. Smith, "The Portrayal of the Church as the New Israel in the Names and Order of the Tribes in Revelation 7.5–8" (1990); Ross E. Winkle, "Another Look at the List of Tribes in Revelation 7" (1989); Albert S. Geyser, "The Twelve Tribes in Revelation Judean and Judeo-Christian Apocalypticism" (1982).

[135] Cf. Marcus, "Twelve Tribes," 434–35. For more on exile/restoration themes in Revelation, see Benjamin G. Wold, "Revelation's Plague Septets: New Exodus and Exile" (2009); Eskola, *A Narrative Theology*, 410–17.

[136] On restoration eschatology in 1 Peter, see Eskola, *A Narrative Theology*, 397–99.

[137] E.g., Acts 2:22; 3:12; 5:35; 13:16; 21:28. As Thiel ("'Israel' and 'Jew' as Markers," 96) explains, "Subsets within this entity [Israel] took on the appellation by synecdoche."

Israel/Israelite is nowhere treated as equivalent to *Ioudaios*. Instead, the term regularly refers to biblical Israel or suggests an eschatological nuance, particularly in the context of the proclamation of the gospel.[138] *Ioudaios*, in contrast, is never used in these contexts. Once one recalls the larger sense of "Israel" as including both Judah and the tribes of northern Israel, the plural in Acts' reference to "the peoples of Israel" (4:27) is also noteworthy.[139]

Nevertheless, if Jesus' gospel message amounted to a proclamation of the end of the age of wrath and the reunification and restoration of all twelve tribes of Israel, there is no avoiding an uncomfortable question in the years after the crucifixion: Where are the twelve tribes?[140] Was Jesus wrong? This question would grow even more urgent as more gentiles became Messiah-followers, further drawing attention to the apparent absence of Israel's restoration since the prophetic promises – and Jesus' proclamations of imminent fulfillment – were made to Israel and Judah, not everyone else.

In many respects, Schweitzer's "undischarged task" referenced in the Introduction is a reformulation of the same question: How did a movement focused on Israel's restoration develop into the primarily gentile phenomenon that came after Paul, and how does one get from Jesus' restoration eschatology to Paul's gospel of gentile incorporation?[141] Remarkably, this is also the question that governs the narrative of Acts, which opens with the disciples asking the risen Jesus, "Is this the time that you restore the kingdom to Israel?" (Acts 1:6).[142] That is, if Jesus came to redeem and restore Israel through his death, when will this restoration take place and why has it not already happened?[143] Paul himself is at pains to answer this question in Romans, and the remainder of this study will focus on how Paul addresses this question by connecting Israel's restoration with the incorporation of faithful gentiles.

---

[138] E.g., John 1:31; Acts 1:6; 9:15; 13:23; 28:20.

[139] Some later scribes seem to have been puzzled by the plural λαοῖς here, as E Ψ 326 and the Syriac tradition correct it to a singular.

[140] See Matthew S. Harmon, review of *Jesus, the Tribulation, and the End of the Exile*, by Brant Pitre, *RBL* (2007), 6.

[141] Schweitzer, *Paul and His Interpreters*, v–vii.

[142] For a recent and thorough examination of the implications of this question, arguing that the continued expectation for Israel's restoration is central to Luke–Acts, see Oliver, *Luke's Jewish Eschatology*. See also David L. Tiede, "The Exaltation of Jesus and the Restoration of Israel in Acts 1" (1986).

[143] For more discussion of Israel's restoration in Acts and how that relates to gentiles, see Richard J. Bauckham, "The Restoration of Israel in Luke-Acts" (2001); David W. Pao, *Acts and the Isaianic New Exodus* (2000); Ravens, *Luke and the Restoration of Israel*; Tiede, "Exaltation of Jesus"; Jacob Jervell, *Luke and the People of God* (1972).

2

Paul and the Israel Problem

> The essence of Paul's antithesis lies in the covenants' respective abilities to empower their members. Ezekiel 36 and Jeremiah 31 promise a time when people will obey God, not because there will be different requirements, but because God will renovate people, supplying them with new resources for fidelity.
>
> Kyle B. Wells[1]

Chapter 1 established that, contrary to the assumption of many scholars today, Paul lived in a world in which it was not assumed that "Israel" was just another way of saying "the Jews." Instead, "Israel" was widely understood to be a category including but not limited to Jews, while the continued presence of Samaritans further underscored the distinction between the subset of Jews (=Judahites) and the larger category of Israel, which by definition includes some who would be classified as neither Jews nor gentiles. Moreover, there was persistent debate about and competition over who exactly comprised Israel – or would at the eschaton. Consequently, if Paul's use of "Israel" and *Ioudaios* terminology corresponds with how these terms were used in his contemporary context, his use of "Israel" should not be understood as synonymous with Jews (*Ioudaioi*), though these categories would be expected to have significant overlap. Indeed, in light of how these terms were used in other Second Temple sources, if it were true that "when Paul says 'Israel,' he means 'Jews,'"[2] he would be anomalous – perhaps even singular – among his contemporaries. Instead, as one might expect, the evidence from the

---

[1] Kyle B. Wells, *Grace and Agency in Paul and Second Temple Judaism* (2014), 280.
[2] Fredriksen, "'Circumcision Is Nothing': A Non-Reformation Reading of the Letters of Paul" (2022), 79.

Pauline corpus follows the same pattern found across other early Jewish literature, and there is no indication that Paul equated Israel with Judah.

First of all, every instance of *Ioudaios* in the Pauline corpus refers to contemporary Jews.[3] Fifteen of these explicitly contrast Jews with non-Jews, either Greeks (Ἕλληνες, 10×) or nations/gentiles (ἔθνη, 5×),[4] as in the phrase "to the Jew first and also to the Greek."[5] Paul also uses cognates of *Ioudaios* on four occasions (all in Galatians) to refer to the Jewish way of life,[6] and the geographical term Ἰουδαία (Judah/Judaea) also appears four times.[7] Paul does not use *Ioudaios* to refer to biblical history or the eschatological people of God, nor does this term occur in the context of prayer or ritual formulas.

In contrast, although Paul regularly sets Jews and gentiles/Greeks opposite one another and uses *Ioudaios* as the typical term referring to his contemporaries, he uses Israel differently and does not treat that term as interchangeable or synonymous with *Ioudaios*.[8] Paul's use of Israel terminology is heavily concentrated in three chapters focused on biblical and eschatological Israel: thirteen of the nineteen uses of Israel/Israelite in the undisputed letters occur in Rom 9–11.[9] Of the six examples outside these chapters, three refer to biblical Israel,[10] two to Paul's own genealogical descent from Israel,[11] and one to "the Israel of God"

---

[3] *Ioudaios* appears twenty-five times in the seven undisputed letters: Rom 1:16; 2:9; 2:10; 2:17; 2:28; 2:29; 3:1; 3:9; 3:29; 9:24; 10:12; 1 Cor 1:22; 1:23; 1:24; 9:20 (3×); 10:32; 11:24; 12:13; Gal 2:13; 2:14; 2:15; 3:28; 1 Thess 2:14. The term occurs once more in the disputed letters (Col 3:11), which follows the same pattern as the other letters.

[4] Jews/Greeks: Rom 1:16; 2:9, 10; 3:9; 10:12; 1 Cor 1:22, 24; 12:13; Gal 3:28. Jews/gentiles: Rom 3:29; 9:24; 1 Cor 1:23; Gal 2:14–15.

[5] E.g., Rom 1:16; 2:9, 10. This statement of Jewish primacy may derive primarily from Zech 12:7a, "YHWH also will save the tents of Judah first." Moreover, in Isaiah, the good news is proclaimed first in Jerusalem and Judah and then goes out to the whole world (see Robert C. Olson, *The Gospel as the Revelation of God's Righteousness: Paul's Use of Isaiah in Romans 1:1–3:26* [2016], 93).

[6] Ἰουδαϊσμός in 1:13 and 14; ἰουδαΐζω and Ἰουδαϊκός in 2:14.

[7] Rom 15:31; 2 Cor 1:16; Gal 1:22; 1 Thess 2:14.

[8] Thus Dunn (*The Theology of Paul the Apostle* [2006], 506): "Strictly speaking, it is not possible to include 'Greeks' within 'Jews'; that is simply a confusion of identifiers. But it might be possible to include 'Gentiles' within 'Israel.' And this is in effect what Paul attempts to do in Romans 9–11." See also Jewett, *Romans* (2006), 575, 599, 601. Contra Graham Harvey, *The True Israel* (1996), 7: "Paul's use of 'Israel' is little different to his use of 'Jew.'"

[9] An additional instance appears in the majority text of Rom 10:1. The term occurs once more in the disputed letters (Eph 2:12).

[10] 1 Cor 10:18; 2 Cor 3:7, 13. See Hans Conzelmann, *1 Corinthians* (1975), 172.

[11] Phil 3:5; 2 Cor 11:22.

(Gal 6:16), a phrase that has engendered significant debate, especially given its apparent contrast with "Israel according to the flesh" (κατὰ σάρκα) in 1 Cor 10:18.[12] Regardless of how one interprets Gal 6:16, the very use of "according to the flesh" as a limiting qualifier when referring to biblical Israel in 1 Cor 10:18 ensures that Paul's addressees not be contrasted with Israel but only "Israel according to the flesh."[13] Even in Rom 9–11, where Paul otherwise uses Israel, when he contrasts gentiles with another category, he uses *Ioudaios* rather than Israel (9:24; 10:12).[14] Paul also opens his discussion of Israel in Rom 9–11 by declaring that "not all who are descended from Israel are Israel" (9:6), a statement that calls attention to the complexity inherent in this term – demonstrating that it can be employed in more than one way – and sets up a sophisticated argument about Israelite status and the composition of Israel.

Paul also calls attention to the tribal nature of Israel in Rom 11:1, highlighting his own Israelite heritage through the tribe of Benjamin. Paul elsewhere similarly betrays this preference of emphasizing his "independent tribal identity"[15] rather than calling himself a Jew, identifying himself as "from the race of Israel, of the tribe of Benjamin" (Phil 3:5). Glenn Snyder explains:

> The perspective of the historical Paul was thus determined by his identity as a Benjaminite, a tribal identification that he used both to identify with a broader ethnic group (*Israēl*, "Israel") and also to differentiate himself from another of its tribes (*Ioudaia*, "Judah") .... It was as a Benjaminite that Paul proclaimed this message to peoples outside the land of *Ioudaia*, in order to call for the reunion of "all Israel."[16]

---

[12] Cf. also Rom 4:1; 9:3. Several options for the "the Israel of God" in Gal 6:16 have been proposed. For a recent treatment including a robust history of scholarship, see Susan Eastman, "Israel and the Mercy of God" (2010), though Eastman's conclusion that the phrase straightforwardly refers to Jews (believing or unbelieving) is unpersuasive in light of how "Israel" is not synonymous with Jews elsewhere in Second Temple literature.

[13] "The very usage [of κατὰ σάρκα], which is otherwise unnecessary, seems to imply that there is another Israel κατὰ πνεῦμα" (Gordon D. Fee, *The First Epistle to the Corinthians* [1987], 470 n. 38)

[14] Rom 9:30–31 is an important exception and will be addressed more substantively below.

[15] Scott W. Hahn, "All Israel Will Be Saved" (2015), 94.

[16] Glenn E. Snyder, "Paul beyond the Jew/Gentile Dichotomy" (2015), 129–30. This explanation better accords with the use of "Israel" in other early Jewish literature than that of Jennifer Eyl, who proposes that Paul prefers "Israelite" as a way to anchor his authority in the primordial past by using the term that implies a "really, *really* ancient Judean" ("I Myself Am an Israelite" [2017], 154–55). As for "Hebrew from Hebrews" (Phil 3:5), this is not a claim to be among the "elite of his race" (Gerald F. Hawthorne and Ralph P. Martin, *Philippians* [2004], 185) or a "Jew's Jew" (Andrew S. Jacobs, "A Jew's

The one exception to this pattern, Paul's rebuke of Peter in Gal 2:15, "we are Jews by nature, not sinners from [the] gentiles," further illustrates the principles in play.[17] If Paul were to distinguish himself and Cephas from gentiles with the term "Israelites" (as the popular insider/outsider model would predict),[18] that would suggest that these former gentiles are effectively outside the boundaries of "Israel." But the question of Israelite status is precisely the matter of debate both in the "Antioch incident" and in Galatians as a whole. Paul therefore necessarily avoids an Israel/gentile dichotomy in his argument, instead employing a Jew/gentile dichotomy, arguing that Jewish and gentile followers of Israel's messiah have equal status in the eschatological *ekklēsia*, implying that both fall under the larger umbrella of Israel, God's chosen people.[19]

In other early Jewish literature, the use of "Israel" is strongly correlated with either historical or restorationist contexts,[20] and Paul's use of the terms corresponds to this larger pattern. It is therefore no coincidence that Paul's use of Israel terminology is primarily concentrated in the three chapters (Rom 9–11) where he systematically discusses Israel's history and the hope of eschatological redemption. Contrary to the assumptions of numerous interpreters who have applied Kuhn's insider/outsider paradigm to suggest that Paul is suddenly speaking "as an insider rather than as one looking in from the outside,"[21] the terminology shifts in these

---

Jew" [2006], 263) but rather a straightforward claim to be a native Hebrew (or Aramaic) speaker born to Hebrew speakers. See Jason A. Staples, *The Idea of Israel in Second Temple Judaism* (2021), 77–80 and D. R. G. Beattie and Philip R. Davies, "What Does Hebrew Mean?" (2011), 73. That Paul's quotations often agree with the LXX says nothing about his facility in Hebrew (*pace* Eyl, "I Myself Am an Israelite," 153 n. 14). It should hardly be surprising that he frequently quotes the most common version in the language in which he was writing, and the numerous examples in which he does otherwise suggest facility beyond knowledge of one Greek version.

[17] Jeremy Hultin, "Who Rebuked Cephas? A New Interpretation of Gal 2:14–17," (2013), has argued that Gal 2:15 is not a claim from Paul himself but rather a quotation of the people from James. Either way, as a Benjaminite, Paul falls under the larger umbrella of *Ioudaios*, though not being from the tribe of Judah.

[18] In "All Israel," 378 n. 36, I explained this exception by citing the insider/outsider context of Paul's remarks, which I now recognize as erroneous.

[19] Cf. Dunn, *Theology*, 506; Jewett, *Romans*, 575, 599, 601.

[20] Staples, *The Idea of Israel*, 339–48.

[21] Dunn, *Romans*, 682; cf. also Douglas J. Moo, *Romans* (1996), 560–61; Jewett, *Romans*, 561–63; John H. Elliot, "Jesus the Israelite Was Neither a 'Jew' Nor a 'Christian'" (2007), 144; Otto Michel, *Römer* (1978), 295; Peter J. Tomson, "The Names Israel and Jew in Ancient Judaism and the New Testament" (1986), 288; Ulrich Luz, *Das Geschichtsverständnis des Paulus* (1968), 26–27, 269–70. Pablo Gadenz (*Called from the Jews and from the Gentiles* [2009], 66–78) observes that Paul's shift in terminology

chapters because, like his predecessors and contemporaries, Paul distinguishes between the Jews and the larger body of Israel of which Jews are a portion, understanding the larger entity of Israel as still awaiting redemption.[22] Although it comes into full focus only in Rom 9–11, this restoration-eschatological perspective is foundational to Paul's theology and gospel proclamation, which are deeply rooted in the hope for Israel's redemption and the conviction that this restoration began with the crucifixion and resurrection of Jesus.[23] Indeed, Paul's characterization of his ministry in "new covenant" terms is itself a strong indicator of the central role of restoration eschatology in his thought.[24]

MINISTER OF A NEW COVENANT

The centrality of the new covenant to Paul's gospel has often been overlooked because of a widely held view that Paul does not operate within a covenantal framework. For example, after observing that in the few places Paul uses the word "covenant" (διαθήκη), the idea tends to be "presupposed" rather than developed, Christopher Stanley concludes that covenant plays a "surprisingly limited" role in Paul's theology.[25]

---

indicates "that he is considering the situation not just of individual Jews but of Israel as a collective whole" (48) and acknowledges the broader twelve-tribe sense of the term "Israel" but nevertheless treats the two terms as fundamentally coextensive for Paul, accepting the insider/outsider view.

[22] David I. Starling, *Not My People: Gentiles as Exiles in Pauline Hermeneutics* (2011), 204.

[23] That Romans is the only letter to an *ekklēsia* Paul did not found and thus required explanation on points he could assume with his own communities probably accounts for why this framework comes into the center of the frame only in Rom 9–11. Restoration eschatology is also foundational in the other letters, but foundations are rarely visible once a building project is further along. Note the similar observation about the centrality of covenantal nomism in early Judaism in E. P. Sanders, *Paul and Palestinian Judaism* (1977), 420–21. For restoration eschatology as foundational for Paul's theology, see Wells, *Grace and Agency*, 209–92; Starling, *Not My People*, 209–12; Gadenz, *Called*, 41–63, 75, 297–303; Guy Prentiss Waters, *The End of Deuteronomy in the Epistles of Paul* (2006), 248–53; J. Ross Wagner, *Heralds of the Good News* (2003), 255–56; Frank Thielman, *From Plight to Solution* (1989); Scott J. Hafemann, "Paul and the Exile of Israel in Galatians 3–4" (1997).

[24] See Wells, *Grace and Agency*, 25–62.

[25] Christopher D. Stanley, *Paul and the Language of Scripture: Citation Technique in the Pauline Epistles and Contemporary Literature* (1992), 169. Stanley Porter, "The Concept of Covenant in Paul" (2003), however, protests that a concept like covenant cannot be linked to one lexical item (such as διαθήκη) alone but must be studied employing semantic-domain methodology to assess the full scope of the concept. Moreover, the fact that the

Although Stanley is correct about the relative infrequency of the term, the fact that the idea of covenant is presupposed suggests the opposite conclusion: namely, that covenant was so foundational to Pauline theology that it could be taken for granted.[26] That is, Sanders' conclusion about Rabbinic Judaism just as easily applies to Paul: "it is the *fundamental nature of the covenant conception which largely accounts for the relative scarcity of appearances of the term "covenant" in Rabbinic literature.*"[27] Sanders notes that "similar observations could be made about most of the rest of the literature" from the period between 200 BCE–200 CE[28] but then startlingly does not apply the same insight to the Pauline corpus.[29] Instead, a better conclusion – based on the reasoning Sanders applies to everything except Paul – is that, just like in other early Jewish literature, covenant is so foundational to the Pauline framework that it rarely needs to be explicitly in view. After all, one typically only sees the foundation of a building if something has gone wrong.

That new covenant language and themes do emerge at crucial points throughout the Pauline letters – precisely in contexts when Paul is most convinced something has in fact gone wrong – is strong evidence that the concept is always present below the surface when not directly in view.[30]

---

most common meaning for διαθήκη in this period was not "covenant" but rather something closer to a "last will and testament" (e.g., *Ant.* 17.53, 78, Heb 9:16–17, etc.) may be another reason this term appears infrequently in Paul's letters, which otherwise employ language fitting the context of covenantal relationship: πίστις (trust/treaty language), χάρις (relational reciprocity), etc.

[26] For example, Van Unnik, "La conception paulinienne de la Nouvelle Alliance" (1973), 111, points out that Paul can cite the "new covenant" in 2 Cor 3 without explanation because his readers were already well aware of its significance.

[27] Sanders, *PPJ*, 420–21, emphasis his.   [28] Sanders, *PPJ*, 421.

[29] Sanders, *PPJ*, 511–15, 543–56. Similarly, Ellen Juhl Christiansen, *The Covenant in Judaism and Paul* (1995), argues that covenant has ceased to serve as a primary category for Paul. Sanders does, however, concede that "one can see already in Paul how it is that Christianity is going to become a new form of covenantal nomism" (513; cf. 552), which raises the question of whether Paul abandoned it at all. In a conversation on March 22, 2010, Sanders acknowledged that in contrast to Romans and Galatians, which are more concerned with outsiders "getting in," Paul's approach in the Corinthian correspondence, which focuses more on "staying in," "look[s] very much like covenantal nomism"; cf. also Sanders, *Paul, the Law, and the Jewish People* (1983), 9.

[30] "Jeremiah ... was a prophetic text he drew on in contexts in which he defended his apostleship" (Lutz Doering, "The Commissioning of Paul: Light from the Prophet Jeremiah on the Self-Understanding of the Apostle?" [2016], 558). For Paul as a covenantal thinker, see Scott J. Hafemann, *Paul: Servant of the New Covenant* (2020); Brant Pitre, Michael P. Barber, and John A. Kincaid, *Paul, a New Covenant Jew* (2019); Morna D. Hooker, "Paul and 'Covenantal Nomism'" (1982); Wells, *Grace and Agency*; Wagner, *Heralds of the Good News*; Richard B. Hays, "Adam, Israel, Christ: The

It is telling that when summarizing his own role and gospel, Paul describes himself as a "servant of a new covenant, not of the letter but of the spirit" (2 Cor 3:6) placing a reference to Jeremiah's new covenant prophecy at the very center of his self-presentation and explicitly positioning his ministry "within a Jeremianic framework."[31] Similarly, Paul's most famous self-appellation, "apostle of gentiles" (Rom 11:13) echoes Jeremiah's calling to be "prophet to the nations" (Jer 1:5),[32] and his description of his authority in terms of "building up" and "tearing down" (2 Cor 10:8; 13:10) echoes Jeremiah's call to tear down and build up (Jer 1:10; cf. 31:28).[33] Like the prophet of the new covenant, Paul was "set apart and called by [God's] grace even from [his] mother's womb" (Gal 1:15; cf. Jer 1:5) and remains unmarried due to his specific call.[34] "By echoing the language of these prophetic texts," Johnson Hodge explains, "Paul links himself to the tradition of Israelite prophets whose task it was to go to the nations.... Thus Paul's work as a teacher of gentiles is a part of the larger story of Israel, not a break from it."[35]

Question of Covenant in the Theology of Romans" (1995); N. T. Wright, "Romans 9–11 and the 'New Perspective'" (2010); *The Climax of the Covenant* (1993); Carol K. Stockhausen, *Moses' Veil and the Glory of the New Covenant* (1989); Scott W. Hahn, "Covenant, Oath, and the Aqedah" (2005); William L. Lane, "Covenant: The Key to Paul's Conflict with Corinth" (1982).

[31] Jeffrey W. Aernie, *Is Paul Also among the Prophets?* (2012), 175. For a fuller assessment of the impact of Jeremiah on Paul's self-presentation, see Doering, "The Commissioning of Paul." The arguments of Dietrich-Alex Koch, *Die Schrift als Zeuge des Evangeliums* (1986), 45–46, and Christian Wolff, *Jeremia im Frühjudentum und Urchristentum* (1976), 134–37, that Jeremiah's new covenant prophecy is not in view in 2 Cor 3:3–6 (particularly Koch's claim that Paul drew the term "new covenant" not from Jeremiah but from the eucharistic tradition) are implausible, especially since Paul not only refers to the "new covenant" but also incorporates several other motifs from that section of Jeremiah in the surrounding context. On other elements of Jer 31–32 (LXX 38–39) in the first four chapters of 2 Cor, see B. J. Oropeza, "New Covenant Knowledge in an Earthenware Jar" (2018).

[32] Cf. also Gal 2:8–9; Rom 15:16, 18. Nevertheless, it should be noted that Paul does not call himself "apostle to the gentiles" as often translated; ἐθνῶν is genitive, not dative.

[33] Doering, "The Commissioning of Paul," 556–57; Hetty Lalleman, "Paul's Self-Understanding in the Light of Jeremiah" (2011), 106–9; Aernie, *Is Paul Also among the Prophets?*, 166–75; Lane, "Covenant," 9.

[34] Echoes of Jeremiah pointed out by Martin Hengel and Anna Maria Schwemer, *Paul between Damascus and Antioch* (1997), 95.

[35] Caroline Johnson Hodge, "Apostle to the Gentiles" (2005), 276. Cf. also Krister Stendahl, *Paul among Jews and Gentiles* (1976), 8–11; Lane, "Covenant," 6–7; A. M. Denis, "L'Apôtre Paul, prophète 'messianique' des Gentiles" (1957). I am not, however, claiming that Paul *exclusively* identified himself with Jeremiah, as he drew upon more than one prophet when constructing his self-presentation, frequently conflating Isaiah and Jeremiah (see Doering, "The Commissioning of Paul," 564–65). Jeffrey Aernie

Not only did Paul present his work as part of Israel's story, the "good news" that Paul preached was specifically that the new covenant promised to Israel was in the process of fulfillment. The distinctive reference to the new covenant in Paul's version of the institution narrative (1 Cor 11:23–25) – language not present in the institution narratives of Mark, Matthew, or the shorter variant in Luke – further confirms its foundational role in Pauline theology,[36] unambiguously embedding a reference to the fulfillment of the new covenant into the ritual most central to community identity practiced every time the community gathered together as an *ekklēsia* (11:18). As Paul's communities "proclaim the Lord's death until he comes" (11:26), they are reminded that Jesus' death specifically inaugurated the new covenant in which they stand.[37]

THE NEW COVENANT AND ISRAEL'S JUSTIFICATION

As for the new covenant promise itself,[38] Jeremiah proclaims:

"See, days are coming," declares YHWH, "when I will make a new covenant with the house of Israel and the house of Judah, not like the covenant I made with their ancestors on the day I took them by the hand to lead them out of the land of

---

explains that although "Paul's purpose is not to define his ministry in terms of individual prophetic figures, but to position himself within the prophetic tradition corporately" (*Is Paul Also among the Prophets?*, 248), he nevertheless "positions his ministry within a Jeremianic framework" (175). See also Kipp Davis, "The Apostle Paul in the Prophetic Matrix of Jeremiah" (2016), 569. For the influence of Isaiah on Paul, see Florian Wilk, *Die Bedeutung des Jesajabuches für Paulus* (1998); "Paulus als Nutzer, Interpret und Leser des Jesajabuches" (2005), esp. 109–13. For the influence of the call of Moses on Paul's self-presentation, see Scott J. Hafemann, *Paul, Moses, and the History of Israel* (2005), 92–109.

[36] Stanley, *Paul and the Language of Scripture*, 169, dismisses the significance of the reference to the new covenant here on the grounds that Paul merely "reflects traditional language," but his case is weakened by fact that none of the parallel institution narratives aside from the Western non-interpolation in the longer reading of Luke 22:20 (a Gospel already in a Pauline tradition) directly mentions the *new* covenant. On the Lukan variant, see Bart D. Ehrman, *The Orthodox Corruption of Scripture* (1993), 198–209. Stanley's case is also weakened by the mention of the "old covenant" in 2 Cor 3:14, further indicating that "new covenant" was a formative category for Paul.

[37] For a more on the centrality of the new covenant to Paul, see Hafemann, *Servant of the New Covenant* and Pitre, Barber, and Kincaid, *Paul, a New Covenant Jew*.

[38] For an extended study of the new covenant promise, see Christoph Levin, *Die Verheissung des neuen Bundes in ihrem theologiegeschichtlichen Zusammenhang ausgelegt* (1985), whose main points are summarized in Hafemann, *Servant of the New Covenant*, 21–27.

Egypt – my covenant which they broke, though I was a husband to them,"[39] declares YHWH. "Because this is the covenant I will make with the house of Israel after those days," declares YHWH: I will put my Torah within them and write it on their heart.[40] And I will be their God and they will be my people. They will not teach again, each his neighbor and his brother, saying, 'Know YHWH,' for they will all know me, from the least of them to the greatest," declares YHWH. "For I will forgive their misdeed, and their sin I will remember no longer." (Jer 31:31–34 [LXX 38:31–34])[41]

This prophecy is manifestly a promise of Israel's reunification and restoration and presumes the basic premises of restoration eschatology:

(1) Israel's covenantal infidelity: The passage explicitly states that the reason a new covenant is needed is that Israel has broken the covenant made at the exodus from Egypt through infidelity and injustice.

(2) The curse of the covenant: Israel consequently no longer stands in a relationship of covenantal favor with YHWH. The LXX reading of Jer 38:32 (MT 31:32) especially emphasizes this aspect of the broken covenant, declaring that "since they did not remain in my covenant," God himself has "neglected them" (ἠμέλησα).[42] Or, as Hosea puts it and Jeremiah echoes, Israel is now "not my people" (Hos 1:9), having been given their "certificate of divorce" (Jer 3:8).[43] Israel "went after the empty things and became empty, and they followed the nations that surrounded them" and became just like the (non-chosen) nations that surrounded them (2 Kgs 17:15). Because they worshiped other gods, Israel will now be scattered and will serve other nations and their gods (Deut 4:27–28). Like the other nations, Israel now stands under God's

---

[39] LXX: "because they did not remain in my covenant, and I neglected them." This wording explicitly declares that "they" are no longer "in" the covenant. For a comparison of the MT and LXX versions of this passage, see Adrian Schenker, *Das Neue am neuen Bund und das Alte am alten* (2006), 17–48.

[40] LXX: "I will surely give my Torahs (νόμους) into their mind (διάνοιαν) and I will write them on their hearts."

[41] The Greek version of Jeremiah is significantly different from the Hebrew version; unless otherwise noted, citations of Jeremiah will use the Hebrew versification.

[42] Jörg Frey, "The Notion of the Spirit in the Dead Sea Scrolls and in Texts of the Early Jesus Movement" (2019), 520, concludes that in the LXX version, "the old covenant is not only broken but completely dissolved, and not only by the Israelites but by the Lord himself."

[43] On Jeremiah's allusions to and reappropriations of the themes of Hosea, see William L. Holladay, *Jeremiah II* (1989), 45–47; Georg Fischer, *Das Trostbüchlein* (1993), 186–204; Jeremiah Unterman, *From Repentance to Redemption* (1987), 151–66.

wrath rather than under covenantal favor until the covenant is renewed.

(3) Future restoration: YHWH will nevertheless renew his covenant with Israel and Judah, reelecting and readopting Israel as his people and restoring them to covenantal relationship and favor: "I will be their God and they will be my people" (Jer 31:33; LXX 38:33), echoing "I will say to those who were not my people, 'You are my people'" (Hos 2:25 MT [2:23 ET]).

But the distinctive focus of the new covenant prophecy is the *mechanism* of this restoration; Jeremiah declares that this renewed covenant will not be like the exodus covenant. Instead, God promises not only to return and restore Israel but also to rectify the root cause of Israel's present plight: the infidelity and injustice that brought Israel under the covenantal curse in the first place.[44] That is, whereas the broken covenant had been contingent on Israel's obedience to external written instructions (Torah), the new covenant will involve YHWH writing his Torah on the heart of Israel, who will then naturally fulfill the parameters of the covenant.

Of course, while the specific language and imagery of the new covenant prophecy is unique, the idea that Israel's restoration will be accompanied by Israel's transformation into a just people is by no means unusual in the prophets. On the contrary, it is a biblical commonplace that since Israel's exile was the result of Israel's infidelity, Israel's restoration will necessarily involve renewed fidelity and justness/righteousness.[45] Restated in more familiar Pauline vernacular, *Israel's restoration requires Israel's justification* – that is, for Israel to be restored, Israel must become a righteous/just people who live according to YHWH's stipulations. This ethical transformation will then ensure that the restoration is permanent, a sentiment

---

[44] "Several passages in Jeremiah and Ezekiel treat an *anthropological renewal* of God's people in the framework of the future salvific condition as an essential element of restoration" (Konrad Schmid and Odil Hannes Steck, "Restoration Expectations in the Prophetic Tradition of the Old Testament" [2001], 78; emphasis original). See also Hafemann, *Servant of the New Covenant*, 24–26.

[45] Cf. Wells, *Grace and Agency*; Lambert, *How Repentance Became Biblical* (2016); "Did Israel Believe That Redemption Awaited Its Repentance? The Case of Jubilees 1" (2006); John M. G. Barclay, "By the Grace of God I Am What I Am: Grace and Agency in Philo and Paul" (2006); VanderKam, "Recent Scholarship on the Book of Jubilees," 425; John C. Endres, "Eschatological Impulses in Jubilees" (2009), 328, 335; Todd R. Hanneken, "The Status and Interpretation of Jubilees in 4Q390" (2012), 427 n. 42; Abraham J. Heschel, *The Prophets* (2001), 253, 310, 333–34, 367.

reflected in the prophetic declaration, "Your people shall all be righteous/ just; they shall possess the land forever" (Isa 60:21).

Whereas some restoration passages are equivocal or ambiguous with respect to how this change will take place,[46] Jeremiah declares that YHWH himself will write his Torah on the heart of Israel such that Torah becomes an intrinsic part of Israelites in the new covenant, resulting in natural obedience. God will thereby fix the problem that had led to the broken covenant and its consequences, changing the inclination of his people and enabling them to obey him perfectly. As such, since each person will directly receive the internal Torah, the new covenant itself will grant each individual the capacity to know and obey God rather than depending on the leaders of the state (priests/kings).[47] This expectation of ethical transformation – framed as the writing of "Torah on the heart" as opposed to external legislation (language unique to this passage) – is the distinctive characteristic of the new covenant promise.

THE SPIRIT AND THE NEW COVENANT

Paul emphasizes exactly this divine transformative activity in 2 Cor 3, where he explains that Messiah has written on the Corinthians themselves, "not with ink but with the spirit of the living God, not on tablets of stone but on tablets of human hearts" (3:3).[48] They have thereby been incorporated in "a new covenant, not of the letter but of the spirit – for the letter kills, but the spirit gives life" (3:6). This passage is especially important not only because it explicitly invokes the new covenant and heart transformation of Jer 31 but also because it reveals how Paul links that promise with Ezekiel's declaration that YHWH would "give you a new heart and a new spirit" (Ezek 11:19; 36:26), connecting the new covenant with the spirit language that so permeates the Pauline epistles.[49]

---

[46] See the discussion in Lambert, "Did Israel Believe," 631–39, and Chapter 6.
[47] Jack R. Lundbom, *Jeremiah 1–20* (1974), 469.
[48] Cf. Hafemann, *Paul, Moses, and the History of Israel*; Wells, *Grace and Agency*, 276–84; Richard B. Hays, *Echoes of Scripture in the Letters of Paul* (1989), 125–40; Lane, "Covenant," 7–8; Starling, *Not My People*, 101; Hans-Joachim Eckstein, "Nahe ist dir das Wort" (1988), 215–17; Gerhard Dautzenberg, "Alter und neuer Bund nach 2 Kor 3" (1999).
[49] "There is no line of argument without the full force of this scriptural background, as the scholarly confusion over Paul's meaning amply attests" (Stockhausen, *Moses' Veil*, 54). On the conflation of Jer 31:31–34; Ezek 11:19; 36:26–27; Exod 34:29–35; and Deut

These prophetic passages are so closely linked thematically and terminologically that some have argued that "the promise of the new heart and new spirit in Ezek 36:26 represents an inner-biblical exegesis of the new covenant in the book of Jeremiah."[50] More significantly, the two passages are frequently interpreted together in other early Jewish literature, most notably in the Dead Sea Scrolls, wherein the Yaḥad sectarians present themselves as members of the new covenant.[51] According to these new covenanters, the original covenant with Israel was broken long ago, leading to an ongoing "age of wrath" in which Israel has been subject to the covenantal curse.[52] But the turn of the eras has arrived, heralded by the sectarians themselves, to whom the "right way" (CD 2:6) has been revealed, and their halakhic revelation and divinely guided praxis is therefore the beginning of the promised restoration. As participants in the new covenant, they have been granted the freedom to "choose what pleases God and hate what he rejects, living perfectly in all his ways, not following the leading of the evil inclination and eyes of fornication" (CD 2:16–17) but rather the "sacred spirit" (e.g., CD 7:4; 1QS 3:7), which they have

---

29–32 in this passage and its implications, see Stockhausen, "2 Corinthians 3 and the Principles of Pauline Exegesis" (1993); *Moses' Veil*, 35–70; James D. G. Dunn, "'The Letter Kills, but the Spirit Gives Life' (2 Cor. 3:6)" (2013); Hafemann, *Paul, Moses, and the History of Israel*, 148–49, 156–73; Otfried Hofius, "Gesetz und Evangelium nach 2 Korinther 3" (1989), 79–81. B. J. Oropeza ("New Covenant Knowledge," 409–12) also rightly connects the "new covenant" of Jer 31 with the "eternal covenant" of Jer 32, which provides another point of contact between these chapters of Jeremiah with Ezek 37:26, especially since the LXX of Jer 32[39]:39 promises "another heart," while the Peshitta has "new heart and new spirit" (MT Jer 32:39 has "one heart and one way"), further harmonizing the passage with Ezekiel 36:26. In any case, the textual evidence of the scribal harmonization of these passages in Jer and Ezek further attest to how they were interpreted together at an early stage within the tradition.

[50] Anja Klein, "From the 'Right Spirit' to the 'Spirit of Truth'" (2009), 176; "Prophecy Continued" (2010), 578–81; *Schriftauslegung im Ezechielbuch* (2008), esp. 100–106; Walther Zimmerli, *Ezekiel II* (1979), 248–50.

[51] CD 6:19; 8:21; 19:33–34; 20:12; 1QpHab 2:3–4. See Stephen J. Hultgren, *From the Damascus Covenant to the Covenant of the Community* (2007), 104; Bilhah Nitzan, "The Concept of the Covenant in Qumran Literature" (2000), 93–98; Klein, "New Material or Traditions Expanded?," 325; and Staples, *The Idea of Israel*, 259–89, and the sources cited there. Whether the term "new covenant" refers specifically to the Qumran sectarians (as argued by Philip R. Davies, *The Damascus Covenant* (1983), 176–86) or to its parent movement (as argued by Hultgren, *From the Damascus Covenant*, 56–62) is immaterial to the present discussion since it is central in either case.

[52] CD 1:5; cf. CD 4:9; 6:10; 6:14; 12:23; 15:7; 16:2; 20:23; 4Q215a 1 2 4; 1QpHab 5:7; 7:7; 4QMMTC 12–14.

received from God himself (1QH^a 4:38; 20:14–15), who engraved the Torah on their hearts (1QH^a 12:11).[53]

As even this short summary demonstrates, the same conflation of Ezekiel's new/sacred spirit and Jeremiah's Torah written on the heart found in 2 Cor 3 is also evident in the scrolls, which treat these as different ways of referring to the same phenomenon of ethical transformation as part of the fulfillment of the new covenant. On closer examination, these two passages are part of a larger pool of restorationist texts linked by common themes and vocabulary that are consistently interpreted together and in light of each other within the scrolls, providing the foundation for the sectarians' self-understanding as participants in the beginnings of Israel's restoration.[54] Elements like the circumcision of the heart/inclination, inscription of Torah on the heart, reception of a new/sacred/right spirit, cleansing by the spirit, and reception of a new heart not only cite or allude to specific individual passages but, as especially highlighted by the degree to which these citations or allusions are often conflated with one another, also serve as hyperlinks to all the related passages in this larger pool of intertextually related restoration promises.[55] These texts are so consistently read together and conflated that citing one can serve as a shorthand way of citing the whole network, as a way to refer to the larger restoration framework as a whole.[56]

---

[53] Julie Hughes, *Scriptural Allusions and Exegesis in the Hodayot* (2006), 109, connects this passage with both Deut 6:6 and Jer 31:33. In this light, Andrew Das' claim that Paul "ignores Jeremiah 31's Law written on the heart" (*Paul and the Stories of Israel* [2016], 91) is baffling even before one considers Rom 2:15. See also Judith H. Newman, "Speech and Spirit: Paul and the Maskil as Inspired Interpreters of Scripture" (2014).

[54] See, e.g., Hultgren, *From the Damascus Covenant*, 104, who lists Deut 4:25–31; 29; 30:1–5; Jer 29–31; and Amos 5:26–27 as especially important to CD, and Klein, "From the 'Right Spirit' to the 'Spirit of Truth,'" who demonstrates the influence of Ps 51 and Ezek 36 (both developing Jer 31:31–34) in this network of texts with respect to 1QS. See also the extended discussion of a host of passages in this larger network in Rodrigo J. [Isaac] Morales, *The Spirit and the Restoration of Israel* (2010), 13–40.

[55] Such linked texts "become mutually explanatory as a whole. Each text may be used to expand the interpreter's understanding of any of the others …. The individual texts become a mutually interpreting group and their individual aspects form a pool around their leading concept" (Stockhausen, "Principles of Pauline Exegesis," 156).

[56] "The repeated exegesis of the same texts sometimes creates interpretive networks" (Gary Edward Schnittjer, *Old Testament Use of Old Testament* [2020], xliii). Further, such "networks emanate a cumulative force over their constituent parts," and allusion or citation of one part of such a network taps into "additional interpretive connotations that may connect themselves to one or more of the exegetically associated scriptural contexts" (875).

As others have observed, the new covenant promised in Jer 31 is the lynchpin of the whole paradigm, sitting at the very center of this foundational network of restoration texts,[57] though the passage itself and Jeremiah in general are seldom directly quoted or cited in the scrolls.[58] Instead, the new covenant idea is more frequently "transmitted indirectly through the transformations of Ezek 36 and especially Ps 51, with an emphasis on the creation of a new spirit and a right inclination which allows one to observe the commandments."[59] That is, rather than works like Isaiah or Deuteronomy, which tend to be cited as scripture with attribution to Isaiah or Moses, Jeremiah traditions – particularly the distinctive new covenant promise – were so thoroughly internalized that they shaped and impacted the interpretation of other scriptural passages and tradition even or especially when not directly in view. Kipp Davis explains:

There is a clear indication from the echoes and allusions to scriptural Jeremiah throughout the Qumran scrolls that their handlers were so immersed in the Jeremianic traditions, in such a way that its expressions and ideals virtually permeated their own.[60]

This strongly parallels Paul's own use of Jeremianic traditions – particularly his foundational application of the new covenant promise.

---

[57] "Jer 31:31–34 is very much at the heart of the 'new covenant' of the Damascus covenant; indeed, it is the linchpin" (Hultgren, *From the Damascus Covenant*, 108). Christoph Levin, *Die Verheissung des neuen Bundes*, argues that the new covenant promise stands at the theological center of the Hebrew Bible. Contra Shemaryahu Talmon, "The Community of the Renewed Covenant" (1994), 13. For a graphical representation of a tightly defined portion of this new covenant network of scriptural texts based on verbal parallels, see Schnittjer, *Old Testament Use of Old Testament*, 878.

[58] See Kipp Davis, *The Cave 4 Apocryphon of Jeremiah and the Qumran Jeremianic Traditions* (2014), 3, 302–3; Eibert J. C. Tigchelaar, "Jeremiah's Scriptures in the Dead Sea Scrolls and the Growth of a Tradition" (2016), 301.

[59] Eibert J. C. Tigchelaar, "Jeremiah's Scriptures in the Dead Sea Scrolls and the Growth of a Tradition" (2016), 300; cf. also Klein, "New Material or Traditions Expanded?," 325; Annie Jaubert, *La notion d'Alliance dans le judaïsme aux abords de l'ère chrétienne* (1963), 238–42.

[60] Davis, *Qumran Jeremianic Traditions*, 305–6. Further: "Jeremiah's reputation as a prototypical prophet, combined with the recollection of his announcement of the 'new covenant' in Jer 31:31 set him apart in a special way for the sectarians as a symbol for covenant obedience. The Jeremianic traditions in the Qumran scrolls in various ways all conform to this feature more than any other; they functioned as vivid depictions of the contrast between covenant 'insiders' and 'outsiders,' and effectively contributed to affirming community identity by what it meant to be participants in the 'new covenant in the land of Damascus'" (302), and "the meaning of Jeremiah's words became secondary to his presentation as the prototypical prophet of exile, and his articulation of the new covenant" (303).

As in the scrolls, Paul rarely directly quotes Jeremiah, but the new covenant is never far below the surface, with the same new-covenant-adjacent language and traditions found throughout the sectarian scrolls also thoroughly permeating Paul's letters. The degree of similarity between Paul's conceptual world and that of the Yaḥad sectarians – both shaped by the same pool of restorationist texts – is evident on even a cursory reading of a text like the Community Rule. The passage typically labeled the Treatise of the Two Spirits (1QS 3:13–4:26), for example, explains that in the time of God's visitation (4:19), the flesh of some will be cleansed "with a spirit of sanctity" (4:21) and sprinkled with the "spirit of truth" because God has chosen them for an "eternal covenant" (4:21–22), in which injustice will be no more (4:22) and they will have the full "glory of *adam*" (4:23) in the resulting "new creation" (4:25).[61] The parallels to Paul's own language and conceptual world are inescapable, as the apostle proclaims the advent of the "last Adam" (1 Cor 15:45), insists that his converts have received the "spirit of sanctity" (Rom 1:4; 5:5; 8:11) and have thereby been cleansed and justified (1 Cor 6:11), and associates all of this with "a new creation" (2 Cor 5:17; Gal 6:15).[62] Both Paul and 1QS also emphasize the sanctifying cleansing of the "sacred spirit" (1QS 3:7–8;[63] Rom 5:5; 15:16) and the importance of the "circumcision of the inclination (יצר)" (1QS 5:5)[64] or "circumcision of the heart" (Rom 2:29) for participation in the new covenant community.

Similar conflations of the same set of new covenant restoration passages appear widely throughout early Jewish literature. For example, in Jubilees 1:5–26, God reveals to Moses that Israel will forsake the covenant (1:5–12) and consequently be "scattered among the nations" (1:13), from which they will eventually be regathered and restored after they

---

[61] The same theme of Adamic glory and new creation through the spirit given to Israel appears in the Hodayot. See Rony Kozman, "Ezekiel's Promised Spirit as *adam*'s Revelatory Spirit in the Hodayot" (2019); Jason Maston, "Anthropological Crisis and Solution in the Hodayot and 1 Corinthians 15" (2016).

[62] "The ministry of the new covenant is a ministry of righteousness/justice .... Accordingly, its effect is to create a righteous/just people" (Michael J. Gorman, *The Death of the Messiah and the Birth of the New Covenant* [2014], 60).

[63] See Klein, "From the 'Right Spirit' to the 'Spirit of Truth,'" 177. On the concept of the "sacred spirit" or "spirit of sanctity" in the scrolls, see Eibert J. C. Tigchelaar, "Historical Origins of the Early Christian Concept of the Holy Spirit: Perspectives from the Dead Sea Scrolls" (2014).

[64] Cf. Deut 30:6; 10:16; Jer 4:4. Intriguingly, the phrase in 1QS is not attested in the MT, but in LXX Jer 31:33, the analogous διάνοιαν is used where "heart" appears in the MT, possibly indicating a Hebrew exemplar with יצר (*yetzer*). In that case, 1QS 5:5 would be conflating Deut 30:6 with Jer 31:33.

recognize God's justice and seek him with their whole heart (1:14–18). On hearing this revelation, Moses begs that God instead "create in them an upright spirit, and do not let the spirit of Beliar rule over them to accuse them before you and ensnare them from all the paths of justice so that they perish from before your face" (1:20). That is, Moses requests that God transform Israel's heart at Sinai, preventing such things from happening.[65] In response to Moses' intercession, God promises to purify Israel and give them a sacred spirit as requested – but only on the other side of Israel's rebellion. This passage is pregnant with numerous new covenant hyperlinks:[66]

> Then the Lord said to Moses: "I know their contrary nature, their way of thinking, and their stubbornness. They will not listen until they acknowledge their sins and the sins of their ancestors. After this they will return to me in a fully upright manner and with all (their) minds and all (their) souls (Deut 4:29; 30:2, 6). I will cut away the foreskins of their minds and the foreskins of their descendants' minds (Deut 30:6). I will create a sacred spirit for them and will purify them (Ps 51:7, 10–11; Ezek 36:25–27) in order that they may not turn away from me from that time forever (Jer 32:40). Their souls will adhere to me and to all my commandments (Ezek 11:20). They will perform my commandments. I will become their father and they will become my children.[67] All of them will be called children of the living God (Hos 2:1)." (Jub 1:22–25a)[68]

Here Jubilees provides yet another example of the conflation of circumcision of the heart, the gift of a "sacred spirit," purification, and the transformation of Israel to a naturally just and obedient people (that is, justification), all in the context of the re-adoption of Israel and the renewal of YHWH's covenant. That Jubilees also presents this revelation

---

[65] 4 Ezra 3:17–20 similarly wonders why God did not remove the people's evil heart and transform them at Sinai. Lambert observes, "Given the prophets' link between new covenant and re-creation of Israel's spirit (see, e.g., Jer 31:31–34), *Jubilees* and 4 Ezra are on solid ground in wondering why such re-creation did not occur already at the time of the Sinai covenant" ("Did Israel Believe," 638).

[66] "We find in *Jub.* 1:15–16 the same kind of connection between Deut 4:29–30; 30:4; and Jer 29–32 that we found lying behind the idea of a 'new covenant' in CD" (Hultgren, *From the Damascus Covenant*, 138).

[67] 2 Sam 7:14; Jer 31:9; Isa 43:6. The messianic promise to David in 2 Sam 7:14 is here corporately applied to eschatological Israel, which will be adopted as God's children as a whole. The same move can be seen in T. Judah 24:1–3. See James M. Scott, *Adoption as Sons of God* (1992), 96–117.

[68] "God revealed to Moses a plan for Israel's redemption, Moses protested the absence of divine re-creation, and God revised the original formulation accordingly" (Lambert, "Did Israel Believe," 639). Translations of Jubilees here and elsewhere are from James C. VanderKam, *The Book of Jubilees: A Translation* (1989).

of Israel's rebellion, punishment, and new covenant – which open the book – as preemptively vindicating YHWH's justice/righteousness and fidelity despite his people's inclination to evil (Jub 1:5–6) is also especially relevant to Paul's argument in Romans, as will be discussed below.

Remarkably, the prevalence of these very concepts of spirit, heart transformation, justification by grace, and new creation in the Pauline epistles have frequently been understood as evidence that Paul has departed from a traditional Jewish covenantal framework. Sanders, for example, claims that Paul does not connect ethics to the concept of a new covenant; instead, for Paul, "ethics are connected above all to receiving the Spirit."[69] This is a puzzling claim in light of other early Jewish evidence that strongly associates the reception of the spirit with the new covenant. Based on that evidence and Paul's own conflation of "new covenant" and "spirit" in 2 Cor 3:3–6, it is apparent that Paul's emphasis on receiving the spirit does not signal a departure from traditional Jewish covenantal theology but instead demonstrates exactly the opposite.[70] In the Prophets, the promise of the spirit is all about Israel being empowered to obey, and Paul's references to the gift of the spirit, circumcision of the heart, and other related concepts are ways of saying that the new covenant has been initiated, with each individual reference effectively activating the whole network of restorationist texts he understands as fulfilled in Messiah. This is why Paul writes to the Thessalonians of his confidence that "you yourselves are taught by God (θεοδίδακτοι) to love one another" because God has "given his sacred spirit to you"[71] – that is, the new covenant promise of intrinsic divine instruction and ethical transformation has come to pass.[72]

---

[69] Sanders, *PPJ*, 513.
[70] See the discussion in Morales, *The Spirit and the Restoration of Israel*, esp. 164–65, 168–71.
[71] 1 Thess 4:8–9; cf. Rom 15:14.
[72] M. V. Hubbard, *New Creation in Paul's Letters and Thought* (2002), 117. Cf. also 2 Cor 2:9; Gal 5:6–7, 22–25. This is also where Schweitzer, *The Mysticism of Paul the Apostle* (1968), 295, is wrong to argue that Paul's ethics is not derived from his conception of justification because "it would have been necessary to show how the man who previously was inherently incapable of producing good works received through the act of justification the capacity to do so. That capacity can only be bestowed upon him through Christ; but according to the doctrine of faith-righteousness, all that Christ does to believers is to cause them to be justified." But Paul did not need to show this because it could be assumed from the prophetic texts from which he is working – the very point of justification is the establishment of Israel's capacity to do justice, and Messiah's justification of believers therefore enables them to do good works.

It is therefore no coincidence that as Paul presents his gospel in Romans, he argues that the new covenant promise is being fulfilled among the followers of Jesus who have received the spirit, a thread of argument that begins with the second chapter's reference to those who manifest "the Torah written on their hearts" (Rom 2:15) and the assertion that the circumcision that matters is "of the heart by the spirit, not by the letter" (2:29). This concept is echoed again near the middle of the argument, as Paul says that those in Messiah "serve in newness of the spirit and not in oldness of letter" (7:6),[73] and finally comes full circle at the conclusion of the argument with yet another reference to the covenant through which Israel's sins would be taken away (11:27).[74]

SPIRITS IN BONDAGE: THE CURSE OF THE TORAH AND ISRAEL'S INFIDELITY

This framework of new covenant restoration eschatology helps explain Paul's assertion that those "from works of Torah are under a curse" (Gal 3:10) and his strident insistence on the inability of the "letter" or "works of Torah" to make God's people just/righteous.[75] The Torah itself prospectively declares Israel's infidelity to be inevitable because even as the new generation prepared to enter the Promised Land, YHWH still had not given them "a heart to know, nor eyes to see, nor ears to hear to this day" (Deut 29:3 [ET: 29:4]).[76] Consequently, when (not if) the covenant has been broken and the people have fallen under the curse, Israel's God will be vindicated for his dealings with his people (Deut 31:16–22).[77]

---

[73] For this passage as especially tied to the new covenant promise, see Wells, *Grace and Agency*, 224–25.

[74] This is widely understood as a reference to the new covenant. See Joseph A. Fitzmyer, *Romans* (1993), 625; Jewett, *Romans*, 705; and the discussion in Chapter 6 below.

[75] E.g., Rom 2:27–29; 3:20; 7:6; 2 Cor 3:6; Gal 2:16; 3:2–5.

[76] Rom 11:8 explicitly refers to this verse, interpreting it with Isa 29:10, "God gave them a spirit of stupor." The passages are linked by the tag "until today" (ἕως τῆς ἡμέρας ταύτης), which is also echoed in 2 Cor 3:14–15. See Jane Heath, "Moses' End and the Succession: Deuteronomy 31 and 2 Corinthians 3" (2014), 41–43; Stockhausen, *Moses' Veil*, 142–43; Hafemann, *Paul, Moses, and the History of Israel*, 375–77.

[77] In their final form, the end chapters of Deuteronomy are unequivocal that it is not a matter of *if* Israel will break the covenant and come under its curses but rather *when* this will happen: "this people will abandon me and break my covenant" (Deut 31:16). LXX Deut 30:1 also removes the ambiguity of that verse by rendering כי with ὡς, ensuring that it is read as a certainty. On the ambiguity of the Hebrew grammar, see Marc Zvi Brettler, "Predestination in Deuteronomy 30:1–10" (1999).

YHWH's justness is all the more demonstrated in that even after Israel's inevitable infidelity, he will yet redeem them, at which time he finally will circumcise their hearts, enabling them to keep the (renewed) covenant henceforth (Deut 30:1–14).[78] The Book of the Torah is therefore given to Israel "as a witness against you" (Deut 31:26), in anticipation of Israel's covenant-breaking, thereby vindicating YHWH in light of what will come.[79] That is, later hearers and readers will be able to recognize that Israel has been unfaithful despite YHWH's fidelity. Similarly, in Jubilees, God commands Moses to write down what he is told so that "when all of these things befall them they will recognize that I have been more faithful than they in all their judgments and in all their actions" (Jub 1:6).[80]

Paul similarly understands the written Torah as a witness to God's faithfulness in spite of Israel's infidelity and a prophetic proclamation of better things to come after Israel has broken the covenant and fallen under "the curse of the Torah."[81] This is effectively the argument of Rom 3, which opens with the claim that "our injustice proves the justness of God" (3:5), supported by a citation of Ps 51:4, "so that you may be justified in your words and prevail when you are judged."[82] God's

---

[78] LXX Deut 30:6 says God will "cleanse your heart" rather than the MT's "circumcise your heart." This cleansing of the heart is precisely what the apostles claim God has done to them *and the nations* in Acts 15:9, further illustrating the centrality of this concept. Thanks to Paul Sloan for reminding me of this.

[79] This passage's presentation of the Song of Moses and the Torah as a whole as a "witness against you" surely underlies John 5:45, "Do not think that I will accuse you before the father; the one who accuses you is Moses."

[80] "Revelation, as contained in Moses' book, does not serve to warn the people, to prevent Israel's sin, but to reassure them in exile, 'that I have not abandoned them,' and to vindicate God at the end of days by constituting an element of Israel's self-knowledge: 'they will know that I was justified, not them.'" (Lambert, *How Repentance Became Biblical*, 132).

[81] On the curse of the Torah, see David Lincicum, *Paul and the Early Jewish Encounter with Deuteronomy* (2010), 142–47; Waters, *End of Deuteronomy*, 80–113; Thielman, *From Plight to Solution*, 65–72; David Brondos, "The Cross and the Curse" (2001), 15; Wisdom, *Blessing for the Nations*, 154–200 (but note the critique of Wisdom's argument by Lincicum, "Paul's Engagement with Deuteronomy" [2008], 49–50); James M. Scott, "'For as Many as Are of Works of the Law Are under a Curse' (Galatians 3.10)" (1993); Terence L. Donaldson, "The 'Curse of the Law' and the Inclusion of the Gentiles" (1986), 102–7; Susan Grove Eastman, "The Evil Eye and the Curse of the Law" (2001); Gadenz, *Called*, 61; Timothy G. Gombis, "The 'Transgressor' and the 'Curse of the Law'" (2007).

[82] The citation elides the first half of the verse, which is nevertheless relevant to Paul's argument: "Against you alone have I sinned, and what is evil before you I did." Lambert observes that Paul, like Jubilees, "seems to have placed its [Psalm 51's] requests for purification into an eschatological framework" (*How Repentance Became Biblical*,

justness is manifest precisely through his response to Israel's injustice, of which the Torah itself stands as a witness:

> Now we know that whatever the Torah says, it says to those in the Torah, so that every mouth may be closed and all the world may become accountable to God, because by the works of Torah all flesh will not be justified, since through Torah is the knowledge of sin. (Rom 3:19–20)

Like Jubilees 1 and Deut 29–32, Paul argues that the purpose of Torah is to justify God over and against unfaithful, covenant-breaking Israel (and thus the whole world), vindicating God's judgment while promising God's ultimate redemptive action on behalf of his people.[83] The knowledge of sin is revealed through Torah precisely because sin had not been removed from the heart of Israel when the Torah was given.[84] But without a command to transgress, that sin lay latent, present but hidden: "where there is no law, there is no transgression" (Rom 4:15). The command is therefore necessary to awaken and reveal sin in order that sin may be dealt with. This is what Paul means when he says "I would not have known sin except through the law" (7:7).[85] Consequently, although "the Torah is sacred, and the command is sacred and just and good" (7:12), because of the presence of sin in the flesh, it is nevertheless an administration of death (2 Cor 3:7), since "the command which was for life, the same was for death" (Rom 7:10).[86] Far from being a shocking

---

148, 216 n. 109). Klein has shown the same is also true of the use of Ps 51 in 1QS ("From the 'Right Spirit' to the 'Spirit of Truth'"). For more on the use of Ps 51 in Rom 3, see Jackson Wu, "Why Is God Justified in Romans?" (2017). Cf. Pss. Sol. 9:2.

[83] Lambert, *How Repentance Became Biblical*, 148–49. Paul elsewhere highlights the instructive function of Torah: "These things befell them as an example, and they were written for our instruction" (1 Cor 10:11).

[84] Lambert observes that Jubilees similarly understands this as the purpose of exile: "Israel needs to suffer exile because it is only there that they can gain an understanding on an ontological level of their depravity, that a sense of sin can enter into their knowledge of themselves" (*How Repentance Became Biblical*, 133).

[85] This meaning works regardless of whether the "I" (ἐγώ) of Rom 7 is autobiographical or refers to Adam or Israel or any of the other options. On the "I" in Romans 7, see Timmins, *Romans 7 and Christian Identity*; Justin King, "Rhetorical Chain-Link Construction and the Relationship between Romans 7.1–6 and 7.7–8.39" (2017). The "I" of the Hodayot in the Dead Sea Scrolls should also be considered as an important parallel, especially given its undertones of Adamic rebellion and redemption. See Kozman, "Ezekiel's Promised Spirit"; Jason Maston, *Divine and Human Agency in Second Temple Judaism and Paul* (2018).

[86] "Paul views the law as that instrument which brought the sentence of death to Israel as a collective body, formed definitively in and through the Sinai experience" (Douglas J. Moo, "Israel and Paul in Romans 7.7–12" [1986], 128).

statement that would have seemed blasphemous to anyone holding a traditional view of Torah,[87] this latter statement recalls Moses' exhortation:

> Look, I have put before you today life and good, death and evil, in that I am commanding you today to love YHWH your God ... so that you may live .... And if your heart turns aside and you do not listen ... I declare to you today that you will surely be destroyed ... I call heaven and earth to witness against you today that I have put before you life and death, the blessing and the curse. So choose life in order that you may live – you and your seed – by loving YHWH your God, obeying his voice, and clinging to him, so that you may live in the land.
> (Deut 30:15–20)

Here Moses explicitly declares that the same command – the love command (note the singular in Deut 30:11) – is both life and death, contingent on the response of the people.[88] But as already mentioned, YHWH himself subsequently declares to Moses that this command will inevitably bring death and not life because of the people's sinful inclination:

> When I bring them into the land ... they will turn to other gods and serve them and despise me and break my covenant. Then, when many evils and troubles find them, this song will testify before them as a witness (for it will not be forgotten from the mouth of their seed), because I know their inclination[89] according to which they are doing today even before I bring them into the land. (Deut 31:20–21)

The problem is not with the command but with the inclination of the people, and the command reveals that problem precisely by "bringing about my death through what is good so that through the command sin would become utterly sinful" (Rom 7:13). That is, since the Torah is good, the fact that the command resulted in death reveals the true source of that death – sin dwelling in the "fleshly" (σάρκινος) inclination of those

---

[87] As suggested by Michel, *Römer*, 228; followed by Jewett, *Romans*, 452.

[88] It is remarkable how many commentators have missed such an obvious allusion, especially given the unusual grammar of Rom 7:10. Neither Deut 30:15 nor Deut 30:19 is included among the list of citations and allusions in NA28 and E. Earle Ellis, *Paul's Use of the Old Testament* (2003), though 30:19 is briefly mentioned in Mark A. Seifrid, "Romans" in Beale and Carson, eds., *Commentary on the New Testament Use of the Old Testament* (2007), 629. Will Timmins (*Romans 7 and Christian Identity*, 124) even declares, "There is no direct allusion to an OT text, but rather a resonance with Jewish writings in which the law is presented as the way to life" (citing Preston M. Sprinkle, *Law and Life* [2008], where the connection is similarly missed). It seems that commentators have been so fixated on Lev 18:5 here that they do not pay sufficient attention to Deut 30, which is never far from the surface in Romans.

[89] Heb: יצר; LXX: πονηρία ("wickedness").

to whom the command was given, who are not only unable to keep the command but inclined to rebel against it (7:8–9, 14; 8:7). For those without the spirit, the external "letter" of the Torah "kills" (2 Cor 3:6) because "the mind set on the flesh is death" (Rom 8:6) and "those who are in flesh cannot please God" (8:8).

The consequence of Israel's obedience to the command would have been life and blessing, but thanks to the presence of sin, the letter cannot bring life but can only condemn. Israel's infidelity therefore resulted in death and the curse, and without circumcision of the heart, that consequence remains.[90] That is, while the command *reveals* that sinful inclination, it cannot *remove* it. That removal, Paul argues, must take place *pneumatically*, on the same "spiritual" plane as the Torah itself, through the circumcision of the heart by the spirit (2:29; cf. Deut 30:6).[91] Since "we know that the Torah is spiritual (*pneumatikos*), but I am fleshly, sold under sin" (7:14), the solution is the writing of the spiritual Torah on the fleshly heart (2 Cor 3:3), at which point "you are not in the flesh but in the spirit" (Rom 8:9). In so doing, God has finally dealt with the "inability of the Torah in which it was weak through the flesh" (8:3) "so that the just statute (δικαίωμα) of the Torah may be fulfilled in us who do not walk according to the flesh but according to the spirit" (8:4). That is, just as promised in Deut 30:6, God has circumcised (dealt with the flesh) of the heart, enabling his people to "love YHWH your God with all your heart and all your soul, so that you may live" – the "just statute" fulfilled is specifically the love command (cf. Deut 30:10, 16).

Paul therefore does not present his gospel as "law-free" but rather as "law-implanted," as the only way to accomplish full, faithful obedience to God, reversing the cause of Israel's current plight.[92] Like his interlocutors, Paul presumes the requirements of Torah must be fulfilled; the question is

---

[90] In this light, the idea that the Torah registers sin and brought a curse resulting in slavery and death *only for gentiles but not for Jews* (as Fredriksen, "What Does It Mean to See Paul 'within Judaism'?" [2022], 377–78) is untenable. On the contrary, the Torah's curse applies specifically to its recipients: Israel.

[91] One suggestion is to label this concept "cardiac righteousness." See John A. Kincaid, "New Covenant Justification by Cardiac Righteousness" (2017); Pitre, Barber, and Kincaid, *Paul, a New Covenant Jew*, 170–79.

[92] On the many problems with depiction of Paul's mission as "law-free," see Fredriksen, "Judaizing the Nations" (2010); "Why Should a 'Law-Free' Mission Mean a 'Law-Free' Apostle?" (2015); Mark D. Nanos, "The Myth of the 'Law-Free' Paul Standing between Christians and Jews" (2009). On Paul's gospel as the means for obedience, see Klyne R. Snodgrass, "Justification by Grace – To the Doers" (1986). On the gospel as the fulfillment of the new exodus, see W. D. Davies, "Paul and the New Exodus" (1997).

how those requirements are to be fulfilled.[93] Here Paul is no different than any other Jewish teacher engaged in halakhic disputes with those from other sects, disputes that similarly concern the proper means of fulfilling the Torah. He does not argue that his opponents' Torah-keeping is the problem but rather that they do not in fact keep the Torah adequately,[94] declaring that faithful obedience to YHWH requires the new heart and the indwelling sacred spirit granted to the followers of the resurrected Messiah.

It is in this respect that Paul can argue that his gospel in no way "discontinues Torah through fidelity" but rather "establishes Torah" (Rom 3:31). He is not arguing that the Torah has been eliminated, nor does he argue against "legalism" or "law-keeping." Instead, he argues for a particular understanding of the written Torah's function. "The works of Torah," he argues, are not a means through which the covenant can be kept or reestablished – the covenant has been broken and cannot be renewed in that manner. Instead, the written Torah, in its proper function, simultaneously serves as a witness to God's justness and fidelity over and against Israel's infidelity and injustice while also pointing forward to the ultimate *pneumatic* justification of God's people via the new covenant after passing through the curse for disobeying the command – that is, after the age of wrath. In this respect, Stephen Hultgren's summary of the perspective of the Damascus Document would apply equally well to Paul's view:

The covenant of the law of Moses *includes* the new covenant within itself insofar as the arrangements that govern the covenant of God include within themselves the promise of restoration of the covenant (Deut 4:29–31; 30:1–5), a restoration that will be a new covenant (Jer 31; cf. Deut 29–30). Thus Jeremiah's new covenant is subsumed under the covenant of the law of Moses.[95]

This understanding of the Torah's function explains why Paul declares that although he himself had previously "become blameless according to the justness which is in the Torah" (Phil 3:6), such blamelessness was inadequate (σκύβαλα; 3:8) in light of the "justness from God" (3:9; cf. Rom 3:21). Blamelessly observing the written Torah could neither bestow the spirit promised by the Torah, nor could it grant life – the very things Paul proclaims may be attained through knowing Messiah and sharing in his sufferings (Phil 3:3, 11). Instead, the Torah itself bears witness to the

---

[93] E.g., Rom 2:13, 25–29; 5:14; 6:2; 8:4; 13:8.   [94] E.g., Rom 2:2–11, 22–25.
[95] Hultgren, *From the Damascus Covenant*, 113.

need for justification "apart from Torah" (Rom 3:21). Thus, Paul gladly "suffers the loss of all things" in order to "gain Messiah and be found in him, not having my own justness which is from Torah but that which is through the fidelity of Messiah, the justness from God based on his fidelity ... if perhaps to attain resurrection from the dead" (Phil 3:8–9, 11).

SMOKE ON THE MOUNTAIN: THE LETTER AND THE VEIL

The same framework sheds light on the complex passage in 2 Cor 3 in which Paul compares his own "new covenant" ministry with Moses' "ministry of death" (3:7) and "condemnation" (3:9), arguing that his gospel provides direct access via the spirit to the glory that is "veiled" in the "old covenant" (3:14). It is noteworthy that Paul does not mention Torah (νόμος) at all in this passage but instead contrasts "letter" (γράμμα) with "spirit," which allows him to distinguish between the old and new covenants without criticizing Torah itself, which he continues to uphold as sacred and good (Rom 7:14). The problem with Moses' ministry was not the Torah but rather that the Torah was given in written form without the spirit,[96] inevitably resulting in condemnation and death for the rebellious people who received it. Indeed, just before his death, Moses himself declares:

I know your rebellion and your stiff neck. You have been rebellious against YHWH as long as I have been alive and with you until today, and how much more after my death! ... For I know that after my death, you will surely be corrupted and turn from the way that I commanded you, and evil will confront you in the latter days, because you will do that which is evil in the sight of YHWH, provoking him to anger with the work of your hands. (Deut 31:27, 29)

This, Paul argues, is why Moses needed to veil himself to shield the people from the glory that reflected from his face (2 Cor 3:7, 13). Because "their minds were hardened" (3:14), they could not endure the glory of God or even stare at Moses' unveiled face (3:7; cf. Exod 34:33–35). It is not, as many have suggested and most English translations assume, that Moses covers his face because he does not want the people to see the glory of his face fade. First of all, καταργέω does not mean "fade away" but rather denotes something closer to

---

[96] Hafemann, *Paul, Moses, and the History of Israel*, 165. See further pp. 94–97.

"discontinue," "annul," "render idle or inactive," or "make inoperative."[97] Secondly, Moses covers his face in Exod 34 not because the glory is fading but because the people cannot bear to look at his face.[98] Nevertheless, although the glory of Moses' face did not fade, it was destined to be *discontinued* (καταργέω) because Moses himself "came to an end" (ἐτελεύτησεν) and died (Deut 34:4–7).[99] Thus, although Moses provides a preview of the glory of the resurrection, in which "the just will shine like the sun in the kingdom of their father" (Matt 13:43) and "shine as lights in the cosmos" (Phil 2:15),[100] that glory was fleeting because of Moses' own eventual death. Paul argues that Moses' own fate mirrors that of his "ministry of death" (2 Cor 3:7), which will likewise come to an end.[101] In the same way that Moses could not bring the people into the promise but left that task to his successor Joshua (LXX: Ἰησοῦς; "Jesus"), so now the "letter" cannot grant life (3:6) but rather gives way to the "ministry of the spirit" (3:8) administered by another Jesus, through whom the promise of life is granted.[102] "Moses" (=the letter) no longer leads those who, following Jesus and having received the spirit (*pneuma*), have entered into the promise.

Stepping further back into the Exodus narrative, it is noteworthy that such veiling only becomes necessary because the people – chosen to be a "kingdom of priests" (Exod 19:5–6) – shrink back from direct interaction with YHWH upon his initial address to all the people (Exod 19:17–20:18), in which the commands are first revealed: "Then they said to Moses, 'You speak with us and we will listen, but do not let God speak with us, lest we die'" (20:19).[103] When Moses recounts this episode in

---

[97] As demonstrated by Hafemann, *Paul, Moses, and the History of Israel*, 301–12. In Paul's usage, "It is almost a technical term, denoting the old age coming to an end" (Sigurd Grindheim, "The Law Kills but the Gospel Gives Life" [2001], 108).

[98] Hafemann, *Paul, Moses, and the History of Israel*, 286–301.

[99] Jane Heath observes that the LXX "uses τελευτάω for what happened to Moses, rather than offering any explicit term for 'death'" ("Moses' End and the Succession," 56), connecting this terminology to the reference to "the end of what was being discontinued" in 2 Cor 3:13 (46, 51–52).

[100] Cf. Jesus' transfiguration, in which "his face shone like the sun, and his clothing became as white as light" (Matt 17:2) and 4 Ezra 7:97.

[101] Heath, "Moses' End and the Succession," 51; Michael Theobald, *Die überströmende Gnade* (1982), 184 n. 79.

[102] Heath, "Moses' End and the Succession," 56–58.

[103] Cf. Song of Songs Rab. 1:2, 13, which reports a teaching of R. Judah that although the Torah was fixed in Israel's hearts when they heard the divine voice (Exod 20:2), they forgot it when they placed Moses as mediator between them and YHWH (20:19), since "Just as Moses is mortal and passes on, so his learning passes away." On recognition of

Deuteronomy, he recalls that YHWH agreed with the people's assessment, longing for a situation in which "their heart would be for them to fear me and always keep my commands, so that it would go well with them and their children forever" (Deut 5:28–29).[104] Consequently, because of their "stiff neck" and "uncircumcised hearts,"[105] God tells Moses to "Warn the people, so that they do not break through to YHWH to stare and many of them perish,"[106] and the tabernacle is established to ensure safe boundaries, shielding mortal, fleshly people from the peril of direct encounter with God's glory. Rather than receiving divine instruction (Torah) directly and in its native pneumatic/spiritual form, Israel would henceforth receive the "letter" through the mediation of Moses, who did receive the Torah (and its glory) directly.[107]

Even greater distance is needed after the flagrant and decisive violation of the covenantal terms in the golden calf incident (Exod 32:1–10), after which YHWH declares, "I will not go up in your midst, because you are a stiff-necked people, and I might destroy you on the way" (Exod 33:3).[108] Scott Hafemann explains:

> their mistake, Moses rebuffs the people's plea for a second chance, "That cannot be now, but it will be in the age to come. For it is said, 'I will put my Torah in their inner part, and on their heart I shall write it' (Jer 31:33)" (Song Rab 1:2, 13G–H). This is immediately followed by a parallel tradition from R. Nehemiah in which the evil inclination "was uprooted from their hearts" (13I) on hearing YHWH's voice but returned at the establishment of Moses as mediator, whereupon Moses again rebuffs the people's request for a second chance, this time with a citation of Ezek 36:26 (Jer 31 and Ezek 36 again interpreted together). Translations from Jacob Neusner, *Rabbinic Narrative: A Documentary Perspective, Vol 3* (2003), 30.

[104] The grammar in Deut 5:29 is awkward, as YHWH seems to ask, "Who will give and there would be for them a heart . . ." (מי־יתן והיה לבבם זה להם), potentially suggesting that the heart to obey must come from another source, but emending והיה to יהוה (an easy scribal mistake) would result in a more straightforward statement in keeping with other analogous passages in Deut: "would that YHWH give a heart in them . . . ."

[105] Cf. Exod 32:9; 33:3, 5; 34:9; cf. Deut 29:2–4; Jer 5:20–29; 7:25; 11:1–14; Ezek 20:1–31; Ps 106; etc. On the "tent of meeting" as a means of attenuating God's glory to spare the people, see Hafemann, *Paul, Moses, and the History of Israel*, 209–11.

[106] Exod 19:21; cf. Num 4:20; 18:22.

[107] As G. Anthony Keddie demonstrates, Paul's argument about the inadequacy of the letter is in keeping with contemporary philosophical positions put forward by Philo (*Prob.* 45–47; *Mos.* 2.49–51) and others in which "written codes of law are cast as insufficient for freedom" ("Paul's Freedom and Moses' Veil" [2015], 278).

[108] Several later rabbinic traditions point to the golden calf episode as the moment when Israel – having been granted eternal life and the glory of Adam through the reception of the Torah – was condemned to die just like Adam (e.g., Mek. Bah. 9; b. Abod. Zar. 5a; Sifre Deut. 320; Lev. Rab. 11:3; Qoh. Rab 8:1.3; Pesiq. Rab. 14:10). Henceforth, Israel would be subject to the cosmic elements and death and placed under guardian angels just

Due to Israel's sin with the golden calf, the earlier promise of God's presence to guide Israel on her way, once the very expression of his blessing, has now become the instrument of his judgment. But that God would consent to withdraw his presence is also an ironic expression of his long-suffering grace. Given the "stiff-necked" nature of the nation, God's withdrawal of his presence from Israel's midst is not only part of his judgment upon the people for their sin (32:34), but also a necessary act of divine *mercy which makes it possible for Israel to continue on as a people.*[109]

At this point in the Sinai narrative, the people have recoiled from the voice of YHWH, demanded that Moses mediate between them and God, and then broken the covenant, resulting in a second giving of the Torah,[110] this time on tablets cut out by Moses (34:1–4) rather than by God himself (32:16).[111] Yet in response to Moses' intercession and plea that God "pardon our wrongdoing and sin and take us as your own possession" (34:9), God promises a new covenant that will come after a future marvelous act apparently even greater than the exodus from Egypt that had just taken place (34:10).[112] It is only after all this that Moses begins to veil himself, shielding the people even from the reflected glory of

---

like the other nations (e.g., Exod. Rab. 32:3–7; cf. Gal 3:19–4:3). See Jerome H. Neyrey, "'I Said: You Are Gods': Psalm 82:6 and John 10" (1989); Terrance Callan, "Paul and the Golden Calf" (1990), 5, 10–12. For more on Paul's use of the golden calf episode and interpretive traditions pertaining to it in 2 Cor 3, see Hafemann, *Paul, Moses, and the History of Israel*, 275–316, 347–418; Alec J. Lucas, "Paul and the Calf" (2018), 112–13; Hays, *Echoes*, 122–53; Wright, *Climax*, 175–92; C. J. A. Hickling, "Paul's Use of Exodus in the Corinthian Correspondence" (1996); Linda Belleville, *Reflections of Glory* (2015); Francis Watson, *Paul and the Hermeneutics of Faith* (2004), 273–313.

[109] Hafemann, *Paul, Moses, and the History of Israel*, 207–8. Heath ("Moses' End and the Succession," 50) similarly observes that "the very narrative motifs that resonate most strongly with [Exod 34:29–35 in 2 Cor 3] ... are contaminated by allusions to both causing and suffering death, when seen and heard without the 'spirit of the Lord,' which is received in gazing upon the glorious icon of God in the face of Christ."

[110] Given the rabbinic tradition ascribed to (second century) R. Jose the Galilean that Moses broke the first tablets lest he condemn Israel to death by delivering them after Israel's adulterous act ('Avot R. Nat. 2.3; cf. similar explanations in Exod. Rab. 43:1; Pesiq. Rab. 20:2 [96b]), the delivery of the second set of tablets might easily be called a "ministry of death." See the discussion in Terrance Callan, "Pauline Midrash: The Exegetical Background of Gal 3:19b" (1980), 562–64.

[111] Exod 34:28 is also ambiguous as to whether Moses or YHWH wrote the words on the second set of tablets, though on the strength of 34:1 it should probably be understood as referring to YHWH's writing. On the other hand, the ambiguity may reflect the idea that Moses now functions as YHWH's presence for the people (as Exod 4:16, "You will be as God to [Aaron]"). On Moses as here becoming the locus of YHWH's presence among the people, see Herbert Chanan Brichto, "The Worship of the Golden Calf" (1983), 36.

[112] On Exod 34:10 as a promise that goes beyond the covenantal/cultic arrangements that follow, see Hultgren, *From the Damascus Covenant*, 133–36. On Moses' intercession

his face (34:29–35) and preventing them from staring at the glory (2 Cor 3:13).[113] From this point forward, Israel would only encounter God's glory through a veil – whether that be the one covering Moses' face, the one in the tabernacle, or (Paul argues by extension) the "letter" or written "Moses" (2 Cor 3:14–15).[114]

The progression in 2 Cor 3 from Moses the lawgiver to "Moses" as a metonymy for the "letter" or written Torah allows Paul to focus his critique on the mediated nature of the "old covenant" (3:14) without criticizing the Torah itself. That is, when reading "Moses" (=the written Torah), a person is not encountering Torah in its unfiltered, spiritual form but only as filtered through its human mediator.[115] Here Paul's representation of (written) "Moses" is strongly reminiscent of Jubilees' distinction between the "heavenly tablets" revealed *to* Moses and their earthly approximation in the written Torah delivered *through* Moses.[116] As Lambert explains, in Jubilees:

The Torah of Moses may be an attenuated, decidedly human affair, mixed in content and, ultimately, incomplete, but it is a reflection of works that are themselves divinely-authorized copies of the heavenly tablets that are the truest, most essential repository of the world's hardwiring, divine law and events.[117]

---

and the subsequent cultic commands and veiling of Moses, see Hafemann, *Paul, Moses, and the History of Israel*, 211–26.

[113] Hafemann, *Paul, Moses, and the History of Israel*, 221–24, 286–316; William J. Dumbrell, "Paul's Use of Exodus 34 in 2 Corinthians 3" (1986), 186.

[114] "The glory suffusing Moses' face seems in these circumstances to express the potential in covenant relationship which had previously been held out to all Israel ... Israel's consequent inability to understand and thus to participate fully in covenant blessings, though addressed by Moses and his successors, is underscored by the veiled face of Moses after they had been addressed" (William J. Dumbrell, "Paul's Use of Exodus 34 in 2 Corinthians 3" [1986], 185).

[115] "The Torah has been filtered through the mediation of Moses, who *veiled* and *wrote*, and thus is limited. The person who follows only the Mosaic law is restricted by a humanly mediated law code, and is therefore a slave according to the Stoic paradox" (Keddie, "Paul's Freedom and Moses' Veil," 281).

[116] Jub 3:10, 31; 5:13; 6:17; etc. For more discussion of the "heavenly tablets" in Jubilees, see David A. Lambert, "How the 'Torah of Moses' Became Revelation" (2016); Leslie Baynes, *The Heavenly Book Motif in Judeo-Christian Apocalypses, 200 B.C.E.–200 C.E.* (2012), 109–34; Martha Himmelfarb, "Torah, Testimony, and Heavenly Tablets" (1999); Florentino García Martínez, "The Heavenly Tablets in the Book of Jubilees" (1997); Hindy Najman, "The Law of Nature and the Authority of Mosaic Law" (1999); Eva Mroczek, *The Literary Imagination in Jewish Antiquity* (2016), 140–44.

[117] Lambert, "Torah of Moses," 49; cf. Himmelfarb, "Torah, Testimony, and Heavenly Tablets," 27–28.

Jubilees was not unique in drawing a distinction between the perfect heavenly Torah and its earthly manifestation,[118] and Lambert's description could just as easily serve as a summary of Paul's own view of the Torah of Moses as put forward in 2 Cor 3. Moses as mediator was a contingency due to Israel's "hardened minds" (3:14), which required Moses to stand between God and the people, attenuating the presence of God and exposure to the heavenly Torah. Since direct exposure to God's presence would have been deadly, Moses veiled himself and established the tabernacle, in which a veil stood between God and the people. This reading also makes sense of Paul's related argument in Galatians, where he declares that the Torah "was added for (χάριν) transgression (παράβασις), having been arranged through angels by the hand of a mediator until the seed would come to whom the promise had been made" (Gal 3:19),[119] becoming a pedagogue to lead to Messiah, through whom the fidelity promised by the Torah would be granted (3:23–29).[120]

Paul therefore presents the Torah revealed *through* Moses (the "letter") as a mediated, earthly, attenuated, ephemeral version of the unmediated, heavenly, spiritual, eternal Torah revealed *to* Moses. It is the latter Torah – the "Torah of fidelity" (Rom 3:27) – that Paul understands as written on the hearts of new covenant members, who no longer must look to "Moses" to see the glory of God filtered through the veil because they now see what Moses himself saw. That is, rather than facing Moses to see the reflected glory, they have "turned (ἐπιστρέψῃ) to the Lord" (1 Cor 3:16),[121] facing the same direction as Moses himself and

---

[118] Heavenly tablets also appear in 1 En 81:1–2; 93:2; 103:2; 106:9. Philo also makes a similar move in presenting the perfect, unwritten, ideal divine law (e.g,. *Opif.* 4; *Abr.* 4–6) as manifested in the written Torah (*Mos.* 2.14; *Leg.* 1.47). Moses' laws are "likenesses and copies" of that ideal reality (*Mos.* 2.11, 2.51–52). See Hindy Najman, "A Written Copy of the Law of Nature" (2003); David Winston, "Philo's Ethical Theory" (1984), 381.

[119] On the textual variants of this verse, see Jason A. Staples, "Altered Because of Transgressions?" (2015). For further discussion of Gal 3:19 in context, see pp. 257–58 in Chapter 6.

[120] For a list of parallels between Gal 3:21–25, 4:1–5 and 2 Cor 3, see Grindheim, "The Law Kills," 112.

[121] Ἐπιστρέφω is the typical LXX translation of שוב, the word most frequently used by the prophets to denote "turning" or "turning back" to YHWH. "Turned to the Lord" (ἐπιστρέφω πρὸς κύριον) is an especially evocative phrase, appearing 13 times in the LXX, including Deut 4:30, which says that after Israel has been scattered "in all the nations" (cf. Rom 1:5; see pp. 26–27) and becomes subject to their gods, they will "turn to the Lord," and Hos 6:1, which after declaring that YHWH will tear his people (Ephraim and Judah) apart and go to his place, exhorts, "Come, let us return to the Lord."

seeing the glory of God in its unfiltered, spiritual form. The expressed wish of Moses has therefore come to pass: "Would that all YHWH's people were prophets, that YHWH would put his spirit upon them!" (Num 11:29).

In making this argument, Paul therefore does not reject Moses or the Torah but rather argues that those who have received the spirit are receiving the heavenly Torah as Moses himself had promised.[122] Just as the Temple Scroll situates its readers in Moses' position on Sinai, hearing God's words directly rather than Moses' words,[123] Paul argues that those who have the spirit stand on the same footing before the Lord as Moses himself, being transformed by God's glory in the same way Moses was (2 Cor 3:16–18).[124] Like those set free in Plato's Allegory of the Cave, those who have received the heavenly Torah written on the heart by the spirit are now facing the Lord, no longer seeing the mediated reflection but the thing itself.[125] Rather than going *through* Moses, they have have become *like* Moses himself.

THE CURSE OF THE TORAH: DEATH (BY EXILE)

It is apparent from the preceding discussion that when Paul refers to the "curse of the Torah," he is referring to death.[126] This should hardly be surprising, as this accords with Moses' identification of the ultimate curse in Deut 30:19, "I have set before you life and death, the blessing and the curse." The blessing, on the other hand, is equated with life – enduring resurrection life facilitated through the reception of the spirit (*pneuma*).

---

[122] 2 Cor 3:10 thus "leaves the distinct impression that Paul sees the old covenant not as having been *abolished* but as having been *subsumed* or built upon, and that the essence of the Sinai covenant had been retained, as Jeremiah had argued that it would be" (Dumbrell, "Paul's Use of Exodus 34," 187).

[123] On the Temple Scroll's systematic "re-voicing" and "de-voicing" of "texts originally attributed to Moses" for a new context that "purports to be the direct discourse of God," see Molly M. Zahn and Bernard M. Levinson, "Revelation Regained" (2002), 335. Cf. Molly M. Zahn, "New Voices, Ancient Words" (2006); Lawrence H. Schiffman, "The Temple Scroll and the Halakhic Pseudepigrapha of the Second Temple Period" (1999); Lambert, "Torah of Moses," 51–52.

[124] Ben Sira similarly suggests that the one who has wisdom has access to the source of Torah. See Benjamin G. Wright III, "Jubilees, Sirach and Sapiential Tradition" (2009).

[125] Cf. Plato, *Republic* 6.514a–20a.

[126] See J. Andrew Cowan, "The Curse of the Law, the Covenant, and Anthropology in Galatians 3:10–14" (2020), 224–25. Pace Wright, *Climax*, 140, who identifies "the curse of all curses" as "exile." For more discussion of the covenantal curse see the sources cited in n. 81 on p. 86.

Unfortunately, modern readers frequently overlook that for Paul, like his Jewish predecessors and contemporaries, death is not solely an individual problem but a corporate one,[127] and this corporate aspect – the death of the people as a nation – gets more attention in the context of Deuteronomy and other scriptural antecedents than the individual aspect.

Indeed, when Moses sets "life and death" before the people, these words come on the heels of Deut 28–29, which does include curses on individuals who break covenant and will be singled out for disaster (e.g., 29:21) but focuses more on the collective punishment of the people as a whole, closing with a prophecy of the death of the nation itself:

> The future generation, your children who rise up (LXX: ἀναστήσονται) after you and the foreigner who comes from a distant land, when they see the plagues of that land ... all the nations will say, "Why has YHWH done this to this land? Why this great wrath of anger?" Then they will say, "Because they abandoned the covenant of YHWH ... therefore the anger of YHWH burned against that land, to bring on it every curse which is written in this book, and YHWH uprooted them from their land in anger, fury, and great wrath, and cast them away into another land, as it is this day." (Deut 29:22–28)

The curses apply to the individual, but the reason the Torah so frequently emphasizes the need to cut off disobedient individuals is that their disobedience threatens the whole people. Just as a disobedient individual is subject to the penalty of death, once the people as a whole break covenant, the nation itself is likewise subject to the curse of death. They had been commanded to "consume all the nations whom YHWH turns over to you" (Deut 7:16),[128] but if they disobey and instead behave like those nations, "You also will perish like the nations that YHWH destroys before you" (8:20). This is the context in which Moses lays out "life and death, the blessing and the curse" (30:19), declaring that if the people do not heed the command, "you (pl.) will perish" (30:18). This curse therefore involves not merely the physical death of individuals but the annihilation or destruction (אבד) of the people as a whole. For the people of Israel as a whole, the curse of the Torah is death – by exile. As any Assyrian statesman knew well, exile and assimilation are a means to bring about the death of a people (*ethnos*), a phenomenon now called genocide.

---

[127] Levenson, *Resurrection and the Restoration of Israel* (2006), x: "Modern individualism has, in fact, been a major impediment to the proper understanding of resurrection in Judaism."

[128] Cf. the fate of Israel itself being "swallowed up" by the nations (Hos 8:8).

The close relationship between death and exile established in these passages warrants further clarification. On an individual level, the punishments of death and banishment were typically treated as equivalent in the ancient Mediterranean world,[129] mainly because a banished individual could customarily be killed with impunity and without pollution (e.g., Num 35:27), which is what necessitated flight from the land.[130] A similar equivalency of death and exile is evident in the first pages of Genesis, where YHWH warns Adam, "on the day you eat from it you will die" (2:17). But when the humans do eat from the tree, they are banished from the garden (3:22–24), signaling the essential equivalence of death and exile from the perspective of the author of this story. Then, when Cain murders his brother Abel, his punishment is banishment to be a wanderer, though measures are taken to ensure that he is not fair game to be killed by anyone who comes across him (4:12–15).

Along the same lines, Hosea not only proclaims the impending exile but declares the death of Ephraim/northern Israel. "Through Baal," the prophet declares, "Ephraim was guilty and died" (Hos 13:1). Israel has consequently been "swallowed up" (8:8; cf. Deut 7:16), "slain by the words of my [YHWH's] mouth" (6:5), and stands in need of "resurrection" (LXX: ἀνίστημι) so that they "may live before him" (Hos 6:2). Similarly, 2 Kgs 17:15 laments the destruction of the northern kingdom, saying that Israel "became empty/ephemeral" (הבל; LXX: ἐματαιώθησαν) because they pursued emptiness/nothingness (ההבל).[131]

Ezekiel likewise portrays "the whole house of Israel" as not only dead in exile but as having been dead so long that their bones have become desiccated (Ezek 37:1–4, 11). The problem in this passage is not that the people have been exiled; the problem is that the exile has resulted in Israel's death. Exile is not the ultimate curse – exile has been the means

---

[129] For a parallel example, Sara Forsdyke concludes that in ancient Greece, "there was an equivalency between sentences of death and sentences of exile" (*Exile, Ostracism, and Democracy* [2005], 11).

[130] See Adele C. Scafuro, "*Atimia*" (2013); Forsdyke, *Exile, Ostracism, and Democracy*, 10–11; Serge Vleminck, "La valeur de ἀτιμία dans le droit grec ancien" (1981); A. R. W. Harrison, *The Law of Athens: Procedure, Volume 2* (1998), 169–76; Douglas M. MacDowell, *Spartan Law* (1986), 73–75.

[131] Similarly, the father of the prodigal son declares that his newly returned son "was dead and is alive again" (Luke 15:24), equating his previous departure with death. In 4Q372 1 15, Joseph's exile "shattered all his bones until he was at the point of death," when he finally cries to God for mercy.

of fulfilling the ultimate curse of death.[132] It is important that Ezekiel prophesies here not about *Judah*, which had been in exile only a few years, but "the whole house of Israel," terminology that usually refers to the northern kingdom, which had been in exile well over a century by the time of Ezekiel's prophetic career.[133] The question, "can these bones live?" (Ezek 37:3) confronts skepticism over whether the seemingly long-dead northern house of Israel could be restored, a point reinforced a few verses later when God promises to reunite the sticks of "Ephraim" and "Judah" into one people (37:15–25).[134]

Despite Israel's lifeless condition, YHWH promises, "I will open your graves and raise you from your graves – my people!" (37:12)[135] and "I will put my spirit in you and you will come to life" (37:14). The resurrection of the dead is not here an individual phenomenon but a corporate phenomenon referring to the people of Israel. After having been put to death for breaking the covenant, the "whole house of Israel" will be resurrected from the dead and given new life. The same is true in each of the other explicit references to the eschatological resurrection in the Hebrew Bible, leading Jon Levenson to conclude:

> Without the restoration of the people Israel ... God's promises to them remained unfulfilled, and the world remained unredeemed. Those who classify the Jewish expectation of resurrection under more universal and individualistic rubrics, such as "life after death," miss the promissory character of the expectation and its inextricable connection to a natural family, [Israel].[136]

Consequently,

> Jewish belief in resurrection was not, thus, only or even primarily about the ultimate destiny of mortal human beings. It was about God's righteousness, the vindication of those loyal to him, and the establishment of justice. The earth

---

[132] Thus, as observed by Hafemann ("Paul and the Exile of Israel," 367–68 n. 73), Paul does not tend to use the Septuagintal vocabulary of "exile" (e.g., αἰχμαλωσία, ἀποικία, μετοικία, διασπορά), though αἰχμαλωτίζω in Rom 7:23 is an exception, referring to captivity to the "law of sin." That this passage includes such a term is likely no accident, however, as John Goodrich has demonstrated that Rom 7:14–25 "echoes several terms and themes from LXX Isa 49.24–50.2" evoking Israel's exile and restoration eschatology, "connecting the allusions to Israel's *early* history in Rom 7.7–13 to images of the nation's *later* history in 7.14–25" ("Sold under Sin" [2013] 477).

[133] A tradition ascribed to Rab in b. San. 92b associates the bones of Ezek 37 with Ephraimites.

[134] See the discussion in Staples, *The Idea of Israel*, 135–38.

[135] Cf. Hos 2:25 [ET 2:23]; Rom 9:26.

[136] Levenson, *Resurrection and the Restoration of Israel*, x.

would give up its dead only in the context of the righting of Israel's wrongs, the punishment of the wicked, the restoration of the lost, the reconstruction of the holy city and the Temple, and the universal recognition of the Lord as the faithful God of justice.[137]

In this light, it is a mistake to assume that Paul's discussion of the "curse of Torah" and the death brought by the Torah is exclusively or even primarily about individuals. In the context of early Jewish restoration eschatology, death and the curse of the Torah are inextricably tied to the fate of Israel; when Israel is restored, the anthropological/individual problem will also be solved and vice-versa. It is therefore not the case that when Paul discusses death or the curse, the scope of death is limited to the anthropological or individual level.[138] Instead, the individual and corporate aspects of the curse are considered together, and the resurrection involves not only individuals but Israel as a whole, as he explains in Romans: "if their casting away is the reconciliation of the world, what is their acceptance if not life from the dead?" (11:15). The individual gains life by participation in God's faithful fulfillment of the corporate promise of life to Israel, the fulfillment of the "blessing of Abraham" (Gal 3:14).[139] Exile was the means of Israel's death, and as Ezekiel promised, the outpouring of the spirit is the means of Israel's resurrection (Ezek 37:14).

DELIVERANCE FROM THE AGE OF WRATH

In summary, when Paul speaks of deliverance "from this present evil age" (Gal 1:4; cf. Rom 12:2) and proclaims that now is the "season of good favor" (2 Cor 6:2), he is operating from within the same framework as the Damascus Document when it refers to "the age of wrath" (CD 1:5),[140]

---

[137] Kevin Madigan and Jon D. Levenson, *Resurrection* (2008), 7.
[138] Contra the larger argument of Cowan, "Curse of the Law."
[139] On the "blessing of Abraham" as eternal life, see David A. Burnett, "'So Shall Your Seed Be': Paul's Use of Genesis 15:5 in Romans 4:18 in Light of Early Jewish Deification Traditions" (2015).
[140] For Paul's conception of "this present evil age" as part of an apocalyptic restoration-eschatological framework, see Dunn, *The Epistle to the Galatians* (1993), 35–36; James R. Harrison, "Paul, Eschatology and the Augustan Age of Grace" (1999), 81–82; Paul Garnet, "Qumran Light on Pauline Soteriology" (1980), 24–32. See also the critiques of L. Ann Jervis, "Did Paul Think in Terms of Two-Age Dualism?" (2020), who does not, however, address Paul's καιρός language despite acknowledging its significance (77 n. 15).

and his understanding of the "curse of Torah"[141] and Israel's current plight is strikingly similar to that found in the Dead Sea Scrolls and in many other early Jewish sources.[142] In this framework, Israel remains under the "ongoing reality of the Deuteronomic curses,"[143] of which death itself is the ultimate curse. Israel came under the curse due to injustice and infidelity to the covenant, the root problem with which Paul is chiefly concerned.[144] For Israel to overcome death – manifest most clearly in the scattering and assimilation of (northern) Israel among the nations – God himself will have to provide the solution to Israel's chronic infidelity.

This traditional connection between Israel's restoration and justification (that is, becoming a righteous/just people) explains why justification is so central in Paul's presentation of his gospel.[145] According to Paul, the messiah died to put an end to the age of wrath characterized by sin resulting in the covenantal curse and to inaugurate a new era of God's favor characterized by fidelity mediated through the spirit and resulting in the blessings promised to God's people of old.[146] Whereas Israel's moral impairment and inclination to sin meant the Torah could never grant what it promised (Rom 8:3), God has acted to fulfill that promise, providing a new heart and new spirit capable of

---

[141] Gal 3:10–13; for further discussion, see Chapter 6.

[142] "As in the Qumran texts, Paul viewed the history of Israel under the Sinai covenant to be characterized by disobedience and hard-heartedness .... Indeed, Israel as a whole still lived under the exilic curse of the Law as prophesied in Deut. 27–32" (Hafemann, "The Spirit of the New Covenant, the Law, and the Temple of God's Presence" [1997], 174). Cf. Waters, *End of Deuteronomy*, 113; Brondos, "The Cross and the Curse," 15.

[143] Thomas Richard Wood, "The Regathering of the People of God" (2006), 55 (cf. 172–73).

[144] Gadenz, *Called*, 49–50; Hafemann, "Paul and the Exile of Israel," 368–70.

[145] In the context of a concern for Israelite redemption through moral transformation, Paul's use of *dik-* words is usually best understood as referring to doing what is right in covenantal terms (see Stephen Westerholm, "The Righteousness of the Law and the Righteousness of Faith in Romans" [2004]; Wright, *Paul and the Faithfulness of God* [2013], 795–815; Charles Lee Irons, *The Righteousness of God* [2015], 56–60). God therefore demonstrates his justness (δικαιοσύνη) by redeeming Israel, while Israel must be "justified" (that is, made morally competent) to be redeemed. For Paul's gospel as centrally concerned with the solution to moral incompetence as the means of redemption, see Wells, *Grace and Agency*, 211–311.

[146] Wells, *Grace and Agency*, 209–89; Brondos, "The Cross and the Curse," 26–32; John M. G. Barclay, *Obeying the Truth* (1988), 106–45; Walt Russell, "The Apostle Paul's Redemptive-Historical Argumentation in Galatians 5:13–26" (1995). See also the discussion of Rom 2 in Chapter 3.

exceeding the justness that could be accomplished through the written Torah (Rom 8:2–4, 9–17; 2 Cor 3:4–18).

But the end of the age of wrath does not mark a discontinuation of Torah (Rom 3:31). Instead, those who have died with Messiah (6:3–4; 7:4) have passed through the death of the curse of the Torah and are no longer under the jurisdiction of the Torah (7:6), which was given to govern life in the flesh, not the pneumatic/spiritual domain. In Paul's own words, "through Torah I died to Torah" (Gal 2:19). In the death of the messiah who fulfilled the Torah's requirements to end the wrath brought about by disobedience to Torah (cf. Rom 4:15; 3:19–31), the Torah has come to its *telos* (Rom 10:4): the curse of death followed by the renewed life promised by the Torah itself.[147] Those who have received the spirit are therefore no longer "under Torah but under favor (χάρις)" (Rom 6:14–15), having moved beyond the age of wrath into the age of favor.[148]

Every piece of this framework is reflective of the central role of restoration eschatology in Paul's thought – he does not challenge or depart from the pattern of religion or restoration eschatological framework of his Jewish contemporaries. Instead, the points of discontinuity and disagreement concern whether those eschatological promises have indeed begun to be fulfilled – and if so, how. Indeed, such views are so thoroughly within the mainstream of Jewish eschatology from this period that if we had only recently discovered the Pauline letters after centuries of reading the Dead Sea Scrolls and other Jewish literature from the Second Temple period, we would in no way be surprised by Paul's statements about justification, the spirit, the role and function of Torah, and the old and new covenants. The inclusion of gentiles is another matter altogether, as will be addressed in detail in the remainder of this book.[149]

---

[147] For more discussion of Rom 10:4 and its meaning in context, see Chapter 6.

[148] For an especially helpful discussion of how Paul understands living under the Mosaic Torah as situating oneself in the wrong era, see Joshua D. Garroway, "Paul: Within Judaism, Without Law" (2019). See also Hafemann, *Servant of the New Covenant*, 18–21.

[149] "Once 2 Cor 3:6a is interpreted in the way suggested above, Paul's understanding of what it means to be living in the new age of the new covenant provides a striking parallel to the central themes associated with the new covenant in the Qumran writings, i.e. that of obedience to the Law from the heart, the role of the Spirit, and the identity of the community with the remnant of the Old Testament" (Hafemann, *Paul, Moses, and the History of Israel*, 153).

In this respect, Sanders' insistence that Paul reasons from solution to plight,[150] while defensible on a *personal* level given Paul's "robust conscience,"[151] stands for revision on a *corporate* level, since restoration eschatology by definition involves a recognition of Israel's plight and the need for a divine solution to that plight, as Sanders himself recognizes elsewhere.[152] Here it should be remembered that Sanders' point about Paul working from solution to plight is specifically engaging with the position of Bultmann and his students that Paul's soteriology originated from his anthropology,[153] and while Sanders argues that the order should be reversed, he sees the overall understanding of the two in Bultmann's framework as otherwise correct.[154] Consequently, even Sanders' corrective program regarding Paul and Judaism, while moving in the right direction, still shares the soteriological assumptions of Bultmannian Protestant Christianity inasmuch as the primary end in view is personal salvation and "the plight of man" in the abstract.[155]

But it is not enough merely to turn things around and argue that Paul's anthropology originated from his soteriology. Instead, we must recognize

---

[150] Sanders, *PPJ*, 442–47. Others, particularly those from the so-called apocalyptic school, have especially emphasized Sanders' solution-to-plight principle, most notably Douglas Campbell, who critiques Sanders for being insufficiently consistent on this point (*The Deliverance of God* [2009], 439–40).

[151] Krister Stendahl, "The Apostle Paul and the Introspective Conscience of the West" (1963), 200.

[152] E.g., Sanders, *Jesus and Judaism* (1985), 77–119. See Thielman, *From Plight to Solution*, esp. 28–45.

[153] Sanders, *PPJ*, 435–42. Cf. Rudolph Bultmann, *Theology of the New Testament* (1951), 1:190, 227.

[154] "Having noted my objections to the analysis of Paul's anthropology by Bultmann and his students – above all the role which it is given in the total scheme – I must now say that otherwise I do not think that it can be improved upon.... I close this discussion of man's plight by referring the reader to the work of Bultmann and his students" (Sanders, *PPJ*, 510–11).

[155] Sanders, *PPJ*, 499. See the critiques of Nils A. Dahl and Samuel Sandmel, review of *Paul and Palestinian Judaism*, *RSR* (1978), 157; Wright, "Romans 9–11 and the 'New Perspective,'" 43–44; Timo Eskola, "Paul, Predestination and 'Covenantal Nomism' – Re-assessing Paul and Palestinian Judaism" (1997). This tendency to see Paul through such lenses is shared widely, especially in more traditional Protestant readings (see the summary of Stephen Westerholm, "Law, Grace and the 'Soteriology' of Judaism" [1991], 69–70). This is likewise true of the so-called apocalyptic school of Pauline interpretation, which, owing to its allergy to "salvation history" (*heilsgeschichtlich*), often produces a disembodied, demythologized, ahistorical Paul who speaks to the human condition in general (particularly as framed by twentieth/twenty-first century philosophical trends) but not so much to a first-century *Sitz im Leben*.

that Paul's soteriology arose from his eschatology.[156] That is, Paul is not writing as a philosopher concerned with the plight of humanity in general but rather from the perspective of a first-century Jew concerned with the plight of Israel,[157] looking forward to Israel's restoration and the fulfillment of Israel's mission to be a "light to the nations" (Isa 42:6).[158] This distinction between personal conscience and Israel's corporate need of redemption helps account for Sanders' recognition that regardless of whether Paul worked from solution to plight, his arguments are nearly always prospective.[159] Rather than positing that Paul's argumentation works in the opposite direction of his reasoning, which Douglas Campbell concedes is "an extremely difficult hypothesis to sustain,"[160] a better solution is to understand Paul's prospective arguments in light of Israel's corporate plight through the lenses of restoration eschatology, in keeping with the evidence of numerous other Jewish authors applying the same types of prospective arguments.

Thus, although Sanders is correct that Paul was not seeking *personal* salvation arising from some deficiency within Judaism or his own inability to keep the Torah, Paul did assume that *Israel* had not kept the Torah and stood in need of the redemption promised by the Prophets. Such a view of Israel's plight, while surely not universal (some groups such as the Sadducees seem not to have shared the popular eschatology of their more

---

[156] Agreeing with Schweitzer, *Paul and His Interpreters* (1912), 54, 216–17, 247–49. Sanders also argues for the primacy of eschatology, but thanks to his retention of a fundamentally Bultmannian conception of Pauline soteriology, he winds up reconstructing a Pauline "participationist eschatology" (*PPJ*, 549) wholly distinct from the early Jewish "restoration eschatology" he recognizes elsewhere (e.g., *Jesus and Judaism*, 90). In this respect, I advocate for the application of a "thoroughgoing eschatology" to Paul along the lines of what Dale Allison, "A Plea for Thoroughgoing Eschatology" (1994), suggests for the historical Jesus.

[157] Contra the position classically articulated by Bultmann, *Theology of the New Testament*, 1:190–352. Along the same lines, Rafael Rodriguez observes that when many "read Paul (and Romans, specifically), they find the apostle waxing philosophically about the human condition" and thus "implicitly cast Paul as a Christian theologian pursuing a metaphysical argument, rather than a culturally situated Jewish author writing to socio-historically located readers" ("Romans 5–8 in Light of Paul's Dialogue with a Gentile" [2016], 102–3).

[158] See Caroline Johnson Hodge, "Olive Trees and Ethnicities" (2004), 88–89; Lloyd Gaston, *Paul and the Torah* (1987), 6.

[159] Sanders, *PPJ*, 488–99; cf. Sanders, *PLJP*, 4.

[160] Campbell, *Deliverance of God*, 439, explaining: "The key contention must fly in the face of the thrust of the text, and is located itself in an uncertain domain (i.e., Paul's underlying reasoning and intentions)."

apocalyptically-minded contemporaries),[161] would hardly have been controversial, as it amounts to little more than a restatement of the basic framework of restoration eschatology presumed in most early Jewish literature.[162] But what *was* controversial was the claim that the eschatological hopes of Israel were already being fulfilled through Jesus, who had been declared Lord and messiah upon his own resurrection (cf. Rom 1:4).[163] Even more controversial was Paul's application of these promises to uncircumcised non-Jews and his insistence that these uncircumcised men could be included as full members of the new covenant, and it is this latter claim and its relationship to those promises that has caused so much difficulty for later interpreters. The distinctive difference between Paul and his Jewish contemporaries is therefore not found in Paul's view of Israel's plight but rather in his distinctive solution to that plight, the details of which will occupy the remainder of this book.

---

[161] Acts 23:6 presents Paul creating a debate among Pharisees and Sadducees over precisely this question of "hope and resurrection" (ἐλπίδος καὶ ἀναστάσεως). Contra Fitzmyer, *The Acts of the Apostles* (1998), 718, this phrase should not be understood as a hendiadys, nor is it "hope in the resurrection." Rather, the "hope" referred to here must be the restoration of Israel, which was "bound up with the resurrection of the dead" (F. F. Bruce, *Acts* [1964], 428). Note the parallel in Acts 26:6–7, where Paul explains that he is on trial "for the hope of the promise to our fathers ... to which our twelve tribes [!] hope to attain."

[162] Thielman, *From Plight to Solution*; Donaldson, "The 'Curse of the Law,'" 102–7; Starling, *Not My People*, 204, 210.

[163] "This emphasis on an inauguration in Christ, short of consummation, is, of course, what separates Paul's view of Israel's restoration from exile from that found in most of postbiblical Judaism on the one hand, and in the Qumran writings on the other" (Hafemann, "Paul and the Exile of Israel," 369 n. 75).

3

The Israel Problem and the Gentiles

I find, in short, no distinctively Pauline imprint in [Rom] 1:18–2:29, apart from the tag in 2:16.... It stands out because it deals directly with salvation and makes salvation dependent on obedience to the law.

E. P. Sanders[1]

The proclamation that the sacred spirit and circumcised heart promised to Israel has been granted through the death and resurrection of Jesus, while controversial, is exactly the sort of thing one might expect from a first-century Jew operating within a new covenant framework. But the second part of Paul's gospel message, the incorporation of uncircumcised gentiles among those being redeemed, is surprising enough that Paul himself labels it a "mystery."[2] After all, the new covenant is not a promise of gentile salvation or incorporation – it does not mention gentiles at all – but is instead a promise of the restoration and reunification of all Israel.[3] The

---

[1] Sanders, *Paul the Law, and the Jewish People* (1983), 129, 132.
[2] On "mystery" (μυστήριον) in the New Testament and early Christianity, T. J. Lang, *Mystery and the Making of a Christian Historical Consciousness* (2015), concludes that the language marks something that was once hidden but is now revealed to the inside group, establishing a framework for new revelation with claims of antiquity. Paul's language here is reminiscent of the "mystery" (רז) language found in the Dead Sea Scrolls in the context of a similar apocalyptic perspective. See also Samuel I. Thomas, *The "Mysteries" of Qumran* (2009); Benjamin L. Gladd, *Revealing the Mysterion* (2008); Markus N. Bockmuehl, *Revelation and Mystery in Ancient Judaism and Pauline Christianity* (1990); David E. Aune, "Charismatic Exegesis in Early Judaism and Early Christianity" (1993); Raymond E. Brown, *The Semitic Background of the Term "Mystery" in the New Testament* (1968).
[3] Although the new covenant is promised to Israel and Judah without any overt mention of those from other nations, the declaration in Jer 31:27 (LXX 38:27) that YHWH would "sow the house of Israel and the house of Judah with the seed of humankind and the seed

new covenant promise itself is part of an extended section of Jeremiah that begins with YHWH's promise to "restore my people *Israel and Judah* from captivity" (30:3; LXX 37:3) and concludes a chapter proclaiming the return of Ephraim, the chief tribe of the northern kingdom, from among the nations (31:1–22; LXX 38:1–22). This is the context in which Jeremiah proclaims YHWH's promise of "a new covenant *with the house of Israel and the house of Judah*" (31:31), language that unambiguously emphasizes both the northern (house of Israel) and southern (house of Judah) parts of the whole people of Israel. This emphasis on northern Israel's restoration appears throughout Jeremiah, who although aware that Ephraim was "no more" (31:15; LXX 38:15) and that Israel had been "divorced" and was therefore "not my people" (note the allusion to Hosea in Jer 3:8), declared that Judah's subsequent disobedience had paradoxically guaranteed Israel's restoration, since Judah made Israel look good by comparison (Jer 3:11–12).[4]

Thus, as previously discussed, for later readers of Jeremiah anticipating the fulfillment of the promises of a new/eternal covenant, the expectation would be for a complete restoration of all Israel, with the restoration of Jews (=Judahites) inextricably linked to that of Ephraim and the rest of the northern, non-Jewish part of Israel. As such, even a restoration of all Jews and the establishment of an independent Jewish kingdom would not adequately fulfill the new covenant promise. Ephraim must also be restored from the destruction wrought by Assyria, even if such a return would require a greater miracle than the exodus from Egypt (Jer 16:14–15). Even if that restoration is limited to "one from a city and two from a family" (3:14), Israel must be complete and reunified once again. Until that happens, the new covenant has not been and cannot be fulfilled.

The same is true of the other prophetic passages frequently interpreted together with the new covenant promise. Ezekiel's parallel promises, for example, are not only fundamentally national in scope but emphasize a

---

of animals" is intriguing in light of how animals often represent various nations in apocalyptic symbolism (see Jason A. Staples, "Rise, Kill, and Eat" [2019]). It is conceivable (albeit speculative) that the "seed of beasts" could have been understood by at least some interpreters as referring to the incorporation of some from other nations (as in 1 En. 91:38), though I am unaware of any exegete of the passage from antiquity who directly makes this case.

[4] See the discussion in Jason A. Staples, *The Idea of Israel in Second Temple Judaism* (2021), 132–35.

similarly comprehensive view of Israel's restoration.⁵ Those to whom it is promised, "I will put my spirit within you and you will come to life,⁶ and I will place you on your own land" (Ezek 37:14) are represented by the two sticks of Judah and Ephraim symbolically joined together in Ezek 37:15–20, an action explained by the prophet as follows:

This is what the Lord YHWH says: "See, I will take the children of Israel from among the nations where they have gone, and I will gather them from every side and bring them into their own land,⁷ and I will make them one nation in the land on the mountains of Israel, and one king will be king of all of them – they will no longer be two nations and no longer be divided into two kingdoms. And they will no longer defile themselves with their idols or their abominations or with all their rebellions, but I will save them from all their offenses which they have sinned and will cleanse them.⁸ And they will be my people and I will be their God. And my servant David will be king over them, and they will have one shepherd, and they will walk in my just requirements and keep my statutes and follow them."⁹ (Ezek 37:21–24)

The restoration passages in Isaiah on which Paul draws are also distinctly nationalistic, specifically promising *Israel's* restoration. The Isaianic servant in Isa 49:1–6, for example, is commissioned "to establish the tribes of Israel and to bring back the dispersion of Israel" (49:6).¹⁰

---

⁵ "In both Ezek 11:17 and 20:34, then, as in Jer 29:10–14, we have very close parallels to Deut 30:3–5. All four of these texts promise that God will gather the exiles from the land to which he has deported them and bring them back to the land of Israel. The first three of these texts are addressed directly to the exiles themselves" (Stephen J. Hultgren, *From the Damascus Covenant of the Community* [2007], 91).

⁶ Note that here Ezekiel explicitly equates Israel's restoration with resurrection from the dead.

⁷ LXX: "into the land of Israel."

⁸ Following the LXX here; as pointed in the MT, this clause says, "save them from their dwelling places which they sinned."

⁹ The LXX of 37:24b is slightly different: "they will walk in my commands and they will guard/keep my judgments and will do them."

¹⁰ The LXX reading is even stronger than the MT reading, as the MT has "it is too light a thing," while the LXX has "it is a great thing." David Baer argues that the Greek translator likely understood the "light to the nations" as referring "to his [the servant's] role in bringing Diaspora Jews back from such distant places" ("It's All about Us!" [2006], 31–32). Lutz Doering, "The Commissioning of Paul" (2016), 552 n. 28, says that "this would evidently not have tied in with Paul's vision of the salvation of both Gentiles and Jews." But both Baer and Doering conflate the "tribes of Jacob" with "Diaspora Jews," missing a key link between this passage and Paul's understanding of his own mission. Jacob is not equivalent to Judah in Isaiah, and once the distinction is understood, the mission to restore Israel makes more sense in a Second Temple period context. Arie van der Kooij's ("The Servant of the Lord" [1997], 394–95) argument that the "servant" is also the one who "shall be gathered" (Isa 49:5) is similarly mistaken;

Similarly, the outpouring of the spirit is promised not to the nations but to "your [Jacob's] offspring" (44:3), specifically "to those in Jacob who turn from wrongdoing" (59:20). When Paul quotes Isa 59:21 in Rom 11:27, "this is my covenant with them," he is pulling from a passage about *Jacob's* reception of the spirit, restoration, and exaltation, not a promise of the outpouring of the spirit on non-Israelite nations.

In this light, if Paul believed the new covenant was being fulfilled as predicted by the biblical prophets, one would expect him to be celebrating the miraculous return of the northern tribes, not proclaiming the "mystery" of the justification and incorporation of gentiles in the new covenant *ekklēsia*. This is a critically important point often missed when discussing Paul's rationale for gentile inclusion. Wright, for example, asserts that "the new covenant is emphatically not a covenant in which 'national righteousness' ... is suddenly affirmed. It is the covenant in which sin is finally dealt with."[11] On the contrary, the new covenant is explicitly, emphatically, and unavoidably national, promising restoration and righteousness to "Israel and Judah" and saying nothing about those outside those national boundaries. Wright gives no explanation for why this national covenant suddenly applies to gentiles, sidestepping a critically important question given the terms stated in the new covenant promise itself. Lutz Doering recognizes this problem when he points out that when Paul draws on such passages, he seems to "disregard the Israel-related aspects,"[12] while the fact that Isaiah's servant engages in "a ministry immediately directed to *Israel* ... run[s] counter to Paul's deployment of the prophetic passages."[13]

It is true that many Jewish restorationists expected that upon Israel's restoration many gentiles would serve YHWH (or be subject to Israel),[14]

---

rather, the servant is the one who does the gathering of *another* group, namely, "Jacob and Israel" and the "tribes of Jacob" (49:6). Kooij may be correct, however, that the servant "is to be equated, within the whole of LXX Isaiah, with 'my people in Egypt'" and "the priest Onias (IV) ... and his followers" (394–95). The "servant" could also be identified as Judah – that is, the Jews – whose job it is to turn back the dispersion of Israel and to be a light to the nations. Such a reading would certainly seem more in keeping with the Judah-as-vanguard perspective of Ezra–Nehemiah, for example (see Staples, *The Idea of Israel*, 142–61).

[11] N. T. Wright, *The Climax of the Covenant* (1993), 251.
[12] Doering, "The Commissioning of Paul," 554.
[13] Doering, "The Commissioning of Paul," 551–52. See also Florian Wilk, *Die Bedeutung des Jesajabuches für Paulus* (1998), 295–96.
[14] See Chapter 6 for further discussion of the anticipated eschatological pilgrimage of the nations to Jerusalem.

but *the incorporation of uncircumcised gentiles as equal members within the covenantal people* is a different story. Given that he claims to be proclaiming the fulfillment of the new covenant, Paul is at pains to explain the incorporation of uncircumcised gentiles into the new covenant *ekklēsia* when the new covenant promises Israel's restoration, not gentile salvation. This question is central throughout Romans, climaxing in Rom 9–11 with Paul's explanation of the mysterious relationship between the incorporation of gentiles and Israel's salvation (11:25–27). Indeed, the fact that Paul begins Rom 9 by acknowledging that "the covenants" belong to Israel (9:4) indicates that he is fully aware of this problem, as Dunn rightly observes that through the use of the "somewhat surprising" plural, Paul is asserting that "Israel has first 'claim' on the new covenant as well as the old. However much more widely the new has been extended, it is still primarily Israel and Judah who were in view when it was first announced (Jer 31:31–34)."[15]

But Israel is not just "primarily" in view in Jer 31:31–34; Israel and Judah are *solely* in view in that passage and therefore have *sole* claim on the new covenant. Paul does not challenge this fact – again, "*theirs* are the covenants" (Rom 9:4) – but he nevertheless insists that gentiles are to be included in Israel's covenant, offering an extended argument that gentile inclusion in the new covenant is a necessary component of the promised salvation of "all Israel" (11:26) and "that his apostolate to the Gentiles is *also* a form of ministry to Israel."[16] Indeed, at its core, Romans is a defense of how gentile incorporation in the *ekklēsia* following Israel's messiah is inextricably linked to Israel's salvation and is paradoxical proof of God's faithfulness to Israel.

Paul ties Israel's restoration together with the redemption of the nations at the very start of Romans, declaring that he was set apart as an apostle of the "good news of God, which he promised beforehand through his prophets" (1:1b–2) in order "to bring about the obedience of fidelity in all the nations for his name's sake" (1:5; cf. 15:18; 16:26).[17] He repeats this connection yet again in his declaration that the gospel "is the power of God for salvation to all who are faithful, to the Jew first and also

---

[15] James D. G. Dunn, *Romans* (1988), 534.
[16] Doering, "The Commissioning of Paul," 552 n. 30.
[17] That the book both begins and ends with reference to bringing about the "obedience of fidelity" underscores its thematic importance to the letter and Paul's understanding of his ministry as a whole. See Don B. Garlington, *Faith, Obedience, and Perseverance* (2009), 10–13.

to the Greek" (1:16).¹⁸ He then lays the foundation for that argument, presenting a traditional restoration eschatological perspective in which disobedient Israel has come under the same wrath as the nations and consequently needs the circumcision of the heart and the new spirit promised in the prophets to attain the life promised in the Torah. This chapter will focus on Paul's presentation of the first half of that paradigm (disobedience and God's impartial judgment), while Chapter 4 will address the second half, namely Paul's distinctive application to the gentiles of the new covenant promises made to Israel.

THE STUMBLING BLOCK OF ROMANS 1–2

After declaring that the good news he proclaims is "the power of God for salvation" and that this salvation applies "to the Jew first and also to the Greek" (1:16), Paul immediately launches into an extended declaration of God's wrath against impiety (ἀσέβεια) and injustice, which he argues also applies "to the Jew first and also to the Greek" (2:9–10) because God is impartial and will judge each person based on works (2:12–13). This section and what immediately follows in Rom 2:14–29 have proven especially difficult for modern interpreters, not only because such condemnations seem like a strange way to follow a declaration of "good news" but also because of their strong emphasis on judgment according to works and the necessity of doing Torah, which many readers have found difficult to square with the apostle's repeated assertion that justification is not "from works of Torah" (e.g., Rom 3:20, 28).

E. P. Sanders, for instance, explains that he "studiously avoided mentioning Rom 1:18–2:29" in his discussion of Paul's view of the fulfillment of the Torah, avoiding systematic treatment of 1:18–32 altogether and relegating Rom 2 to an appendix because "the treatment of the law in chapter 2 cannot be harmonized with any of the diverse things which Paul says about the law elsewhere."¹⁹ Observing that the chapter does not

---

[18] For Rom 1:16–17 as the letter's thesis, including a list of commentators who have taken it as such, see Robert Jewett, *Romans* (2006), 135. See also Rikki E. Watts, "For I Am Not Ashamed of the Gospel" (1999); Jacob Neusner, "The Premise of Paul's Ethnic Israel" (1995), 51; Jean-Noël Aletti, "La présence d'un modèle rhétorique en Romains" (1990); Ernst Käsemann, *Romans* (1980), 21–32. Nevertheless, J. R. Daniel Kirk, *Unlocking Romans* (2008), 49, rightly observes, "The 'thesis' that Paul takes up in 1:16–17 is none other than the 'topic enumerated' in the expansion of the letter opening [in 1:2–5]." See also Stephen L. Young, "Paul's Christological Use of Hab 2.4 in Rom 1.17" (2012).

[19] Sanders, *PLJP*, 123; see also Sanders' recitation of alleged contradictions between 1:18–2:29 and the rest of Romans (35–36).

"naturally lead up to the conclusion that no one keeps the law – much less that the law cannot be kept" but instead argues that the law can and must be kept, Sanders sees no way to correlate the views represented in this section with the rest of Pauline theology. He therefore concludes that the whole section must have been a "synagogue sermon ... written from a Jewish perspective" and only lightly edited by Paul for its new context in Romans.[20] More recently, Douglas Campbell has built on Sanders' foundation, arguing that most of Rom 1:18–3:20 should be regarded not as Paul's own view but rather as a parodic speech-in-character recitation of the theological perspective of Paul's opponents in order to demonstrate its absurdity.[21]

In many respects, Sanders and Campbell have only said the quiet part out loud. Even among less radical interpreters, the arguments of Rom 1:18–2:29 and their law-positive perspective have frequently been treated as little more than a foil for the *real* salvific message of Romans ("justification by faith apart from works of law") beginning in chapter three.[22] "Even where this text has been discussed," Klyne Snodgrass observes, "more time has been spent explaining the text *away* than explaining it."[23] As such, although Rom 1:18–2:16 emphasizes that final judgment will be based on each individual's works, and both Rom 2:14 and 2:25–29 indicate that keeping the Torah is not only possible but necessary for final vindication, most interpreters have glossed over such statements as superseded by later sections presumed to mean that keeping Torah is impossible and therefore unnecessary. "Commentators are so

---

[20] Sanders, PLJP, 129.
[21] See Campbell, *The Quest for Paul's Gospel* (2005), 233–61; *The Deliverance of God* (2009), 530–93. Campbell was anticipated in many particulars, especially as pertains to Rom 1:18–32, by Thomas Schmeller, *Paulus und die 'Diatribe'* (1987), 225–86 and Calvin L. Porter, "Romans 1.18–32: Its Role in the Developing Argument" (1994). Here it is worth noting that the primary impetus of assigning portions of these chapters to an interlocutor is not formal or grammatical but theological, specifically the idea that Paul could not have agreed with the statements in question. Consequently, such rescriptings of the alleged dialogue in these chapters are methodologically circular, wherein statements that seem "unpauline" are assigned to an interlocutor and then potential formal features are identified (or not!) post hoc. In this respect, these dialogical approaches are little different from the older approach of hypothesizing interpolations wherever apparent theological inconsistencies were detected, as each solves the problem not by questioning the model but rather by eliminating inconvenient data as non-Pauline. Not coincidentally, the dialogue is always divided such that Paul agrees with the distinctive theology of his modern interpreter against a bigoted or legalistic (usually Jewish) interlocutor.
[22] N. T. Wright, "The Law in Romans 2" (1996), 131.
[23] Snodgrass, "Justification by Grace – To the Doers" (1986), 73, emphasis his.

clear," Stanley Stowers explains, "about their destination at 3:9 ('all are sinners in need of Christ') that they tend to fly over chapter 2 quickly and at a high altitude, seeing only the message of 3:9 being worked out."[24]

But Romans 1–2 and their emphasis on works and Torah-obedience are not only thoroughly Pauline, these chapters are foundational to Paul's gospel, establishing the link between new covenant restoration eschatology and the inclusion of gentiles in Israel's promises, without which the rest of Romans cannot be fully understood. Moreover, once the centrality of restoration eschatology to Paul's gospel is recognized, these chapters no longer need to be treated as puzzle pieces that do not fit with the larger image or as the views of Paul's opponents. Instead, they snap into place within the framework of Paul's gospel, both further clarifying the larger argument of Romans and requiring a reconsideration of Paul's perspective on the Torah and Israel.

PARADISE LOST: JUDGMENT AGAINST IMPIETY AND IMMORALITY

Paul opens his argument with a declaration of God's wrath against "all impiety and injustice of humans" (Rom 1:18) – that is, the violation of the two great commands of the Torah: love God (Deut 6:5; 30:16) and love neighbor (Lev 19:18). In what follows, Paul tells a narrative of decline in which breaking the first command (impiety) inevitably leads to failure to do the second (injustice), resulting in death (Rom 1:32). This narrative of impiety and its consequences tracks very closely with that found in the Wisdom of Solomon 13–14,[25] with each following a similar progression:

(1) a failure to properly worship God in light of the wonders of creation (Wis 13:1–9; Rom 1:19–20)
(2) idolatry/impiety, including worship of animals (Wis 13:10–14:11; 15:7–13; Rom 1:21–23)

---

[24] Stowers, *A Rereading of Romans* (1994), 126. Cf. also the similar sentiment of Wright, "The Law in Romans 2," 131.
[25] The Wisdom of Solomon is a Jewish work of exhortation focused on the theme of wisdom. The book was composed in Greek, most likely in Alexandria. The date is uncertain, with the consensus placing it between about 220 BCE and 50 CE, most likely in the early Roman period. See Moyna McGlynn, *Divine Judgement and Divine Benevolence in the Book of Wisdom* (2001), 1–24; Jonathan A. Linebaugh, *God, Grace, and Righteousness in Wisdom of Solomon and Paul's Letter to the Romans* (2013), 28–30.

(3) the decline into immorality occasioned by idolatry/impiety (Wis 14:12–14, 22–29; Rom 1:24–31)
(4) the appropriate divine judgment that awaits those guilty of idolatry/impiety and immorality (Wis 14:30–31; Rom 1:32).[26]

Given the presence of numerous thematic and verbal parallels between these passages,[27] it is difficult to escape the conclusion that this section of Romans is borrowing from and engaging with Wisdom. Most commentators have therefore treated this passage as a "theologically faithful representation of *Wisdom* 13–14," a stereotyped condemnation of gentile idolatry and immorality.[28] This narrative of a decline from aniconic worship to the use of images in worship also appears in non-Jewish sources from the era, giving it additional force for a Roman audience aware of such critiques of contemporary Roman practices.[29]

In this light, despite the general language of "humanity" in verse 18, Rom 1:18–32 has frequently been read as specifically condemning *gentile* impiety and injustice, with Israel not included in the critique.[30] But in Rom 2:1, Paul's argument sharply breaks from the narrative progression of Wisdom, as the latter follows the fourth stage of its polemic against idolatry by pausing to reflect on how "we" are not subject to such judgments but instead have the knowledge of God, which ensures justness and protects against idolatry:

But you, our God, are kind (χρηστός) and true, patient (μακρόθυμος) and managing all things in mercy. For if we sin, we are yours, knowing your power. But we will not sin, knowing that we are reckoned as yours. For to know you is complete justness (δικαιοσύνη), and to know your power is the root of immortality. For

---

[26] Note, however, that Paul's version includes divine judgment at every step, not just at the end. For more detailed discussion of each of these steps, see Linebaugh, *God, Grace, and Righteousness*, 97–100 and the earlier version in Linebaugh, "Announcing the Human" (2011), 218–20. It should also be observed that a similar progression of sin and consequent judgment also appears in 1 Cor 10, where Paul recounts the sins of Israel in the wilderness: idolatry, sexual immorality, testing the Lord, and grumbling (10:7–10), concluding that "these things happened to them as an example and were written for our instruction, upon whom the ends of the ages have come. Therefore, let the one who thinks he stands watch out so that he does not fall" (1 Cor 10:11–12).

[27] For a detailed list of verbal parallels, see Timo Laato, *Paul and Judaism* (1995), 94–95.

[28] Linebaugh, *God, Grace, and Righteousness*, 94.

[29] As observed by Thiessen, *Paul and the Gentile Problem* (2016), 49, citing especially Plutarch's *Life of Numa* 8.8.

[30] E.g., Thiessen, *Paul and the Gentile Problem*, 43–52; Paula Fredriksen, "Circumcision Is Nothing" (2022), 85; Brian Rainey, *Religion, Ethnicity and Xenophobia in the Bible* (2018), 230–35; Stowers, *A Rereading of Romans*, 83–125;

neither has the evil intent of human art misled us, nor the fruitless toil of painters.... (Wis 15:1–4)

Paul, on the other hand, takes this moment in the progression to do exactly the opposite. Rather than concluding that "*we* are distinct from *them*," he suddenly turns on his audience with the second person: "therefore you are indefensible" (2:1), censuring his hearer for doing the same things for which he (rightly) judges others while imagining that he will "escape God's judgment" (2:3). Many readers have therefore understood these chapters as first condemning gentile impiety and immorality with a traditional litany of accusations in 1:18–32 before suddenly springing a rhetorical trap on his judgmental but hypocritical Jewish addressee with parallel condemnations in Rom 2, departing from Wisdom in surprising fashion.[31] Others, however, have contested this reading, pointing out that the addressee of 2:1–16 is not identified as a Jew and proposing that this judgmental figure should be understood as a gentile who agrees with the judgments against other gentiles' idolatrous and unjust practices as outlined in 1:18–32.[32]

In any case, these close affinities with Wisdom and the general tenor of condemnation in Rom 1:18–32 are why some have concluded that this passage cannot represent Paul's own views but must rather represent the position of his theological rivals, whose theology depends on these sections of Wisdom,[33] while Paul will refute "both the content of the discourse and the practice of using such discourses" in the immediately following passage.[34] "Is it more likely," Campbell asks, "that Paul, the preacher of a law-free Gospel to the Gentiles, is citing traditional Jewish Propaganda Literature like the Wisdom of Solomon, or that his law-observant opponents, the Teachers are? Clearly the latter."[35]

---

[31] See the fuller summary of this position in Linebaugh, *God, Grace, and Righteousness*, 93–94.

[32] E.g., Stowers, *A Rereading of Romans*, 126–34. Those arguing that the addressee(s) of Rom 2 is a circumcised convert to Judaism usually agree with Stowers in referring to this hypothetical figure as a "gentile," despite that label being misleading as applied to proselyte to Judaism (e.g., Runar M. Thorsteinsson, *Paul's Interlocutor in Romans 2* [2003]; Matthew Thiessen, *Paul and the Gentile Problem*; Rodríguez, *If You Call Yourself a Jew* (2014); Joshua D. Garroway, *Paul's Gentile-Jews* [2012]). For further discussion, see pp. 23–24 and 150–54.

[33] See especially Campbell, *Deliverance of God*, 542–93, building on the position of Sanders, PLJP, 123–35 (quote 129). Similarly, John C. O'Neill, *Paul's Letter to the Romans* (1975), 52–53, concludes that 1:18–2:29 is "a traditional tract which belongs essentially to the missionary literature of Hellenistic Judaism."

[34] Porter, "Romans 1.18–32," 215.   [35] Campbell, *Quest*, 258.

But it is too rarely noticed that Paul does not replicate Wisdom's polemic in a straightforward fashion but has instead made a series of subtle changes throughout his account that systematically undermine Wisdom's traditional conclusion that Israel stands apart from the just condemnation of the nations – exactly the opposite of what one would expect if the passage were a straightforward representation of his opponents' views.[36] That Rom 9 similarly subverts Wisdom's arguments about Israel's election further reinforces the function of his engagement with Wisdom in these chapters.[37] Rather than Rom 1:18–32 targeting "the pagan gentile world alone,"[38] this passage weaves together the transgressions of Adam and Israel to indict all humanity – Israel and the nations alike – as under sin and therefore subject to the curse of death, an assessment then made explicit in Rom 2 and then again in Rom 3.[39]

THE DISCARDED IMAGE: IDOLATRY, IMMORALITY, AND THE KNOWLEDGE OF GOD

The first hint that Rom 1:18–32 is not merely reproducing Wisdom's stereotypical condemnations of gentile impiety and immorality is found in the repeated claim that the subjects in question "knew God" before they rebelled against him (1:19, 21, 25, 28, 32). This is in stark contrast to the argument of Wisdom, in which the idolators are "empty by nature," "ignorant of God," and "unable to know the one who is" (13:1). Here Wisdom stands on traditional ground; it was a truth universally acknowledged in early Jewish literature that God had *not* revealed knowledge of himself to the other nations, which therefore persist in darkness and ignorance, but only to Israel, which was established to be a nation of priests and a light to the nations. "You alone have I known among all the families of the earth," declared Amos, "therefore I will punish you for all your misdeeds" (Amos 3:2). This theme of the theological ignorance and blindness of gentile polytheists appears in a variety of Hellenistic Jewish

---

[36] Linebaugh, *God, Grace, and Righteousness*, 106 n. 43; Charles E. B. Cranfield, *Romans* (1979), 104 n. 1; Dunn, *The Theology of Paul the Apostle*, 93. See also Alec J. Lucas, *Evocations of the Calf?* (2014), 169–211; "Distinct Portraits and Parallel Development of the Knowledge of God in Romans 1:18–32 and Wisdom of Solomon 13–15" (2011).

[37] See Chapter 5 for more discussion of Paul's engagement with Wisdom in Romans 9.

[38] Thiessen, *Paul and the Gentile Problem*, 47.

[39] On Rom 1 as weaving together the stories of Adam and Israel, see Linebaugh, *God, Grace, and Righteousness*, esp. 111–15.

sources in addition to Wisdom, including Josephus, Philo, and the Sibylline Oracles.[40]

As already seen in Wisdom 15:1–4, Israel was different from the ignorant gentile nations precisely because Israel had been given revelation and knowledge through the gift of the Torah, as Deuteronomy itself declares: "The hidden things belong to YHWH our God, but the revealed things belong to us and to our children forever" (Deut 29:28 [ET: 29:29]).[41] The book of Baruch,[42] for example, proclaims that the "rulers of the nations" (3:16) "did not know the way of knowledge" (3:20) and that because God did not choose the original inhabitants of Canaan, "he did not give them the way of knowledge, and they perished because they did not have wisdom" (3:26). Israel, however, is different:

> Who has gone up into heaven and taken her and brought her down from the clouds? Who has crossed over the sea and found her and will bring her in exchange for choice gold? [Deut 30:12–14] ...
> This is our God. No other will be counted before him. He discovered the whole way of knowledge and gave her to his servant Jacob and to Israel who was loved by him. After this she appeared on earth and associated among humans. She is the book of the commands of God and the Torah that remains forever. All who seize her gain life, but those who forsake her will die. Turn, Jacob, and take hold of her. Pass through toward the shining in the presence of her light. Do not give your glory to another and your benefits to another nation. Blessed are we, Israel, because what is pleasing to God is known to us. (Bar 3:29–30, 3:36–4:4)

In contrast to the standard Jewish polemical argument that Israel has been set apart from the theologically ignorant pagans by the reception of the Torah, the account of Rom 1:18–32 "offers a completely distinct explanation."[43] In Paul's account, Kathy Gaca explains, the idolators are "not theologically blind outsiders but something far more reprehensible in biblical terms. They are knowledgeable about God ... yet have

---

[40] E.g., Josephus, *Ap.* 2.168–169, 2.224, 2.250–54; Philo, *Spec. Leg.* 1.15–21, 3.97–99; *Opif.* 45; *Ebr.* 42–45; *Decal.* 52–56, 66–81; *Contempl.* 10–11; and *Sib. Or.* 3.669–70, 207–8, 300–62. See the discussion in Kathy L. Gaca, "Paul's Uncommon Declaration in Romans 1:18–32 and Its Problematic Legacy for Pagan and Christian Relations" (1999), 167–71; cf. John M. G. Barclay, *Jews in the Mediterranean Diaspora* (1996), 186.

[41] Cf. LXX Exod 2:24, "And God looked upon the children of Israel, and he became known to them (ἐγνώσθη αὐτοῖς)"; Ps 75:2, "God is known in Judah; in Israel his name is great."

[42] The dating of Baruch is uncertain, with most placing it somewhere between 200–60 BCE but with little precision. For a general introduction to the book, see Daniel J. Harrington, "Baruch, Book of" (2010); Francis Watson, *Paul and the Hermeneutics of Faith* (2004), 456–58.

[43] Gaca, "Paul's Uncommon Declaration," 171.

become rebels."[44] This is not a minor change. Right from the start, the alert reader familiar with traditional Jewish polemics will be startled by the assertion that "what is knowable about God is revealed among them, for God has revealed it to them" (1:19). Since when has the knowledge of God been revealed among the pagans? Is not the knowledge of God granted through the Torah the very thing that has set Israel apart?

Unlike Wisdom's ignorant idolaters who failed to realize the knowledge of God through extrapolating from creation to creator, Paul tells a narrative in which the explicit revelation from creator to creation is realized but rejected.[45] As such, like Adam,[46] the subjects of Romans are "without excuse" or "indefensible" (ἀναπολογήτους) precisely because they knew better and rebelled against the revelation of God.[47] Not only did they have access to divine revelation, they "understood" (νοούμενα) the "unseen things" (τὰ ἀόρατα; 1:20).[48] Rom 1:18–32 does not speak "of people who should have known God's attributes through the creation around them"[49] but rather of people who *did* know God's attributes through the revelation God gave them. By implication, the knowledge of God and divine revelation is not in fact a safeguard against impiety and sin as Wisdom suggests (15:2) but rather is the very reason the rebels of Rom 1 stand without excuse for impiety and injustice. In Jonathan Linebaugh's words, "*Wisdom's* polemic targets idiots; Paul aims at apostates."[50]

But Paul does not argue that *gentiles* are apostates having started from the knowledge of God and willingly rejecting God in favor of idolatrous impiety; indeed, he makes exactly the opposite point in Rom 5, where he explains:

Just as through one human, sin entered the world and death through sin, and thus death spread to all humanity, because all sinned – for until the Law, sin was in the world, but sin is not reckoned when there is no law. But death reigned from Adam

---

[44] Gaca, "Paul's Uncommon Declaration," 171.
[45] Linebaugh, *God, Grace, and Righteousness*, 111; cf. Richard H. Bell, *No One Seeks for God* (1998), 94.
[46] Cf. Hos 6:5: "Like Adam (LXX: ὡς ἄνθρωπος) they have transgressed the covenant."
[47] This again strongly contrasts with Wisdom, which declares that "those who have been taught [sacred things] will find a defense" (6:10). Cf. also the denunciation of the senseless idolators in Let. Jer. 40–41.
[48] The claim of Rom 1:20 that God's attributes have been "understood through what has been made" echoes T. Naph. 3:4, which declares that unlike the nations which went astray, Israel will "recognize in the firmament, in the earth, and in the sea, and in all created things, the Lord who made all things."
[49] As Frank Thielman, *Paul and the Law* (1994), 168.
[50] Linebaugh, *God, Grace, and Righteousness*, 110.

until Moses even over those who had not sinned in the likeness of the transgression of Adam. (Rom 5:12–14)

The key point here is that because there was no Torah between Adam and Moses, there is a qualitative difference between the rebellious act of Adam, who sinned with full knowledge of the command, and the sins committed in ignorance rather than "in the likeness of the transgression of Adam" (5:14). An act of rebellion comparable to that of Adam could not be replicated until the arrival of the Torah, giving Israel the unique distinction of sinning in the same fashion as Adam.[51] In Rom 2:12–14, we find that the same principle still applies to at least some gentiles who "do not have the Torah" (2:14) and thus could not know it; such persons will "perish without the Torah" while all who have "sinned in Torah will be judged by Torah" (2:12).[52] In this light, it is all the more significant that Paul's excoriation of impiety starts not from ignorance but from knowledge – a situation shared by Adam and Israel but not the stereotypical gentile, who is to a large degree a victim of ancestral sin resulting in the empty reasoning, foolishness, and depraved minds that ensure they remain captive to sin and subject to death (Gal 4:8; cf. Eph 4:17–19).

Paul is not, however, the only early Jewish author to give an account of impiety or idolatry that does not begin from ignorance but instead outlines a turn from the knowledge of God to impiety resulting in impurities, immorality, and divine punishment. The other example is found in Philo's *On Rewards and Punishments*, which refers to:

the curses and the punishments which are suitable for those persons who have disregarded the sacred laws of justice and piety and have gone off to polytheistic opinions, the end of which is ungodliness through forgetfulness of the instruction of their relatives and ancestors, which from their earliest life they were disciplined to know the nature of the One, the highest God, to whom alone it is necessary to join those persons who pursue sincere truth instead of fabricated fables."[53] (*Praem.* 162)

---

[51] As observed by Linebaugh, *God, Grace, and Righteousness*, 112–13. A similar rabbinic tradition paralleling the sin of Israel with that of Adam can be found in Num. Rab. 16:24. See Jerome H. Neyrey, "'I Said: You Are Gods': Psalm 82:6 and John 10" (1989), 657–59.

[52] Linebaugh, *God, Grace, and Righteousness*, 113–14, points out that the sins of Adam and Israel in the wilderness are also associated in Rom 7, where the command against coveting links both stories. In that chapter, Paul takes the perspective of a person with knowledge of the Torah of God who is nevertheless enslaved to sin in the flesh and therefore comes under the curse of death because of disobedience, recapitulating the knowledge, sin, death progression of Rom 1:18–32 from a different angle. For more on the connection between the sins of Adam/Eve and Israel in Rom 7, see John K. Goodrich, "Sold under Sin" (2013), 487–94.

[53] Another Philonic parallel concerning the descent of idolatry into increasingly disgusting forms can be found in *Decal.* 52–56, 66–81, but in that case such idolators are presumed

But it is telling that this passage is not about *gentile* idolatry; instead, this passage refers to *Israel's* turn from the covenant to impiety and the resulting covenantal curses, which Philo has just outlined in the previous section (*Praem.* 126–61), where he offers his interpretation of Deut 28–29. In keeping with Deut 30, the following passage then declares that if those who have fallen under such curses receive them "not as for their destruction but rather for their warning and improvement ... and change their ways," they will once again receive favor from God, who will then bestow upon them a great gift – close relationship to his word (*logos*) accompanied by "restoration to freedom" and regathering "from the ends of the earth" (*Praem.* 163–165).[54] On the other hand, the "noble-born" who does not repent in response to these calamities will be cut off, while the faithful foreigner (ἔμπηλυς) who has "come over to God of his own accord" will receive "a sure and firm heavenly habitation" (152; cf. Rom 2:6–11).

That Paul, like Philo, also has Israel in view in Rom 1:18–32 becomes all the more evident in 1:23, which describes the behavior of these rebels against revelation with a striking reference to the account of the golden calf episode in Psalm 106:20:

And they exchanged their glory (καὶ ἠλλάξαντο τὴν δόξαν) for (ἐν) the likeness (ὁμοίωμα) of a grass-eating ox. (Ps 106[105 LXX]:20)

And they exchanged the glory (καὶ ἤλλαξαν τὴν δόξαν) of the immortal God for (ἐν) the likeness (ὁμοίωμα) of an image of mortal humanity and of birds and quadrupeds and creeping things. (Rom 1:23)[55]

The verbal parallels are especially strong, including an unusual grammatical construction in which the verb for "exchange" (ἀλλάσσω) takes the preposition ἐν ("in"; an artifact of translating the Hebrew ב), which further signals that this is a reference to the Psalm rather than merely coincidental or familiar language.[56] By recalling this psalmic passage as

---

to have begun from ignorance (59), though some especially impious persons do practice "willful forgetfulness" (62). See Barclay, *Jews in the Mediterranean Diaspora*, 186.

[54] Cf. Rom 2:4. On Philo's restoration eschatology, particularly as shown in *On Rewards and Punishments*, see Staples, *The Idea of Israel*, 239–52.

[55] Jewett, *Romans*, 160–61, notes that Paul's formulation "avoids the LXX's ambiguity in the use of δόξα ("glory") by a formulation closer to the MT" and that the curious expression "likeness of an image" reflects "an image twice removed, a distortion."

[56] The usual preposition with verbs of exchange is not ἐν but ἀντί. See Hubert Weir Smyth, *Greek Grammar* (1920), §1373. One might also expect a genitive without a preposition representing the thing obtained by the trade, as in Aesch, *PB*, 967 (Smyth, §1372). Another example of the unusual ἀλλάσσω + acc + ἐν + dat is found in Sir 33:21, also a

he engages in what his hearers would surely recognize as the form of a stereotypical Jewish polemic against idolatry,[57] Paul remarkably puts Israel itself forward as the chief illustration of impiety.[58] Moreover, the language of exchange in this verse not only serves as an unmarked citation of Ps 106 but also connects closely with Jer 2:11–13,[59] where the prophet declares that Israel's impiety was of a special quality precisely because – unlike the impiety of the nations as summarized in typical Jewish polemics – it entailed exchanging the true God for false ones:

> Has a nation exchanged their gods (ἀλλάξονται ἔθνη θεοὺς αὐτῶν) when they were not gods? But my people have exchanged their glory (ὁ δὲ λαός μου ἠλλάξατο τὴν δόξαν αὐτοῦ) for that which is no benefit.... For my people have done two evils: They forsook me, the fountain of living water. And they dug out for themselves cisterns, cracked cisterns that cannot hold water. (Jer 2:11, 13)

Whereas the nations never had "the glory of the immortal god" in the first place and therefore could not exchange that glory for something worthless, that is exactly what Jeremiah says Israel did, making Israel doubly guilty.[60] Paul's use of the very same "exchange" language here is therefore especially significant,[61] sharply contrasting with Wisdom's

---

translation from Hebrew where it presumably renders ב. Thorsteinsson ignores this telltale signal when he argues that "although there are some verbal similarities ... it is to be noted that Paul in no way indicates that he is alluding to scripture. Such allusion would not have been evident to his readers, either" (*Paul's Interlocutor*, 170). His second objection, that "it is beyond a reasonable doubt that neither Paul nor his readers would have understood these latter [the verses surrounding v. 23] descriptions as referring to Jews," runs aground on the numerous other indications in those verses that more than just gentiles are in view, most notably that these idolaters do not begin from ignorance (Thorsteinsson does not engage with Gaca's work).

[57] Dunn, *Romans*, 72.

[58] Cf. Dunn, *Romans*, 73. Similarly, 1 Cor 10:1–22 highlights Israel's idolatry in the golden calf episode, suggesting that for Paul, "idolatry is the basic sin of Israel, encompassing all others" (Terrance Callan, "Paul and the Golden Calf" [1990], 3).

[59] Thorsteinsson, *Paul's Interlocutor*, 170 n. 49, and Emma Wasserman, *The Death of the Soul in Romans 7* (2008), 119–20 n. 2, object that Jer 2:11 and Ps 106:20 refer to the people exchanging *their* glory rather than God's glory. But Lucas, *Evocations of the Calf*, 127, points out that this objection both overlooks that the calf was made from the people's jewelry and misses the point, since Israel's glory *was* the glory of God in their midst. Cf. Deut 10:21; Ps 3:3; Isa 62:2.

[60] This concept of double guilt also appears in Hos 10:10 and accounts for why Israel and Judah receive double punishment for their sins (Isa 40:2; Jer 16:18; cf. Rev 18:6).

[61] Similar language appears in T. Naph. 3–4, which says that "nations wandered and abandoned the Lord and changed (ἀλλοιόω) their order and obeyed trees and stones" (3:3). The passage then declares that despite recognizing the Lord through creation, "my children" (=Israel/Naphtali) will similarly "depart from the Lord, walking according to all the lawlessness of the nations and will do according to all the wickedness of Sodom"

claim of Israel's innocence by citing the very episode elided from Wisdom's contrast between Israel and pagan idolators.⁶² As Francis Watson remarks, "Paul faces the fact that the author of *Wisdom* strives to suppress: that the holy nation is itself deeply complicit in the idolatry and ungodliness that it prefers to ascribe to the Gentiles."⁶³ It is probably not mere coincidence that in another Pauline passage referring to the golden calf episode, namely 2 Cor 3, "the motif of glory, or rather loss of glory, is prominent."⁶⁴

But Paul does not limit his critique to the golden calf episode; rather than the psalm's explicit reference to the "grass-eating ox," Paul's apostates worshiped "the likeness of an image of mortal humanity and of birds and quadrupeds and creeping things," broader language pulled from the injunctions against images in Deut 4:16–18 and the Genesis creation narrative – again connecting Israel's sin with Adam's sin.⁶⁵ In so doing,

---

(4:1), whose distinctive sin is "exchanging (ἐναλλάσσω) the order of their nature" (3:4). That is, whereas the nations ignorantly *changed* their order, Israel will knowingly *exchange* their proper order for impiety, resulting in twice-repeated captivity and diaspora, "until the compassion of the Lord comes, a man doing justice and doing mercy to all who are far off and all who are near" (4:5). T. Naph. therefore explicitly argues that Israel has not been distinct from the nations but has engaged in the same sorts of behavior characteristic of the nations, exactly the undercurrent of Paul's argument in Rom 1:18–32.

⁶² On Wisdom's suppression of the golden calf narrative and its implications, see Linebaugh, *God, Grace, and Righteousness*, 68–80, 102–4; John M. G. Barclay, "I Will Have Mercy on Whom I Have Mercy" (2010), 91.

⁶³ Watson, *Hermeneutics of Faith*, 411.

⁶⁴ Alec J. Lucas, "Paul and the Calf" (2018), 112 n. 6. Contra the suggestion that Paul (in Rom 9:4) "also claims that even now the glory belongs to Israel, suggesting that he does not think contemporary Jews have exchanged it or lost it" (Thiessen, *Paul and the Gentile Problem*, 47; cf. Stowers, *A Rereading of Romans*, 130). If Paul believes that his fleshly kin do in fact still have the glory of God, it is puzzling that in the preceding verse (9:3) he is so grieved for them that he, like Moses in the very narrative in which Israel exchanges the glory for an image, presents himself as asking God to cut him off for the sake of his people. That the glory rightfully belongs to Israel is not in question. But that does not imply that all Israelites (or Jews) actually possess what rightly belongs to them. Paul's grief only makes sense if it is on behalf of those who presently lack what ought to be theirs (rightly pointed out by Joshua W. Jipp, "What Are the Implications of the Ethnic Identity of Paul's Interlocutor?" [2016], 201 n. 57). But even if 9:3 could be explained away, 3:23 explicitly says, "*all* have sinned and lack the glory of God," and unless Jews or other Israelites are somehow excluded from the "all," it seems most natural to identify 1:23 as including Israel's idolatrous history in the larger framework of *human* (1:18) impiety and injustice.

⁶⁵ Deut 4:16–18 prohibits making an engraved likeness of "male or female" (presumably humans) as well as animals, birds, creeping things, or water creatures. On the echoes of the Genesis creation story in Rom 1:23, see Lucas, *Evocations of the Calf*, 127–31; Linebaugh, *God, Grace, and Righteousness*, 112 n. 65, 114; Jouette M. Bassler, *Divine*

Paul invokes not only the single episode of the golden calf but the repeated pattern of idolatry begun with the calf and including a variety of images, from the bronze serpent (Num 21:9; 2 Kgs 18:4) to "every form of creeping thing and animals and abominations" worshiped in the Jerusalem temple in Ezekiel 8:10.[66]

The reference to Israel's idolatry in Rom 1:23 sheds more light on the already allusively evocative language of 1:21, as there are, in addition to the Eden story, two scriptural instances of those who "knew God" but "did not glorify him as God." The first and most obvious is in Mal 2, where the priests who "should preserve knowledge" (2:7) have come under the curse because they did not "give glory to my name" (2:2). The second is when the northern Israelites scornfully reject Hezekiah's appeal five years before the fall of Samaria: "Do not harden your necks but give glory to the Lord God[67] ... and be subject to the Lord your God, and he will remove from you the anger of his wrath" (2 Chr 30:8).[68]

The consequence of such knowing refusals to glorify God, Paul says, is that these apostates "became empty (ἐματαιώθησαν)." Here Paul uses not only the same word but exactly the same form found in the lament over northern Israel after Samaria's fall in 2 Kgs 17, which declares that Israel "did not keep his testimonies ... and they went after the empty things and became empty (ἐματαιώθησαν) and went after the nations that were around them, of whom he had commanded them not to imitate" (17:15). The only other place this form appears in the Greek Bible is in a parallel passage in Jer 2:5, where YHWH declares to the "house of Israel" that their ancestors "went far from me and went after empty things and became empty (ἐματαιώθησαν)."[69] Again, in contrast to the

---

Impartiality (1982), 195–97. On echoes of Deut 4:15–19, see David A. Burnett, "A Neglected Deuteronomic Scriptural Matrix for the Nature of the Resurrection Body in 1 Cor 15:39–42" (2019), 202, 205; Joseph A. Fitzmyer, *Romans* (1993), 283.

[66] MT: כל־תבנית רמש ובהמה שקץ. LXX Ezek 8:10 lacks the reference to the animals and creeping things, instead referring to the "empty abominations" (μάταια βδελύγματα) and "idols" (εἴδωλα). Nevertheless, the LXX passage still refers to the worship of numerous images in the Jerusalem temple.

[67] Translating the LXX; MT has "give a hand to YHWH" rather than "give glory to."

[68] Although it is rarely noticed that Hezekiah's invitation precedes the final destruction of the northern kingdom, 2 Kgs 18:10 places the fall of Samaria in the sixth year of Hezekiah, while Chronicles puts this invitation in his first year (2 Chr 29:37; 30:2). See Staples, *The Idea of Israel*, 114–15; Sara Japhet, "Exile and Restoration in the Book of Chronicles" (1999), 40 n. 19.

[69] The verb ματαιόω is rare, appearing only in the Septuagint (7×), Rom 1:21, and the work of grammarians and scholiasts. The form Paul uses appears only here and 2 Kgs 17 and Jer 2:5. The use of such a rare form – particularly such unusual and specialized

idolators of Wisdom, the willful apostates of 2 Kings, Jeremiah, and Rom 1 did not start in futility and ignorance but rather, "though they knew God," they *became* empty through exchanging their glory for dishonor, their fullness for emptiness, and their wisdom for foolishness.

Lest these allusions to Israel's idolatrous past prove too subtle, Paul brings his invective to a close with the startling declaration that these immoral idolators not only "knew God" (Rom 1:21) and the "truth of God" (1:25), they also "knew the just statute (δικαίωμα) of God" (1:32). Although this word (δικαίωμα) can refer to "acts/requirements of justice" in a general sense, it is difficult to escape the biblical resonance of "δικαίωμα of God" as referring to the revelation of those requirements in the Torah (e.g., Deut 30:10, 16),[70] especially since Paul uses it explicitly in that sense in Rom 2:26 and 8:4.[71] The next clause strengthens this resonance, as Paul specifies that the "δικαίωμα of God" is "that those who do such things are worthy of death" (1:32). But idolatry, homosexual acts, and the rest of the vices Paul has just listed (excepting murder) were not capital offenses in gentile law codes,[72] a fact that has led to significant difficulties as interpreters have (sometimes rather creatively) attempted to establish on what basis Paul could argue that these deeds are recognized as worthy of death.[73] But once one recognizes that Rom 1:18–32 conflates the stories of Adam and Israel, that problem is moot, as both Adam and Israel are given specific commands that if violated will result in death. Specifically, Moses presents the choice between obeying and disobeying God's statutes (δικαιώματα) as a choice between "life and death" (Deut 30:19),[74] and those who know the Torah are the ones who know that persons who do such things come under its curse – that is, death.[75]

---

vocabulary from such a well-known passage as 2 Kgs 17 – gives this echo high intertextual volume. On intertextual volume, see Richard B. Hays, *Echoes of Scripture in the Letters of Paul* (1989), 30.

[70] Δικαίωμα appears 134 times in the LXX, including 28 in Deuteronomy, 34 in Psalms, and 17 in Ezekiel. The vast majority of these (and all 79 in Deuteronomy, Psalms, and Ezekiel) refer to the "statute(s)" of God/YHWH as revealed specifically to Israel. Cf. also Luke 1:6; Heb 9:1, 10.

[71] Rom 2:26 and 8:4 both refer to the "δικαιώματα of the Torah," and the two occurrences in Rom 5:16, 18 reflect back on this verse with the additional filter of 2:26, as Paul parallels Adam's transgression with Jesus' δικαίωμα (that is, the fulfillment of Torah, as is further clarified in 8:4).

[72] Thielman, *Paul and the Law*, 169.   [73] See Jewett, *Romans*, 190–91.

[74] Thielman, *Paul and the Law*, 169.

[75] Contra Dunn's argument that "in using this word he is not thinking of requirements of the law as normally understood in Judaism (2:26; and see further on 8:4)" (*Romans*, 69).

Nevertheless, by referring to the "just statutes of God" rather than "the just statutes of the Torah" (as in 2:26), Paul retains sufficient ambiguity to apply to the transgressions of both Adam and Israel, thereby including all humanity as having come under the penalty of death. That is not to say, however, that "Paul speaks of what all people, whether blessed with special revelation or not, can know of God's just judgment,"[76] since Paul has emphasized special revelation throughout the passage. Unlike Wisdom, Paul is not making an *empirical* argument from natural law but rather an *exegetical* argument linking the rebellion of Adam and Israel, with all humanity subject to the ignorance, immorality, and death wrought by the disobedience of their forebears, who in each case *did* have access to special revelation. Moreover, as will be shown below, the argument of Rom 2 that "obedience to what the law requires is possible to those who do not know the law as such" is not (as is often assumed) the result of natural law among gentiles in the absence of special revelation.[77] On the contrary, inasmuch as such obedience requires the "work of the Torah written on the heart" (2:15), it is instead proof that such persons are indeed participants in the new covenant and therefore recipients of special revelation.

Finally, these apostates not only know the "just statute of God" and do the things worthy of death anyway, they also "approve those who do the same" (1:32). Some commentators have questioned why the approval of such things is framed as even worse than doing them, but a look at Paul's scripture again helps clarify his point. Such approval of evil hearkens back to strong prophetic condemnations of the wicked in Israel who not only commit injustice but also suppress the truth they were appointed to deliver and teach others to do evil.[78] Malachi, for example, denounces wicked priests for saying, "Everyone who does evil is good before YHWH, and he delighted in them.' And 'Where is the God of justice?'" (2:17). Isaiah similarly condemns Israel's leaders, "who call evil good and good evil ... who are wise in themselves and knowledgeable in their own sight" (5:20–21).[79] Perhaps the most pointed parallel is found in Hos 4, where the prophet declares:

---

[76] Douglas J. Moo, *Romans* (1996), 121; similarly, Dunn, *Romans*, 69.

[77] Contra Dunn, *Romans*, 69.

[78] It therefore cannot be concluded that when Paul refers to "humans who suppress the truth" in Rom 1:18 that this could only refer to gentiles, as argued by Rainey, *Religion, Ethnicity and Xenophobia*, 233. If anything, it suggests the opposite since such suppression requires knowing the truth in the first place.

[79] Cf. Rom 1:22. An even closer parallel appears in T. Ash. 6:2.

My people have become like one without knowledge. Because you have rejected knowledge (ἐπίγνωσις), I also will reject you from being my priest. As you forgot the Torah (νόμος) of your God; I also will forget your children ... I will turn their glory (δόξα) into dishonor (ἀτιμία). (Hos 4:6–7)

Once again, it is not the ignorant nations that the prophet condemns for rejecting knowledge but Israel. The result is Israel's forfeiture of its glory and its status as the chosen people. God warns Israel that he will forget their children, and as Hosea has already declared, (northern) Israel is now "not my people" and YHWH is "not your God" (Hos 1:9). That is, they are now no different from the other (non-elect) nations, having exchanged their glory for emptiness. By this point, it is evident that, unlike Wis 13–15, Israel does not stand apart from Paul's condemnation of impiety, injustice, and immorality.[80] Indeed, as Gaca explains, "Paul's accusation in Rom 1:18–32 has a specific and technical biblical force.... Paul strenuously reiterates that the people are rebellious Israel through pointed allusions he makes to the Septuagint of Deuteronomy, Psalms, and Jeremiah."[81] Or, in David Starling's words:

Crucially, it is the sin of Israel that is depicted as abolishing the distinction between Jew and Gentile (3:9, 19–20, 22b–23; 4:5–10; 11:30–32), the 'wrath' that Israel has incurred under the curses of the law that is depicted as corresponding with the impending wrath hanging over the heads of the Gentiles (e.g., 1:24, 26, 28; 2:5, 12; 3:5–6; 4:15; 9:22), and the promised 'mercy' of God to Israel that is depicted as corresponding with his mercy in the Gentiles' calling and salvation (e.g., 9:23–24; 11:30–32).[82]

Whereas Wisdom presents Israel as innocent of idolatry thanks to God's revelation (15:1–4),[83] Paul presents Israel as the paradigmatic example of idolatrous rebellion in the face of divine revelation and glory. Although "idolatry was the fundamental sin of the gentiles and the root of the gentile problem,"[84] Israel "followed the nations that surrounded them" (2 Kgs 17:15) and engaged in the same fundamental sin to the point that Ezekiel declares that Jerusalem "became more wicked than the

---

[80] "In *Wisdom* 13–15, the ignorant idolaters do not include Israel (15.2b–4). Paul's polemic permits no such limitations" (Linebaugh, *God, Grace, and Righteousness*, 112).
[81] Gaca, "Paul's Uncommon Declaration," 172.
[82] David I. Starling, *Not My People* (2011), 163.
[83] Cf. Linebaugh, *God, Grace, and Righteousness*, 115; Barclay, "I Will Have Mercy," 93; Watson, *Hermeneutics of Faith*, 411.
[84] Thiessen, *Paul and the Gentile Problem*, 47.

nations (ἔθνη) and countries around her" (Ezek 5:6).[85] Similarly, when Moses explains that YHWH is displacing the nations of Canaan "because of the impiety (ἀσέβεια) of these nations," he warns Israel, "Do not say in your heart, 'it is because of my justness that YHWH has brought me to inherit this good land'" (Deut 9:4, cf. Rom 10:6). Far from being distinct from the nations, Moses declares that Israel had been "unfaithful with respect to the things of YHWH from the day he knew you" (Deut 9:24). Pointing to the golden calf incident and other instances of infidelity in the wilderness, Moses reminds Israel that he had to appeal to YHWH to overlook their "impious acts" (ἀσέβημα; 9:27) so that they would not be utterly destroyed, "thus recalling the reason just given for the Gentiles' destruction."[86] Idolatry and impiety are therefore no less the root of the Israel problem than the gentile problem.[87] Indeed, a central premise of traditional Jewish restoration eschatology is the conviction that due to its

---

[85] The account in 1 Cor 10:1–22 of Israel's idolatry beginning with the golden calf episode indicates that just as with gentiles, "idolatry is the basic sin of Israel, encompassing all others" (Callan, "Paul and the Golden Calf," 3). Thiessen's objection that Israel could not be in view in Rom 1 because "Paul's fellow Jews believed that they worshiped the true God and that the majority of gentiles worshiped idols" (*Paul and the Gentile Problem*, 47) misses the point because Paul's fellow Jews also believed that past Israel had chronically engaged in idol-worship and that some Jews continued to engage in illicit practices that placed them outside the bounds of Israel (e.g., 1 Macc 1:11–15; Philo, *Praem.* 162). Paul does, however, make it clear in 1 Cor 10:7–10 and Rom 11:4–5 that not all Israelites did in fact engage in such practices.

[86] Alec J. Lucas, "Reorienting the Structural Paradigm and Social Significance of Romans 1:18–32" (2012), 136.

[87] Thiessen argues that Ephesians' exhortation that "you must no longer walk as the gentiles walk in the futility of their minds" (4:17) is evidence that the similar language in Rom 1:18–32 must "portray gentiles, and only gentiles, in this way"(*Paul and the Gentile Problem*, 50). But this overlooks both the echo of 2 Kgs 17:15 and the fact that *Ephesians does not say that only gentiles walk like gentiles* – nor, given the witness of Israel's scriptures, could it plausibly make that claim. If someone tells a group to "stop behaving like children," it does not imply that the group includes only children – if anything, it tends to imply the opposite. As even a cursory reading of the Torah (e.g., Deut 4:15–20) or Prophets demonstrates, the exhortation not to walk like gentiles applies just as well to Jews (or other Israelites) as gentiles. Eph 4:17–19 therefore cannot be understood as a confirmation that the critique of Rom 1:18–32 is limited to gentiles. Similar problems emerge in Thiessen's analysis of other early interpretations of Rom 1:18–32. For example, the fact that Tatian cites Rom 1:20 in his *Oration against the Greeks* (4.2) is certainly not proof that he thinks it would not apply to Egyptians or Persians, so it is hardly evidence that it applies solely to gentiles, either. The same is true of Clement of Alexandria's use of the passage in *Exhortation to the Greeks* 8. More damaging is that whereas Thiessen cites *On the Incarnation* 11 as evidence that Athanasius interpreted Rom 1:25 as solely about gentiles, if one keeps reading to *Incar.* 12:5–6, it becomes apparent that Athanasius includes the Jews – and the knowledge of God through the Torah – in this expanded discussion of Rom 1:18–32 and human rebellion. So although Athanasius certainly

own idolatry and rejection of God's revelation and failure to keep the command to love YHWH, Israel is no longer separate and distinct from the rest of humanity but rather stands under the same judgment. Paul simply builds on this principle, arguing that all humanity is therefore in the same situation, under sin and the curse of death, with God's mercy the only hope.

PRIDE AND PREJUDICE: ISRAEL AND THE NATIONS UNDER SIN

In light of the thick network of citations and allusive language recalling Israel's impiety and idolatry in Rom 1:18–32 and the fact that no other Jewish polemic against gentiles suggests that they once possessed the knowledge, glory, and just statute of God, it is remarkable that the passage has been so frequently interpreted as a condemnation solely of gentile sin.[88] Given the familiar form and traditional stereotypes, the

---

regards 1:18–32 as applicable to the "non-Jewish Greco-Roman world" (as demonstrated in *Against the Pagans*), he does not treat it as *exclusive* to that subset of humanity but instead applies it to all humanity, Jews and non-Greco-Romans alike. Thus, although some interpreters (e.g., Chrysostom, *Homilies on Romans* 3, 5) did read Rom 1:18–32 as specifically addressing Greeks, the early interpreters are not univocal on this point as Thiessen suggests. Moreover, appeal to early interpretation cuts both ways for Thiessen, since the earliest interpreters of Rom 2 *are* nearly univocal in applying it to Jews, a reading Thiessen resists.

[88] Contra Thorsteinsson, Thiessen, and Rodríguez, "Paul's Interlocutor," 21: "Arguments that Paul includes Jews within at least parts of his rhetoric are very weak ... Paul, however, describes the gentile world in 1:18–32, and the numerous third-person references suggest that Paul does not intend to indict all of humanity in the sins he catalogues there." But the third person in 1:18–32 is hardly proof that the passage refers strictly to gentiles or even that "with this language of otherness, Paul's portrayal of these people fits the gentile world best" (Thiessen, *Paul and the Gentile Problem*, 47). It is a pity that Thorsteinsson, Thiessen, Rodríguez and others arguing for a strictly gentile reading of 1:18–32 do not substantively engage with the work of Bassler, Gaca, Linebaugh, and Lucas in their assessments of the evidence. Indeed, the only chapter in Rodríguez and Thiessen, eds., *The So-Called Jew in Paul's Letter to the Romans* (2016) to mention any of these important studies is Joshua Jipp's response essay ("What Are the Implications," 184 n. 2), which briefly observes that the work of Lucas and Linebaugh in particular deserves more engagement in this discussion. It is insufficient to dismiss the reference to Jer 2:11 and Ps 105:20 LXX in Rom 1:23 as though that were the only argument or evidence that Israel is included in the indictments of the passage. For the "gentile only" reading of 1:18–32 to obtain, one must also explain why, unlike every other extant example of early Jewish polemic against gentile idolatry, Paul's subjects begin from knowledge rather than ignorance – and how/when he imagines gentiles ever had knowledge of the "just statute of God" (1:32). If, for example, one proposes that Paul introduces the idea of pagan knowledge to avoid depicting God's judgment as cruel and

audience could be forgiven for initially assuming that such condemnations of idolatry and immorality apply to gentiles but not to Israel (as in Wis 13–15). But this is exactly the assumption Paul undermines throughout the passage by subtly altering the content to include Israel as the paradigmatic example of such impiety. The *form* is therefore that of a traditional Jewish polemic against gentiles, but the *voice* is that of Jacob's infidelity.[89]

That Israel does not stand apart from such indictments has been hiding in plain sight; it is too infrequently noticed that Rom 1:18–32 never actually mentions gentiles.[90] The opening statement of judgment in 1:18 does not say that God's wrath is revealed against "all impiety and injustice of *gentiles*" but of "humans" – had Paul intended to limit his target to gentiles, it is remarkable that he missed such an easy opportunity to make that clear. The passage then builds on the universal condemnation of 1:18 by characterizing idolators as apostates starting from the knowledge and glory of God and repeatedly alluding to Israel's own idolatry before concluding with the explicit declaration that such judgment applies "first to the Jew, and also to the Greek" (2:9, 10). It is surely significant that non-Jews are only singled out in formulas emphasizing that the judgments of 1:18–32 apply equally to Jews who do the same things.[91] Remarkably, the first time the word "gentiles" (ἔθνη) is mentioned in the discussion is 2:14, which refers not to gentile idolatry but surprisingly to gentiles who "do the Torah." It is therefore not the case, as Joseph Fitzmyer suggests, that Paul "is simply extrapolating from such incidents in the history of the chosen people and applying the ideas to the

---

monstrous, one must then address why no other extant Jewish polemic against pagan sinfulness exhibits the same concern.

[89] "Although he employs an argument traditionally directed against the Gentiles, he clearly signals that it was also, if not primarily, appropriate to the Jews" (Bassler, *Divine Impartiality*, 122).

[90] One commentator who does highlight this fact and its implications is Thomas H. Tobin, *Paul's Rhetoric in Its Contexts* (2004), 110.

[91] The idea that "the references to homoerotic behavior in Rom 1:24–27 were, from a Jewish perspective, actions that only gentiles were involved in" (Thorsteinsson, Thiessen, and Rodríguez, "Paul's Interlocutor," 21) does not adequately appreciate the rhetorical force of typical Jewish condemnations of such "gentile" behaviors. Is it really plausible that no Jews of this period engaged in such homoerotic practices? On the contrary, condemnations of such behaviors as "outsider" practices serve a pedagogical function for insiders, effectively marking insiders who do such things as de facto outsiders. In any case, Judges 19 is sufficient evidence that historical Israel did not escape the lures of even the most egregious "gentile" sins.

pagan world"[92] but rather that he uses the incidents of idolatry in the history of the chosen people to show that the just condemnation of the pagan world applies equally to the chosen people.[93]

Again, it is imperative to remember that the idea that Israel stands under the wrath of God was not a marginal perspective in the Second Temple period. For the many Jews operating within a restoration eschatological framework in this period, it could be taken for granted that Israel broke the covenant by turning from God to impiety and injustice, thereby falling under the curse of the covenant and becoming "nothing" (2 Kgs 17:15), indistinguishable from the other nations that likewise stand condemned for their sins. Jubilees provides an especially poignant example of this view, summarized by Ronald Charles as follows:

> The present situation of the world is one of corruption and sin. Every being on earth had been corrupted/contaminated. Israel has turned away from the directives of Torah to follow the ways of the wicked peoples of the nations. The temple cult has become so corrupt that it can no longer be considered as authentic. Israel has forsaken the festivals, the covenant, and God himself.[94]

In this paradigm, Israel has long been in the "age of wrath" (CD 1:5) precisely because of its "impiety and injustice" (Rom 1:18), and when Paul opens with the statement that "God's wrath is revealed from heaven," these restoration eschatological overtones are already present. It is also surely no accident that Paul concludes the extended theological argument of Romans by quoting Isaiah's promise that the deliverer "will remove impiety (ἀσεβεία) from Jacob" (11:26; Isa 59:20) – the removal of the very impiety first identified in Rom 1:18.

This context accounts for what Douglas Campbell calls "the awkward temporality of v. 18," which speaks of the present disclosure of God's wrath, when "all that follows builds toward its *future* revelation."[95] But the passage does not in fact present God's wrath solely as a matter of future judgment or revelation; instead, it shows how the Torah and the history of Israel have revealed God's wrath to the present day – God *gave* them over, not *will give* them over (1:24, 26, 28). That is, God's wrath has

---

[92] Fitzmyer, *Romans*, 271.
[93] "At the very least, then, it can be said that in the matter of idolatry Paul conceived of an Israel which was at one with the rest of humanity – as startling a notion as that must have been for his Jewish compatriots" (Don B. Garlington, "ἹΕΡΟΣΥΛΕΙΝ and the Idolatry of Israel (Romans 2.22)" [1990], 144). For 1:18–2:11 as directed at both Jews and gentiles, see Jewett, *Romans*, 152.
[94] Ronald Charles, ed., *Paul and Matthew among Jews and Gentiles* (2020), 62.
[95] Campbell, *Deliverance of God*, 543.

been a present reality for both Israel and the nations throughout the age of wrath. Nevertheless, Paul also looks forward to the "day of wrath" (2:5) in which God will judge humanity and bring about justice (according to Paul's gospel; 2:16!), including the granting of eternal life, glory, and honor to those worthy of it (2:7, 10).

Rather than condemning exclusively gentile sin before targeting his fellow Jews (or proselytes) in the next chapter, Rom 1:18–32 combines traditional indictments of stereotypical gentile behaviors with the restorationist commonplace of Israel's status as under the curse of the Torah for doing the same things, thereby collapsing the distinction between Israel and the nations with respect to sin. In this presentation, Israel is no longer distinct from the nations; Israel's story is the story of the nations in a microcosm, and the story of the nations is Israel's story. Even beyond that, whereas repentance is sufficient for those inside the functioning covenant,[96] because the covenant has been broken, both Israel and the nations are beyond repentance and given over to the power of sin, from which only divine rescue can deliver.[97] Those appointed to give sight to the blind have themselves exchanged their glory for darkness, and with the blind leading the blind all have fallen into the same ditch.

THE ABOLITION OF MAN: GOD'S IMPARTIAL JUSTICE

That Israel is in view throughout Rom 1:18–32 explains the inferential force of the "therefore" (διό) of 2:1, "*therefore* you have no excuse, every human who judges." Commentators have frequently found this transition especially troublesome.[98] Wright, for example, confesses that he finds this

---

[96] Cf. Sanders, *Judaism: Practice and Belief 63 BCE–66 CE* (1992), 271–73.

[97] The idea that repentance is not efficacious in the period of the covenantal curse is not unique to Paul but is already present in Isa 1 and Jer 11, among other prophetic passages. The idea is reiterated by Josephus in *Ant.* 4.312–14, which says that Moses had declared that if Israel transgressed the covenant, "their repentance would in no way profit them in their sufferings." Thanks to Paul Sloan for the Josephus reference. Beverly Gaventa is therefore correct to conclude, "Paul needs the relentless argument of 1:18–3:20 in order to show the depth of human oppression by suprahuman powers. Since humanity is incapable of repenting or changing its mind or reforming its behavior (we are 'weak' enemies of God, as he puts it in 5:8–10), humanity must be rescued" ("Rescue Mission" [2010], 36).

[98] Thorsteinsson, *Paul's Interlocutor*, 177–88, spends eleven pages on what he calls the "διό debate." See also Lucas, *Evocations of the Calf*, 6–7, 119–21. Although some have suggested that διό has no inferential weight here (e.g., Käsemann, *Romans*, 54), Thorsteinsson has convincingly shown that this suggestion is "no more persuasive than

start to 2:1 "puzzling, since the person addressed is *ex hypothesi* not guilty of the charge at the end of 1:32."⁹⁹ But the "therefore" is not nearly so puzzling without the assumption that there is a major shift in thought at the chapter break.¹⁰⁰ Instead, the "therefore" in 2:1 is the third and final of a series of "therefores" (διό in 1:24 and διὰ τοῦτο in 1:26),¹⁰¹ marking the conclusion of the narrative progression of impiety and its consequences and revealing that the Torah-knowledgeable addressee is no less "without excuse" (ἀναπολόγητος, 1:20; 2:1) than those excoriated in the preceding polemic.¹⁰²

The condemnation of 2:1-2 is therefore not a break in thought but rather a natural and emphatic extension of the argument, finally making

---

attempts to explain away the problem, for instance, by arguing that διό is a scribal error for δίς or that 2:1 simply is a secondary gloss," since every other use of the particle in the Pauline epistles "marks a conclusion drawn from the preceding" (*Paul's Interlocutor*, 178). Thorsteinsson's own conclusion, however, is hamstrung by the fact that he shares the assumption that "it cannot be convincingly maintained that the indictment against gentiles in 1:18-32 tells something about Jewish conduct" (178, 167-77). But once one recognizes that 1:18-32 is not merely "an indictment against gentiles" and is nowhere marked as such, the problem disappears entirely.

⁹⁹ N. T. Wright, "The Letter to the Romans" (2002), 438.

¹⁰⁰ Despite the rhetorical shift, the chapters are closely linked verbally and thematically: e.g., "without defense" (ἀναπολόγητος, 1:20; 2:1); "wrath" and "reveal/revelation" (ὀργή/ ἀποκαλύπτω/ἀποκάλυψις, 1:18; 2:5); "wrath, injustice, truth" (1:18; 2:8); "to the Jew first and also the Greek" (1:16; 2:9-10). Bassler has argued that 1:16-2:11 functions as a discrete thought unit structurally characterized by the technique of inclusion (ring-structure) and word chains (*Divine Impartiality*, esp. 121-55; more succinctly argued in Jouette M. Bassler, "Divine Impartiality in Paul's Letter to the Romans" [1984], esp. the diagram at 47). But see the criticisms of Thorsteinsson, *Paul's Interlocutor*, 156-59, who persuasively shows that the thought unit does not end at 2:11 but continues to at least 2:16.

¹⁰¹ See Lucas' analysis demonstrating that the polemic is organized in a threefold cycle with an A-BA-BA-B structure, in which (A) idolatrous *exchange* (1:22-23, 25, 26b-27) results in (B) being *given over* (1:24, 26a, 28-32) to injustice and impurity, which is tied to the next exchange, with the effect that "to suggest that idolatry ultimately creates a vortex in which acts become indistinguishable from consequences" (*Evocations of the Calf*, 117-19 [quote 119]; "Reorienting the Structural Paradigm," 132-34). But the threefold "therefore" suggests that 2:1 should be considered as part of the final stage of consequences (B). It should nevertheless be acknowledged that the διό in 2:1 "cannot mark a conclusion being drawn directly and solely from the preceding sentence, since it clearly does not follow from Paul's charge against those who *approve* of others' vices (1:32) that the one who *judges* others is 'therefore' without excuse (2:1)" (Thorsteinsson, *Paul's Interlocutor*, 179). The third "therefore" marks a conclusion drawing from the whole process, carrying the cycle established in 1:18-32 forward to its logical conclusion for those who recognize the Torah's condemnations of the behavior of both Israel and the nations.

¹⁰² Lucas, *Evocations of the Calf*, 121-22.

explicit what has been allusively implicit and forcing the hearer to retrospectively reconsider the significance of the numerous signals to Israel's history in the preceding polemic.[103] The basic point – the inference signaled by the "therefore" – is that if one agrees with the preceding discourse, then no one stands aloof from God's judgment. Specifically, those who know the Torah and were paying attention to the signals to Israel's history in 1:18–32 know that Israel committed the same offenses and is therefore subject to the same wrath as the rest of the nations. Those who agree that such things are worthy of condemnation – that is, those who have received the Torah and agree with its judgments – are no less under God's wrath than those from the nations. Indeed, the one who agrees with the Torah is self-condemned because the Torah condemns its hearers and declares that its own function is to be a "witness against you" (Deut 31:26).

It is important to recognize that Paul is making an *exegetical* case about Israel and the nations, not an empirical one.[104] That is, the passage indicts Israel from the witness of scripture as guilty of the same sins as the nations, but Paul nowhere asserts that all his Jewish contemporaries are guilty of such behavior. The point is not that the actual or implied addressees of the letter actively worship creepy-crawly images or engage in sexual immorality but rather that scripture testifies that all

---

[103] "Functionally, then, the indictment of Romans 1.18–32 becomes, at least retroactively, an indictment of the Jew as much as the Gentile" (Linebaugh, *God, Grace, and Righteousness*, 95). On διό as emphatic, see Thorsteinsson, *Paul's Interlocutor*, 179–80. Thorsteinsson objects that adjusting one's understanding of 1:18–32 based on what follows violates the principle that letters are designed to be read forward rather than in reverse (180–82). But Thorsteinsson underestimates the impact of such rhetorical turns as one finds in 2:1, which demand retrospective adjustments to the reader's understanding of foreshadowed signals in prior passages. Literary examples of this phenomenon abound; readers of the *Harry Potter* series, for example, are famously forced to retrospectively adjust their understanding of previous passages – even prior books in the series – after plot turns overturn the reader's expectations and suddenly shine new light on likely overlooked subtle hints and foreshadowing in earlier episodes. See Shira Wolosky, "Well-Spotted: Plots and Reversals" (2010); Fabian Firman Elmar and Maria Ananta, "Creature Symbols to Foreshadow Harry's Confrontation with his Past in J. K. Rowling's Harry Potter and the Prisoner of Askaban" (2017). Such retrospective adjustment requires that the preceding have elements that take new meaning after the later revelation; in the case of Rom 1:18–32, the numerous allusions to Israel's rebellion and the insistence that these idolaters sinned in defiance of revelation and knowledge are clarified in 2:1–16, requiring hearers to consider how the preceding in fact (surprisingly) applies to them regardless of their social situation.

[104] Lucas, *Evocations of the Calf*, 24; contra Simon J. Gathercole, *Where Is Boasting?* (2002), 211–12.

humanity – Israel foremost of all – has engaged in impiety and injustice and is therefore subject to God's wrath. Contemporary Jews may not be actively worshiping idols but are still subject to the circumstances resulting from Israel's historical impiety and idolatry, still awaiting the renewal of God's covenantal favor, as it is written, "Our ancestors sinned and are no more, and we bear their misdeeds" (Lam 5:7).

It should also be noted that despite the second-person address, the passage does not yet involve a distinct interlocutor,[105] let alone one with a specific social location, since there has been no formal introduction of a second voice before this point in the discourse.[106] Instead, the addressee is "every human who judges,"[107] inclusively placing the addressee among the "humans" of 1:18 and working against any efforts to stand apart

---

[105] Thorsteinsson is correct that "the tradition of reading a Jewish interlocutor in Rom 2:1–5 is a relatively recent phenomenon" since ancient interpreters do "not even mention such a reading" ("Paul's Interlocutor," 5). But reading a distinct interlocutor *at all* in Rom 2:1–5 is a recent phenomenon, since ancient interpreters consistently read these verses as addressed to anyone in the audience of the letter, "including not only the gentile but also the Jew" (Augustine on Rom 7–8; see Paula Fredriksen, *Augustine on Romans* [1982], 4).

[106] Even in Rom 3, it is not clear that there is any interlocution from a second character, as all the questions and responses work at least as well if read in Paul's voice. After all, do rhetorical questions and responses require speech-in-character or a voice distinct from that of the author? Surely not! Notably, Paul clarifies in 3:5 that he is "speaking as a 'human,'" connecting the questions of ch. 3 with the "human" perspective of the addressee of 2:1 and distancing himself from the idea that God could be unjust. That Paul here clarifies when he is not speaking from his own perspective works against the idea that the previous chapters repeatedly shift between Paul's own voice and that of an interlocutor without such overt indications, as most notably argued by Douglas Campbell, *Deliverance of God*, 530–41, depending on Stowers' arguments that speech-in-character need not be formally marked ("Apostrophe, ΠΡΟΣΩΠΟΠΟΙΙΑ and Paul's Rhetorical Education" [2003], arguing against the critiques of R. Dean Anderson, *Ancient Rhetorical Theory and Paul* [1996]). The dialogical approach to Romans is further called into question by the significant divergence among its proponents on how to script the voices in these chapters. If the distinct voices are so difficult to identify, either Paul did an especially poor job of marking them or – as seems more likely – Paul is the speaker throughout, raising leading questions for himself. For a blistering critique of modern speech-in-character reconstructions in Romans, see Will N. Timmins, "Romans 7 and Speech-In-Character" (2016); *Romans 7 and Christian Identity* (2017), 12–47. The most devastating argument against these readings is that no ancient reader of Romans identifies multiple characters/voices in these passages but instead reads them as Paul's own voice throughout (contra Stowers' misreading of Origen in *A Rereading of Romans*, 264–69 and "Romans 7.7–25 as a Speech-in-Character (προσωποποιία)" [1994], 193–98; on that misreading, see Timmins, *Romans 7 and Christian Identity*, 27–32).

[107] On the translation of ὦ ἄνθρωπε πᾶς ὁ κρίνων and its implications, see Bo Frid, "How Does Romans 2.1 Connect to 1.18–32?" (2006), 126.

from that categorization,[108] a fact that works against efforts to identify the addressee at this point as specifically either a Jew or a gentile.[109] Rather than specifically targeting Jews or gentiles, the point is that the condemnations of 1:18–32 apply to "every human" who does such things; whoever practices impiety or injustice stands condemned whether Jew or Greek and without any regard for that person's knowledge of or agreement with Torah.[110]

JUSTICE AND MERCY HAVE KISSED

Notably, the addressee is not condemned for judging – the passage does not argue that such condemnatory judgment is wrong – but rather for hypocrisy, for doing the very things known to be worthy of condemnation.[111] Contrary to Campbell's objection that the retributive justice in these chapters stands at odds with Paul's understanding of "the essential nature of the God of Jesus Christ" as characterized by compassion rather than judgment,[112] there is no indication that Paul in any way disagrees with the traditional Jewish portrayal of God's character, in which the

---

[108] Timmins, *Romans 7 and Christian Identity*, 19–20.
[109] Jae Hyun Lee, *Paul's Gospel in Romans* (2010), 109–10. Significant effort has been exerted to identify the "interlocutor(s)" of Rom 2–3 as either a Jew or gentile, with most commentators since antiquity reading Paul as addressing a Jew in Rom 2 or at least from 2:17 forward. Stowers argues that 2:1–11 is targeted at a gentile interlocutor and 2:17–3:9 is in dialogue with a Jewish interlocutor (*A Rereading of Romans*, 100–109, 143–62). Others have argued that the whole of Rom 2 is targeted at a gentile-born convert to Judaism, whose status as a Jew would be dubious to some other Jews, perhaps including Paul (e.g., Thorsteinsson, *Paul's Interlocutor*; Thiessen, *Paul and the Gentile Problem*; Joshua D. Garroway, "Paul's Gentile Interlocutor in Romans 3" [2016]). Rodríguez identifies two interlocutors, the first a gentile (2:1–16) and the second a proselyte to Judaism (2:17–29), though the first apparently never gets the opportunity to make an interlocution (*If You Call Yourself a Jew*, 32–61). See pp. 150–54 for further discussion.
[110] Contra Rainey, *Religion, Ethnicity and Xenophobia*, 233, who argues that Paul's "seemingly general reference to humans" in Rom 1:18 is a "kind of rhetorical hyperbole" that really only refers to gentiles, since only gentiles are idolators – a premise that would surely surprise the biblical prophets.
[111] Contra Porter, "Romans 1.18–32," 215.
[112] Campbell, *Deliverance of God*, 543. Campbell's argument here draws remarkably close to Marcion's antithesis between Paul's merciful God and the God of Israel. Linebaugh *God, Grace, and Righteousness*, 106, observes that Campbell has "put asunder what Paul has joined together." It is also unclear what Campbell means by mercy or compassion in the absence of a retributive framework for justice since mercy presumes a prior notion of desert. It is nonsense, for example, to forgive someone for having a toothache or a congenital disease. Campbell's emphasis on the divine rescue/deliverance

opposite of justice is not mercy but arbitrariness or partiality.[113] This traditional image of God's character is deeply rooted in the Torah, where YHWH's self-revelation to Moses places compassion and mercy alongside retributive justice at the core of YHWH's character (Exod 34:6–7). Paul's emphasis on mercy is therefore far from unique. Instead, God's mercy is a point of emphasis in countless early Jewish texts (cf. also Jas 2:13),[114] and the Torah and prophets frequently treat mercy and justice as interdependent rather than as opposites.[115] In sharp contrast to Campbell's suggestion that Paul is in conflict with the very bedrock of Jewish theology, Abraham Joshua Heschel's summary of the perspective of the biblical prophets applies equally well to Paul:

There are few thoughts as deeply ingrained in the mind of biblical man as the thought of God's justice and righteousness. It is not an inference but an a priori of biblical faith, self-evident; not an added attribute to His essence but given with the very thought of God. It is inherent in His essence and identified with His ways.[116]

It is on this basis that Paul opens his argument by appealing to the shared foundation of God's impartial justice, assuming that his hearers will surely agree that, as Heschel puts it, "The Lord is long-suffering, compassionate, loving, and faithful, but He is also demanding, insistent, terrible, and dangerous."[117] Or, to use Paul's own words: "See then the kindness and severity of God" (Rom 11:22). The first-person plural of 2:2 therefore communicates a fundamental point of *agreement* between Paul and his hearers: "And *we know* that the judgment of God on those practicing such things is in keeping with truth."[118] That is, Paul and his

---

of humanity is to be commended, but in the absence of a retributive framework, it is unclear from what humanity is being delivered (see Gaventa, "Rescue Mission," 36).

[113] As demonstrated by Sanders, *Paul and Palestinian Judaism* (1977), 126–28, 182, 234. See also the extended treatment of God's impartiality as a core Jewish axiom in Bassler, *Divine Impartiality*, 7–120.

[114] Sanders, *PPJ*, 123–25.

[115] E.g., Exod 20:5–6; Mic 6:8; Isa 30:18; Jer 9:24–25 (25–26 ET).

[116] Abraham J. Heschel, *The Prophets* (2001), 255. Heschel emphasizes the contrast between the just God of Israel, with whom one could know where one stands based on behavior, and the capricious divinities known throughout the ancient Mediterranean (254; cf. 299–317). See also Heschel's magisterial treatment of the Hebrew prophets' portrayal of God's justice, which he ties to a distinctively Hebrew conception of divine pathos (249–81; on divine pathos: 285–357). See also the discussion on the potter-clay metaphor in Chapter 5.

[117] Heschel, *The Prophets*, 366.

[118] Jewett, *Romans*, 198, notes the "rhetorical subtlety" in such an opening that guarantees agreement from his hearers, only to turn this agreement back on them later in the chapter. Thorsteinsson, *Paul's Interlocutor*, 190, rightly observes that "we know" in

Torah-knowledgeable addressees know and agree that God "will repay each person corresponding to his works" (2:6; Ps 62:12), judging impartially on the basis of corresponding retribution rather than showing favoritism or caprice.[119]

Such emphasis on judgment based on works is by no means out of character for Paul. On the contrary, Paul's thinking is dominated by the impending eschatological judgment in which God will finally mete out justice based on what people deserve. This theme of God's judgment is so foundational that it appears in every undisputed Pauline letter except Philemon, being significantly more pervasive in that respect than justification by faith. A few examples should suffice to show that the view of judgment in Rom 2 is by no means outside of the Pauline norm:

For we must all appear before the judgment seat of Messiah, so that each may receive corresponding to what he has done in the body, whether good or bad, and so, knowing the fear of the Lord, we persuade people. (2 Cor 5:10–11)

I forewarn you just as I previously forewarned you that those who do such things will not inherit the kingdom of God. (Gal 5:21)

Or do you not know that the unjust will not inherit the kingdom of God? Do not be deceived. (1 Cor 6:9a)

Do not be deceived, God is not mocked, because whatever a person sows, this he will also reap. (Gal 6:7)

Each one's work will become evident, for the day will show it, because it will be revealed with fire, and the fire will test the quality of each one's work. (1 Cor 3:13)

Do everything without grumbling or arguing so that you will become blameless and innocent children of God above reproach in the midst of a crooked and perverse generation ... holding firmly the word of life, so that on the day of Messiah I can take pride because I did not run or labor for nothing. (Phil 2:14–16)

We will all stand before the judgment seat of God . . . . So then each one of us will give an account of himself to God. (Rom 14:10, 12)

It is especially noteworthy that Paul in no way suggests that believers will be excused from such judgment; he never reassures his audience that their belief in Jesus' death and resurrection has saved them from being judged by

---

2:2 infers not only the hearers but also Paul's opponents. George Carras, "Romans 2,1–29: A Dialogue on Jewish Ideals" (1992), 190–91, compares the rhetoric of Paul's opening with that of Amos.

[119] See Bassler, "Divine Impartiality," 45–49. The Gospels also attest that, like other Jews, Jesus held a similar view of God's impartiality and corresponding retribution (e.g., Luke 12:47–48; Matt 23; 25:32–46).

their works or that Jesus' works will be substituted for their own. Instead, he repeatedly and emphatically says the opposite, reminding his readers of the impending judgment and warning them to remain obedient.

Recognizing the progression of the argument here reveals an important insight about Paul's rhetorical approach. Rather than opening by challenging his opponents' preconceptions, Paul takes a "yes ... and" rhetorical approach. That is, Paul's strategy is to start by appealing to common ground, building his arguments on the shared foundation of restoration eschatology and the impartial justice of God, who will ultimately judge the world and set things right in accordance with what each person and nation deserves. He then builds on this foundation to argue that his gospel is the most natural consequence of those shared priors, with God mercifully providing the means to become just/righteous and therefore pass unscathed through the impartial judgment of God. The aim is therefore not merely to defeat his opponents but to win them over, convincing them that their own theological foundation requires them to agree with Paul's conclusions.[120] This reading also helps make sense of the first person plurals not only in Rom 2:2 but also in 3:5; 3:9, and 4:1, as Paul speaks on behalf of all parties involved in the discussion, in each case implying that all now agree.[121] This move is especially forceful by the time one reaches Rom 3:9, where the first-person plural suggests that Paul and his hearers – including his implied opponents – are now agreed that "both Jews and gentiles are all under sin."

CRIME AND PUNISHMENT: IMPARTIAL JUDGMENT FOR JEWS AND GREEKS ALIKE

The emphasis on God's impartiality in Rom 2:1–10 contradicts Wisdom's claim that God treats Israel differently than the "impious" (ἀσεβεῖς) who

---

[120] In this respect, Paul's strategy is in keeping with the rhetorical advice of Epictetus, who notes that Socrates "would force his interlocutor to be his [Socrates'] witness ... he would make the consequences which followed from the [shared] presuppositions so clear that everyone recognized the contradiction involved and therefore abandoned it." (*Disc.* 2.12.4–5; e.g., Plato, *Symposium* 199d–201c).

[121] On this rhetorically inclusive use of the first-person plurals in Romans, see Stowers, "Paul's Dialogue with a Fellow Jew in Romans 3:1–9" (1984), 720, who calls it a "dialogical 'we.'" But as we all know, this function of the first-person plural need not depend on fictive dialogue within a speech or letter, as it just as easily refers to the presumed agreement between Paul and his audience/addressees. Contra Garroway, *Paul's Gentile-Jews*, 84, there is no reason to assign this question to a gentile interlocutor, as it applies equally well to Jews and gentiles, each of whom may have that question at this stage of the argument.

"were tormented when judged with wrath" (Wis 11:9), while Israel was instead "tested as a parent does for a warning" (11:10). Wisdom's distinction is in keeping with what Thorsteinsson calls a "well known characteristic of many Jewish writings from antiquity that God deals differently with the sins of the Jewish people ... than with the sins of non-Jews."[122] An even clearer expression of this idea is found in 2 Maccabees:

> For the Lord does not deal with us just like the other nations, for whom he waits patiently to punish until they have reached the full measure of their sins, so that he may not take vengeance on us afterward, when our sins have reached their height. (2 Macc 6:14–15)

In contrast, Paul declares that the same standard of justice applies to Jews and Greeks alike (2:9, 10) because "there is no partiality with God."[123] The fact that God has shown patience with his people's sins in the past (cf. Wis 11:9–10) does not mean retribution has been permanently suspended. Instead, Wisdom's explanation that God did not wipe out the Canaanites with a single word because "by judging them little by little you gave them an opportunity to repent" (12:10)[124] applies equally to Jews and Greeks. Those who imagine God's kindness will exempt them from the principle of retributive justice are instead "storing up (θησαυρίζω) wrath" to be revealed "on the day of wrath and revelation of the just judgment of God" (Rom 2:5). Indeed, the purpose of God's "kindness, restraint, and patience" is not to exclude from judgment but rather to "lead you to repentance" (2:4).[125] Throughout this passage, Paul's

---

[122] Thorsteinsson, *Paul's Interlocutor*, 192.
[123] "Partiality" is literally "accepting of face" (προσωπολημψία). Cf. Pss. Sol. 2:18, "God is a just judge and will not admire a face." The importance of God's impartiality throughout the first chapters of Romans has been persuasively argued by Bassler, "Divine Impartiality," 45–49; *Divine Impartiality*, 121–70. In addition, Neil Elliott, *The Rhetoric of Romans* (2006), 122, points out that "the argumentative flow is not from other premises toward 'impartiality' but *from* God's impartiality *as* an axiom ... *toward* the main thesis, "there is no excuse before God's judgment." In keeping with traditional Jewish theology, Paul treats God's impartiality as an axiomatic first principle, not something that needs to be defended.
[124] Paul returns again to the same passage in Rom 9:19b, citing Wisdom 12:12 and again reconfiguring what Wisdom applies to the Canaanites to apply to Israel. See Chapter 5 for more discussion.
[125] That God's "kindness" leads to repentance is a delightful pun, as χρηστός (kindness) would have sounded almost identical to χριστός (messiah) in typical first-century pronunciation. The same pun appears again in Rom 11:22 (cf. also 3:12). Philo may be engaging in the same wordplay when using χρηστός in the context of Israel's messianic deliverance in *Praem.* 166.

language and argument are strongly reminiscent of Pss. Sol. 9,[126] which discusses the relationship between God's just judgment, God's kindness, and repentance:

> In your justness you visit the children of human beings. The one who does justness stores up (θησαυρίζω) life for himself with the Lord, and the one who does injustice is responsible for the destruction of his own person, for the judgments of the Lord are in justness for each man and household. To whom will you show kindness, O God, if not to those who call on the name of the Lord?" (cf. Rom 10:13). You will cleanse a person from sins in confession, in acknowledgement (cf. Rom 10:9–10). For shame is on us and our faces concerning all these things …. And your kindness is upon sinners in repentance. (Pss. Sol. 9:4c–9:6, 9:7c)

This psalm is not referring to the sins or confession or repentance of the nations but is instead specifically addressing Israel's apostasy and appealing for reconciliation. The first verses of the psalm make this explicit:

> When Israel was led away in exile to another place, when they apostatized from the Lord who redeemed them, they were expelled from the inheritance which the Lord had given them. The diaspora of Israel was among every nation according to the word of the Lord, so that you may be justified, O God, in your justness on our lawless acts (cf. Rom 3:4), because you are a just judge over all the peoples of the earth. (Pss. Sol. 9:1–2)

In the same way, in Rom 1–2, Paul appeals to Israel's history to demonstrate that the theological bedrock of God's impartial justice undermines any idea that God's mercy means Jews will be judged by a separate standard from everyone else.[127] Whether Jew or Greek, the one who knows the Torah and agrees with the condemnations of the

---

[126] On the background of the Pss. Sol., which were composed sometime between the invasion of Pompey in 63 BCE and the early first century CE, see Eberhard Bons and Patrick Pouchelle, eds., *The Psalms of Solomon* (2015); Kenneth R. Atkinson, "Solomon, Psalms of" (2010); *I Cried to the Lord* (2004).

[127] Thorsteinsson's conclusion that "there is no apparent sign of Paul turning this aspect of Jewish belief 'on its head'" (*Paul's Interlocutor*, 193) is baffling. If the assertion that God judges all by the same standard does not oppose the idea that God deals differently with the sins of Jews and gentiles, what *would* constitute such opposition? Thorsteinsson's treatment of the implications of 2:6–16 gives no indication of how he reconciles these ideas (192–94; cf. the structural analysis at 153–59). More recent work following Thorsteinsson's proposal has not provided clarity here; these verses are only mentioned in a single line in Thiessen, *Paul and the Gentile Problem*, 56, and receive only a paragraph's worth of attention in all the essays of Rodríguez and Thiessen, *The So-Called Jew* combined (Thorsteinsson, Thiessen, and Rodríguez, "Paul's Interlocutor," 24, and Jipp, "What Are the Implications," 200).

preceding verses is not exempt from the same punishments for impiety and injustice. Indeed, the judgment upon the nations for their ignorant offenses applies all the more to those who have the Torah but do "the same things" (2:1; 2:13, 21–25),[128] since unlike ignorant gentiles who had no such advantage, those who have received the Torah and had the knowledge of God are without excuse and will be judged accordingly.[129]

Paul does not say, however, that all Jews and Greeks will be condemned. Instead, only the disobedient who "do such things" (2:2) stand condemned. Such persons should not imagine that they will escape judgment by virtue of knowing the Torah or being (or being called) Jews since the same standard of behavior and judgment applies to all humans. But those who do not practice such things are not condemned – those who both hear and obey, "persevering in good works" will receive "glory, honor, and immortality" (2:7). The point is that having and approving the Torah – that is, knowledge of the revelation of God – does not grant judicial immunity. The rest of the chapter builds on this point, making it clear that possession of the Torah, birth, and circumcision provide no security against God's impartial judgment if one does not behave justly. If God judges without favoritism, then a disobedient Jew will receive the same punishment as a sinful gentile. But the converse equally holds true: gentiles who do such things are rightly condemned, but a gentile without Torah who "does the things of Torah" (2:14) will receive the same "glory, honor, and peace" as an obedient Jew (2:10).

---

[128] Lucas, *Evocations of the Calf*, 22–24; Bassler, *Divine Impartiality*, 195–97.

[129] Romans 3 similarly explains that although Jews do have an advantage over the gentiles who lack the "very words of God" (3:2), that advantage is forfeited in the absence of obedience. Contra Justin King, *Speech-in-Character, Diatribe, and Romans 3:1–9* (2018), 254, who bases his rescription of chapter 3 largely on the conviction that "only one voice most appropriately speaks 3:2 – and it is not Paul's," other passages show that Paul *does* believe Jews are at an advantage. To mix the metaphors of Rom 9–11, they are natural branches with a head start that the gentiles lacked (2:14), and they remain beloved due to the ancestors (11:28). Such continued advantage is also evident from Gal 2:15 and Rom 9:1–4, not to mention the repeated statement of priority "to the Jew first" (Rom 1:16; 2:9, 10). Moreover, the middle/passive προεχόμεθα without a direct object in 3:9 is best taken as a passive, "are we [Jews] surpassed/worse off?" (see Jewett, *Romans*, 256–58 and Garroway, "Paul's Gentile Interlocutor," 87–90, though the question need not be asked by a gentile as Garroway suggests, since it follows the statements about the "infidelity" and "injustice" of some [τινες] Jews in 3:3–5). The point is that although Jews start with an advantage, infidelity and injustice obviate any advantage, leading to the question of whether Jews are therefore at a *disadvantage*, which Paul denies because *all* are under sin. There is therefore no contradiction between 3:9 and 3:2, obviating the need to put 3:2 in any voice other than Paul's own and calling into question the very foundation for rescripting Rom 3.

In this respect, whether one identifies the addressee as a Jew or gentile is irrelevant to the central point of Rom 2:1–16, which is that every human will be repaid "corresponding to his works" (2:6; cf. Ps 62:12).[130] The same standard of judgment applies "first to the Jew and also to the Greek" (2:9, 10), and those who practice the things discussed in 1:18–32 will receive the corresponding punishment with no exceptions. Jews (whether natural-born or proselytes) are no less subject to God's judgment, and if the addressee is a gentile, becoming a Jew does not change anything or confer any advantage in judgment.[131] Instead, "those who sinned without Torah will perish without Torah, and whoever sinned in Torah will be judged via Torah" (2:12). The same condemnation applies to both those outside the covenant by nature and those who broke the covenant and came under its curse: death reigns over those without Torah whose sin was not like that of Adam and over those who received the command and therefore sinned "in the likeness of the transgression of Adam" (5:14).[132]

Hearing the Torah is of no advantage if it does not lead to obedience "because the hearers of Torah are not righteous/just before God but the doers of Torah" (2:13). This dictum, which Paul's opponents would surely approve,[133] applies not to the "lawless [gentiles] who have never

---

[130] "Though Paul uses the second singular to address this figure, it is not as though he actually calls out a specific person, true-to-life or imaginary. Once again, that adjective that is already so significant in Paul's argument returns – πᾶς [all] . . . . What is more, in 2:1–16, Paul never addresses this interlocutor in ethnic terms. Paul talks about Jews and Greeks (2:9–10) and 'nations who do not have Torah' (2:14), but he resists applying these terms to his addressee. The scope of Paul's argument, and the identity of his addressee, is as broad and ethnically vague as ever" (King, *Speech-in-Character*, 238–39).

[131] "The principle of desert, when it is strictly applied is *peculiarly destructive to historical and elective concerns*" (Campbell, *Deliverance of God*, 551, emphasis his). But contra Campbell, Paul is not making an absurdity of his opponent's position to oppose the idea of retributive justice but rather presses the point to its logical conclusion to illustrate Israel's plight in a restoration eschatological framework.

[132] There is therefore no need to choose between understanding the curse of the Torah as "Israel's corporate curse" or the "anthropological inability of sinful humans to fulfill the law" (as discussed in J. Andrew Cowan, "The Curse of the Law, the Covenant, and Anthropology in Galatians 3:10–14" [2020]). Since Israel's corporate curse is the result of anthropological inability, and since all Israel is under that corporate curse, all humans are subject to the same consequence: death.

[133] Cf. Jas 1:22–24; M. *Abot* 1:17; Josephus, *Ant.* 20.24; Peter Stuhlmacher, *Romans* (1994), 42; Neusner, "Paul's Ethnic Israel," 88; Simon J. Gathercole, "A Law unto Themselves" (2002), 32–33; Peter J. Tomson, "'Die Täter des Gesetzes werden gerechtfertigt werden' (Röm 2,13)" (2005); Campbell, *Deliverance of God*, 554.

heard God's word" (*Sib. Or.* 3.70) but rather to the hearers to whom the Torah was addressed (cf. Deut 6:4).[134] In contrast to the lawless gentiles, Israel rebelled after hearing, as recounted by another first-century writer:

> For who heard and rebelled but those who came out of Egypt via Moses? ... And to whom did he swear that they would not enter his rest if not to those who were disobedient? And so we see that they were unable to enter because of infidelity. (Heb 3:16, 18–19)

This phenomenon of hearing but not obeying is the very problem that the Prophets declare must be solved for Israel to be restored. Again it is to be emphasized that Paul is standing firmly within the mainstream of early Jewish theology and restoration eschatology here, gesturing to the prophetic commonplace that Israel's distinction from the nations always depended on covenantal obedience.[135] The Torah had revealed God's just requirements (cf. Rom 3:20), but because Israel did not in fact obey, Israel came under God's wrath, being scattered and becoming indistinct from the nations as a consequence of behaving like the nations. But this is only the first half of the restoration eschatological paradigm, and one would therefore expect Paul's argument to progress to the promise of Israel's renewal, including the transformation to obedient justness that had previously eluded them. This is precisely what follows as the argument develops in Romans.

---

[134] The connection of "hearing" the Torah with the Shema has been noted by numerous commentators, e.g., Jewett, *Romans*, 211; Neusner, "Paul's Ethnic Israel," 88. As Gathercole notes, the irony here is that the "doers of Torah to be justified are actually not hearers of Torah at all" ("A Law unto Themselves," 33).

[135] E.g., in Jubilees, "The end of the exile and the coming of a new creation involve judgment upon the Gentiles and unfaithful Israelites alike, as well as blessings to those who are faithful and obedient" (Ronald Charles, "The New Creation Motif in Romans 8:18–27 in Light of the Book of *Jubilees*" [2020], 63).

4

Salvation through Justification

Jews and Gentiles Alike

My hunch is that Sanders' reforms in Pauline studies have not yet, in fact, gone far enough ... and that Romans 2, for so long the Achilles heel of schemes on Paul and the law, may make a vital contribution to some eventual solutions, both to the theological questions which surround all of Paul's writings and, of course, to the exegesis of Romans itself.

N. T. Wright[1]

Chapter 3 examined how Paul's strict application of a traditional Jewish restorationist paradigm in light of God's impartiality results in a situation in which all idolatrous and unjust humans – whether from Israel or the nations – are subject to God's wrath. Whereas gentiles could be assumed to be under sin, the Torah and the history of Israel – that is, scripture rather than experience – testify that Jews are no less under sin.[2] But the traditional restorationist paradigm does not end with Israel permanently under judgment. Instead, the prophets had not only declared that Israel had lost its distinction from the nations due to covenantal disobedience, they also promised that God would deliver Israel by fixing the cause of Israel's plight: the stubborn and unrepentant hearts (Rom 2:5) that the Torah revealed but could not repair.[3] God will finally enable Israel to

---

[1] N. T. Wright, "The Law in Romans 2" (1996), 132. See Luke 4:21b.
[2] Agreeing here with Matthew V. Novenson, "The Self-Styled Jew of Romans 2 and the Actual Jews of Romans 9–11" (2016), 152, though he does not recognize that Rom 1–2 are already engaged in demonstrating the latter.
[3] Kyle B. Wells, *Grace and Agency in Paul and Second Temple Judaism* (2014), 25–62; David A. Lambert, *How Repentance Became Biblical* (2016), 148–49. Alec J. Lucas persuasively argues that Rom 2:5 "subtly conflates Deut 9:27b; 10:16" to highlight Israel's disobedience, building on the foundation already established with the reference

receive the good promises of the Torah by circumcising Israel's hearts (Deut 30:6), writing the "Torah on their hearts" (Jer 31:33), and giving them "a new heart and a new spirit" (Ezek 36:26), finally enabling them to keep the command and "love YHWH your God with all your heart and all your soul, so that you may live" (Deut 30:6).

In this framework, God's mercy does not involve changing the standard of judgment to accommodate the people but instead changing the people to accommodate to the standard of judgment. That is, rather than unjustly judging the unjust to be just, God will transform the unjust into "doers of Torah" who can then be justly judged "just before God" (2:13). Rather than eliminating Torah, God will transform people, and these justified people will obey God, having been given the fidelity needed to fulfill Torah.[4] But until that transformation takes place, Israel stands in the same position as the nations, having fallen under the curses of the covenant due to disobedience and awaiting the promised restoration. It should not be surprising that after establishing the fundamental premises of restoration eschatology with respect to the plight of all humanity, Paul proceeds to present his gospel as the fulfillment of exactly those prophetic promises of ethical transformation, pointing to those who have been empowered to fulfill the Torah's requirements. But in a startling move, at precisely the point in his argument that one would expect Paul to refer to the ethical transformation and reconciliation of *Israel*, he asserts that *gentiles* are exhibiting the transformation promised to Israel:

For whenever gentiles who do not have Torah by nature do the things of the Torah,[5] these not having Torah are a Torah to themselves in that they exhibit the work of the Torah [ἔργων τοῦ νόμου] written on their hearts, their conscience bearing witness and the reasonings within themselves alternately accusing or even defending them, on the day when God will judge the hidden things of humans according to my gospel through Messiah Jesus. (Rom 2:14–16)

Here Paul refers to the possibility of gentiles, who naturally lack the Torah, becoming natural doers of "the things of the Torah," thereby manifesting "the work of the Torah written on their hearts." At first glance, this application of scripture about Israel's restoration to gentiles

---

to Ps 106 (LXX 105):20 in Rom 1:23 (*Evocations of the Calf?* [2014], 24–25, 28–30, 133–49).

[4] Wells, *Grace and Agency*, 224–75 (esp. 280).

[5] The placement of φύσει ("by nature") is syntactically ambiguous, allowing it to do double duty, (i.e., "do not have Torah by nature" *and* "by nature do ..."). The parallels in 2:26–27 and 8:4 suggest that the nature by which the gentile in 2:14–15 is "doing Torah" is one that has been renewed by the spirit.

seems like a radical departure from the restoration eschatological framework he has set up so far. But the logic here is not only coherent with this framework but depends upon it, pressing the typical assessment of Israel-under-the-curse to its limit. In building his argument on God's impartial justice, Paul has also surprisingly laid the groundwork for the inclusion of the nations in Israel's redemption. That is, if, as the prophets declared, Israel has become indistinct from the nations due to sin, do not the nations now have an opportunity to partake in Israel's transformation and deliverance from that condition? "Everyone who calls on the name of YHWH will be saved" (Joel 2:32; Rom 10:13), and everyone means *everyone*.

The parallelism in Paul's argument is unmistakable: just as Israel became indistinguishable from gentiles through disobedience and behaving like the other nations, gentiles are now being incorporated into the new covenant community through the Torah written on their hearts and behaving like faithful, obedient Israelites.[6] Because Israel became like the nations, their fates are interconnected.[7] Israel's redemption is also Adam's redemption (that is, humanity's redemption), a new creation.[8] As will be further discussed below, Paul later brings this parallelism and the theme of interconnected destinies into the center of the frame in Rom 9–11, particularly in the conclusion of 11:11–36.

The stunning import of this passage and its function as a hinge between what comes before and after it in the larger restorationist argument of Rom 1–2 has often been missed because interpreters have so frequently overlooked or ignored the connection between these verses and the new covenant promise of the Torah written on the heart.[9] Instead, many have interpreted these verses as putting forward a theology of natural law in

---

[6] On the new covenant in Rom 2, see Akio Ito, "Romans 2: A Deuteronomistic Reading" (1996); Wright, "The Law in Romans 2"; Simon Gathercole, "A Law unto Themselves" (2002). Ernst Käsemann's objection, "Since no eschatological facts are made known, the promise of Jer 38:33 LXX is not at issue .... Even a reminiscence is doubtful" (*Romans* [1980], 64) is nonsense in light of the eschatological framework of the argument throughout. The point is that the eschatological gift of obedience has been granted.

[7] Cf. Otto Michel, *Römer* (1978), 344; Pablo T. Gadenz, *Called from the Jews and from the Gentiles* (2009), 238.

[8] On Israel's restoration by the spirit as a new creation of humanity as it should be, see Rony Kozman, "Ezekiel's Promised Spirit as *adam*'s Revelatory Spirit in the Hodayot" (2019) . Contra Paula Fredriksen, "What Does it Mean to See Paul 'within Judaism'?" (2022), 376, it is not just Paul's "eschatological gentiles" who are a new creation but "anyone who is in Messiah," including Jews like Paul himself.

[9] Rom 2:14–16 is not even listed among the passages with quotations or allusions to scripture in E. Earle Ellis, *Paul's Use of the Old Testament* (2003).

which every person's conscience serves as an inward law, with all therefore responsible to follow their conscience.[10] Dunn, for example, suggests that Paul "is simply noting that there are Gentiles who, despite their ignorance of the law, give evidence of a moral sensitivity which one would sooner expect to find in the people of the law."[11]

But it is difficult to fathom Paul using such loaded language as "Torah written on their hearts" to represent the concept of natural law among gentiles, especially on the heels of Rom 1:18–32, which narrates a descent from the knowledge of God that could be "understood by what has been made" (1:20) to "a depraved mind" (1:28). Moreover, these gentiles do not merely "give evidence of a moral sensitivity" but in fact "do the things of the Torah" (2:14).[12] They are distinctive precisely because in doing so they "exhibit the work of the Torah written on the hearts" (2:15), which has given them the capacity to obey God – the very function of the Torah written on the heart in the new covenant promise.[13] Torah obedience resulting from the Torah written on the heart is manifestly a new covenant concept. The effect of such a heart transformation is that the description of Rom 1:18–32 is reversed. These gentile Torah-doers are not "defenseless" (ἀναπολόγητος; 1:20) or "empty in their reasonings" (διαλογισμός; 1:21). Instead, their "reasonings" (λογισμός) are the very things that will give them a defense (ἀπολογέομαι) in the judgment (2:15).[14]

This then leads to the next question of whether these Torah-doing gentiles should be understood as a hypothetical scenario to be considered in the abstract or as real persons highlighted as an example.[15] The answer

---

[10] See the discussions in Gathercole, "A Law unto Themselves"; Simon Gathercole, "A Conversion of Augustine: From Natural Law to Restored Nature in Romans 2:13–16" (2002), 149–52. For a modern example of this reading, see John W. Martens, "Romans 2.14–16: A Stoic Reading" (1994).

[11] James D. G. Dunn, *Romans* (1988), 105. Dunn differentiates his view from a typical natural law reading inasmuch as "the law in question is still the Jewish law," but the result is effectively the same.

[12] The language of the "things of the Torah" denotes fulfilling the Torah in its entirety. See Simon Gathercole, *Where Is Boasting?* (2002), 127 n. 53; Heikki Räisänen, *Paul and the Law* (1987), 103.

[13] Despite taking a natural law reading in his earlier work, Augustine's later works shift to understanding these verses as representing the fulfillment of the new covenant. See Gathercole, "A Conversion of Augustine," 153–62.

[14] See Jane Heath, "The Righteous Gentile Interjects (James 2:18–19 and Romans 2:14–15)" (2013), 283.

[15] For a fuller discussion of the debate, see James D. G. Dunn, "In Search of Common Ground" (1996), esp. 321.

depends on whether one is reading forward with only knowledge of the preceding or reconsidering the question retrospectively as the argument continues to unfold throughout Romans. Grammatically, the use of "whenever" (ὅταν) with the subjunctive suggests a hypothetical scenario, effectively arguing that, were such gentiles to exist, their doing Torah-things would be evidence of the work of the new covenant, since otherwise they would not have the knowledge of Torah. But Paul then proceeds to argue in the following chapters that this hypothetical scenario is precisely what is happening: that is, "gentiles who did not pursue justness/righteousness attained it" (Rom 9:30).[16] Or, as he tells the Galatians, "Messiah redeemed us from the curse of the Torah ... so that in Messiah Jesus the blessing of Abraham would come to the nations, so that we would receive the promise of the spirit through fidelity" (Gal 3:13–14). Reflecting on the latter passage, John Levison muses:

It is difficult to identify which promise Paul recalls here. The promise of outpouring upon sons and daughters, old and young, male and female slaves in Joel 3:1–4 (Eng. 2:28–32), which is cited in Acts 2:17–21, could be construed as a promise to the nations, though its context in Joel is centered upon Israel, and even Peter, in the Pentecost sermon in Acts, appears to interpret its fulfillment exclusively in relation to Israel (Acts 2:38–39).[17]

The reason the promise is difficult to identify is that it does not refer to a single passage but to the whole network of new covenant restoration promises read together, with the gift of the spirit understood as equivalent to the circumcised heart, Torah written on the heart, and other related metaphors. Reading "the just will live from fidelity" (Gal 3:11; Hab 2:4) together with the promises of justification through the gift of the spirit results in the idea of "receiving the promise of the spirit through fidelity" (Gal 3:14). Likewise, Paul argues in Galatians that the spirit is what enables the fulfillment of "the whole Torah" (5:14) because the one who "walks by the spirit ... will not carry out the desire of the flesh" (5:16; cf. Rom 8:4–17).

But Levison is correct to observe that this promise is always centered on Israel, and his puzzlement about Paul's application of the promise to gentiles reflects exactly what made Paul controversial in his own day and

---

[16] As noted by Roland Bergmeier, "Das Gesetz im Römerbrief" (2000), 52–53, and Gathercole, "A Law unto Themselves," 31–32, close parallels between the language of Rom 2:14 and 9:30 suggest the gentiles of 2:14 are the same group of gentiles as that of 9:30.
[17] John R. Levison, *Filled with the Spirit* (2009), 270 n. 18.

continues to cause difficulty for modern interpreters. That is, although he builds on the same restoration eschatological foundation as his contemporaries, Paul takes the additional step of arguing that the restoration promises to Israel also apply to uncircumcised gentiles who can (and do!) receive the spirit, thereby becoming equal members in restored Israel's new covenant.[18] For Paul, because God is impartial and Israel has become indistinct from the nations by behaving like the nations, the promise to Israel is also a promise to the nations. This is exactly the move that makes Paul's argument distinctive among his contemporaries and led to the circumcision debate among the earliest followers of Jesus. It is also exactly the argument he is making in Rom 2, as he puts forward the possibility of gentiles having the Torah written on their hearts. The first argument in Romans for the inclusion of gentiles without physical circumcision rests on an extension of the new covenant promise to gentiles who then do the things the Torah requires, which will result in a good judgment "on the day when God will judge the hidden things of humans according to my gospel through Messiah Jesus" (2:16).

JEWISH IDENTITY AND GOD'S IMPARTIALITY

Paul then turns to consider the other side of the coin, addressing the implications of God's impartiality and the new covenant promise for those who are recognized as Jews who rely on the Torah (2:17), observing that although the Torah informs and instructs (2:18–20; cf. 3:20), reliance on the Torah has never guaranteed obedience to its dictates.[19] Instead, the Torah convicts those who violate its commands (2:21–27).[20] Structurally speaking, although verse 17 is often treated as beginning a new thought unit, it is both grammatically (δέ) and thematically continuous with the immediately preceding content.[21] Specifically, verses 14–16 and 17–25 develop the thesis laid out in verse 12, "Whoever sinned without Torah

---

[18] For more on Paul's application of Israel's promises to Israel in Galatians, see Frank Thielman, *Paul and the Law* (1994), 135–38. Cf. C. Marvin Pate, *The Reverse of the Curse* (2000), 224–26.

[19] "The possession of the law, and even some expertise in it, can actually count for nothing. The most outrageous sins can still take place – and did!" (Douglas A. Campbell, *The Deliverance of God* [2009], 562).

[20] Note the parallels to Jer 7 and 9 in these verses discussed in Timothy W. Berkley, *From a Broken Covenant to Circumcision of the Heart* (2000), 82–90.

[21] See the discussion in Justin King, *Speech-in-Character, Diatribe, and Romans 3:1–9* (2018), 247–49.

will also perish without Torah (14–16), while whoever sinned in Torah will be judged via Torah (17–24)." This statement is then immediately followed by examples for each side of the equation: "Whenever gentiles not having Torah ... but (δέ) if you are called a Jew and rely on Torah." Paul therefore lays out both possibilities, and in each case all that matters is whether the person does what the Torah requires – whether a person is called a Jew, studies and teaches Torah, or is circumcised is inconsequential on the day of judgment.

As mentioned above, some have argued that this passage does not in fact pertain to natural-born Jews but rather addresses a proselyte who was born as a gentile and *calls himself* a Jew, though Paul, not regarding adult circumcision as efficacious, does not privilege him with that label.[22] This proposal develops from the observation that in 2:17 Paul avoids referring to the addressee as a Jew, an important point observed as early as Origen.[23] But it does not follow that the addressee must therefore be understood as a convert to Judaism,[24] whereas natural-born Jews who transgress the Torah are exempt from such judgment. In addition to the problem that this interpretation depends on a lexically improbable reflexive reading of the middle/passive form ἐπονομάζῃ,[25] this interpretation problematically depends on reading 1:18–32 as exclusively applying to gentiles and then, based on the inferential force of the "therefore" (διό) in 2:1, concluding that the address of 2:1–5 is also exclusively targeted at a

---

[22] Suggested by David Frankfurter, "Jews or Not? Reconstructing the Other in Rev 2:9 and 3:9" (2001), 419–20, and then more thoroughly argued by Runar M. Thorsteinsson, *Paul's Interlocutor in Romans 2* (2003) and adopted by Joshua D. Garroway, *Paul's Gentile-Jews* (2012), 91–95; Rafael Rodríguez, *If You Call Yourself a Jew* (2014); Matthew Thiessen, "Paul's Argument against Gentile Circumcision in Romans 2:17–29" (2016); *Paul and the Gentile Problem* (2016). This perspective and its potential implications are further explored in the essays of Rafael Rodríguez and Matthew Thiessen, eds., *The So-Called Jew in Paul's Letter to the Romans* (2016). For a thorough critique of this reading, see Paul T. Sloan, "Paul's Jewish Addressee in Rom 2–4: Revisiting Recent Conversations" (forthcoming).

[23] Origen, *Commentary on Romans* 2.11.4–13.7.

[24] The suggestion that the addressee of 2:17–24 "might be a Jew *religiously* but is a gentile *ethnically*" (Rodríguez, *If You Call Yourself a Jew*, 51) requires an anachronistic distinction between religion and ethnicity.

[25] As discussed on pp. 23–24, evidence across other Greek literature demonstrates that the middle/passive form of ἐπανομάζω consistently represents the passive ("if you are called a Jew") rather than the reflexive middle ("if you call yourself a Jew"). Asserting that the reflexive meaning should be favored because "Paul's emphasis lies heavily upon the interlocutor's perception of himself, not other people's perceptions of him" (Thiessen, *Paul and the Gentile Problem*, 199 n. 80) assumes the conclusion. See Lionel J. Windsor, "The Named Jew and the Name of God" (2021), 235–37.

gentile. But as demonstrated in Chapter 3, a gentile-exclusive reading of 1:18–2:11 is untenable. Instead, this opening section uses the familiar form of Jewish condemnations of gentile vices to undermine and ultimately collapse the distinction between Jew and gentile typically maintained in those polemics, demonstrating that because of God's impartiality both Jews and gentiles are equally subject to judgment. This reading then better accounts for the ethnic ambiguity of the addressee in 2:1–5, in which Paul does not address "every *gentile* human who judges" but rather "every human who judges" (2:1). A gentile-only reading simply does not take the comprehensive language of those passages seriously enough.

This leads to a second problem, namely that understanding 2:17–29 as specifically targeted at a convert to Judaism misconstrues the rhetorical function of the qualifying phrase "if you are called" as a way to *narrow* the scope as compared to saying "if you are a Jew." But the phrase does exactly the opposite, including *not only* native-born Jews *but also* any circumcised proselyte or anyone else who might self-identify as or be called a Jew.[26] For example, no one would assume the statement, "If you call yourself a Canadian, you must know how to skate," applies only to people not born in Canada. Instead, such a statement would refer *primarily* to natural-born Canadians while also applying to all others identifying themselves as Canadians (perhaps to avoid other stereotypes while abroad). Similarly, there is no indication in Romans of any attempt to distinguish native-born Jews from gentile Judaizers identifying themselves or identified by others as Jews; instead, inasmuch as both native-born Jews and proselytes would identify as Jews, the language of 2:17 applies to both. The phrasing of Rom 2:17 therefore does not limit the scope to a small subset of self-identified Jews who were born as gentiles but rather addresses anyone who might be identified as a Jew. It thereby casts the widest possible net for those who might be associated with that label.

A third problem applies not only to the "so-called Jew as gentile" reading but also to any other reading that requires a distinct and identifiable interlocutor (or interlocutors): such readings do not adequately account for the "if" (εἰ) that opens the address. Paul does not say

---

[26] Contra Frankfurter's statement: "We might well ask, who 'calls oneself' a Jew anyway? Certainly not someone who is *recognized* as Jewish by birth or by community" ("Jews or Not?," 419). That someone recognized as Jewish by others would not also self-identify as a Jew is puzzling to say the least, and this argument is mooted by the fact that this form of ἐπανομάζω is better read as a passive.

"*although* you call yourself a Jew" but rather "*if* you are called a Jew." This is a significant difference, as it indicates that despite the second person singular, Paul is not introducing or addressing a distinct individual interlocutor who calls himself a Jew. Instead, the conditional implies that there are other addressees who are not identified as Jews, serving a rhetorical function roughly equivalent to, "This will not apply to some of you, but . . ." As such, the address of Rom 2:17 is similar to that of 2:1 in that neither introduces a distinct interlocutor but rather addresses the audience of the letter or a subset thereof – in 2:17, those who are identified as Jewish. So while in 2:17 Paul withholds the label "Jew" from at least some otherwise recognized as such, the determining factor is not natural birth or timing of circumcision but rather, as will be established at the end of the chapter, whether their hearts are circumcised. That is, in parallel with the example of gentiles in verses 14–16, the question is whether a person otherwise identified as a Jew has received the spirit and properly keeps the Torah. If so, then that person's Jewishness is valid. If not, Paul argues that such a person is no different from disobedient gentiles and will receive the same condemnation.

Despite its ancient pedigree dating back at least to Origen, Matthew Novenson has objected that "this is a strange line of reasoning" because "'Jew,' unlike 'philosopher' or 'free person' or 'good person' is a conventional ethnic name, not a claim of merit such as those disputed in philosophical dialogues."[27] But it is unclear why debate about the authenticity of an individual's ethnic status would be strange, especially given an ethnos so strongly identified with specific cultural traditions (Torah). The very name of the "no true Scotsman" argument is based on the fact that even today certain behaviors can cause some to regard specific individuals as not authentically part of the ethnos into which they were born. Ethnic status is always socially negotiated and constructed, and being born a Jew was no guarantee that all Jews would regard one as authentically Jewish. As Fredriksen explains, in this period "*ethnic distinctiveness and religious distinctiveness are simple synonyms, and native to all ancient peoples,*"[28] and further, "Peoples inherited their protocols for showing respect, and these protocols defined what we call 'religion.' At the same time, these protocols also designated ethnicity."[29] Novenson himself recognizes that in Roman antiquity "while the name 'Jews' obviously attaches to people of

---

[27] Novenson, "The Self-Styled Jew of Romans 2," 140.
[28] Paula Fredriksen, "Judaizing the Nations" (2010), 234, emphasis original.
[29] Fredriksen, "Judaizing the Nations," 235.

Judean extraction, it is also regularly used of [those who] choose to follow the laws and customs of the Jews."[30] In such a context, dispute about one's ethnic status (closely tied to the laws and customs of the ethnic group) is hardly strange. Moreover, the evidence from Philo, the Dead Sea sect, 1 Maccabees, and others from the era strongly indicate that it was by no means unusual to believe that a person born a Jew could cease to be Jewish through disobedience or covenantal infidelity. Paul appears no different from his contemporaries in this respect, arguing that Jews (whether native-born or otherwise) who do not obey the Torah have thereby forfeited their Jewishness and their place within the covenant.

THAT HIDEOUS STRENGTH: THE THREE TRAPS OF BELIAL

This continued focus on the need for obedience helps explain the function of the statements about the instructive use of Torah (2:18–20) and the litany of questions posited to establish whether the teacher of Torah in fact practices what he preaches:

So then, you who teach another, do you not also teach yourself?[31] You who preach, "Do not steal," do you steal? You who say, "Do not commit adultery," do you commit adultery? You who abominate idols, do you rob sacred things (ἱεροσυλέω)?[32] You who boast in the Torah, do you dishonor God by transgressing the Torah?[33] (Rom 2:21–23)

---

[30] Novenson, "The Self-Styled Jew of Romans 2," 140, citing Dio Cassius, *Roman History* 37.17.1. But Dio does not say such individuals "call themselves 'Jews' in this sense," as Novenson suggests, but rather that the name "applies to those humans who adopt their customs [νόμιμα]." For Dio, such persons are not just self-identified Jews, they *are* Jews.

[31] Rodríguez, *If You Call Yourself a Jew*, 54, observes that the first question anticipates an affirmative answer by using οὐ rather than μή. The implied answer is therefore, "yes, I do also teach myself." This does not, however, imply that the addressee must be guiltless of the next three potential sins as Rodríguez suggests (54–56). On the contrary, the following three questions test whether the one who answers the first affirmatively is in fact obedient to Torah, and their rhetorical force depends on their potentially revealing a contradiction with the answer to the first question.

[32] At least six options have been proposed for the translation of ἱεροσυλέω. See J. Duncan M. Derrett, "'You Abominate False Gods; but Do You Rob Shrines?' (Rom 2.22b)" (1994). Etymologically, it combines the roots for "sacred" (*hiero-*) and "strip off" or "pillage" (*sul-*), resulting in the common translation "rob temples" (e.g., NRSV, NASB). But that rendering is over-specific because ἱερός is not limited to a temple proper, which would usually be ναός ("temple"), and the *hierosul-* cluster is used not only of temple robbery but general sacrilege or misuse/plundering of sacred, devoted things.

[33] Matthew Thiessen, "Paul's So-Called Jew and Lawless Lawkeeping" (2016), 76, argues that 2:21–22 should not be read as questions but accusations and translates them as such. But although the final four sentences could function as either indicatives or interrogatives,

Interpreters have typically found the specific sins mentioned in verses 21–22 perplexing, especially the third, "sacrilege" or "sacred robbery," which seems both oddly specific and atypical. Is Paul really suggesting that those reliant on Torah have a habit of robbing temples or committing sacrilege? A variety of unsatisfactory explanations have been put forward, illustrating the difficulty interpreters have had with the passage. Among the proposed options, some have suggested that Jews may have rationalized theft from pagan temples on the basis of the falsity of the gods in question,[34] though even proponents of this view concede such an offense could hardly have been common enough to have been stereotypical.[35] Others have suggested that Paul indicates that despite detesting idols, some Jews hypocritically involved themselves with pagan temples or profited from idol worship.[36] Another option is that "sacred robbery" refers to reviling or blaspheming pagan gods and thereby violating the Hellenistic Jewish tradition of respect for non-Jewish religion.[37] One especially creative suggestion is that the passage refers to a specific event decades earlier in which a few Jewish men had swindled a Roman noblewoman named Fulvia of her donation to the Jewish temple.[38] More recently, Matthew Thiessen has argued that Paul is accusing a convert to Judaism of committing all three sins by attempting to steal the heritage of Israel through his conversion. That is:

> At least some ancient Jews thought gentiles who adopted the Jewish law were guilty of taking what did not belong to them. If one viewed the law as an inheritance or gift from God to Israel, then gentiles who adopted it were guilty of theft. If one viewed the law as Israel's marital partner, then gentiles who adopted it were guilty of adultery. ... Either way, the gentile who takes what is sacred and belongs to Israel is guilty of sacrilege and breaks the very law in which he boasts (Rom 2:23).[39]

---

the οὐ ("not") grammatically marks the first sentence as a question rather than an indicative statement. (In making his case for an indicative reading, Thiessen ignores the οὐ in the first sentence, resulting in "The one who teaches another, teach yourself!") Given that the first sentence is unambiguously a question, the sentences that follow are also best understood as questions on both syntactic and rhetorical grounds (see Robert Jewett, *Romans* [2006], 227–29).

[34] E.g., Gottlob Schrenk, "ἱερός κτλ.," *TDNT* 3:256; Dunn, *Romans*, 115; Douglas J. Moo, *Romans* (1996), 164.

[35] "Paul would be accusing his Jewish target of an offense that was, at best, rare" (Moo, *Romans*, 164).

[36] E.g., Thomas R. Schreiner, *Romans* (1998), 133; Frank J. Matera, *Romans* (2010), 73.

[37] E.g., Jewett, *Romans*, 229, following Edgar Krentz, "The Name of God in Disrepute: Romans 2:17–29 [22–23]" (1990), 433–35.

[38] *Ant.* 18.81–84. See Francis Watson, *Paul, Judaism, and the Gentiles* (2007), 203–5; followed by Campbell, *Deliverance of God*, 561.

[39] Thiessen, "Paul's So-Called Jew," 83.

To defend this proposal, Thiessen cites Wis 14:23–27, suggesting that it "corresponds strikingly to the three actions Paul notes in Rom 2:21–22."[40] On this basis, Thiessen concludes that "Paul still has in mind stereotypically gentile vices .... Paul's statements elsewhere suggest that he thinks these vices are peculiar to gentiles alone."[41] But Wis 14:23–27 is an extended list of about twenty sins including "ritual child murder ... corruption, infidelity, tumult, perjury, forgetfulness of favors, perverse lineages, disordered marriages" and the like. It is hardly surprising that such a lengthy list of sins would contain adultery, murder, and idolatry, nor does such an extended list "strikingly" correspond to the limited list of Rom 2:21–22, making the argument for a parallel less than compelling.[42]

A bigger problem with this proposal is that the third vice in Rom 2:22 is not idolatry but rather sacrilege or sacred robbery (ἱεροσυλέω), of which there is no parallel in Wisdom's list. Moreover, the suggestion that Paul imagines that stealing or adultery are strictly gentile sins is implausible, especially in light of 1 Cor 10, where his summary of the sins of Israel in the wilderness includes idolatry, sexual immorality (πορνεία), testing the Lord, and grumbling (10:7–10). To be fair, Thiessen does acknowledge that "Paul might be making the uncontroversial claim that some of his contemporary Jews failed to lead exemplary moral lives."[43] But once that possibility is acknowledged, it cannot be maintained that such sins are "peculiar to gentiles alone" – unless one also argues that Jews who commit such sins thereby become gentiles.

Fortunately, several much closer parallels to Rom 2:21–22 can be found that help explain why Paul cites these three specific vices. The first is found in the Damascus Document, which refers to three sins especially associated with Israel:

> Its interpretation concerns the three traps of Belial, in which Levi the son of Jacob said Belial would catch Israel .... The first is sexual immorality (הזנות); the second is wealth (הון); the third is defiling the sanctuary (טמא המקדש). The one who escapes

---

[40] Thiessen, "Paul's So-Called Jew," 76–78; previously Thiessen, "Paul's Argument," 381.
[41] Thiessen, "Paul's Argument," 381.
[42] The same criticism can be applied to the other "examples of vice lists that contain references to theft, adultery, and sacrilege/temple robbery" cited in Thiessen, "Paul's So-Called Jew," 77 n. 54. For striking parallels, one should not be looking for vice lists that *contain* references to these three sins but rather for lists that are limited or nearly limited to these three.
[43] Thiessen, "Paul's Argument," 380.

from one is caught in the next, and whoever escapes from that is caught in the other. (CD 4:15-18)

The passage goes on to castigate the sect's priestly enemies ("shoddy wall-builders," 4:19) for falling into two of these traps: sexual immorality and pollution of the sanctuary. Shortly thereafter, CD implies that the opponents of the sect also have not kept themselves removed from "wicked unclean wealth taken from what is vowed or consecrated to God or found in the temple funds" but have instead "robbed the poor of God's people" (6:15-16) – that is, they have engaged in temple robbery and theft. This passage therefore helps clarify what is meant by the second trap: wealth obtained by robbery and theft, particularly as pertains to sacred things.[44] The three traps CD regards as specifically laid out for Israel are therefore strikingly similar to the three sins Paul cites in Rom 2:21-22, certainly a much closer match than the extended vice list of Wis 14:23-27.

The Damascus Document's list appears to depend on a passage in the Testament of Levi, in which the patriarch predicts that his descendants

will be darkened by impiety (ἀσέβεια) and will bring curses upon our family, for which the light of the Torah was given to you to be a light to every person, although you wish to destroy this by teaching commands opposed to the just statutes (δικαίωμα) of God. You will rob (ληστεύω) the offerings of the Lord and you will steal (κλήπτω) from his portion, and before the time of the sacrifice to the Lord, you will take a chosen portion and eat it in disdain with prostitutes. In greed will you teach the commands of the Lord, you will profane married women and pollute the virgins of Jerusalem, and you will join together with prostitutes and adulteresses ... and you will be puffed up because of your priesthood, rising up against people – and not only that but also against the commands of God. Being puffed up, you will mock the sacred things, laughing in disdain. Because of these things, the temple which the Lord will choose will be desolate in impurity, and you will be captives to all the nations. (T. Lev 14:4-15:1)

Although less succinctly stated, the vices in this passage match even more closely to Paul's list: robbery of the Lord's offerings, stealing, and sexual immorality/adultery – not to mention false/greedy teaching, which further accords with the context of Rom 2:17-20. As in the Damascus Document, these are not regarded as gentile vices but are sins especially associated with Israel – specifically with the corrupt priestly class. Moreover, the result of these transgressions is that the sacred things are

---

[44] A similar (albeit fragmentary) list of the wicked deeds of God's people is found in 4Q390 .2 i 4-10.

mocked, the temple is desolated, and Israel subjected to the nations. These consequences closely match the next statements of Rom 2:23–24, in which God is dishonored (2:23) and God's name is blasphemed among the nations (2:24).

Similarly, the Psalms of Solomon accuses the leaders of its generation of the same three categories of sin: sexual immorality (8:10), plundering God's sanctuary (8:11), and temple/sacrificial sacrilege (8:12), concluding that "they did not neglect a sin which they did not do more than the nations" (8:13).[45] For this, "God was justified in his judgments among the nations of the earth," (8:23 cf. 8:7) since through God's action against these wicked leaders in Jerusalem, "all the earth knew the just judgments of God" (8:8), statements that closely parallel Paul's argument in Rom 3 about how God is justified through his actions against sin and infidelity. Philo also lists prohibitions against adultery, sacrilege/sacred robbery (ἱεροσυλία), and stealing as the first three commands of the second tablet of the *Decalogue* (*Decal.* 121–37), explaining that murder is in fact sacrilege, robbing God of his most sacred possession and offering – the human life (*Decal.* 133; cf. *Spec.* 3.83). He also lists the same three vices together in *Conf.* 163 and *Spec.* 2.13, while two of the three (ἱεροσυλία and stealing) occur together in his allegorical reading of Joseph fleeing from the third (adultery) in *Leg.* 3.241. In all these cases, these three vices are at least as applicable to Israel (the recipient of the *Decalogue*) as to anyone else and are by no means understood as uniquely gentile vices. It is also probably not insignificant that Paul employs a word for sacrilege (ἱεροσλέω) that sounds so much like the Hellenistic form of Jerusalem (Ἱεροσόλυμα) that at least one gentile polemicist known in Paul's day had suggested the city had been named for the sacrilegious propensities of its inhabitants.[46]

The same sins appear together in indictments of Israel and Judah found in the Prophets. Jeremiah, for example, declares that the people of Jerusalem "are trusting in deceptive words for no purpose" (7:8) imagining that they will be delivered despite their sin, asking, "will you steal,

---

[45] See Sloan, "Paul's Jewish Addressee in Rom 2–4" (forthcoming). Criticisms of the same sins also appear in Pss. Sol. 2:3, 11–13.

[46] Josephus, *Ap.* 1.309–19 ascribes this idea to Lysimachus, who must have written prior to the middle of the first century, since Apion appears to have built on his work (cf. *Ap.* 2.20; see Lucia Raspe, "Manetho on the Exodus: A Reappraisal" [1998], 140–43). On the different Greek forms of "Jerusalem," (Ἱερουσαλήμ and Ἱεροσόλυμα), each of which appears in the Pauline corpus, see Frederick E. Brenk, "*Hierosolyma*: The Greek Name of Jerusalem" (2011).

murder, commit adultery ... has this house which is called by my name become a den of robbers?" (7:9–11).[47] Similarly, Malachi sequentially impugns Israel for four major sins: polluting the sanctuary with defiled offerings (1:6–14), idolatry (2:10–12),[48] marital infidelity (2:14–16), and "robbing God" through withholding properly devoted tithes and offerings (3:8–10; cf. Deut 26:12–14). To make matters worse, Malachi declares that these violations were committed by the priests who were set apart to "guard knowledge" and deliver Torah (2:7) but "turned aside from the way and made many weak in Torah" (2:8).[49] Consequently, because these priests refused "to give glory to my name" (2:2), showed partiality in judgment (2:9; cf. Rom 2:11), approved evildoers (Mal 2:17; cf. Rom 1:32), and impugned God's justice, they will not stand in the day of fiery judgment when God distinguishes between the just and unjust among his people (Mal 3:13–23 [ET 3:13–4:3]) – a thematic progression closely matching that of Rom 1:18–2:11.

In light of these parallels, it is apparent that the sins of Rom 2:21–22 were selected not because they are peculiar to gentiles but for the opposite reason: because these are the temptations traditionally associated with Israel. There is also no reason to suspect that Paul is referring to specific instances with his terminology of ἱεροσυλέω. It is not necessary to posit, for instance, that "Paul envisions someone here who claims to abhor idols, but then desires and steals the valuable objects which are used in cultic worship of these idols"[50] or that he refers specifically to the swindlers of Fulvia, though both would certainly qualify as instances of ἱεροσυλία, as would inadequate tithing practices that "rob God" (Mal 3:8–12; cf. Deut 26:12–14), improper handling of offerings, or stealing devoted things like Achan in Josh 7. A litany of temple robberies is also recounted in 2 Maccabees, one of which led to the murder of the legitimate high priest, Onias III (2 Macc 4:32–34), after which one of the perpetrators, the

---

[47] See B. J. Oropeza, "Paul's Use of Deutero-Isaiah in Romans 2:24 and in the Gospel of Romans" (2021), 33, 44 n. 18. The end of this passage is famously recited by Jesus in his demonstration at the Jerusalem temple (Mark 11:17; Matt 21:13; Luke 19:46).

[48] The language of "Judah abominating the sacred things of the Lord" (διότι ἐβεβήλωσεν Ιουδας τὰ ἅγια κυρίου) through idolatry in Mal 2:10–12 helps account for the parallelism between "abominating idols" (βδελυσσόμενος τὰ εἴδωλα) and "robbing the sacred" (ἱεροσυλέω) in Rom 2:22. Even if idolatry has been rejected, ἱεροσυλία in its many forms amounts to the same class of violations.

[49] Translating the LXX here (MT: "caused many to stumble in Torah"). The idea of many becoming "weak in Torah" interfaces intriguingly with Rom 8:3; 14:1–2; 1 Cor 8:11–12.

[50] Thiessen, "Paul's Argument," 380.

(illegitimate) deputy high priest Lysimachus, is explicitly called a "temple robber" (ἱερόσυλον; 2 Macc 1:42).

An additional intriguing thematic parallel is found in Deut 29:18 LXX, in which a person hearing the curse, will nevertheless say, "May sacred things (ὅσια) become mine, because I will walk in the stubbornness of my heart." Such a person, Moses declares, will not be pardoned by God but will instead be the reason the nations witness Israel's destruction (29:20–28). Similarly, Brian Rainey observes that the Holiness tradition of Leviticus counterposes abomination, characteristic of the Canaanites, with sacrilege (מעל), for which Israel will be exiled from the land. On this basis, Rainey suggests that Paul here refers to sacrilege as opposed to idolatry or abomination because it remained applicable to Paul's Jewish contemporaries, who had rejected idolatry.[51] The point is therefore less about specific identifiable instances of sacrilege than that Israelite and more recent Jewish history reveals repeated and flagrant violations in this category.

This conclusion is further reinforced by the fact that these verses are immediately followed not by a condemnation of gentiles (of which there is no scriptural shortage) but rather by a recitation of the prophetic indictment of Israel's lawless behavior: "The name of God is blasphemed among the nations because of you" (Rom 2:24).[52] Far from being a condemnation of outsiders wrongly claiming to be Jews, this quotation of Isa 52:5 is pulled from a passage that declares Israel's infidelity and consequent exile has led to the nations regarding YHWH as impotent and blaspheming his name.[53] The rest of that passage explains that YHWH

---

[51] Brian Rainey, *Religion, Ethnicity and Xenophobia in the Bible* (2018), 234, cf. 186–89.
[52] For a fuller analysis of Rom 2:24 and its use of Isaiah, see Oropeza, "Paul's Use of Deutero-Isaiah." That this citation applies so poorly to a gentile addressee likely accounts for why v. 24 gets so little attention from proponents of the interlocutor-as-gentile hypothesis. Thiessen, for example, brushes past v. 24 in a single sentence in each of his defenses of a "judaized gentile" reading (Thiessen, "Paul's Argument," 83–84; "Paul's So-Called Jew," 83), in neither case explaining how this prophetic indictment of Israel would apply to a gentile claiming to be a Jew.
[53] Contra Richard Hays, who suggests that Paul's use of Isa 52:5 here is, "from the standpoint of critical exegesis, a stunning misreading of the text" because in Isaiah, "the quoted passage is part of [YHWH's] *reassurance* of Israel in exile" (*Echoes of Scripture in the Letters of Paul* [1989] 45). That is, "Paul transforms Isaiah's oracle of promise into a word of reproach," though this "provocative misreading of Isa. 52:5 is only provisional" since Paul does emphasize God's ultimate deliverance of Israel. But this reading overlooks that Isaiah has already established that Israel's defeat and exile – the situation addressed in Isa 52 – is the consequence of Israel's infidelity and violation of the covenant (see Shiu-Lun Shum, *Paul's Use of Isaiah in Romans* [2002], 179). As is also the

will restore Israel specifically to stop the blasphemy of the nations. A closely related prophetic passage that has been in view throughout Rom 2:17–25 is worth citing in full,[54] as that passage specifically highlights the ethical transformation associated with Israel's return:

> Therefore, say to the house of Israel, thus says YHWH: "It is not for your sake, house of Israel, that I am about to act, but for my sacred name, which you have desecrated among the nations where you went. I will vindicate the sanctity of my great name which has been desecrated among the nations. Then the nations will know that I am YHWH," declares Lord YHWH, "when I prove myself sacred among you in their sight. For I will take you from the nations, gather you from all the lands ... I will sprinkle clean water on you and you will be clean. I will cleanse you from all your uncleanness and from all your idols. Moreover, I will give you a new heart and put a new spirit within you ... I will put my spirit in you and cause you to walk in my statutes and you will be careful to observe my ordinances.... So you will be my people, and I will be your God." (Ezek 36:22–28)

By now it should be clear that Paul's use of scripture in these chapters is not haphazard; instead, he combines related passages to present his gospel as the fulfillment of the promises to Israel in the wake of Israel's disobedience.[55] Whereas Israel's vocation was to be a "light to those in

---

case in Ezek 36, this is the context in which YHWH reassures his people that he will act such that not only the nations but his own people will "know his name" (52:5), vindicating himself through his restoration of his undeserving people, who are to blame for his name being blasphemed. Isa 52:5 is thus *both* a word of reproach (as recognized by Paul) *and* a promise of deliverance. Thorsteinsson similarly misunderstands the context of this saying in Isaiah and its function in Romans by claiming that the verse in Isaiah is "an indirect accusation against *gentiles*" (*Paul's Interlocutor*, 220; cf. Runar M. Thorsteinsson, Matthew Thiessen, and Rafael Rodríguez, "Paul's Interlocutor in Romans" [2016], 28, wrongly assigning this claim to Hays). On the contrary, Isa 52:5 is direct accusation against *Israel* – all the second-person pronouns and imperatives, including the attribution of blame ("because of you") are directed toward Israel. To put it bluntly, Paul is not the one engaged in a "stunning misreading" in this case.

[54] Oropeza observes that Paul's quotation makes two adjustments (τὸ ὄνομα preceding δι' ὑμᾶς and omission of διὰ παντός) that more closely match Ezek 36:20–23 than Isa 52:5, suggesting that "although the partial content of Isaiah 52:5 is evident in Paul's quote, the content of Ezek 36:20–23 also seems to be present" ("Paul's Use of Deutero-Isaiah," 34–35). For more discussion of the correspondences between Rom 2:17–29 and Ezek 36:16–27 and their use in Rom 2:24, see Berkley, *From a Broken Covenant*, 90–94, 136–40.

[55] Contra James Aageson's claim that "there appears to be little or no direct evidence that the larger scriptural contexts were thematically important for Paul" ("Paul's Use of Scripture" [1984], 111). In contrast, Stockhausen concludes, "A fourth element of Paul's use of both focus and related texts is his consistent attention to the context of cited passages. It seems to me that this is an extension of his narrative interest" ("2 Corinthians 3 and the Principles of Pauline Exegesis" [1993], 144). See also the larger discussion of Paul's incorporation and interpretation of broken/restored covenant

darkness,"[56] the breaking of the covenant and its consequences had the opposite effects, which now require divine action to reverse.[57] Since Israel's rebellion is, according to the prophets, the cause of the nations blaspheming God's name, God will solve that problem with the Torah written on the heart, the circumcision of the heart, the new heart and new spirit. Moreover, through his application of these scriptures, Paul suggests that just as Israel's disobedience had resulted in gentile blasphemy, Israel's redemption will now result in gentile praise (cf. Rom 15:8–12) – even, as the next verses argue, to the point of the inclusion of gentiles among those receiving the promised transformation.[58]

THE VALUE OF CIRCUMCISION

Paul is not, however, making the claim that the typical Jew is individually guilty of one or all of the activities mentioned in Rom 2:21–22.[59] The three questions about specific sins do not imply a specific answer, whether affirmative or negative, and many in the audience (whether implied or actual) could presumably answer that they did not in fact steal, commit adultery, or plunder sacred things. Indeed, the next verses emphasize that the circumcised, so-called Jew who does *not* engage in such behaviors but keeps Torah correctly retains the value of his circumcision and is approved by God. But even if the addressee can answer that he has not engaged in these sins, the fact that Israel has been so plagued by "the three traps of Belial" means even the one trusting and proclaiming Torah is

---

material from the prophets throughout this section in Berkley, *From a Broken Covenant*, 170–77. Cf. also Richard B. Hays, *The Conversion of the Imagination* (2005), 2; *Echoes*, 71; Brian J. Abasciano, *Paul's Use of the Old Testament in Romans 9:1–9* (2005), 5–26; David I. Starling, *Not My People* (2011), 6–21.

[56] Rom 2:19; cf. Isa 42:6, 49:6, 51:4; 60:3.

[57] Lionel L. Windsor, *Paul and the Vocation of Israel* (2014), 140–94, argues that Rom 2:17–29 as a whole concerns the nature of Israel's vocation to be a light to the nations.

[58] For further discussion of Rom 15:8–12 and Paul's use of Ps 18:49 (17:50 LXX; 18:49 ET), Deut 32:43, Ps 116:1, and Isa 11:10 to clinch his argument for the union of Jews and gentiles in Messiah, see Novenson, "Jewish Messiahs," 367–72, which observes that all four passages "have in common the mention of the ἔθνη in connection with the people of Israel" (367) See also Hays, *Echoes*, 71–72; Abasciano, *Romans 9:1–9*, 6–7. Note that here Paul suggests that Israel's disobedience caused the nations to blaspheme, whereas in 11:11 he asserts that Israel's misstep led to gentile salvation. But as will be demonstrated below, Paul's argument is that Israel's misstep resulted in gentile inclusion precisely through God's redemptive action on behalf of Israel, such that gentiles are now participating in Israel's restoration.

[59] As rightly argued by Thiessen, "Paul's Argument," 380.

relying on a broken covenant and proclaiming Israel's judgment (explicitly brought up in 2:24), which is why the promised new covenant is needed in the first place.⁶⁰ The point is that no one who engages in such practices is exempt from judgment by virtue of birth, reliance on Torah, or circumcision,⁶¹ the last of which becomes the focus of the final section of Rom 2:

> For circumcision is indeed beneficial if you practice Torah, but if you are a transgressor of Torah, your circumcision has become a foreskin.⁶² And so if the foreskin[ned man] keeps the just statutes of the Torah, will not his foreskin be counted as circumcision? And he who is physically foreskinned, if he fulfills the Torah, will judge you who through letter and circumcision are a transgressor of Torah. For the [Jew] in visible things (ἐν τῷ φανερῷ) is not a Jew nor is circumcision in the visible things in flesh, but the Jew in the hidden things (ἐν τῷ κρυπτῷ) [is a Jew] and his circumcision of the heart in spirit not letter, whose approval is not from humans but from God.⁶³ (Rom 2:25-29)

The reference to the foreskinned man keeping "the just statutes of the Torah" echoes Deut 30:10 and 30:16, each of which enjoin Israel to "keep his just statutes,"⁶⁴ connecting the uncircumcised man with the promise of redemption.⁶⁵ That echo suggests that the same is probably more subtly echoed in 2:14, "the things [=just statutes] of the Torah." Paul's interpretation of Deut 30:10 and 30:16 may have been influenced in this respect by Ezek 5:6 LXX, which orders the proclamation of "my just statutes to the lawless from the nations/gentiles"⁶⁶ – precisely what Paul claims to be doing in Romans.⁶⁷

---

⁶⁰ "By applying LXX Isaiah 52:5 to this figure, Paul paints his fellow countryman *in exile*.... As in Deuteronomy, themes of exile are immediately followed by obedience to the Law, heart-circumcision and praise from God (vv 26, 29)" (Kyle B. Wells, "The Vindication of Agents, Divine and Human" [2012], 88).

⁶¹ "Paul is concerned less with these individual vices than he is with the pattern that his examples establish" (Thiessen, "Paul's Argument," 383).

⁶² On the terms here and their likely polemical nuances for a Roman audience, see Joel Marcus, "The Circumcision and the Uncircumcision in Rome" (1989).

⁶³ The NA28 text is as follows: οὐ γὰρ ὁ ἐν τῷ φανερῷ Ἰουδαῖός ἐστιν οὐδὲ ἡ ἐν τῷ φανερῷ ἐν σαρκὶ περιτομή, ἀλλ' ὁ ἐν τῷ κρυπτῷ Ἰουδαῖος, καὶ περιτομὴ καρδίας ἐν πνεύματι οὐ γράμματι, οὗ ὁ ἔπαινος οὐκ ἐξ ἀνθρώπων ἀλλ' ἐκ τοῦ θεοῦ. Thanks to Stephen Carlson for more than one helpful conversation working through the difficult syntax of these verses.

⁶⁴ Gk. φυλάσσεσθαι τὰ δικαιώματα αὐτοῦ.

⁶⁵ Cf. Wells, "The Vindication of Agents," 87, 90.

⁶⁶ Gk. δικαιώματά μου τῇ ἀνόμῳ ἐκ τῶν ἐθνῶν.

⁶⁷ The precision of the wording in 2:26 is also intriguing for another reason, as the uncircumcised man keeps "the just statutes of the Torah" (2:25) while Paul elsewhere warns that "every man who has himself circumcised is obligated to keep the whole Torah" (Gal 5:3). One might initially conclude that Paul therefore maintains a

The final line of Rom 2:27 is difficult, as the preposition διά could be rendered instrumentally, resulting in "through letter and circumcision," or as referring to attendant circumstance, resulting in "while/in the state of [having] letter and circumcision."[68] Thiessen has put forward a strong argument in favor of the instrumental reading, but his conclusion that Paul is therefore criticizing circumcisions performed after the eighth day is unpersuasive.[69] For one thing, regardless of how one reads Gen 17, the Torah still authorizes – even mandates – adult circumcision for the resident alien (גר) who wishes to participate in Passover, after which he is to be regarded "like a native of the land" (Exod 12:48). Thiessen argues that such circumcision does not grant full Israelite status, observing that the many cases in which the Torah specifies that the resident alien and native Israelite are to follow the same law demonstrate that the two categories are not in fact equal.[70] But even if one grants that conclusion, the fact that adult circumcision in this case grants cultic inclusion within the "congregation of Israel" (עדת ישראל; Exod 12:19) represents a serious challenge to the idea that adult circumcision for that purpose would amount to a transgression of Torah.

The bigger problem with the proposal that Rom 2:27 refers to circumcisions conducted after the eighth day is that such circumcisions would be objectionable not because they transgress "through the letter" but because they transgress the letter itself. That is, those objecting to such circumcisions would argue that they are misguided not because they properly follow the letter but because they *violate* the letter, working against the instructions in the written Torah. To describe such transgression, one would expect something more like διά περιτομῆς παρά γράμματος ("through circumcision against the letter"). But Paul instead says transgression is not only "by/through circumcision" but "by/through the letter," which, if understood instrumentally, suggests that the

---

distinction between what is required of Jews (the whole Torah) and non-Jews (the Torah statutes specifically pertaining to justice). But later in the same passage of Galatians, Paul argues that "the whole Torah is fulfilled in one word: 'You will love your neighbor as yourself'" (5:14) and argues that such is done by walking by the spirit. He also argues that Cephas, "being a Jew, live[s] like the nations and not like the Jews" (2:14), which also works against the idea of maintaining separate standards for the two groups in Messiah. Instead, it is better to understand the "just statutes" (δικαιώματα) as the love commands.

[68] See the discussion of the options in Jewett, *Romans*, 234.
[69] Thiessen, *Paul and the Gentile Problem*, 65–67; Thiessen, "Paul's Argument," 388. Cf. Rodríguez, *If You Call Yourself a Jew*, 56–61.
[70] Matthew Thiessen, *Contesting Conversion* (2011), 60–63.

transgression is happening *by means of the letter itself* – that is, the letter in this case actually results in transgression. This idea accords with Rom 5:13–14; 7:6; and especially 2 Cor 3:6 ("for the letter kills, but the spirit gives life"), each of which suggest that the letter itself engenders transgression.[71] On the other hand, Rom 4:10–11 says that Abraham was reckoned just/righteous prior to his circumcision "in order that he might be the father of all who trust while foreskinned (δι' ἀκροβυστίας)," employing the same διά + genitive construction that appears in 2:27. But in Rom 4:11, this διά + genitive construction is definitely not instrumental but rather refers to attendant circumstance ("while"/"in the state of"), suggesting the parallel in 2:27 should be construed similarly.

The final two verses (28–29) are highly elliptical, and at the risk of even more technical grammatical discussion, it is worth pausing a moment to consider their syntax given their importance at the conclusion of the argument of Rom 1–2. One recent proposal is that these verses should be rendered as follows: "For it is not the outward Jew, nor the outward circumcision in the flesh, but the hidden Jew, and the circumcision of the heart in spirit and not in letter, whose praise [is] not from humans but from God."[72] This translation, although initially attractive due to its economy (requiring fewer words added for sense) and how it integrates with the relative pronoun in 29b, is syntactically untenable. The problem is that the enclitic ἐστιν ("is") in 2:28 must occur in the second position of its unit, which marks *Ioudaios* as the predicate and establishes a grammatical break between *Ioudaios* and the preceding.[73] As such, regardless

---

[71] Thanks to Paul Sloan for calling attention to the connection between these passages. Dunn's explanation (*Romans*, 123) that Paul refers to the ethnocentric use of circumcision and other boundary markers is unpersuasive due to its being built on the "Paul versus ethnocentrism" model that doesn't hold elsewhere.

[72] Proposed by Hans Arneson in an unpublished manuscript and adopted by Thiessen, "Paul's Argument," 377; *Paul and the Gentile Problem*, 58; and closely followed by Novenson, "The Self-Styled Jew of Romans 2," 137–38, 149–50. A similar rendering is also proposed by Ben Witherington III and Darlene Hyatt, *Paul's Letter to the Romans* (2004), 86.

[73] An enclitic is a word or particle that attaches itself (or "leans on") the preceding word and is then pronounced as though it were part of that preceding word. Enclitic attachment is prosodically determined, resulting in attachment to the first phonological word – that is, the first non-enclitic and non-proclitic that bears an accent – within an intonational phrase. In the case of Rom 2:28, ὁ ἐν τῷ φανερῷ is one phonological word, while Ἰουδαῖος is another. The attachment of ἐστιν to the latter is what marks Ἰουδαῖος as the first word in its unit and therefore as the predicate. On the second-position rule for enclitics, see Ann Taylor, "A Prosodic Account of Clitic Position in Ancient Greek" (1996); Mark Janse, "The Prosodic Basis of Wackernagel's Law" (1993); David Goldstein, *Classical Greek Syntax: Wackernagel's Law in Herodotus* (2016), 52–53,

of how one construes the rest of the sentence, the syntax requires the rendering "... is a Jew" (or "... is Jewish") for the predicate. The alternative rendering, which treats "the outward Jew" as the subject in a cleft sentence, would require ἔστιν ("it is") at the beginning of the sentence, resulting in οὐ γὰρ ἔστιν ὁ ἐν τῷ φανερῷ Ἰουδαῖος.[74] As such, although this proposal renders the Greek *words* in an elegant sentence that makes sense in English, the way it combines those words significantly misrepresents the Greek *syntax*.

Because of the enclitic ἐστιν, verse 28 syntactically provides a predicate while eliding an implied subject, most naturally a second *Ioudaios*, presumably elided to prevent repetition: οὐ γὰρ ὁ ἐν τῷ φανερῷ [Ἰουδαῖος] Ἰουδαῖός ἐστιν.[75] As written, the combination of the article preceding the prepositional phrase and the attached ἐστιν signal that the single explicit *Ioudaios* is grammatically doing double duty for an implicit doubling of the word, serving both as subject and (explicit) predicate.[76] Interestingly, the first two clauses (verse 28) provide the predicates but elide the subjects, while the second two (verse 29) do the opposite.[77] The syntax does not, however, demand the addition of words such as "real" or "true," which are unfortunately often added in English translation. Instead, all that is needed is to recognize that the syntax signals the elision of *Ioudaios* in the first clause, which then informs the hearer how to understand the elisions in the parallel clauses as well.

In any case, in this passage Paul denies that circumcision has no value in the same way that in Rom 3:2 he denies that Jews have no advantage. In both cases, the continuation of that advantage is contingent on obedience (cf. 3:3, 9). These verses explain why Paul previously withheld

---

61–65; and the classic study of Jakob Wackernagel, "Über ein Gesetz der indogermanischen Wortstellung" (1892).

[74] As in, for example, Rom 2:11; 3:22; 6:14; 10:12; 13:1; 14:17; 1 Cor 11:8; 14:33; 2 Cor 2:17.

[75] In the same chapter in which he advocates for a version of Arneson's alternative translation of 2:28–29 on the basis of its lack of "numerous explanatory additions," Novenson has no objections to the need for explanatory additions in elliptical sentences elsewhere, as he recognizes that Rom 9:32a "is elliptical, having neither stated subject nor stated verb" ("The Self-Styled Jew of Romans 2," 156), therefore requiring an implied subject and verb to be added to the English translation for sense.

[76] This is in keeping with Pauline tendencies toward a sparse style and avoiding repetition when pivotal placement can allow one word to do double duty. The φύσει of 2:14, for example, similarly functions as a single word that grammatically works both with the preceding and following material.

[77] As observed by Frédéric Louis Godet, *Commentary on St. Paul's Epistle to the Romans* (1883), 130–31.

The Value of Circumcision

the label "Jew" from some who might be called Jews (2:17).[78] Such a claim to Jewishness, he argues, is only valid if the claimant keeps the Torah correctly.[79] The one who refuses to obey should be regarded as a gentile (cf. Matt 18:17). Contrary to those who argue that this critique applies solely to converts to Judaism, the passage makes no special provision for those who were born to Jewish parents and were properly circumcised at the prescribed time.[80] It does not say, "circumcision is indeed beneficial if it was properly performed at the right time, and other transgressions of the Torah do not invalidate the Jewishness of natural-born and rightly circumcised Jews."

Instead, the same rule applies to all who understand themselves to be Jews, whether native-born or a convert: if a so-called Jew does not practice Torah, he is not approved by God as a Jew. If a man born to Jewish parents and circumcised on the eighth day does not "practice Torah" (2:25), that man, Paul argues, has become – and will be judged as – an uncircumcised gentile. Even a properly timed circumcision loses its value for the transgressor of Torah. Disobedience invalidates the benefit of circumcision to the point that God regards physically circumcised transgressors of Torah as having foreskins, having effectively undergone epispasm of the heart.[81] The point is that although such persons may be called Jews and be physically circumcised, from God's perspective they are uncircumcised gentiles. This statement explicitly brings to the surface what these chapters have been establishing all along: transgression of the

---

[78] "But if Paul is not redefining Jewishness, why will he not concede that his interlocutor is Jewish? Why does he distance himself from this claim?" (Thiessen, "Paul's Argument," 379).

[79] Nor is Rom 2 the only place Paul suggests that some so-called Jews or Israelites are not properly reckoned as such. See, e.g., Rom 9:6 (where "not all from Israel are Israel" is both similarly grammatically elliptical and a close conceptual match to "the Jew in outward things is not a Jew"); 11:17–24; Phil 3:2–3.

[80] For the claim that Paul's argument here is specifically targeted at wrongly timed circumcisions, see Thiessen, *Paul and the Gentile Problem*, 64–102. That Paul objects to physical circumcision of adults as a means to enter the covenant people is beyond question. But for Paul even eighth-day circumcision (whether of a person born to Jewish parents or otherwise) is insufficient to ensure one's status in the covenant, which is contingent on obedience. The passage here therefore cannot be limited to a criticism of adult circumcision. Instead, Paul believes that the fleshly covenant had already been broken and that, because God is just, all that matters is obeying the just commands (δικαίωμα) of God, especially since one has no control over birth, childhood circumcision, etc.

[81] Epispasm was a surgical process of foreskin restoration for a circumcised man sometimes undergone by Jewish men aiming to apostatize and become gentiles. See 1 Macc 1:15; T. Mos. 8:1–3.

covenant breaks down any distinction between Jew and gentile with respect to God's judgment.

One may nevertheless object that because the "Torah itself provided the mechanisms for repentance, atonement, and (in the case of stealing), restitution," it is implausible that Paul could claim that "transgression of this or that commandment of Torah (e.g., stealing) nullified circumcision."[82] But this objection both presumes an unbroken, functioning covenant and ignores that Paul has already highlighted the lack of repentance in 2:4–5, suggesting that like the one Moses warns in Deuteronomy 29:18 (ET: 29:19), the transgressor imagines that because of God's mercy he will prosper despite walking in the stubbornness of his heart.[83] The precise terminology should also be noted: it is telling that Paul uses the term "transgressor" (παραβάτης), which applies to willful and rebellious disobedience such as Adam's sin, Israel's covenant-breaking,[84] and adultery,[85] rather than "sinner" (ἁμαρτωλός), which can represent sin "not in the likeness of the transgression of Adam" (Rom 5:14).[86] Paul does indeed argue that such transgression nullifies circumcision, meaning that the circumcised man cannot rely on circumcision because (in light of Israel's prior rebellion), it only represents a broken covenant.[87] But Paul also argues that repentance and reception of the spirit restores otherwise nullified circumcision and establishes one's place in the covenant as approved by God.

As such, Paul is effectively making a "no true Scotsman" argument that Jews who do not adequately fulfill the Torah (according to his halakhic understanding) are not in fact Jews. Only the Torah-keeper retains the value of his circumcision and has rightful claim to the label "Jew." In the same way that gentiles stand condemned unless they manifest the "work of the Torah written on their hearts" through "doing the things of the Torah" (2:14–15), Jews are condemned if they are transgressors of the Torah. It should be noted that Paul is by no means singular among his Jewish peers in

---

[82] Rodríguez, *If You Call Yourself a Jew*, 57.

[83] Wells, "The Vindication of Agents," 87–88, observes that Rom 2 matches Deut 29:18–30:20 in theme and progression, beginning with the one who presumes God's mercy despite disobedience, followed by God's judgment not only on that person but on the whole nation (Deut 29:19–27), followed by obedience to Torah, heart-circumcision, and life granted by God (30:1–20), to whom the hidden things belong (29:28 [ET 29:29]).

[84] Exod 32:8; Deut 9:12, 16.   [85] Num 5:12, 19, 29.

[86] "The 'transgression' committed is nothing less than forsaking the covenant." (Wells, "The Vindication of Agents," 90).

[87] "Apostasy forfeits the efficacy of cultic elements" (Wells, "The Vindication of Agents," 91 n. 88). See also p. 132 n. 97. Cf. Gathercole, *Where Is Boasting*, 206, 210.

taking such a view; the Dead Sea sectarians, for example, would surely have agreed that those who do not keep the Torah correctly are thereby not reckoned as the people of YHWH regardless of how or when their circumcisions were performed, though they would surely have been less amenable about the conclusions Paul draws about gentiles (e.g., 4Q372 3 8).[88] There is also strong warrant in the prophets for the distinction Paul draws here, as Jeremiah declared, "The days are coming, says YHWH, 'when I will examine their foreskins upon all the circumcised ... because all the nations are uncircumcised in flesh and all the house of Israel are uncircumcised in their hearts'" (Jer 9:24–25 [ET 25–26]).[89]

THE HIDDEN JEW BELONGS TO GOD

The dichotomy between the "visible" (φανερός) and "hidden" (κρυπτός) in verses 28–29 alludes to Deut 29:28 (ET 29:29), which declares, "the hidden things (κρυπτός) belong to YHWH our God, but the visible things (φανερός) belong to us and our children forever, so that we may do all the words of this Torah."[90] This verse serves as the hinge between the

---

[88] A similar condemnation of "those who say they are Jews but are not" can be found in Revelation (2:9; 3:9), which similarly seems most likely to be a group of Jews who, by virtue of not following Jesus, Revelation rejects as Jews. See Adela Yarbro Collins, "Insiders and Outsiders in the Book of Revelation" (1975); "Vilification and Self-Definition in the Book of Revelation" (1986).

[89] Rendering the LXX. The MT has "I will judge those who are circumcised in/by their foreskins" and lacks "in flesh." Rodríguez objects to the connection between this passage and Romans because those rebuked by Jeremiah "have not merely transgressed this or that statute of Torah but have abandoned Torah altogether!" (*If You Call Yourself a Jew*, 57). But Paul's argument similarly involves not just sin but "transgression" (παράβασις; note the difference in Rom 5:14), that is, breach of covenant. Thiessen points out the difference between the nations who are "uncircumcised in flesh" despite having just been labeled as circumcised and Israel being "uncircumcised in heart" and concludes that the distinction has to do with the "mechanics of gentile circumcision" (*Paul and the Gentile Problem*, 68–70 [quote 69]). On this basis, he argues that when Paul says that the transgressor's "circumcision has become a foreskin" (Rom 2:25), this is specifically claiming that "gentiles who undergo circumcision are truly uncircumcised ... on the basis of the timing of their circumcision" (69). But even if this is what Jeremiah meant, Paul's assertion that circumcision becomes a foreskin is saying something different, since the claim that circumcision only counts if one keeps Torah applies no less to Jews than gentiles. Instead, Paul is making what Thiessen acknowledges is "the uncontroversial claim that physical circumcision and Jewish descent do not make a Jew pleasing to God" (70), which Paul then claims applies equally to gentiles since God is impartial.

[90] This is the only place in the LXX that κρυπτός and φανερός appear together, with the unusual and specialized vocabulary calling attention to the parallel (see Wells, "The Vindication of Agents," 87, 93–95; Berkley, *From a Broken Covenant*, 99). Philo cites

rehearsal of the covenantal curses in Deut 29 and the promise of restoration in Deut 30,[91] and Paul connects the "hidden things" of this statement to the circumcised heart promised six verses later (Deut 30:6). Those approved (that is, recognized as covenantal members) by humans due to what is externally visible are not necessarily those who truly belong to YHWH, who judges "the hidden things of humans" (cf. Rom 2:16). That is, while physical circumcision may result in human praise and acceptance by those who can only see what is external, "God knows who are his and who are sacred" (Num 16:5). For this reason, Paul elsewhere exhorts, "do not judge before the time until the Lord comes, who will bring to light the hidden things (τὰ κρυπτά) of darkness and reveal (φανερώσει) the purposes of the hearts, and then approval (ἔπαινος) will come to each person from God" (1 Cor 4:5).

Paul draws a similar distinction between human approval and divine approval in Gal 1:10, while Jesus in Matthew also counsels against visibly (φανερός) doing actions for human approval rather than doing them in secret (ἐν τῷ κρυπτῷ), which will then be rewarded not by humans but by God (Matt 6:5–6). Thus, while physical circumcision may result in acceptance and recognition by humans, who do not have the authority to grant eternal life, God's approval at the judgment – and the everlasting reward that comes with it – depends on the circumcision of the heart, which results in true covenantal obedience.[92] Of course, by now it should be no surprise that the "circumcision of the heart by the spirit" is cited only a few verses after a reference to the "work of the Torah written on the heart," as both concepts derive from core restoration passages naturally

---

this verse in a discussion of the difference between outward actions (knowable by all) and the intentions underlying those actions, which can be known only by God, before whose judgment seat the soul will appear (*Cher.* 15–17). John M. G. Barclay observes that although this word pair is familiar from Platonic thought (referring to the "contrast between noetic, incorporeal truths and sensible, corruptible matter"), Paul does not use the pair in this way but rather to refer to what is and is not "(presently) accessible to human eyes" ("Paul and Philo on Circumcision" [1998], 553). The parallel to LXX Deut 29:28 (which Barclay surprisingly does not mention) therefore better explains Paul's use of the dichotomous pair. It is also noteworthy that CD 3:12b–17a interprets the revelation of the "hidden things" together with Lev 18:5/Ezek 20:11–21, which Paul cites in Rom 10:5. See Preston M. Sprinkle, *Law and Life* (2008), 58–62.

[91] Duane L. Christensen, *Deuteronomy 21:10–34:12* (2002), 729.
[92] 1 Cor 4:5 confirms that God's "approval" (ἔπαινος) should be understood as positive eschatological judgment. Some have wondered how, if approval here refers to eschatological reward, it could be thought to have come "from humans" (Jewett, *Romans*, 237), but that is precisely the point – humans do not have this power, so the approval they can confer is fleeting, whereas God's approval is what truly matters.

read together in a new covenant context. And as previously discussed, Paul treats each as synonymous with the reception of the spirit, which enables the followers of Jesus to fulfill the Torah (cf. Gal 5:13–6:2). Those who have the spirit are therefore members of the new covenant, whether physically circumcised or not.

There are close connections in theme and vocabulary between this passage and Rom 8:4, which says that Jesus died so that "the just statute of the Torah might be fulfilled in us who do not walk according to flesh but according to spirit,"[93] and the reference to fulfilling (τελοῦσα) the Torah in 2:27 is also closely linked to the assertion that "Messiah is the *telos* of Torah" in Rom 10:4.[94] These passages are further connected by their use of Deut 30 in similar settings, with this earlier passage helping establish a foundation for how to understand the later citation of Deut 30 in Rom 10:6–8.[95] These links strongly suggest that these uncircumcised Torah-keepers of Rom 2:14–15 and 2:26 should be understood as Messiah-followers who have received the spirit promised to new covenant Israel rather than as wholly theoretical contrary-to-fact examples.[96] Nor is it the case that Paul believes that gentiles who attempt to keep the Torah are thereby guilty of stealing, adultery, and sacrilege by virtue of attempting to claim what is rightfully Israel's.[97] Instead, as the later

---

[93] J. R. Daniel Kirk, "Reconsidering Dikaiōma in Romans 5:16" (2007), argues that δικαίωμα is best rendered "reparation" rather than "just statute" in Rom 5:16, referring specifically to a specific action performed that justifies the defendant. Rom 5:16 does have this nuance, but since the justifying action performed is specifically the fulfillment of Torah's requirements, I have rendered it as "just statute."

[94] George Carras' objection that "[*telein*] is not used elsewhere by Paul in association with [*nomos*]" and therefore does not help resolve the question of gentile Torah-keeping ("Romans 2,1–29" [1992], 204) is therefore mistaken. For more discussion of Rom 10:4, see Chapter 6.

[95] Noting these parallels, Guy Prentiss Waters suggests that "the Pauline patterns of reading Deut 27–30, 32 may inform some of the difficult exegetical issues surrounding this section in Romans" (*The End of Deuteronomy in the Epistles of Paul* [2006], 253). See further David Lincicum, *Paul and the Early Jewish Encounter with Deuteronomy* (2010), 150–51 and Chapter 6. This is only one of many scriptural connections between Rom 1–2 and 9–11, as the latter chapters revisit many of the same sections of scripture to further establish Paul's case.

[96] Contra Carras, "Romans 2,1–29," 203; Käsemann, *Romans*, 63–64; Marie-Joseph Lagrange, *Saint Paul, Épitre aux Romains* (1950), 56.

[97] Contra Thiessen, "Paul's So-Called Jew," 83. Practical considerations must also be weighed. For example, given his thoughts on table fellowship and insistence on the equal status of pagan converts, there is little indication that Paul would have objected to a marriage between an uncircumcised Jesus-follower and a Jesus-following Jewish woman (despite advising them against marriage in general; 1 Cor 7:7–8, 25–40). If such marriages would be permitted, would that not require that the gentile husband participate

arguments of the book make clear, the point is precisely that gentiles who receive the promise of the "Torah written on the heart" – and therefore walk by the spirit – can and do "keep the just statutes of the Torah" (2:26) and have been included in the promises and heritage of Israel by God himself. In light of God's impartial justice, "circumcision is nothing and foreskin is nothing; all that matters is keeping the commands of God" (1 Cor 7:19).[98]

CIRCUMCISED JEWS, UNCIRCUMCISED ISRAELITES

It is surely significant, however, that Paul stops short of saying that the uncircumcised man who "fulfills the Torah" (2:27) thereby becomes a Jew.[99] While it is true that the gentile doers of Torah in 2:14–15 correspond to the foreskinned man who keeps the Torah in verses 26–27, many commentators make little or no distinction between such gentiles and the "hidden Jew" discussed in verses 28–29, resulting in a redefinition of Jewishness that does not include physical circumcision.[100] John Barclay, for example, argues that "Paul's remaining grip on Jewish election privilege must not be allowed to obscure the fact that what he argues in 2.25–9 thoroughly redefines the terms 'Jew' and 'circumcision' in a way which preserves their honorific status but cancels their normal denotation."[101] Such a reading results in Paul calling Jesus-following uncircumcised men "Jews,"[102] which is implausible given how he uses these terms in the remainder of Romans and the rest of his letters.

---

in Israel's heritage without transgressing in the process? One also wonders how Paul might have answered the question of whether such a couple should circumcise their son. I suspect he would have advised circumcision on the eighth day "for the sake of conscience" (Rom 13:5; 1 Cor 10:28–29) while also maintaining that it was neither mandatory nor salvific.

[98] This statement, which Sanders calls "one of the most amazing sentences [Paul] ever wrote" (*Paul, the Law, and the Jewish People* [1983], 103), leads to the obvious question of "what 'circumcision' *is* if not 'obedience,'" since "the circumcision of a Jewish male on the eighth day *is* obedience" (Rodríguez, *If You Call Yourself a Jew*, 60). But the very fact that circumcision is performed on the eighth day of life means circumcision has nothing to do with the obedience of the one *receiving* it but rather the one(s) *performing* it. For Paul, "keeping the commands of God" involves obeying what one is responsible to obey, and one's own circumcision is out of one's hands, so to speak.

[99] Contra Garroway, *Paul's Gentile-Jews*, 92.

[100] E.g., Wright, "The Law in Romans 2," 139; Jewett, *Romans*, 236; Käsemann, *Romans*, 74–75; Daniel Boyarin, *A Radical Jew* (1994), 94–95.

[101] Barclay, "Paul and Philo on Circumcision," 546.   [102] E.g., Käsemann, *Romans*, 75.

The key is to recognize that there are not two or three categories of persons in Rom 2 but four: unjust Jews, unjust gentiles, just gentiles, and just Jews, and the passage does not in fact say that the uncircumcised man becomes a "hidden Jew" but rather that the obedient foreskinned man will judge the circumcised transgressor. And just as the Torah-keeping foreskinned man is not condemned with the disobedient gentiles, so also not all of those who are circumcised will be condemned as transgressors. Recall that Paul has already declared that circumcision is indeed of value for the one who keeps the Torah (2:25), and he does not dispense with that assertion in verses 28–29. That is, although Paul argues that physical circumcision does not *by itself* make a man a Jew but instead must be combined with the "circumcision of the heart by the spirit" (v. 29), he does not conversely argue that heart circumcision makes a physically uncircumcised man a Jew. In other words, Paul argues that being a Jew is a "both ... and" proposition.[103]

It therefore appears that Paul retains the traditional definitions of "Jew" and "circumcision" but tightens the boundaries, counting as "Jews" only those who are circumcised *and* true Torah-keepers as defined by Paul's own halakhic standard. The God-approved Jew in verses 28–29 is not the same as the uncircumcised participant in the new covenant (2:14–15, 25).[104] Rather than calling obedient gentiles "true Jews" in verses 28–29, these verses instead refer to others like himself who are both physically circumcised and circumcised in heart by the spirit. Here again it is helpful to recall that, for Paul and his contemporaries, not all Israelites are Jews. As will be discussed in the following chapters, Paul's argument is that the physically uncircumcised but Torah-fulfilling person (2:13–14, 26) is incorporated into new covenant *Israel* by receiving the spirit but without becoming a *Jew*, and the two groups together then comprise "all Israel" (11:26).[105]

---

[103] Barclay, "Paul and Philo on Circumcision," 546. Paul's position is therefore similar to what Thiessen attributes to Jeremiah: "Jeremiah does not suggest that physical circumcision is unimportant for Judah; rather, he stresses that it is insufficient. In addition to practicing physical circumcision, Judah needs to be circumcised of heart" (*Paul and the Gentile Problem*, 69).

[104] Contra Wright, "The Law in Romans 2," 139.

[105] In Fredriksen's words, they "share the same heavenly father κατὰ πνεῦμα, but κατὰ σάρκα they remain distinct" ("Judaizing the Nations," 244). It is worth noting how carefully Paul finesses his argument in Romans, which was written to an *ekklēsia* he did not found. Unlike Galatians, where he openly refers to the "Israel of God" (6:16) without explanation, in Romans, he avoids "Israel" language until his argument is well established, waiting to fully reveal his hand until Rom 11.

DOING TORAH BY THE SPIRIT: GRACE AND WORKS

Romans 2 therefore argues that eschatological salvation – that is, "glory, honor, and immortality" (2:7) – is contingent on works, specifically on doing the "just statutes (δικαιώματα) of the Torah" (2:25). Moreover, the basis for the inclusion of gentiles is not a rejection of Jewish legalism, ethnic particularity, or the need for works but rather that they "do the things of the Torah" (2:14). More than anything else in Rom 1–2, this is the claim that so many find incompatible with Paul's other statements about the Torah.[106] If the central and most distinctive premise of Paul's gospel is, as is widely assumed, that a person is "justified by fidelity apart from works of Torah,"[107] how can he also insist that final judgment and salvation are contingent on doing what the Torah requires?

The confusion on this point derives from the persistent attempt to read not only Rom 2 but the Pauline epistles as a whole outside a traditional Jewish eschatological framework, as though the apostle stood opposed to foundational premises of traditional Jewish theology. But Paul is not engaged in an abstract, universalizing theological argument about individual salvation, nor is he writing on the basis of introspective assessments of his own inability to keep Torah.[108] His arguments are not based on the modern virtue of inclusiveness as opposed to ethnic exclusivity, nor is he trying to ensure that gentile Christians understand that Jews will be saved regardless of whether they follow Jesus. Instead, he is working from the traditional restorationist perspective of a first-century Jew who believes the new covenant is being fulfilled through the gift of the spirit granted to the followers of Jesus, the Messiah of Israel. Though less familiar or fitted to modern concerns, this framework is more compatible with Paul's first-century context, and the arguments of Romans 2 – nearly all of which appear in different verbiage elsewhere in the Pauline letters – fit naturally within such a framework.

Thus, when Paul elsewhere says justification cannot come through "works of Torah," he is not, as some have suggested, rejecting the need for human actions due to a conviction that God's grace must operate in "sovereign, splendid isolation."[109] Nor is it the case that Paul emphasizes the concept of grace (χάρις) to emphasize "the unilateral character of

---

[106] E.g., Sanders, *PLJP*, 125–31; Räisänen, *Paul and the Law*, 101–9.
[107] Rom 3:28; cf. 3:20; Gal 2:16.
[108] Krister Stendahl, "The Apostle Paul and the Introspective Conscience of the West" (1963).
[109] Stephen Westerholm, "Torah, Nomos and Law" (1991), 55.

Doing Torah by the Spirit

God's righteousness and justifying act" or to protect "the covenantal language of righteousness – which is inherently bilateral – against the idea of a reciprocity between God and his people, just as it protects the obedience of faith against the idea of synergism."[110] On the contrary, if this were the aim, the use of χάρις ("grace") terminology itself would be exceedingly strange, since that word functions as a term of reciprocity when used by any other Greek author or speaker. Indeed, in classical works, where modern theological concerns are not in view, the word is sometimes rendered as "reciprocal gift-giving."[111] Far from protecting against a covenantal perspective, the nuance of reciprocity inherent to χάρις makes that term especially compatible with the covenantal language of justness, as God freely gives a gift (χάρις) without regard to the recipient's merit and then expects gratitude (χάρις), fidelity, and obedience in response.[112] Paul does not advocate a grace that operates in sovereign isolation but rather one that works in relationship and facilitates obedience.

Specifically, Paul teaches that the gift of the spirit brings transformation into the likeness of Messiah (whose *pneuma* is the gift),[113] which then initiates the gracious response of those having been brought into gracious and faithful relationship with God. Unlike so many of his later readers, Paul's aim is not to establish the philosophical principle of the unilateral sovereignty of God but rather to argue that the promises to Israel are being fulfilled through the gospel he preaches. But Moses and the prophets do not promise that God will save the unjust by declaring

---

[110] J. Christiaan Beker, *Paul the Apostle* (1980), 264.

[111] Linda McNeil, for example, refers to "the aesthetics and ethics of fifth-century Athenian notions of reciprocal gift-giving (*kharis*)" ("Bridal Cloths, Cover-Ups, and Kharis" [2005], 2). Cf. Gabriel Herman, *Ritualised Friendship and the Greek City* (2002); Bonnie McClachlan, *Age of Grace: Charis in Early Greek Poetry* (1993); Richard Seaford, *Reciprocity and Ritual* (1994); and Francis Cairns, "'ΕΡΟΣ in Pindar's First Olympian Ode" (1977), which discusses "the [ancient Greek] notion that it was a lover's duty to repay his beloved's χάρις" (32).

[112] See especially the important work of John M. G. Barclay, *Paul and the Gift* (2015). See also John Milbank, "Can a Gift Be Given?" (1995), esp. 136–37; David A. deSilva, *Honor, Patronage, Kinship & Purity* (2000), 95–156; James R. Harrison, *Paul's Language of Grace in Its Graeco-Roman Context* (2003); Jason Whitlark, "Enabling χάρις: Transformation of the Convention of Reciprocity by Philo and in Ephesians" (2003); Zeba A. Crook, *Reconceptualising Conversion* (2004), 132–47; John M. G. Barclay, "By The Grace of God I Am What I Am" (2006); Troels Engberg-Pedersen, "Gift-Giving and Friendship" (2008); B. J. Oropeza, "The Expectation of Grace" (2014).

[113] Thomas D. Stegman, "Paul's Use of *dikaio-* Terminology" (2011), 511; Pitre, Barber, and Kincaid, *Paul, a New Covenant Jew*, 180–81.

them to be just despite their continued injustice, eliminating his just statutes and rewarding the unjust as though they were just. On the contrary, they promise that God will make the unjust just, giving them the desire and capacity to do the justice he requires. That is, as Deut 30:6 promises, "YHWH your God will circumcise your heart ... to love YHWH your God with all your heart and all your soul so that you may live." The promise is that God will change the heart so that the people will fulfill the love command, which is identified with the "just statutes" in Deut 30:10, 16. The consequence of fulfilling the love command as a result of that heart circumcision will be life – the very thing Paul says is the outcome of fulfilling the "just statutes of the Torah" (2:25).[114] This is the framework within which Paul argues that justification only comes through God's grace and not through works of Torah. This is why John Barclay explains that grace for Paul is best understood as "empowerment"[115] or "energism"[116] – that is, exactly the power to do right promised to Israel.[117]

Rather than arguing against the principle of retributive justice or the need for works for a good judgment, Paul is instead addressing what one might call the *paradox of justification*: a person cannot become just through the works of Torah because only a just person will properly fulfill the just things of the Torah – that is, the love commands. Instead, to fulfill Torah a person must first *become* just (=be justified; δικαιόω). Attempting to do it the other way around is to put the cart before the horse, akin to asking a fig tree to produce olives. Or, as Rom 3:20 puts it, "through works of Torah no flesh will be justified."[118] The morally incompetent must first be made morally competent through the reception

---

[114] "In Deuteronomy 30, Life is given to those who turn and obey God, 'to keep and to do all his commandments and his righteous decrees' (φυλάσσεσθαι καὶ ποιεῖν πάσας τὰς ἐντολὰς αὐτοῦ καὶ τὰ δικαιώματα αὐτοῦ, v. 10). Following Deuteronomy, Paul reasons that only those who keep the righteous decrees of the Law ... are finally counted (λογισθήσεται as God's people and given Life ([Rom] 2:26, 29)" (Wells, "The Vindication of Agents," 89).

[115] John M. G. Barclay, "Grace and the Transformation of Agency in Christ" (2008), 384; see also John Nolland, "Grace as Power" (1986).

[116] Barclay, "Transformation of Agency," 388 n. 38.

[117] Pitre, Barber, and Kincaid, *Paul, a New Covenant Jew*, 162–210.

[118] Paul is working with a specific concept of the verb "justify" (δικαιόω) derived primarily from Second Isaiah, which repeatedly declares that God will make previously unjust Israel just (43:25–26; 45:25; 50:8; 53:11) so that they may ultimately be vindicated in judgment. On the pervasive influence of Isaiah on Paul's conception of righteousness/ justification and Israel's redemption, see Robert C. Olson, *The Gospel as the Revelation of God's Righteousness* (2016), esp. 102–14.

of a new heart and new spirit as promised by the prophets; only then can the newly competent moral agent do the required morally upright things.[119] The contrast is subtle but significant: whereas a person cannot be justified "through works of Torah" (3:20), justification through the "work of the Torah written on the heart" (2:15) enables a person to do the works of justice the Torah requires.[120] It is not that God saves unrighteous people by merely judging them as though they were righteous. Rather, Paul's message is that God graciously takes unjust people and makes them just, thereby satisfying both God's mercy and justice in judgment. Again, it must be emphasized that Paul is not proclaiming a "Torah-free" gospel but rather a "Torah-implanted gospel."[121]

Moreover, the (written) Torah was "added because of transgression" (Gal 3:19) and is no longer necessary for those who have become just/righteous through the Torah written on their hearts and walk by the spirit. Such persons will naturally produce the fruit of the spirit (Gal 5:13–26; Rom 2:14–16), works that fulfill what the Torah requires (Rom 8:4) and "against which there is no law/Torah" (Gal 5:23). Because the one in Messiah is no longer a transgressor and already naturally does the things the Torah teaches,[122] the written Torah is superfluous and unnecessary. This reading explains why, after so energetically arguing against circumcision and "works of Torah" as a means to justification, Paul is so adamant about the necessity of works in the last two chapters of Galatians, including a warning that would fit just as well in Rom 2: "Do not be deceived: God is not mocked, for whatever a person sows, this he will also reap. For the one who sows to his own flesh will from the flesh reap destruction, but the one who sows to the spirit will from the spirit reap eternal life" (6:7–8).

The point is that if a person no longer "walks by the spirit" but instead "walks according to the flesh" and does injustice, that person comes once again under the domain of the Torah, which will judge that person's

---

[119] Wells, *Grace and Agency*, 211–311.
[120] "For Paul, reception of grace must be what might be called an 'activated reciprocity' rather than an active reception... It is therefore only through an operation of restructuring grace that humans can be active recipients, participants in the circle of gift that substantiates relationships, vertical and horizontal" (Wells, *Grace and Agency*, 310 n. 58).
[121] See Chapter 2.
[122] As observed by Beker, *Paul the Apostle*, 216–17, Luther's *simul iustus et peccator* is antithetical to Paul's understanding, which is better summarized *tunc peccator, nunc iustus* ("once a sinner, now justified"). See also Hans Windisch, "Das Problem des paulinischen imperativs" (1924).

wrongdoing (Gal 5:18). That is, those in Messiah are not under Torah so long as they walk by the spirit and thereby "fulfill the whole Torah" (5:14), but the disobedient will be judged by the Torah. Paul objects to treating the Torah as the means to becoming just/righteous, arguing that since the Spirit gives both the volition and the power to fulfill what the Torah requires, a return to the works of Torah that give neither will only lead to imprisonment under sin once again.[123] When Paul argues that such justness can only come through God's grace, this is not over and against desert or the need for works, nor does he ever argue that a person is saved "by faith alone."[124] Instead, "in Messiah Jesus, neither circumcision nor foreskin matters, only fidelity working through love" (Gal 5:6). That is, fidelity must be worked out (the "justified" person must do justice), and God's grace is what brings transformation, empowering and motivating the works of justice necessary for a good judgment justly based on works. "Therefore," he says, "earn (κατεργάζεσθε) your salvation with fear and trembling, for it is God who works in you both to will and to work for his good pleasure" (Phil 2:12–13).

Paul therefore draws exactly the distinction Stephen Westerholm finds "inconceivable," distinguishing "an anticipatory justification based on faith … from a final justification based on a different criterion,"[125] namely, works. Justification and salvation must not be conflated – rather than being synonymous, the former facilitates the latter, which is in accordance with justice and requires justness.[126] For Paul, justification amounts to the forgiveness of past sins, freedom from the human propensity to sin (slavery to the power of sin), and the power to obey God fully.[127] Moreover, Paul does not present justification as a merely substitutionary affair, as though Jesus dies in the place of sinners, for whom

---

[123] Gal 5:4, 18; cf. Rom 7.
[124] The only place the phrase "by faith alone" appears in the New Testament or any other early Jewish literature is in Jas 2:24, where it is preceded by the word "not." Surprisingly, even otherwise careful scholars have often succumbed to imprecision in suggesting that Paul taught salvation "by faith alone" (e.g., James D. G. Dunn, *The New Perspective on Paul* [2007], 25, 51, 56, 87–88).
[125] Stephen Westerholm, *Justification Reconsidered: Rethinking A Pauline Theme* (2013), 84.
[126] "Justification by faith does not amount to salvation at the last judgment. To be forgiven of their past sins and freed from the power of evil is, for sinners, an important step on the path to salvation, but it is not a guarantee of future salvation at the last judgment, where only deeds will be assessed. Justification is not sin insurance or a blank check ready to be filled at any time" (Gabriele Boccaccini, *Paul's Three Paths to Salvation* [2020], 122).
[127] Chris VanLandingham, *Judgment & Justification in Early Judaism and the Apostle Paul* (2006), 335.

God's justice and the penalty of death then no longer apply. On the contrary, Paul declares that God's justice against sin is satisfied inasmuch as the sinner *participates in Messiah's death*. That is, the "old human was crucified with him so that the body of sin would be made inoperative (κατεργέω), so that we would no longer be enslaved to sin, for someone who has died has been liberated from sin, and if we died with Messiah, we believe that we also will live with him" (Rom 6:6–8). Having thus died to past sins and being empowered by the spirit to do justice, each person will eventually stand before God to be "repaid corresponding to works" (Rom 2:6). This final judgment will be based on whether a person has in fact practiced justice and persevered in good works as empowered by the spirit provided through Messiah's death. "If so, eternal life will be the reward; if not, damnation."[128]

RESTORATION VIA THE SPIRIT IN ROMANS

Reading Rom 2 in light of the new covenant promises of Israel's moral transformation by the spirit and the extension of that promise to gentiles therefore not only resolves apparent contradictions within Rom 2 but sheds further light on other supposedly troublesome passages throughout the Pauline epistles.[129] In this light, Sanders is mistaken when he asserts that the material in Rom 2 seems neither Jewish nor Pauline,[130] nor is it the case that this material represents the views of Paul's opponents in contrast to his own.[131] Far from being "the joker in the pack,"[132] Romans 2 sits at the very core of the Pauline framework, establishing the foundational premises to be taken for granted in the building of the rest of the edifice. The chapter the exegetes have rejected is the chief cornerstone of Romans.

---

[128] VanLandingham, *Judgment & Justification* (2006), 335.
[129] This reading's capacity to resolve apparent contradictions raised by other alternatives has been a major factor in the growth in its scholarly support in recent years. See Watson, *Paul, Judaism, and the Gentiles*, 208–16; Gathercole, "A Law unto Themselves"; Bergmeier, "Das Gesetz im Römerbrief," 53–54; Ito, "Romans 2"; Wright, "The Law in Romans 2"; Charles E. B. Cranfield, *Romans* (1979), 155–59; "Giving a Dog a Bad Name" (1990), 80–81, 84–85 n. 3; Felix Flückiger, "Die Werke des Gesetzes bei den Heiden (nach Röm 2, 14ff)" (1952).
[130] Sanders, *PLJP*, 130–31.
[131] Contra Douglas A. Campbell, *The Quest for Paul's Gospel* (2005), 233–61; *Deliverance of God*, 530–47.
[132] Wright, "The Law in Romans 2," 131.

Romans 1–2 establishes a foundation of restoration eschatology and presents Paul's gospel as the fulfillment of the new covenant promise of the spirit sent to justify the people of God, a message of salvation through justification. These two opening chapters thus serve as the front bookend of an argument about Israel's restoration and its relationship to the incorporation of gentiles in the promises to Israel, an argument concluded in Rom 11, where Paul fully unveils the mystery of his gospel. As such, Paul does not introduce the question of Israel's redemption afresh in Rom 9; on the contrary, that question is central from the very beginning of the book, with Rom 9–11 developing the themes of new covenant restoration already established in the first two chapters of the book. Moreover, Paul's argument here and throughout Romans rests on a foundation of restoration eschatology, as he presents his gospel as the solution to the condition ascribed to Israel throughout the prophets and other early Jewish literature ("under the power of sin," cf. Rom 3:9) and therefore as the means of Israel's restoration through the fulfillment of the new covenant promise.

From this point forward, Paul argues that the Torah can only be fulfilled by fidelity through the indwelling spirit. Paul therefore argues that his gospel is the only possible Torah-observant gospel and that the gentiles coming into the community through the work of the spirit are themselves fulfilling Torah, having become participants in the promised new covenant by the spirit. Although a detailed discussion of chapters 3–8 is beyond the scope of this study, they are by no means insignificant but rather extend the apostle's thinking as the book moves towards chapters 9–11. A brief sketch of that content (in addition to what has already been addressed in the preceding discussion) before progressing to chapters 9–11 is therefore in order.

Romans 3 further develops the restoration eschatological foundation of Israel's infidelity and disobedience, arguing that the Torah did not – and could not – transform anyone into a just/righteous people. Instead, the function of the Torah is to convict the unjust of injustice and vindicate God for his judgments while also promising the rectification of injustice beyond itself.[133] Consequently, Rom 4 argues, justification must come through another source – as a gift to those who rely on God in the manner of Abraham, whether circumcised (either as infants or, like Abraham, as adults) or uncircumcised. Romans 5 then argues that this gift has been

---

[133] For more on this point, see pp. 85–91 in Chapter 2.

provided through the death of Jesus, which has brought an end to the age of wrath, reconciled those previously under the wrath of God for sin (whether outside or under the Torah), and facilitated the outpouring of the spirit.

In Rom 6, Paul then argues that those who have pledged to follow Israel's messiah and have received the spirit are reckoned as having already died through participation in Messiah's death and are therefore no longer under the jurisdiction of the Torah or its curse. And because they have already died, they are no longer subject to the inclination to sin rooted in the (now dead) flesh – the very thing that had led to disobedience in defiance of Torah – and have the freedom to obey God fully.[134] Romans 7 explains this in greater depth, explaining death-in-messiah in terms of a marriage covenant that extends to the grave but has no jurisdiction after death. But (as explained in Chapter 1) it is not the Torah from which freedom was needed but rather the enslaving power of sin in the flesh, which took advantage of the command – which promised life to the obedient and death to the disobedient – to bring death to the sinner.[135] But the Torah was not equipped to bring transformation and was only capable of revealing and cursing sin, leading to the need for *pneumatic* deliverance (7:24).[136] Romans 8 then argues that the spirit of Jesus has provided the moral transformation the Torah could not, finally enabling those who have received the spirit to fulfill the "just statute (δικαίωμα) of the Torah" (8:2–4).[137] But it is the final thread of Paul's restoration eschatological argument – how this justification by the spirit corresponds to the promise of Israel's salvation – that will draw our focus for the remainder of this study.

---

[134] See especially the discussion in Michael J. Gorman, *Inhabiting the Cruciform God* (2009), 40–104.
[135] Here Paul's argument works along the lines of a common Hellenistic conception of the self as divided, with the irrational, appetitive part of the self overpowering the reasoning part and capturing the will, resulting in immoral behavior and inner turmoil. See Emma Wasserman, "The Death of the Soul in Romans 7" (2007).
[136] See especially Wells, *Grace and Agency*, 224–53.
[137] See Wells, *Grace and Agency*, 253–69. Cf. Brendan Byrne, "Interpreting Romans Theologically in a 'Post-New Perspective' Perspective" (2001), 236–38; "Living out the Righteousness of God" (1981).

5

"Not My People"

Israel's Infidelity and God's Fidelity

> A look at the literature confirms: One of the main problems of Rom 9–11 is that sometimes it is hard to tell who Paul is talking about when he says "Israel."
>
> Wolfgang Reinbold[1]

Paul's argument that the ethical transformation promised by the prophets is being granted to followers of Jesus raises a significant problem: what about the restoration of Israel that was supposed to accompany the circumcision of the heart? That is, if God is fulfilling the promise of making his people just and obedient, why is this not accompanied by the fulfillment of the related promises of all Israel being regathered from the nations and reunited, no longer subservient to the nations? Even more troubling, why are gentiles participating through the spirit in what are rightfully Israel's promises? By the time he gets to Rom 9, Paul is therefore at pains to explain how the incorporation of gentiles for which he has been arguing in the previous eight chapters does not invalidate but rather reinforces God's faithfulness to his promises to Israel. As such, these chapters, once widely regarded as an appendix or an unrelated treatise appended to the first eight chapters, constitute the conclusion of the larger argument Paul has been making from the start: namely, that the gospel he proclaims is in fact the fulfillment of the promises of Israel's redemption.[2]

---

[1] Wolfgang Reinbold, "Zur Bedeutung des Begriffes 'Israel' in Römer 9–11" (2010), 401; cf. "Israel und das Evangelium: Zur Exegese von Römer 10,19–21" (1995).

[2] "The allusions to chapters 1–8 indicate that chapters 9–11 were written for the letter, and are not simply Paul's previously preached sermon 'On the Rejection of Israel' as Dodd... proposed" (Leander E Keck, *Romans* [2005], 226; citing C. H. Dodd, *The Epistle of Paul to the Romans* [1932], 149). For Rom 9–11 as the climax of the letter, see Krister Stendahl,

As previously discussed, although Paul regularly uses the term *Ioudaios* ("Jew") elsewhere, Rom 9 marks a sudden shift to "Israel" terminology, which appears only six other times in the undisputed letters but thirteen times in Rom 9–11. Unfortunately, the scholarly discussion of these chapters has been muddled by the assumption that "Israel" simply means "the Jews."[3] For example, Dunn opens his treatment of Rom 9 by reminding the reader, "Whatever is made of Paul's talk of 'Israel' in v 6, it should not be forgotten that he prefaces the whole discussion with the firm statement, 'the Jews are *Israelites*.'"[4] But this is a curious admonition since Paul does not in fact say this. Indeed, Paul never refers "*the* Jews" at all in Romans, only to "Jews" without the definite article, and that only twice (9:24; 10:12). To understand Paul's arguments in this tightly argued section, it is imperative to pay attention to Paul's precise word choices, including close consideration of what he does *not* say.

This scholarly tendency to conflate Israel with "the Jews" is further complicated by the fact that most readers have interpreted Rom 9–11 from the perspective of later gentile-dominated Christianity, a context in which "the ongoing and exasperating presence of those thorough unbelievers, the Jews" represented "an acute challenge to their [Christians'] increasingly triumphalist theological posture."[5] From this retrospective view, the problem to be explained is the persistent presence of Jewish unbelievers with a competing claim to Israel's covenantal heritage. As such, many have treated Rom 9–11 as a quasi-independent excursus on what some have called the "Jewish question" – that is, the

---

Paul among Jews and Gentiles (1976), 4, 28; Charles E. B. Cranfield, *Romans* (1979), 445–50; James D. G. Dunn, *Romans* (1988), 519–21; Joseph Fitzmyer, *Romans* (1993), 541; Douglas J. Moo, *The Epistle to the Romans* (1996), 548; Ben Witherington III and Darlene Hyatt, *Paul's Letter to the Romans: A Socio-Rhetorical Commentary* (2004), 237; Christoph Stenschke, "Römer 9–11 als Teil des Römerbriefs" (2010).

[3] Matthew Novenson, for example, suggests that "We stand to gain, therefore, from a close comparison of the self-styled Jew of Romans 2 with the actual Jews of Romans 9–11" and that "Paul characterizes the 'one who calls himself a Jew' in one way and 'the Jews' in a quite different way" ("The Self-Styled Jew of Romans 2 and the Actual Jews of Romans 9–11" [2016], 134). But Paul does not refer to "the Jews" in Rom 9–11 at all, where he instead discusses "Israel" and "Israelites," with the only mentions of "Jews" (sans article) in these chapters coming in 9:24 and 10:12, each of which pairs "Jews" with "Greeks" exactly as is done in Rom 1:16 and 2:9–10. Consequently, not only do Rom 1–2 and Rom 9–11 take the same view with respect to the status of Jews and gentiles, one cannot look to Rom 9–11 to find Paul's characterization of "actual Jews" in the first place.

[4] Dunn, *Romans*, 526.   [5] Jacobs, "A Jew's Jew," 262.

fate of the Jews in light of their rejection of the gospel.[6] Or more precisely, since not all Jews have rejected the gospel, Paul must explain "that the saving work of the one God is incomplete and remains unfinished as long as the majority of the chosen people of God are rejecting the gospel."[7] Others have suggested that the problem was the relative success of the outreach to gentiles in comparison to the Jewish mission.[8]

But Paul did not write in a context in which he could assume the "relative success" of the gentile mission,[9] nor did he share the perspective of his later Christian readers, for whom the question of gentile incorporation was no longer a live debate. Instead, he is writing as a restorationist Jew at a time when the Jesus movement was still overwhelmingly Jewish, as is evident by the very fact that he has to fight so hard for the inclusion of the uncircumcised.[10] Indeed, as Terence Donaldson observes, "if his

---

[6] E.g., "the 'Jewish question'" (J. Christiaan Beker, "The Faithfulness of God and the Priority of Israel in Paul's Letter to the Romans" [1986], 11); "the Jews' No to the Gospel" (Keck, *Romans*, 224); "The topic is the Jewish people" (E. P. Sanders, "Paul's Attitude Toward the Jewish People" [1978], 176); "The love song [of Rom 8] is abruptly interrupted and potentially, if not implicitly, contradicted by this urgent question: 'What about the Jews?'" (Susan Grove Eastman, "Israel and Divine Mercy in Galatians and Romans" [2010], 147). In contrast, Beverly Gaventa rightly points out that "the question that logically follows on 8:39 is *not* why does most of Israel not believe Jesus to be the Messiah of God" ("On the Calling-Into-Being of Israel" [2010], 257).

[7] Peter Stuhlmacher, *Romans* (1994), 142. There is near universal agreement on this reading of Rom 9–11. Cf. Elisée Ouoba, "Paul's Use of Isaiah 27:9 and 59:20–21 in Romans 11:25–27" (2010), 187; Otfried Hofius, "Das Evangelium und Israel" (1986), 297–98. Despite the popularity of this view, it is exceedingly implausible that Paul imagined that God's saving work would be complete only once more than 50 percent of Jews believed the gospel.

[8] "Paul wants to deny that the law-free mission to the Gentiles, and its relative success in comparison to the Jewish mission, represents the failure of God's covenantal promises to historic Israel. But the route he traces out to reach it is virtually unnavigable" (Terence L. Donaldson, "'Riches for the Gentiles' (Rom 11:12): Israel's Rejection and Paul's Gentile Mission" [1993] 89). Cf. A. Katherine Grieb, "Paul's Theological Preoccupation in Romans 9–11" (2010), 393.

[9] Contra C. K. Barrett, "Romans 9:30–10:21: Fall and Responsibility of Israel" (1982), 137, we should *not* conclude "that he showed exceptional foresight in seeing, when many of his contemporaries could not do so, that before long Jewish Christians would be no more than a small and not very highly regarded minority in the church."

[10] It is not clear what the ratio of Jews to gentiles was even in Paul's own groups, nor can that question be answered by evaluating the names in his letters, as Jews did not necessarily go by Semitic or traditionally Jewish names. Paul's own name, for example, is a Roman surname (Latin *Paulus*) and would not in itself suggest a Jew; similarly, Apollos and Paul's relatives Andronica and Junia have names that would not otherwise indicate Jews. For the intriguing suggestion that Junia is the Latinized name of Joanna the wife of Herod's steward Chuza (Luke 8:3; 24:10), see Richard J. Bauckham, *Gospel Women* (2002), 165–86.

career as a persecutor tells us anything, we can be assured that Paul's experience to that point had been of the success of the gospel within Judaism, not its failure; one does not attempt to suppress a message that has been 'rejected.'"[11] Moreover, it is not as though Paul's gentile ministry was resulting in mass conversions of gentiles wherever he went. A few households in each city does not amount to "incredibly successful Gentile churches."[12] After all, most Jews *and* gentiles rejected the gospel. And even if the movement was having more success among gentiles than Jews by the time Paul wrote Romans, one wonders what ratio would have been sufficiently acceptable – or what percentage of Jews would need to believe – to make Rom 9–11 unnecessary. Such questions may seem absurd, but the point is that in the absence of specifics, such explanations make no clear claims about what is really at issue in these chapters.

Methodologically speaking, Paul's arguments must be evaluated without presuming the later success of Christianity, as though his efforts had ended with the same results as the Dead Sea sect. Only such hermeneutical agnosticism with respect to the later outcome allows a reasonable assessment of how the apostle is participating in the discourses of his day. The next step after establishing a plausible reading in that context is to examine how that reconstruction fits with later trajectories in Christianity as the movement carried forward. The mistake – altogether too common in Pauline scholarship – is to conflate the two steps, reading Paul from the perspective of later gentile-dominated Christianity as though such an end were an obvious or foregone conclusion assumed by Paul himself.

In any case, from Paul's restorationist perspective, the fact that many of his fellow Jews did not believe the gospel is unlikely to have been especially problematic.[13] After all, Israel's chronic infidelity could be taken for granted as an essential part of a restoration eschatological framework,[14] and the idea that disobedient Israelites will be (or have been) cut off even as Israel itself is preserved is a common motif

---

[11] Donaldson, *Paul and the Gentiles* (1997), 21, a reversal of his argument in "Riches for the Gentiles," 89.
[12] The phrase is that of Grieb, "Paul's Theological Preoccupation," 393.
[13] On Israel's unbelief as not the problem at issue in Rom 9–11, see Brian J. Abasciano, *Paul's Use of the Old Testament in Romans 9:1–9* (2005), 33.
[14] Pablo T. Gadenz, *Called from the Jews and from the Gentiles* (2009), 57–63, shows that Rom 9–11 shares many formal and thematic features of postexilic prayers of appeal that are similarly characterized by restoration eschatology and covenantal theology.

throughout biblical and other early Jewish literature.[15] The Dead Sea sectarians, for example, had no theological qualms about the majority of contemporary Jews being swept away in judgment when God finally restores the remnant of Israel,[16] while Philo expects that many Jews will not participate in Israel's salvation and even suggests that proselytes may take their place.[17] The Gospels record John the Baptist warning his fellow Jews that the "axe is laid at the root of the trees" (Matt 3:10; Luke 3:9), with God poised to remove the wicked "brood of vipers" (Matt 3:8; Luke 3:7) and preserve the people as a whole through the salvation of a righteous remnant. Descent from Abraham is no guarantee of (or obstacle to) salvation, since "God is able to raise up children for Abraham from these stones" (Matt 3:9; Luke 3:8). In Acts, Peter cites the warning of Deut 18:19 that "every person who does not listen to that prophet shall be utterly destroyed from among the people" (Acts 3:23), explicitly identifying "that prophet" with Jesus. Even the Mishnah allows that some Israelites, such as Epicureans or those who do not believe in the resurrection, may disqualify themselves from partaking in Israel's ultimate salvation in the age to come (m. Sanh. 10:1). In a later development of that discussion recorded in the Babylonian Talmud, R. Simai observes that only two out of six hundred thousand in the exodus from Egypt ultimately enter the land, and Rava, citing Hosea 2:17 (ET 2:15), says that it will be "likewise in the messianic age" (b. Sanh. 111a). That Israel's redemption would not include everyone descended from Israel was not controversial, and it is unclear why Paul should be expected to differ from his contemporaries in this respect.

What *was* controversial, however, is the incorporation of *any* uncircumcised men as equal members of the covenantal people of God. As such, Rom 9–11 is not concerned with proportions of Jews versus gentiles or the phenomenon of Jewish unbelief; instead, these chapters aim to explain (1) why the uncircumcised are being incorporated *at all* and (2) why the reunification and restoration of all twelve tribes of Israel seems

---

[15] "The idea that Israel will need to be purged of sinners is common enough in the post-biblical literature (e.g., Ps. Sol 17:26), and even where it is not expressed it can hardly be ruled out. Will God save those who reject him?" (E. P. Sanders, *Jesus and Judaism* [1985], 97). See also Talmon, "Emergence of Jewish Sectarianism," 601.

[16] Cf. Annette Steudel, "Die Texte aus Qumran als Horizont für Römer 9–11" (2010), 120.

[17] E.g., *Det.* 107–108; *Virt.* 156–157; *Praem.* 172. See also Jason A. Staples, *The Idea of Israel in Second Temple Judaism: A New Theory of People, Exile, and Israelite Identity* (2021), 256–58 and Chapter 7. Cf. Peder Borgen, "There Shall Come Forth a Man" (1992), 348; Betsy Halpern-Amaru, "Land Theology in Philo and Josephus" (1986), 83.

not to be happening as anticipated. Put together, the problem Paul must explain is how his gospel – including the counterintuitive incorporation of gentiles – fulfills the promises of Israel's redemption despite not *looking* like Israel's restoration. In light of the apparent absence of Israel's restoration combined with gentile reception of the spirit the prophets promised to Israel and Judah, Paul must defend against the charge that God has been unfaithful to his promises to Israel.

In response to this problem, Paul insists that despite Israel's unfaithfulness (cf. Rom 3:3), God has remained faithful and has by no means rejected Israel,[18] nor does the incorporation of the uncircumcised represent an abandonment of the promises to Israel. Instead, the declaration of Rom 9:6a governs the argument throughout the next three chapters: despite appearances, "it is not as though God's word has failed."[19] Paul argues that God has in fact been over-faithful, going so far as to extend redemption to the gentiles as a means to fulfill his word and redeem "all Israel" (11:26). Thus, throughout Rom 9–11, Paul attempts to explain why gentiles are partaking in the promises associated with Israel's redemption – and how that redemption will ultimately be fulfilled – from the larger perspective of Israel's story, arguing for the interdependence of gentile incorporation and Israel's salvation.[20] Moreover, Paul explains that God not only has been able to accomplish his redemptive purposes in spite of Israel's disobedience, God has paradoxically used Israel's disobedience as a key ingredient in the recipe of redemption.

"NOT ALL FROM ISRAEL ARE ISRAEL"

The section opens with another allusion to the golden calf narrative, as Paul likens himself to Moses interceding for the rebellious Israelites at

---

[18] Paul not only nowhere suggests that God has rejected Israel, he expressly denies such an idea in Rom 11:7. See Herman N. Ridderbos, *Aan de Romeinen* (1959), 240.

[19] For Rom 9:6 as the section thesis (*subpropositio*) governing at least chapter 9, see Jean-Noël Aletti, "La dispositio rhétorique dans les épîtres pauliniennes" (1992), 392–94. I agree with Johann D. Kim, *God, Israel, and the Gentiles* (2000), 121–22, and Scott J. Hafemann, "The Salvation of Israel in Romans 11:25–32" (1988), 43–44, that 9:6a governs not only Rom 9 but 9–11 as a whole.

[20] Contra David Starling's assertion that "a motif that is noticeable by its almost complete absence from Paul's arguments from Scripture in Rom. 1–4 and 9–11 is the appeal to the Gentiles' incorporation into Christ, effected and evidenced by the Spirit, as the hermeneutical warrant for their inheritance of the scriptural promises [as in Galatians]" (*Not My People* [2011], 162). Chapter 4 showed otherwise with respect to Rom 2, and a close reading of Rom 9–11 will find this appeal to gentile incorporation underlying nearly every argument in Rom 9–11.

Sinai: "I was praying that I be anathema from the messiah on behalf of my siblings, my relatives according to the flesh, who are Israelites" (9:3–4a).[21] The implication is that just as Moses delivered the covenant with much of Israel already in breach of that covenant at the very moment of its delivery, so also Paul stands in the place of Moses administering a new covenant – and interceding for the disobedient – in similar circumstances. In Exodus, Moses' intercession ensures that Israel is not entirely destroyed, but Moses cannot reverse the judgment upon those Israelites who continue to resist YHWH, as some are killed shortly after the golden calf event (Exod 32:35; cf. Jub 1) and then the entire generation save for Joshua and Caleb is barred from the Promised Land and doomed to die in the wilderness for their infidelity. Elsewhere, Paul explicitly uses these events as a warning for Jesus-followers, for whom the behavior of that earlier generation serves as a warning (1 Cor 10:1–22).

Similarly, Paul emphasizes that although these fleshly kin are in fact "Israelites" (9:4), even "my siblings" (ἀδελφῶν μου), language otherwise reserved for those in Messiah,[22] and lists the blessings that are rightfully theirs (9:4–5), Israel's salvation is not contingent on their participation. Moo rightly points out that in Rom 11:26, "Paul writes 'all Israel,' not 'every Israelite' – and the difference is an important one."[23] In the same way, here Paul does not write, "they are Israel" but rather "they are Israelites," and the difference is equally important. Paul argues that just as most Israelites in Moses' day did not enter into the promise but were rejected due to their infidelity and disobedience, the unfaithful Israelites of his own day cannot be equated with Israel as a whole: "But it is not such that the word of God has failed, for not all who are from Israel are Israel" (Rom 9:6).[24] With this statement Paul clarifies that his lament is not for

---

[21] Cf. Exod 32:30–32; Deut 9:18–19, 25–29. On the allusion to the golden calf episode and Paul's identification with Moses here, see Johannes Munck, *Christ and Israel* (1967), 29; Scott W. Hahn, "All Israel Will Be Saved" (2015), 89–90; J. Ross Wagner, *Heralds of the Good News* (2003), 45; John M. G. Barclay, "I Will Have Mercy on Whom I Have Mercy" (2010); Jonathan A. Linebaugh, *God, Grace, and Righteousness* (2013), 182. Panagiotis Bratsiotis, "Eine exegetische Notiz zu Röm. IX 3 und X 1" (1962), hears additional echoes of LXX Esth 4:17 here. The LXX uses ἀνάθεμα to render the Hebrew חרם, "devoted to destruction."

[22] E.g., Rom 1:13; 7:1; 8:12; 10:1; 11:25; 12:1; 1 Cor 1:1, 10, 26. Cf. Dunn, *Romans*, 533.

[23] Moo, *Romans*, 722.

[24] The textual tradition witnesses to the difficulty of this verse at a very early stage, as P46, the Old Latin, Syriac, and Ambrosiaster omit the second Ἰσραήλ, while D F G and the Vulgate read οὗτοι Ἰσραηλῖται. Some recent commentators have suggested taking the οὐ not with the first phrase (πάντες οἱ ἐξ Ἰσραήλ) as does my translation but with the second

Israel, which will indeed be saved in its entirety (11:26), but for those disobedient *Israelites* who stand in danger of being excluded from Israel.[25]

Again, it should be emphasized that the defining problem Paul confronts is therefore neither Israel's unbelief nor (*especially not!*) God's rejection of Israel. Rather, the question at hand concerns God's faithfulness to Israel in light of the exclusion of some Israelites from Israel's salvation and the inclusion of some from the nations in that salvation. Throughout these three chapters, Paul endeavors to demonstrate that far from God having rejected Israel, such a pruning of Israel is in accord with the previous faithful activity of God and does not endanger the fulfillment of the promises to the whole. On the contrary, he says, it has always been the case that only "the remnant" will be saved (9:27; cf. Isa 10:22). Nevertheless, Paul expresses his grief that not all of his fleshly kin (though Israelites) will participate in Israel's salvation (cf. 11:17–23), acknowledging that he hopes through his ministry to "save some of them" (11:14). In this respect, Rom 9:6 says nothing new or unusual – certainly no more radical more than Hosea's declaration that the Israelites to whom he preached were "not my people" (Hos 1:9) – but instead restates a core component of traditional covenantal theology: God will always preserve Israel, but individual participation in those blessings is not guaranteed.

To illustrate this point, Paul points to Ishmael and Esau, each of whom was directly descended from Abraham but did not inherit the promise.[26] If Abraham's son and grandson were not included, neither can distant descendants of Israel presume that they will be included by virtue of biological descent. Instead, "it is not the children of the flesh who are children of God but the children of the promise are reckoned as [Abraham's] seed" (Rom 9:8). In Beverly Gaventa's words, "the entity known as 'Israel' ... is not a biological but a theological category."[27] Furthermore, God chose Isaac and Jacob to be Abraham's heirs even before they were born, demonstrating

---

(οὗτοι Ἰσραήλ), resulting in "All those who are from Israel, these are not Israel" (e.g., John Piper, *The Future of Justification* [2007], 48, followed by Moo, *Romans*, 573; Richard H. Bell, *The Irrevocable Call of God* [2005], 210). Gaventa has argued that the entire statement is negated, producing, "For it is not the case that all those who are from Israel (i.e., Israelites by birth), these people are (i.e., they constitute) Israel" ("Calling-Into-Being," 259). Regardless of how the phrase is rendered in English, the basic meaning is not difficult to ascertain: Israel is not equivalent to those genealogically descended from Israel.

[25] Cf. Karl-Wilhelm Niebuhr, "'Nicht alle aus Israel sind Israel' (Röm 9,6b)" (2010), 434.
[26] Alan F. Segal, "Paul's Experience and Romans 9–11" (1990), 58; N. T. Wright, *The Climax of the Covenant* (1993), 238, But see Lloyd Gaston, *Paul and the Torah* (1987), 94.
[27] Gaventa, "Calling-Into-Being," 59.

that they were not chosen for their special qualities or their justness/righteousness (9:9–12). With the latter point, Paul once again opposes the position staked out in the Wisdom of Solomon, which programmatically explains God's choice of the patriarchs and Israel as corresponding to their justness/righteousness (Wis 10:3–11:14). Wisdom presents the exodus, for example, as the rescue of "a sacred people and a blameless seed from a nation of oppressors" (10:15), whereas the wicked Canaanites "were an accursed seed from the beginning" (12:11). In contrast, Paul's argument carries forward Deuteronomy's emphasis on the incongruity of God's choice in light of Israel's unworthiness:

Do not say in your heart, "It is because of my justness that the Lord has brought me into this land to inherit it." ... And you will know today that it is not because of your justness that the Lord your God is giving you this good land to inherit, because you are a stiff-necked people. (Deut 9:4, 6)

These verses, to which Paul alluded in Rom 2 and directly quotes in Rom 10:6, are then followed by a recounting of the golden calf debacle, at which "YHWH was angry enough with you to exterminate you" (Deut 9:8), leading to the intercession of Moses to which Paul has just alluded in Rom 9:3 (Deut 9:18–19), followed by a recitation of Israel's other rebellious behavior, leading to their deaths in the wilderness (9:20–29).[28] Similarly, Ezekiel declares that Israel's redemption from the nations is not only undeserved but is exactly the opposite: God will redeem Israel to repair the damage Israel did to his good name:

It is not for your sake that I will act, house of Israel, but for the sake of my sacred name, which you have desecrated among the nations where you went .... Be ashamed and humiliated for your ways, house of Israel! (Ezek 36:22, 32)

It is surely not accidental that each of these subtexts is also prominent in Rom 2, which similarly deals with Israel's history of rebellion and infidelity and the consequences of that history: namely, that all humanity – Jews and Greeks alike – are under sin, subject to just condemnation, and dependent on God's mercy. Moreover, as illustrated by God's selection of the patriarchs and Israel itself, no one can presume special access to that mercy. The patriarchs and Israel were not chosen because of their justness/righteousness, and the Torah did not restrain Israel from doing the things the nations did. Instead, Israel has been sustained only by God's

---

[28] Rom 2:5 also alludes to Deut 9; see Alec J. Lucas, *Evocations of the Calf?* (2014), 133–41, 146–47.

undeserved mercy all along, and even despite that mercy many from Israel have not inherited the promise to Abraham.[29]

GOD IN THE DOCK: POTTER, CLAY, AND DIVINE PATHOS

Despite its scriptural and traditional pedigree, the potential exclusion of some Israelites from the covenantal promise raises the question of divine injustice (ἀδικία; Rom 9:14), especially in light of corresponding gentile inclusion, which could be – indeed sometimes has been – understood as God having abandoned his covenant people in favor of others.[30] Paul counters by again returning to the paradigmatic golden calf episode to which he has already alluded in 1:23 and 9:3, this time quoting God's response to Moses' intercession: God will have mercy on whomever he chooses (Exod 33:19).[31] In contrast to Wisdom, which deletes this moment from its narrative of Israel's history,[32] Paul reminds the reader that Israel was by no means "blameless" (Wis 10:15). Instead, in light of Israel's flagrant infidelity, God would have been justified condemning all, just as he initially declared to Moses that he would do (Exod 32:10; Deut 9:8; cf. Rom 3:23, 5:12). Consequently, rather than being based on God's obligation to the people, Israel's salvation depends on God extending mercy far beyond the requirements of justice and his obligation to the covenant, as the covenant was already broken at its very inception. Indeed, by implication, God has the right not only to pardon but also to harden (σκληρύνω), as he did with Pharaoh during the Exodus (9:17–18).[33]

---

[29] In this respect, Paul turns Wisdom's argument on its head and is much closer to the view expressed by Philo in *Sacr.* 54–57.

[30] "If historical Israel was the recipient of God's promises to Abraham (vv. 4–5), and if God has now rejected her in favor of a new and multi-racial people, does that not impugn the faithfulness and reliability of God?" (John A. Ziesler, *Paul's Letter to the Romans* [1989], 234).

[31] For the golden calf narrative as underlying Rom 9:15–16, see Barclay, "I Will Have Mercy"; Wagner, *Heralds of the Good News*, 50–53. Note also the allusion to Tob 4:19 in Rom 9:18 as pointed out by Alexander A. Di Lella, "Tobit 4,19 and Romans 9,18" (2009).

[32] "For Paul, however, divine mercy is scripturally defined in the event *Wisdom* deletes from Israel's history – namely, the Golden Calf debacle" (Linebaugh, *God, Grace, and Righteousness*, 186–87).

[33] Wagner, *Heralds of the Good News*, 54, points out that the verb "harden" does not appear in the verse Paul cites but does appear in the immediate context, a good illustration of Paul's "exegetical interest in the elements of the narrative not explicitly cited."

This hardly solves the problem, however, as Paul anticipates the objection that God's choices are therefore arbitrary or capricious: "So you will say to me, 'Why does he still find fault? For who has resisted his will?'" (9:19).[34] This question echoes the complaints of Job 9:19 and 33:10 and the declarations of Wis 11:21 and 12:12 but with a subtle alteration of the traditional formula. Whereas Job and Wisdom use the gnomic future "who will resist" (ἀνιστήσεται) to cast doubt on the possibility of human resistance, the question here is in the perfect: "Who has resisted?" (ἀνθέστηκεν).[35] This detail has been ignored by most interpreters, who have treated the question as a matter of capability equivalent to its scriptural analogues, assuming that "the perfect tense has no past-referring significance here"[36] and is functionally equivalent to the scriptural analogues it echoes.

But the change from the future to the perfect is by no means insignificant; in contrast to the future or other gnomic options, the force of such an "empirical perfect" is that the truth claim is "expressly based on a fact of experience."[37] That is, rather than asking whether resisting God is *theoretically* possible, Rom 9:19 asks the *empirical*, historical question of whether anyone has in fact resisted God, which fits better in the discussion of Israel's history to this point. Like its scriptural antecedents, the question is framed expecting an obvious negative answer, but Paul subverts that expectation by appealing to the traditional image of a potter working with clay to illustrate the "mercy" and "hardening" of the preceding discussion:

> Rather, who are you, human, who talks back to God? Will the molded thing will say to the molder, "Why did you make me like this?" Or does the potter not have a right over the clay to make from the same lump a vessel for honorable use and another for dishonorable? (Rom 9:20)

This rebuke introduces a passage resounding with scriptural echoes,[38] as the potter/clay relationship is frequently used as an image for God's dealings with humanity in general and Israel in particular.[39] Although

---

[34] See Wagner, *Heralds of the Good News*, 56–57. The following sections borrow from Jason A. Staples, "Vessels of Wrath and God's Pathos" (2022), which goes into significantly more detail on these points.

[35] The force of the phrase is "Who has ever resisted," as rightly argued by Robert Jewett, *Romans* (2006), 591; cf. Fitzmyer, *Romans*, 568.

[36] Moo, *Romans*, 600. [37] Hubert Weir Smyth, *Greek Grammar* (1920), §1948.

[38] Wagner, *Heralds of the Good News*, 70 n. 88; Richard B. Hays, *Echoes of Scripture in the Letters of Paul* (1989), 65. Rom 9:20–23 draw upon at least Hos 8:8, 13:15; Wis 15:7–8; Isa 8:5, 10:5, 29:16, 45:9, 64:8; Jer 18:1–11, 50:25 (LXX 27:25); Job 9:12, 33:13; Dan 4:35; Sir 27:4; Ps 2:7–10; 31:12 (30:13 LXX).

[39] "To anyone familiar with Israel's scriptures, however, it would be evident that Paul is drawing on a traditional metaphor for God's relationship to creation, and, more specifically, to his people Israel" (Wagner, *Heralds of the Good News*, 57–58). Paul's

many have assumed the lump (φύραμα) here refers to humanity as a whole,⁴⁰ the context still concerns God's dealings with Israel, governed by the thesis of 9:6 that not all descended from Israel share the same fate. In this light, the single lump is best understood as representing Israel (like the lump in 11:16),⁴¹ with the analogy representing how God has handled Israel, from which he has made vessels for both honorable and dishonorable use.⁴² The language of the clay's question to the potter especially recalls Isaiah 29:16/45:9, of which Ross Wagner observes:

> Both of these Isaianic passages set the clay's challenge to the potter in the context of Israel's confrontation with God over his chosen means of redemption. Israel is portrayed as blind and deaf, doubting God's wisdom and resisting his appointed means of redemption, either by relying on their own schemes for salvation or by questioning God's plan of deliverance.⁴³

In keeping with this larger context, Paul follows his own version of the potter/clay analogy by making precisely the same point about Israel's resistance to God's appointed means of redemption, arguing that this resistance led to Israel stumbling over the stumbling stone (Rom 9:31-33). But before that, not content to let the potter/clay analogy stand on its own in the abstract, Paul makes its application explicit:

> And⁴⁴ if God, wishing to demonstrate his wrath and to make his power known, produced [ἤνεγκεν] with much patience vessels of wrath reshaped [κατηρτισμένα] for destruction, so that he might also make known the riches of his glory toward vessels of mercy, which he prepared beforehand for glory – us whom he also called not only from Jews but also from gentiles. (Rom 9:22-24)

---

argument can of course be expanded to apply to humanity in general (as also in other biblical potter/clay passages), but that is not his central concern here.

⁴⁰ E.g., Dunn, *Romans*, 557.

⁴¹ On the lump in 11:16 as representing Israel, see James W. Aageson, "Typology, Correspondence, and the Application of Scripture in Romans 9–11" (1987), 21 n. 56; Otto Michel, *Römer* (1978), 347–48; N. T. Wright, "The Messiah and the People of God" (1980), 186; Gadenz, *Called*, 193–94, 260. Note also that Paul uses φύραμα to refer to Messiah-followers in 1 Cor 5:7.

⁴² Gadenz, *Called*, 193–94. If the lump is Israel, the suggestion of John A. Battle, "Paul's Use of the Old Testament in Romans 9:25-26" (1981), 125–27, that the "vessels of wrath" of v. 22 refer to gentile oppressors of Israel is impossible, as these vessels also derive from the same lump as the vessels of mercy. For the sense of honor and dishonor here as referring to differing functions, see Dunn, *Romans*, 557; Jewett, *Romans*, 594–95.

⁴³ Wagner, *Heralds of the Good News*, 67–68, noting similar themes in 1QS 11, further supporting such an understanding of Paul's similar metaphor (68–71).

⁴⁴ Contra Cranfield, *Romans*, 492, the particle δέ here does not indicate that God's ways are different from a potter's ways but that God has behaved like a potter (corresponding to Jer 18:1-11).

This passage is syntactically and lexically difficult, and it is worth discussing a few important details. First, the syntax is elliptical, as verse 22 provides the first half (protasis) of a conditional clause ("And if ...") to which there is no explicit conclusion (apodosis). My translation retains the anacoluthon, leaving an implied conclusion unexpressed (e.g., "then God is justified").[45] The second and more significant difficulty has to do with how to understand certain specific vocabulary in the passage. Under the assumption that the potter/clay analogy serves to defend God's sovereign right to arbitrary choice,[46] most interpreters have understood verse 22 as suggesting that God "has endured with much patience the objects of wrath" (NRSV), which are either "made" (NRSV) or "prepared" (ESV, NIV) for destruction. But this reading is flawed on the grounds of sense, lexical precision, and its inconsistency with Paul's expressed sentiments elsewhere.

The first problem is that the "endured with much patience" reading does not make sense in the context of the analogy; it is unclear what it would mean to "patiently endure" a vessel. Many commentators have expressed their confusion or frustration with how the metaphor seems to break down at this point, observing that Paul could have more clearly made his point about God's right to arbitrarily predestine some to destruction.[47] But he does not make that point clearly because that is not in fact what he argues at all. Once the precise terminology of the passage is better understood, it becomes clear that this verse says nothing of "enduring" vessels nor of predestination to destruction.

Specifically, the verb φέρω (here in the form ἤνεγκεν), which appears nowhere else in the Pauline corpus, has been poorly understood in this

---

[45] It is also possible to construe v. 23 as the apodosis introduced by καί (assuming the καί is original, as it is lacking in a few minor MSS). For a defense of this reading, see Folker Siegert, *Argumentation bei Paulus, gezeigt an Röm 9–11* (1985), 132–33. Others have argued that 22–23 is the protasis with 24 supplying the apodosis (e.g., Dieter Zeller, *Juden und Heiden in der Mission des Paulus* (1973), 203–8). I have also taken θέλων as denoting purpose rather than in a causal or concessive sense. For further discussion of the grammar in these verses, see Günther Bornkamm, ed., *Das Ende des Gesetzes: Paulusstudien* (1952), 90–92; Cranfield, *Romans*, 492–98; Jewett, *Romans*, 595; Moo, *Romans*, 604. The language of these verses strongly echoes that found in key verses throughout Rom 1–8, as discussed by Gaventa, "Calling-Into-Being," 266.

[46] E.g., Piper, *Future of Justification*, 193–202.

[47] "It is difficult to account for the expression Paul uses: God *bears with much longsuffering* unbelieving Jews, who are fitted for destruction. How does this patience toward the Jews display God's wrath or power? Would it not be better to say: he *judges, punishes,* or *oppresses* vessels of wrath?" (Battle, "Paul's Use of the Old Testament," 126). To which I say, μὴ γένοιτο!

God in the Dock 195

passage, with most modern interpreters seeming to have derived its sense from the nearby word for "long-suffering" or "patience" (μακροθυμία).⁴⁸ While φέρω often does mean something like "carry" or "bear" and, by extension, to "endure" something, it can also mean something closer to "fetch" or even "produce." As a rule of thumb, when Paul's vocabulary or syntax seem especially obscure, it is often a signal that he is alluding to or borrowing scriptural language, so it should not be surprising that the phrase with which so many have struggled is lifted directly from Jer 27:25 LXX (50:25 MT), which says God "has brought out the instruments of his wrath" with which he will destroy the land of the Chaldeans (Table 5.1).⁴⁹

Table 5.1 *Vessels of wrath in LXX Jeremiah 27:25 and Romans 9:22*

Jer 27:25 LXX (50:25 MT)	κύριος ... ἐξήνεγκεν τὰ σκεύη ὀργῆς αὐτοῦ	Lord ... brought out his vessels of wrath
Rom 9:22	ὁ θεὸς ... ἤνεγκεν ... σκεύη ὀργῆς	God ... produced ... vessels of wrath

On the basis of this intertextual reference, one could understand Rom 9:22 as referring to God "carrying" or "conveying" the vessels, which would conform closely to the sense in the source passage. But Paul has altered Jeremiah's "bring out" by removing the prefix from the verb, which facilitates another meaning of the verb φέρω better suited to the context of the formation of clay vessels: "produced" or "formed."⁵⁰ This

---

⁴⁸ E.g., Michel, *Römer*, 315 n. 22.
⁴⁹ A similar reference to "vessels of wrath" (σκεύη ὀργῆς αὐτοῦ) appears in Codex Marchalianus and Symmachus' version of Isa 13:5 (though most LXX MSS have οἱ ὁπλομάχοι αὐτοῦ), referring to the instruments of the Lord's wrath which he will summon "from a far country" and with which he will destroy the whole land of Babylon (not, as Munck, *Christ and Israel*, 67, "the whole earth"). Anthony T. Hanson, "Vessels of Wrath or Instruments of Wrath? Romans ix. 22–3" (1981), 434–35, points out that the evidence from the targumim suggests the two prophetic passages were connected in the tradition. Note also the intriguing interpretation in a later rabbinic text reflecting on the merciful purpose of God in scattering Israel: "Of course the owner (i.e., God) knows where he put his tools (i.e., the people of Israel); when he returns to his house (i.e., the Land, or the Temple) he will restore the tools to his house" (Seder Eliyahu Rabbah 10); translation from Isaiah Gafni, *Land, Center and Diaspora* (1997), 32, based on the edition of Meir Friedman, ed., *Seder Eliyahu Rabbah ve-Seder Eliyahu Zuta (Tana de-ve Eliyahu)* (1969), 54.
⁵⁰ E.g., Philo, *Mos.* 2.62; *Leg.* 2.95; 3.30; *Mos.* 2.62; *Opif.* 78, 167; Mark 4:8; John 12:24; 15:2; Plato, *Tim.* 24d; cf. also T. Naph. 2:2). Cf. LSJ, s.v. "φέρω," V and IV.3; BDAG, s.v. "φέρω," 1052 #10, though the latter is mistaken that "produced" only applies in the context "of a plant and its fruits."

reading makes significantly more sense in the context of the metaphor, as it represents the potter showing "much patience" in the process of *producing* vessels of wrath. That is, rather than passively waiting and enduring the clay, the potter is actively and patiently involved in the process of trying to change the clay's shape. An active reading of God's patient formation of the clay also corresponds nicely with Paul's arguments about God's justice elsewhere in Romans, where he has already declared that God's "patience" is intended to lead to repentance (Rom 2:4).[51]

This understanding of divine patience in the process of the formation of these vessels helps shed light on the nuance of the final part of that clause, the phrase typically translated "made/prepared (καταρτίζω) for destruction" and interpreted as though it "expresses a nuance of predestination (damnation)."[52] But if Paul intended to communicate that the potter had planned all along to make these vessels for destruction, it is curious that he uses a word that does not carry a nuance of predestination or planning, especially since he does just that in the parallel clause in verse 23, where the "vessels of mercy" are "prepared beforehand" (προητοίμασεν). In contrast to the προ- prefix in verse 23, which clearly establishes a prospective sense, the κατα- prefix of καταρτίζω denotes the "completion of the action of a verbal idea."[53] In keeping with this sense, καταρτίζω typically means something closer to "mend," "repair," or "make good," including every other Pauline occurrence, such as his exhortation that those who are spiritual "restore" anyone caught in trespass (Gal 6:1) or his desire to "fix" what is lacking in the faith of the Thessalonians (1 Thess 3:10).[54]

Elsewhere in the New Testament, καταρτίζω is the term used to denote the disciples "fixing" their nets (Mark 1:19), a disciple becoming "fully trained" (Luke 6:40), and the final work of God to "establish" those who have "suffered for a little while" (1 Pet 5:10) or "equip" believers to do his will (Heb 13:21). The same nuances of restoration or repair emerge in other Greek corpora, including in the Septuagint and later Christian writings,[55] and the Latin translation of Rom 9:22 (*aptata*) carries the

---

[51] David A. Lambert, *How Repentance Became Biblical* (2016), 148, also observes that the theme of patience here connects with the need (established earlier in Rom 2–3) for God to display his own justness in the face of human stubbornness and rebellion: "As in Jubilees, it is this concern for the disclosure of God's righteousness that paradoxically necessitates delaying rectification of human nature."

[52] Fitzmyer, *Romans*, 570.   [53] Smyth, *Greek Grammar*, §1648.

[54] See also 1 Cor 1:10; 2 Cor 13:11.

[55] See the examples in Staples, "Vessels of Wrath and God's Pathos," 207–8.

God's Patience and Divine Pathos

same nuance of adjustment or adaptation, suggesting the ancient translator understood the Greek term in this sense. In contrast to the "vessels of mercy," which have been shaped in accord with what was planned beforehand, the "vessels of wrath" have been patiently "fixed." One set of vessels is *prepared*; the other is *repaired*.

GOD'S PATIENCE AND DIVINE PATHOS

The upshot of recognizing these nuances of divine patience and adaptation is that it depicts a more dynamic relationship between the potter and clay than is typically assumed by modern interpreters who arrive at this passage under the presumption that the potter/clay imagery serves as a defense of God's arbitrary choice. That presumption has led many to recognize an apparent inconsistency between the image of God as arbitrary potter and Paul's insistence on divine justice elsewhere. Reinhard Feldmeier, for example, speaks for many when he asks, "How can the God whose devotion and fidelity is so consistently unfolded in Rom 1–8 be reconciled with the arbitrary potter?"[56] The answer is that such a reading of the potter and clay gets the point of the analogy backwards. Paul employs this metaphor not to *defend* God's arbitrary choices but rather, in keeping with clay's reputation as an especially stubborn and willful material,[57] to *rebut* the idea that God's choices are unilateral and arbitrary.

Specifically, by calling attention to God's patience and the process of amendment in v. 22,[58] Paul alludes to Jer 18:1–11, where the potter and clay metaphor is used to teach the remarkable lesson that although YHWH shapes the destiny of people and nations, he does not do so

---

[56] Reinhard Feldmeier, "Vater und Töpfer? Zur Identität Gottes im Römerbrief" (2010), 388, continuing: "Why does Paul then write Rom 9 as he does, as a text that has provided the crucial *dicta probantia* for the doctrine of the *gemina praedestinatio*, and therefore also for the predestination to damnation?"

[57] For clay being notorious for having "a mind of its own," see Staples, "Vessels of Wrath and God's Pathos," 209–10.

[58] "To appreciate the force of μακροθυμία here it must be recalled that God's patience with his chosen people was one of Israel's most common refrains" (Dunn, *Romans*, 558). Wisdom 12:20–21 similarly refers to God's patience in granting time to repent, though it complains of God's strictness toward his own people. Paul previously brought up God's patience (μακροθυμία) in Rom 2:4, where God patiently provides an opportunity for repentance.

unilaterally or arbitrarily.[59] Instead, just as a master potter improvises and changes his plans based on the response of the clay, so also God declares, "Can I not do the same to you as this potter, O house of Israel? ... See, you are in my hand like the clay in the potter's hand" (Jer 18:6). The fundamental lesson of the potter and clay analogy is not that God works arbitrarily but rather that although God ultimately decides the fate of humans and nations, those decisions are contingent on his interactions with human beings who can and do resist his will.[60] That is, Jeremiah appeals to what Abraham Heschel calls divine pathos, portraying a God who is flexible and responsive to human action and capable of being *affected* by his creation:

> The All-wise and Almighty may change a word that He proclaims. Man has the power to modify his design. Jeremiah had to be taught that God is greater than His decisions. The anger of the Lord is instrumental, hypothetical, conditional, and subject to his will. Let the people modify their line of conduct, and anger will disappear.[61]

This characteristic of Israel's God is no less foundational than the presumption of God's impartial justice. Indeed, when YHWH reveals himself to Moses in Exod 34:6–7, he opens his self-presentation not by declaring his impartiality but rather by declaring that he is "compassionate" (רחום), a word connoting a sense of deep attachment and affection corresponding closely to Heschel's concept of pathos. This is the characteristic that makes Israel's God sensitive to their entreaties even when justice would seem to demand otherwise. It is God's compassionate pathos – and concern for his great name – that keeps him from simply destroying Israel due to disobedience. As Heschel explains, "Divine pathos may explain why justice is not meted out in the world .... Above reward and punishment is the mystery of His pathos. Sin does not inevitably bring about punishment."[62]

---

[59] Jacob Thiessen, *Gott hat Israel nicht verstoßen* (2010), 52. Cf. Dunn, *Romans*, 565; Hays, *Echoes*, 65–66; J. Ross Wagner, "Who Has Believed Our Message?" (1999), 81–84.

[60] Jeremiah reveals that human beings "can actually, by their choice of evil or carelessness concerning right, frustrate God's purposes of grace, just as by penitence and self-reform they can avert a doom that is impending" (R. Waddy Moss, "A Study of Jeremiah's Use (xviii. 1–17) of the Figure of the Potter" [1891], 274). "Life is clay, and righteousness the mold in which God wants history to be shaped. But human beings, instead of fashioning the clay, deform the shape" (Abraham J. Heschel, *The Prophets* [2001], 253).

[61] Heschel, *The Prophets*, 367.   [62] Heschel, *The Prophets*, 305–6.

In keeping with this conception of a relational God of pathos, Paul suggests that God does not set out to condemn but patiently works with stubborn clay to achieve his purposes.[63] By definition, patience/longsuffering (μακροθυμία) implies not getting one's own way, and the implication of the analogy is that if anyone resists God's initial plan, God will patiently find another way for that person or nation to serve God's larger, overarching purpose in history.[64] But such reshapings, although still ultimately serving God's purposes, may not result in the most honorable outcome for that individual vessel.[65] Moreover, as Heschel points out, Israel's resistance to God's purpose to transform the world through his people is a primary theme of the biblical narrative and central to the message of the prophets:

Israel's history comprised a drama of God and all men. God's kingship and man's hope were at stake in Jerusalem. God was alone in the world, unknown or discarded. The countries of the world were full of abominations, violence, falsehood. Here was one land, one people, cherished and chosen for the purpose of transforming the world. *This* people's failure was most serious.[66]

The similarity of this assessment to Paul's own summary in Rom 1–3 is striking. But Paul argues throughout Rom 9–11 that God is nevertheless accomplishing his redemptive purposes through and for Israel by other, previously unforeseen means. Indeed, although Israel has been obstinate and stubborn, God has responded by patiently reshaping and forming instruments for his ultimate redemptive purposes, including making of some of that clay into "vessels of wrath."[67] Paul's use of the potter/clay analogy therefore provides a surprising answer to the question, "Who has resisted his will?": "We have."

---

[63] "Paul's argument in Romans 9:22–23 is thoroughly grounded in a traditional Jewish conception of how God works in history to make even ungodly nations serve his purposes" (Wagner, *Heralds of the Good News*, 73).
[64] Heschel, *The Prophets*, 222–23.
[65] Kylie Crabbe, "Being Found Fighting against God: Luke's Gamaliel and Josephus on Human Responses to Divine Providence" (2015), sees a similar principle at work in Josephus' *War* and the book of Acts, in which divine providence is "an unstoppable force" (22) but "human responses to divine providence have eschatological consequences …. [B]y failing to embrace divine providence, characters can become fighters of God and, in so doing, bring disaster upon themselves" (39).
[66] Heschel, *The Prophets*, 17, emphasis original.
[67] "Even the less honorable pot is used for something" (Gaventa, "Calling-Into-Being," 265).

VESSELS OF WRATH

The "vessels of wrath" in LXX Jer 27:25 are instruments God uses against his enemies, and in this context of God's adaptive reshaping of his people for redemptive purposes, the "vessels of wrath" in verse 22 are best understood primarily as *instruments* rather than as *objects* of God's wrath, especially since the prior verse has already established that the potter is making different kind of vessels, each with a particular *function*, whether honorable or dishonorable.[68] Dunn, however, dismisses the parallel to LXX Jer 27:25 as "interesting but of doubtful relevance here,"[69] and although he concedes that in the previous verse "the more natural sense of the metaphor is of vessels put to differing uses within history,"[70] like most commentators, he immediately drops this instrumental reading for the "vessels of wrath" in verse 22.[71] That is, "since the following phrase has more clearly in view final destruction and its cause, σκεύη ὀργῆς [vessels of wrath] here is probably intended in the sense 'vessels which are objects of God's wrath now.'"[72] But if this is the case, it is unclear why Paul chose the word σκεῦος ("vessel"), which represents a functional instrument. A "vessel of water," for example, does not mean "a vessel which is the object of water now," either in English or Greek.[73] Instead, a "σκεῦος of X" typically represents something serving as an instrument with respect to something else, such as a vessel filled with or conveying something (e.g., Paul as a "chosen vessel" in Acts 9:15; cf. 2 Cor 4:7),

In keeping with the larger metaphor, it is more likely that a potter would make vessels to serve a useful function rather than solely for the purpose of immediately destroying them.[74] This reading also better fits

---

[68] Thiessen, *Gott hat Israel nicht verstoßen*, 52. Cf. Christian Müller, *Gottes Gerechtigkeit und Gottes Volk* (1964), 27.

[69] Dunn, *Romans*, 559. [70] Dunn, *Romans*, 557.

[71] Similarly, Battle, "Paul's Use of the Old Testament," 127. Cranfield also suggests, "σκεῦος ... is used in vv. 22 and 23 ... without any special thought of the literal use of the word in v. 2" (*Romans*, 495 n. 4), which seems implausible given the grammatical (δέ) and thematic connections between the two verses.

[72] Dunn, *Romans*, 559. Similarly, Simon Légasse, *L'épître de Paul aux Romains* (2002), 609–10; Ouoba, "Paul's Use of Isaiah," 177; Jewett, *Romans*, 596–97; Moo, *Romans*, 609; Ernst Käsemann, *Romans* (1980), 270; Michel, *Römer*, 313–15.

[73] I suspect that some interpreters have been led astray by the verbal quality of ὀργῆς, thereby interpreting the phrase as an objective genitive (e.g., Starling, *Not My People*, 119 n. 44). But an objective genitive requires that the head noun include or imply a verbal idea; a verbal noun in the genitive is irrelevant. See Evert Boas et al., *The Cambridge Grammar of Classical Greek* (2019), §30.28; Smyth, *Greek Grammar*, §1328–§1335. The genitive here must therefore be understood as attributive rather than verbal. See Daniel B Wallace, *Greek Grammar beyond the Basics* (1996), 86–88.

[74] As Hanson, "Vessels of Wrath," 440. Similarly, Cranfield, *Romans*, 492 n. 2: "The potter does not make ordinary, everyday pots, merely in order to destroy them!"

"Not My People"

with the material in 9:6–18, in which Pharaoh, Ishmael, and Esau are all persecutors used by God for redemptive purposes.[75] Similarly, the "vessels of mercy" in v. 23, though also recipients of God's mercy, should be understood in an instrumental sense of God's mercy to the world, thereby fulfilling Israel's role as a "light to the nations."[76] Johannes Munck rightly notes that an instrumental reading of "vessels of honor" and "vessels of mercy" brings out a theme of interdependent redemption:

> In this connection, a peculiar feature of Paul's thought in Romans 9–11 may be noted, namely that none of the participants in *Heilsgeschichte* are saved or lost for themselves alone. The hardening of the one has as its redemptive motive the salvation of the other, and again, the salvation of the other leads to the salvation of the first after all.[77]

An instrumental sense – that is, that God is working out his wrath *through* these vessels – is therefore in the foreground.[78] And as Gaventa observes, "the instrumental reading of σκεύη [vessels] here better serves to lay the groundwork" for the upcoming arguments about the interdependence of the salvation of Israel and the gentiles in Rom 11.[79]

"NOT MY PEOPLE," ETHNIC MIXTURE, AND VESSELS AMONG THE NATIONS

The theme of the interdependence of the salvation of Israel and the gentiles is further brought into the foreground as Paul identifies the "vessels of mercy" as

> us,[80] whom he has called not only from Jews but also from gentiles, as he also says in Hosea, "I will call 'my people' those who were 'not my people,' and she who

---

[75] As pointed out by Munck, *Christ and Israel*, 67–68. Cf. Hanson, "Vessels of Wrath"; Gaventa, "Calling-Into-Being," 266.
[76] Munck, *Christ and Israel*, 67–68. Cf. Hanson, "Vessels of Wrath"; Gaventa, "Calling-Into-Being," 266. Pace Starling (*Not My People*, 119 n. 44), the phrase in v. 23 is not support for the objective reading in v. 22 but rather should also be understood instrumentally in light of the pottery metaphor Paul has been employing through the entire passage.
[77] Munck, *Christ and Israel*, 67–68.
[78] Contra Jacob Thiessen (*Gott hat Israel nicht verstoßen*, 51–55), who acknowledges an instrumental aspect ("Werkzeug") is present in the phrase as used in the verse but regards an objective aspect ("Gefäß") as in the foreground (54). See also Christian Maurer, "σκεῦος," *TWNT* 7:359–68, who also sees both senses, with God working out his wrath both on and through these vessels.
[79] Gaventa, "Calling-Into-Being," 267.
[80] Niebuhr, "Nicht alle aus Israel," 435 notes that the anacoluthon emphasizes the "us" (ἡμᾶς) here.

was not beloved, I will call beloved. And it will be in the place where it was said to them, 'you are not my people,' there they will be called children of the living God." (Rom 9:24b–26)[81]

Many have flagged this passage as an especially egregious example of "arbitrary hermeneutics on Paul's part," since Hosea's prophecy concerns "a renewal of God's mercy toward the rebellious northern tribes of Israel: those whom God rejected and named *lō-ruḥamah*, 'not pitied,' and *lō-ami*, 'not my people' ... are again shown mercy and adopted again as God's people."[82] But in this passage, Paul "appears to wrench Hos 2:25 and 2:1 from their historical contexts to apply them to gentiles rather than Israel."[83] C. H. Dodd goes even further:

When Paul, normally a clear thinker, becomes obscure, it usually means that he is embarrassed by the position that he has taken up. It is surely so here .... It is rather strange that Paul has not observed that this prophecy referred to Israel, rejected for its sins, but destined to be restored .... But if the particular prophecy is ill-chosen, it is certainly true that the prophets did declare the calling of the Gentiles.[84]

On the contrary, as has been demonstrated throughout this study, when Paul appears to be obscure, it usually signals engagement with scriptural intertexts. Moreover, this use of Hosea and the application of the "not my people" (Hos 1:9) motif to gentiles at this point in the argument is neither arbitrary nor obscure. Instead, the scriptural background of the citation – namely, that Hosea's promises were made to northern Israel – is instrumental to the argument.[85]

---

[81] For a fuller evaluation of Paul's alterations of his source material and their significance, see Starling, *Not My People*, 110–14; Wagner, *Heralds of the Good News*, 79–92. For a thorough rhetorical analysis of the passage, see Gadenz, *Called*, 91–102.

[82] Moo, *Romans*, 612; cf. Eduard Lohse, *Der Brief an die Römer* (2003), 281–82.

[83] E. Elizabeth Johnson, *The Function of Apocalyptic and Wisdom Traditions in Rom 9–11* (1989), 150. Cf. Hays, *Echoes*, 66–67; J. Ross Wagner, "Not from the Jews Only, But Also from the Gentiles" (2010), 422; Bruce D. Chilton, "Romans 9–11 as Scriptural Interpretation and Dialogue with Judaism" (1988), 29; Ouoba, "Paul's Use of Isaiah," 188 n. 133.

[84] Dodd, *Romans*, 159–60.

[85] Foster, *Renaming Abraham's Children*, esp. 151–215, persuasively argues that in this section "Paul wrestles with the meaning of Hosea on a level more profound than is usually acknowledged" (191), citing prophetic texts "not as independent texts arbitrarily selected but as hermeneutical lenses that reveal the mystery of Abraham's family" (184). Specifically, Paul "brings Genesis and Hosea together in order to decipher the eschatological mystery that Gentiles have become children of Abraham" (191). See also Nils A. Dahl, *Studies in Paul* (2002), 146; Romano Penna, *Lettera ai Romani II* (2006), 283; Cranfield, *Romans*, 499–500; Starling, *Not My People*, 117, 120, 163–65; Wagner,

It should first be recalled that although many scholars treat 9:24 as the beginning of a new unit,[86] this citation of Hosea's prophecy grammatically and thematically serves as the conclusion of the potter/clay analogy, as the relative clause of verse 24 depends on the "vessels of mercy" in the prior verse, further developing the argument of the metaphor.[87] The surprising inclusion of gentiles among "vessels of mercy" did not come out of nowhere. Instead, the imagery of God making "vessels for dishonorable use" (9:21) has already recalled Hosea's lament that "Israel was swallowed up; they are now in the nations like a worthless vessel" (Hos 8:8)[88] and Jeremiah's declaration that recently exiled king Jeconiah/Jehoiachin "is dishonored (ἀτιμώθη) like a useless vessel, for he is hurled out and cast into a land which he did not know" (Jer 22:28 LXX).[89]

These echoes call attention to the past consequences of Israel's infidelity and the fact that God has always reserved the right to respond to Israel's disobedience in this manner.[90] God has previously made vessels for dishonor from unfaithful Israel and cast them among the nations as

---

Heralds of the Good News, 86–89. The argument of Gadenz, *Called*, 107–8, that Paul may have in mind here the (non-Israelite?) children of Gomer *in addition to* the northern kingdom of Israel, thus allowing him to apply the passage to gentiles is implausible. It is unclear why Gomer's children would be any less Israelite than any other northern Israelite children in their generation. The point in Hosea is that the whole people has been divorced, and this is the point Paul stretches to its limit in his application of this passage.

[86] E.g., Gadenz, *Called*, 94: "Formal criteria ... such as the change of actors (from the imaginary interlocutor in vv. 19–20 to the 'us' in v. 24) and the change of vocabulary (from 'mercy' back to 'call') suggest that v. 24 begins a new unit." Cf. Dunn, *Romans*, 569–76; Fitzmyer, *Romans*, 571–75; Moo, *Romans*, 609–16; Penna, *Romani II*, 280.

[87] Cf. Thomas H. Tobin, *Paul's Rhetoric in Its Contexts* (2004), 334; Starling, *Not My People*, 115–16.

[88] LXX: κατεπόθη Ἰσραηλ, νῦν ἐγένετο ἐν τοῖς ἔθνεσιν ὡς σκεῦος ἄχρηστον. That Hos 8:8 calls Israel ἄχρηστον (a homonym of ἄχριστον, "without Messiah") may have drawn attention to the verse (cf. Rom 2:4; 3:12; 11:22). That Israel is here said to have come to be (ἐγένετο) "in the nations" (ἐν τοῖς ἔθνεσιν) is relevant to the address of Rom 1:5 (see n. 121 on p. 96 and pp. 26–27).

[89] As noted by William L. Holladay, *Jeremiah I* (1986), 610, the phrase "useless vessel" in Jer 22:28 is itself "a quotation from Hos 8:8 .... Now, therefore, Jehoiachin will suffer the same fate as the northern tribes." Though not mentioning the parallels with Hosea or Jeremiah, Jewett, *Romans*, 595 n. 72, observes that Epictetus also employs the same language of a person as a "worthless vessel" in *Disc.* 2.4.4, 6; 3.24.33.

[90] This historical foundation of the argument helps account for the striking chronological order of Paul's scriptural citations in Rom 9, which begin with Genesis and end with Isaiah and Israel's exile. On that chronological progression, see Watson, *Hermeneutics of Faith*, 23; cf. N. T. Wright, "Romans 9–11 and the 'New Perspective'" (2010), 42. Pace Starling, *Not My People*, 151 n. 170, it is irrelevant whether Hosea or Isaiah came first in

(apparently) useless vessels, and those dishonored Israelites of the past were scattered by those who served as God's instruments of wrath at that time.⁹¹ But dishonor and wrath is nevertheless not God's final word for the northern tribes or for Jehoiachin's descendants. Although Israel was "swallowed up," "came to be in the nations," and was declared "not my people," they will nevertheless be re-adopted and made "my people" again.⁹²

In this larger context, the point of this conclusion is precisely that God is now calling vessels of mercy from the nations among which Israel was sown (Zech 10:9; cf. Hos 2:25 [ET 2:23]), with these previously dishonored vessels being redeemed and transformed into instruments of God's mercy and being used for God's purpose of transforming the world through his people after all. As William Campbell notes,

> It would be most unlikely for Paul to use the Hosea citation with reference to Gentiles when this was not its original purpose and especially since it is immediately followed by two other Scripture citations that clearly apply to Israel. I would maintain that the Hosea citation is taken by Paul to apply *primarily* to Israel and thus the three citations [in Rom 9:25–29] all have the same point of reference, Israel. Rejected Israel, like the northern tribes, will be restored. This is Paul's primary thesis, but in and with the restoration, another "non-people," the Gentiles, will also be blessed. Paul does apply the Hosea citation in a secondary sense, typologically, to Gentiles also, but only after he has used it to refer to Israel. Like Hosea, he envisages the reuniting of the twelve tribes into one people.⁹³

Campbell's insight about how all three of these citations of scripture apply primarily to Israel is fundamentally correct, but he stops short of recognizing the full significance of that insight. Paul's primary thesis is indeed that Israel will be restored, but these gentiles are not *another* non-people at all. Although many treat "the gentiles" as a distinct group analogous to "the Jews" and suggest that Paul here is arguing that God has now chosen "the gentiles," the absence of the definite article here is

---

Paul's scripture collections since both prophets were associated with the fall of northern Israel, with Hosea slightly preceding Isaiah chronologically.

[91] E.g., Assyria, "the rod of my anger" (Isa 10:5) and Babylon, "my vessel (σκεῦος) of war" (Jer 51[28]:20).

[92] "Paul continues his retelling of Israel's story by first alluding to the exile in his pottery metaphor, and then by directly citing Hosea and Isaiah (9,19–29). His key point is that God does not destroy the vessel, but remakes it, and this is a metaphor for exile and return" (Matthew W. Bates, "Beyond 'Stichwort'" (2009), 404).

[93] William S. Campbell, "Divergent Images of Paul and His Mission" (2000), 199. See also Battle, "Paul's Use of the Old Testament."

"Not My People" 205

significant.[94] It is not "the gentiles" as a class of people who are called but rather some "from gentiles" (ἐξ ἐθνῶν).[95] The language of persons being called "from nations" is also especially evocative of a panoply of restoration texts in which Israel is gathered and restored "from (the) nations."[96] That the same phrase was also commonly used to refer not to those *among* the nations but to gentiles themselves[97] makes it surprisingly easy to read the passages about Israel's restoration from the nations (that is, being regathered from *among* the nations) as prophesying the *incorporation* of some gentile individuals into Israel.[98]

Moreover, as Wagner points out, by reversing the clauses in Hosea and placing the reference to "not my people" first, Paul gains the leverage to wrest from it "the astounding conclusion that the promise of return from exile and national restoration for Israel in Hosea is really an announcement of [some] *Gentiles* as God's own people."[99] But he does not apply this Hosea citation to gentiles merely in a secondary or typological sense. The key is to remember that the message of Hosea is that having "forsaken YHWH, because they have given birth to illegitimate children" (Hos 5:7), Ephraim has been cut off and "mixed among the peoples" (7:8).[100] Once part of God's chosen people, "[northern] Israel was swallowed up; they are now in the nations/gentiles like a worthless vessel" (8:8),[101] thereby becoming "not my people" (1:9), indistinct from the

---

[94] This is a remarkably common mistake among interpreters. E.g., Ouoba, "Paul's Use of Isaiah," 175: "God has chosen ... some Jews and the Gentiles to be vessels of his mercy." John K. Goodrich also makes the same mistake in his critique of my position when he says there is "no need for the Gentiles to occupy the role of Ephraim" and "because the Gentiles have already been allocated the role of Ephraim" ("Until the Fullness of the Gentiles Comes In" [2016], 20).

[95] As recognized by Dunn, *Romans*, 580. See also Cranfield, *Romans*, 506, on Rom 9:30.

[96] "From nations" (ἐξ ἐθνῶν; Ezek 38:8); "from the nations" (ἐκ [τῶν] ἐθνῶν; 1 Chr 16:35; Ps 106:47; Ezek 11:17; 28:25; 34:13; 36:24; 39:27; T. Naph. 8:3).

[97] E.g., 1 Kgs 11:12; Acts 26:17; Gal 2:15; Josephus, *Ant.* 9.253; 13.196.

[98] A similar play on the phrase occurs in Acts 15:14, where James refers to God "taking a people for his own name from gentiles (ἐξ ἐθνῶν)," again echoing prophetic language about God restoring his people from among the nations but interpreting it as referring to gentiles. Cf. Gadenz, *Called*, 99 n. 55.

[99] Wagner, *Heralds of the Good News*, 81.

[100] Hosea's point is that Ephraim has become (νῦν ἐγένετο; 8:8) ethnically mixed with non-Israelites through the exile. In contrast, the *Ioudaioi* remain ἄμικτον ("unmingled"), which becomes a point of contention and accusation by their enemies (cf. Josephus, *Ant.* 11.212).

[101] See Hans Walter Wolff, *Hosea* (1974), 132, 142. Note also the same phrase in Jer 22:28; 48:38.

other nations. In other words, *these Israelites have become gentiles – after all, what does "not my people" mean if not "gentiles"?*

The fact that Deut 32:21 (which Paul cites in Rom 10:19) uses the title "not people" specifically to refer to gentiles outside the covenantal people provides a natural lens through which to interpret Hosea's "not my people" as a declaration that the northern house of Israel *has become* gentiles. Indeed, since the words *goy* and *ethnos* did not yet have the nuance of "gentile" in the Torah and Prophets that they eventually gained in the postbiblical period, "not my people" is a clear way to communicate what would later be represented by the term "gentile" – that is, someone outside the covenant with Israel.[102] What makes Paul's argument distinctive here is that he takes one more logical step: if these Israelites have indeed become gentiles ("not my people"), their redemption by definition requires inclusion of gentiles.[103] As he has already hinted as far back as Rom 2, Paul takes the radical step of identifying uncircumcised gentiles who "manifest the work of the Torah written on their hearts" as members of new covenant Israel. They are the "not my people" being re-adopted like Hosea promised to northern Israel, which would be scattered, mixed, and absorbed "in the nations" before God showed them mercy once again. Paul therefore applies Hosea's promise to gentiles not in a secondary or typological sense but as a necessary part of the promised redemption of once-rejected Israel. That is, for Hosea's promise to be fulfilled, "not my people" (=gentiles) must be transformed into "my people" (=Israel).[104]

This reading is further strengthened by the immediately following citation of Isa 10:22–23, "If the number of the children of Israel should be like the sand of the sea, a remnant of them will be saved, for the Lord will execute his word on the earth completely and quickly" (Rom 9:27–28). This quotation is drawn from a passage addressing the fate of the northern house of Israel in the wake of its destruction by Assyria, promising that a remnant of that people will ultimately be preserved.[105]

---

[102] On גוי/ἔθνος and relevant terms in the Hebrew Bible and beyond, see Ophir and Rosen-Zvi, *Goy* (2018).

[103] Cf. Starling, *Not My People*, 164. Pace Dunn, *Romans*, 575.

[104] "The phrase 'not-people' thus enables Paul to associate the salvation of the nations with the restoration of Israel, an association he will further develop in Rom 11" (Gadenz, *Called*, 108–9).

[105] Cf. Ouoba, "Paul's Use of Isaiah," 188–89; Wagner, *Heralds of the Good News*, 102–10. See also Staples, *The Idea of Israel*, 122–28. For more discussion of the "remnant" concept and its application here, pp. 299–301.

"Not My People" 207

Interestingly, the variations between Rom 9:27–28 and the source text in Isa 10:22–23 suggest that Paul reshaped his quotation under the influence of Gen 45:7 and Hos 2:25 (ET 2:23), which concern Joseph and the northern kingdom, respectively.[106] Then, in the third citation of the series, Paul asserts that Isaiah foretold exactly this situation, in which God has demonstrated his mercy by leaving a "seed" for his people after Assyria's ravaging of Israel and Judah, which left "Zion like a shelter in a vineyard ... like a besieged city" (Isa 1:8 LXX), rather than destroying them like Sodom and Gomorrah (Rom 9:29; cf. Isa 1:9).[107] As John Battle points out:

> The remarkable thing about these quotations from the prophets [in Rom 9:20–33] is that, with the exception of Isa 45:9, every quotation comes from the same period in Israel's history – the time of impending Assyrian conquest.... It is more significant that in each case the Assyrian judgment of Israel is the subject of the prophecy.[108]

Campbell is therefore correct that Paul does not shift his point of reference from gentiles in 9:25–26 to Israel in the succeeding citations – Israel's restoration has been in view all along. But Paul draws the surprising conclusion that the harvest from the Israelite seed that God sowed for himself in the land (cf. Hos 2:25 [ET 2:23]) is being reaped from gentiles,[109] since Israel's sin broke down the distinction between Israel and

---

[106] See Foster, *Renaming Abraham's Children*, 167–69, who points out that "In the entire Greek Bible, only Gen 45:7 and Rom 9:27–28 promise that a remnant will be preserved *on the earth* [ἐπὶ τῆς γῆς]" (169).

[107] The reference to "seed" in Isa 1:9 may have suggested the quotation to Paul, not only because of his arguments about "seed" in Rom 4:16–18 and again in 9:8 but also because of his immediately prior use of Hos 2:25, in which God "will sow" those who were "not my people" in the land/earth, after which he will say to them "my people." A similar connection between Hos 2:25 and Isa 8:14, 28:16 in 1 Pet 2:6–10 suggests Paul was not alone in interpreting these passages together (see Wagner, *Heralds of the Good News*, 131–36). As noted by Starling, *Not My People*, 151, if the chronological sequencing followed by Paul to this point continues through the end of the chapter, it suggests Paul reads Isa 1:9 as chronologically subsequent to the Isa 10:22 quotation. Based on his use of the same concept in Gal 3:16, Paul also probably identifies the singular "seed" here first and foremost with the messiah, through whom Israel's redemption takes place.

[108] Battle, "Paul's Use of the Old Testament," 124.

[109] On the ambiguity of Hebrew ארץ and Greek γῆ in verses like Hos 2:25 allowing later readers to take references to the "land" as referring to the whole "earth" (and Paul's tendency to do just that), see Esau McCaulley, *Sharing in the Son's Inheritance* (2019); Daniel R. Schwartz, "The End of the ΓH (Acts 1:8)" (1986); W. D. Davies, "Reflections on Territory in Judaism" (1992).

the nations, who – absent the life-giving spirit – are equally "not my people."[110]

On the one hand, this is a startling argument, as Paul "extends the logic of reversal at work in the text well beyond the referential sense envisioned in the original."[111] On the other hand, if gentiles who have received the spirit are indeed incorporated into the people of God as Paul has been arguing all along, it is difficult to avoid the conclusion that they are Israelites, since for Paul as for any other Jew, Israel is the people of God.[112] Paul strongly resists any indication that God has substituted a new people in Israel's place, and as will be further discussed below, he consistently depicts those called from the nations as adopted into the already-existing people of God – that is, Israel.

It is noteworthy that multiple rabbinic discussions similarly apply these passages of Hosea to non-Jews and even non-Israelites. For example, in b. Pesaḥ 87b, R. Eliezer argues on the basis of Hos 2:25 (ET 2:23) that God "exiled the Israelites among the nations so that strangers (*gerim*) would join them," because "someone sows a *seah* to harvest many *kor*," while R. Yoḥanan comes to a similar conclusion, since "not my people" and those on whom God previously "had no compassion" must surely refer to (gentile) converts.[113] The underlying framework of Paul's argument is also strikingly similar to that of R. Joshua about the incorporation of an "Ammonite" proselyte into the assembly of Israel:

---

[110] That the harvest is being reaped where the seed was sown helps account for Paul's inclusion of the spatial reference ἐν τῷ τόπῳ ... ἐκεῖ (9:26). This is a better explanation than "instead of" (e.g., Cranfield, *Romans*, 501; Lohse, *Römer*, 283; Jewett, *Romans*, 601) or the idea of an eschatological pilgrimage (e.g., Munck, *Christ and Israel*, 72–73; Dahl, *Studies in Paul*, 146).

[111] Hays, *Echoes*, 120.

[112] Penna, *Romani II*, 297, points out that 9:25–26 is the first time in Romans that Paul explicitly refers to the concept of a corporate people of God, in which gentiles are surprisingly included. *Pace* Battle, "Paul's Use of the Old Testament," esp. 129, who seems to forget that Paul applies vv. 24–26 to both Jews and gentiles. Cf. A. Andrew Das, *Paul and the Jews* (2003), 111–13.

[113] The larger discussion of Hos 1–3 in b. Pesaḥ 87a–b grapples with the possibility that Hosea prophesies Israel's divorce and the subsequent adoption of gentiles. In this discussion, the prophet is characterized as initially suggesting to God, "exchange them [Israel] for some other nation," (87a), at which point God chooses to teach Hosea mercy through his own experience with Gomer, after which the prophet "annulled the decrees" through the counter-prophecies of "not-my-people" being called "my people" once again. Foster, *Renaming Abraham's Children*, 194, argues that this discussion "almost demands to be read as a rejoinder to an interpretation similar to that found in Rom 9:25–26."

Judah, an Ammonite proselyte came and stood before them in the house of study. He said to them, "Am I allowed to enter the assembly?" Rabban Gamaliel said to him, "You are forbidden." R. Joshua said to him, "You are permitted."

Rabban Gamaliel said to him "It is written: 'An Ammonite or a Moabite shall not enter into the assembly of the Lord, even to the tenth generation.'" [Deut 23:4 (ET: 23:3)] R. Joshua replied to him, "And are there Ammonites and Moabites in this place? Sennacherib, king of Assyria, already came up and mixed up (בלל) all the nations, as it says, 'I have removed the borders of the peoples and plundered their provisions and have brought down as a mighty man those who sit on thrones'" [Isa 10:13].

Rabban Gamaliel said to him, "Look, it says: 'But afterwards I will bring again the return (שוב) of the children of Ammon' [Gen 49:6], and they have indeed returned." R. Joshua said to him, "The scripture says: 'And I will bring about the return (ושבתי את שבות) of my people Israel and Judah, says the Lord' [Amos 9:14]. And they have still not returned." So they permitted him to enter the assembly. (m. Yad. 4:4)

R. Joshua presumes that Israel and Judah have not (yet) been restored from exile and, more significantly, presumes that the consequence of Sennacherib's conquest and deportation was the amalgamation of the various people groups. On this basis, R. Joshua concludes that there are no longer distinct "Ammonites" or "Moabites," since those peoples intermingled among "all the nations." This is the rationale for permitting the outsider to "enter the assembly" (that is, marry into the group). Since Sennacherib came and "mixed" everyone, it is no longer possible for humans to know who is who and draw such clear distinctions. For his part, Paul applies the converse of same argument with his application of Hosea's prophecy: northern Israel also mixed together with "all the nations" in the wake of the Assyrian invasions such that Israel *literally* became "not my people" by assimilating into the nations among which they were scattered.

NOTES FROM THE UNDERGROUND: DISHONORED VESSELS REDEEMED

In the context of the larger argument about God's justice and mercy toward his people, the point is that even vessels for dishonorable use ultimately serve God's redemptive purposes. Like Isaiah's Suffering Servant, whose form was "without honor" (ἄτιμον; cf. Jer 22:28) and who was "dishonored and not esteemed" (Isa 53:3 LXX) – God is using those who were dishonored as instruments of mercy so that both the vessels of honor and of dishonor can be redeemed.[114] The incorporation of transformed gentiles is the means by which formerly rejected Israel is being restored from its dishonored, broken state. Far from representing God's departure from Israel, the incorporation of gentiles in the new covenant community therefore serves as proof of God's continuing fidelity to unfaithful Israel. God's mercy for his people runs so deeply that he has begun incorporating gentiles to ensure the redemption of those Israelites who assimilated into the nations.

The implications of this redemptive action also cuts the other way, as those who are now unfaithful and disobedient stand in danger of the same dishonorable consequences experienced by disobedient Israel in the past (e.g., Hos 8:8; Jer 19, 22:28). They may even be reshaped to serve as vessels of God's wrath akin to the gentile kings and empires of old. And as suggested by the concluding "for destruction" in Rom 9:22, the typical fate of such utensils of wrath after completing their purpose was – as for Pharaoh in Exodus – their own destruction (e.g., Isa 10:12).[115] It should be noted, however, that Paul portrays the clay not as finished and hardened but rather as still in the molding process. That is, he says nothing of the potter "breaking the flawed pot to reconstruct it" as though the pot were already formed.[116] Rather, the process of reshaping takes place before the pot is "hardened" (9:18), Once the clay has been fired in the kiln, it can no longer be reshaped but only destroyed once it is no longer of use.[117]

Along these lines, "hardening" (σκληρύνειν; 9:18) therefore is best understood here as the final step of judgment at which point the vessel is set in its given shape and is hardened to remain that way permanently.[118] "Hardening" does not involve reshaping; it involves

---

[114] See Hays, *Echoes*, 63; Wagner, *Heralds of the Good News*, 335.
[115] Cf. Ps 31:12 (30:13 LXX): "I was forgotten like one who is dead; I became like a broken vessel (σκεῦος ἀπολωλός)."
[116] Dunn, *Romans*, 559; cf. also Jewett, *Romans*, 596.
[117] This difference can be observed in the contrast between Jer 18, in which the clay is still on the wheel and the people still have the opportunity to repent to avoid destruction, and Jer 19, in which the hardened clay jar is smashed (19:10–12), representing the judgment of the city, which has now missed its opportunity for repentance.
[118] The nominal form of the term for "hardening" in 9:18 (σκληρύνειν; cf. Exod 4:21; 7:3, 22; etc.) appears elsewhere in reference to clay hardened in a kiln (Plutarch, *Publ.* 13.2.4 [103]; cf. Aristotle, *Mete.* 383a25 [figs rather than clay]; 386a24; *Gen. an.* 743a15; Ps. Aristotle, *Probl.* 12.10.1–2 [931a]), providing a linguistic link to the potter/clay metaphor in the succeeding verses.

permanently setting the clay in the state in which it already exists. But in Rom 9:20–24, the potter is depicted as still working with the clay, which has not yet become hardened. God's mercy entails showing patience with the clay trying to form it into a better vessel prior to hardening it in its final state. In light of God's pathos and mercy, the potter/clay imagery therefore serves as a call to repentance for those vessels that are as yet unfinished and unhardened, as one second-century Christian explains:

> For we are clay in the hand of the craftsman. As in the case of a potter: if he makes a vessel that is turned or crushed in his hands, he can reshape it again. But if he has already put it into the kiln, he can no longer rescue it. Thus also with us. As long as we are in this world, we should repent from the evil that we did in the flesh. (2 Clem. 8:2)

In this respect, the lesson of the potter and clay is that although God does have the autonomy to show mercy to whomever he chooses,[119] God does not act arbitrarily but always in responsive relationship with the vessel being formed.[120] Each is therefore "to submit in creaturely humility before the divine potter, and perhaps by implication, to submit thereby also to his power to remake."[121] Paul therefore does not regard his contemporary fleshly kin as already hardened beyond repair but rather as not-yet-fired clay still having the opportunity to repent, hoping through his ministry "to save some of them" (11:14).

But his redemptive hopes stretch still further: even if they do not heed the message, Paul still appeals to God's redemptive action among the gentiles as proof that God's mercy may still prevail. If God has made such redemptive use even of Israel's past disobedience as to result in the extension of the promise to gentiles, God can use present disobedience for similarly redemptive purposes. That is, just as God is now redeeming previously dishonored vessels through such an extreme step as the transformation and inclusion of gentiles, so also he may show mercy to those currently resisting his purposes. God's redemption of the former group demonstrates his continued concern for the latter also. Thus all stand on equal footing before a God whose intention is to show mercy to all, and the present incorporation of the gentiles paradoxically serves as the prime proof of God's overarching mercy and faithfulness to Israel.

---

[119] J. L. de Villiers, "The Salvation of Israel according to Romans 9–11" (1981), 202.
[120] Thiessen, *Gott hat Israel nicht verstoßen*, 53. [121] Dunn, *Romans*, 565.

HAVE GENTILES ATTAINED RIGHTEOUSNESS?

Paul follows the startling application of Hosea's prophecy to gentiles by further developing the point (first made in Rom 2) that some gentiles have indeed become participants in the promises of justification:

> What will we say then? That gentiles,[122] who were not pursuing justness,[123] overtook justness – even the justness which is from fidelity, but[124] Israel pursuing a Torah of justness,[125] did not reach Torah [εἰς νόμον οὐκ ἔφθασεν]. Why not? Because [they pursued] not from fidelity but as though [it were reached] from works. They stumbled over the "stone of stumbling," as it is written "See, I am laying in Zion a stumbling stone, a rock for trapping, and whoever trusts upon it will not be put to shame." (Rom 9:30–33)

This passage is almost universally treated as Paul addressing "the present situation of his fellow Jews [sic] in relation to the Gentiles,"[126] specifically, "the irony and tragedy that while Gentiles who never sought that righteousness are now attaining it, Israel as a whole has failed to reach it."[127] Nevertheless, as Dunn points out, "Oddly enough, however, throughout [this] section Paul has never stated explicitly the problem with which he is wrestling, viz., Israel's failure to believe in the gospel of the Messiah Jesus, the Son of God."[128] Interpreters have also struggled with why the parallelism breaks between verses 30 and 31, as one would expect the object of Israel's pursuit to be "justness" in parallel to what

---

[122] Note that ἔθνη is again anarthrous, denoting *some* gentiles, not "the gentiles" as a whole. Cf. Dunn, *Romans*, 580; Cranfield, *Romans*, 506.

[123] Gk. τὰ μὴ διώκοντα δικαιοσύνην. The present participle with the aorist verb requires an imperfective sense, though "most English language commentaries carelessly translate this with 'Gentiles who do (or did) not pursue righteousness'" (Jewett, *Romans*, 609 n. 19). E.g., Dunn, *Romans*, 580; Ziesler, *Romans*, 249, 252; Fitzmyer, *Romans*, 577.

[124] The δέ in this second clause serves to emphasize the implausibility of the statement – that is, how could gentiles be faithful when they did not have the covenant? To what or whom were they faithful? The point is that not only have gentiles attained justness, they have attained *covenantal* justness.

[125] Wagner, *Heralds of the Good News*, 122, highlights the parallels between Paul's wording here and Isa 51:5 LXX, "those pursuing what is just" (οἱ διώκοντες τὸ δίκαιον), with Paul amending the target of Israel's pursuit to "a Torah of justness" (νόμον δικαιοσύνης). Paul's emendation is reminiscent of the polemical phrase, "seekers of smooth things" (דורשי הלקות), in 4QpNah 3–4 ii 2 (itself derived from Isa 30:10), suggesting that Paul is making a similar polemical move here. My translation aims to retain the ambiguity of "pursuing a Torah of justness," which can be understood as an attributive adjectival phrase ("Israel-pursuing-a-Torah-of-justness") or as a concessive verbal idea ("Israel, [despite] pursuing a Torah of justness"). On the grounds of both syntax and sense, I favor the attributive adjective reading, which could be understood to mean that only the portion of Israel pursuing a Torah of justness failed to attain it.

[126] Tobin, *Paul's Rhetoric*, 341.   [127] Dunn, *Romans*, 592.   [128] Dunn, *Romans*, 591.

the gentiles have attained despite not pursuing it.[129] But instead, v. 31 refers to Israel pursuing a Torah of justness and says they fell short not of justness but of Torah.[130] This has "become a storm center of debate,"[131] with numerous interpreters at least as far back as Chrysostom amending or glossing the passage from "a law of righteousness" to "righteousness from the law" to arrive at a more parallel construction.[132]

One key is in recognizing that v. 31 does not in fact say "Israel has not attained the law,"[133] as if the verb were in the perfect, though nearly every translation and scholarly treatment renders the verse this way on the assumption that Paul is speaking of contemporary Jews.[134] Instead, the verse says, "Israel *did not* attain (ἔφθασεν) Torah."[135] The use of the aorist reinforces that Paul is once again referring to Israel in its fuller, biblical sense, pointing to the broken covenant of the past.[136] Dunn is therefore correct that Paul's "choice of [Israel] rather than [*Ioudaioi*]

---

[129] Per Jarle Bekken, *The Word Is Near You* (2007), 158–61.

[130] Walter C. Kaiser, "Leviticus 18:5 and Paul" (1971), 25–26; Godet, *Romans*, 368. Novenson misses the contrast between the two verses when he says, "they pursue a law of righteousness, as indeed they should do" ("The Self-Styled Jew of Romans 2," 155).

[131] Moo, *Romans*, 622; see 622–28 for further discussion of the various options.

[132] E.g., *Hom. Rom* 16:10 (PG 60.563); John Calvin, *Calvin's Commentaries on the New Testament* (1961), 8.217; Käsemann, *Romans*, 277; Stephen Westerholm, "Law, Grace and the 'Soteriology' of Judaism" (1991), 68: "righteousness which is based on the law." Fitzmyer, *Romans*, 578, observes that this interpretation has rightly been abandoned by most contemporary exegetes. Thomas R. Schreiner, "Israel's Failure to Attain Righteousness in Romans 9:30–10:3" (1991), 212, suggests the objective genitive "law for righteousness," but the head noun νόμος is not a verbal or "action" noun, which would be required for an objective genitive (Boas, *Cambridge Grammar*, §30.28; Smyth, *Greek Grammar*, §1328–§1335). To get Schreiner's suggested meaning, one would expect νόμος εἰς δικαιοσύνην.

[133] As rendered by Dunn, *Romans*, 578.

[134] E.g., Goodrich, "Until the Fullness of the Gentiles Comes In," 19.

[135] Recall Philo's explanation that although Israel's redemption remains a future hope, "attaining (φθάνουσα) announces good news (εὐαγγελίζεται) of the things about to come – even a full good" (*Praem.* 161). In proclaiming that Israel did not attain (ἔφθασεν) what it sought, Paul appears to be using familiar or stereotypical language concerning Israel's restoration.

[136] Cf. the aorists in Rom 11:30–31, which also refer to past (perfective) disobedience both on the part of gentiles and Israel without regard to the continuation of such a state of disobedience into the present, such that mercy toward one means mercy toward all – again the theme of interconnected fates appears throughout these chapters. There is nothing in this passage to suggest a gnomic aorist, which would imply that Israel always falls short of what it seeks and therefore has no hope for redemption. Such would be the exact opposite of what Paul ultimately argues. Rather, all contextual markers suggest a historical (perfective) understanding of the verb as applied to biblical Israel, which has been the subject of the discussion to this point.

(cf v 24) is probably significant," but the significance is not (as Dunn suggests) that Paul "is against his people's self-understanding of what it means to be the covenant people."[137] On the contrary, Paul by no means opposes such a self-understanding in these passages or anywhere else. Instead, by combining "Israel" with the aorist verb in this passage at the end of a chronological retelling of Israel's biblical history, Paul is again restating a basic tenet of mainstream Jewish restorationist theology: Israel did not keep the covenant but fell short of the Torah they had been given.[138]

The problem, Paul explains, was pursuing Torah as though justness could be attained through Torah.[139] But those who lack justness cannot obtain it from Torah, which cannot confer justness/righteousness but can only condemn the unjust or confirm justness already obtained from another source – namely, fidelity.[140] Consequently, not understanding the end (*telos*) to which the Torah was a means, Israel not only did not attain justness but fell short of the Torah itself.[141] Nevertheless, by breaking the parallel and stating that Israel fell short of Torah rather than justness, Paul still leaves open the possibility that Israel may yet attain justness in the same manner as the gentiles.[142]

The premise that Israel had failed to keep the Torah was not in dispute – Paul is merely reminding his readers of what they already know from the scriptures on this point. Paying closer attention to the grammar thus resolves several interpretive problems with this passage, including why Paul has not specifically brought up "Israel's failure to believe in the gospel" to this point: he is still establishing the basic facts of God's previous dealings with Israel and how those facts have led to the current circumstances, including the gentile ingathering. Of course, by framing God's past dealings with Israel in this way, Paul is making an *implicit* argument concerning his contemporaries who have not believed the gospel, but he has not yet reached into the present to make that connection *explicit*. At this point in the argument, he is still reminding the reader

---

[137] Dunn, *Romans*, 581.
[138] Barrett, "Fall and Responsibility," 138. Contra Schreiner ("Israel's Failure," 213), "justness" (δικαιοσύνη) is not the implied object of φθάνω; such a reading would obviate the distinction made in the first half of the verse, which establishes Torah as the object of Israel's pursuit.
[139] "Israel pursued the Law in a wrong manner" (Bekken, *The Word Is Near You*, 160).
[140] See the discussion on pp. 85–91 in Chapter 2, pp. 174–79 in Chapter 4, and pp. 255–64 in Chapter 6.
[141] Contra Goodrich, "Until the Fullness of the Gentiles Comes In," 19.
[142] John Paul Heil, "Christ, the Termination of the Law (Romans 9:30–10:8)" (2001), 487.

of Israel's past according to the scriptures, with the present infidelity of some contemporary Israelites a strong undercurrent to be brought to the surface later.

This reading also makes sense of the shift from gentiles attaining "justness" to Israel falling short of Torah, since biblical Israel's failure to keep the Torah is what resulted in Israel's need for redemption after coming under the Torah's curses. In contrast, gentiles "who do not have the Torah" (Rom 2:14) cannot be said to have pursued it, but nevertheless some gentiles (through Messiah) attained the justness to which the Torah testifies (Rom 2:15; 9:30).[143] This is the surprising claim in need of explanation at this stage of the story – again, recall the immediately preceding context, where Paul has just identified the incorporation of these gentiles with the promised redemption of "not my people." Israel's infidelity and failure is neither surprising nor does it require explanation. But that *gentiles attained the justness attested by Torah and are partaking in Israel's promises* is scandalous. How could gentiles who did not have the Torah and thus could not pursue justness have succeeded where Israel, which was specially chosen to receive the Torah, failed?

Here, Paul returns to the theme of fidelity. In contrast to Israel, whose infidelity is well established in the biblical accounts, these gentiles have attained the justness that comes from fidelity (ἐκ πίστεως). Paul summarizes the source of Israel's past failure as the attempt to accomplish desired ends "from works" (ἐξ ἔργων) rather than trusting and obeying God. Traditional readings, assuming "Israel" here refers to contemporary

---

[143] Pace Dieter Zeller, *Der Brief an die Römer* (1985), 184, Rom 2:14–15 is not "long forgotten" but fully in view here, as this passage picks up the thread started in Rom 2 and developed throughout the book – namely, that gentiles transformed by the spirit are being made righteous in keeping with the promises of Israel's renewed covenant. To draw a distinction here between "moral righteousness" and "righteous status in God's sight" (Cranfield, *Romans*, 506) or "covenant righteousness" (Dunn, *Romans*, 580) or "forensic righteousness" (Moo, *Romans*, 621), is to miss the point entirely, as Paul has already established in Rom 2:1–11 that such a distinction is inappropriate in light of divine impartiality (Rom 2:11). For Paul, God's judgment is just, meaning right status in God's sight requires moral righteousness, and no other factors (possession of the Torah, descent from Israel, etc.) will obscure that. Paul systematically undermines the distinction between "forensic righteousness" and "moral righteousness" from the start. Thus, the objection that because "Paul well knows that many Gentiles in his day were earnest and diligent in their pursuit of moral 'uprightness'" (Moo, *Romans*, 621) he cannot here mean righteousness in its moral sense misses the mark. Rather, the statement here presumes that gentiles are by default unrighteous and, not having the law to instruct them, do not pursue righteousness. Nevertheless, through the spirit, they have attained the justness that comes through the new covenant (ἐκ πίστεως reinforces the covenantal sense of the language here). Contra Michel, *Römer*, 319–23.

Jews, have tended to take "from works" as a reference either to Jewish legalism ("works-righteousness") or ethnocentrism,[144] but the reference to the "stumbling stone" of Isaiah 8:14 and the following (conflated) citation of Isaiah 28:16 suggest something else is in view. As Wagner explains, both of the "stumbling stone" passages occur at the climax of prophetic rebukes about Israel's attempts to save itself in the face of the Assyrian threat through political machinations, foreign treaties, and military strength rather than by trusting in YHWH.[145] In contrast, those who instead trust in the stone placed in Zion as their foundation will not be put to shame. That stone is specifically identified as YHWH, who will be a refuge for those of his people who trust in him but a stone of stumbling for those who do not:

It is YHWH of hosts you should regard as sacred .... Then he will become a sanctuary, but to both houses of Israel, a stone to strike and a rock to stumble over. (Isa 8:13–14 MT)[146]

By citing these passages, Paul reminds the reader that God has historically been a "stumbling stone" for the unfaithful among his people while saving those who trust him. Given the thematic undercurrent of Paul's citations to this point in the discussion, it is surely no accident that each of these passages also occurs in the context of the fall of the northern kingdom.[147] It is also noteworthy that each of these citations refers to a

---

[144] E.g., Dunn, *Romans*, 581–82; Kim, *God, Israel, and the Gentiles*, 130.
[145] Wagner, *Heralds of the Good News*, 153.
[146] The LXX differs significantly from the MT here, but Paul's citations here are closer to the Hebrew than the LXX (see Frank Thielman, "Paul's View of Israel's Misstep in Rom 9.32–3" [2018], 365). This corresponds with a tendency of the citations in this section "toward a Hebrew exemplar," as noted by Wagner, *Heralds of the Good News*, 134 (cf. 129–30). It is obviously impossible to know exactly what kind of exemplar(s) Paul knew in these cases, but in this case, it seems likely that Paul knew a version of Isa 8:13 that included "YHWH Sabaoth," connecting his citation of Isa 1:9 to his reference to the "stumbling stone" three verses later. The LXX also lacks the reference to "both houses of Israel," instead referencing "the house of Jacob," but the basic takeaway of the passage – trust in YHWH or he will become a stumbling block – is the same. For more analysis of this passage in the LXX and discussion of Paul's exemplar, see Wagner, *Heralds of the Good News*, 126–57. For another example of a variant closer to the MT than the LXX possibly underlying Paul's arguments in these passages, see Enno Edzard Popkes, "Jes 6,9f. MT als impliziter Reflexionshintergrund der paulinischen Verstockungsvorstellung" (2009).
[147] These citations are not haphazard but are held together by a series of linguistic and thematic ties. Hos 2:25 is linked with Isa 10:22–23 and 1:9 via the theme of (northern) Israel's destruction and the preservation of a remnant and also by specific catchwords. The "sowing" (σπερῶ) of Hos 2:25 links with the remaining "seed" (σπέρμα) in Isa 1:9,

Have Gentiles Attained Righteousness? 217

division and reduction of Israel in the past, specifically the destruction of the northern kingdom and accompanying reduction of Judah that led to Israel being scattered and intermingled among the nations in the first place. Isaiah 28 is specifically directed at "the drunkards of Ephraim,"[148] while Isa 8 serves as a warning not to follow the example of those who have put their trust in the Syro-Ephraimite coalition that will soon be destroyed. Only those who trust in YHWH as their foundation will be preserved, while the rest will be shattered by YHWH himself. This reading helps make sense of the theological/christological ambiguity of the "stumbling stone" in Rom 9:32–33.

Again, it is too rarely noticed that Paul has not yet explicitly brought up the failure of many of his contemporaries to believe the gospel;[149] the focus throughout Rom 9 has not been Messiah but rather Israel's history. Reading forward in the context of the argument to this point, the stumbling stone is therefore not primarily christological but rather theological.[150] In context, the most likely reference point for Israel's stumbling block is the Torah, which Israel pursued but did not

---

where "YHWH Sabaoth" links to the "stone of stumbling" in Isa 8:14. The stone of stumbling then connects to the stone in Zion of Isa 28:16, which draws out the theme and language of trust/fidelity, such that "the one trusting in him will not be put to shame" (ὁ πιστεύων ἐπ' αὐτῷ), as opposed to the unfaithful who will be swept away in each of these passages (e.g., Isa 28:1–22; 8:1–22). Within Romans itself, not being "put to shame" of course links to Paul's opening statement in Rom 1:16, while gentiles becoming just/righteous links to Rom 2:14–16. Remarkably, the verbal connections between some of these verses are in the portions Paul does not quote (e.g., the "sowing" of Hos 2:25, the reference to YHWH Sabaoth in Isa 8:13). This is similar to the phenomenon of secondary citation, in which the interpretation of one passage is guided by another passage operating below the surface, discussed with respect to the pesharim in Shani L. Berrin [Tzoref], "The Use of Secondary Biblical Sources in Pesher Nahum" (2004). On Paul's use of catchwords to link citations and allusions, see Carol K. Stockhausen, "2 Corinthians 3 and the Principles of Pauline Exegesis" (1993). See also M. Mielziner, *Introduction to the Talmud* (1969), 142–52. On Pauline techniques resembling later Rabbinic interpretive practices, see Dan Cohn-Sherbok, "Paul and Rabbinic Exegesis" (1982), esp. 127–28; Pasquale Basta, *Gezerah Shawah* (2006), (esp. 85–104). But see also the warning of Philip S. Alexander, "Rabbinic Judaism and the New Testament" (1983), 242–44, about applying later Rabbinic rules of interpretation to Paul.

[148] The LXX has μισθωτοί, "hirelings," vocalizing the Hebrew differently. Other Greek versions match the vocalization found in the MT, translating μεθύοντες, "drunkards." See John D. W. Watts, *Isaiah 1–33* (2005), 426.

[149] As rightly observed by Gadenz, *Called*, 103.

[150] Gadenz, *Called*, 102; Mark A. Seifrid, "Romans" (2007), 650–52. Contra Moo, *Romans*, 620, "Israel's failure is ultimately christological: by failing to believe in him, he has become for Israel the cause of her downfall (vv. 32b–33)"; and Dunn, *Romans*, 594; Jewett, *Romans*, 611–12; Joseph A. Fitzmyer, *Tobit* (2003), 579; Frank Schleritt,

attain.¹⁵¹ As he further explains in the next chapter, the pursuing of Torah as a means of bringing about their own restoration rather than depending on God for justness attained neither Torah nor justness.¹⁵² And the reason they did not attain Torah or justness is that pursuing the Torah itself "as if from works" rather than pursuing justness itself effectively made the *means* into the *end* (*telos*), stumbling over the Torah itself and falling short of both (9:32).¹⁵³ He then proceeds to identify the proper *telos* of Torah a few verses later: Messiah (Rom 10:5). This reading corresponds especially well with Paul's explanation of the role of Torah elsewhere, as "the command which was for life, the same was for death" (Rom 7:10; cf. Deut 30:15, 19).¹⁵⁴

Of course, Paul's point in citing this warning from the past is to apply it to the present, as many "from Israel" (9:6) are in danger of following the example of their forebears, refusing to trust the agent of YHWH's salvation and thinking they must first bring about their own justness to initiate God's promises, a connection he proceeds to make explicit in 10:1–4. Thus the stumbling stone is theological while reading forward and then christological when considered retrospectively, in light of what Paul says afterwards.¹⁵⁵ This passage thus serves as the boundary between Paul's account of Israel's history and contemporary events, and Paul's discussion of the past easily bleeds into the present as the reader is invited to identify the present situation with the biblical precedent. This

---

"Das Gesetz der Gerechtigkeit" (2010), 288–89; Goodrich, "Until the Fullness of the Gentiles Comes In," 19.

[151] As argued by Paul Meyer, "Romans 10:4 and the 'End' of the Law" (1996), 64, who observes, "There is no more striking example in the Pauline letters of a crucial exegetical tradition made on grounds extrinsic to the text itself" than the interpretation that the stone of stumbling in 9:32 is Christ. Cf. Barrett, "Fall and Responsibility," 144–45.

[152] See Thielman, "Paul's View of Israel's Misstep," 367–71, who argues that the "stumbling stone" here borrows from an early Christian tradition portraying the Jerusalem leadership stumbling "over Jesus' approach to the Jewish law, including the law's regulation of the temple" (371).

[153] Thus Thomas Rhyne, "Nomos Dikaiosynēs and the Meaning of Romans 10:4" (1986), 489, is correct that the problem highlighted in v. 31 is not the Torah but rather that "they falsely imagined that they could attain to the law simply by performing its works (see 10:5) rather than by faith (see 10:6–8)." But he is incorrect in asserting that Paul "does not fault Israel with pursuing the law per se but with pursuing it as though the righteousness it promises could be reached by works" (490). Instead, the pursuit of the Torah as a *telos* in itself is precisely what results in attaining neither justness nor Torah itself.

[154] See the discussion on pp. 87–89.

[155] Barrett, "Fall and Responsibility," 144. Cf. also 1 Cor 10:4, where Paul interprets the rock in the wilderness christologically.

discussion of Israel's past failings therefore does have strong implications regarding Paul's contemporary fleshly kin, but a solely christological reading of the stumbling stone puts the cart before the horse and misses the force of Paul's rhetoric throughout this section: those from Israel who are now resisting the gospel are repeating and persisting in their biblical forebears' infidelity, which is what led to Israel's present need for redemption in the first place, and without changing course, those who refuse to submit to Israel's messiah will end up like their unfaithful predecessors.

THE BUSINESS OF HEAVEN: REDEMPTIVE REVERSAL

The entire ninth chapter of Romans therefore applies both sides of "the logic of redemptive reversal already present in Hos 1–2,"[156] starting from the premise already established in Rom 1–2 that some Israelites have become gentilized and then concluding that the promise to restore Israel therefore requires the incorporation of gentiles. The chapter is organized chronologically, working sequentially from Abraham to exiled Israel in Paul's day. Throughout the chapter, Paul's logic consistently works on two levels, looking to biblical history and prophecy for insight into the present, reading the ancestral narratives of Genesis through the lenses of Hosea and Isaiah to reveal how the fates of Israel and the nations are mutually related.[157]

It has too rarely been noticed that the opening discussion of the younger son being chosen to inherit the promise – Isaac over Ishmael, Jacob over Esau – in Rom 9:7–13 sets up the themes of reversal and mutuality that emerge in the last portion of the chapter. In Genesis, each time one son inherits the blessing over another, the chosen son must then undergo a "symbolic death."[158] By being designated the covenantal heir, "The beloved son is marked for both exaltation and for humiliation. In his life the two are seldom far apart."[159] Isaac must pass through the Aqedah (Gen 22), Jacob is effectively exiled to Mesopotamia and later bows before Esau seven times (27:42–45; 33:3), Joseph is cast into a pit, sold into slavery, and reckoned as dead (37:18–35).[160] Of those marked as chosen heirs of the promise in Genesis, Ephraim (48:14–20) is the only

---

[156] Wagner, "Not from the Jews Only," 422.
[157] Foster, *Renaming Abraham's Children*, 185.
[158] Jon D. Levenson, *The Death and Resurrection of the Beloved Son* (1993), 59.
[159] Levenson, *Death and Resurrection*, 59.
[160] See Foster, *Renaming Abraham's Children*, 170–72.

one whose dereliction and symbolic death or exile is not narrated, a lacuna filled for Paul by Hosea, who proclaims Ephraim's destruction, exile, and subsequent restoration and exaltation.

According to Hosea as filtered through Paul's lenses, many who were descended from Israel are no longer Israel, having become gentiles ("not my people"), which by implication suggests contemporary descendants of Israel can be cut off from Israel just as those in the past had been, a point Paul later makes explicit in Rom 11:17–24. But does this mean that those who are being cut off and separated from Messiah are therefore permanently lost? To this, Paul would say: absolutely not (μὴ γένοιτο)! Instead, this is where the two threads of the argument converge, as Paul presents God's incorporation of gentiles as evidence of God's mercy toward Israel such that even God's punishments bend toward salvation. That is, if those who had become "not my people" through Israel's past disobedience can now be restored through the work of the spirit extended even to the nations, hope still remains for those who have stumbled over the stumbling stone.

6

God's Justice and the End of the Torah

The debate over whether Jesus was the messiah is therefore also an argument about the inherent ability of man. For Christians, repentance is impossible if the messiah has not yet come; for Jews, the messiah cannot come if repentance has not yet occurred.

Meir Soloveichik[1]

After reiterating his heartfelt desire for Israel's salvation (10:1),[2] Paul argues that he himself is a "witness on their behalf" to their authentic but misguided zeal for God, surely alluding to his own past as a zealous persecutor (10:2). At this point, he finally makes explicit what was implicit in the previous chapter, bringing the discussion out of the scriptural past to discuss Israel's messiah. Having already established that Israel had pursued but not attained a Torah of justness, he further explains that this resulted in not submitting to the messiah:

For not knowing the justness (δικαιοσύνη) of God and seeking to establish their own, they did not submit themselves to the justness of God – for Messiah is the *telos* of Torah for (εἰς) justness in everyone who is faithful.[3] (Rom 10:3–4)

---

[1] Meir Soloveichik, "Redemption and the Power of Man" (2004), 57.
[2] Grammatically, the direct address ("Siblings") is not connected to the preceding passage, signaling a new section in much the same way as 9:1.
[3] The substantive participle πιστεύοντι lacks an explicit object, leading E. P. Sanders to render 10;4, "to *all* who *faith*" (*Paul, the Law, and the Jewish People* [1983], 39). The lack of an object suggests that the word refers to a posture of allegiance or fidelity – that is, Messiah grants justness to those who "give allegiance" or "are faithful" to him (cf. 10:9). See Matthew W. Bates, *Salvation by Allegiance Alone*, 77–100; Douglas A. Campbell, *The Quest for Paul's Gospel* (2005), 178–207.

Romans 10:4 has "received as much attention as any single verse in Paul,"[4] and there is significant disagreement about what exactly Paul means by *telos* here. Some have argued that *telos* means "end" or "termination," such that the Torah has effectively been abolished or abrogated as a means to righteousness.[5] Others, recognizing that Paul himself protests the accusation that his gospel invalidates the Torah (3:31), argue instead that *telos* should be understood as the "goal" of Torah, the object of pursuit as reflected in the metaphorical language of racing throughout the section, most notably in 9:30–10:3 and 11:9.[6] Of course, if the goal of a race or object of pursuit has been achieved, the race has also ended, so some have concluded that the nuance of *telos* must include both of these senses, with Messiah both the goal to which the Torah led and also terminating the Torah as a means to justness.[7]

In any case, he then proceeds to contrast the "justness from the Torah" (10:5) represented in Lev 18:5 with the "justness from fidelity" (10:6–13) represented by Deut 30:12–14. This section, in which Paul lays out his case for the redemptive role of the messiah, has been called "hermeneutically the most significant of the entire letter."[8] Nevertheless, despite the pithy, quotable nature of the individual statements throughout Rom 10, this passage is also one of the most difficult, complex, and controversial in

---

[4] Sanders, *PLJP*, 38. The secondary literature on this verse and the larger passage is too extensive to even approximate here. For detailed discussions of Rom 10:4 and previous scholarship thereupon, see Per Jarle Bekken, *The Word Is Near You* (2007), 153–228; Robert Badenas, *Christ: the End of the Law* (1987).

[5] E.g., Sanders, *PLJP*, 39–40; Hans Hübner, *Gottes Ich und Israel* (1984), 135, 138, 148; Robert Jewett, "The Law and the Coexistence of Jews and Gentiles in Romans" (1985), 349–54; James D. G. Dunn, *Romans* (1988), 589; John Paul Heil, "Christ, the Termination of the Law (Romans 9:30–10:8)" (2001); Thomas R. Schreiner, "Paul's View of the Law in Romans 10:4–5" (1993); Lothar Wehr, "Nahe ist dir das Wort" (2006), 194.

[6] E.g., George E. Howard, "Christ the End of the Law" (1969), 331–37; C. Thomas Rhyne, "Nomos Dikaiosynēs and the Meaning of Romans 10:4" (1986); Badenas, *End of the Law*, 81–115; Charles E. B. Cranfield, *Romans* (1979), 515–20; Glenn N. Davies, *Faith and Obedience in Romans* (1990), 185–89; Joseph A. Fitzmyer, *Romans* (1993), 584; Edith M. Humphrey, "Why Bring the Word Down?" (1999); Leander Keck, *Romans* (2005), 249; William S. Campbell, "Christ the End of the Law: Romans 10.4" (1978); N. T. Wright, "Romans 9–11 and the 'New Perspective'" (2010).

[7] E.g., C. K. Barrett, *Romans* (1991), 197–98; Morna D. Hooker, "Christ: The 'End' of the Law" (2005); Bekken, *The Word Is Near You*, 169–93.

[8] Mark A. Seifrid, "Romans" (2007), 652. See also the structural analysis of Matiaž Celarc, "Christ as the Goal of the Law (Rom 10,4)" (2019), 442–45, who shows 9:30–10:21 to be the centerpiece of the argument in Rom 9–11, with 10:4 effectively reintroducing the overall thesis of 1:16.

God's Justice and the End of the Torah

the Pauline corpus, serving as ground zero for significant debates about Paul's view of Torah, his understanding of salvation, and the gospel in general. How one understands what Paul means by "the justness of God" (δικαιοσύνη θεοῦ), "seeking their own justness," and "the *telos* of Torah" both shapes and reflects how one understands the larger framework of Paul's gospel.[9]

Beyond the specific question of whether *telos* means "end" or "goal" or both, since the rise of the New Perspective most debates about Rom 10 have concerned whether the chapter presents the gospel as opposed to self-righteous Jewish legalism or Jewish ethnic particularism. In the former and more traditional view, the reference to those "seeking to establish their own justness" (10:3) refers to the "attempt of individual Jews to establish a relationship with God through their own efforts."[10] This has then been universalized by some to suggest that Paul's objection is that seeking to live by the Torah leads to "self-righteousness" that paradoxically "has precisely the effect of making [the law-keeper] a sinner"[11] because "it is already fundamentally sinful to wish to insure oneself righteousness and life; indeed this is the human sin par excellence."[12] In contrast, God's justness is obtained only by faith in Messiah, who is "the end of using the law to establish one's own righteousness."[13] Among this group, some have additionally argued that Messiah is the end of the law *only for those who believe* – that is, "Christ is the goal of the law with respect to God's plan to redeem the gentiles"[14] – while it remains possible for unbelieving Israel to be reckoned righteous via "righteousness from the Torah" (10:6).[15]

---

[9] "Scholars will continue to interpret this verse in accordance with their general understanding of the law and righteousness in Paul and in conformity with their construction of the immediate context" (Sanders, *PLJP*, 39).

[10] Douglas J. Moo, *Romans* (1996), 634. Others holding this view include Thomas R. Schreiner, "Israel's Failure to Attain Righteousness in Romans 9:30–10:3" (1991), 215–18; Ernst Käsemann, *Romans* (1980), 281–83; Stephen Westerholm, "Righteousness of the Law and the Righteousness of Faith in Romans" (2004), 259–61.

[11] Herman N. Ridderbos, *Paul: An Outline of His Theology* (1975), 139.

[12] Ridderbos, *Paul*, 142.

[13] Schreiner, "Paul's View of the Law," 121. "Christ is an end to legalism for the attainment of righteousness" (C. F. D. Moule, *An Idiom Book of New Testament Greek* [1959], 70).

[14] Stanley K. Stowers, *A Rereading of Romans* (1994), 308. Stowers does not, however, take a firm position on Paul's understanding of salvation for Jews (see his comments at 205).

[15] E.g., Franz Mussner, "Christus [ist] des Gesetzes Ende zur Gerechtigkeit fur jeden, der glaubt" (1977), esp. 40–44; Lloyd Gaston, *Paul and the Torah* (1987), 33; John

In contrast, many other interpreters have tended to read "their own justness" as referring to "the righteousness available to the Jew *alone* on the basis of observing the law,"[16] which by its very nature excludes gentiles. On this reading, Paul is not opposing "legalism" but rather Jewish ethnic particularism and pride in their own special status,[17] arguing instead for a righteousness based on faith that is available to all – Jew and gentile alike and on even footing.[18] The primary distinction between Paul's gospel and the position of his opponents is therefore between the limited scope of "their own" and "*everyone* who trusts" (10:4), a contrast that continues into the scriptural quotations of verses 5–8: whereas Moses wrote that the justness from the law leads to life (for Jews alone), the justness from faith leads to salvation to *all* who trust in Messiah, with no distinction between Jews and gentiles.

I propose, however, that these readings ultimately fall short because they look at the chapter through the wrong end of the telescope – backwards from later Christian theology as though the passage is centrally about individual salvation in light of Jewish unbelief rather than forwards from the perspective of early Jewish eschatology. Read from the latter perspective, this passage is neither about faith versus legalism nor about inclusiveness versus ethnocentrism. Instead, in this section Paul is participating in a long-established debate within early Judaism about the relationship between Israel's repentance/justness and Israel's full restoration, arguing that Jesus is God's solution to Israel's predicament. With that foundation in mind, we can cut through these long-standing debates and gain a better understanding of the chapter by reading Rom 10:1–13 inside-out, starting from Paul's use of Deuteronomy in Rom 10:6–8 and then working outwards to the rest of the chapter.

G. Gager, *Reinventing Paul* (2000), 60. See the helpful discussion and critiques of Terence L. Donaldson, "Jewish Christianity, Israel's Stumbling and the *Sonderweg* Reading of Paul" (2006).

[16] Sanders, *PLJP*, 38, emphasis his. Similarly, Dunn, *Romans*, 595: "Paul is thinking of Israel's claim to a righteousness which was theirs exclusively, shared by no other people, possessed by them alone." Cf. Howard, "Christ the End of the Law," 336; Robert Jewett, *Romans* (2006), 617–19; Mary Ann Getty, "An Apocalyptic Perspective on Rom 10:4" (1982), 97, 100; François Refoulé, "Romains, X, 4" (1984), 339.

[17] Jewett, *Romans*, 618. Similarly, N. T. Wright, "Romans" (2002), 654–55: "a covenant membership for Jews and Jews alone." John M. G. Barclay, *Paul and the Gift* (2015), 541, critiques this view as too narrow in its focus on ethnicity and Jewish exclusivity but arrives at a similar but more universal conclusion: the problem is "the natural assumption that when God acts in saving benevolence, he distributes his gifts to those we consider fitting or worthy."

[18] Sanders, *PLJP*, 37–38.

BRINGING THE MESSIAH: RIGHTEOUSNESS AND REDEMPTION

It may seem strange to start with verses 6–8, since Paul's use of Deuteronomy here has baffled interpreters for generations. In these verses, Paul seems to cite the "justness from fidelity" as a contrasting voice to the "justness from Torah" represented in Lev 18:5:

> For Moses writes of the justness which is from Torah that "the one who does these things will live by them." And the justness from fidelity speaks thus: "Do not say in your heart, 'Who will ascend into heaven?'" That is, to bring Messiah down – nor "who will descend into the abyss?" That is, to bring Messiah up from the dead. But what does it say? "The word is near you, in your mouth and in your heart." That is, the word of fidelity which we proclaim. (Rom 10:5–8)

The distinction between what is written and spoken recalls the letter/spirit contrast of 2 Cor 3, Rom 2:27–29, and Rom 7:6, as Moses *writes* about the justness from Torah while the "justness from fidelity" *speaks*.[19] In addition to the possibility that Paul cites Torah against itself to produce an apparent contradiction,[20] the primary difficulty is that Paul quotes a passage from Deut 30 about the accessibility of the command Moses has given Israel as though it were about the messiah. In that passage, Moses declares:

> because this command which I am commanding you today is not too difficult, nor is it far away. It is not in heaven, to say, "Who will ascend to heaven and get it for

---

[19] Others have emphasized the centrality of this distinction, most recently Yael Fisch, "The Origins of Oral Torah: A New Pauline Perspective" (2020), 57–59, who sees this passage as evidence that Paul held a notion of a "twofold torah," one written and one oral, akin to but differently directed than the later Tannaitic distinction between written and oral Torahs. Fisch argues that Paul sees the written Torah as uniquely for Jews and the oral Torah (derived from the written) as a separate path for gentiles. This distinction is implausible because, although Paul does appear to distinguish between two Torahs, he repeatedly argues that the " letter" is unable to grant life to *anyone*, whether Jew or gentile, in contrast to the heavenly/spiritual Torah mediated by the spirit. As more fully discussed below, it is not accidental that the "justness from fidelity speaks" from the very chapter of Deuteronomy that promises that God will transform the hearts of *Israel*. See Akio Ito, "The Written Torah and the Oral Gospel" (2006), 251–60. Paul's preference for orality over the letter (cf. Fisch, "Origins of Oral Torah," 61) thus derives from the internal quality of the new covenant he is proclaiming, not a distinction between Jews and gentiles.

[20] *Pace* Fisch, "Origins of Oral Torah," 56, who rightly observes that it would be "truly exceptional" for a first-century Jewish exegete to present such an antithesis and leave it unresolved and then concludes that this is exactly what Paul has done, it will be demonstrated below that Paul does not present Lev 18:5 as antithetical to the gospel, nor does he present these two quotations as irreconcilably opposed.

us and proclaim it to us so that we may do it?"²¹ Nor is it beyond the sea, to say, "Who will cross the sea for us and get it for us and proclaim it to us so that we may do it?"²² On the contrary, the word is very near you, in your mouth and in your heart, that you may do it. (Deut 30:11–14)

That the very passage Paul cites as an apparent contrast to "justness from Torah" is about keeping Moses' command only further complicates matters. Moo ably summarizes the problem: "How, then, can Paul take a passage that is about the law of God and find in it the voice of righteousness by *faith*? And how, in his explanatory comments, can he claim that what the text is talking about is not the commandment but Christ?"²³ The connection between the quotation and its interpretation seems so tenuous that many have concluded that Paul's exegesis here is arbitrary and unjustified, with the apostle simply lifting key phrases from a passage not well suited for the point he is making.²⁴ Some have even tried to solve the problem by arguing that despite the verbatim agreements, he is not interpreting Deut 30 at all but is instead just borrowing biblical language from the passage.²⁵ This is, however, implausible given the pesher-style interpretations that follow each quoted line.²⁶ Another proposal is that Paul typologically identifies Messiah with the command in Deut 30 and interprets the passage from that assumption, with both Messiah and the command serving as examples of God graciously bringing his word near to the people.²⁷ But this still leaves the problem of why the command in Deut 30 should be seen as somehow different from the apparently contrasting quotation of Lev 18:5.

The first step to understanding Paul's interpretations is recognizing that although verses six and seven are typically rendered "to bring Christ up/down," the word "Christ" is not used as an alternative proper name for Jesus, who is conspicuously not mentioned between Rom 9:5 and 10:9, where he is finally explicitly identified and declared to be

---

[21] LXX: "And when we hear it, we will do it."
[22] LXX: "And when we hear it, we will do it."   [23] Moo, *Romans*, 651.
[24] E.g., C. H. Dodd, *Romans* (1932), 165–66; Richard B. Hays, *Echoes of Scripture and the Letters of Paul* (1989), 79–82; R. David. Kaylor, *Paul's Covenant Community* (1988), 167; Fitzmyer, *Romans*, 588; Francis Watson, *Paul and the Hermeneutics of Faith* (2004), 330–31, 335–40, 437–38.
[25] Fitzmyer, *Romans*, 588.
[26] See Moo, *Romans*, 651–52; cf. Christopher D. Stanley, *Paul and the Language of Scripture* (1992), 128–33. On Paul's interpretive use of τοῦτ'ἔστιν here and its differences from "the *pesher* technique of Qumran," see Mark A. Seifrid, "Paul's Approach to the Old Testament in Rom 10:6–8" (1985), 27–34.
[27] E.g., Cranfield, *Romans*, 524. Cf. Dunn, *Romans*, 614–15; Moo, *Romans*, 652–53.

"Lord." Instead, like the reference to "the Christ" being of Israelite descent in Rom 9:5, these verses use *Christos* as a title referring more generally to the messiah, the one anointed to bring about Israel's redemption.[28] As such, these verses are better rendered "to bring [the] messiah," which carries a different connotation to ears accustomed to treating "Christ" as essentially Jesus' surname. The point is that the passage is not criticizing attempts to bring *Jesus* up or down, nor is it arguing against individual efforts to earn salvation or God's favor. Instead, when Paul argues that Deut 30:12–14 warns against efforts to "bring messiah," he is opposing a common early Jewish idea that the coming of the messiah – and therefore Israel's restoration – is contingent on Israel's repentance and proper Torah observance.[29]

RIGHTEOUSNESS AND RESTORATION IN THE TORAH AND PROPHETS

As discussed in Chapter 2, biblical literature consistently links Israel's redemption with Israel's repentance; inasmuch as Israel broke the covenant through infidelity and disobedience, the renewal will be marked by covenantal fidelity and obedience.[30] Nevertheless, while these concepts

---

[28] On "Christ" as an honorific title more akin to "Caesar" rather than a name, see Matthew V. Novenson, *Christ among the Messiahs* (2009), esp. 64–178; "The Jewish Messiahs, the Pauline Christ, and the Gentile Question" (2009). See also Joshua Jipp, *Christ Is King* (2015), esp. 1–11, 139–210; Adela Yarbro Collins and John J. Collins, *King and Messiah as Son of God* (2008), esp. 122.

[29] "The Messiah has appeared, and it is therefore impossible to hasten his coming (as some devout Jews thought to do) by perfect obedience to the law and penitence for its transgressions" (Barrett, *Romans*, 199). Cf. Badenas, *End of the Law*, 131; Jewett, *Romans*, 626–27; Jan Heller, "Himmel- und Höllenfahrt nach Römer 10,6–7" (1972), 484–85.

[30] The fact that the word for "return" (שוב) comes also to mean "repent" shows just how linked these concepts became in the tradition. On the development of שוב in this respect, see David A. Lambert, *How Repentance Became Biblical* (2016), esp. 152–87, though Lambert distinguishes "repentance," which he defines as a mental act that "utilizes an *emotion of sorrow*" (154, emphasis original), from the biblical concept of "cessation of sin" (154–55), while I regard the latter as the definition of repentance. The frequent rendering of the Hebrew concept of שוב with μετανοέω in the New Testament reflects a distinctive interpretation of the transformation promised in the Prophets – the Greek concept of a "change of mind" (νοῦς) corresponds to the more idiomatic Hebrew notion of a change of "heart." John the Baptist's message and proclamation of a "baptism of repentance" (Mark 1:4) should therefore be understood in eschatological terms, as a proclamation of the fulfillment of the prophetic promises of transformation (see *How Repentance Became Biblical*, 143–44).

are unambiguously linked in the tradition, there is significant ambiguity about how Israel's newfound fidelity and obedience will come about. Specifically, will Israel's restoration and transformation be initiated by repentance, or will that repentance be the result of God's action initiating Israel's restoration and transformation?[31] Although there are many passages (such as the new covenant prophecy) that emphasize God's transforming role in bringing about Israel's justification, many restoration passages can be read as suggesting that Israel's redemption is contingent on repentance.

Leviticus 26, for example, lists a variety of punishments for covenantal disobedience broken up by the refrain, "If after all these things you still do not obey me, then I will punish you seven times more for your sins" (26:18; cf. 18:21, 24, 28). The chapter concludes with the promise that after being punished with exile, "They will confess their iniquity and that of their forefathers, which they committed against me in their infidelity ... then their uncircumcised heart will be humbled and then they will redeem their iniquity,[32] and then I will remember my covenant" (26:40–42).[33] Similarly, Deuteronomy declares that after Israel is exiled for disobedience, "from there you will seek YHWH your God, and you will find him when you search for him with all your heart and all your soul" (Deut 4:29). It would be easy for postexilic readers of such passages to conclude that the long-overdue restoration had been delayed due to inadequate repentance.

This is, of course, exactly the argument of Dan 9, which aims to explain why Israel has not been restored despite the fact that the seventy years of Jeremiah's prophecy have concluded.[34] After a prayer of confession and intercession in response to this realization (his own personal

---

[31] See Lambert, "Did Israel Believe That Redemption Awaited Its Repentance?" (2006), 631–39.

[32] LXX: "approve their sin" (ὑδοκήσουσιν τὰς ἁμαρτίας αὐτῶν). The idea is that they will recognize that what they have done is sinful and that God's judgment was just.

[33] Many English versions render these verses as conditional statements, with the NRSV, for example, rendering 26:40, "But if they confess ..." But there are no conditional particles in these verses (unlike the refrain in Lev 26:18 and parallels), suggesting that 26:40–42 should be taken as temporal (that is, as a promise) rather than conditional and contingent.

[34] See John S. Bergsma, "Persian Period as Penitential Era" (2009), 60–62; Michael A. Knibb, "The Exile in the Literature of the Intertestamental Period" (1976), 255; Brant Pitre, *Jesus, the Tribulation, and the End of the Exile* (2005), 60.

fulfillment of Lev 26:40–42),[35] Daniel receives the explanation that Jeremiah's seventy years have been multiplied sevenfold – an obvious allusion to Lev 26 – meaning another sixty-three "sevens" stand between the construction of the Second Temple and Israel's full redemption (Dan 9:24–27).[36] It is difficult to read Dan 9 as anything but a tacit acknowledgment that Israel's restoration is contingent on Israel's obedience, the absence of which has caused the delay. Similarly, Malachi concludes with the declaration that the prophet Elijah will come before the "great and terrible day of YHWH," to "turn the hearts of the fathers to their children" and vice-versa "lest I come and strike the land with a curse" (3:23–24 [ET 4:5–6]), implying that "if Elijah does not accomplish his mission, then God will curse the land."[37]

Ezra–Nehemiah, which presents the returnees to the land as the vanguard of Israel's restoration "engaged in the task of re-establishing the broader historical and theological reality of 'Israel,'"[38] similarly presumes that inadequate obedience and sanctity is the reason its protagonists did not succeed.[39] In this context, things like exogamy and the failure to keep the Sabbath are so disastrous precisely because they threaten the final restoration that depends on "turning to YHWH" (Neh 1:9) in obedience and sanctity, ensuring that wrath remains on Israel and even adding to it (Neh 13:18, 23–29; cf. Ezra 9:13–14).[40] For things to be set right, these returnees must further repent, purify, and separate themselves, and each failure in the book prompts ever more rigorous efforts to purify the "sacred seed," establish proper cultic observances, and separate from

---

[35] The fact that God's promise of redemption comes as a response to Daniel's confession and intercession is similar to Moses' intercession in Jubilees 1 (not to mention Exod 33–34) and illustrates the paradox of an intercessor instigating a sovereign God to take action. Cf. Lambert, "Did Israel Believe," 643–44; *How Repentance Became Biblical*, 33–50, 130–32.

[36] Cf. John S. Bergsma, *The Jubilee from Leviticus to Qumran* (2007), 225–27, countering John E. Goldingay, *Daniel* (1989), 267.

[37] Dale C. Allison, "The End of the Ages Has Come" (1982), 341.

[38] Christopher Mark Blumhofer, *The Gospel of John and the Future of Israel* (2020), 17.

[39] For a detailed discussion, see Jason A. Staples, *The Idea of Israel in Second Temple Judaism* (2021), 143–61.

[40] J. Gordon McConville, "Ezra-Nehemiah and the Fulfillment of Prophecy" (1986), 216–17, 222–24. Similar conceptions about the contingency of Israel's restoration are reflected in Hezekiah's declaration to the northern remnant that if those living in the land "return to YHWH" wholeheartedly, even those living in exilic captivity abroad will be returned to the land (2 Chr 30:6–9).

the nations.[41] As such, Ezra–Nehemiah represents the beginning of the restorationist Jewish sectarianism that characterizes the later Second Temple period, with competing groups attempting to establish the correct halakha and thereby initiate Israel's restoration and the end of the age of wrath.[42]

THE YAḤAD AS RIGHTEOUS VANGUARD OF ISRAEL

The Dead Sea Scrolls attest to a sect contemporary with Paul that envisioned itself as doing what the protagonists of Ezra–Nehemiah failed to accomplish, having established correct obedience to Torah and thereby initiating Israel's impending restoration.[43] The Damascus Document says:

> In the age of wrath, 390 years after delivering them into the hand of Nebuchadnezzar, [God] visited them and caused to grow from Israel and from Aaron a root of planting to inherit his land and to become fat with the good things of his soil. And they recognized their iniquity and knew they were guilty, but they were like blind persons and like those groping for a path over twenty years. And God considered their deeds, because they sought him with a whole heart [cf. Deut 4:29],[44] and raised up for them a teacher of justice to guide them in the way of his heart. He taught to later generations what God did to the generation deserving wrath. (CD 1:5–12)

After an extended discourse recounting the punishments of God against the wicked of Israel (CD 1:13–5:1) and the preservation of a remnant (3:12–4:6), the sect presents itself as having withdrawn from the wicked in the land of Judah, effectively rejoining the larger body of Israel that has remained in exile for centuries (6:2–7:21).[45] In that exilic

---

[41] "This remnant stands on the threshold of restoration, contingent on their faithfulness in obeying God's law" (Bradley C. Gregory, "The Postexilic Exile in Third Isaiah" [2007], 491).

[42] Later examples include the Maccabean *Hasidim*, the Pharisees, the Dead Sea Scroll sect, and the sects led by John the Baptist and Jesus. For Ezra and Nehemiah as the origin of Jewish sectarianism, see Shemaryahu Talmon, "Emergence of Jewish Sectarianism in the Early Second Temple Period" (1987), 593–601.

[43] For a more detailed discussion of Israel's restoration and the sectarians' self-representation in the Dead Sea Scrolls, see Staples, *The Idea of Israel*, 259–89.

[44] The fact that God raised up the teacher after twenty years of seeking with their whole heart works against Lambert's ("Did Israel Believe," 646–50) claim that the sectarians take a wholly deterministic perspective. On the contrary, the initiative seems to be shared, as their repentance and seeking seems to have preceded the granting of justness.

[45] My conclusions in this respect are similar to those of Shemaryahu Talmon, "The New Covenanters of Qumran" (1971); "Emergence of Jewish Sectarianism," 605–7.

context, these sectarians understand themselves as the vanguard of Israel, with their proper Torah observance fulfilling the requirements of repentance on behalf of the rest of exiled Israel and initiating the end of the age of wrath. The Community Rule further explains:

> They are to walk with everyone by the standard of truth and by the regulation of the age. When these exist in Israel, the council of the Yaḥad will be founded on truth, an eternal planting, a sacred temple for Israel, and a secret holy of holies for Aaron, a true witness for justice, c[ho]sen by grace (רצון) to atone for the land and to repay the wicked their recompense. (1QS 8:4–7a)

> They shall separate from the dwelling of the men of iniquity to go to the wilderness to prepare the way of truth there, as it is written, "in the wilderness prepare the way of YHWH; make straight in the desert a highway for our God." (1QS 8:13–14)

This suggests that the group understands their function and role as atonement for the rest of Israel through the "interpretation of the Torah which he commanded by the hand of Moses, to act in keeping with what has been revealed age by age" (1QS 8:15). Their mediation and intercession are to lead to the restoration of the rest of Israel. That final restoration will take place when the "the sons of light return from the wilderness of the peoples" to join the "sons of Levi, Judah, and Benjamin" in the climactic battle against the forces of darkness (1QM 1:2–3). The idea that there are specific Torah strictures for each age also appears in CD 6:14, which says, "they must take care to act in keeping with the exact interpretation (כפרוש) of the Torah for the age of wickedness." That is, there is a specific way in which the Torah must be kept in the "age of wickedness," while the praxis of the age of favor after the restoration may differ.[46] Devorah Dimant explains:

> One of the fundamental characteristics of all the sect's writings is the peculiar eschatological tension, created by the special place in history the sect ascribed

---

[46] This conception of specific Torah praxis for specific time periods may support the suggestion that Paul understood Torah observance in the messianic era to be different from that required prior to that era, an idea posited but also acknowledged to be based on scanty evidence in the Second Temple period by W. D. Davies, *Paul and Rabbinic Judaism* (1955), 52; *Torah in the Messianic Age And/or the Age to Come* (1952), esp. 90–91. Cf. also Richard N. Longenecker, *Paul, Apostle of Liberty* (2015), 116–41; Frank Thielman, *From Plight to Solution* (1989), 28–45. The Tanna debe Eliyahu cited in b. Sanh. 97a is also of note in this respect: "The world is to exist six thousand years. In the first two thousand was desolation; two thousand years the Torah flourished; the next two thousand years is the age of the messiah." This source is late, but its similarity to the six thousand year eschatological schemes of Barn. 15:4 and 2 Pet 3:8 suggest a comparable tradition may well have existed in the late Second Temple period.

to itself. The theoretical means by which this place is defined, is the teaching of the periods .... Through it, the sect established its own special role on the threshold of the *eschaton*, which determines all its activities. The radical break with the past by repentance is at the same time a return to a purified, idealized past; the strict practice of the Law of Moses implies an uncompromising separation from the present wickedness and evil. Yet by these very elements, the sect announces the approaching End, and initiates the beginning of the eschatological process.[47]

The sectarian scrolls therefore portray Israel's restoration as first and foremost involving a return to justness and obedience that will ultimately culminate in an eschatological reunion of all twelve tribes in the land, the sweeping away of all the disobedient among Israel (CD 7:9–13), and the subjugation of the nations to Israel. They identify themselves as the vanguard of this return to virtue, which has already happened for them through the revelation of the Teacher of Justice, which was itself the indication that the restoration was imminent.[48] In the process, these "repentant/returnees of Israel"[49] are already participating in the new covenant promised by Jeremiah (CD 6:19), having received the "spirit of sanctity" (1QS 4:21) and being transformed by the divine presence in their midst. Their community, set aside for obedience by God and instructed by divine revelation, has thus become the necessary atonement in exile to bring about the final eschatological restoration of all Israel. Their existence and obedience are the final steps necessary for Israel's restoration outlined in Leviticus and Deuteronomy.[50] The end result will be the rise of "the prince of the whole congregation," the scepter promised in Num 24:13, who will destroy the enemies of Israel (CD 7:20–21; cf. 1QM 5:1).[51]

---

[47] Devorah Dimant, "Qumran Sectarian Literature" (1984), 539.
[48] "This was the function performed by the Teacher of Righteousness. The knowledge he imparted to the sect unveiled to its members the fact that they are living in the final generation, on the threshold of the Eschatological Era" (Dimant, "Qumran Sectarian Literature," 536).
[49] That is, שבי ישראל (CD 4:2; 6:5; 8:16). The phrase is ambiguous and can mean several things, though its primary sense seems to be "those of Israel who have turned." See Staples, *The Idea of Israel*, 264–65 n. 25.
[50] "They entered this 'new covenant' in anticipation of the return to and repossession of the land, which would be the result of their seeking God. That the return to and the repossession of the land were the ultimate purpose of the 'new covenant' is confirmed not only by the connections between Jer 31:31–34, Jer 29:10–14 and Jer 30, read in conjunction with Deuteronomy, but also by CD 1,7–8" (Stephen J. Hultgren, *From the Damascus Covenant to the Covenant of the Community* [2007], 105).
[51] "The Essenes in Qumran anticipated that a priestly and a political messiah would be ushered in by a holy war when God was satisfied with the preparation of the new priestly

THE CONTINGENCY OF ISRAEL'S RESTORATION

Numerous other early Jewish materials from the Second Temple period further attest to the idea that Israel's restoration depends on repentance and justness.[52] For example, 2 Baruch promises that "if you destroy vain error from your heart ... if you thus do these things" then God will "with much mercy gather together again those who were dispersed" (78:6–7). On the other hand, 4 Ezra rebuts the idea that "all of us who are full of ungodliness" (4:37) are the reason the restoration ("threshing of the just," 4:38) has been delayed – with this opposition providing strong evidence that at least some first-century contemporaries *did* believe that the restoration had been delayed due to injustice/unrighteousness and that it must be initiated by repentance.[53] Philo also seems to regard restoration as contingent, declaring of those who have been scattered as punishment (*Praem.* 115), "If they change their ways, reproaching themselves for their errors and openly declaring and confessing (ὁμολογήσαντες) all the sins they have committed ... they will then meet with a favorable acceptance from God, their merciful savior" (163). At that time, he says, "they shall all be restored to freedom in one day" and exalted above all the nations (164–72).[54]

---

community" (Jewett, *Romans*, 627). See especially Shemaryahu Talmon, "Waiting for the Messiah" (1987).

[52] In addition to the instances already mentioned, Dale C. Allison, *The End of the Ages Has Come* (2013), 155–56, lists T. Dan 6:4; T. Sim 6:2–7; T. Jud. 23:5; As. Mos. 1:18. Others not mentioned by Allison include T. Sim 3:4; 4:2 and T. Jud. 19:2 (see Lambert, *How Repentance Became Biblical*, 167, 220–21 n. 70 and n. 78). E. P. Sanders, *Paul and Palestinian Judaism* (1977), 92–97, 146– 47, 234–37, 371, 422–23, also stresses that obedience is the condition for salvation or redemption throughout early Jewish thought. In light of these sources, the objection of Lambert, "Did Israel Believe," 650, that notions of restoration as contingent on repentance "only became foundational after the Second Temple Period" because Jews of earlier periods tended to view the world as "largely determined by divine fiat" is unsustainable. Lambert himself moderates this position in *How Repentance Became Biblical*, 126, 212 n. 17.

[53] Cf. Allison, "End of the Ages," 344–45.

[54] Some have expressed doubt about whether Philo expected Israel's restoration at all, suggesting that as an allegorist he no longer held to such concrete eschatological hopes. E.g., Burton L. Mack, "Wisdom and Apocalyptic in Philo" (1991); Betsy Halpern-Amaru, "Land Theology in Philo and Josephus" (1986), 85; Erich Gruen, "Diaspora and Homeland" (2002), 40 n. 50. But the two levels of interpretation are inseparable for Philo, who emphasizes in *Praem.* 93–97 that the promised eschatological blessings are contingent on the people's obedience to the commands and their embodiment of the virtues found in the Torah and elsewhere criticizes those who embrace the allegorical meaning to the exclusion of the natural meaning, which he says is "equally" (ἴσως) true (*Conf.* 190; cf. *Migr.* 89–93). Thomas Tobin, "Philo and the Sibyl" (1997), 97–98, has

Even the New Testament includes indications of the idea that Israel's restoration is contingent on obedience, starting with John the Baptist's "baptism of repentance" to prepare the way for the coming of the kingdom (Mark 1:4–8) and Jesus' own teachings about repentance.[55] Dale Allison has observed that Jesus' lament over Jerusalem is also intriguing through this lens: "How often I longed to gather your children together ... but you were unwilling. See, your house is left to you desolate, for I say to you that you will not see me until you say, 'blessed is he who comes in the name of the Lord.'" (Matt 23:37–39).[56] But the most telling example comes from Peter's sermon in Acts 3:19–20, in which the apostle declares, "Change your minds (μετανοήσατε) and return (ἐπιστρέψατε) ... so that times of refreshing may come from the presence of the Lord, and so that he may send Jesus, the messiah appointed for you." Peter's exhortation remarkably suggests that repentance would result in the coming of the messiah (!) and the "restoration of all things" (3:21). Of course, Peter's sermon presumes that the messiah had already come once, leading to the outpouring of the spirit narrated in the second chapter of Acts, providing the capacity for repentance that would lead to the times of refreshing proclaimed in the sermon.[57] Romans 11 also suggests that Paul himself may have regarded his own mission as part of that process.

REPENTANCE AND RESTORATION IN RABBINIC TRADITIONS

The view that Israel's restoration is conditional on repentance is also widely attested in rabbinic literature and later Jewish thought.[58] Among

---

persuasively shown that rather than abandoning restoration eschatology, Philo instead revises the militant nationalist eschatology evident in sources like the Sibylline Oracles 3 and 5 toward a more quietistic emphasis on Torah observance and the practice of virtue as the means of restoration. We can therefore safely conclude that "Philo, despite his allegorizing, maintained the traditional hope for the restoration of Israel" (E. P. Sanders, *Jesus and Judaism* [1985], 86). See also Staples, *The Idea of Israel*, 239–52; James M. Scott, "Philo and the Restoration of Israel" (1996), 537; John J. Collins, *Between Athens and Jerusalem* (2000), 136–37.

[55] See Allison, "End of the Ages," 347–76; *End of the Ages*, 155–60.
[56] See Allison, "End of the Ages," 358–69.
[57] Similarly, 2 Pet 3:11–12 enjoins its recipients to behave with "sacred conduct and godliness, looking for and hastening the coming of the day of God," implying that the timing of that day could be impacted by their behavior.
[58] E.g., Maimonides, *Mishneh Torah*, Laws of Repentance 7:5. Cf. Dale C. Allison, "Matt. 23:39 = Luke 13:35b as a Conditional Prophecy" (1983), 77; Soloveichik,

several early examples, a saying ascribed to second-century R. Shimon b. Yoḥai declares, "If Israel would keep two Sabbaths as prescribed, they would be delivered immediately" (b. Šab. 118b; cf. Isa 58:13–14). About a century later, R. Levi cuts this standard in half: "If Israel would keep only a single Sabbath as prescribed, the messiah would come immediately" (y. Ta'an. 64a). Similarly, Rav (third century) concludes, "all predestined dates have passed, and the matter now depends solely on repentance and good works" (b. Sanh. 97b).[59] More significantly, the Babylonian Talmud includes two versions of a dispute between two rabbis from the second half of the first century. In the first version,

> R. Eliezer says, "If Israel repents, they will be redeemed. And if not, they will not be redeemed." R. Joshua replied, "If they do not repent, will they not be redeemed? On the contrary, the Sacred One (blessed be he) will raise up for them a king whose decrees are as harsh as those of Haman, and the Israelites will repent and be restored to a good path." (b. Sanh. 97b)

Notably, R. Joshua does not challenge the idea that Israel's redemption requires repentance. Instead, he tacitly agrees with the first statement of his interlocutor but argues that there is no possibility of the second because God will ensure Israel's repentance, thereby ensuring their redemption.[60] In the second and more extended version of this debate (97b–98a), R. Joshua ends the debate by citing Dan 12:6–7 ("a time, times, and half a time") as evidence that God will ensure that Israel's repentance and redemption comes at the appointed time.[61] This second version further demonstrates that the dispute does not concern whether redemption requires repentance but rather whether Israel's repentance ultimately depends on Israel's initiative or God's. That is, will Israel's repentance precede and initiate the restoration, or will God initiate Israel's repentance as the first step in the process of redemption?[62] Meir Soloveichik summarizes the implications of the former position as

---

"Redemption and the Power of Man," esp. 51–57, 74 nn. 6–7. This is, of course, by no means the only position represented in rabbinic traditions, as will be discussed below.

[59] On the eventual dominance in the rabbinic tradition of the view that Israel's restoration is contingent on repentance, see Soloveichik, "Redemption and the Power of Man."

[60] Ephraim E. Urbach, "Redemption and Repentance in Talmudic Judaism" (1970), 191.

[61] R. Eliezer's silence after this point may suggest an unwillingness to engage with such apocalyptic timetables. See Urbach, "Redemption and Repentance," 191–92.

[62] Both opinions "assume that the redemption will not take place before repentance occurs; the debate focuses merely on whether there is a guaranteed date by which the Jews, because of historical circumstance, will be motivated to repent, or if, in Rav's words, 'all predestined dates [for redemption] have passed'" (Soloveichik, "Redemption and the Power of Man," 75 n. 6; cf. Urbach, "Redemption and Repentance," 191–92).

follows: "Faith in the messiah is faith in ourselves, in our ability to bring the messiah by becoming worthy of his arrival."[63]

THE GRAND MIRACLE: DIVINELY INITIATED JUSTNESS

This, I propose, is precisely the position Paul is opposing in Rom 10, specifically in 10:3–9, where his pesher-style interpretation of Deut 30:12–14 rejects any efforts to "bring messiah" (Rom 10:6–7) through the "justness of their own" pursued in 10:3. In this passage, Paul is participating in an established early Jewish debate about the relationship between Israel's obedience and redemption. Paul does agree that Israel's redemption depends on Israel's justness; without repentance, there will be no return. The debate has to do with the source and nature of that repentance and justification. The question is whether Israel must become sufficiently righteous/just to bring the messiah or whether the messiah will come to make Israel sufficiently just. Paul takes the latter view. Put simply, Paul's argument boils down to this: rather than Israel's justness bringing the messiah, the messiah already came to make Israel just.

In contrast to the eschatology of the Yaḥad sectarians, who understand the creation of the new covenant community as taking place prior to the coming of messianic deliverance, for Paul the coming of the messiah precedes and facilitates the outpouring of the spirit and establishment of the new covenant community.[64] Whereas the new covenant of the Yaḥad is a foretaste of the new era as the group stands on the threshold of redemption practicing Torah in keeping with the requirements of the age of wrath, Paul argues that the new age has already been inaugurated, with Jesus as both "teacher of justice" and messianic deliverer, first from sin through the spirit and then from the consequences of sin at his return. And since the messiah has already come, any effort to usher in Israel's restoration or the messianic age by repentance, Torah-observance, or zealous political or military campaigns is misguided.[65]

Paul is not unique in arguing that the messiah's arrival precedes and facilitates Israel's repentance; he is instead taking a position widely

---

[63] Soloveichik, "Redemption and the Power of Man," 53.
[64] Scott J. Hafemann, *Paul, Moses, and the History of Israel* (2005), 163–64.
[65] Barrett, *Romans*, 199; Jewett, *Romans*, 625–27; Robert Jewett, "The Basic Human Dilemma" (1997); Heller, "Himmel- und Höllenfahrt"; Kyle B. Wells, *Grace and Agency in Paul and Second Temple Judaism* (2014), 272; Bekken, *The Word Is Near You*, 178–80; David I. Starling, *Not My People* (2011), 152–54.

represented elsewhere in early Jewish and later rabbinic traditions. For example, while many rabbis argued that the messiah would only come once Israel repented, others argued that the messiah will come when things are at their worst, at which time he will set things straight. These seemingly contradictory answers often appear alongside one another within the tradition, as in the summary statement of R. Yoḥanan (180–279 CE): "The son of David will come to a generation that is either entirely righteous or entirely wicked" (b. Sanh. 98a). As a whole, the opinions about the coming of the messiah recorded in the Babylonian Talmud can be grouped into four basic categories.[66] In the first three, the messiah will either come (1) once Israel repents and is adequately just, (2) when Israel is completely apostate,[67] or (3) at an appointed time based on an apocalyptic eschatological timetable not contingent on Israel's justness.[68] A fourth opinion attributed to R. Joshua b. Levi instead suggests that the *manner* of the messiah's coming will depend on whether Israel is righteous or not: "If they have merit, it will be 'with the clouds of heaven' [Dan 7:13], but if they do not have merit, it will be 'lowly and riding on an ass' [Zech 9:7]" (b. Sanh. 98a). Paul's position essentially combines all four options: the messiah came at the appointed time (Gal 4:4; Rom 5:6) for an apostate and unjust people (Rom 1–3), and the humble manner of his coming was in accord with Israel's impiety and injustice. He came the first time to bring justification and repentance through his death and resurrection, and he will return in the clouds (1 Thess 4:17) when Israel has been fully transformed and justified by the spirit.

Within the Second Temple period, the aforementioned discussion in 4 Ezra 4:38–42, for example, explicitly opposes the idea that Israel's restoration to obedience depended on Israel's justness. Similarly, Jubilees (esp. 1:22–25) declares Israel's incapacity to obey and promises that God will transform Israel and facilitate their wholehearted turn to him, circumcising their hearts and creating a sacred spirit in them to cause them to

---

[66] Not every opinion fits neatly into these categories. R. Hillel II (fourth century), for example, argues that there is no future messiah at all, "for they have already enjoyed him in the days of Hezekiah" (b. Sanh. 99a). Nevertheless, these categories do account for the bulk of the discussion of the advent of the messiah in the Talmud.

[67] E.g., R. Isaac (third/fourth century): "The son of David will come only when the entire kingdom has turned to heresy" (b. Sanh. 97a).

[68] Lambert, *How Repentance Became Biblical*, 154, argues that the notion of repentance "as a technology of the self" is a later rabbinic development. One might conclude that this development is related to the general rabbinic rejection of apocalypticism, which tends to be associated with divine-priority eschatological positions.

obey – all concepts central to Paul's own gospel proclamation. Lambert explains that Jubilees thus presents the human role in transformation as limited to crying out to God in awareness of their vulnerabilities and need for transformation, whereby they "urge God to repair humanity, but the actual work of repair is God's alone."[69] It is difficult to read this and not immediately think of Rom 10, where Paul argues against the attempt to "establish justness of their own" (10:3) rather than receiving God's work of repair through the messiah by calling on the name of the Lord (10:9–13).

At bottom, Paul's argument assumes that since Israel's covenant has been broken, Israel cannot renew it without divine help. Instead, God has to re-call his people from their broken state (Rom 9:24–26). That Paul's quotation of Deut 30:12–14 is preceded by and conflated with a quotation of Deut 9:4a (a passage repeatedly echoed in Romans) further reinforces this reading,[70] alluding to a warning against Israel imagining that God has worked on their behalf due to their own justness:

Do not say in your heart, "It is because of my justness (δικαιοσύνη) that the Lord has brought me into this land to inherit it" .... And you will know today that it is not because of your justness that the Lord your God is giving you this good land to inherit, because you are a stiff-necked people. (Deut 9:4, 6)

Together with the quotation of Deut 30:12–14, the point is that God's action on behalf of his people is not due to their obedience or because they deserved it, making any effort to initiate the restoration (that is, "bring the messiah") through Torah observance misguided at best and "at worst a supreme form of ingratitude."[71] Instead, Paul argues, the messiah already came to bring the faithful obedience promised as part of the restoration. In the process, Paul evidently reads Deut 30:11–14 as subsequent to the promise of transformation in Deut 30:1–10 that has been in the background throughout Romans.[72] That is, he presents Deut

---

[69] Lambert, "Did Israel Believe," 644. Lambert moderates this emphasis on agency in his updated discussion of these themes in Jubilees in *How Repentance Became Biblical*, 123–33, 211–17.

[70] "The association would be an easy one because only here and in the closely related [Deut] 8:17 do the words Paul uses μὴ εἴπῃς ἐν τῇ καρδίᾳ σου occur in the LXX" (Moo, *Romans*, 651 n. 26; cf. Hays, *Echoes*, 78–79; Jewett, *Romans*, 625–26).

[71] Kyle B. Wells, "The Vindication of Agents, Divine and Human" (2012), 96 n. 113. See also Barrett, *Romans*, 199; Jewett, *Romans*, 626–27.

[72] In addition to the discussions above on the centrality of Deut 30:1–10 to Romans, see Wells, "The Vindication of Agents," esp. 70–81.

The Grand Miracle

30:11–14 as referring to the time after God has circumcised the hearts of the people, giving them the capacity to obey that they previously lacked.[73]

Some have argued that Paul simply could not have read Deut 30:1–14 in this linear, sequential fashion because, as Moo argues, "there is a clear transition from the prophecy of future restoration in [Deut 30] vv. 1–10 to the situation of Israel as she prepares to enter the promised land."[74] Leaving aside the question of whether that would preclude a first-century interpreter like Paul from reading the passage sequentially, that transition is not in fact clear in the Hebrew version of the passage. The primary basis of this allegedly clear transition is that verses 11–14 lack the future-oriented (vav-consecutive) verbal forms that appear through Deut 30:1–10.[75] But the problem with that reasoning is that there are no finite verbs at all in verses 11–14 aside from the (future-oriented) imperfects representing reported speech (e.g., "who will go up," 30:12). Instead, verse 11 is linked to the preceding by the conjunctive particle כי, continuing a string of כי clauses beginning in 30:9b.[76] Like the Greek ὅτι that translates it in Deut 30:11 LXX, this particle is ambiguous, as it can represent temporal ("when"), causal ("for/because"), and sometimes conditional ("if") meanings. A look at the transition in context and how the other כי clauses in the series function can help inform how one should understand verse 11:

And YHWH your God will prosper you in every work of your hand ... because [כי] YHWH will again rejoice over you for good, just as he rejoiced over your ancestors, because [כי] you will obey YHWH your God,[77] to keep his commands and his statutes which are written in this book of the Torah, because [כי] you will turn to YHWH your God with all your heart and soul,[78] because [כי] this command I am commanding today [is/will not be] too difficult for you ...

---

[73] See Wells, "The Vindication of Agents," esp. 82–97; Steven R. Coxhead, "Deuteronomy 30:11–14 as a Prophecy of the New Covenant in Christ" (2006); John H. Sailhamer, *The Pentateuch as Narrative* (2017), 473–74; Thielman, *From Plight to Solution*, 113–14.

[74] Moo, *Romans*, 652, depending on the arguments of Samuel Rolles Driver, *Deuteronomy* (1902), 330–31.

[75] Driver, *Deuteronomy* (1902), 330–31. The "today" of Deut 30:11 does not mark a transition to the present capacity of the people since it refers to Moses' delivery of the command (happening in the "today" of the passage) rather than to the people's obedience. That is, the passage does not say, "This command is not too difficult for you today" but rather refers to the "command I am commanding you today."

[76] Wells, "The Vindication of Agents," 82; Coxhead, "Deuteronomy 30:11–14," 305–8; Driver, *Deuteronomy*, 31.

[77] LXX: "If (ἐάν) you should obey."   [78] LXX: "If (ἐάν) you should be turned back."

because[79] [כי] the word [is/will be] very near you, in your mouth and in your heart for you to follow it.[80] (Deut 30:9–11, 14a)

The כי of verse 11 therefore ties verses 11–14 together with verses 1–10, and given that context, the tense-neutral participles and prepositional phrases of the nonverbal clauses of 11–14 would typically take their tense from the previous (imperfect/future) statements.[81] It is true that in the Greek the כי clauses of 30:10 are rendered as conditionals: "if (ἐάν) you should obey ... if you should be turned back," and the implied verbs of vv. 11–14 are rendered in the present tense (as also in Paul's quotations), but 30:11–14 is still not treated as an independent passage that has moved the attention back to the wilderness generation as opposed to the immediately preceding future-oriented passage. Instead, verses 11–14 are connected to the preceding verses with ὅτι ("when/because"), like the Hebrew indicating a causal or temporal relationship to the preceding statements.

The Septuagint also renders Deut 30:1 as an unconditional promise rather than a conditional statement, therefore establishing that Israel will eventually have no difficulty fulfilling the "ifs" of verse 10 precisely because the word is in their hearts and mouths after the guaranteed transformation of Deut 30:1–9. The extant Targumim also connect verses 11–14 with the preceding passage in a causal sense,[82] which should also not be ignored since Paul's wording "descend to the abyss" (Rom 10:7) corresponds to the readings of Deut 30:13 in the Fragmentary Targum and Targum Neofiti against the extant Hebrew and Greek versions, suggesting that he was familiar with a tradition akin to that witnessed by these later Aramaic versions.[83]

---

[79] This כי is left untranslated in the LXX.

[80] It is possible to interpret these כי clauses as conditional (as the LXX does for some of them), but there is evidence that at least some in the Second Temple period read these passages as unconditional (causal or temporal) promises. See, for example, the discussions of the unconditional interpretation of Deut 30 in the Dead Sea Scrolls in Wells, "The Vindication of Agents," 84–85 and Hultgren, *From the Damascus Covenant*, 110–11.

[81] Cf. Coxhead, "Deuteronomy 30:11–14," 306.

[82] E.g., Onqelos: ארי תפקידתא הרא ("because this command"); Neofiti: ארום מצוותה הדה ("because this command").

[83] For Deut 30:13, Neofiti has "And it [the Torah] is not beyond the Great Sea for you to say, 'Oh that there would be for us one like the prophet Jonah, who will descend to the depths (יחות לעמקוי) of the great sea and bring it up for us, so that he will cause us to hear the commands so that we will do them." The Fragmentary Targum has: "And not beyond the great sea for you to say, "Oh that there would be one prophet for us like Jonah, who will descend to the depths (יחות לעימקי) of the Great Sea and bring it to us so that he will cause us to hear the commands so that we will do them." These readings and their

Thematically, reading Deut 30:11–14 as continuous with and subsequent to the immediately prior verses also resolves an apparent contradiction in Deuteronomy. Taken independently, the declaration that "this command which I am commanding you is not too difficult" because "the word is very near you, in your mouth and in your heart, so that you may do it" (30:11, 14) seems strongly at odds with Moses' previous assertion that God had not given Israel a heart to know him (Deut 29:3 [29:4 ET]) and the pronouncement of the next chapter that they will therefore certainly fall under the curse for disobedience (31:16–27).[84] Throughout the rest of Deuteronomy, Israel's problem is precisely that they do *not* have the word in their heart or in their mouth, meaning that the command *was* too difficult for them. But this is the problem Deut 30:6 promises to solve through the circumcision of the heart, which will cause the people to fulfill the love command "so that you may live." If the word "in your mouth and in your heart" of 30:14 refers to the epoch after the divinely initiated ethical transformation promised in the immediately preceding verses, any potential contradiction is resolved.[85]

That said, the application of these verses not to the command but to the messiah still begs explanation. Some have posited that Paul identifies the Torah or command with wisdom (as Bar 3:29–30), and because he

---

potential implications are discussed in Stanislas Lyonnet, "Saint Paul et l'exégèse juive de son temps" (1957). The association of Deut 30:13 with Jonah in these Targumim also raises intriguing questions about the parallels between Jesus and Jonah in Matt 12:39–41; 16:4; and Luke 11:29–32. Pace Bekken, *The Word Is Near You*, 5, the fact that the word "abyss" does not appear in the targumim does not refute the possibility of Paul's knowledge of such traditions, as one would hardly expect a specific Greek word in an Aramaic translation, and לעמקוי effectively means the same thing. In any case, both Paul's quotation and these targumim conflate Deut 30:12–13 with Ps 107:26 (LXX 106:26), which are also more similar in the LXX than in the MT.

[84] "A related paradox is the affirmation both that obedience and loyalty to God seem *very difficult* for Israel to maintain (29:22–28) and yet the statement that the commandments [sic] are *not difficult* and very near to the heart" (Dennis T. Olson, "How Does Deuteronomy Do Theology?" [2003], 209).

[85] For the equivalence of the Torah in the heart (Jer 31:33) and the word in the heart (Deut 30:14) and the consequences of obedience/justness, see Ps 37:31; 119:11; Isa 51:7. Cf. Coxhead, "Deuteronomy 30:11–14," 309. Thus Nachmanides reads Deut 30:11–14 eschatologically, arguing that the promise "is put in participial form to hint at the promise that the future of the matter will be thus" (*Miqraot Gedolot*, 5:355). See the discussion in Coxhead, "Deuteronomy 30:11–14," 311 n. 17. Similarly, Wells concludes, "But when one takes into account that 30:6 falls between 29:22 and 30:11, the paradox disappears. The anthropological optimism of 30:11–14 could simply be based upon Yhwh's work in 30:6. Thus ... the Divine-Priority reading might actually *resolve* a tension that is already present in the text if one does not read the text in a linear fashion" ("The Vindication of Agents," 83–84, emphasis original).

also associates wisdom with the messiah, he can then seamlessly substitute one for another.[86] A better solution considers the implications both of the passage in its context in Deuteronomy and of Paul's interpretation of "descend to the abyss" (Rom 10:7). When Deuteronomy says that the people will not need someone to cross the sea/descend to the abyss or ascend into heaven to get the command, it should not be forgotten that this is exactly what Moses had done on their behalf, walking the floor of the (Red) sea and going into the heavens (on Sinai/Horeb) to obtain the Torah.[87] But after the redemptive actions of Deut 30:1-10, no such mediation will be necessary because the command will be "very near you, in your mouth and in your heart" (30:14).[88]

In this context, Paul's interpretation of "descend to the abyss" (Rom 10:7) reflects his view that the messiah did descend and ascend in order to gain the authority to put the command in the hearts of the people as promised in Deut 30. Just as Moses crossed the sea and ascended to the heavens to reveal the Torah, the messiah has descended to the abyss in death and then ascended to the heavens in exaltation to give the spirit, putting the Torah in the mouths and hearts of the faithful.[89] Just as it was in the case of Moses, it was not the people who ascended to obtain the Torah but rather the one chosen by God to mediate on their behalf. And since the promise is already being realized through the spirit, the question of how to bring the messiah or gain the total obedience promised in Deut 30 is therefore rendered senseless.[90] Moreover, inasmuch as Paul has declared that the "justness of God" manifest in the death and resurrection of Jesus is "witnessed by the Torah and the Prophets" (Rom 3:21), by reading Deut 30:12-14 as a reference to the messiah's death and resurrection, Paul has found in the Torah exactly such a witness.[91] Paul's interpretation of these

---

[86] This is the position of M. Jack Suggs, "The Word Is Near You" (1967) and is accepted at least as part of the picture by Dunn, *Romans*, 614; Seyoon Kim, *The Origin of Paul's Gospel* (1981), 130-31; Hays, *Echoes*, 78-81.

[87] Targum Neofiti and the Fragmentary Targum further witness to this interpretation in their renderings of Deut 30:12, which explicitly refer to Moses' action of ascending to heaven to "take it for us" (Tg. Neo.) or "to bring it to us" (Frg. Tg.).

[88] "The content of vv. 12-13 speaks as if the mediation of Moses either was no longer necessary in the present or else would not be necessary at some time in the future" (Coxhead, "Deuteronomy 30:11-14," 310).

[89] Cf. Acts 5:31: "This one God exalted to his right hand as leader and savior to give repentance to Israel and release from sins."

[90] See Wells, "The Vindication of Agents," 95-96.

[91] "Only by finding in the law a witness to God's raising of Jesus from the dead can Paul also claim that the law is a witness to the gospel he has articulated in Romans (beginning in 1:2-4)" (J. R. D. Kirk, *Unlocking Romans* [2008], 169).

verses therefore suggests that the messiah is the prophet like Moses that Israel must follow (Deut 18:15-22), and the proof of that authority is the resurrection – the very thing Paul cites in the next verse.

THE ONE WHO LIVES: MESSIAH AND THE JUSTNESS OF GOD

If Paul understands Deut 30:12-14 as speaking from the perspective of the new era of fidelity wrought by God's redemptive action through the messiah,[92] that accounts for why he cites these verses as a declaration of "the justness from fidelity" in contrast to the "justness from Torah" represented by Lev 18:5, which represents the age prior to the covenantal renewal and internal transformation of Deut 30:1-14.[93] Inasmuch as Messiah has already died once and for all (Rom 6:2-7), he and those unified in him by having received his spirit are no longer under the domain of sin and subject to death. Having brought "the present evil age" (Gal 1:4) to its end, Messiah has inaugurated a new era and domain of covenantal favor and fidelity over which he himself is Lord and into which the person joined to him also can participate with confident hope for fullness of life and freedom from sin and death.[94]

But there is also another reason for the contrast. Working outwards from verses 6 to 8, the juxtaposition of the promise of life to "the human who does these things" (Rom 10:5) and the confidence in verse 9 that Jesus did in fact rise from the grave has too often gone unnoticed, as these two elements stand on either side of the pesher-citation of Deut 30:12-14, which also explicitly refers to the resurrection. The relationship between these verses – the promise to the doer of Torah[95] and Jesus' resurrection from the dead – suggests that Paul reads Lev 18:5b as a messianic

---

[92] On Philo's use of Deut 30:11-14 in an eschatological framework, see Bekken, *The Word Is Near You*, 155, who further observes "against such a Jewish referential background, it becomes more intelligible why Paul could use Deut 30:12-14 within a literary context dealing with the 'Messianic' salvation" (155).

[93] Contra Dunn (*Romans*, 613), who argues that the contrast is "the law and commandment *understood in terms of works* (9:32) in terms of national righteousness (10:3)."

[94] See Kirk, *Unlocking Romans*, 115-16.

[95] It is well established that many Jewish readers in this period interpreted Lev 18:5 as a conditional promise of eternal life to anyone who properly "does these things" (e.g., Pss. Sol. 14:1-10; Bar 3-4; 2 Bar 41-51). See Preston M. Sprinkle, *Law and Life* (2008), 195; Simon J. Gathercole, "Torah, Life, and Salvation" (2004). Jesus himself seems to have shared this view given his answer to the question of how to obtain eternal life: "If you want to enter life, keep the commands" (Matt 19:16-17). The concept of "repentance to life"

prophecy in which "the human who does these things will live by them" refers to one person who will attain (eternal) life through properly fulfilling the requirements of the Torah.[96] That is, whereas verses 6–8 argue that Messiah has activated the promise of transformation in Deut 30:12–14, the preceding use of Lev 18:5 puts forward the *means* of that redemption: the obedient work and resurrection of the messiah.

Some have objected that a messianic reading of Rom 10:5 "completely misses the point ... [since] it would make Jesus an exemplar of Israel's nationalist righteousness – the very opposite of Paul's intention."[97] But this argument assumes its conclusion, namely that Paul's chief aim was to undermine "Israel's nationalist righteousness." But that is not in fact Paul's target. Instead, the question all along has been *how Israel will become righteous* in accordance with the promises of the scriptures, and Rom 10 is opposed not to "legalism" or "nationalist righteousness" but rather to the attempt to initiate Israel's restoration through "justness from Torah" (10:5). Against this idea, Paul asserts that Israel's messiah, whose justness was validated by the resurrection (Rom 10:5, 9), has the power to grant the moral transformation promised by the prophets to those who trust him (10:6–13).

The presence of the definite article (lacking in the LXX) in Paul's citations of Lev 18:5 is especially instructive, as it ensures that Lev 18:5 can be read as applying to a specific person rather than as a conditional statement applying to everyone. Such a reading corresponds well with Paul's "penchant for describing Christ with articular substantives,"[98] not to mention his insistence in Gal 3:16 that the promise made to Abraham and his (singular) seed refers to the messiah destined to be Abraham's heir.[99] It should also be noted that, in contrast to the Greek version, the

---

granted to both Jews and gentiles in Acts 11:18 suggests the same idea, with spirit-enabled repentance resulting in the eternal life granted to the obedient.

[96] See Cranfield, *Romans*, 521–22; Stowers, *A Rereading of Romans*, 308–9; Markus Barth, *The People of God* (1983), 39; Andrew J. Bandstra, *The Law and the Elements of the World* (1964), 103–5; Campbell, "Christ the End of the Law," 77–78.

[97] Dunn, *Romans*, 601; followed by Jewett, *Romans*, 624–25.

[98] See the discussion in Jipp, *Christ Is King*, 255. In addition to the examples noted by Jipp, Paul also interprets "the one who arises" (ὁ ἀνιστάμενος) in Rom 15:12 (from Isa 11:10) christologically. Kirk, *Unlocking Romans*, 113–16, has also argued that "the human who has died" in Rom 6:7 also refers specifically to the messiah, in whose death others participate by the spirit. Kirk's reading is strengthened by Rom 8:34, which explicitly says, "Messiah Jesus is the one who died (ὁ ἀποθανών)."

[99] See Richard B. Hays, "'The Righteous One' as Eschatological Deliverer" (1989), 210–11; *The Faith of Jesus Christ* (2002), 136–37; Max Wilcox, "The Promise of the 'Seed' in the

Table 6.1 *Leviticus 18:5b and Paul's citations*

Rom 10:5	ὁ ποιήσας αὐτὰ ἄνθρωπος ζήσεται ἐν αὐτοῖς	the human who does these things will live by them
Gal 3:12	ὁ ποιήσας αὐτὰ ζήσεται ἐν αὐτοῖς	the one who does these things will live by them
Lev 18:5 LXX	ἃ ποιήσας ἄνθρωπος ζήσεται ἐν αὐτοῖς	which by doing a human will live by them
Lev 18:5 MT	יעשה אתם האדם וחי בהם	the human [*adam*] will do them and will live by them

Hebrew of Lev 18:5b lends itself remarkably well to a messianic reading due to its lack of a clear conditional marker ("if"/אם), which allows it to be read not as a conditional blessing of anyone observing Torah but rather as a prophecy about and promise to a future individual: "the human [*adam*] will do them and will live by them (see Table 6.1)."[100] This absence of a conditional marker is further emphasized by the striking transition from the second person plural addressed to Israel in Lev 18:2–5a to the third person singular in 5b.[101]

Reading Rom 10:5 as referring to the messiah also makes sense of its relationship to the prior verse, which declares that "Messiah is the *telos* of Torah." In this context, 10:5–9 explains what Paul means by "*telos* of Torah," namely that the Torah itself points to the messiah as the agent of God's justness, to whom and through whom the life promised in the Torah is granted. Taken together, the basic argument is therefore that Torah is not an end in itself (cf. 9:31, 10:3); instead, the Torah points

---

New Testament and the Targumim" (1979); Nils A. Dahl, *Studies in Paul* (2002), 130 n. 12. Paul seems to have read this promise to Abraham's seed together with the promise to David that "I will raise up (ἀναστήσω) your seed," understood as a reference to the resurrection of the Davidic messiah, who is also Abraham's seed and heir. See Dennis C. Duling, "The Promises to David and their Entrance into Christianity" (1973), 73; Matthew Thiessen, *Paul and the Gentile Problem* (2016), 124–25; Novenson, *Christ Among the Messiahs*, 141–42. Cf. also b. Sanh. 98b, which records an analogous tradition that the world was created solely for the messiah (or David or Moses).

[100] Most translations – both modern and ancient – render Lev 18:5b as a conditional blessing, which is the most natural reading in context, but the grammar does not require it. In any case, Paul's version in Rom 10:5 is closer to the Hebrew than the LXX, suggesting that he either knew the Hebrew version or was working from a different, Hebraizing version of the Greek.

[101] As noted by Sprinkle, *Law and Life*, 28. Cf. also the discussion in Klaus Grünwaldt, *Das Heiligkeitsgesetz Leviticus 17–26* (2014), 35.

beyond itself to the redemption and justness wrought by Messiah, through whom the purposes of Torah are fully realized.[102]

Here it is helpful to recall that the final verses of Deuteronomy – the literal end of the Torah – narrate the passing of authority to Joshua (LXX: Jesus) and the *telos* of Moses (LXX 34:7) before concluding with the statement that "since that time, no prophet has risen in Israel like Moses" (34:10). The Torah therefore ends by pointing back to the unfulfilled promise (and attached command) of Deut 18 that "YHWH your God will raise up for you a prophet like me from your brothers: to him you shall listen" (18:15). Notably, these passages do not merely promise the emergence of this prophet but that he will "rise" (ἀνίστημι), the most common word for resurrection in the New Testament.[103] The resurrection is therefore the proof that Jesus is "the prophet like Moses" and "the human who [did] these things," having therefore received the power over the ultimate curse of the Torah: death. As such, Jesus now has the authority to grant the justness, restoration, and life promised in Deut 30, bringing about the transition to the age of fidelity and favor promised in the Torah.[104]

This reading brings Rom 10 into striking correspondence with the arguments earlier in the letter about Jesus' redemptive obedience and its justifying consequences. Specifically, the reference to a particular human (ὁ ἄνθρωπος) who "does these things" in Rom 10:5 hearkens back to Rom 5:15–21, which tells of "the one human (τοῦ ἑνὸς ἀνθρώπου) Jesus Messiah" (5:15) and his "one act of justice (ἑνὸς δικαιώματος) for the justification of life for all humans" (5:18).[105] The same logic also appears in Rom 3, which explains that "now apart from Torah the justness of God has been revealed ... the justness of God through the fidelity of Jesus Messiah" (3:21–22). The parallels between Rom 3 and 10 are striking, especially since the phrase "the justness of God" (δικαιοσύνη θεοῦ), so

---

[102] See Kirk, *Unlocking Romans*, 168.

[103] This passage – and the language of the prophet "rising" – is explicitly connected with Jesus and the resurrection in Acts 3:22–26 (note also the summary in 4:2) and echoed again in Acts 7:37. Other examples of ἀνίστημι/ἀνάστασις as denoting the resurrection include 1 Thess 4:14, 16; Mark 8:31; 9:9–10, 31; 10:34; 12:23–25; Luke 24:46; John 6:39–40, 44, 54; 11:23–24; 20:9; Acts 2:24, 32; 13:33–34; 17:3, 31. Cf. also Mark 5:42; 9:27; Heb 7:15.

[104] "Verse 5 describes the Messiah's faithfulness, and 6 extends the discourse by personifying the righteousness that results from the Messiah's faithfulness" (Stowers, *A Rereading of Romans*, 309–10).

[105] "Paul retains *anthrōpos* in 10:5 as he does not in his use of the quotation in Gal 3:12, because he wants to point to the messianic obedience of the one man" (Stowers, *A Rereading of Romans*, 308).

Table 6.2 *God's justness, the Messiah, and fidelity*

Rom 3:22	δικαιοσύνη δὲ θεοῦ διὰ πίστεως Ἰησοῦ Χριστοῦ εἰς πάντας τοὺς πιστεύοντας	the <u>justness</u> of God through Jesus <u>Messiah</u>'s fidelity <u>for all who trust</u>
Rom 10:4	τέλος γὰρ νόμου Χριστὸς εἰς δικαιοσύνην παντὶ τῷ πιστεύοντι	for Messiah is the *telos* of Torah for justness to all who trust

prominent at the beginning of the letter, does not appear after Rom 3 until 10:3, where Paul again explicitly identifies the "justness of God" with the Messiah whose purpose is "justness for all who trust" (10:4). The themes and vocabulary of the passages are strikingly similar, as can be seen through a comparison of Rom 10:4 and Rom 3:22 (see Table 6.2).

The explicit argument of Rom 3 is that Messiah's faithful fulfillment of the Torah's requirements – culminating in the crucifixion – has secured justness for those who share his fidelity. That is, "Messiah Jesus ... was displayed publicly ... for the demonstration of his [God's] justness at the present time, so that he would be just and the justifier of the one who is of the fidelity of Jesus" (3:24–26). Similarly, in Rom 10, the "justness of God" is revealed in the messiah, who by fulfilling Lev 18:5 has received life and granted fidelity to those who trust in him. The logic of all three passages is the same: the messiah's complete justness and obedience to the requirements of Torah has facilitated the justification of those previously under the Torah's curse.

DIVINE DEADLIFTING: THE RESURRECTION OF THE JUST ONE[106]

This reading of Rom 10:5 also accords with Paul's treatment of the resurrection as proof of God's justness and Jesus' messianic identity at the very beginning of the letter, where he says that Jesus "was declared the son of God in power corresponding to a spirit of sanctity by the resurrection from the dead" (1:4), a development "promised beforehand through his prophets in the sacred writings" (1:2).[107] A few verses later, Paul gives an example of one of these prophetic promises, declaring that in his gospel,

---

[106] The language of divine deadlifting is pilfered from Paul Sloan, https://bit.ly/deadliftingsloan.

[107] See Stephen L. Young, "Paul's Christological Use of Hab. 2.4 in Rom. 1.17" (2012), 279–82; Kirk, *Unlocking Romans*, 39–49; Jipp, *Christ Is King*, 248–49.

"the justness of God is revealed" in keeping with Hab 2:4, "the just one from fidelity will live."[108] In isolation, one might doubt that this citation of Habakkuk should be understood as referring specifically to Jesus and the resurrection, but in addition to the instances later in Romans in which the revelation of the "justness of God" is identified with the crucifixion and resurrection of Jesus, there is strong evidence from other contemporary sources that "the just one" (ὁ δίκαιος) should be understood here as technical terminology designating a messianic figure.[109]

In the Similitudes of Enoch (1 En 37–71), for example, "the just one" is one of the primary titles for the messianic deliverer also called "the elect one" (e.g., 53:6, "the just and elect one") and the "son of man" (e.g., 46:3, "son of man, to whom belongs justness and with whom justness dwells"; cf. 48:2; 62:5).[110] The appearance of this "elect one of justness and faith" (39:6) will result in the vindication of the just, the destruction of the unjust, and the establishment of justness for all those who are just (39:6; 38:1–6; 53:1–6). As such, "the just one" of the Similitudes is, as Joshua Jipp explains, "quite simply, the mediator and agent through whom God executes justice"[111] – a role that accords closely with what Paul assigns to Jesus throughout Romans.

---

[108] My translation renders the prepositional phrase as modifying the verb, in keeping with the arguments of D. Moody Smith, "Ο ΔΕ ΔΙΚΑΙΟΣ ΕΚ ΠΙΣΤΕΩΣ ΖΗΣΕΤΑΙ" (1967). Although the prepositional phrase could modify the noun, resulting in "the just one from fidelity [is the one who] will live," in that case one would expect the prepositional phrase between the article and the noun rather than following the noun. Either way, J. Louis Martyn observes on the basis of Gal 3:21 "that the two readings would mean the same thing to Paul, for in that verse he equates rectification with making alive" (cf. also Rom 4:17) (*Galatians* [1997], 314). Paul's citation also differs from both the LXX and the MT. The Hebrew includes the third-person pronoun: "the just one will live by his fidelity," leaving some ambiguity about whether the fidelity is God's or the just one's. Most LXX MSS distinctly choose the divine option, rendering the pronoun "his" with "my" (perhaps the result of orthography, as י and ו are difficult to distinguish in some scribal hands), resulting in "the just one will live by my fidelity." In keeping with his penchant for ambiguity, grammatical constructions that allow words or phrases to do double duty (e.g., Rom 2:14, 28), and "both-and" arguments, Paul's version here and in Gal 3:11 splits the difference, removing the pronoun entirely and resulting in a version at least as ambiguous as the MT. See Hays, *Faith of Jesus Christ*, 133–34, 138–41.

[109] See Jipp, *Christ Is King*, 256–57; Hays, "Eschatological Deliverer," 193–206; and the extensive study of the history of interpretation of Hab 2:3–4 in August Strobel, *Untersuchungen zum eschatologischen Verzögerungsproblem* (1961). Compare b. B. Bat. 75b, "Said R. Samuel bar Nahmani said R. Yohanan: 'There are three called by the name of the Sacred One, blessed be he: the just ones, the messiah, and Jerusalem.'"

[110] See Hays, "Eschatological Deliverer," 193–94; Jipp, *Christ Is King*, 256.

[111] Jipp, *Christ Is King*, 256; cf. See Hays, "Eschatological Deliverer," 194.

Divine Deadlifting 249

Within the New Testament, Acts explicitly refers to Jesus as "the just one" in three separate passages, two of which deserve special attention here.[112] The first instance is in Peter's speech, in which he declares, "But you denied the sacred and just one (τὸν ἅγιον καὶ δίκαιον) ... and killed the ruler of life, whom God raised from the dead" (3:14-15). The parallels to Paul's use of Hab 2:4 are striking here, as both passages associate "the just one" with life – and that specifically understood as referring to the resurrection. The second instance comes in Stephen's speech before the Sanhedrin:

> You stiff-necked people, uncircumcised in heart and ears always resist the sacred spirit – you are just like your ancestors. Which one of the prophets did your ancestors not persecute? They killed those who announced beforehand the coming of the just one, and you have now become his murderers and betrayers – you who received the Torah as decrees through angels and did not keep it. (Acts 7:51-53)

The connections between this passage in Acts and Paul's arguments in both Romans and Galatians are striking, though this is not the place for a fuller exploration of those parallels.[113] More significant is that the reference to the "coming" (ἔλευσις) of the "just one" suggests a reading of Hab 2:3-4 as a messianic prophecy.[114] These verses in Habakkuk are easily read this way, since God responds to the prophet's complaint about divine silence "when the wicked swallow up those more just than they" (Hab 1:13)[115] with the promise of a future deliverer:

> For the vision is still for the appointed time: he groans (פוח; LXX: ἀνατελεῖ) toward the goal and will not fail. If he delays, wait for him! For he will certainly come and not be late. If it is puffed up,[116] his breath is not upright in him. But the just one by his fidelity will live. (Hab 2:3-4)

---

[112] The third is in Acts 22:14, where Paul recounts Ananias' words, "The God of our fathers appointed you to know his will, to see the just one, and to hear a voice from his mouth." Hays, "Eschatological Deliverer," 198-206, also discusses 1 Pet 3:18; 4:18; Jas 5:6; 1 John 2:1b; 2:29; 3:7b; and Heb 10:35-39, concluding that "there was an early convention of applying the epithet *ho dikaios* to Jesus" (205).

[113] See further Hays, "Eschatological Deliverer," 196.

[114] Hays, "Eschatological Deliverer," 195. Cf. also Radu Gheorghita, *The Role of the Septuagint in Hebrews: An Investigation of Its Influence with Special Consideration to the Use of Hab 2:3-4 in Heb 10:37-38* (2003), 214; Christian Rose, *Die Wolke der Zeugen: Eine exegetisch-traditionsgeschichtliche Untersuchung zu Hebräer 10,32-12,3* (1994), 53; Strobel, *Verzögerungsproblem*, esp. 47-56; Dietrich-Alex Koch, "Der Text von Hab 2.4b in der Septuaginta und im Neuen Testament" (1985), 73 n. 25.

[115] "The verse from Habakkuk had had a rich history prior to Paul's quoting it. Originally, it was a salvation oracle (a vision of the way things will in fact be) in which God makes an indelible promise" (Martyn, *Galatians*, 312).

[116] The Hebrew syntax is difficult. I am translating הנה as a conditional (roughly equivalent to הן) and עפלה as referring to נפשו (his soul/breath) in the next clause. See Wolfgang

The ease with which this passage lends itself to a messianic reading has often been obscured because most modern interpreters have understood the implied subject of the verbs in verse 3 to be the "vision" mentioned in the first line.[117] But this reading makes little sense; the prophet has just been given the vision (Hab 2:2) – how then can he be told to wait for what he has already received and written down?[118] The Greek translator of the passage certainly did not read the verbs of verse 3 as referring to the vision, as demonstrated by the fact that whereas the Greek for "vision" (ὅρασις) is feminine, the pronoun in 3b is masculine: "wait for him!"[119] Consequently, one natural reading that seems to have gained significant currency by the first century – certainly among followers of Jesus – is to identify the one who was to come (cf. Luke 7:19) with the "just one" mentioned in the next verse, who by fidelity would set things right and live.

Acts also gives strong evidence that this promise of life was understood in an eschatological sense as referring to the resurrection. Not only does Acts explicitly identify Jesus as "the just one," it also points to the resurrection as the proof of Jesus' status as God's "sacred one" (Acts 2:27; Ps 16:10), for whom "it was impossible to be held in [death's] power" (2:24). Like Paul, Acts here interprets the promise of life in Ps 16:11 to a singular figure – in this case "your sacred one" (τὸν ὅσιόν σου) – as a messianic prophecy realized in the resurrection of Jesus, confirming Jesus' status as that messianic deliverer. Later, Acts has Paul make a similar appeal to the resurrection as the proof of Jesus' status, declaring that God "will judge the world in justness through a man whom he has appointed, having provided proof by raising him from the dead" (17:31). Moreover, having been resurrected, Jesus "is the one whom God exalted to his right hand as a ruler and savior to grant repentance to Israel and forgiveness of sins" (Acts 5:31) – precisely the function of Messiah as the

---

Kraus, "Hab 2:3–4 in the Hebrew Tradition and in the Septuagint, with its Reception in the New Testament" (2009), 105–6. The LXX has ἐὰν ὑποστείληται (if it shrinks back).

[117] E.g., Ralph Lee Smith, *Micah–Malachi* (1984), 104–8.

[118] As pointed out by Francis Andersen, *Habakkuk* (2001), 205, who also observes that a vision also does not "hurry," "delay," "come," or "be late." The messianic interpretation of Hab 2:3–4 therefore need not "have arisen in communities that read the prophecy in the LXX translation rather than in the Hebrew" (Hays, "Eschatological Deliverer," 205).

[119] It is also possible to read "end" (קץ) or "appointed time" (καιρός) as the subject of the verbs in v. 3 in the MT and LXX, respectively. See Kraus, "Hab 2:3–4," 103–4, 107–9. Nevertheless, that possibility does not preclude a messianic reading, which is evident in the quotation of Hab 2:3–4 in Heb 10:37–38 (Kraus, "Hab 2:3–4," 113–16).

revelation of the "justness of God" in Rom 3:21–26, 5:15–21, and 10:1–13. These elements of obedience/justness and consequent resurrection/exaltation are put together even more plainly in Phil 2:8–9, where Jesus "humbled himself, becoming obedient to the point of death – death on a cross. And for this reason God highly exalted him and gave him the name above every name" – the very thing Paul expects his audience to confess in Rom 10:9, "Jesus is Lord."

In light of this evidence and the relationship between the quotation in Rom 1:17 and the preceding verses, the most reasonable conclusion is that Paul understands Jesus' resurrection as the fulfillment of Habakkuk's prophetic promise of resurrection to "the just one."[120] The opening of the letter therefore establishes that in Paul's gospel, the "justness of God" (δικαιοσύνη θεοῦ, 1:17) is revealed through the resurrection of God's son, Jesus (Israel's) Messiah, who has been made "Lord" and to whom all the nations owe their obedience (1:4–5).[121] In this context, the resurrection serves as the confirmation that Jesus is in fact the deliverer of Habakkuk's vision, having come as promised to rectify the injustice about which the prophet was complaining.[122] Once again, Paul's use of scripture is not haphazard but rather reflects deep engagement with the context of the passage – interpreted through distinctly messianic lenses – while presenting his gospel as the fulfillment of the promises to Israel found in his scriptures.[123]

That Paul read the promise of life to "the just one" in Hab 2:4 as a promise of resurrection to the messiah further informs his reading of Lev 18:5b, which contains the same promise of life, this time to "the human who does these things." Whereas Habakkuk provides evidence that the resurrection was "promised beforehand through his prophets" (Rom 1:2), Leviticus serves as the witness from the Torah (cf. Rom 3:21), with both prophecies about one individual who is truly faithful and just and

---

[120] See Young, "Paul's Christological Use," 279–82; Kirk, *Unlocking Romans*, 39–49; Jipp, *Christ Is King*, 248–49. Others taking this view include Anthony T. Hanson, *Studies in Paul's Technique and Theology* (1974), 39–45; Douglas A. Campbell, "Romans 1:17 – A Crux Interpretum for the πίστις Χριστοῦ Debate" (1994); Stowers, *A Rereading of Romans*, 198–202; Desta Heliso, *Pistis and the Righteous One* (2007).
[121] See Jipp, *Christ Is King*, 249; Mark A. Seifrid, "Unrighteous by Faith" (2004), 111.
[122] "Christ is depicted as the righteousness of God, because he was vindicated as *righteous* through his resurrection" (Heliso, *Pistis and the Righteous One*, 101, emphasis original).
[123] Once one realizes "that Paul is setting out in Romans to address the question of God's faithfulness to the covenant with Israel, the aptness of the quotation from Habakkuk immediately stands forth" (Hays, "Eschatological Deliverer," 207).

consequently "will live."[124] The fulfillment of these promises is the ultimate manifestation and revelation of the "justness of God" (Rom 10:3), the *telos* of Torah (10:4), and the beginning of a new era of fidelity (10:6–8) in keeping with the "spirit of sanctity" (1:4), since "if the spirit of him who raised Jesus from the dead dwells in you, the one who raised Messiah from the dead will also make your mortal bodies live through his spirit dwelling in you" (8:11).[125]

THE JUST ONE AND REDEMPTION FROM THE CURSE OF THE TORAH

One significant objection to reading Rom 10:5 as a messianic reference is that such a reading allegedly would, as Moo explains, "put Paul's application of Lev. 18:5 here in conflict with his application of the same text in Gal. 3:12. And while not impossible, a difference between the two would be unlikely because the texts have a great deal in common."[126] Both passages do have much in common, and Paul's application of Lev 18:5 does not conflict with his application of the same in Gal 3:12 – not because neither refers to Messiah's fulfillment of Torah but rather because both do. Indeed, although not widely recognized, Gal 3 is governed by the same logic observed in Rom 1, 3, 5, and 10, specifically that the messiah's obedient justness, death, and resurrection have provided justification for those previously under the Torah's curse. This is the context in which Paul cites both Hab 2:4 and Lev 18:5 together to explain how Messiah has brought the curse of the Torah to an end and inaugurated a new era of fidelity:

For whoever are from works of Torah are under a curse, for it is written: "Cursed is everyone who does not abide by all the things written in the book of the Torah to do them." That by Torah no one is justified before God is evident, because "the just one will live from fidelity."[127] The Torah, on the other hand, is not from

---

[124] Agreeing with Stowers, *A Rereading of Romans*, 308.
[125] "God's righteousness (10:1) is not based on law (10:3) but on that to which the law points (10:4): the coming and resurrection of Christ (10:6–7)" (Kirk, *Unlocking Romans*, 167–68).
[126] Moo, *Romans*, 647. It is well established that Gal 3:11–12 and Rom 1:16–17 and 10:1–8 "move in the same orbit of thinking" (647 n. 9; cf. Hays, "Eschatological Deliverer," 206–11; and Strobel, *Verzögerungsproblem*, 190–92).
[127] Andrew Wakefield, *Where to Live* (2003), 162–67, punctuates v. 11 differently, resulting in: "Because by Torah no one will be justified before God, it is evident that …" If one prefers Wakefield's punctuation of 3:11, the δέ of 3:12 would just as

fidelity, yet "he who does these things will live by them." Messiah redeemed us from the curse of the Torah, having become a curse for us, for it is written: "Cursed is everyone who hangs on a tree," so that the blessing of Abraham would come to the nations in Messiah Jesus, so that we would receive the promise of the spirit through fidelity. (Gal 3:10–14)

The logic of this passage is extremely compressed, as Paul assumes his audience is familiar enough with his gospel and his reading of these passages to be able to follow his argument without substantial clarification.[128] That is, Richard Hays explains, "Rather than having to explain the meaning of the quotation, Paul can use it to argue a point ... he appears to be citing a famous text that serves at once as rubric and clincher of his argument."[129] This is little help to Paul's modern interpreters, however, who do not enjoy such familiarity with the apostle's preaching.

Like Rom 10, this passage is often read as though Paul cites Leviticus only to invalidate it with an opposing citation about faith/fidelity, thereby contrasting "two mutually exclusive principles" of faith and law.[130] J. Christiaan Beker, for example, explains, "In a daring move, Paul opposes Scripture to Scripture (cf. Rom. 10:5–9) and thus splits Scripture apart, because Lev. 18:5 is antithetical to God's will in Christ. The law then seems indeed an antidivine agency."[131] J. Louis Martyn goes even further, declaring that Paul cites Hab 2:4 "to disqualify the Law before he quotes from the Law," revealing that "the Law speaks a false promise"[132] because "God had no role of any kind in the genesis of the Law,"[133] though "God was able to use to his purposes *even* the Law in whose genesis he played no role."[134] The point, Martyn concludes, is to

---

easily be rendered "and," still setting up the contrast between the life granted to the doer of Torah and the statement that the Torah is not from fidelity.

[128] See Strobel, *Verzögerungsproblem*, 191; C. H. Dodd, *According to the Scriptures* (1965), 51.
[129] Hays, "Eschatological Deliverer," 211.
[130] Normand Bonneau, "The Logic of Paul's Argument on the Curse of the Law in Galatians 3:10–14" (1997), 74. Similarly, Nils A. Dahl, "Contradictions in Scripture" (2002), 170: "The whole train of thought in Gal 3:1–12 rests on the presupposition that Hab. 2:4 and Lev. 18:5 contradict one another, and that the two corresponding principles 'by faith' and 'by (works of) the law' mutually exclude one another as qualifications for justification and life."
[131] J. Christiaan Beker, *Paul the Apostle* (1980), 54.
[132] Martyn, *Galatians*, 332; J. Louis Martyn, "The Textual Contradiction between Habakkuk 2:4 and Leviticus 18:5" (1997), 188.
[133] Martyn, *Galatians*, 366.   [134] Martyn, *Galatians*, 366.

emphasize "the gulf between the voice of the cursing Law and the voice of the blessing God."[135]

But Paul was not Marcion. The very idea that the Torah should be understood as "an antidivine agency" or that the voice of the Torah is contradictory to the voice of God would be anathema to the apostle who so strongly protested, "Do we then nullify Torah through fidelity? Absolutely not! Rather, we establish Torah" (Rom 3:31). It bears repeating that Paul did not preach a "law-free" gospel or denigrate the Torah but instead proclaimed a specific vision of the Torah's fulfillment through the outpouring of the spirit as part of the new covenant initiated through the work of Israel's messiah.[136] He remained committed to the truth of Torah and continued to build his arguments on the conviction that the Torah did *not* speak false promises but rather pointed to the messianic deliverer he proclaimed.[137]

Nevertheless, it is still necessary to explain how Paul's scriptural citations relate to his argument here, as many have concluded that his scriptural proofs "affirm the opposite of what he asserts,"[138] because they uphold rather than undermine the importance of doing Torah. The possibility that Paul understands himself as aiming to uphold rather than undermine the Torah has unfortunately rarely been given serious consideration. But once it is understood that Paul, working within a framework of new covenant restoration eschatology, reads both Hab 2:4 and Lev 18:5b as messianic prophecies fulfilled by Jesus' faithful obedience and consequent resurrection, the logic of Gal 3:10–14 is significantly clarified. The relationship between the argument and the scriptural quotations makes considerably more sense, and the argument as a whole is shown to cohere closely with what we have already observed in Romans.

---

[135] Martyn, *Galatians*, 333.   [136] See the discussion in Chapter 2, esp. pp. 84–91.

[137] Martyn, *Galatians*, 329, citing Quintilian, *Inst. Orat.* 7.7.2, rightly observes that, as a rule, when such seemingly contradictory passages from an authoritative body of literature (e.g., law or sacred writ) are cited in the context of debate, all parties "take for granted that the law (or scripture) cannot ultimately be in conflict with itself" and that such seemingly contradictory passages would be cited "to find a resolution that affirms both texts." The key to winning such a debate is "giving a new interpretation to [the] opponent's text, being thereby able not only to honor both texts as aspects of the invisible law but also to show that, correctly read, both texts support his own assertion." Remarkably, Martyn follows this insight with the startling declaration that it does not apply to Paul in this case, alleging that Paul no longer expected such consistency from the scriptures but instead rejected the Torah entirely as not originating from the true God.

[138] Jarvis J. Williams, *Galatians* (2020), 91.

THE LOGIC OF GALATIANS 3

First, by arguing that those "from works of Torah" are under a curse, Paul builds on the foundation of restoration eschatology established at the very beginning of Galatians, which proclaims that Jesus "gave himself for our sins so that he might rescue us from this present evil age" (1:4).[139] Because Israel itself is under the curse of the Torah, becoming part of Israel through works of Torah brings one under the very curse from which Israel itself needs redemption. To support his point, Paul cites the concluding curse from Deut 27, which unlike the other curses from that section of Deuteronomy, does not refer to specific actions but is instead comprehensive, explicitly cursing "everyone (πᾶς) who does not abide in *all the words of this Torah*" (27:26).[140] Moreover, this curse not only applies to the distinct individuals who break the Torah but also has corporate downstream effects, as Deut 28:58–59 declares, "if you do not follow all the words of this Torah written in this book ... the Lord will cause extraordinary plagues on you and on your seed." Specifically, he "will disperse you into all nations," where "you will be subject to other gods" (Deut 28:64; cf. Gal 4:3).[141] The curse is therefore laid not only on those who disobey but also on their descendants, who remain under that

---

[139] See pp. 101–6. Contra Timothy Gombis, "The 'Transgressor' and the 'Curse of the Law'" (2007), 84 n. 10, who argues that "there is nothing in the context of Galatians that points toward an exile/restoration dynamic," Paul's opening immediately puts that dynamic at the very center of the discussion.

[140] Gal 3:10 agrees with the LXX and Samaritan readings of Deut 27:26, which harmonize the language with 28:58, while the MT lacks "everyone" and "all." Unlike the MT, the LXX and Samaritan readings suggest that the Torah does in fact require perfect obedience. The objection that such a reading is impossible because the Torah itself provides the means of atonement for specific sins neglects to account for the problem of a broken covenant – once the covenant is broken, the curse impacts the whole people, and the efficacy of the means of atonement provided in the Torah are called into question, as is evident from the attitude of the Dead Sea Scrolls sect toward the Jerusalem temple. See pp. 231–32 and n. 97 on p. 132.

[141] "Israel's plight is that she is under, not foreign domination, but the law and the curse that this entails" (Donaldson, "The 'Curse of the Law,'" 102). Gombis' objection that Deut 27:26 "has to do with a curse on individuals who commit heinous sins, such that they are to be cut off from Israel" ("The Transgressor," 84 n. 10) overlooks the conflation with Deut 28:58 and its corporate application of the curse to the whole of the people culminating in exile, as illustrated in narrative form throughout the Former Prophets. Others who have recognized that Paul's citation of Deuteronomy here refers to the downstream and continuing effects of that curse on Israel include James M. Scott, "'For as Many as Are of Works of the Law Are under a Curse' (Galatians 3.10)" (1993); N. T. Wright, *The Climax of the Covenant* (1993), 141–47; Joel Willitts, "Context Matters: Paul's Use of Leviticus 18:5 in Galatians 3:12" (2003).

curse. That is, they remain under slavery (Gal 3:19–4:31) until the redemption promised in Deut 30:1–14, the very thing Paul proclaims has been wrought in and through Jesus' death and resurrection.

It bears repeating yet again that this understanding of Israel's plight under the curse of Torah was by no means unique to Paul among his contemporaries; indeed, this was a point on which Paul could presume agreement with his interlocutors. The point of disagreement between Paul and his opponents at Galatia was not Israel's covenantal status – all parties seem to have agreed on the basic framework of new covenant restoration eschatology and Israel's need for redemption and a new covenant. Nor was Jesus' role as messiah and redeemer of Israel in dispute; Paul's opponents also proclaimed Israel's redemption through Messiah Jesus. Instead, the dispute concerns the proper practices for those participating in Israel's redemption and what was necessary to be part of the renewed Israel of the new covenant. That gentiles could worship Israel's God and show honor to Israel's messiah was hardly in dispute – the Prophets were clear enough that the nations would also serve Israel's God after Israel's restoration.[142] But actual *membership in Israel* would surely require submission to Torah, especially since the capacity to fully obey God – the Torah written on the heart – is the central feature of the new covenant. It therefore stands to reason that uncircumcised men would need to be circumcised in order to become full members of Israel; after all, did not Gen 17:14 declare that the uncircumcised male has no part in the Abrahamic covenant?[143]

This is where Paul parts company with his opponents, arguing that those relying on "works of Torah" for their incorporation into Israel are not gaining justification but are instead being brought under the curse, no less dependent on the redemption provided by the messiah than before coming under the Torah since, as he argues in Romans, "both Jews and Greeks are completely under sin" (Rom 3:9). Underlying this premise is Paul's very next statement: "that by Torah no one is justified before God is evident" (Gal 3:11). Here again the problem is the paradox of

---

[142] E.g., Ps 18:43; Dan 7:14. Novenson highlights a set of prophetic "royal-ideology texts" focused on the eschatological expectation "of political and military rule of the scion of the house of David over the pagan nations" ("Jewish Messiahs," 366). Others have pointed to the prophetic expectation of an eschatological pilgrimage to Jerusalem to do homage to Israel's God. See esp. Terence L. Donaldson, "Proselytes or 'Righteous Gentiles'?" (1990); Fredriksen, "Judaism, the Circumcision of Gentiles, and Apocalyptic Hope" (1991); Sanders, *PLJP*, 171–206; and the discussion in Chapter 7.

[143] For more discussion on this point, see Chapter 8.

justification: a person cannot become just (δίκαιος) or vindicated before God "from (ἐκ) works of Torah" because only a just person will do the just things (δικαίωμα) required by the Torah (cf. Rom 2:26–29).[144] The justness the Torah requires must therefore come from a different source than the Torah itself. As proof, Paul cites Hab 2:4, "the just one from fidelity will live." Here the prophet explicitly identifies the source of the just one's justness and life: it comes not from the Torah itself but rather "from fidelity" (ἐκ πίστεως).

"On the other hand," Paul explains, "the Torah is not 'from fidelity'" (Gal 3:12) but was instead, as he clarifies a few verses later, the consequence of *infidelity*: "the Torah was added for (χάριν) transgression (παράβασις), having been arranged through angels by the hand of a mediator until the seed would come to whom the promise had been made" (3:19).[145] Contrary to the suggestion of some, this does not imply that God had no role in the giving of the Torah or that the Torah is antithetical to God's promises or the gospel itself.[146] Instead, as Paul argues in less compressed fashion elsewhere, the point is that a mediated Torah was given through Moses because the people were disobedient and hard-hearted (cf. 2 Cor 3) and rejected direct access to God in favor of a mediated, attenuated revelation of divine presence (cf. Exod 20:19).[147] The Torah is indeed from God and an extension of mercy toward his people, but that mercy establishes a measure of divine *distance* and, through the guidance provided by the pedagogy of the Torah, "a form of limited safety from the full brunt of sin's enslaving power for God's people, which differentiated them from the other nations (cf. Gal 2:15), and preserved them until the time of God's intervention."[148] The Torah does not justify the unjust – it cannot compel obedience – but rather reveals and condemns sin (cf. Rom 7:7–14), which under Torah becomes transgression, for "where there is no law/Torah, there is no transgression" (Rom 4:15; cf. 5:14).[149] The written Torah was therefore God's

---

[144] See pp. 176–77. In this respect, Gombis' observation that the twelve curses of Deut 27:15–26 are all upon "sins committed in secret, demonstrating a heart of treachery" ("The Transgressor," 91) further reinforces the focus on the need for heart transformation.

[145] See Robert A. Bryant, *The Risen Crucified Christ in Galatians* (2001), 176–77. This reading of ἐκ πίστεως in Gal 3:12 also sheds light on Rom 3:30, which distinguishes between the circumcised being justified ἐκ πίστεως (from fidelity) and the foreskinned διὰ τῆς πίστεως (through fidelity).

[146] As argued by Martyn, *Galatians*, 332, 366.   [147] See pp. 91–97.

[148] Christopher Zoccali, "What's the Problem with the Law?" (2015), 398.

[149] See pp. 85–91 and 175–79.

temporary response to the problem of infidelity that can only be resolved by a transformation of the people from a source beyond the "works of Torah." Whereas the Torah was arranged through angels, those who have the spirit "will judge angels" (1 Cor 6:3), having been transformed and elevated above the angels who oversee the fleshly domain.

In the absence of that pneumatic/spiritual transformation, the Torah's promise of life is inaccessible, because only "the just one" will do the just things the Torah requires. The problem is, as Paul says elsewhere, that "there is none who is just, not one person" (Rom 3:10b). Consequently, "the command which was for life, the same was for death" (Rom 7:10),[150] which is why "as many who are from works of Torah are under a curse" (Gal 3:10a). That is not to say that the Torah makes a false promise or is opposed to the gospel, a conclusion Paul explicitly repudiates a few verses later: "So then, is the Torah opposed to the promises? Absolutely not! For if a Torah had been given that could make alive, then justness would indeed have been from Torah" (Gal 3:21). Instead, "the scripture has imprisoned everyone under sin so that the promise from the fidelity of Jesus Messiah might be given to the faithful" (3:22). That is, all humanity is imprisoned under the sentence of death *except for "the just one,"* the "one to whom the promise had been made" (3:19).[151] That promise is exactly the one specified in both Hab 2:4 and Lev 18:5b: "He will live." The Torah's promise of life to "the one who does these things" therefore applies specifically to "the just one" who "from fidelity" accomplishes "these things."

RECONSIDERING A SO-CALLED ANTITHESIS

Unfortunately, the way the two citations work together has been widely missed because most interpreters have treated the quotation of Lev 18:5 as a proof text to demonstrate that "the Torah is not by faith" since "the law has to do with 'doing' and 'living by its prescriptions' and not with

---

[150] Lev 18:5 is similarly followed by a series of prohibitions and admonitions warning that anyone who does not "do these things" will be either subject to the death penalty (cf. 20:10–20) or extirpation and exclusion from the people Israel, effectively paralleling the warnings of "life and death" from Deut 30:15–20. For the meaning of the punishment of extirpation (כרת), see Jacob Milgrom, *Leviticus 1–16* (1991), 457–61; *Leviticus 17–22* (2000), 1733–34, 1767. For a study of expulsion from the community (in various forms) in the Torah, Dead Sea Scrolls, Rabbinic Judaism, and early Christianity, see Göran Forkman, *The Limits of the Religious Community* (1972).

[151] Agreeing here with Jipp, *Christ Is King*, 253–54.

Table 6.3 *Parallelism in Galatians 3:11–12*

Gal 3:11	ὅτι δὲ ἐν νόμῳ οὐδεὶς δικαιοῦται παρὰ τῷ θεῷ δῆλον	ὅτι	ὁ δίκαιος ἐκ πίστεως ζήσεται
	Postulate: "That by Torah no one will be justified before God is evident"	*Proof*: "because"	"The just one from fidelity will live."
Gal 3:12	ὁ δὲ νόμος οὐκ ἔστιν ἐκ πίστεως	ἀλλ'	ὁ ποιήσας αὐτὰ ζήσεται ἐν αὐτοῖς
	Postulate: "The Torah is not 'from fidelity'"	*Contrast*: "but/yet"	"The one who does these things will live by them"

faith."[152] But such a distinction between fidelity (πίστις) and obedience puts asunder what Paul joins together – the apostle explicitly states that his mission is to bring about "the obedience of fidelity" (Rom 1:5; cf. 15:18; 16:26), indicating that he understands fidelity as *defined* by obedience.[153] As Christopher Zoccali observes, "obedience to God's commands is not optional in Paul's thought any more than it is/was for other Jews, and remains equally critical to one's place among God's people in his gospel (cf. Gal 6:7–8)."[154] Moreover, despite the widespread assumption that Lev 18:5 serves as a proof text for the postulate that the Torah is "not by faith," the grammar of verse 12 does not allow for such a reading. If Lev 18:5 were cited as evidence that "the Torah is not from fidelity," one would expect it to be preceded by a proof statement like "because" (ὅτι) in parallel to the preceding verse.[155] Instead, the citation of Lev 18:5 is preceded not by ὅτι but by the strong adversative ἀλλά ("but"/"yet"; see Table 6.3) .

Rather than introducing a proof text that the Torah is not "from fidelity," the force of the adversative conjunction is to set the quotation

---

[152] Dunn, *Romans*, 120; cf. Martinus C. de Boer, *Galatians: A Commentary* (2011), 207–8; Donaldson, "The 'Curse of the Law,'" 103.
[153] Zoccali, "What's the Problem with the Law?," 380, points out that Paul "simply does not contrast an abstract, quasi-Platonic concept of 'believing' over against 'doing' (or, for that matter, 'being' in Christ over against 'doing'). Paul demonstrates no reservation in requiring from Messiah-followers strict obedience to God as inextricable from their salvation."
[154] Zoccali, "What's the Problem with the Law?," 81, continuing, "In short, perfect obedience is not an obstacle his gospel overcomes, but a goal that is thereby obtained."
[155] Regardless of which reading one chooses for verse 11, one ὅτι (whether the first or the second) still functions as a proof statement ("because"/"since"), the opposite of the adversative ἀλλά in verse 12. In neither case does the citation of Lev 18:5 serve as the proof of the statement in Gal 3:12a, nor is it cited as contradictory to Hab 2:4.

in contrast to the immediately preceding statement that the Torah did not arise out of fidelity. Nevertheless, seemingly under the influence of the ὅτι clause of the previous verse, most interpreters have read 3:12 as though it said ὅτι rather than ἀλλά, interpreting the two verses as contrasting statements supported by contrasting citations of scripture.

But Paul does not set Lev 18:5 against Hab 2:4. Instead, these verses contain not one but two contrasts. The first, weaker (δέ) contrast is between v. 11 and 12a, contrasting the origins of the justness implied in Hab 2:4 and the Torah itself: one is "from fidelity" and the other is "not from fidelity." The second, stronger (ἀλλά) contrast is between the two halves of verse 12, between the Torah not being "from fidelity" and the Torah's own promise of life to "the one who does these things." Structurally and grammatically, the promise of life is not cited as proof that the Torah is not "from fidelity" but rather as a promise that holds *despite* the Torah not being "from fidelity."[156] The two scriptural quotations are not opposed to one another but are instead parallel to one another, each held in contrast to the same statement sandwiched between them: that the Torah is not "from fidelity." That statement and the adversative conjunction ἀλλά serve as the center, the hinge point, of the passage:

Fidelity: "Abraham trusted God, and it was credited to him as justness." (3:6)
  Blessing: "In you all the nations will be blessed." (3:8–9)
    Curse: "Cursed is everyone ..." (3:10)
      Justification: "No one justified by Torah" (3:11a)
        Life: "The just one from fidelity will live" (3:11b)
          Torah/Infidelity: "The Torah is not from fidelity, but ..." (3:12a)
        Life: "He who does these things will live by them" (3:12b)
      Redemption: "Messiah redeemed us from the curse of the Torah" (3:13a)
    Curse: "Cursed is everyone who hangs on a tree" (3:13b)
  Blessing: "So that the blessing of Abraham would come to the nations" (3:14a)
Fidelity: "So that we would receive the promise of the spirit through fidelity." (3:14b)[157]

---

[156] *Pace* Wakefield, *Where to Live*, 159, who recognizes the possibility that the disjunctive ἀλλά "could function rhetorically to extend some point already made by adding contrast" but then concludes that "Lev 18:5 appears to be cited in order to counter any suggestion that law could be of faith," offering "deductive proof that 'the law is not of faith.'" Despite recognizing the significance of the ἀλλά, Wakefield still arrives at a meaning that reinforces rather than contrasts the immediately preceding statement, a reading that would better accord with ὅτι than ἀλλά.

[157] This chiasm is mostly derived from Wakefield, *Where to Live*, 136, though Wakefield does not observe that 3:12a sits at the center between the two scripture quotations about receiving life.

The point of verse 12 is that although the Torah did not arise from fidelity, it yet (ἀλλά) promises life to "the one who does these things" – that is, "the just one" already mentioned in the quotation of Hab 2:4 in the previous verse. The function of citing Hab 2:4 and Lev 18:5 together is therefore not that the fidelity spoken of by Habakkuk invalidates the Torah's promise of life to the doer, nor that, as some have suggested, Paul understands "doing" as incompatible with "faith."[158] Instead, as is also the case in Rom 10, the argument is about the *source* of justification and deliverance from the Torah's curse. Rather than citing Hab 2:4 and Lev 18:5 as a scriptural contradiction, Paul cites them as concurring witnesses to the messiah to whom life is promised. Together they provide the witness of the Torah and Prophets to the resurrection of "the just one," whose fidelity enabled him to "do these things" and receive (resurrection) life, resulting in the dispensation of the spirit to all of God's people.[159]

This identification of "the one who does these things" helps account for the juxtaposition between the quotation of Lev 18:5 and the work of "Messiah" in relation to the Torah in both Romans and Galatians. In Romans, the citation of Lev 18:5 is immediately preceded by the statement that "Messiah is the *telos* of Torah" (10:4). In Galatians, the citation – which again includes the definite article – is immediately followed by the declaration that "Messiah redeemed us from the curse of the Torah" (3:13). The asyndeton ensures special emphasis on the juxtaposition as the very next word after the quotation in Gal 3:12 identifies "the one who does these things" and therefore lives: "Messiah."

The logic here is that when "the just one" submitted to death and "became a curse for us," he effectively activated the escape clause for the Torah's curse. Because the Torah promises life to "the person who does these things," "it was impossible for him to be held in [death's] power" (Acts 2:24), resulting in the resurrection. And since "the one who has died

---

[158] E.g., Donaldson, "The 'Curse of the Law'," 103, "the problem ... is with the 'doing' itself: justification is based on faith, while law is based on the (presumably incompatible) principle of 'doing.'"

[159] By now many readers will have noticed the significance of this reading to the seemingly interminable debate about whether πίστις χριστοῦ (*pistis christou*) and analogous phrases should be understood as subjective ("fidelity of Messiah") or objective ("faith in Messiah"). In brief, "Messiah's fidelity" should be understood as applying *first* to Jesus' faithful obedience *and then* to those who receive his spirit and therefore share in his fidelity. That is, in fulfillment of the new covenant promise, the "Messiah-fidelity" dispensed via the spirit enables obedience for all "in Messiah." For more on the pistis Christou debate, see Matthew C. Easter, "The Pistis Christou Debate" (2010) and Kevin Grasso, "A Linguistic Analysis of πίστις χριστοῦ: The Case for the Third View" (2020).

is free from sin" (Rom 6:7) and "the Torah has jurisdiction over a person only as long as he lives" (7:1), the risen Messiah is no longer under the jurisdiction of Torah and its curse and has the authority to dispense "the promise of the Spirit through fidelity" (Gal 3:14).[160] That is, the Torah's curse is superseded by the life it promises to "the one who does these things." Consequently, "the just one," having become accursed, now has power over the Torah and its curse, and those having received the "spirit of fidelity" (2 Cor 4:13) from Messiah have therefore been rescued "from this present evil age" and brought into a new era of fidelity, as demonstrated by their obedience facilitated by the spirit.[161]

As a final reinforcement of the argumentative structure in Gal 3 and Rom 10, it is helpful to recognize that Paul's quotation not only recalls Lev 18:5b but also the citation of that promise in Neh 9:29 and the repeated quotations of Lev 18:5b in Ezekiel.[162] In the latter, God declares that Israel "did not walk in my statutes and did not keep my judgments (LXX: δικαίωμα), 'which the human will do them and he will live by them'" (20:21). Instead, they were "unfaithful"[163] (20:27) because "their eyes were on the idols of their fathers" (20:24)." Consequently, God "swore to them in the wilderness that I would scatter them among the nations and disperse (LXX: διασπείρω) them among the lands" (20:23) and "also gave them statutes that were not good and judgments by which they could not live" (20:25). That is, since Israel chose not to do the things that would lead to life, God gave them laws by which they *could not* live; here divine judgment involves handing the people over to their own desires in exactly the fashion outlined in Rom 1:18–32.[164] As the psalmist

---

[160] Contra Donaldson, "The 'Curse of the Law,'" 103, it is therefore not the case that "the apparently divergent arguments in vv. 10–12, however, may be nothing more than clever but transient debating points which have no real bearing on the place of the 'curse of the law' in Paul's thought. Perhaps in his view the law brings a curse only because the law is not Christ." On the contrary, these verses are foundational in establishing how Messiah fulfills the Torah and brings about justification for those under the curse.

[161] Being "in Messiah" through participation in the spirit is therefore the only way one can "do these things" (Gal 3:12; cf. "the things of Torah" Rom 2:14). See Zoccali, "What's the Problem with the Law?," 406–8.

[162] See Willitts, "Context Matters"; Rodrigo J. [Isaac] Morales, *The Spirit and the Restoration of Israel* (2010), 101–4.

[163] Translating MT: מעל; the LXX has παρέπεσον ("fell away").

[164] This view of divine judgment as giving people over to their own corrupt desires and actions is a prominent theme in Ezekiel. The people profane the temple, so YHWH does it all the more (Ezek 9:7). The people refuse to listen to the truth, so YHWH sends them false prophets (14:9). They insist on idolatry, so God releases them with the command, "Go, everyone serve his idols" (20:39). See Sprinkle, *Law and Life*, 35. Note also that

laments, "Israel did not obey me, so I gave them over to the stubbornness of their heart, to walk by their own counsels" (Ps 81:13 [ET 81:12]).[165]

Nevertheless, the end result after the people are scattered and have served idols among the nations will be a new exodus, including a new time in "the wilderness of the peoples" (Ezek 20:35; cf. 1QM 1:3), where God will judge them. He will force everyone to "pass under the rod," alluding to the tithing protocol in which every tenth animal is marked as sacred (Lev 27:32), and "will purge the rebels from you" but will bring the rest into a new covenant, restoring them from the nations (Ezek 20:37–44). The language of Ezek 20 is also closely linked with Ezek 36–37, which promises that God will finally cause Israel to "walk in my statutes and observe my judgments" (36:27) – the first time this phrase appears after Ezek 20 – and will establish a Davidic king who will enable them to do so (37:24).[166] The consequence of that will be that the "dry bones" of "the whole house of Israel" will indeed "live."[167] On the basis of Lev 18:5, Ezekiel therefore promises that God will ultimately take the initiative to ensure that Israel will indeed do his "statutes and judgments" and "live by them" through the "new heart and new spirit" (Ezek 36:27; 37:1–14).[168] The correspondences with Paul's use of Lev 18:5 in both Gal 3 and Rom 10 are immediately apparent. Paul believes that what Ezekiel

---

when Lev 18:5b is cited elsewhere in scripture, it is consistently in the context of Israel *not* doing the things that lead to the life promised by the Torah.

[165] This psalm is, of course, immediately followed by Ps 82, in which God declares, "I said, 'you are gods, and all of you are children of the Most High.' Nevertheless, you will die like Adam" (82:6–7). In several later rabbinic traditions (e.g., Mek. Bak. 9; b. Abod. Zar. 5a; Sifre Deut. 320; Lev. Rab. 11:3; Qoh. Rab 8:1.3; Pesiq. Rab. 14:10), this judgment is connected with the golden calf incident, at which point Israel – previously having gained the immortality of Adam at Sinai – lost that immortality because of their sin with the golden calf. This reading of the psalm (connecting Ps 81 and 82) also likely underlies Jesus' use of Ps 82 in John 10:34–35, in which he observes, "If he called those to whom the word of God came gods . . . ." See Jonathan A. Draper, "If Those to Whom the W/word of God Came Were Called Gods." (2015); Jerome H. Neyrey, "I Said: You Are Gods" (1989); James S. Ackerman, "The Rabbinic Interpretation of Psalm 82 and the Gospel of John" (1966). Adam and Israel are, of course, similarly correlated in Rom 5–7.

[166] On the Davidic king facilitating obedience in Ezekiel, see Thomas Renz, *The Rhetorical Function of the Book of Ezekiel* (1999), 115–16;

[167] Ezek 37:3–6, 9, 10–11, 14. See Sprinkle, *Law and Life*, 37–40.

[168] Contra Sprinkle, *Law and Life*, 40, Ezekiel's treatment is less a transition to divine agency from "what was previously conditioned upon human agency – '*if* the person does these things he will live by them'" than it is a reading of Lev 18:5 as an unconditional promise (again, there is no clear conditional marker in Lev 18:5) and then looking to how that promise will be fulfilled by the gift of a new heart and new spirit.

promised is being fulfilled as God's people receive the "promise of the spirit through fidelity" (Gal 3:14), enabling them to produce the "fruit of the spirit" (Gal 5:22) – that is, "to will and to work for [God's] good pleasure" (Phil 2:13).

Messiah as the End of the Torah

Romans 10 and Galatians 3 therefore mutually inform one another. Jesus' redeeming action of submitting to death on a cross and subsequent resurrection is the *telos* of Torah (cf. Deut 34:10),[169] and Jesus is the "prophet like Moses" anticipated and attested to by the Torah itself. Rather than Israel fulfilling Lev 18:5b to bring the messiah and redemption, the messiah fulfilled Lev 18:5b and now has the authority to justify Israel and extend the blessing of Abraham to the nations. Acting as though justification comes "from works of Torah" (Gal 3:10) effectively denies this redemption wrought by the messiah and mediated through the spirit in favor of "establishing their own justness" (Rom 10:3) under the jurisdiction of the Torah, effectively turning the calendar back to the age of wrath (cf. Gal 5:1–6).[170] Such efforts are, Paul argues, profoundly misguided, as justification and life cannot come through the Torah but only through the fidelity of the spirit of Messiah.[171] The question, as Paul asks the Galatians, is "did you receive the spirit from works of Torah or from hearing with fidelity?" (3:2). Israel's justification depends on the spirit, and the spirit comes from Israel's faithful messiah, not from "works of Torah."

Messiah is the one who has fulfilled "the whole Torah" (Gal 5:3), the one who "did these things and lives by them." And because the promise of Deut 30:1–10 has been "eschatologically realized in the Christ event,"[172] the promise of Deut 30:11–14 is now being fulfilled. The Torah has not

---

[169] See Gal 3:13–14, 21–29; cf. Rom 3–5.
[170] Cf. Hays, "Eschatological Deliverer," 210.
[171] For an analogous tradition in which the Davidic Messiah has the power to grant life, see b. Sukkah 52a, "To the messiah, son of David ... the Sacred One, blessed be he, will say, 'Ask something of me, and I will give it to you ....' When he sees the messiah, son of Joseph, killed, he will say, 'Lord of the age, I ask of you only life.' He will say to him, 'Life? Before you spoke of it, your father David had already prophesied about you, as it is said, "He asked life of you, you gave it to him" (Ps 21:5 [ET: 21:4]). The next line (unquoted) of that verse is, of course, "length of days forever and ever," identifying the promise of "life" to the Davidic Messiah as *eternal* life.
[172] Wells, "The Vindication of Agents," 95.

been abrogated but has rather reached its purpose, the total justification of the people, as promised in the Torah and Prophets alike. Those "in Messiah" are "God-taught" (1 Thess 4:9; cf. Jer 31:34), without need to ascend to heaven, descend to the abyss, or even depend on the written Torah itself to obey God fully. Having brought "the present evil age" (Gal 1:4) to its end, Messiah has inaugurated a new era and domain of fidelity over which he himself is Lord and into which the person pneumatically joined to him also can participate with confident hope for fullness of life and freedom from sin and death.[173] Through "Messiah's fidelity" (Gal 2:16), "fidelity has come" (3:25),[174] and "the word is near you, in your mouth and in your heart – that is, the word of fidelity that we are preaching" (Rom 10:8), with the spirit instilling Messiah's fidelity within all who pledge their fidelity to him and acknowledge him as Lord (Rom 10:9–13).

HE'S THE MESSIAH! PLEDGING FEALTY TO THE LIVING LORD

That pledge, Paul says, is the means of attaining salvation:

> If you pledge agreement[175] with your mouth: "Lord Jesus," and trust in your heart that God raised him from the dead, you will be saved. For with the heart one trusts for (εἰς) justness, and with the mouth one pledges agreement for (εἰς) salvation. For the scripture says, "Whoever trusts in him will not be put to shame." For there is no distinction between Jew and Greek, since the same one is Lord of all, rich towards all who call on him – for "everyone who calls on the name of the Lord will be saved." (Rom 10:9–13)

This pledge of allegiance to the dominion of Jesus is akin to the initiation oath in 1QS, in which the initiate commits to the authority of the Yaḥad, those who "together will circumcise the foreskin of this [lower] nature" (1QS 5:5):

> Whoever enters the council of the Yaḥad is to enter the covenant in full view of all who have decided freely (המתנדבים). He will swear with a binding oath to return to the Torah of Moses, according to all that he commanded, with whole heart and

---

[173] See Kirk, *Unlocking Romans*, 115–16.   [174] See Bryant, *Risen Crucified Christ*, 153.
[175] The usual English translation "confess" is misleading, as it tends to carry the connotation either of guilt (e.g., "confess his crimes") or concession (e.g., "he confessed that he might not know the answer"), while the Greek ὁμολογέω ("agree") in this kind of context tends to denote public acknowledgment (e.g., Luke 12:8; Acts 24:14) or a pledge of agreement or allegiance, as in the formula frequently encountered in the Greek papyri, ἐπερωτηθεὶς ὡμολόγησα ("I pledge agreement"). On this phrase, see Matthew R. Crawford, "Confessing God from a Good Conscience" (2016), esp. 25; Bo Reicke, *The Disobedient Spirits and Christian Baptism* (2005), 184.

self, in compliance with all that has been revealed of it to the sons of Zadok .... He will swear by the covenant to separate from all unjust men. (1QS 5:7-10)

Those who are thus initiated into the community become part of the covenant (cf. CD 6:19: 19:33; 20:12), gaining access to the "sacred spirit" (1QS 3:7; cf. CD 7:4), and have the Torah engraved on their hearts (1QH^a 12:11).[176] Lambert observes that this oath "marks a public embrace of sectarian identity, an official adoption of sectarian law .... Now the initiate can be expected to uphold the norms of his new group and can be punished accordingly."[177] The parallels to Rom 10:9–13 are inescapable, as Paul is likewise laying out the means of initiation into a "new covenant" community through which justification and salvation are facilitated by the spirit.

Paul's initiates, however, do not pledge themselves to "to return to the Torah of Moses" in compliance with Zadokite/sectarian interpretation but rather pledge fealty to Jesus as Lord in confidence that Jesus has been raised from the dead. But like the oath of 1QS, Paul is not suggesting that mere words or belief in the resurrection are all that is required for salvation. Instead, the reason belief in Jesus' resurrection is important is that the resurrection is the confirmation that Jesus is the divinely authenticated "just one" who has been "highly exalted and given the name above every name" (Phil 2:9) – that is, the covenantal name YHWH.[178] The resurrection is the proof of Jesus' authority and his capacity to justify and deliver those who submit themselves to him.[179] The confession that "Jesus is Lord" therefore serves as a public embrace of a new identity, an official acknowledgment of Jesus' authority and a commitment to submit to that authority – that is, to live according to Jesus' teachings as mediated via the spirit. Now the initiate into the messianic *ekklēsia* can be expected to uphold the norms of this new group and – as evident in 1 Cor 5 – may be punished accordingly.

In the process, Paul emphasizes that the same applies to both Jews and Greeks – *whoever* trusts in him and *everyone* who invokes the name will be saved. Paul's reading is similar to that of Philo in this respect, as Philo draws on Deut 30:11–14 to argue that those who obey from the heart are

---

[176] See further pp. 78–81 in Chapter 2.
[177] Lambert, *How Repentance Became Biblical*, 137.
[178] On κύριος ("Lord") as a circumlocution for YHWH among Greek-speaking Jews and early Christians in this period, see Jason A. Staples, "'Lord LORD': Jesus as YHWH in Matthew and Luke" (2018).
[179] Cf. Jewett, *Romans*, 630.

"those whose most sacred prayers God hears, and to whose invocations he gladly draws near" (*Praem.* 84).[180] It is therefore not the case, as some have argued, that Paul believes gentiles are saved through faith in Jesus while Jews are saved by virtue of their covenant membership.[181] Instead, from the very beginning of Romans, Paul has been arguing that because of Israel's covenantal disobedience, Jews are under the curse of the Torah and require the same redemption and justification needed by gentiles – justification and redemption provided to those who submit to Israel's messiah.

Lack of such submission is the very thing brought up at the beginning of Rom 10, which explains that, "not knowing the justness of God and seeking to establish[182] their own, they did not submit themselves to the justness of God" (10:3). Many have read this statement as referring to a general refusal of Jews to believe the gospel in favor of attempting to attain their own justness "by performing works of pious achievement."[183] Others have argued that the reference is to a general Jewish commitment to the Torah as granting "that righteousness which the Jews alone are privileged to obtain."[184] But it does not say, "they have not submitted"[185] or "are not submitting" but rather "they did not submit"

---

[180] Contra Bekken, *The Word Is Near You*, 154, Philo does not here "characterize the Jewish nation as the people which invokes God, unlike the other nations." In fact, Philo never refers to "Jews" or the "Jewish nation" at all in this tractate, and this passage refers to an idealized (post-restoration) context in which Israel – which includes proselytes who imitate Abraham's example but not the native-born who disobey and are cut off (*Praem.* 152, 172) – is obedient and its prayers are therefore answered.

[181] E.g., Mussner, "Christus [ist] des Gesetzes Ende," esp. 40–44; Gaston, *Paul and the Torah*, 33; Gager, *Reinventing Paul*, 60; Fisch, "Origins of Oral Torah," 52; Boccaccini, *Paul's Three Paths*.

[182] Jewett argues that the nuance of στῆσαι here is "make or consider valid" rather than 'establish,' which would falsely imply that Jewish believers had not already been granted a firm relationship within the covenant" (*Romans*, 617). But Paul's argument all along has been that the covenantal relationship is *not* firm in the absence of Messiah, and this verse refers not to "Jewish believers" but to those who "did not submit to God's justness." As such, "establish" is a better rendering that more adequately represents the situation Paul is addressing.

[183] The summary phrase of Bekken, *The Word Is Near You*, 164 n. 39, representing the views of Käsemann, *Romans*, 281; Cranfield, *Romans*, 515; etc.

[184] Sanders, *PLJP*, 38. Similarly, Howard, "Christ the End of the Law," 336; Räisänen, *Paul and the Law*, 174–77; Dunn, *Romans*, 595. Jewett further universalizes this into a principle in which "Christ countered the universal human tendency to validate the status of one's group.... By grace alone rather than by conformity to the ethos and laws of the group" (*Romans*, 618–19).

[185] As in the NRSV or as paraphrased by Moo, *Romans*, 633.

(ὑπετάγησαν).[186] As in Rom 9:30, the use of the aorist rather than a primary tense verb indicates that Paul is referring to a specific moment in the *past* in which "they" – that is, those in position to subject themselves to Jesus – did not do so.

Again it is imperative to remember that Rom 9–11 as a whole is not about the "problem of Jewish unbelief" or Jews' commitment to their own "collective righteousness, to the exclusion of Gentiles."[187] but rather aims to explain how, despite appearances, God has in fact remained faithful to his promises to Israel. The primary problem is not the unbelief of many Jews – surely no surprise to a sectarian restorationist like Paul. The problem is that the kingdom seems not to have been restored to Israel (cf. Acts 1:6). If Jesus is indeed Israel's messiah, why has Israel's restoration not happened? Where are the reunified tribes? Why does Jerusalem remain subject to a foreign empire rather than being crowned with glory and exalted above the nations, who should be doing obeisance to Zion and its king? The problem, Paul explains, is that when "the justness of God" came, they did not recognize nor did they submit to him, instead "seeking to establish their own justness" to initiate their own deliverance (Rom 10:3). That is, when Israel's messiah came, he was rejected by the authorities in Jerusalem,[188] resulting in God's rejection of those authorities and guaranteeing the impending destruction of Jerusalem (cf. 1 Thess 2:14–16).[189] Just as their ancestors had stumbled over the stumbling

---

[186] See Munck, *Christ and Israel* (1967), 79–84; Cranfield, *Romans*, 515; Frank Thielman, "Paul's View of Israel's Misstep in Rom 9.32–3" (2018). Moo objects, "The aorist is constantive, summing up the rejection of the gospel by many Jews since the cross and resurrection" (*Romans*, 643). But such a meaning would be better represented by the perfect than the aorist in this case, and understanding the aorist as a past fits better with 9:30 and the rhetoric of the passage as a whole.

[187] Howard, "Christ the End of the Law," 336.

[188] See Munck, *Christ and Israel*, 79–84 and Thielman, "Paul's View of Israel's Misstep".

[189] Agreeing here with Thielman, "Paul's View of Israel's Misstep," 371–77, this reading makes sense of the difficult passage in 1 Thess 2:14–16, often thought to be a post-Pauline interpolation (e.g., Birger A. Pearson, "1 Thessalonians 2:13–16: A Deutero-Pauline Interpolation" [1971]). But Paul's expectation of judgment on Jerusalem and its authorities coheres not only with Jesus' own prophecies against Jerusalem and its temple (e.g., Mark 13:2) but also Paul's understanding of the death and resurrection of Jesus and its consequences. It should be emphasized that the prepositional clause in 2:14–15 must be read as a restrictive rather than a descriptive clause, referring to "the Jews who killed Jesus and the prophets" – a specific subgroup of Jews – rather than "the Jews, who killed Jesus." As Thielman points out, "Everyone Paul refers to in this long sentence was Jewish, so it would be odd for Paul to say that 'the Jews' persecuted the churches in Judea and killed both Jesus and the Prophets" (371). For a fuller defense of this rendering, see Frank D. Gilliard, "The Problem of the Antisemitic Comma Between

stone in Isaiah's day (cf. Rom 9:33), they too refused to submit to the means of deliverance provided by God and will receive the same consequences as their ancestors.

But, Paul argues, God's plan for Israel will not be foiled, as the crucified and resurrected messiah is now justifying all who pledge fealty to him, and all Israel will indeed be saved (Rom 11:26) through the mysterious and surprising gospel Paul now proclaims. Here one is reminded of the saying attributed to the third-century Rabbi Joshua b. Levi, who said of the messiah that "if they have merit, [his coming] will be 'with the clouds of heaven' [Dan 7:13], but if they do not have merit, it will be 'lowly and riding upon an ass' [Zech 9:7]" (b. Sanh. 98a). Paul's argument is effectively that the latter has already happened, and that in the absence of merit, the messiah came to bring the merit that was lacking to those who trust in him and receive the spirit. Paul of course also expects Jesus to return "in the clouds" at a later time (cf. 1 Thess 4:17). Like the Yaḥad sectarians, John the Baptist, and Jesus himself, Paul therefore argues that God has rejected the authorities in Jerusalem and is restoring Israel without them and those who follow them rather than the messiah God has appointed. God is "raising up children for Abraham from these stones" (Matt 3:9 // Luke 3:8) replacing hearts of stone with the life-giving spirit of Israel's messiah, and now that justification has come, the final restoration is only a matter of time.

As such, Rom 10:1-13 epitomizes Paul's gospel: since Israel failed to keep Torah and rejected God's deliverance (Rom 10:1-3), Messiah Jesus fulfilled the Torah and was resurrected (10:4-5) and now has the power and authority to grant the fidelity and justness promised by the Torah itself (10:6-8) to those who acknowledge and submit to his authority (10:9-10), delivering them from the Torah's curse. Moreover, this deliverance is not only available to Jews but to gentiles also, since "the same one is Lord of all" (10:12) and the promises apply to "all" and "whomever" (10:11, 13). Just as in the biblical past, Israel's deliverance therefore once again depends on trusting the foundation stone placed in Zion rather than stumbling over it in the effort to accomplish that salvation. The "good news" is that the agent of justification and merit has come to bring about the justness upon which the fuller restoration of Israel is contingent.

---

1 Thessalonians 2.14 and 15" (1989). Jesus and Paul were by no means alone among their contemporaries in predicting the destruction of Jerusalem and the Herodian temple, as discussed in Craig A. Evans, "Predictions of the Destruction of the Herodian Temple in the Pseudepigrapha, Qumran Scrolls, and Related Texts" (1992).

Nevertheless, as in the past, "not all heeded the good news" (10:16),[190] but a portion remained "a disobedient and obstinate people" (Rom 10:21; Isa 65:2).[191] Israel's deliverance is therefore not only a matter of restoration but of pruning; "all Israel will be saved" (11:26), but in the process, God will do as he promised through the prophet Ezekiel: "I will purge from you the impious (LXX: ἀσεβεῖς) and those who rebel against me" (Ezek 20:38). This combined process of incorporating of the newly faithful and cutting off the impious and unfaithful in order to bring about the promised deliverance of the whole of Israel comes into focus as Paul brings his argument to its climax in the next chapter.

---

[190] The echo of the Shema's call to "hear/heed" (LXX: ἀκούω; Deut 6:4) is notable in Rom 10:16, as not all in fact "heeded" (ὑπακούω) or "trusted" (πιστεύω) "the heard thing" (τῇ ἀκοῇ).

[191] For more discussion of Rom 10:19–21 and the significance of the scriptural citations there, see J. Ross Wagner, *Heralds of the Good News* (2003), 187–213; Guy Prentiss Waters, *The End of Deuteronomy in the Epistles of Paul* (2006), 185–98.

7

The Mystery of Israel's Salvation

Who the "all Israel" are who will be saved, and what that fullness of the nations will be, only God knows, along with his only-begotten and perhaps any who are his friends.

Origen of Caesarea[1]

Romans 10 concludes with a citation of Isa 65:2 about Israel's chronic infidelity: "all day long I have held out my hands to a disobedient and obstinate people" (10:21), leading naturally to the incredulous question that opens the next chapter: "I say then, God did not reject his people, did he?" (11:1).[2] The answer is emphatic: "Of course not!" (μὴ γένοιτο!). The evidence of God's continued fidelity can be found in Paul himself: "I too am an Israelite from the seed of Abraham, of the tribe of Benjamin" (11:2).[3] Even in the days of historical Israel, he explains, only a remnant

---

[1] Origen, CER 4.304. See Caroline P. Hammond Bammel, ed., *Der Römerbriefkommentar des Origenes* (1998), 702: 68–70. If Origen is correct, the present discussion may result in attaining the status of *qui amici eius sunt*. For a look at the early interpretation of this passage, see Jeremy Cohen, "The Mystery of Israel's Salvation" (2005).

[2] Echoing 1 Sam 12:20–23; Ps 94:14 (93:14 LXX). See Richard B. Hays, *Echoes of Scripture in the Letters of Paul*, 69–70; Pablo T. Gadenz, *Called from the Jews and from the Gentiles* (2009), 227–30.

[3] Note again that Paul highlights his precise tribal lineage here, emphasizing Israel's larger, tribal nature. Cf. Scott W. Hahn, "All Israel Will Be Saved" (2015), 94. Paul's emphasis on this tribal distinction reinforces from the start that the "remnant" of which he speaks is not just "the Jewish believers in Christ" (as suggested by Shayna Sheinfeld, "Who Is the Righteous Remnant in Romans 9–11?" [2016], 44) but also includes a remnant from the rest of Israel. Given his past as an "Israelite" who violently opposed the gospel at first, Paul's example is especially relevant to the immediately preceding discussion of misplaced zeal (Robert Jewett, *Romans* [2006], 653).

was preserved (11:2–4), using the Elijah narrative to show that biblical Israel was profoundly divided between the idolatrous majority and the minority God reserved for himself (11:4).[4] He then explicitly brings these historical lessons into the present, declaring, "So also *in the same way in the present season*[5] there has come to be a remnant in keeping with a choice of grace" (11:5). That is, God has continued to deal with his people in the same manner displayed in all these past examples. Israel remains an incomplete, divided people, and although the unfaithful will again be cut off in the same way they were in the past, God will preserve Israel as a whole through the portion that remains – the "remnant."

Returning to the themes established in 9:30–33, he develops his argument that although not all of Israel has received the promise, it is not the case that all of Israel has failed or been cast off: "As for what Israel seeks,[6] this it did not obtain. The election obtained it, but the rest were made insensible (ἐπωρώθησαν)" (11:7). Here the typical rendering, "the rest were hardened," can cause confusion, suggesting a repetition of the "hardening" (σκληρύνω) motif in 9:18. But the two concepts are distinct; the hardening of Rom 9 represents a final hardening like clay in a kiln,[7] while the concept here (πωρόω) denotes something more like

---

[4] Hahn, "All Israel," 94–96, points out the connections between Elijah and Moses as intercessors for the people (cf. Rom 9:1–5). See also Gadenz, *Called*, 231–34; J. Ross Wagner, *Heralds of the Good News* (2003), 238.

[5] The eschatological nuance of the phrase ἐν τῷ νῦν καιρῷ is difficult to get across in English, as this phrasing suggests that the present is in fact a new era – probably best understood as the "age of the messiah" or "age of favor" that follows the "age of wrath." Other Pauline examples of this combination refer specifically to the eschatological age (Rom 3:26; 8:18; 2 Cor 6:2 [2×]).

[6] Stanley E. Porter *Verbal Aspect in the Greek of the New Testament* (1989), 197, argues that the present-tense ἐπιζητεῖ here is an example of a historical imperfective (though he then puzzlingly renders it with a perfective, "Israel sought"). The verb of the relative clause is dependent on the aorist verb of the subsequent main clause, suggesting a past orientation. Porter argues that in such cases the present form marks "a discourse unit selected for special significance, such as a climactic turning point" (196). Kenneth McKay, "Time and Aspect in New Testament Greek" (1992), 212, acknowledges that the verb could be read as a historical present but observes that a present sense cannot be ruled out, suggesting the verb is best rendered with "an all-embracing *has been seeking*" (his emphasis). Either way, the verb is imperfective, such that Israel's "seeking" is depicted as an incomplete process – that is, the promises to Israel remain unfulfilled. Scribal difficulties with the present form are attested by the alteration to the imperfect ἐπεζήτει in F G 104 1836 *pc* latt sy. The point is the same in either case and even strengthened in the variant – Israel did not obtain (perfective aspect) the promises that were/are being sought (imperfective aspect). For the relative ὅ as meaning "as to/for what," see Hubert Weir Smyth, *Greek Grammar* (1920), §2494.

[7] See the discussion on pp. 210–11.

"insensibility," "obtuseness," or "blindness," better corresponding with the scripture citations in 11:8–10.[8] By using a different term and a different metaphorical concept in 11:7, Paul avoids making a direct parallel to 9:18.[9] The obtuseness in 11:7 may lead to a final hardening as in 9:18, but these two concepts should not be regarded as synonymous, as the insensibility (πώρωσις) of 11:7 is not necessarily decisive (cf. 11:11–26). Therefore, to retain the distinction that would have been evident to a Greek reader, this concept is better rendered as "insensibility" or "callous."[10]

Under the assumption that Paul is referring to contemporary Jewish unbelief,[11] this verse is also usually interpreted as though the verbs for "obtain" and "made insensible" were in the perfect (e.g., "What Israel is seeking, this she has not obtained ... the rest have been hardened").[12] Like 9:31, however, these verbs are in the aorist, again denoting Israel's *past* failings and divisions,[13] though the lasting *consequences* of that hardening remain "through everything" (διὰ παντός; 11:10).[14] As Gadenz points out, "these hardened others in Paul's time are juxtaposed with the idolatrous Israelites in the time of Elijah."[15] That is, both those from the northern kingdom in the past who "became insensible" and

---

[8] A problem already noted by J. Armitage Robinson, "ΠΩΡΩΣΙΣ and ΠΗΡΩΣΙΣ" (1901), 92.

[9] As observed by Thomas H. Tobin, *Paul's Rhetoric in Its Contexts* (2004), 358. Contra Gadenz, who objects that "Paul himself seems to suggest such a parallel by using the verb σκληρύνω in 9,18 and πωρόω in 11,7" and concludes "the common translation 'harden' for πωρόω is not that misleading" (*Called*, 207–8 n. 144).

[10] Following Wagner, *Heralds of the Good News*, 240 n. 68. The argument of Mark Nanos, "'Callused,' Not 'Hardened'" (2010), that the sense of the term is "protected" is unpersuasive, as that runs counter to the theme of judgment in the explanatory catena of 11:8–10. Nanos' analogy to the formation of a callus on a plant is intriguing, but as he admits, Theophrastus does not use the same terminology in his description of that process. Nevertheless, for Paul the insensibility of 11:7 is a state that can be healed through Messiah. For an assessment of the same matter with respect to German translation, suggesting the rendering "Nicht-Erkennen," see Marie-Irma Seewann, "'Verstockung', 'Verhärtung' oder 'Nicht-Erkennen'" (1997).

[11] E.g., Douglas J. Moo, *Romans* (1996), 679–80; Charles E. B. Cranfield, *Romans* (1979), 548.

[12] Moo, *Romans*, 670; cf. NASB, "it has not obtained." Even when the translation itself is correct, commentators regularly *interpret* the passage (including a restatement of the translation) as though the verbs were in the perfect, e.g., Peter Stuhlmacher, *Romans* (1994), 164; Wagner, *Heralds of the Good News*, 240–41.

[13] Note the parallel use of the verb with reference to historical Israel in 2 Cor 3:14 and see Margaret E. Thrall, *2 Corinthians* (1994), 262. The point both there and here is that the insensibility that characterized Israel in the past can be healed through turning to Messiah; the aorist implies that past insensibility need not apply to the present.

[14] See Florian Wilk, *Die Bedeutung des Jesajabuches für Paulus* (1998), 144; cf. Guy Prentiss Waters, *The End of Deuteronomy in the Epistles of Paul* (2006), 205.

[15] Gadenz, *Called*, 235.

those descended from Israel who are currently characterized by insensibility stand outside the promises to Abraham's seed.

It is again important to note Paul's careful language here as he speaks not of "the Jews" but of *Israel*, nor does he suggest that Israel as a whole was made insensible. Once again, the central problem he is addressing is not that "the Jews" have resisted the gospel but rather that the anticipated elements of *Israel's* restoration seem to be lacking. It must not be forgotten that *even if every Jew alive in Paul's day had embraced the gospel, that would still fall far short of the traditional expectations of Israel's restoration unless the other (non-Jewish) tribes returned in fidelity and unity with the Jewish remnant*, with the nations also subjugated to Israel and its God. But Israel's situation remains characteristically divided, with some standing within the promise and "the rest" (οἱ λοιποί) outside due to unfaithfulness. This divergence from the comprehensive expectations of Israel's restoration is only further underscored by the unexpected incorporation of gentiles within the redeemed community, and this is the situation that requires explanation. The rest of the chapter aims to show how, despite appearances, God is in fact fulfilling his promise of redemption to Israel.

DISOBEDIENCE, MERCY, AND JEALOUSY

Paul's response is that just as in the past, Israel's restoration involves a double edge – redemption for some, judgment and condemnation for "the rest." To support this, he cites a series of scriptures as witness to the divine response to Israel's disobedience, beginning with a conflation of Deut 29:3 (ET: 29:4) and Isa 29:10 to show that God did not repair the people's stubborn and rebellious nature but actively "gave them a spirit of stupor, eyes not to see and ears not to hear" (Rom 11:8), ensuring that they remained under judgment for their disobedience.[16] This condition need not be permanent,[17] however, as Paul explains:

---

[16] As in Paul's application of the potter/clay metaphor, it is noteworthy that both Isa 29:10 and Deut 29:3 (ET: 29:4) are divine *responses* to prior disobedience rather than the cause of that prior disobedience. God again is *responding* to his people's stubbornness rather than initially *causing* their disobedience. For more on the scriptural catena in 11:8–10, particularly its covenantal resonances and the continued emphasis on divine response to Israel's disobedience, see Wagner, *Heralds of the Good News*, 240–65; Waters, *End of Deuteronomy*, 199–205; Gadenz, *Called*, 235–37; Enno Edzard Popkes, "Und David spricht." (2010).

[17] The expression διὰ παντός in 10:10 should therefore be rendered "continually" or "through everything" rather than "forever." See the discussion in Jewett, *Romans*, 665.

Disobedience, Mercy, and Jealousy 275

I say then, did they stumble in order to fall? μὴ γένοιτο! But by their misstep/trespass,[18] salvation [came] to the nations to make them jealous. And if their misstep was riches for the world and their loss riches for the nations, how much more their fullness (τὸ πλήρωμα αὐτῶν)! I am speaking to you who are gentiles. On the other hand,[19] inasmuch as I am indeed an apostle of gentiles I glorify my service, hoping that somehow I may make my flesh jealous and save some of them.[20] For if their casting away[21] is the reconciliation of the world, what is their reception[22] if not life from the dead? (11:11–15)

Paul here adds another layer to the relationship between Israel and the nations, explaining that the trespass or misstep of "the rest" (οἱ λοιποί) – that is, the non-remnant, the portion that did not remain – resulted in salvation for the nations to make them jealous. Interpreters have found this passage difficult in many respects, in large part because so many have misidentified the antecedent as "Israel" and then compounded that mistake by then conflating "Israel" with the Jews of Paul's day.[23] But the most natural antecedent is "the rest," which also serves as the antecedent for the citations in the immediately preceding catena. Adding to the

---

[18] Typically rendered "trespass" or "transgression," the sense of παράπτωμα is that of a stumble or false step from which one can recover (Gal 6:1; Ps 18:13; Pss. Sol. 3:7; 13:5, 10), and given the motif of stumbling and the race metaphor of Rom 9:16, 30–33, etc., Paul is drawing on the literal sense of the term. See Wagner, *Heralds of the Good News*, 266 n. 151; Gadenz, *Called*, 239–40; Jewett, *Romans*, 673; Jean-Noël Aletti, "Romains 11" (2009), 201 n. 7. The same language of "misstep" is applied to Adam and humanity in general in Rom 5:15–17, again reinforcing the point that Israel, having the Torah, "sinned in the likeness of Adam's transgression (παράβασις)" (5:14).

[19] Following Cranfield, *Romans*, 559, μὲν οὖν likely carries the sense of "contrary to what you might think," rather than a concessive sense as suggested by Marie-Joseph Lagrange, *Saint Paul, Épitre aus Romains* (1950), 277.

[20] Here I take both παραζηλώσω and σώσω as aorist subjunctives marking intention following Gadenz, *Called*, 240, but they can also be read as future indicatives, as argued by Richard H. Bell, *Provoked to Jealousy* (1994), 116. In either case, the meaning is the same.

[21] Ἀποβολή is often translated as "rejection" here in parallel with 11:1, but the term alludes to Israel's having been cast out among the nations (cf. Deut 29:27–28; Hos 9:15; Jer 12:14, 15; 22:28). Paul has already strongly denied that God has in any way rejected (ἀποθέω) his people (11:1). Like the distinction between the terms for "hardening" in 9:18 and 11:7, it is important to distinguish between the different terms used in 11:1 and 11:15. See Gadenz, *Called*, 251–54.

[22] The terminology of πρόσλημψις refers to God's action of taking up, choosing, or receiving his people for himself (echoing 1 Sam 12:22). Every other time Paul uses this term, it refers to the acceptance of people (Rom 14:1, 3; 15:7; Phlm 17; see Gadenz, *Called*, 251–52 n. 309), and all but three of the twenty biblical occurrences of προσλαμβάνω refer to receiving or accepting people.

[23] E.g., James D. G. Dunn, *Romans* (1988), 670; Moo, *Romans*, 688; Joseph A. Fitzmyer, *Romans* (1993), 612; Jewett, *Romans*, 680–81.

difficulty is the fact that Paul does not here explain why the misstep of "the rest" should lead to gentile salvation in the first place. The logic of that progression is assumed rather than explained in this passage.

Many have also found it perplexing that Paul would imagine "jealousy" or "zealous rage"[24] should bring about salvation or the desire to emulate the behavior of believing gentiles. Sanders, for example, wonders, "Does he really think that jealousy will succeed where Peter failed?"[25] A final problem has to do with what seems like Paul's attempt to have it both ways, as Donaldson muses, "Why if the world is blessed through Israel's failure should it also be blessed through its success?"[26] As for why "their misstep" would result in salvation for the nations, many have, leaning on the accounts in Acts,[27] assumed that Paul here alludes to "the way in which he and other preachers of the gospel would turn to the gentiles after being spurned by the Jews."[28]

Aside from the methodological problems inherent to reading Acts into Romans, this interpretation still does not explain why being rejected by Jews would be a necessary precursor to gentile inclusion. If the Jews of the synagogue accepted the message, surely it would be even easier to persuade the gentiles in the synagogue, exactly the situation in Berea according to Acts 17:10–12. Moreover, this explanation still does not explain the theological rationale for the focus on gentiles in the first place; Paul and his coworkers could easily have excluded the uncircumcised and focused on the small number of Jews they did manage to persuade. The Yaḥad sectarians, for example, did not turn to the gentiles after most of their contemporaries rejected their distinctive sectarian teaching. Others have suggested that Jewish rejection was necessary so that Jewish customs would not be an obstacle in the path of gentile faith/fidelity.[29] But in

---

[24] As suggested by Jewett, *Romans*, 675; cf. John C. O'Neill, *Romans* (1975), 179. Stuhlmacher, *Romans*, 167, suggests "angry jealousy," also adopted by Winfrid Keller, *Gottes Treue, Israels Heil* (1998), 185–87.

[25] E.g., E. P. Sanders, *Paul, the Law, and the Jewish People* (1983), 198. Cf. Jewett, *Romans*, 644–47, 674–75; Ernst Käsemann, *Romans* (1980), 304–7; Gadenz, *Called*, 249. Fitzmyer's condemnation is especially remarkable: "Paul's motivation in seeking to make Israel "jealous" is not of the highest level; he argues from a very human consideration" (*Romans*, 611).

[26] Terence L. Donaldson, "'Riches for the Gentiles' (Rom 11:12)" (1993), 91.

[27] E.g., Acts 8:1; 13:44–48; 18:4–7; 19:8–10; 28:23–29. See C. H. Dodd, *Romans* (1932), 176; Pierre Benoit, "Conclusion par mode de synthèse" (1977), 288; Francois Dreyfus, "Le Passé et le présent d'Israël (Rom 9,1–5; 11,1–24)" (1977), 149; William Sanday and Arthur C. Headlam, *Romans* (1902), 321.

[28] Moo, *Romans*, 687.

[29] E.g., Lagrange, *Romains*, 275; H. L. Ellison, *The Mystery of Israel* (1966), 80–81.

addition to the problem that Paul nowhere says anything of the sort, this theory again begs the question by assuming that gentile fidelity should be a priority in the first place. Why should gentile fidelity be such a priority that some among Israel need to be made obtuse to facilitate it?

Others have suggested that the Jews' rejection of Jesus himself, which led to his crucifixion and thereby the redemption of the world, is the specific misstep in view,[30] but Paul clearly views Jesus' death as salvific for Israel in addition to the rest of the nations, and it is again unclear why Paul would presume the death of the messiah should lead to salvation for the gentiles rather than Israel. Attempting to explain this problem, Wright has noted parallels between Paul's portrayal of Israel in Rom 11:11-15 and the death and resurrection of Messiah in Rom 5, suggesting that Israel needed to be cast aside, descending into death to bring salvation to the nations, thereby imitating the death and resurrection of the messiah.[31] But the plight of "the rest" is the result of disobedient misstep (παράπτωμα), which sharply contrasts with Messiah's obedient death and consequent resurrection. These parallels therefore do not explain why "the rest" would need to be cast aside to conform to the fate of the Messiah, nor do they explain why salvation would go to the nations to make disobedient Israelites jealous.[32]

In any case, most readings as far back as the *adversus Judaeos* traditions in late antiquity have interpreted Rom 11:11 as making salvation a zero-sum proposition with respect to Jews and gentiles.[33] As Paul Achtemeier explains, "There is almost a spatial analogy here. Only if some Israelites have been cleared out will there be room for gentiles."[34]

---

[30] Karl Barth, *A Shorter Commentary on Romans* (2007), 87; accepted by Cranfield, *Romans*, 556.

[31] N. T. Wright, "The Messiah and the People of God" (1980), 180-82; *Paul and the Faithfulness of God* (2013), 1206-7. See also Hays, *Echoes*, 61.

[32] Bell, *Provoked to Jealousy*, 111-12; Jewett, *Romans*, 674 n. 70. Despite these objections, Wright's insight with these parallels is on the right track, though falling short of a full explanation for the passage itself. With respect to the obedience/disobedience contrast, the key is returning to the potter/clay analogy, where Paul explains that God will accomplish his purpose either through obedience (as with Messiah) or disobedience ("the rest" of 11:11), though the ultimate fate of each individual instrument may be different depending on whether it was through obedience or disobedience. This accounts for Paul's concern for his disobedient fleshly kin – they will be used salvifically either way, but their own fates are contingent on incorporation in the new covenant via the faithfulness mediated by the spirit.

[33] E.g., John Chrysostom, *Homilies on Romans* 19 (on Rom 11:18): "For it is into their place that you have been set and their goods that you enjoy."

[34] Paul J. Achtemeier, *Romans* (1985), 180.

This view, however, falters in that verses 12 and 15 clearly suggest that "their" success and fullness leads to even greater results than their defeat, and 11:25–26 clearly states that there is plenty of salvific "space" for both the fullness of the nations and all Israel. Another alternative is that Paul is instead thinking *temporally* rather than spatially. That is, Jewish rejection of the gospel has delayed the parousia, which would mark the "termination of Gentiles' opportunity for salvation,"[35] thereby providing the time delay necessary for gentile salvation.[36] But again, this approach still does not explain why the gospel should go to the gentiles at all, nor does it explain the function of jealousy as a motivation for gentile salvation or means of Israelite repentance. Owing to these difficulties, most interpreters have effectively equivocated on the passage, appealing to a vague "salvation-historical aspect,"[37] "apocalyptic scenario,"[38] or "plan of salvation"[39] underlying Paul's statements here. Donaldson goes so far as to suggest that the apostle's argument is circumstantial and shows a "startling lack of logical consistency,"[40] such that "scholarly investigation of these verses should be concerned not to ascertain any logical consistency but to use the cracks in the argument as windows into the underlying structure of Paul's convictional world."[41]

JEALOUS GOD, JEALOUS PEOPLE

On the contrary, Paul's argument here is not only coherent and logically consistent but relatively straightforward. The key is to read this passage in light of Paul's citation of Deut 32:21 in Rom 10:19. The close proximity of that quotation is what allows him to use the shorthand "in order to make them jealous" without explanation in 11:11, since he has already provided the contextual explanation a few lines earlier. By citing the Song

---

[35] Donaldson, "Riches for the Gentiles," 94.
[36] Donaldson, "Riches for the Gentiles," 92–98. Others holding this temporal view include Seyoon Kim, *The Origin of Paul's Gospel* (1981), 96–97; Sanders, *PLJP*, 195; Stanley Stowers, *A Rereading of Romans* (1994), 315; Murray Baker, "Paul and the Salvation of Israel" (2005), 478–79; Aletti, "Le développement de l'argumentation," 218–19; Gadenz, *Called*, 250.
[37] Käsemann, *Romans*, 304.   [38] Jewett, *Romans*, 674.
[39] James W. Aageson, "Typology, Correspondence, and the Application of Scripture in Romans 9–11" (1987), 282.
[40] Donaldson, "Riches for the Gentiles," 88.
[41] Donaldson, "Riches for the Gentiles," 91. Nils A. Dahl, "The Future of Israel" (2002), 150: "We should not overstress the correlation of cause and effect …. Paul interprets what actually happened."

of Moses, which was widely read "as a prophecy of Israel's future ... [and] widely understood as itself predicting Israel's restoration after exile,"[42] Paul again appeals to the framework of restoration eschatology and Israel's present plight, and this section of Deut 32 proves especially useful for his argument in that it explicitly links Israel's disobedience with benefit for the nations.[43]

In Deut 32:21, YHWH declares, "They made me jealous by what is not a god; they provoked me to anger with their idols, so I will make *them* jealous with a not-nation;[44] I will provoke *them* to anger with a senseless nation."[45] The logic here is that God will turn the tables on unfaithful Israel by acting like a spurned lover, pursuing another to induce his adulterous beloved into a jealous rage and drive her back to him.[46] That is, in Wagner's words, "One good spurn deserves another."[47] To further induce this jealousy, YHWH will also "heap disasters on them

---

[42] Richard J. Bauckham, "Tobit as a Parable for the Exiles of Northern Israel" (2006), 142. For more on Deut 32:21 and its influence on Paul, see especially Wagner, *Heralds of the Good News*, 191–201. Waters, *End of Deuteronomy*, 147, 243–44, argues that Paul (along with T. Moses and *Sifre Deut.*) saw Deut 32 as having an "eschatological expansiveness." Cf. Matthew Thiessen, "The Form and Function of the Song of Moses (Deuteronomy 32:1–43)" (2004); Steven Weitzman, *Song and Story in Biblical Narrative* (1997); Bell, *Provoked to Jealousy*, 209–85. See also the discussion in Jason A. Staples, *The Idea of Israel in Second Temple Judaism* (2021), 98–102.

[43] "For Paul, the disobedience of Israel, the inclusion of the Gentiles, the provoking to jealousy of Israel, and the final salvation of Israel all belong together. They belong together because the themes are linked in Dt. 32" (Bell, *Provoked to Jealousy*, 112–13).

[44] The MT has "not-people" (לא־עם) rather than the LXX's "not-nation" (οὐκ ἔθνει), making a connection with the Hosea passages Paul cites in 9:25–27 even more natural. Wagner, *Heralds of the Good News*, 197 n. 229, notes that the Peshitta translates Deut 32:21 based on Hos 2:1, 25, suggesting that these verses were linked in the interpretive tradition. See also Umberto Cassuto, "The Prophet Hosea and the Books of the Pentateuch" (1973), 96–100.

[45] Translated from the LXX. As such, Paul's slightly altered quotation of Deut 32:21 in Rom 10:19 should probably be understood emphatically: "I will make *you* jealous by a non-nation, and with a senseless nation I will make *you* angry" (note the emphatic ὑμᾶς in each clause).

[46] Contrary to the suggestion of Bell, *Provoked to Jealousy*, 39, cf. 113; followed by Waters, *End of Deuteronomy*, 208–9, that it be understood here "in the good sense, 'provoke to emulation,'" there is no reason to think παραζηλόω means anything different in 11:11, 14 than it does in 10:19 (and Deut 32:21). For a full critique of a "positive" reading of the term, see Gadenz, *Called*, 245–49. The suggestion that the function of jealousy is to indicate that the gentile mission is still ongoing is equally unpersuasive, as that serves no function with respect to Israel and results in circular logic: the mission to the gentiles is ongoing to make Israel jealous in order to demonstrate that the mission to the gentiles is ongoing. Contra Gadenz, *Called*, 250–51; Aletti, "Le développement de l'argumentation," 221; Baker, "Paul and the Salvation of Israel," 476–79.

[47] Wagner, *Heralds of the Good News*, 190, punctuation slightly amended.

[disobedient Israel]" (Deut 32:23), pouring out the covenant curses upon them while showing favor to a "not-nation" so that they will see the difference between God's favor and his wrath.[48] As such, according to the Song of Moses, God's fidelity to Israel is paradoxically the reason he extends favor (grace) to a "not-nation" and wrath toward his people – it is all in service of stoking desire and repentance in his people.[49] But in time, when YHWH "sees that their strength is gone" (32:36), he will yet again raise his people up, thereby demonstrating that he is the one who "puts to death and gives life" (32:39; cf. Rom 11:15), the one who wounded and will heal. The Song of Moses therefore concludes: "Rejoice, nations, with his people!" (32:43), a conclusion Paul quotes in the close of this letter (Rom 15:10). In Paul's reading, the end result is therefore not only Israel's restoration but that the nations who have been shown favor because of Israel's disobedience can now rejoice among YHWH's redeemed people. Paul's argument through Rom 11 thus follows the same progression from disobedience to jealousy to redemption as the Song of Moses.[50]

Contrary to Thomas Tobin's curious assertion that "the Deut 32:21 motif of God making Israel jealous is not found elsewhere in the Scriptures or elsewhere in Judaism during this period,"[51] the fact that the non-people/foolish nation and jealousy motifs of Deut 32:21 were applied to the Samaritans in Paul's day adds an extra layer to the argument, since Samaritan claims to Israelite status as descendants of the northern tribes was precisely what rankled their Jewish rivals.[52] Samaritan claims to (non-Jewish) Israelite status therefore serve as a ready parallel for Paul's faithful gentiles and his claim that they should be received as full covenant members.[53] Paul's appeal to the jealousy motif

---

[48] Recall Josephus' appeal to the same pattern in his explanation of why the "rod of empire" currently rests in Rome. See Paul Spilsbury, "Flavius Josephus on the Rise and Fall of the Roman Empire" (2003), 21; Staples, *The Idea of Israel*, 210–32.

[49] See Wagner, *Heralds of the Good News*, 198.

[50] As observed by Wagner, *Heralds of the Good News*, 198–201; Bell, *Provoked to Jealousy*, 285. Cf. Hays, *Echoes*, 164.

[51] Tobin, *Paul's Rhetoric*, 361.

[52] Recall the use of Deut 32:21 with reference to the Samaritans in 4Q372 1 10–11, 14–15 and Josephus' views of the Samaritans as Israelite pretenders who were the result of Assyrian repopulation of the land (depending on 2 Kgs 17; see Staples, *The Idea of Israel*, 272–75). *Sifre Deut.* 331 also interprets this verse as referring to the Samaritans, indicating that this tradition persisted even at a much later date. See Waters, *End of Deuteronomy*, 71–75. For a more general summary of the use of Deut 32 in the Dead Sea Scrolls, see Bell, *Provoked to Jealousy*, 217–21.

[53] It is probably no coincidence that the Samaritans serve a similar symbolic function as the halfway point between the Jews and the nations in the Gospels and Acts. On the significance of the Samaritans in Luke–Acts, see the sources cited in n. 127 on p. 64.

therefore yet again recalls the fate of northern Israel, never far below the surface throughout Rom 9–11. Nevertheless, although Deut 32:21 says God will make his people jealous by a not-nation, it does not in fact say this not-nation will be saved or participate in Israel's redemption, though Deut 32:43 could easily be interpreted in that direction.[54] To arrive at this conclusion, Paul interprets Deut 32:21 together with the earlier-referenced promise of Hosea to "not my people," applying both of them together to the gentiles now participating in the promise of the spirit.[55]

IMPARTIAL JUSTICE, MERCY TO ALL

The connection between the "not-people" of Deut 32:21 and the "not-my-people" of the northern kingdom brings into play yet another prophetic passage, which introduces the idea that the rebellion of one people leads to the salvation of another. In Jer 3, Judah's abhorrent behavior serves as the rationale for the redemption and return of the northern kingdom: "Faithless Israel has proved herself more just than treacherous Judah. Go and proclaim these words toward the north and say, 'Return, faithless Israel, declares YHWH; I will not cause my face to fall on you in anger'" (Jer 3:11–12). To shame Judah, YHWH declares that he will restore Israel from divorce (3:8; alluding to Hosea's declaration of divorce), while still pleading with Judah to repent and be saved itself. This theme then carries through much of the rest of Jeremiah, particularly in Jer 31 (38 LXX), where the promise of a new covenant for both houses of Israel occurs at the end of an extended passage calling for Ephraim's return.[56] The logic throughout is that if Judah will ultimately be shown mercy in spite of its treachery then Israel must also be shown mercy for its previous rebellion.[57]

Paul suggests Israel's insensibility (πώρωσις) has resulted in salvation for the nations in precisely the same manner that Jeremiah says Judah's treachery has enabled Israel's redemption. The logic is the same: God's

---

[54] E.g., 4Q372 1 20–22, which interprets the Song of Moses such that the "enemy" dwelling in Joseph's land will be destroyed when Joseph is finally restored.
[55] Francis Watson, *Paul and the Hermeneutics of Faith* (2004), 448. Cf. also David I. Starling, *Not My People* (2011), 163–64; Bell, *Provoked to Jealousy*, 185 n. 84; Gadenz, *Called*, 109–10. If Paul knew the Hebrew reading ("not people," לא־עם), such a connection would have been even more natural.
[56] See the discussion in Chapter 5.
[57] See Chapter 3 and the discussion in Staples, *The Idea of Israel*, 132–35. Remarkably, according to Isa 11:13, Ephraim's jealousy (LXX: ζῆλος) of Judah is ultimately what led to its destruction, from which a remnant will ultimately return (11:11).

impartial justice demands that if mercy is shown to one, it must be extended to the other (cf. Rom 2:9–11). This is, of course, in keeping with what Paul has already argued in Rom 1–3, where he establishes that because Israel behaved like the nations, the same judgment applies to both Jews and Greeks – all are under sin and subject to death. Consequently, he argues, this also means that the nations now have access to the same mercy promised to Israel. That is, Israel's misstep eliminated their head start and put Israel in the same position as the nations (11:11–15; cf. 3:1–9), so now the nations may share in the redemption by the spirit promised to Israel (cf. Gal 3:14).

Again it is important to note that here Paul does not speak of the misstep or insensibility of *Jews*; instead, he refers to *Israel* (11:7), the larger group including but not limited to Jews, and the reference to Elijah's appeal "against Israel" explicitly brings *northern* Israel into view since Elijah's prophetic career was in the north.[58] This reminder that "Israel" not only concerns Judah ("Jews") but also those from apparently rejected northern Israel further reinforces Paul's scriptural and historical focus – including repeated citations of passages about northern Israel – throughout Rom 9–11. In that framework, "Israel's" stumbling, insensibility, judgment, and redemption is significantly more expansive than the fact that some contemporary Jews had not accepted Paul's proclamation of the gospel. That is, in this larger context, it is not just the insensibility of some from *Judah* (that is, Jews) but of *both* houses of *Israel* that has led to salvation for the nations. First, those of the northern kingdom who became insensible were cast away among the nations, becoming "not-my-people" (Hos 1:9) and a "non-nation" (Deut 32:21), effectively sowing Israel among the nations (Hos 2:25 [ET: 2:23]).[59] Then Judah's misstep set Ephraim's return in motion (Jer 3), opening the door for the redemption of "not-my-people" – that is, the nations in which these insensible Israelites had been sown (Rom 9:25–26).

Because Israel was scattered among – and assimilated by – the nations, Israel's salvation paradoxically depends on salvation coming to the gentiles (11:11), and like a master potter, God has used Israel's misstep not for destruction but to accomplish the very purpose for which Israel was chosen in the first place: riches for the world (11:12) and the blessing of Abraham for all nations (Gal 3:14). "The rest" who were cast out as

---

[58] "The remnant of 7000, in the context of 1 Kings 19, is clearly a remnant of *northern* Israel" (Hahn, "All Israel," 95).

[59] See the discussion in pp. 201–9 in Chapter 5.

dishonored vessels (cf. Hos 8:8; Jer 22:28) have brought blessing for the nations into which they were cast, and the nations are now participating in the promises made to Israel. But the fact that salvation has come to the gentiles makes it clear that even if much of Israel was previously cast away, the portion that was cast away among the nations can still be redeemed (11:15). The ingathering of the nations means that even "the rest" are not hopelessly lost; redemption is possible even for those who are now cut off from the remnant of Israel, a point further emphasized in the olive tree metaphor a few verses later.

In keeping with this hope, Paul explains that he hopes his ministry to the gentiles stirs his unfaithful kin ("my flesh"; 11:14) to zeal in fulfillment of Deut 32:21. Like the presence of Samaritans in the land, God's favor among the gentiles is proof of God's judgment and the need to turn to God for redemption.[60] Paul seems to allude here to his own experience in which his violent zeal – presumably in the defense of the halakhic fidelity necessary to initiate Israel's redemption – climaxed in a revelation of Messiah (cf. Gal 1:13–16).[61] Indeed, Paul himself is evidence that "the rest" may yet be restored; just as he was previously insensible in his ignorant zeal but is that no longer, so also God has provided for the healing of the insensibility of "the rest."[62] But Paul's example is not a guarantee that all will have the same outcome, as Paul apparently only expects "some" (τινάς) to be saved.[63]

But as much as the stumbling enabled deliverance for the nations, the fulfillment of the promises (Israel's fullness) is even greater: "For if their casting away [is] the reconciliation of the world, what [is] their acceptance if not life from the dead?" (11:15). The precise language in this grammatically elliptical verse has often been misunderstood. Paul does not here refer to "Israel's rejection,"[64] which he has already categorically denied in

---

[60] Matthew Thiessen, "4Q372 1 and the Continuation of Joseph's Exile" (2008), 395.
[61] Jewett, Romans, 675.
[62] Note again that Paul *was* insensible (which Acts 9:18 represents through literally hardened eyes), but that condition does not necessarily imply continuation into the present, illustrating why rendering the aorists as perfects in 11:7 is potentially misleading.
[63] Gadenz, Called, 249–51, argues that Paul is speaking of two separate groups here, one stirred to jealousy and another who are saved, but this is difficult to sustain since Paul himself fits in both groups. It is instead better to see jealousy as the motive for the inclusion of gentiles, with some (like Paul) potentially passing through that jealousy into salvation.
[64] E.g., Moo, Romans, 685–88, 693–94.

Rom 11:1, or "the Jews' rejection of the gospel,"[65] since he nowhere refers to Jews (still less "*the* Jews") in this passage, let alone their rejection of the gospel. Nor does the second half of the verse denote a temporal shift to refer to some future event (perhaps at the parousia) when the Jews will accept the gospel en masse.[66] Indeed, the clauses in 11:12, 13, and 15 are all nonverbal, meaning any temporal shift must be imported by the reader rather than being explicit in the text itself.[67] Instead, the relationship between these statements should be understood as primarily logical rather than chronological, setting the stage for the reveal in 11:25–26, where Paul finally unveils how and why Israel's destiny is so thoroughly wrapped up with the fate of the nations.[68]

The sense of the verse is more easily understood if viewed in the context of the restoration framework in which Paul has been working all along. In that context, the "casting away" (ἀποβολή) of "the rest" (οἱ λοιποί), echoes Deut 29:26–27 (ET: 29:27–28), where Moses declares that as the culmination of the covenantal curse, God will "cast them out" (LXX: ἐχέβαλεν) into another land.[69] The very next verse, already recalled in Rom 2:28–29,[70] declares that "the hidden things belong to the Lord"

---

[65] Contra Fitzmyer, *Romans*, 612, who argues that because 11:1 explicitly says that God has not rejected his people, the genitive here must be taken in a subjective sense, referring to "the Jews' rejection (of the gospel)." Cf. Jewett, *Romans*, 680–81. This ignores the argument of the intervening verses in which Paul establishes that although God has by no means rejected (ἀποθέω; 11:1) his people as a whole, *some* ("the rest") had been excluded while God preserved a "remnant" of his people. This is in keeping with the numerous biblical references to God "casting away" (e.g., Deut 29:26–27 [ET: 29:27–28]) his people; it was a historical fact that God had cast his people among the nations, though he never abandoned the remnant. Romans 11:15 addresses the "casting away"; Rom 11:1 addresses the question of rejection or abandonment. The subjective reading also must supply an object (such as the gospel) since no such language appears in the context. See Verena Jegher-Bucher, "Erwählung und Verwerfung im Römerbrief?" (1991), 329. Moreover, Gadenz, *Called*, 251–52, points out that since the apodosis almost certainly refers to God's action of receiving his people, the protasis should be taken objectively in reference to God's action as well. Nevertheless, the ambiguity of the genitive does allow the reader to associate God's rejection of disobedient Israelites with their rejection of God and his justness.

[66] As held by Jewett, *Romans*, 676; Käsemann, *Romans*, 307; and others holding to what Christopher Zoccali, "And So All Israel Will Be Saved" (2008), 290–93, labels the "eschatological miracle" position.

[67] Contra Gadenz, *Called*, 250.

[68] That is not to suggest that they *cannot* be read chronologically or that Paul denies any sort of historical/chronological aspect to the process he outlines, but the *primary* relationship between these terms is logical. See the section on 11:25–27 below for more explanation.

[69] Cf. also Hos 9:15; Jer 12:14, 15; 22:28. [70] See pp. 169–72 in Chapter 4.

(Deut 29:28 [ET: 29:29]),[71] leading into the promise of restoration from the curse in Deut 30:1–14. Paul will unveil his interpretation of those "hidden things" (the mystery) of Israel's restoration a few verses later in Rom 11:25–26, a solution toward which he has been building since the very first chapter of Romans.

In any case, the point here is that the consequence of Israel's covenantal punishment, its "casting away" [ἀποβολή] among the nations, is paradoxically the reconciliation of the world – including Israel itself. Through the inclusion of gentiles, whom Paul likewise portrays as formerly dead and raised to new life in Messiah (cf. Rom 6:4; 7:4; 8:10–11), those formerly cast away are now becoming partakers in the covenant community. And if Israel is truly being received back again from assimilation among the nations, how is it anything but life from the dead? The "very dry" bones of the "whole house of Israel" (Ezek 37:2, 11) are being resurrected through "a spirit of life" (37:5). Once again, Paul argues that Israel's salvation is inextricably interdependent with that of the nations, and salvation coming to gentiles is the proof that even those who are now insensible may yet be saved through the new life of the spirit. Salvation has come to the gentiles precisely to bring Israel back from the dead as the prophets had promised.

JEALOUSY, NOT-MY-PEOPLE, AND A NON-NATION

At this point, one may ask how, if transformed gentile believers are becoming "Israelites," their inclusion would make Israel jealous. It is obviously nonsense to suggest that these new Israelites would make themselves jealous. But Paul does not say "to make Israel jealous" but "to make *them* (αὐτούς) jealous" (11:11) and "move *my flesh* to jealousy" (11:14). That is, he again refers not to the whole of Israel but rather to "the rest" (οἱ λοιποί) of Israel who were made insensible and currently stand outside the fulfillment of the promises. Those who have submitted to Israel's Messiah and received the spirit are no longer *them* (that is, those outside) but rather have become "us" (Rom 9:25).[72] This continues Paul's careful language throughout Rom 9–11. Nowhere has he suggested that Israel as a whole remains disobedient, and he actively goes out of his

---

[71] That is, even after Israel is cast out, God will not lose track of them but will transform and restore them. Cf. Seder Eliyahu Rabbah 10 (see n. 49 on p. 195).

[72] Contra John K. Goodrich, "Until the Fullness of the Gentiles Comes In" (2016), 19–20.

way to deny that Israel is not participating in the promised redemption, using himself as a prime example against such an idea (11:1–2). Instead, he consistently uses pronouns or refers specifically to his *fleshly* kin as a way to represent the *portion* of Israel that has become insensible, and he has consistently characterized such divisions between the just and unjust *within* Israel as typical throughout Israel's history.

Secondly, this objection does not sufficiently appreciate what Paul is suggesting when he employs the "not my people" and "non nation" motifs. Paul does not suggest that there are "disguised" Israelites among the nations who have simply forgotten their true ethnic heritage and are now being restored through recognition of their Israelite lineage. The nations/gentiles are not unknown Israelites. On the contrary, just as was the case in Rom 9:24–25, the point is that the bulk of northern Israel *has actually become* "not my people" (=gentiles). That is, a large portion of Israel has become gentiles, having been divorced from the covenant (cf. Jer 3:8) and fully assimilated by the nations among which they were scattered (cf. Hos 8:8). Israel's redemption is therefore not a matter of finding and identifying unknown Israelites among the nations – perhaps by combing through "endless genealogies" (1 Tim 1:4) in search of a distant Israelite ancestor – but rather involves *recreating* Israel from the gentiles through the transformative work of the spirit.

These non-Israelites must therefore be adopted and transformed to become "my people," a process that involves not merely recognition and reunion but *resurrection*, life from the dead (Rom 11:15), and new creation.[73] The significance of "adoption" language in this context must not be downplayed. These are neither fleshly children nor foster children but adoptees – legitimate, legal children and heirs (Rom 8:15–23; Gal 4:5) with the same "adoption" that belongs to "Israelites" (Rom 9:4).[74] They have *become* Israelites through the same process of selection from among the nations that created Israel in the beginning, fulfilling the prophetic promises that previously divorced Israel, swallowed up among the nations (Hos 8:8), would not be forgotten or permanently rejected but rather would be redeemed and called out from among the nations. Again, the logic of Paul's argument is that because Israel behaved like the gentiles and thereby became gentiles (cf. Rom 1:18–2:11, 3:9), now Israel's

---

[73] Cf. 2 Cor 5:17; Gal 6:15; 1QS 4:25.
[74] On the concept of "adoption" in this context and Paul's use of it, see Caroline Johnson Hodge, *If Sons, Then Heirs* (2007), 28–36, 67–77; James M. Scott, *Adoption as Sons of God* (1992).

redemption includes gentiles who become Israelites by receiving the spirit, becoming children of God and the promised pneumatic seed of Abraham.⁷⁵

The contemporary application of the jealousy motif to the Samaritans is again instructive on this point, as Jewish anti-Samaritan polemics rejected their claims to be Israelites on the basis of alleged intermarriage between the remaining northern Israelites and the gentile peoples imported into Samarian territory by the Assyrians.⁷⁶ The problem with the Samaritans in this respect is not only their locus of worship outside Jerusalem but that they have "gentilized." Paul effectively turns typical anti-Samaritan polemic on its head, arguing that Israelite intermarriage among and assimilation by the nations – through which Israel literally became "not my people" – requires the incorporation of actual gentiles who may or may not have a single Israelite ancestor (truly "not my people") as full covenant members of restored Israel. The inclusion of such gentiles (or Samaritans) in Israel's covenant is what stirs up outraged jealousy on the part of natural born Israelites.⁷⁷ Nevertheless, what brings the argument full circle is the paradox that these non-Israelites must be incorporated for Israel to be complete, since a significant portion of Israel has become inseparably intermingled among and assimilated into the nations.

CONSECRATED BY INCORPORATION

The full covenantal status of these adoptees from the nations incorporated into the sacred people of God is exactly the subject of the next section,

---

⁷⁵ Note the seven references to divine sonship of Messiah and those in him in Rom 8 (vv. 3, 14, 15, 16, 17, 19, 21, 23, 29) and the three references to the divine sonship of Israel in 9:4, 8, 26. Matthew D. Ketterling, "God's Sons and the Logic of the Covenant" (2018), 130–211, rightly observes that Paul equates the category "children of God" with the "seed of Abraham" such that "divine sonship connotes covenant membership in Romans" (131; cf. 210). On Abraham's pneumatic seed, see David A. Burnett, "So Shall Your Seed Be" (2015).

⁷⁶ See, for example, Jesus' labeling of a Samaritan as a "foreigner" (ἀλλογενής) in Luke 17:18.

⁷⁷ The situation is analogous to granting large-scale expedited citizenship to undocumented immigrants in the United States; even the suggestion of such has kindled outrage among many xenophobic natural-born citizens. But that outrage would not mean that such newly granted citizenship is not real; on the contrary, their new citizenship is precisely what would spur outraged zeal and efforts to tighten national boundaries.

introduced by verse sixteen: "If the firstfruits are sacred, so is the lump;[78] and if the root is sacred, so also are the branches." This short pair of halakhic rulings serves as a bridge between the discussion of 11:11–15 and the olive tree allegory immediately following, for which it also functions as a thesis statement.[79] The two rulings of Rom 11:16 have, however, been poorly understood by most interpreters. The first, about the firstfruits and lump, has typically been understood as an allusion to the practice of setting aside a small portion of dough for the priest when baking bread, in keeping with Num 15:18–20.[80] Working from this assumption, Gadenz comes to the remarkable conclusion that "the biblical principle itself does not support the conclusion which Paul draws from it, but … the important thing is that the premise in the metaphor be accepted by Paul's audience in order for it to be persuasive."[81] But even if Paul's audience were to accept the premise in the metaphor, Benjamin Gordon has pointed out an additional and even more serious problem:

> The sanctification of the loaf, once the offering is set aside from it, would run precisely counter to Paul's message regarding the inalienability of Israel's heritage to the church. (Applying its logic to the metaphor that follows would result in the sanctification of the olive tree only after its sacred root is removed from it.) Rather, most fitting to the context would be a saying that illustrates how something is sanctified when it is added to a holy entity, not detached from it, such as branches sanctified once they are grafted into a sacred tree.[82]

Unsurprisingly, the problem lies not with Paul's misapplication of a biblical principle but with modern scholars' misidentification of the practice from which Paul is drawing. Rather than the practice outlined in Num 15:18–20, Paul's metaphor refers to "mixtures of unsacred and sacred produce,"[83] in which unconsecrated dough has been added to the consecrated firstfruits (ἀπαρχή), becoming sacred through integration with the previously consecrated material. The basic logic is the same as "a little leaven leavens the whole lump" (Gal 5:9; 1 Cor 5:6), only in this case

---

[78] The use of φύρασμα recalls the lump of clay in 9:21. Paul here shifts the metaphor to dough rather than clay, but the imagery is linked by the lump, which represents Israel in each case. See Gadenz, *Called*, 193–94.
[79] See Gadenz, *Called*, 195–96.
[80] E.g., Gadenz, *Called*, 218; Jewett, *Romans*, 681–82; Dunn, *Romans*, 659, 671.
[81] Gadenz, *Called*, 2018. Similarly, Jewett, *Romans*, 682; Dunn, *Romans*, 659.
[82] Benjamin D. Gordon, "On the Sanctity of Mixtures and Branches: Two Halakic Sayings in Romans 11:16–24" (2016), 358.
[83] Gordon, "Mixtures and Branches" (2016), 358. For the rabbinic principles concerning such mixtures, see m. Terumot 3:1–2, 5:1–9. For a case specifically addressing an admixture of dough, see m. Ṭ. Yom 3:4, t. Ṭ. Yom 2:7, b. Niddah 46b.

sanctity is transmitted rather than impurity. This reading of the metaphor obviously corresponds well with Paul's arguments about the incorporation of non-Jews into the new covenant people of Israel – the point is that gentiles are consecrated/sanctified via integration into consecrated Israel.[84]

THE OLIVE TREE

The second statement about the root and branches is similar, though again "lack of familiarity with the ancient Jewish practice of dedicating agricultural property to God has led scholars to assume that Paul must be speaking figuratively here."[85] On the contrary, the second half of 11:16 simply cites another halakhic commonplace to establish the principle that sanctity is transferable via incorporation. In the same way that mixing ordinary dough with the sacred portion makes the whole batch sacred, previously common branches become sacred when joined to the root and stump of a dedicated tree.[86] This second halakhic saying therefore leads naturally into the more extended allegory of the olive tree:

But if some of the branches were broken off, and you, being from a wild olive tree, were grafted in among them, becoming co-partakers of the root, of the fatness of the olive tree,[87] do not boast against the branches. But if you do boast against them: it is not you who supports the root – the root supports you. You will say then, "Branches were broken off so that I might be grafted in." Fine. They were broken off for infidelity, but you stand by fidelity. Do not be proud but be afraid, for if God did not spare the natural branches, neither will he spare you. See then the kindness[88] and severity of God: severity toward those who fell, but toward you, kindness – if you remain in his kindness. Otherwise, you also will be cut off. And those ones also – if they do not remain in infidelity – will be grafted in, for God is able to graft them in again. For if you were cut off from the wild olive tree

---

[84] Benjamin D. Gordon, "Sacred Land Endowments and Field Consecrations in Early Judaism" (2013), 254–55.

[85] Gordon, "Mixtures and Branches," 359. Recognizing the halakhic nature of the saying does not reduce the allegorical application of the halakha in the passage or the biblical echoes implied in the image of an olive tree.

[86] Gordon, "Mixtures and Branches," 368.

[87] Following Franz Mussner, "Mitteilhaberin an der Wurzel" (1987), 157 n. 10, translating τῆς πιότητος τῆς ἐλαίας epexegetically, in apposition to τῆς ῥίζης, rather than adjectivally ("the rich root") as do most modern versions (e.g., NRSV, NASB, NAB; cf. Moo, *Romans*, 702 n. 28). Rom 11:17 contains a text-critical problem likely due to the awkwardness of the phrase τῆς ῥίζης τῆς πιότητος τῆς ἐλαίας (ℵ* B C Ψ). Some MSS omit τῆς ῥίζης (P46 D* F G) or introduce a καί after ῥίζης (ℵ² A D²), each of which clarifies the reading. See Gadenz, *Called*, 264.

[88] Paul again appears to be punning on χρῖστος with χρηστότης (cf. Rom 2:4; 3:12).

to which you belonged by nature[89] and contrary to nature were grafted into a cultivated olive tree, how much more will these who are natural [branches] be grafted into their own tree?[90] (Rom 11:17–24)

Having just cited the rule that the sacred root sanctifies the branches, Paul extends this principle to the preservation of Israel through the analogous process of cutting off the unfaithful and incorporating faithful outsiders. Paul's specific imagery here is borrowed from Jeremiah,[91] which depicts Israel as an olive tree with branches being cut away:

> The Lord called your name a well-shaded olive tree, beautiful in form. A fire was kindled against it toward the noise of its cutting (περιτομῆς), and great is the affliction coming upon you – her branches have become worthless. And the Lord who planted you pronounced evil against you because of the evil of the house of Israel and the house of Judah. (Jer 11:16–17a LXX)

Hosea uses the same image to portray Israel after redemption from being not-my-people: "I will be like dew to Israel ... his branches (κλάδοι) will spread and he will be like a fruitful olive tree" (Hos 14:7).[92] Olive trees were famous in antiquity for their regenerative properties, making a revitalized olive tree an especially suitable image for Israel's renewal. Pliny, for example, explains, "An olive tree, even after being completely burned, rejuvenates."[93] In this light, the consecrated olive tree of Rom 11 surely

---

[89] Κατὰ φύσιν is often translated as though it modifies the olive tree (i.e., "from that which is by nature a wild olive tree"; as NRSV, NASB, Käsemann, *Romans*, 303–4, etc.), but the phrase is best understood in in light of the immediately following clauses, such that the branch is being removed from the tree to which it naturally belongs and engrafted into another through outside intervention, as opposed to the natural branches which would be grafted into the tree to which they belonged by nature. See Cranfield, *Romans*, 571–72; J. C. T. Havemann, "Cultivated Olive – Wild Olive" (1997), 102–3. Although many commentators have suggested that παρὰ φύσιν implies that Paul is signaling an impossible or ridiculous process, the phrase is better understood as a reference the fact that the transplantation of branches involves interfering with nature and is by no means a natural process. See A. G. Baxter and John A. Zeisler, "Paul and Arboriculture" (1985), 29; Cranfield, *Romans*, 566, 571.

[90] The φύσις terminology here recalls the language of 1:28; 2:14, 27.

[91] Agreeing with Matthew Thiessen, *Paul and the Gentile Problem* (2016), 118. Zechariah 4:3, 11–14 also offers an interesting parallel in that it presents a picture of two olive trees before the Lord, but given the thematic differences that passage seems not to be in view here. On Rom 11:17–24 as an allegory, see Lancy Rodrigues, "Rom 11:16–24 in the Context of Rom 9–11" (2003), 89–90; Philip F. Esler, "Ancient Oleiculture and Ethnic Differentiation" (2003), 106–7.

[92] See Dongsu Kim, "Reading Paul's καὶ οὕτως πᾶς Ἰσραὴλ σωθήσεται (Rom. 11:26a) in the Context of Romans" (2010), 320.

[93] *Oliva in totum ambusta revixit.* Pliny, *Nat.* 17.241. Cf. Alison Burford, *Land and Labor in the Greek World* (1993), 130, 231–32.

represents Israel, the preservation and salvation of which has been in view throughout Romans as a whole and chapters 9–11 in particular.[94] Any other meaning would require a sudden and unannounced shift of subject, and any reader familiar with traditional prophetic imagery would naturally assume the olive tree represents Israel.[95]

BROKEN OFF AND GRAFTED IN

That God stands ready to break off the disobedient is jarring to modern sensibilities, but Paul and his contemporaries had no trouble maintaining what today may seem an irreconcilable juxtaposition: "See then the kindness and severity of God" (11:22). Indeed, such a view of God's preservation of Israel (kindness) through the removal of unfaithful Israelites (severity) is reflective of mainstream early Jewish theology. This logic persists throughout the Prophets, wherein Israel's restoration is typically presented as "a process that usually entails the violent removal of whatever cuts Israel off from [the deity] ... often through the elimination of a portion of the people."[96] The basic idea is that the preservation

---

[94] Others have suggested the olive tree refers to Messiah (cf. Gal 3:16; John 15:5; e.g., Maria Neubrand and Johannes Seidel München, "'Eingepfropft in den edlen Ölbaum' (Röm 11,24)" [2000], 70) or the church (e.g., Myles M. Bourke, *A Study of the Metaphor of the Olive Tree in Romans XI* [1947], 103, 111), but most interpreters agree that it best represents Israel. See the discussion in Rainer Schwindt, "Mehr Wurzel als Stamm und Krone" (2007), 71–91. The root has been variously identified as equivalent to the tree itself (=Israel; Wagner, *Heralds of the Good News*, 274); the patriarchs (Schwindt, "Mehr Wurzel"; Gadenz, *Called*, 262–63; W. D. Davies, *Jewish and Pauline Studies* [1984], 154–57; Bourke, *Metaphor of the Olive Tree*, 65–111), the promise itself (Dieter Sanger, "Rettung der Heiden und Erwählung Israels" [1986], 118), and even faith, peculiarly resulting in branches standing in the root by the root (Holger Zeigan, "Die Wurzel des Ölbaums (Röm 11,1)" [2006], 128). Given that Paul explicitly identifies Jesus as "the root" in Rom 15:12 (the only other place in Romans "root" terminology appears), the best option is that the root should be identified as the messiah. See Svetlana Khobnya, "'The Root' in Paul's Olive Tree Metaphor (Romans 11:16–24)" (2013); Anthony T. Hanson, *Studies in Paul's Technique and Theology* (2002), 117–21; N. T. Wright, "Romans" (2002), 683–84. The point is that one's status in Israel comes from being "in Messiah" (Rom 3:24; 6:23; 8:1; 12:5; etc.).

[95] Caroline Johnson Hodge, "Olive Trees and Ethnicities" (2004), 80–86; *If Sons, Then Heirs*, 143, highlights the metaphor's affinities to the figure of the "family tree," showing the relationship between generations, with each succeeding member the continuation of preceding progenitors.

[96] David A. Lambert, "How the Torah of Moses Became Revelation" (2016), 97. One especially relevant example comes from a passage Paul has quoted only a few verses above in Rom 10:15, "Look! On the mountains the feet of him who brings good news .... Because the Lord has turned away the hubris of Jacob" (cf. Rom 11:26) just as the hubris

of the covenant people requires cutting off those Israelites like Achan, whose infidelity endangers the covenant and therefore the people as a whole (Josh 7:22–26).[97] And if Israel does not do so as prescribed by the Torah,[98] God himself ultimately takes the initiative to prune his people, excising those who are not faithful to the covenant.[99] The time of Israel's redemption is also the time of judgment, when the wicked will be removed from Israel, leaving a righteous remnant as the purified whole of Israel. This is certainly the view of Jubilees, for example, summarized by Peter Enns as follows:

> *Israel as a people* will always remain because God is faithful. Transgression of eternal commands, however, will result in individual punishment and forfeiture of one's individual covenant status. The fact of Israel's election, however, remains sure. In fact, it is precisely the fact that God destroys individuals while maintaining the whole that demonstrates to the people that he is *faithful to the covenant*: the actions of individuals cannot affect God's purpose and plan – Israel's existence is his doing.[100]

Similar images are employed in the Gospels by both John the Baptist (Matt 3:10; Luke 3:9) and Jesus (Matt 7:19; John 15:4–10), who warn that those who do not bear good fruit will be excised and eventually burned.[101] John's additional assertion that descent from Abraham is no safeguard since "God can raise up children for Abraham from these stones" (Matt 3:9; Luke 3:8) further corresponds to Paul's image in which branches are grafted into the tree from outside. Philo also uses a similar

---

of Israel, because they have completely shaken them off and have destroyed their branches (Nah 2:1a, 3 [ET 1:15], 2:2 [ET 2:1]). Cf. also Deut 4:27, "you will be left few in number"; Mal 3:18–21 (ET 3:18–4:3); 2 Chr 36:20; and Isa 27:11, which says Jacob's lawlessness and sin will be removed (cf. Rom 11:27) by a process including the breaking off of branches.

[97] The incorporation of faithful Canaanite Rahab and her family into Israel (Josh 6:25) serves as a sharp contrast to the cutting off of unfaithful Achan and his entire household; the paradigmatic story of Israel's entry into the promised land thus includes both the cutting off the unfaithful natural born and the inclusion of the faithful outsider.

[98] See Exod 12:15, 19; 30:33, 38; 31:14; Lev 7:20–21, 25, 27; 17:4, 9, 14; 18:29; 19:8; 20:5, 17–18; 22:3; 23:29; Num 9:13; 15:30–31; 19:13, 20. See also n. 150 on p. 258.

[99] That God is cutting off (כרת) the unfaithful among his people is an especially common prophetic motif: see Ps 37:9, 22, 28, 34, 38; 101:6–8; Prov 2:21–22; Isa 48:18–19; Jer 6:2; 44:7–12; Hos 8:1–4; 10:1–15; Nah 2:1 [ET 1:15]; Zeph 1:4–6; Zech 13:8–9. See also 1 Kgs 9:7; 14:10, 14; 21:21; 2 Kgs 9:8; 10:32; 2 Chr 22:7. The LXX typically renders כרת terminology with ἐξολεθρεύω, though the terminology of cutting off is retained in some instances (e.g., ἀπαιρέω in LXX Jer 6:2; ἐκκόπτω in LXX Jer 51:7).

[100] Peter Enns, "Expansions of Scripture" (2001), 97 (emphasis original).

[101] Cf. Isa 27:11. Reinhard Feldmeier, "Vater und Töpfer?" (2010), 389, observes this similarity between the Baptist's message and Paul's.

metaphor for the same purpose, explaining that the "well born" (εὐπατρίδης) who do not obey are cut off, leaving only the roots of the tree (*Praem.* 172), while the "foreigner" (ἔπηλυς) who imitates Abraham's example can be incorporated in their place, as God "disregards his original roots ... because he has changed and become cultivated for fruitfulness" (152).[102]

Similarly, in the context of the halakhic statement concerning a consecrated tree in Rom 11:16b, Gordon observes that "the grafting of new branches would have as its primary goal, on a literal level, the sustenance and rejuvenation of the dedication and, on a symbolic level, the joining of all Israel together as a holy community regardless of the stock from which its branches derive."[103] Grafting of unconsecrated branches into sacred olive trees appears to have been practiced in Classical Athens, for example, as a means of propagating the μορίαι, olive trees sacred to Athena supposedly derived from the original olive tree planted by the goddess herself on the sacred rock of the Acropolis.[104] It also can no longer be disputed that the grafting of scions of the wild olive (ἀγριέλαιος) into cultivated olive trees was practiced in antiquity to make an unfruitful cultivated tree more fruitful.[105] In this light, there is little reason to

---

[102] Philo further explains that through new shoots from the root of a tree that has been cut down, "the old tree flourishes again" (*Praem.* 172). Elsewhere, Philo declares that converts are to be received "as friends and kinsmen" since "even if they were previously blind, they have now received their sight" (*Virt.* 179, alluding to Isa 61:1 LXX) – an especially noteworthy statement given Philo's definition of Israel as "seeing God" (e.g., *Praem.* 44; *Her.* 78; *Leg.* 2.34).

[103] Gordon, "Mixtures and Branches," 365.

[104] See S. C. Todd, *A Commentary on Lysias, Speeches 1–11* (2007), 482–87. Cf. also Nikolaos Papazarkadas, *Sacred and Public Land in Ancient Athens* (2011), 260–84. Gordon ("Mixtures and Branches," 361) also notes a related anecdote in m. Pesaḥ. 4:8, which discusses caprification branches attached to consecrated sycamore trees, declaring such to be sacred by their attachment to the consecrated trees.

[105] The first-century Roman writer Columella writes that well-established but unproductive trees can be rejuvenated by engrafting wild olive shoots (*De re rustica* 5.9.16–17) See William M. Ramsay, "The Olive-Tree and the Wild-Olive" (1905); Baxter and Zeisler, "Paul and Arboriculture"; Jewett, *Romans*, 684–85. Remarkably, despite his awareness of the statements of Paul's contemporary about this practice, Esler, "Ancient Oleiculture," 112–20, nevertheless argues that Paul would not have been aware of such a practice because he "had spent his life in the Eastern Mediterranean," where the practice was unknown. To demonstrate this, Esler (113–16) appeals to the earlier Greek writer Theophrastus (371–287 BCE), who outlines the usual practice of grafting cultivated branches onto wild trees and notes that the reverse will not result in quality fruit (τὸ δὲ καλλικαρπεῖν οὐχ ἕξει; *De causis plantarum* 1.6.10). But Theophrastus neither denies that such is done, nor do his comments prove that such practices were not performed in the eastern Mediterranean three centuries later. Esler then notes that

suppose that Paul was a townsman ignorant of arboriculture[106] or that he is deliberately talking botanical nonsense by reversing the usual process to emphasize a specific point about Jewish superiority.[107] Instead, the allegory suggests that God is engaged in the maintenance of the consecrated tree, ensuring its longevity and productivity for sacred purposes by the insertion of previously unconsecrated wild branches,[108] and the primary point is that these engrafted branches are indeed sanctified by incorporation into the sacred tree (11:16b).

God is effectively adding new branches to the family tree,[109] with these newly engrafted branches fully incorporated into the corporate body of "all Israel" as part of the rejuvenation and reviving of the tree. The practice of grafting was already a familiar metaphor for describing the important institution of legal adoption in the Roman world, so the imagery here fits closely with the language of "adoption" Paul uses elsewhere (Rom 8:15, 23; 9:4; Gal 4:5; cf. Eph 1:5).[110] The same image of grafting is also used in later rabbinic literature to symbolize

olive trees were generally raised in nurseries in Italy rather than by grafting (117–18), a detail hardly relevant to the discussion. Moreover, by Esler's own admission (118), Columella visited Cilicia and Syria and would thus have been aware of Eastern Mediterranean practices. Esler's case is further damaged by Philo, *Agr.* 6, "Those which do not produce good fruit, he wishes to improve by insertion of other kinds into their roots, grown together in union." Finally, Esler argues that Columella's procedure is inapplicable because Paul nowhere says anything about the tree being unfruitful (120–21). But Paul does say the broken branches are "unfaithful" (ἀπιστίᾳ), which implies unfruitfulness (or bad fruit) and suggests that the unnatural branches need to produce good fruit to remain in the tree and that the natural branches are more naturally fruitful provided they are faithful.

[106] E.g., Dodd, *Romans*, 180: "[Paul] had not the curiosity to inquire what went on in the olive-yards which fringed every road he walked" (a signal example of a modern interpreter ascribing inconsistency or ignorance to the ancient author rather than to himself). Commentators as ancient as Origen have objected to the impossibility of the practice (*Commentary on Romans* 8.10).

[107] Esler, "Ancient Oleiculture." See also W. D. Davies, "Paul and the Gentiles" (1984); Havemann, "Cultivate Olive – Wild Olive"; Sigurd Grindheim, *Christology in the Synoptic Gospels* (2012), 158–68; Mark D. Nanos, "'Broken Branches': A Pauline Metaphor Gone Awry?" (2010).

[108] Gordon, "Mixtures and Branches," 365–66. The objection of Esler, "Ancient Oleiculture," 119, to the language of "rejuvenation" because Roman society so valued antiquity misses the point, since the object of such rejuvenation is to keep the older plant strong and productive, not to make it younger.

[109] Johnson Hodge, "Olive Trees and Ethnicities," 89.

[110] E.g., Seneca the Elder, *Controversiae*, 2.4.14. Cf. Joshua D. Garroway, *Paul's Gentile-Jews* (2012), 153; Michael Luke Peppard, *The Son of God in the Roman World* (2011), 51–57; Scott, *Adoption as Sons of God*, 81; Johnson Hodge, "Olive Trees and Ethnicities," 83.

intermarriage and the ethnic incorporation resulting from it.¹¹¹ These newly engrafted branches are brought in for the purpose of bearing sacred fruit, but there is some irony in that wild olive trees do not produce worthwhile fruit,¹¹² so the allegory depicts unproductive natural branches being broken off and previously fruitless (or poor-fruited) wild branches being grafted into the tree.¹¹³ By including that detail, Paul emphasizes that these newly engrafted branches were not selected due to their superiority; as already stated in 11:16b, they derive their sanctity (and eventual fruitfulness) from the root of the consecrated tree. The newly engrafted wild branches must also be faithful (=produce good fruit) to remain in the tree, or they will share the fate of the removed natural branches.¹¹⁴

That Paul here says these unfaithful wild branches would be "cut off *also*" (11:22) implies that the broken branches were indeed cut off, which works against Mark Nanos' argument that the natural branches have not been excised but are instead "damaged" and being protected by God. Nanos concedes the problem but suggests that Paul's allegory "goes awry" here and that "the tree allegory has proven unable to communicate this nuanced perspective effectively – it is itself broken."¹¹⁵ Given the force of Paul's arguments to this point and the venerable prophetic tradition of Israelites being cut off from Israel due to infidelity, it is more

---

¹¹¹ Marc Rastoin, "Une bien étrange greffe (Rm 11,17)" (2007), has suggested a connection between Paul's allegory and b. Yebam. 63a, which describes the engrafting of Ruth and Naomi into Israel, though the metaphor there is that of vine cultivation rather than that of an olive tree. Gordon, "Sacred Land Endowments," 272–73, points to an interesting midrash on Ps 128:3 by R. Levi in y. Kil. 27b that says Jewish families should never be adulterated through foreign intermarriage "just as there is no grafting with olives," which Gordon suggests may be an example of anti-Christian polemic: "In sharp contrast to Paul, where foreign branches sustain the tree, R. Levi has them polluting it" (273). On Ps 128:3 and how it "presupposes an astonishing familiarity with the cultivation of olive trees on the part of the poet as well as the hearers of our Psalm," see Frank-Lothar Hossfeld and Erich Zenger, *Psalms 3* (2011), 401–3 (401). See also Helga Weippert, "Deine Kinder seien wie die Schößlinge von Ölbäumen rund um deinen Tisch!" (2001).
¹¹² As noted by Theophrastus, *De causis plantarum* 1.6.10. See also Esler, "Ancient Oleiculture," 122, though again his fuller argument depends on the idea that Paul aims "deliberately to diverge from accepted horticultural practice, in a manner that would be immediately recognized by his eastern Mediterranean audience as a divergence." Why Esler considers the recipients of Romans to be an eastern Mediterranean audience remains a mystery.
¹¹³ On Israel as unfruitful or producing bad fruit, see, e.g., Jer 2:21; Isa 5:1–2.
¹¹⁴ Paul may have considered the gentiles' material contribution to the poor in Jerusalem (15:27) an example of good fruit already being produced.
¹¹⁵ Nanos, "Broken Branches," 368, 369.

probable that Paul is not making the argument Nanos wishes he were. Nevertheless, in another twist of the usual prophetic trope, Paul unexpectedly explains that previously excised branches can be restored into the tree, a striking alteration for a reader accustomed to prophetic warnings about branches being cut off and burned. Thus, the newly engrafted branches should not boast against the broken branches not only because they themselves stand in danger of being removed but also because those branches can be reincorporated. Indeed, the incorporation of gentiles is itself proof of the extent of God's mercy, which applies all the more to the natural-born.

This reminder about God's capacity to reincorporate previously pruned branches is made even more poignant by the realization that the unnatural branches now being grafted in are not branches of other types of trees, a practice also known in antiquity, but wild *olive* branches.[116] Although interpreters have regularly discussed the meaning of the cultivated olive tree, the source of the uncultivated branches has typically not been considered. Recall, however, that many branches have *previously* been excised from Israel and scattered among the nations. Inasmuch as most Roman olive trees were grown from cuttings from older trees,[117] one might expect that these previously excised branches had resulted in uncultivated olives – that is, non-Israelites derived from branches that had previously been cut off from the tree. But now, as evidenced by the incorporation of unconsecrated, non-Israelite branches, even the descendants of previously excised branches may now be incorporated into the cultivated tree.[118]

---

[116] On interspecific grafting, see Varro, *Res rustica*, 1.40.5. Interspecific grafting is prohibited in m. Kil. 1:7 based on Lev 19:19, further attesting to the practice.

[117] Varro, *Res rustica*, 1.41.6; Theophrastus, *Caus. plant.* 5.1.3–4; *Hist. plant.* 2.1.4 (the latter of which says olives grow in more ways than any other plant). Since olives do not grow well from seed, cuttings of one sort or another were the typical method for growing new trees. Ovules (trunk growths) seem to have been preferred by Greek farmers due to the lower water supply, while cuttings from branches were more typically used by Roman husbandmen. See Lin Foxhall, "Olive," *OCD* ; Burford, *Land and Labor*, 130–31.

[118] Goodrich, "Until the Fullness of the Gentiles Comes In," 21, objects on the grounds that "the very branches that have been cut-off are … the *natural* branches (οἱ κατὰ φύσιν κλάδοι, 11:21), and they will remain *natural* when regrafted into *their own* olive tree." But Goodrich does not account for the difference between natural branches recently removed and still capable of being grafted back into their own tree and branches removed and discarded generations earlier, resulting in the uncultivated branches now being engrafted. In any case, while an intriguing possibility that fits well with Paul's

In any case, the branches being grafted into the tree (even the wild ones!) are transformed into members of the consecrated tree by virtue of their connection with the root – that is, all the branches become constituent parts of Israel, including those unnatural branches that were not so prior to their incorporation. And if God can incorporate these wild branches, the branches more recently broken off can obviously be reincorporated even more easily through the same process since they remain elect "according to nature" (cf. 11:28–29).[119] God is therefore calling his people back, not only from the Jews but also from the nations among which Israel had assimilated (cf. 9:24–26), and the fact that God is incorporating outside branches is both proof of his continuing faithfulness to Israel and evidence that those who are currently broken can themselves be reincorporated. Nevertheless, that reincorporation remains contingent on the response of the broken branches, who must not remain unfaithful, or they will not be grafted back in despite God's ability to do so.[120]

Once again, Paul's arguments do not call into question the foundational assumptions about the covenant or Israel's restoration. Instead, he is participating in the larger discourse about the nature of Israel's restoration and where the proper boundaries should be drawn in light of the work of Israel's Messiah – that is, what constitutes fidelity or infidelity to the covenant and what a proselyte must do to become a full member of Israel. For Paul, those "natural branches" who refuse to submit to Messiah are by definition unfaithful to the Torah's command of obedience to the "prophet like Moses," thereby forfeiting their covenantal position in Israel. On the other hand, all who have received the spirit from Messiah – whether circumcised or uncircumcised – and fulfill the "just statutes of the Torah" (2:26) are thereby confirmed as the redeemed people of God through their participation in the new covenant promise. They stand in the tree by fidelity, though they too can be removed if they become disobedient.[121]

Paul's application of the olive tree analogy therefore confirms that he has by no means abandoned the basic principles of covenantal nomism: whereas some (e.g., Jews) are born into the tree by nature and are elect

---

overall argument, identifying these wild branches as derived from branches previously removed is not necessary to the larger argument.

[119] Garroway, *Paul's Gentile-Jews*, 155–56.
[120] Garroway, *Paul's Gentile-Jews*, 145–46.   [121] Garroway, *Paul's Gentile-Jews*, 152.

from birth but can be removed for infidelity,[122] others must come into the tree by an "unnatural" process (i.e., proselytism) and can likewise be cut off for infidelity.[123] Consequently, these newly engrafted gentiles have no basis for celebration or boasting against the broken branches – the inverse of the boasting of the *Ioudaios* chastised in Rom 2–3.[124] Paul thus again warns these unnatural branches that *election is no guarantee of salvation*.[125] That is, neither natural birth nor unnatural adoption guarantee permanent standing in the covenant, which must be sustained by fidelity (cf. 9:30–32; 10:6).[126] The promises ultimately regard the preservation of the tree and those remaining in it, not the individual branches. As he will reinforce in 11:25–26, Paul reminds the unnatural branches that they depend on the root – they are participating in Israel's salvation and their own salvation is part of Israel's story.[127] There is no supersession or replacement here, only incorporation into God's one people Israel, the remnant of which will be saved (9:27; 11:5). Ultimately, both non-Jewish and Jewish branches must coexist equally in the olive tree, the whole of Israel.

---

[122] *Pace* Sanders, *PLJP*, 207–8.

[123] Based on 1 Cor 7:14, Paul explains that the children of uncircumcised Messiah-followers are naturally born into the covenant (ἅγιος), which further indicates that he regards their transformation as what we would call ethnic – since the parents have become Israelites, their children are born with that status. Remarkably, Paul seems to regard *either* a male or female parent as sufficient, which differs from later Rabbinic developments. See Stephen C. Barton, "Sanctification and Oneness in 1 Corinthians with Implications for the Case of 'Mixed Marriages' (1 Corinthians 7.12–16)" (2017); Gordon, "Mixtures and Branches," 364; Yonder Moynihan Gilligan, "Jewish Laws on Illicit Marriage, the Defilement of Offspring, and the Holiness of the Temple" (2002).

[124] The motif of boasting also recalls Jer 9:23–24 (ET 22–23).

[125] The conflation of election and salvation has long been a problem in studies of Paul and early Judaism. Enns, "Expansions of Scripture," 98, observes, "It might be less confusing to say that *election* is by grace but *salvation* is by obedience …. The point still remains, however, that the final outcome is based on more than initial inclusion in the covenant." The distinction between "grace" (χάρις) and "obedience" is also problematic, however, given the reciprocal quality of χάρις, which would include obedience as a response to the initial gift. Nevertheless, the distinction between election and salvation is an important one, as Paul himself distinguishes between the two throughout Rom 9–11. For more analysis of election in this period, including the reminder that "election" language frequently refers to being chosen for specific purposes rather than for salvation, see A. Chadwick Thornhill, *The Chosen People* (2015). On the concept of apostasy in the New Testament, see B. J. Oropeza, *Jews, Gentiles, and the Opponents of Paul* (2012).

[126] Cf. Gadenz, *Called*, 261–62; Garroway, *Paul's Gentile-Jews*, 152.

[127] Kim, "Reading Paul's καὶ οὕτως," 321.

JUDGMENT AND THE REMNANT

It is important to recognize here that the "remnant" is not part of Israel but is instead the whole tree that remains after the pruning process. This reading is contrary to the popular view that Rom 11 moves from the salvation of the *remnant* to the salvation of "the rest," such that "all Israel" (11:26) represents "the sum of the remnant and the [rest]"[128] or "both the remnant and those with hardened hearts combined."[129] Nor is it the case that for Paul "the existence of the remnant is a temporary phenomenon, to be superseded when God's work is complete."[130] Instead, Paul's conception of the remnant corresponds with that of his scriptural source material, in which the "remnant" is simply what remains of Israel after divine judgment and punishment has pared down the community.[131] In the same way, for Paul, the remnant is "all Israel" that remains; the branches that have been cut off are no longer part of "all Israel" but are instead those "from Israel" who are "not Israel" (9:6). Thus "all Israel will be saved" (11:26) and "the remnant will be saved" (9:27) are equivalent statements.

The same basic conception of the "remnant" as the whole people who remain after God's judgment is common in early Jewish literature. In the Damascus Document, for example, God "caused a remnant to remain for Israel" (CD 1:4–5) during the events of destruction and exile and eventually "caused to sprout ... a shoot of a plant" (1:7), from which the "new covenant" community arose (CD 1:8–2:1), and future judgment will come upon those who have turned away during the age of wrath, while those from the community will survive that judgment and be part of the remnant preserved in that time. This combination of the rejection of some and narrowing of God's people to a remnant is explicitly portrayed as a persistent pattern of God's dealing with his people (2:11–13). Similar expectations of a limited remnant surviving the upcoming judgment and comprising the whole of Israel appear elsewhere in Qumran literature

---

[128] Gadenz, *Called*, 276, cf. 78, 263.
[129] Sheinfeld, "Who Is the Righteous Remnant," 46, continuing: "once the full number of gentiles believe, the rest of Israel will join" (47).
[130] Lester V. Meyer, "Remnant" (1992), 671.
[131] For example, in Jer 31(38):7–8, the totality of Israel that is saved is called "the remnant" (that is, the ones who remain after others are removed). That this is the basic conception in the Prophets is recognized by Sheinfeld, "Who Is the Righteous Remnant," 34–35; Meyer, "Remnant," 671. Cf. also Ronald E. Clements, "'A Remnant Chosen by Grace' (Romans 11:5)" (1980); Adi Ophir and Ishay Rosen-Zvi, *Goy* (2018), 65.

(e.g., 1QpHab 5:2–6; 4Q171 2:19; 4:10). But it is not the case that the sectarians therefore regard their "new covenant" as only for a remnant as opposed to the whole nation of Israel as though they understood these as distinct.[132] Instead, the covenant is explicitly stated to be "for all Israel" (CD 15:5) precisely because the remnant *is* "all Israel" that remains after the judgment.[133]

Attempts to contrast the "remnant" with the whole ("all Israel") in Rom 11 are therefore misguided, working against the very language and scriptural/prophetic content employed throughout this discussion. It is nonsense to contrast a newly trimmed tree with the "whole tree," as though the latter referred both to the tree and the branches recently removed from it. On the contrary, the remnant of the tree after it is pruned is the whole tree, though that whole is now smaller than it once was. "All that remains" (=remnant) is indeed different from the previous "all," though after the reduction there is no longer another "all" or "whole" with which to contrast the remnant.[134]

Part of the confusion on this point owes to Paul's insistence that the remnant is still not finalized – broken branches can still be reincorporated into the tree through repentance, being thereby once again included in the remnant that ultimately will be saved. As such, the *present* remnant (cf. 11:5) – that is, those who presently stand within the faithful community and *would* be saved if the judgment were today – is not identical to the *final* remnant that *will* be saved at the eschatological judgment. Instead, the remnant is still under construction, subject to continued expansion, growth, and further pruning until it reaches its fullness. Nevertheless, Paul does not suggest that *all* broken branches will be reincorporated, only that they *can* be reincorporated "*if they do not persist in infidelity*"

---

[132] "The idea that the covenant is for all of Israel and the idea that only a few enter it could, and apparently did, stand side-by-side in the thought of the author and of others who belonged to the same movement" (Stephen J. Hultgren, *From the Damascus Covenant to the Covenant of the Community* [2007], 108–9 n. 55).

[133] The sectarians did not, however, identify themselves as the whole of the remnant or as the "true Israel," as suggested by Sheinfeld, "Who Is the Righteous Remnant," 37. Instead, the sect has positioned themselves to be part of the remnant after divine punishment (see E. P. Sanders, *Paul and Palestinian Judaism* [1977], 249–57). Even then, the sect is not the whole remnant but only a part, as they will be joined by those currently scattered among the nations (see Staples, *The Idea of Israel*, 259–89).

[134] "So the 'remnant' was not merely *one* link in God's salvation history. It was *the* group of the saved" (Timo Eskola, "Paul, Predestination, and 'Covenantal Nomism'" [1997], 99).

(11:23); he therefore hopes to "save *some* of them" (11:14).[135] That distinction is an important one, as Paul is again clear that only the remnant will be saved, though the size of the remnant may still be increased because the process is not yet final and excised branches can still be reincorporated.

With the olive tree analogy, Paul is therefore employing a familiar image to illustrate what he has been arguing throughout Rom 9–11: God's way of dealing with his people has not changed, nor has God rejected Israel. Instead, just as God has always cut off the unfaithful while preserving a remnant in his past dealings with Israel (e.g., 9:26–30), so also now a remnant remains (11:2–5) while not all from Israel are Israel (9:6). The survival of the whole tree does not require the persistence of specific branches but only a remnant attached to the root – the tree remains the whole of itself even after some branches are removed, though the branches must remain attached to the life-giving root to survive.[136] Indeed, just as in the past the disobedient were removed for their infidelity, so also those unfaithful in the present (whether natural or unnatural branch) will likewise be removed to ensure the preservation of the whole – that is, the salvation of "all Israel" (cf. 11:26).[137] Put simply, the remnant *is* all Israel.

PAUL'S MYSTERY REVEALED

Paul concludes the olive tree metaphor by bringing his entire argument to its climax,[138] finally unveiling the "hidden things" (τὰ κρυπτά) of Deut

---

[135] Garroway, *Paul's Gentile-Jews*, 145–46.
[136] Cf. Nanos, "Broken Branches," 369, who observes that individual branches are not Israel but rather Israelites. It is, however, unnecessary to speak of the trunk of the tree (which Paul does not explicitly mention), as does Franz Mussner (*Traktat über die Juden* [1979], 68–74; "Mitteilhaberin an der Wurzel," 153–55), especially since olive trees often do not have a distinct trunk and branches can be grafted directly into the root-shoot (see Klaus Haacker, *Der Brief des Paulus an die Römer* [1999], 233; Aletti, "Le développement de l'argumentation," 205). One might draw some comparison with the venerable "Ship of Theseus" thought experiment wherein the question is whether an object that has had all its constituent parts replaced is in fact the same object. The key difference for Paul is that the root is never replaced, nor are all the natural branches removed.
[137] See Garroway, *Paul's Gentile-Jews*, 150.
[138] The γάρ links Paul's conclusion to the olive tree imagery and, "more specifically, to the claim that God can and will again graft severed Israel[ites] onto the tree" (T. J. Lang, *Mystery and the Making of a Historical Consciousness* [2015], 44 n. 52).

29:28 (ET 29:29), explaining the mystery of the connection between the ingathering of gentiles and Israel's salvation:

For I do not want you to be ignorant, siblings, of this mystery (lest you become high-minded yourselves)[139] that a partial[140] insensibility[141] has come upon Israel until[142] the fullness of the nations has entered – and thus all Israel will be saved,[143]

---

[139] Gk. ἵνα μὴ ἦτε ἑαυτοῖς φρόνιμοι, probably echoing LXX Prov 3:7. Cf. Jewett, *Romans*, 699.

[140] Some have argued ἀπὸ μέρους should be taken adjectivally with Israel, meaning "a part of Israel," (e.g., Jewett, *Romans*, 699–700; Käsemann, *Romans*, 312–13; C. K. Barrett, *Romans* [1991], 206; Anders Nygren, *Romans* [1949], 404). Others have argued that the phrase should be taken adverbially with γέγονεν, rendering "a partial hardening has come upon Israel" (Cranfield, *Romans*, 575; Dunn, *Romans*, 679; Fitzmyer, *Romans*, 621; Moo, *Romans*, 717). Oddly, although Cranfield argues for the adverbial usage, he then translates and treats the phrase adjectivally (Cranfield, *Romans*, 572–75). Although I translated the phrase adjectivally in Staples, "What Do the Gentiles Have to Do with 'All Israel'?" [2011], 371, I have become persuaded that the adverbial reading is grammatically preferable, mostly because it is adverbial in every other Pauline example (Rom 15:15, 24; 2 Cor 1:14, 2:5; see Richard B. Hays, "Hope for What We Do Not Yet See" [2018], 552–54). Taken adverbially, it could either be temporal (modifying γέγονεν and interacting with ἄχρι οὗ; as in the Peshitta) or partitive, "by portion" or "in part" (modifying πώρωσις). Given Paul's previous emphasis that only part ("the rest") of Israel has been made insensible and how ἀπὸ μέρους serves as a natural parallel to the πᾶς Ἰσραήλ in the next verse (see Michael Wolter, "Ein exegetischer und theologischer Blick auf Röm 11.25–32" [2018], 126), I have rendered the phrase as partitive. Both senses may be in play, with the hardening both temporary and partial (that is, a limited portion with respect to both time and space). The partitive adverbial meaning also approaches the meaning of the adjectival reading, which underscores that the phrase is perhaps more easily understood than translated.

[141] Paul brings the πώρωσις theme begun in 11:7 to its conclusion here.

[142] The ἄχρι οὗ here is durative, emphasizing "not the event that follows Israel's blindness, but the duration of Israel's blindness" (Joshua D. Garroway, "The Circumcision of Christ" [2012], 203 n. 22). Cf. 1 Cor 11:26, 15:25; Heb 3:13.

[143] Since Paul's language is ambiguous, I have chosen an equally ambiguous translation ("thus"). Moo, *Romans*, 719–20, lists four options for the sense of the καὶ οὕτως here, choosing the fourth: temporal ("and then"), consequential (referring backwards), consequential (referring forwards), and manner ("in this manner"). Pieter van der Horst, "Only Then Will All Israel Be Saved" (2000), 521–39, has shown (rare) lexical support for the temporal option, leading Jewett, *Romans*, 701, and Scott, "And Then All Israel Will Be Saved (Rom 11:26)" (2001), 492–93, to favor such a meaning here (in conjunction with ἄρχι οὗ). But even if a temporal sense is possible for the phrase, the primary sense seems to be modal – the default Pauline usage for οὕτως (e.g. Rom 1:15; 4:18; 5:12, 15, 18–19, 21; 6:4, 11, 19; 9:20; 10:6; 11:5, 31; 12:15; 15:20) As Zoccali, "All Israel," 309, points out, for a temporal sense Paul would more easily have written καὶ τότε, an alteration that often appears in the patristic period (see Scott, "All Israel," 491–92). Lang, *Mystery*, 44 n. 56, rightly emphasizes that what matters here is that Israel's salvation is presented as the *logical consequence* of the first two factors, whether it should be construed as temporally posterior or causative. Cf. also Judith M. Gundry Volf, *Paul and Perseverance* (1990), 179–81.

just as it is written: "The deliverer will come from Zion;[144] he will remove impiety from Jacob. And this is my covenant with them when I take away their sins." (Rom 11:25–27)

Perplexed interpreters through the ages have agreed with Origen's declaration that "only God – and his only begotten and perhaps any who are his friends" understands this passage.[145] Nearly every word in 11:25–26 has been the subject of significant debate, as the unveiling has been found more inscrutable than the mystery itself.[146] To understand this passage, one must satisfactorily answer three primary interpretive questions: (1) how Paul defines "all Israel," (2) what Paul means by "the fullness of the nations/gentiles," and (3) how the salvation of the former is connected (καὶ οὕτως) to the incoming of the latter.[147] These questions can be further boiled down and framed as follows: what does the entrance (into what?) of "the fullness of the nations/gentiles" have to do with the salvation of "all Israel"?

A MYSTERIOUS SEQUENCE?

Despite identifiable scriptural analogues for each of the three elements of the mystery, most interpreters have nevertheless found the relationship between each element and especially the sequence of Paul's revelation mystifying.[148] Why is Israel's salvation contingent on the incoming of the fullness of the nations and how are those two elements related? Gadenz speaks for most interpreters when he says, "There are no texts which

---

[144] Paul's reading (ἐκ Σιών) differs from every other ancient reading of Isa 59:20, which portrays the deliverer's victorious return *to* Zion or "for Zion's sake." See Wagner, *Heralds of the Good News*, 284–886 and the discussion below.

[145] Origen, CER 4:304. Origen then gives a very Philonic interpretation of "Israel," suggesting that it cannot attain salvation as long as it remains fleshly but only if it becomes a "true Israelite" according to the Spirit through "gazing on God," though he still takes no defined position as to what the "all" means. See Thomas P. Scheck, ed., *Origen: Commentary on the Epistle to the Romans, Books 6–10* (2002), 184; Cohen, "Israel's Salvation."

[146] For a fuller look at the history of interpretation over the past century, see Zoccali, "All Israel"; Christopher Zoccali, *Whom God Has Called* (2010), 91–117.

[147] Scott, "All Israel," 490. For a similar but slightly different breakdown of the necessary interpretive questions, see Franz Mussner, "Ganz Israel wird gerettet werden (Röm 11,26)" (1976), 241.

[148] E.g., Seyoon Kim, "The 'Mystery' of Rom 11:25–26 Once More" (1997), 415–20; Jewett, *Romans*, 698–99. Moo, *Romans*, 716, lists several difficulties in the passage in addition to the sequence itself.

support the three clauses of the mystery together .... The mystery is thus not revealed as such in the Scriptures."[149] Regarding Paul's sequence as a non sequitur, most modern interpreters have added a fourth element between the incoming of the nations and all Israel's salvation: a future mass conversion of Jews, perhaps out of jealousy in response to the gentile ingathering.[150] That a fourth element has been added to the sequence is frequently overlooked because so many conflate conversion and salvation, but Paul does not say "all Israel will be converted" or "all Israel will believe the gospel" but rather "all Israel will be saved." Others, presuming that Jews are saved through another path, have denied any connection at all between the incoming of the fullness of the nations and Israel's salvation.[151] But Paul makes a clear connection (καὶ οὕτως) between the first two elements and the consequent result, and it is precisely this logical progression that he labels a "mystery" – a previously hidden but newly revealed knowledge of the eternal design and plan of God for Israel's salvation.[152]

The primary difficulty with Paul's sequence is that the entrance of the gentiles (into a destination left implicit) apparently precedes the salvation of Israel, an inversion of the order expected in prophetic and apocalyptic

---

[149] Gadenz, *Called*, 210 n. 149. See also Jacob Neusner, "The Premise of Paul's Ethnic Israel" (1995), 283.

[150] "He seems to have quoted Scripture to prove what he had just said, that all Israel would be saved as a consequence of the Gentile mission" (Sanders, *PLJP*, 196). "The first mystery is that Israel will be saved as a result of the Gentile mission. The second would be that at the end Israel will be saved apart from the work of the apostles" (206 n. 92). Paul, however, only mentions one mystery, nor does he suggest Israel will be saved "apart from the work of the apostles."

[151] E.g., Lloyd Gaston, *Paul and the Torah* (1987); John G. Gager, *Reinventing Paul* (2000). The idea itself is usually traced back to Stendahl, *Paul among Jews and Gentiles* (1976), though Stendahl distanced himself from this interpretation (*Final Account: Paul's Letter to the Romans* [1993], x–xi). For critiques, see Reidar Hvalvik, "A 'Sonderweg' for Israel: A Critical Examination of a Current Interpretation of Romans 11.25–27" (1990); Sanger, "Rettung der Heiden"; Terence L. Donaldson, "Jewish Christianity, Israel's Stumbling Block and the *Sonderweg* Reading of Paul" (2006). A newer subgroup of scholars (e.g., Pamela Eisenbaum, *Paul Was Not a Christian* [2009]; Gabriele Boccaccini, *Paul's Three Paths to Salvation* [2020]) has also presented a "two-ways salvation" reading that avoids the language of two covenants but still argues that Paul regards all Torah-observant Jews as saved whether or not they follow Jesus. The primary problem with this view is that Paul seems to equate proper Torah observance with following Jesus.

[152] Lang, *Mystery*, 44. Lang's larger project demonstrates how Paul and other early Christians use this type of "once hidden/now revealed" schema and language of "mystery" to imbue new revelation with old authority. Cf. Sanger, "Rettung der Heiden," 115.

literature, wherein Israel's restoration is often followed by gentiles making an eschatological pilgrimage to worship YHWH in Jerusalem.[153] Sanders goes so far as to argue that "Paul's entire work, both evangelizing and collecting money, had its setting in the expected pilgrimage of the Gentiles to Mount Zion in the last days,"[154] though the success of the gentile mission and corresponding failure of the Jewish mission caused him to conclude that "the eschatological scheme has been reversed; Israel will be saved not first, but as a result of the Gentile mission."[155] Along the same lines, Seeyoon Kim concludes that Paul's mystery must have been the result of a personal revelation since there is no scriptural source for such a sequence of events:

> Is it not strange that Paul explicitly substantiates the inference from the "mystery" proper with the Scriptures but does not do the same for the "mystery" proper itself? Had he obtained the "mystery" from the exegesis of the Scriptures, is it not to be expected of him to substantiate it with reference to those Scriptures?[156]

But if Paul did in fact have a personal revelation that the anticipated order of eschatological events would be inverted, it seems especially strange that he opens Romans by declaring that the gospel is "to the Jew first and also to the Greek" (1:16). In response to this problem, Kim argues that Paul did not actually follow the order he states in 1:16, since there is "little evidence for Paul's ever having concentrated on a mission to

---

[153] Thus, in his critique of my paradigm as laid out in Staples, "All Israel," Goodrich notes that "numerous passages in Jeremiah ... do in fact forecast the conversion/pilgrimage of the nations" and asks "what role Paul would have assigned to those nations in his New Covenant appropriation of Jeremiah's prophecy, because the [sic] Gentiles have already been allocated the role of Ephraim" ("Until the Fullness of the Gentiles Comes In," 20). The problem (as noted below) is that Paul nowhere references those passages, whereas he does frequently cite passages about northern Israel in relation to his gentile converts. (Note Goodrich's use of the definite article with "gentiles" in this context, whereas Paul nowhere refers to the salvation of "the" gentiles but rather of *some* gentiles, specifically "the fullness of the nations/gentiles.")

[154] Sanders, *PLJP*, 171.

[155] Sanders, *PLJP*, 195. Similarly, Dunn, *Romans*, 682, along with many others. On early Jewish gentile eschatological pilgrimage traditions, see esp. Terence L. Donaldson, "Proselytes or 'Righteous Gentiles'?" (1990). Cf. Paula Fredriksen, "Judaism, the Circumcision of Gentiles, and Apocalyptic Hope" (1991); Rainer Stuhlmann, *Das eschatologische Mass im Neuen Testament* (1983), 166–73.

[156] Kim, "Mystery," 416–17. Similarly, Gadenz, *Called*, 210–11: "Since it is something new, the mystery in 11:25b–26a is not contained as such in the (OT) Scriptures. The mystery itself goes beyond the Scriptures (but not against them), and indeed, the Scriptures can be re-read in light of the revealed mystery." Cf. Otfried Hofius, "Das Evangelium und Israel" (1986), 324.

the Jews, or, at least, for his having worked for the Jewish mission as much as for the gentile mission."[157] Such a statement ignores Paul's own testimony, as the fact that Paul "received thirty-nine lashes from the Jews five times" (2 Cor 11:24) indicates considerable activity in and around synagogues,[158] though one wonders on what basis one could judge whether such efforts amount to "as much as for the gentile mission." Of course, if Paul understood his gentile mission as part and parcel of a mission to Israel for Israel's restoration, that would provide a natural explanation for why some synagogue authorities might have taken exception to his activities. In any case, one must still account for why, if he had personal revelation that the sequence had been reversed, Paul explicitly states that the gospel is "to the Jew first and also to the Greek."

Moreover, if Paul were suggesting that the eschatological pilgrimage of the gentiles was being fulfilled through his gentile mission, why is it that he "never cites pilgrimage texts, despite plenty of opportunities"?[159] For that matter, the verb εἰσέρχομαι ("enter" or "come in"), which Paul associates with the "fullness of the nations," does not appear in a single eschatological pilgrimage text, making it an especially odd word choice if Paul were connecting the faithful gentiles of his *ekklēsias* with these passages.[160] To make matters worse, such an inversion of the sequence of these passages abandons the logical foundation of the tradition itself, since the gentile pilgrimage is consistently depicted as the nations' awed response to Israel's redemption and the glorification of Zion.[161] It is simply implausible that Paul understood his gentile mission as the fulfillment of the prophecies of the eschatological pilgrimage of the nations

---

[157] Kim, "Mystery," 418–19, 428; cf. Jewett, *Romans*, 698.   [158] See p. 25.
[159] Donaldson, "Riches for the Gentiles," 92.
[160] As acknowledged by Bell, *Provoked to Jealousy*, 132, though he believes this "is not an insuperable difficulty."
[161] As noted by Donaldson, "Riches for the Gentiles," 92. Donaldson had previously taken the eschatological pilgrimage view in "The 'Curse of the Law' and the Inclusion of the Gentiles" (1986), 94–112. Scott, "All Israel," 495, on the other hand, argues that Isa 49:22; 60:4, 9; 66:20 imply that "the nations will become devotees *before* the exiles are brought back to Jerusalem" and concludes that Paul believed in a "two-stage process of Israel's restoration" (further 492–96, 524–25). Similarly, Richard J. Bauckham, "The Restoration of Israel in Luke-Acts," 457 (cf. 472): "In Isaiah it is the Gentile nations, drawn by the light of the gloriously restored Jerusalem, who will bring mother Zion's exiled children back to her." But the nations do not precede Israel's restoration in these passages but rather respond to the glorious restoration of Jerusalem/Zion and then aid in the return of the exiles. Moreover, this reading ignores that in Isaiah, the gentiles do not *precede* but rather *join together with* Israel – these events are concurrent rather than subsequent to one another (see Hahn, "All Israel," 102).

despite (1) reversing the order of events, (2) not citing or alluding to any such passages in his discussion of the matter in question, and (3) nowhere encouraging his converts from the gentiles to make a pilgrimage to Jerusalem.

PAUL'S MYSTERY: THE FULLNESS OF THE NATIONS

Fortunately, a more robust explanation is available, as Paul does in fact substantiate the mystery from the scriptures, citing what he apparently regards as the final, conclusive proof at precisely the transition between Israel's partial insensibility and salvation: the incoming of "the fullness of the nations" (τὸ πλήρωμα τῶν ἐθνῶν). The meaning of this peculiar phrase has proven especially elusive. Some have suggested the phrase represents the completion of the gentile mission – that is, when gentile salvation reaches its "fullest extent" or the gospel has gone out to the whole gentile world[162] – while others have suggested it denotes a predestined but unspecified number of elect gentiles (or nations) in keeping with an unspecified apocalyptic scheme.[163] But the reason this phrase has been so difficult to explain is that its scriptural underpinnings have consistently been overlooked.

The key to understanding this passage is recognizing the connection between Paul's peculiar phrase "the fullness of the nations" and Jacob's use of the same phrase in his blessing of Joseph's sons, where the aged patriarch explains that he is placing his right hand on the younger Ephraim's head because:

> [Manasseh] will also become a people and he will also be great. However, his younger brother [Ephraim] will be greater than he, and <u>his seed will be the fullness of the nations.</u>[164] (Gen 48:19)

---

[162] E.g., Johannes Munck, *Christ and Israel* (1967), 134–35; Hans Hübner, *Gottes Ich und Israel* (1984), 112–13.

[163] See especially Stuhlmann, *Das eschatologische Mass*, 164–78; Hans Hübner, "πλήρομα," *EDNT* 3:110–11. Cf. Jewett, *Romans*, 700; Dunn, *Romans*, 691; Moo, *Romans*, 718–19; Fitzmyer, *Romans*, 621–22; Neusner, "Paul's Ethnic Israel," 349; Roger D. Aus, "Paul's Travel Plans to Spain and the 'Full Number of the Gentiles' of Rom. XI 25" (1979); Gadenz, *Called*, 243, 274. For ἔθνη as "nations" rather than individual gentiles here, see James M. Scott, *Paul and the Nations* (1995), 127; Gadenz, *Called*, 243 n. 269; Arland J. Hultgren, "The Scriptural Foundations for Paul's Mission to the Gentiles" (2006), 35.

[164] Following the translation of John Skinner, *Genesis* (1930), 506, who notes that מלא־הגוים is "a peculiar expression for populousness." Philo (*Leg.* 3.88–94) interprets Gen 48:19 together with the Jacob/Esau story of Gen 25:21–23 (cf. Rom 9:10–13); likewise,

Table 7.1 *Ephraim's seed: The fullness of the nations*

Rom 11:25b	ὅτι πώρωσις ἀπὸ μέρους τῷ Ἰσραὴλ γέγονεν ἄχρι οὗ <u>τὸ πλήρωμα τῶν ἐθνῶν</u> εἰσέλθη	... that an insensibility has come upon Israel for awhile until <u>the fullness of the nations</u> enters.
Gen 48:19b MT	ואולם אחיו הקטן יגדל ממנו וזרעו יהיה <u>מלא־הגוים</u>	... however, his younger brother [Ephraim] will be greater than he, and his seed will be <u>the fullness of the nations</u>.
Gen 48:19b LXX	ἀλλὰ ὁ ἀδελφὸς αὐτοῦ ὁ νεώτερος μείζων αὐτοῦ ἔσται καὶ τὸ σπέρμα αὐτοῦ ἔσται εἰς <u>πλῆθος ἐθνῶν</u>	... but his younger brother will be greater than he, and his seed will be <u>a multitude of nations</u>.

At the very climax of his argument, Paul alludes to yet another passage about the northern Israelites,[165] only this time the cited passage explicitly identifies Israel/Ephraim as the ancestor of gentiles/nations (ἔθνη). It is remarkable that interpreters have so consistently missed the scriptural antecedent of such a singular and difficult phrase.[166] The most likely reason is that Paul's wording differs slightly from the LXX, as seen in Table 7.1.

The phrase "the fullness of the nations" (τὸ πλήρωμα τῶν ἐθνῶν) is a word-for-word rendering of the odd Hebrew phrase מלא־הגוים, which is nearly as baffling in its original context as in Paul's own use of the phrase.[167] The Septuagint harmonizes this phrase with the "multitude/tumult of nations" (המון גוים) promised to Abraham in Gen 17:4,[168]

Barn.13 connects these two Genesis passages (using them to argue that the covenant is "ours" and not "theirs"), suggesting Paul is referencing texts already connected in prior tradition.

[165] Recall that Ephraim is used in synonymous parallelism with Israel in Hos 5:3, 5; 6:10; 7:1 and represents the whole northern nation in Hos 4:17; 5:11; 7:8; 8:11.

[166] Even those focusing on the use of scripture in the New Testament or Paul specifically have regularly missed it, as the connection to Gen 48:19 goes unmentioned in E. Earle Ellis, *Paul's Use of the Old Testament* (2003); Walter C. Kaiser, *The Uses of the Old Testament in the New* (2001); and the discussion of this passage in Mark Seifrid, "Romans" in Beale and Carson, eds., *Commentary on the New Testament Use of the Old Testament* (2007), 672–78.

[167] "This last phrase occurs only here and is difficult to interpret" (Gordon J. Wenham, *Genesis 16–50* [1994], 466). Cf. Edwin C Kingsbury, "He Set Ephraim Before Manasseh" (1967).

[168] That the LXX uses the same phrase in both passages suggests the two passages were often interpreted together. Paul himself cites Gen 17:4 in Gal 3:7–8 to argue that justified gentiles are children of Abraham.

though it nowhere else translates מלא ("fullness") as πλῆθος ("multitude"), which more typically translates words from the רבב root.[169] Paul's use of πλήρωμα, however, accords with the usual LXX translation for מלא elsewhere.[170] This variance should hardly be surprising, as Paul's quotations often differ from the LXX (particularly in Rom 9–11),[171] and he frequently tends "toward a Hebrew exemplar."[172] Paul's claim to be a native "Hebrew" speaker (Phil 3:5; 2 Cor 11:22) is obviously relevant here,[173] though given the usual Greek translation of מלא, it is also possible that his Greek exemplar already contained this reading. In any case, πλήρωμα is a word often carrying an apocalyptic or eschatological connotation, fitting nicely into the apocalyptic context of this passage.[174]

Some may object that such a short phrase is insufficiently recognizable as a reference to Gen 48:19, but the peculiarity and uniqueness of the phrase – a *hapax legomenon* and interpretive puzzle in both Romans and Genesis – militates against accidental coincidence of language and gives the allusion an especially high intertextual volume.[175] Even one word can easily be evocative given the right context and setup among a group sharing the same cultural capital. For example, among the right group of people, the exclamation "Inconceivable!" is enough to draw knowing laughter based on immediate recognition of the source material. In such cases, Wagner, notes, "We should not underestimate the close knowledge of [scripture] possible for ancient readers – particularly those with

---

[169] E.g., Gen 16:4; 27:28; 30:30; 32:12; 36:7; 48:16; Exod 1:9; 15:7; 19:21; 23:2; it occasionally translates המון (Gen 17:4; Judg 4:7; 2 Sam 18:29).

[170] E.g., 1 Chr 16:32; Ps 23:1; 49:12 [50:12 MT]; 88:12 [89:12 MT]; 95:11; 97:7; Eccl 4:6; Jer 8:16; 29:2 [47:2 MT]; Ezek 12:19; 19:7; 30:12.

[171] Cf. Anthony T. Hanson, "Vessels of Wrath or Instruments of Wrath?" (1981), 443. The citations in Rom 9:9, 13, 17, 20, 25, 27, 28, 33; 10:5, 7, 11, 15, 19, 20; 11:2, 3, 8, 9–10, 25a, and 26b–27 all differ from the LXX, while those in Rom 9:7, 20; 11:2, 11:34, 35 appear without introductory formulae. For more on Romans' use of scripture and the relationship between Paul's citations and the LXX, see Christopher D. Stanley, *Paul and the Language of Scripture* (1992), 83–184; Wagner, *Heralds of the Good News*, 341–52; Timothy H. Lim, *Holy Scripture in the Qumran Commentaries and Pauline Letters* (1997), 140–60.

[172] Wagner, *Heralds of the Good News*, 16 n. 40, 126–36, 170–74, 340–51 (quote from 16 n. 40). See also Lim, *Holy Scripture*, 140–60.

[173] See Staples, *The Idea of Israel*, 78–80.

[174] On πλήρωμα as a specialized apocalyptic term, see Jewett, *Romans*, 677–78, 700–701; Hans Dieter Betz, *Galatians* (1979), 206; Stuhlmann, *Das eschatologische Mass*, 164–78; Heinrich Schlier, *Der Brief an die Galater* (1989), 340–41; Hübner, "πλήρωμα," 3:110–11. There is, however, no need to read πλήρωμα quantitatively in Rom 11:25.

[175] For the concept of intertextual volume, see Hays, *Echoes*, 30.

scholastic interests – who regarded it as a sacred text."[176] In any case, the echo of Gen 48:19 is significantly stronger than any echoes to the "eschatological pilgrimage" traditions often alleged to be detectable in this passage, such as Aus' suggestion that the phrase is a modification of LXX Isa 60:5,[177] which shares only "nations" (ἐθνῶν) – hardly a rare word – with Paul's phrase here.

If the phrase "the fullness of the nations" were the only data point, one might dismiss its significance as an interesting but insignificant or even coincidental echo. But this reading is in elegant continuity with everything Paul has argued to this point, continuing a clear pattern of applying scripture about the northern kingdom (Ephraim) to the nations throughout Romans, especially in chapters 9–11. More than that, the reference to the blessing of Ephraim brings the argument of Rom 9–11 full circle. The argument begins in Rom 9 by calling attention to Isaac and Jacob/Israel as the heirs of the promise to Abraham, rooting his defense of gentile inclusion in the ancestral narratives of Genesis. In so doing, he builds on the foundation established in Rom 4, which discusses the nature of Abraham's seed, arguing that the covenantal promise establishes Abraham as the father of both circumcised and uncircumcised (4:10–12). That covenantal promise is specifically that Abraham will be "father of many nations" (Rom 4:17; Gen 17:4–5), in whose seed "all the nations of the earth will be blessed" (Gen 22:18). That promise is then inherited by Isaac (Gen 26:4) and Jacob, to whom God promises that "a nation and an assembly (קהל) of nations will come from you" (Gen 35:11; cf. 28:3; 48:4), especially evocative language in the context of Paul's inclusion of gentiles within the messianic *ekklēsia* (cf. Rom 16:4, ἐκκλησίαι τῶν ἐθνῶν).[178]

But Jacob is not the final patriarch in Genesis to inherit this specific blessing pertaining to the nations. Instead, he explicitly passes this blessing to the next chosen heir: Ephraim, the son of Jacob's beloved son

---

[176] Wagner, *Heralds of the Good News*, 147–48.   [177] Aus, "Paul's Travel Plans," 251.
[178] The LXX translates קהל with συναγωγή in Gen–Num but defaults to ἐκκλησία elsewhere. In the three blessings of Jacob/Israel in Gen 28:3; 35:11; 48:4, the singular קהל is rendered with a plural, producing "synagogues/gatherings of peoples/nations." This rendering effectively actualizes the prophecy for its diaspora readers, who would have naturally identified their own synagogues among the nations as at least a partial fulfillment of the promise to Israel. See Ralph J. Korner, *Origin and Meaning of Ekklēsia in the Early Jesus Movement* (2017), 95–96. On the actualization of prophetic texts in the LXX, see Staples, *The Idea of Israel*, 191, 195. Paul surely understood this promise to Jacob/Israel as being fulfilled in and through his ministry, though in a very different fashion from that suggested by the LXX translators.

Joseph. In Genesis, the blessing of Ephraim therefore serves as an extension of YHWH's promise to Jacob/Israel and Abraham *as it specifically pertains to the nations*. It should therefore come as no surprise that Paul pulls from that blessing for his concluding statement on the matter, closing the narrative loop begun in Rom 9. The first section of the argument focuses on three of the four patriarchs of Genesis linked to the promise of blessing to the nations: Abraham, Isaac, and Jacob/Israel. The argument then concludes with allusive reference to the blessing given to the fourth, thereby linking the incorporation of gentiles to the fulfillment of the covenantal promise.[179]

This is the emphatic concluding statement to which Paul has been building from the very beginning of the book. The physically uncircumcised people displaying the "work of the Torah written on their hearts," (Rom 2:14–15) are God's way of resurrecting the house of Israel, which must be united with the faithful from the house of Judah.[180] Dishonored and useless vessels previously cast among the nations (Hos 8:8; Jer 22:28) are becoming vessels of mercy (Rom 9:23). God is redeeming "not my people" from among the nations as promised, but in a surprising twist, that redemption involves calling vessels of mercy "not only from Jews but also from gentiles" (9:24). Israel is being resurrected through those who are literally "not my people" – gentiles outside the covenant people – becoming "children of the living God" (9:26). Branches were broken off from the olive tree of Israel due to infidelity (Jer 11:16–17), but now wild olive branches are being grafted into the tree by fidelity (Rom 11:17–24). Israel was rendered partly insensible (11:7, 11:25) but only until Ephraim's seed ("the fullness of

---

[179] Notably, although that promise is extended to Joseph and Ephraim, the ruler designated to receive "the obedience of the peoples" will come from Judah (Gen 49:10). The reference to "the seed ... to whom the promise had been made" in Gal 3:19 alludes to this passage, presumably reading the textual variant שלה, "which is to him," another example of Paul citing this portion of Genesis at a key moment in his argument. On Gal 3:19 as containing a messianic reading of Gen 49:10, see Dahl, *Studies in Paul*, 172; Donald H. Juel, *Messianic Exegesis* (1988), 86. Thanks to Logan Williams for reminding me of this connection.

[180] Cf. Rom 2:28–29; Ezek 37:15–23; John 10:14–16; 11:51–52. Eusebius, *Eclogae propheticae*, PG 22.1172, explicitly ties this phrase to the restoration of Israel, identifying the ten tribes of the "stick of Ephraim" (Ezek 37:16) with "the fullness of the nations" in Rom 11:25. See Joel Marcus, "'The Twelve Tribes in the Diaspora' (James 1.1)," 444–46, though *pace* Marcus, "the fullness of the nations" is not a second group apart from "the lost sheep of the house of Israel" in this passage but instead stands in appositional relationship, identifying "the fullness of the nations" not only with the stick of Ephraim but also with the "discovery of the lost sheep of the house of Israel."

the nations") comes into the assembly of YHWH (11:25).[181] This is how Israel is brought to its fullness (11:12; τὸ πλήρωμα αὐτῶν) – and "what is their acceptance," Paul asks, "if not life from the dead" (11:15)?[182] In keeping with Ezekiel's prophecy, the resurrection of the "whole house of Israel" (πᾶς οἶκος Ἰσραηλ; Ezek 37:11) from the dead through the indwelling of the spirit (37:14) also means uniting the "stick of Joseph, which is in the hand of Ephraim, and the tribes of Israel, his companions" together "with the stick of Judah," making them "one stick in [YHWH's] hand" (Ezek 37:19). This is how *all* Israel will be saved as promised.

"ALL ISRAEL": ISRAEL AND JUDAH

With the phrase "all Israel," Paul reminds the reader that God promised not only to redeem and restore the Jews (=Judahites) but all twelve tribes of Israel, including the non-Jewish northern tribes rendered insensible and cut off for breaking covenant. Unfortunately, because most modern interpreters have presupposed that "when Paul says 'Israel,' he means 'Jews,'"[183] this nuance has been consistently missed, as interpreters have attempted to understand how Paul suddenly pivots to the claim that "all Jews" will be saved.[184] But such a meaning for "all Israel" not only would

---

[181] Paul's use of "entered" (εἰσέρχομαι) likely derives from "enter the assembly of YHWH" (Deut 23:4, 9 [ET 23:3, 8]), which accounts for why he can leave the object unstated. Cf. m. Yad. 4:4, discussed on p. 209. To enter the assembly of YHWH is to be received as a legitimate Israelite. See also the discussion in n. 125 on p. 32.

[182] The parallel between "their fullness" (τὸ πλήρωμα αὐτῶν) in Rom 11:12 and "the fullness of the nations/gentiles" (τὸ πλήρωμα τῶν ἐθνῶν) 11:25 is also often noted, but most have agreed that "there is not a complete parallel between the two uses of πλήρωμα" (Gadenz, *Called*, 243 n. 269), because v. 12 is most likely not quantitative (contra Jewett, *Romans*, 700). But none of Paul's other uses of πλήρωμα are quantitative (Rom 11:12; 13:10; 15:29; 1 Cor 10:26; Gal 4:4), and it is unlikely that 11:25 is an exception in that respect. Once the full import of 11:25 is understood, 11:12 takes on even more significance: through the ingathering of gentiles, God is resurrecting Israel (cf. Ezek 37). Contra Goodrich, "Until the Fullness of the Gentiles Comes In," 21, Rom 11:12 by no means invalidates the allusion to Gen 48:19 in 11:25. On the contrary, Paul surely employs this wording in 11:12 specifically to set up 11:25–26.

[183] Paula Fredriksen, "Circumcision Is Nothing" (2022), 79; cf. Fredriksen, "What Does It Mean to See Paul 'within Judaism'" (2022), 376. Fredriksen recognizes that "'all Israel' means all twelve tribes, itself an eschatological idea" (95) but does not explain why Paul would then idiosyncratically limit "Israel" to Jews alone, nor what Paul thought about the apparent absence of many non-Jewish tribes in his own day.

[184] For surveys of past views on the meaning of "all Israel," see Zoccali, "All Israel"; Keller, *Gottes Treue, Israels Heil*, 223–41; William Chi-Chau Fung, "Israel's Salvation" (2004), 19–34, 190–210.

be at odds with Paul's own argument to this point in Romans, it would be unique to Paul among the Jewish literature of the Second Temple period, wherein, as discussed in Chapter 1, "Israel" is not identical with "Jews" but is the superset of which Jews are a subset. Indeed, Jewish sources throughout the Second Temple period attest to an expectation of a restoration of the full twelve-tribe people of God, including both Jews and non-Jewish Israelites from the northern tribes.

Recall, for example, that Josephus distinguishes between the Jews (*Ioudaioi*) who returned from Babylon and "all the people of Israel" (ὁ πᾶς λαὸς τῶν Ἰσραηλιτῶν) who "remained in that country," explaining that "only two tribes came to Asia and Europe and are subject to the Romans, but the ten tribes are beyond the Euphrates until now" (*Ant.* 11.132–33). For his part, in case the reader might be misled by the ambiguity of the unmodified term "Israel," Paul goes out of his way to emphasize this larger scope of the term by adding the qualifier "all," effectively removing all doubt that he, like Josephus, is referring to the larger, twelve-tribe ethnic group including but not limited to Jews.[185] For Paul to employ "all Israel" here to mean something else would surely prove confusing to his audience, who would have no reason or precedent to expect this phrase to mean "all Jews."

Instead, by employing the phrase "all Israel," Paul signals that, like other apocalyptic Jews of his day, he expected not only the salvation of "the Jews" but also the larger redemption of the full twelve-tribe people of Israel in accordance with the promises of the prophets. That larger-scale restoration has been in view all along in Romans, and his conclusion naturally resolves the question of how Israel's fullness (cf. 11:12) will be restored. Paul proclaims that through the combination of faithful Jews with the entrance (engrafting) of "the fullness of the nations," not only Judah but *all* Israel – that is, the entire sacred olive tree from 11:16–24 – will be saved. Note that the emphasis here falls on the "all" rather than the "Israel." It is a given that Israel will be saved, but Paul's argument all

---

[185] "In the OT, the expression 'all Israel' relates exclusively to the *tribal structure* of the descendants of Jacob/Israel" (Scott, "All Israel," 507). See also James W. Flanagan, "The Deuteronomic Meaning of the Phrase 'kol yiśrā'ēl'" (1976). Ferdinand Hahn, "Zum Verständnis von Römer 11.26a" (1982), 229, argues that the phrase indicates that in percentage terms the number of saved Israelites will surpass the number of saved gentiles, but this requires Paul to have said something other than what he meant. Understanding "all Israel" as denoting the whole people (including all the tribes) despite some individuals being cut off from that people is the most natural solution, especially following the olive tree metaphor.

along has been that the non-Jewish part of Israel is being miraculously included in this salvation, ensuring that *all* Israel – not just one or two tribes – will be saved.

The previously puzzling connection between the ingathering of "the fullness of the nations" and the salvation of "all Israel" suddenly makes sense, since "all Israel" must include Ephraim's seed. It should be noted that the Joseph tribes are an especially suitable illustration of the incorporation of outsiders into Israel through intermarriage because Ephraim and Manasseh are the product of Joseph's marriage to the daughter of an Egyptian priest (Gen 41:45–52), a fact that apparently required some creative explanation among later readers potentially scandalized by such things.[186] Moreover, the eschatological significance of the "fullness" (πλήρωμα) concept may have also led Paul to conclude that since Ephraim did not just become "gentiles" but "the fullness of the gentiles," representatives from every nation – corresponding with the seventy nations of Gen 10 – must be included for Ephraim's restoration to be complete.[187]

In any case, because *all* Israel must include not only Jews but the remnant of both houses of Israel, Paul argues that the inclusion of "the fullness of the nations" into Israel is necessary for all Israel to be saved. This reading therefore also clarifies the implied object of the verb "enter" or "come in" (εἰσέρχομαι) in v. 25,[188] a puzzle that "has long vexed interpreters who think the destination is anything but God's people Israel."[189] But if the gentiles are coming into Israel (that is, God's

---

[186] See Esau McCaulley, *Reading While Black* (2020), 100–103. That Joseph's marriage was problematic for later Jewish audiences is evident from Joseph and Aseneth, which takes great pains to clarify that Aseneth was divinely transformed in order to marry the patriarch. See Jill Hicks-Keeton, *Arguing with Aseneth* (2018); Matthew Thiessen, "Aseneth's Eight-Day Transformation as Scriptural Justification for Conversion" (2014); Ross Shepard Kraemer, *When Aseneth Met Joseph* (1998).

[187] On the significance of the "table of nations" tradition to Paul's ministry, see Scott, *Paul and the Nations*. This understanding of the "fullness of the nations" would also correspond to the need for the gospel to go to "all the nations" (Rom 16:26; cf. Mark 13:10; Matt 28:19; Luke 24:47) and the significance of "every nation" in Acts 2:5, 10:35; Rev 7:9.

[188] Cranfield, *Romans*, 576, observes that the verb is "seldom used by Paul, and he uses it in this pregnant sense nowhere but here."

[189] Garroway, "Circumcision of Christ," 144. See n. 181 on p. 312. Despite his awareness of gentiles being incorporated into Israel in the past, Wright, *Paul and the Faithfulness of God*, 1243, wrongly sees such entry of gentiles into Israel as at odds with an "ethnic" definition of Israel, characterizing it as a "polemical redefinition indeed." Others have suggested that the destination is inclusion in the gentile eschatological pilgrimage. E.g., Tobin, *Paul's Rhetoric*, 371–72; Wilk, *Die Bedeutung*, 68–70; John A. Ziesler, *Romans*

"All Israel" 315

kingdom), the difficulties inherent to other options fall away. It is therefore best to understand this verse as carrying forward the metaphor of being grafted into the olive tree and in keeping with the argument for full gentile incorporation in the new covenant throughout Romans,[190] indicating the full inclusion of gentiles into the covenant people of Israel.[191] The point is that the fullness of the nations must enter (εἰσέλθῃ) Israel for *all* Israel to be complete. Paul has not inverted the order of Israel's salvation and the gentiles turning to YHWH, he has *combined* them – they are happening simultaneously through the work of the spirit.

By invoking "the fullness of the nations" at the climax of his argument, Paul makes explicit what he has been arguing since the opening chapters: because Israel disobeyed and behaved like the gentiles, Israel had been gentilized, becoming indistinct from the nations (literally in the case of most of the northern tribes), and now God has begun to restore Israel *from the gentiles*.[192] In accordance with Jacob's prophecy, Ephraim's seed

---

(1989), 284; Stuhlmann, *Das eschatologische Mass*, 166–67; Aus, "Paul's Travel Plans," 251–52; Heikki Räisänen, "Römer 9–11" (1987), 2922; Dieter Zeller, *Römer* (1985), 198; Ulrich Wilckens, *Römer* (1980), 254–55; Christoph Plag, *Israels Wege zum Heil* (1969), 56–58. But εἰσέρχομαι is not used in any eschatological pilgrimage passages, and Paul nowhere else uses those passages. Jewett, *Romans*, 700–701, argues, "The implied logic is more likely to be the eschatological church containing the predestined full number of Jews and Gentiles." But this begs the question, as the relationship of the "eschatological church" (or the "kingdom") to Israel is left undefined. Others have argued that Paul is likely drawing from earlier tradition and refers to entrance into the kingdom of God (or some analogous concept), e.g., Dunn, *Romans*, 680; Sanday and Headlam, *Romans*, 335; Käsemann, *Romans*, 313; Heinrich Schlier, *Der Römerbrief* (1977), 339; Leon Morris, *The Epistle to the Romans* (1988), 420; Stuhlmacher, *Romans*, 172: "eschatological city of God"; Fitzmyer, *Romans*, 622: "community of salvation." For his part, Paul seems not to envision "salvation" outside of Israel, which *is* God's kingdom, ruled by the Messiah. It is therefore no coincidence that Paul's εἰσέρχομαι matches closely with the entrance into the kingdom found in Matt 23:13, Mark 9:47, etc. (see Cranfield, *Romans*, 576).

[190] Notably, despite the fact that these verses are explicitly (γάρ) linked to the olive tree passage, Jewett, *Romans*, 700, dismisses the connection to the grafting metaphor as "a less likely option," referring the reader to "the critique by Dunn [(*Romans*, 680)]," who merely states without argument that this reading is "less natural."

[191] Mary Ann Getty, "Paul and the Salvation of Israel" (1988), 459. Note the language of entering the covenant community in the Dead Sea Scrolls (see pp. 265–66). Cf. Hofius, "Das Evangelium und Israel," 313; François Refoulé, "...*Et ainsi tout Israël sera sauvé*": *Romans 11.25–32* (1984), 82–83; Annie Jaubert, *La notion d'Alliance dans le judaïsme aux abords de l'ère chrétienne* (1963), 183.

[192] Thus Dieter Sanger, "Rettung der Heiden," 115, is correct that Rom 11:25–27 does not reveal a mystery that has not already been covered in the preceding chapters; these verses only make the content of the prior chapters more explicit, concluding the larger argument with a striking summary statement.

has indeed become "the fullness of the nations," and God is now effectively resurrecting Israel from the nations by the incorporation of foreskinned gentiles receiving the spirit promised to Israel and Judah in the new covenant. The *ethical* transformation of Paul's former gentiles is therefore also an *ethnic* transformation, restoring Israel through the process of gentile transformation and adoption into the eschatological people of God. The rationale behind gentile inclusion therefore relies on the notion that because Ephraim's seed had been mixed among the nations, gentiles must now be incorporated into Israel to ensure the promised restoration of *all* Israel. God's promise to restore not only those from Judah but from all of Israel ultimately opens the door for – even requires – the inclusion of gentiles in the new covenant for Israel to be complete.

It should be emphasized that Paul does not suggest that all the gentiles following the messiah are physical descendants of ancient Israelites who simply do not know their Israelite heritage, nor does this reading preclude the possibility that Paul imagined that some natural-born members of other tribes were "out there" somewhere awaiting restoration. On the contrary, the argument is simply that the bulk of Israel was assimilated into the nations, becoming "not my people" and ethnically *ceasing to be Israelites*. "The whole house of Israel" (πᾶς οἶκος Ἰσραηλ; Ezek 37:11) had passed away and become "dry bones" and must now be resurrected (37:1–14), being re-adopted from among the nations among which these insensible Israelites had been scattered and assimilated. These spirit-filled gentiles are not just religiously converted but are in fact *ethnically transformed* into Israelites through the process of adoption by incorporation into the body of Messiah.

In this light, Beker is right to say that "Paul does not envision Israel's eschatological salvation as its absorption into the Gentile-Christian church."[193] Instead, Paul's vision is exactly the opposite. The very existence of a "gentile church" or even a church of Jews and gentiles as an entity distinct from Israel is anachronistic and would have been incomprehensible to Paul. "Rather the point," Rodríguez explains, "is that Gentiles find themselves included alongside Jews within the covenantal label 'Israel.'"[194] The eschatological salvation of gentiles comes through their being grafted into the assembly of Israel, and the eschatological salvation of the whole of Israel depends in part on the incorporation of gentiles,

---

[193] J. Christiaan Beker, *Paul the Apostle* (1980), 334–35.
[194] Rafael Rodríguez, *If You Call Yourself a Jew* (2014), 222.

effectively reversing the process of Israel's assimilation among the nations. "All Israel will be saved," and gentiles can share in Israel's salvation through incorporation into Israel. The reverse is a non sequitur.

SURPRISED BY JOY: MERCY TO ISRAEL, MERCY TO ALL

In his explanation of the "mysterious" means by which God is saving "all Israel," Paul therefore argues that God's plan for Israel's redemption has been more comprehensive than anyone had foreseen: Ephraim's return has become the means not only for mercy toward Israel but mercy toward all, fulfilling the promise to Abraham that all nations would be blessed not "through" his seed (i.e., as outsiders) but by inclusion and incorporation *in* his seed (Gal 3:7–8; cf. Gen 17:4). Paul's mystery is that Israel's salvation paradoxically depends on the incorporation and *ethnic transformation* of the gentiles. Just as the fates of Israel and Judah are interconnected, because of Israel's disobedience, the fates of Israel and the nations have become interconnected. Israel's insensibility (πώρωσις) was the means of mercy toward the gentiles, and that mercy toward the gentiles is in turn the means of Israel's own redemption. To save Ephraim, gentiles are saved, and by saving "the fullness of the nations," Ephraim is redeemed. Israel's redemption is the redemption of the cosmos. These concluding verses thus succinctly summarize the argument of Romans as a whole:

Verse 25: "*For I do not want you to be ignorant, siblings, of this mystery (lest you become high-minded yourselves).*" To conclude the olive tree allegory, Paul explains that a fuller understanding of the purpose of gentile incorporation into Israel should keep the gentiles in his audience from an attitude of superiority. They have not been called because they were worthier than native-born Israelites. On the contrary, they are participating in Israel's salvation, and their participation is for the express purpose of bringing about the salvation of all Israel and is the direct result of God's continuing fidelity to Israel.

"*...that a partial insensibility has come upon Israel.*" As observed throughout Rom 9–11, this insensibility has worked on multiple levels over Israel's history. First, the northern kingdom became insensible and was consequently intermingled with the nations. Then, on the second level, the north's restoration is the direct result of Judah's insensibility, which led to God restoring Israel from divorce in order to shame Judah (cf. Jer 3:11–12). But since Ephraim has assimilated among the nations and is no longer ethnically distinct, the twofold insensibility of the whole of diachronic Israel has combined to open the door to the gentiles in order to restore Ephraim through the incorporation of the fullness of the nations.[195] Although Ephraim's punishment appeared to be permanent, God used even that punishment for redemptive purposes, raising Ephraim to life from gentiles/not-my-people who were previously dead in their trespasses and cut off from the covenant blessings by nature. Moreover, the mercy now being shown to the northern house through the incorporation of gentiles is the guarantor of mercy toward unfaithful Israelites in the present, who although in danger of being cut off for disobedience can – and Paul continues to hope that they will – be grafted in again. The incorporation of branches from outside the tree is akin to life from the dead (11:15), a new creation (2 Cor 5:17).

"... *until the fullness of the nations has entered [the assembly of YHWH]."* Gentiles are entering into Israel through the reception of the spirit, and the reference to Gen 48:19 draws attention to their new identity as the reconstituted "seed of Ephraim" – as children not only of Abraham but of Israel (cf. 1 Cor 10:1). Uncultivated olive branches from outside the cultivated tree are now being grafted into the olive tree of Israel. Paul here proclaims both the ingathering of gentiles and the revival of the previously insensible northern kingdom as occurring in the same redemptive action by the spirit. Wagner is therefore right to say that Paul is concerned with "the full inclusion of 'the rest' who have in the present time been rendered insensible," but that inclusion is precisely what Paul argues is already happening through the ingathering of the fullness of the nations.[196] Similarly, although Fredriksen is right to emphasize that these incorporated ex-pagans do not become Jews,[197] they *do* become *Israelites.*[198] Since not all Israelites are Jews, equating the two is a category error.

---

[195] Contra Goodrich, "Until the Fullness of the Gentiles Comes In," 19, this twofold hardening by no means "overwhelms 11:25 with complexity of meaning." It is very simple: both houses of Israel broke covenant, leading to the whole people of God falling under the curses of the Torah. Rather than "two distinct groups of Israelites separated by some eight centuries," this refers to the diachronic people such that the events of eight centuries prior are still relevant not as distinct groups but as part of the same group and events.

[196] Wagner, *Heralds of the Good News,* 279.

[197] Paula Fredriksen, "Judaizing the Nations" (2010), 242; "Apocalyptic Hope," 547.

[198] "I would nuance Fredriksen's formulation by saying that Gentiles do not become Jews .... Nevertheless, they certainly lay claim to the title of 'Israel,' though of a specific kind" (Christine E. Hayes, *What's Divine about Divine Law?* [2017], 147 n. 13).

Verse 26: "and thus all Israel will be saved." In keeping with the analogy leading into this conclusion, the entire olive tree will be saved.[199] And since "all Israel" requires more than Judah alone and includes both houses of Israel, the incorporation of "the fullness of the nations" is a necessary mechanism to bring about the salvation of "all Israel," which requires the restoration of "Ephraim's seed." Thus, to restore all Israel, God is calling his people from among both Jews and those who were "not my people" (=gentiles). Israel's fullness (11:15) now paradoxically includes even the fullness of the nations (cf. Isa 49:6), which amounts to life from the dead since the house of Israel, which had been dead so long its bones were dry, is now being reconstituted by the spirit (cf. Ezek 37). Many from Israel had ceased to be Israel, but "when God acts to save the people he has elected, Israel becomes Israel."[200]

Verse 27: "just as it is written: 'The deliverer will come from Zion; he will turn away impiety from Jacob. And this is my covenant with them when I take away their sins.'" Here Paul returns to the mechanism of Israel's salvation: justification through the new covenant, provided by the redeemer who came from Zion to redeem the whole people of Jacob. All those who have the "Torah written on the heart" (Jew or gentile) become part of the renewed, eschatological *ekklēsia* of Israel. Notably, Paul's quotation of Isa 59:20 diverges from all extant ancient versions, which say the "deliverer will come *to* Zion" or "for Zion's sake" rather than "from Zion."[201] Although some have argued that this alteration should be understood as referring to "Christ's parousia *from* the heavenly Zion,"[202] it is more likely that Paul (or the version from which he is quoting) has assimilated Isa 59:20 with psalmic passages proclaiming deliverance for the people of Israel scattered among the nations.[203] For example:

---

[199] "The Septuagint frequently uses σῴζω of the ingathering and bringing home of the dispersed from the whole world" (Scott, "All Israel," 520; see further 519-24).
[200] Jennifer A. Glancy, "Israel vs. Israel in Romans 11:25-32" (1991), 191.
[201] See Wagner, *Heralds of the Good News*, 284-886.
[202] Gadenz, *Called*, 284. Moo, *Romans*, 728; Donaldson, "Riches for the Gentiles," 93-94.
[203] The phrase ἐκ Σιών occurs only twelve times in the LXX (Ps 13:7; 19:3; 49:2; 52:7; 109:2; 127:5; 133:3; 134:21; Isa 2:3 [ἐκ γὰρ Σιών]; Amos 1:2; Mic 4:2; Joel 4:16 [3:16 ET]) and nowhere else in extant early Jewish literature. Each of these passages "is always about Israel's salvation" (Wolter, "Röm 11.25-32," 132) - exactly the subject of Rom 11:26-27. Hays is therefore likely right that whether or not Paul intended to change the wording here, "the language of these psalms was embedded in Paul's bones, and ... the wording of these texts rose spontaneously to his mind" ("Hope for What We Do Not Yet See," 566). Wagner, *Heralds of the Good News*, 285-86, observes that this change

Who will give the salvation of Israel from Zion? When the Lord turns back (ἐπιστρέφω) the captivity (αἰχμαλοσία) of his people, let Jacob rejoice and Israel be glad. (Ps 14:7 [13:7 LXX]; par. 53:7 [52:7 LXX])

By changing the wording to "from Zion," Paul is able to connect Isaiah's promise of the removal of Jacob's impiety (cf. Rom 1:18–32) to the promise of restoration from captivity and "confirms his contention that God has fulfilled his promises to Israel by extending a gospel of faith to those Gentiles who were always meant to be part of Israel in its final form."[204] Also, whereas the MT and other ancient versions of Isa 59:20 say the redeemer will come "to those who turn from transgression in Jacob," Paul's citation agrees with the LXX, in which the redeemer turns away Jacob's impiety, reinforcing the emphasis of Rom 10 that the redeemer brings justification rather than repentance bringing the redeemer.[205] Jacob's impiety – that is, Israel's persistent violation of the first command to love YHWH – has now been solved by the redeemer (Deut 30:6). Paul then concludes with a final elaboration of his thesis,[206] yet again emphasizing the cosmic scale of Israel's redemption:

With respect to the gospel, they are enemies for your sake, but with respect to election they are beloved for the sake of the fathers, for the gifts and the callings of God are never taken back. For just as you were once disobedient to God but now have been shown mercy because of their disobedience, so also these disobeyed now, so that because of the mercy shown to you they may also now be shown mercy. For God has shut up all in disobedience to show mercy to all. (Rom 11:28–32)

The preceding unveiling of the mystery has shown that God has by no means rejected his people but has been so faithful as to even incorporate gentiles to facilitate Israel's salvation.[207] Israel's past punishments, including Ephraim's incorporation among the nations, which appeared to be a

---

"coheres admirably with the similar alterations made to his citations of Isaiah 52:7 (Rom 10:15) and Hosea 1:10 (Rom 9:26)."

[204] Garroway, *Paul's Gentile-Jews*, 147. Cf. J. R. Daniel Kirk, "Why Does the Deliverer Come ἐκ Σιών (Romans 11.26)?" (2010); Berndt Schaller, "ΕΞΕΙ ΕΚ ΣΙΩΝ Ο ΡΥΟΜΑΝΟΣ" (1984).

[205] See Ephraim E. Urbach, "Redemption and Repentance in Talmudic Judaism" (1970), 192.

[206] On Rom 11:28–32 as an elaboration of 11:25–26a, see Getty, "Paul and the Salvation of Israel," 461–64.

[207] Cf. the parallels between 5:6–11 and 11:25–32 noted in Gadenz, *Called*, 287–88, though he assumes an unnecessary difference in the scope of the two passages.

total and final rejection, has been used to accomplish the very task for which Israel was initially appointed – the redemption and "transformation of the world."[208] In the same way, contemporary unfaithful Israelites have in no way lost their election.[209] They remain God's chosen despite their opposition to the gospel, which (like historical Israel's unfaithfulness) is itself being used for redemptive purposes (cf. 9:21–26). Paul thus argues that the covenantal promises to Israel are being fulfilled in the present – the redemption of the nations together with Jews witnesses to the fidelity of God to the whole people of Israel.[210]

God has not turned back from his promises, nor will he repent of his choices. God will continue to use his chosen instruments to serve his redemptive purposes – with or without their cooperation, whether through their obedience or their disobedience. Since Israel failed to be a "light to the nations" through obedience (cf. Rom 2:19–20), God caused them to fulfill this mission through their disobedience. Those now in Messiah are the proof of this very truth, having themselves been redeemed from the disobedience in which the unfaithful elect now persist. Israel's disobedience has not foiled God's redemptive purposes but rather has been used for the redemption of the nations, which is itself the means of mercy for Israel. The extension of mercy to the one guarantees the extension of mercy toward the other, for the ultimate good of all.[211] The master potter continues to achieve his merciful purposes despite the uncooperative nature of the clay. Israel has been intermingled with the nations, but God's gifts and callings are irrevocable, so even the nations are now being incorporated in the people of God, fulfilling God's promises to Israel. The mystery has been revealed, and God's purposes are far deeper than anyone ever imagined – even God's rejections prove salvific. It is no wonder Paul breaks into praise at this point,

---

[208] Abraham J. Heschel, *The Prophets* (2001), 17. "This is not the first time that Paul has suggested that rejection could be a path leading to salvation. There was a notorious sinner at Corinth who was to be handed over to Satan 'that his spirit may be saved in the day of the Lord Jesus' (1 Co 5:5). The whole Corinthian Church had been warned that if any man's work should be destroyed by the testing fire of judgment 'he will suffer loss, though he himself will be saved, but only as through fire' (1 Cor 5:15)" (George B. Caird, "Expository Problems: Predestination – Romans ix.-xi" [1957], 327).

[209] Recall, however, that for Paul *election* does not guarantee *salvation*, which requires fidelity (see pp. 297–98). The elect will still be judged and therefore still remain at risk of condemnation if they do not live in accordance with fidelity.

[210] Getty, "Paul and the Salvation of Israel," 461.

[211] The "mercy" language of Hosea again pervades this passage.

waxing poetic at the hidden wisdom, the unsearchable and unfathomable plan of God:

> Oh, the depth of the riches
> > both of the wisdom and the knowledge of God!
> How unsearchable are his judgments,
> > and untraceable are his ways!
> For who knows the mind of the Lord
> > or who became his counselor?
> Or who first gave to him
> > so that it should be paid back to him?
> For from him and through him and to him are all things.
> > To him be the glory forever. Amen.
> > > (Rom 11:33–36)

8

The End of the Matter

> Those who have faced the recognition that the teaching of Jesus is eschatologically conditioned ... will naturally endeavour to find out how far the exclusively eschatological conception of the Gospel manifests its influence in the thoughts of the Apostle to the Gentiles.
>
> Albert Schweitzer[1]

By the end of Rom 11, the apostle has turned the question of God's rejection of Israel on its head by reminding the reader that "all Israel" is a larger entity than the Jews alone. Contrary to the widespread presumption of modern interpreters that Paul "did not conceive of categories beyond 'Jew' and 'Gentile,'"[2] Paul did in fact presume a third category prevalent throughout early Jewish discourse: "Israelite."[3] That is, like his predecessors and contemporaries, Paul understood Israel to be a category that includes Jews and non-Jews – Judah is not all of Israel. The presumption that "Israelite" equals "Jew" and "non-Jew" equals "non-Israelite" has caused much confusion for modern interpreters, who then naturally identify "non-Jew" with "gentile." But for Paul and his contemporaries, not all non-Jews are necessarily gentiles – they could be Israelites not from Judah like Samaritans or the Naphtalite protagonists of the book of Tobit.

---

[1] Albert Schweitzer, *Paul and His Interpreters* (1912), x–xi.
[2] Joshua D. Garroway, *Paul's Gentile-Jews* (2012), 5.
[3] The Samaritans had already long been understood by some Jews to be a *tertium quid*, something between Israelite (the larger category including Jews) and gentile (e.g., Matt 10:5). See Gary N. Knoppers, *Jews and Samaritans* (2013), 220–21.

God's promises to Israel therefore apply not only to Judah (=Jews) but to the rest of Israel as well – *all* Israel will be saved, not just one part. The question, of course, is how the rest of Israel would be restored. When Paul observed uncircumcised Jesus-followers receiving the spirit – the very thing promised not to gentiles but to Israel as part of the new covenant – he turned to his scriptures to understand this unexpected development, concluding that gentile participation in the promises to Israel is a surprising part of Israel's redemption. Specifically, Paul argues that after being divorced from the covenant for infidelity and behaving like the nations, the bulk of non-Jewish Israel had effectively become *gentilized*, having assimilated among the non-Israelite nations. As such, the bulk of non-Jewish Israel could be reckoned as ethnically dead, having been assimilated and consumed by the nations, no longer ethnically distinct as a people. But the God who brings life from the dead is now doing just that by calling gentiles – truly "not my people" – his people as Hosea had prophesied.[4] The promise that God would call his people "from the nations" (ἐξ [τῶν] ἐθνῶν) meant not only "from *among* the nations" but "from gentiles."[5] Where Israel had become *gentilized*, now gentiles are effectively being *Israelitized*, transformed from one ethnicity to another and integrated into the ethnic people of Israel. As Isaiah promised, "your brothers from all the nations" (66:20; cf. Rom 12:1; 15:16) are being incorporated into Israel,[6] and the eschatologically restored ethnic Israel is composed of those "called from Jews [=Judahites] and gentiles" (9:24).

The inclusion of physically uncircumcised persons in the promise is therefore not a rejection or replacement of Israel but rather the means by which God is reaching out and saving more of Israel than anyone anticipated, a process analogous to resurrection from the dead. God has not replaced Israel with a new people but is calling, gathering, revivifying, and reconciling even those thought irretrievably lost, having been fully consumed and absorbed by the nations. Paul thus argues that God's

---

[4] Hos 2:1 [ET: 1:10]; 2:25 [ET: 2:23].
[5] E.g., Ezek 28:25; 34:13; 36:24; 38:8; 39:27. Cf. Rom 9:24 and the discussion in Chapter 5.
[6] Paul would thus identify himself with the "survivors" sent "to the nations" (Isa 66:19; cf. Rom 15:16; Gal 2:9). The prophet goes so far as to say YHWH will take some of these "brothers from all the nations" for "priests and Levites" (66:21). See Jill A. Middlemas, "Trito-Isaiah's Intra- and Internationalization: Identity Markers in the Second Temple Period" (2011), 122; Christophe Nihan, "Ethnicity and Identity in Isaiah 56–66" (2011), 95; Joseph Blenkinsopp, "Second Isaiah – Prophet of Universalism" (1988); Dongsu Kim, "Reading Paul's καὶ οὕτως πᾶς Ἰσραὴλ σωθήσεται (Rom. 11:26a) in the Context of Romans" (2010), 322–23.

covenant-keeping power extends beyond the grave, capable even of bringing life from the dead (Rom 11:15), of producing *Israelites* from the nations (ἐξ ἐθνῶν). Paul's "Israel" is therefore no less ethnic than that of his peers, remaining a specific ethnic, national, and theological entity, though incorporating the ethnically transformed within those boundaries.[7]

In this light, the epistle to the Romans is an extended argument for the inclusion of gentiles as a necessary component of Israel's redemption and evidence of God's fidelity. Paul's statements regarding Israel and his arguments about the equal status of uncircumcised followers of Israel's messiah are not contradictory but reflect a nuanced argument about Israelite identity in light of Paul's belief that the restoration promised by the Prophets had been initiated by Jesus' obedient death and subsequent resurrection. The incorporation of physically uncircumcised but divinely transformed persons into the eschatological *ekklēsia* does not undermine but rather vindicates God's overarching fidelity to his people. Indeed, the gentiles now receiving circumcised hearts are proof that God has begun to fulfill the promises of Israel's transformation and consequent restoration, not for Jews alone but for "*all* Israel."

The scope of redemption has therefore been larger than anyone imagined, and God has accomplished his purposes even when his people have not cooperated and have resisted God's hand. Even the chastening and punishments of the past have served a redemptive purpose, and the vessels previously declared worthless have still served the purpose for which God chose and appointed Israel from the beginning: light and redemption for the nations, who are now being blessed in Abraham's seed.[8] Indeed, God has used Israel's *disobedience* to bring about the purpose for which Israel was chosen, and the salvation available to the nations is also paradoxically the means of Israel's own salvation. That is, "in Messiah Jesus the blessing of Abraham has come to the gentiles so that we would receive the promise of the spirit through faith" (Gal 3:14). The Israel problem and the gentile problem are ultimately one and the

---

[7] John K. Goodrich, "Until the Fullness of the Gentiles Comes In" (2016), 18, has wrongly categorized me as an opponent of the "ethnic" interpretation of Israel in Paul. On the contrary, my argument is that Paul never departs from a fundamentally ethnic conception of Israel – my paradigm is rigorously ethnic. The problem is that Goodrich conflates "ethnic" with "Jewish," whereas Paul understands the ethnic boundaries of Israel differently than Goodrich and many other modern interpreters.

[8] For Israel's vocation as a "light to the nations" as foundational to Paul's apostolic identity, see Lionel J. Windsor, *Paul and the Vocation of Israel* (2014).

same, and God has solved both at once through the fulfillment of his promises to Israel wrought by the fidelity of Israel's messiah.

THE LAST BATTLE: DEATH, RESURRECTION, AND THE VINDICATION OF YHWH

The scope of Paul's gospel is not limited to the horizontal sphere of Israel and the nations, however. Instead, the whole drama functions on a larger, cosmic level; Israel and the nations are the battleground in which the God of Israel has been vindicated, vanquishing his enemies through the hidden wisdom unveiled in Paul's gospel. Paul's argument works within a cosmic framework including many heavenly or divine beings, often identified with the celestial bodies.[9] This framework is established most clearly in Deuteronomy, where the Song of Moses explains the special status of Israel as follows:

> When the Most High gave the nations their inheritance,
>   When he separated the sons of Adam,
> He fixed the boundaries of the peoples
>   According to the number of the sons of God.[10]
> For YHWH's portion is his people,
>   Jacob is the allotment of his inheritance.
>   (Deut 32:8–9)

As YHWH's portion, Israel is forbidden from worshiping the heavenly bodies, "which YHWH your God has allotted to all the peoples under all the heavens" (Deut 4:19). The idea is that the nations were divided from one another and each placed under a specific heavenly body or deity, while Israel was set apart by YHWH to be his own people. This framework is readily visible in Daniel, where the heavenly messenger explains to the prophet that although his prayer had been heard immediately, the response had been delayed because "the prince of the kingdom of Persia was standing against me for twenty-one days," until finally "Michael, one

---

[9] Emma Wasserman, *Apocalypse as Holy War* (2018), esp. 108–72; David A. Burnett, "A Neglected Deuteronomic Scriptural Matrix for the Nature of the Resurrection Body in 1 Cor 15:39–42" (2019), esp. 190–95. See also Daniel I. Block, *The Gods of the Nations* (2013); Ellen White, *Yahweh's Council* (2014); Michael S. Heiser, "The Divine Council in Late Canonical and Non-Canonical Second Temple Jewish Literature" (2004), 68–89.

[10] Following the reading of 4QDt^q and 4QDt^j. MT: "sons of Israel." Most LXX MSS have "angels of God"; a few agree with 4Q37 and have "sons of God." For a full text-critical analysis, see Michael S. Heiser, "Deuteronomy 32:8 and the Sons of God" (2001).

of the chief princes, came to help me" (Dan 10:13). The messenger then says that he will "now return to fight against the prince of Persia, so I am leaving – and the prince of Greece is about to come" (Dan 10:20). Here the various deities assigned to each ethnic group are depicted as warring with one another in a cosmic battle mirroring earthly geopolitical engagements.[11]

This image of cosmic, heavenly war is further developed in Revelation, which depicts "war in heaven," with "the dragon" and one-third of the stars of heaven ultimately being thrown down by "Michael and his angels" (Rev 12:3–9). The horsemen of Rev 6:1–8 similarly depict lower deities, of which two figures (Thanatos/Death and Hades) are explicitly named and a third is easily recognizable as Mars, the god of war. Thanatos and Hades are then vanquished and thrown into the lake of fire in Rev 20:13–14. Large portions of 1 Enoch also depict a cosmic framework involving various celestial/heavenly forces,[12] and the Dead Sea Scrolls are replete with such cosmic imagery, such as Belial ultimately being vanquished by YHWH and the forces of light (e.g., 1QM 18:1–3).[13]

Inasmuch as this image of cosmic order and the heavenly realm was widely assumed in early Judaism,[14] it should be no surprise that Paul held to the same revelatory framework, especially given the centrality of Deuteronomy in Paul's theology.[15] Thus he can say, "even if there are many so-called gods in heaven and on earth – as indeed there are many gods and many lords – for us there is only one God" (1 Cor 8:5–6). These "many gods" to which the nations are subject are not gods at all but are instead inferior *daimonia* who are themselves subject to the God of Israel (1 Cor 10:20–21).

But as hinted in Daniel, the gods of the nations have not ruled justly, nor have they remained within their proper domains of authority. Instead, the psalmist declares, "The rulers (ἄρχοντες) conspire together against

---

[11] Wasserman, *Apocalypse as Holy War*, 80–85; Emma Wasserman, "Beyond Apocalyptic Dualism: Ranks of Divinities in 1 Enoch and Daniel" (2014).

[12] Wasserman, *Apocalypse as Holy War*, 65–80; "Beyond Apocalyptic Dualism".

[13] Wasserman, *Apocalypse as Holy War*, 92–105. Wasserman emphasizes the apparent contradiction between the concept of conflict in the divine realm and the total supremacy of YHWH, meaning "depictions of war and conflict … tend to become highly asymmetrical affairs" (205).

[14] E.g., Sir. 17:17, "He appointed a governor for every nation, but Israel is the Lord's portion"; Philo, *Spec.* 1.13–19. See Paula Fredriksen, "Philo, Herod, Paul, and the Many Gods of Ancient Jewish 'Monotheism'" (2022); Wasserman, *Apocalypse as Holy War*, 1–107.

[15] Wasserman, *Apocalypse as Holy War*, 108–72.

YHWH and against his messiah" (Ps 2:2 LXX). These rulers acted violently and removed the boundaries that had been established, resulting in the mixture of the various peoples, consuming Israel among them.[16] In the process, Israel became subject to these gods through exile and assimilation (Deut 28:64), and YHWH was apparently defeated and dethroned through the exile and assimilation of YHWH's people. Although YHWH had used other nations as agents of wrath against his disobedient people, those nations had exceeded their mandate and overstepped their proper boundaries (e.g., Isa 10:5–19). The enemies had "conspired together against your hidden ones;[17] they said, 'come, let us destroy them as a nation, so that the name of Israel will no longer be remembered'" (Ps 83:4). For this reason, YHWH declares, "I am extremely angry with the nations who attacked together, because I was only a little angry, but they attacked together for evil" (Zech 1:15 LXX).[18] YHWH therefore promises that he will act to vindicate his name and rescue his own reputation,[19] and the psalmist proclaims that the gods themselves will be judged:

> God stands in the assembly of the gods,
>   In the midst of the gods he renders judgment.
> How long will you judge unjustly
>   And show partiality to the wicked? Selah.
>   (Ps 82(81 LXX):1–2)

Paul adds a surprising twist to this cosmic drama: rather than marking YHWH's defeat, Israel's destruction as a nation and mixture among the nations is part of the mystery, the hidden plan of YHWH's vindication and victory.[20] By unjustly crossing their spheres of authority, tearing Israel apart and incorporating Israel within their own peoples, the rulers of the nations have given YHWH claim to all the nations. That is, since YHWH has claim to Israel and Israel has been mixed among the nations, YHWH now has claim to all the nations into which Israel has been mixed.

---

[16] Philo, *Post.* 89 explicitly associates the command "you will not move your neighbor's boundaries, which your fathers set up" (Deut 19:14; cf. Prov 22:28) with the establishment of "boundaries of nations according to the number of the angels of God" (Deut 32:8).

[17] Following the MT (צְפוּנֶיךָ); LXX: ἁγίων σου ("your sacred ones").

[18] This immediately follows the description of four horses representing "the ones whom YHWH sent to walk around through the earth" (Zech 1:8–11)

[19] E.g., Deut 32:26–43; Isa 10:5–11:16; 48:11; Jer 14:21; Ezek 20:9–44; 36:22.

[20] Rom 11:25–26; 16:25; 1 Cor 2:7–9; 15:50–57; Eph 1:8–11; 3:1–12; Col 1:26–27. On "mystery" language in Paul, see p. 107 n. 2 and the sources cited there.

Because the allotted boundaries of the nations were moved, the rulers of the nations have forfeited their authority and ceded their rule to YHWH, whose inheritance of Israel now extends to include all the nations, as the psalmist concludes: "Arise (ἀνάστα), O God, judge the earth, for you will inherit all the nations" (Ps 82[81]:8).[21]

Paul associates this "arising" with the resurrection of Jesus, the one appointed to overthrow the unjust celestial rulers, liberating the nations from their oppressive rule and inaugurating the kingdom of Israel's God.[22] Jesus' resurrection proves that he is the one spoken of by the psalmist, the one to whom YHWH has declared: "You are my son, today I have fathered you. Ask of me, and I will give the nations as your inheritance, and the ends of the earth as your possession" (Ps 2:7–8; cf. Isa 9:7 LXX). Now, having arisen in heavenly glory, Messiah Jesus "must reign until he has put all his enemies under his feet" (1 Cor 15:25), as promised to the Melchizedek figure in Ps 110:1.[23] Every "ruler, authority, and power" will be discontinued (καταργέω),[24] the last among them being death itself.[25] Paul claims a role in this process, "having received grace and apostleship to bring about the obedience of fidelity among all the nations" (Rom 1:5) and proclaiming liberation from slavery "to those that by nature are not gods" (Gal 4:1–9).[26] Having received the spirit of Messiah, the "children of God" are no longer under the domain of "the

---

[21] Translation following the LXX.
[22] Burnett, "A Neglected Deuteronomic Scriptural Matrix," 204.
[23] 11QMelch 2:9–13 identifies this Melchizedek figure with the "god" of Ps 82:1, who will "accomplish God's judgments," freeing the just from "Belial and from the hand of all the spirits of his lot." See Burnett, "A Neglected Deuteronomic Scriptural Matrix," 199, who observes that the "lot" language draws on the language of Deut 4:19 and 32:8–9. See also Matthew W. Bates, "Beyond 'Stichwort'" (2009), esp. 397–99.
[24] "Taking the 'principalities and powers' of 1 Cor 15:24 as gentile gods makes sense of a number of difficult features of 15:23–28. Like numerous other writers, Paul conceives of a divine hierarchy in which all other deities fit somewhere in the lesser ranks" (Wasserman, *Apocalypse as Holy War*, 124).
[25] 1 Cor 15:24–26; cf. Ps 82:7–8; Dan 10:10–21; 12:1–3; 11QMelch 2:9–13. "If death is clearly associated with the sin of Adam (Gen 2–3), who or what are the *other* enemies associated with? The answer [is] the gods/angels of the nations, as we have seen above. In early Jewish perspective, the gods/angels' rule over the nations was the outcome of the rebellion of Adam's sons at Babel resulting in God's disinheritance of the peoples. This was understood as the origin of the nations (ἔθνη), when God subjected them to the rule of the principalities and powers" (Burnett, "A Neglected Deuteronomic Scriptural Matrix," 200).
[26] "Our struggle is not against flesh and blood, but against the rulers, against the powers, against the world-rulers of this darkness, against the pneumatic things of wickedness in the heavenly places" (Eph 6:12).

rulers of this age" (1 Cor 2:8) – including the Torah itself (Gal 3:19–4:7) – but have come under the direct rule of God, whose spirit is in their midst (1 Cor 3:16; 6:17–19).

Paul therefore proclaims "God's wisdom in a mystery ... which none of the rulers of this age has understood, for if they had understood it, they would not have crucified the Lord of glory" (1 Cor 2:7).[27] That wisdom is power in weakness, victory through death and resurrection not only of Israel's Messiah but of the whole people: "Messiah the firstfruits, after that those who are Messiah's at his coming" (1 Cor 15:23).[28] Jesus' resurrection is only the "firstfruits" of the larger resurrection event, which also includes the resurrection of all Israel, the judgment of the gods/rulers of the nations, and the inheritance of the cosmos/kingdom of God.[29] This is why Paul can rebuke the Corinthians by reminding them, "Do you not know that we will judge angels?" (1 Cor 6:3).

In this larger cosmic context, Jesus' death and resurrection is mirrored by the death and resurrection of the people of Israel as a whole, who have been "swallowed up and are now in the nations" (Hos 8:8 LXX) and are like "dry bones" (Ezek 37:11). Hosea declares that Ephraim "became guilty and died" (Hos 13:1) but nevertheless proclaims that Israel/Ephraim will be brought back from the grave:

> I will ransom them from the power of Sheol,
>   I will redeem them from death.
> O Death, where are your thorns?
>   O Sheol, where is your sting?
> (Hos 13:14; cf.1 Cor 15:55–56)

This is precisely the good news Paul proclaims. Death and resurrection is not only the story of Israel's messiah but the story of Israel itself and the vindication of Israel's God. God has sown Israel among the nations in death to be raised in victory.

This cosmic framework of Israel's death and resurrection and the extension of YHWH's reign to all the nations further highlights the significance of Paul's reference to his converts from the nations as

---

[27] The reference to the rulers' lack of understanding echoes Ps 82:5, which says of the "gods" being judged, "they do not know, nor do they understand; they walk in darkness."

[28] "In Paul's narrative of the 'resurrection,' the ruling principalities and powers must first be destroyed, and then death" (Burnett, "A Neglected Deuteronomic Scriptural Matrix," 200).

[29] Burnett, "A Neglected Deuteronomic Scriptural Matrix," 198.

former gentiles/pagans: "You know that *when you were gentiles* (ἔθνη), you were led astray, being carried away to mute idols" (1 Cor 12:2). Like their Israelite forefathers – a lineage they now share (1 Cor 10:1–2) – they have experienced an exodus, having been brought out from the nations by passing through the waters of baptism and receiving the spirit. As such, they are no longer gentiles allotted to or subject to the "rulers of this age" (1 Cor 2:8; cf. Eph 1:20–30). Instead, they have been transferred into the allotment of the God of Israel and placed under the rule of YHWH and his Messiah. They represent the resurrection of Israel itself from its "death" among the nations. Having received the firstfruits of the spirit, they now await the conclusion of the drama, the ultimate defeat of death and the final resurrection to heavenly glory and rule (1 Cor 15:50–58), the fulfillment of the promise to Abraham.[30]

PAUL'S COHERENT CORE: ISRAEL'S RESURRECTION

Once one recognizes that Paul understands uncircumcised Jesus-followers as neither Jews nor gentiles but instead as restored, resurrected Israelites, Rom 2 and 9–11 go from being puzzles on the anomalous periphery of Pauline thought to providing the hermeneutical keys to the whole argument. This model not only provides a coherent reading of Romans, it solves many of the biggest puzzles throughout the Pauline corpus and Pauline thought in general. Many passages that have been regarded as anomalous, contradictory, or even non-Pauline are fully coherent if Paul understood physically uncircumcised Jesus-followers as having become regenerated non-Jewish Israelites through their reception of the new covenant promise of circumcised hearts.

Paul's inclusion of gentile believers among the descendants of the Israelite patriarchs (1 Cor 10:1; Gal 3:29), his reference to them as former gentiles (1 Cor 12:2), and his assertion that they are "the circumcision" (Phil 3:3) alongside his insistence that they nevertheless are not – nor should they aim to become – Jews is no contradiction. It is instead a reflection of his identification of these people as newly engrafted non-Jewish Israelites. Likewise, Paul's repeated application of Israelite restoration passages to gentiles – particularly since his selections in these cases

---

[30] On the promise to Abraham as divinization and heavenly, imperishable seed ruling over the nations, see David A. Burnett, "So Shall Your Seed Be" (2015). On deification in the Pauline epistles, see M. David Litwa, *We Are Being Transformed* (2012).

refer to the northern kingdom with surprising frequency – is not merely metaphorical or typological but literal.[31] If anything, Paul's interpretation of his scriptures is hyper-literal to the point that he argues that his gentile converts are becoming transformed into ethnic Israelites, complete with circumcisions not performed with human hands.[32]

Similarly, Paul's positive statements about the Torah are not at odds with his assertions that those who have received the spirit are no longer under the Torah or its curse. He nowhere suggests that the Torah is abrogated through Messiah but rather argues that the spirit is performing the justification of Israel promised in the Torah itself, resulting in an Israel that does the will of God through the Torah written on the heart. In this way, the written Torah is *obviated* rather than *abolished* for these pneumatically empowered, naturally obedient covenant members. Those in Messiah are reckoned as having already died and are therefore no longer under the jurisdiction of the written Torah and are no longer subject to its curses, being instead "children of God" who live and work in the realm of the spirit.[33] Participation in Messiah's death kills the "old human," and the Torah's curse no longer applies to those who have the *pneuma* of Messiah. But those who have not received the spirit or persist in disobedience remain under the written Torah and its curses for disobedience. The Torah remains in force in the fleshly domain, and participation in Messiah's death and the reception of the spirit is both the fulfillment of the Torah's ultimate promises and the means by which its just requirements are fulfilled.

On this front, it should also be emphasized that Romans does not end with chapter 11. Instead, the theological argument of Rom 1–11 informs the ethical instruction in the next three chapters, in which Paul demonstrates how to make halakhic decisions in the framework established by Jesus and as led by the spirit.[34] Ultimately, all are to live according to conscience (13:5; cf. 2:15) and the love command (13:9), the combination of which can answer every potential ethical problem because "love is the fulfillment of Torah" (13:10). The reader has accordingly come full circle from Rom 1:18, which started with God's wrath against the opposite of the love commands. Now, impiety is no longer a problem for those who

---

[31] See, for example, the analyses of Paul's use of restoration passages with reference to the gentiles in David I. Starling, *Not My People* (2011).
[32] Joshua D. Garroway, "Circumcision of Christ: Romans 15.7–13" (2012).
[33] Cf. Rom 8:14, 19; 9:26; Gal 3:26, 4:6; Matt 17:26.
[34] See Scot McKnight, *Reading Romans Backwards* (2019).

have the spirit, who will naturally "love YHWH your God, so that you may live" (Deut 30:6). All that remains is to fulfill the command to love neighbor (justice) as empowered by the spirit.

These arguments about the Torah and the centrality of justification in Paul's gospel therefore ultimately owe to a common Jewish eschatological framework in which Israel's restoration must include Israel being made into a just people. Like his contemporaries at Qumran, Paul believes Israel's justification is now underway, marking the end of "this present evil age" (Gal 1:4) and the beginning of the process of redemption and the age of God's favor promised in the Prophets (2 Cor 6:2). As such, Paul's arguments about justification and Torah by no means entail the rejection of the importance of obedience or "works." Instead, his argument depends on the idea that Israel needed spiritual (*pneumatic*) empowerment to fully please God, empowerment he believes has been granted through the faithful obedience of Messiah Jesus. The "obedience of fidelity" (Rom 1:5) he proclaims among the nations is the very fidelity promised by the Prophets to redeemed and restored Israel,[35] the divinely initiated and provided transformation of unjust people into those who do justice, love mercy, and walk humbly with their God (Mic 6:8).

INCORPORATION, NOT SUPERSESSION

Paul's mission to the gentiles is therefore paradoxically and inextricably linked with Israel's restoration.[36] In this respect, most interpreters have read Romans backwards, looking for how Paul imagines Israel can be saved in light of his message about gentile salvation, while Paul is looking at things exactly the other way around. For the apostle, as with any restorationist Jew of his day, everything starts with the presumption of Israel's salvation and the fulfillment of the promise to Abraham inherited by Israel. Gentiles receiving the spirit undergo not only an *ethical* but an *ethnic* conversion, being unnaturally grafted into Israel. As natural

---

[35] See Don B. Garlington, *"The Obedience of Faith"* (1990), 233–54.
[36] Matthew V. Novenson, "The Jewish Messiahs, the Pauline Christ, and the Gentile Question" (2009), 363, notes that early Jewish messianic traditions were concerned with the fate of Israel and provided "a framework in which Jews could make sense of the role of the Gentiles in the world." That is, "the messiah not only restores the fortunes of Israel but brings the whole οἰκουμένη under his rule" (364). Paul's proclamation of Messiah Jesus does just that, providing a single elegant solution to both the gentile problem and the problem of Israel's restoration.

members of Israel, Jews (*Ioudaioi*) have no need for such an ethnic transformation; the engrafting of gentiles neither threatens nor diminishes their Israelite status, nor do Jews need to be integrated into a separate gentile church (which did not exist in Paul's day) to be saved.[37] Quite the opposite! Instead, gentiles must be integrated into Israel to share in Israel's salvation.[38]

Both Jews and gentiles, however, can find themselves cut off from Israel because of infidelity (as frequently the case in past, biblical Israel), though reconciliation and restoration remains possible even then. Paul therefore envisions a renewed Israel *expanding* through incorporation, not a transfer of Israelite status from one group to another.[39] For Paul, even gentile inclusion itself is in continuity with ancient Israel, since much of Israel has been ethnically assimilated among the nations, requiring gentile inclusion for Israelite restoration. As such, rather than, "God is Jewish, but the Gentiles don't have to be,"[40] Paul's argument is that God is not only *Jewish* but *Israelite* – the God of all Abraham's seed – and gentiles can be incorporated into *Israel* without becoming Jews by following Israel's messiah and receiving the spirit promised to Israel. Moreover, it should be noted that Paul never objects to Jews continuing to engage in their own traditional practices, including circumcision or dietary restrictions, nor does he suggest that these practices should be abandoned. Instead, he argues that non-Jews are to make allowances for those for whom specific foods might violate conscience, preferring to "never eat meat again so that I will not cause my sibling to sin" (1 Cor 8:13). Nevertheless, he argues that Jews are to regard non-Jewish believers as equal heirs to Israel's heritage even when they do not themselves follow those same traditional practices.

Any suggestion of the church superseding or replacing Israel is therefore nonsense. In Paul's idiom, the *ekklēsia* is not a separate entity but rather a shorthand reference to the eschatologically restored Israel, the assembly of YHWH,[41] including (as Israel always had) both Jews and

---

[37] "Jews do not cross ethnic boundaries by virtue of their commitment to Christ; they do not change their God, their ancestry, or their ancestral customs. Gentiles do . . . . To be in Christ, gentiles give up their gods and religious practices, profess loyalty to the God of Israel, accept Israel's messiah, Scriptures, and ancestry" (Caroline Johnson Hodge, "The Question of Identity" [2015], 172).

[38] Cf. Terence L. Donaldson, *Paul and the Gentiles* (1997), 298.

[39] Similarly, Notger Slenczka, "Frage nach der Identität Israels" (2010), 476.

[40] Paula Fredriksen, "God Is Jewish, but Gentiles Don't Have to Be" (2019), 3.

[41] Deut 23:2, et al.; cf. also קהל ישראל, Deut 31:30; 1 Kgs 8:14; et al.

non-Jews.⁴² Former gentiles have become ethnically transformed into members of Israel via the spirit, effectively brought to life from the dead. It is incoherent to suggest that gentile *incorporation into* Israel represents a *replacement of* Israel. Paul does not present himself as a "former Jew" or suggest that the *ekklēsia* constitutes a "third race" distinct from Israel,⁴³ nor does he redefine Israel as a universal, non-ethnic entity. Instead, he continues to assert that ethnic Israel will be saved in its entirety, though the boundaries of that ethnic group are ultimately defined by inclusion and participation in the covenant with the God of Israel mediated by the spirit given by Israel's Messiah, to whom the Torah itself witnesses.

It is therefore not the case that Paul constructs two linked but discrete peoples of God⁴⁴ or that gentiles are incorporated into Abraham but not Israel.⁴⁵ For Paul, the idea of two peoples of God would be nonsense; there is only one people of God and only one heir to Abraham's promises: Israel. Nor is there any indication that Paul conceives of two paths of salvation for separate Israels, a "spiritual" Israel defined by commitment to Jesus and open to gentiles and a parallel ethnic or fleshly Israel defined by traditional Torah observance independent of following Jesus.⁴⁶ Moreover, for Paul, a focus on Jesus is not at odds with a focus on Torah.⁴⁷ Rather, since Torah commands obedience to the "prophet like Moses" (Deut 18:15-22), Torah can now only be fulfilled by obeying Jesus and receiving the spirit granted by Israel's Messiah.⁴⁸ In Paul's own

---

⁴² See Jennifer Eyl, "Semantic Voids, New Testament Translation, and Anachronism" (2014), 323 and the discussion on p. 32.
⁴³ As suggested by Love L. Sechrest, *A Former Jew: Paul and the Dialectics of Race* (2009), esp 157–164.
⁴⁴ As Caroline Johnson Hodge, *If Sons, Then Heirs* (2007).
⁴⁵ As Pablo T. Gadenz, *Called from the Jews and from the Gentiles* (2009), 82.
⁴⁶ See Garroway, *Paul's Gentile-Jews*, 155.
⁴⁷ Cf. Garroway, *Paul's Gentile-Jews*, 168 n. 9.
⁴⁸ The suggestion of Gabriele Boccaccini, *Paul's Three Paths to Salvation* (2020), that Paul puts forward *three* distinct paths of salvation, one for Jews through adherence to Torah, one for righteous gentiles who live by their conscience and natural law, and a third path for sinners who are saved by Jesus' eschatological gift of forgiveness is therefore untenable. Paul's explicit charge "that both Jews and Greeks are all under sin" (Rom 3:9), effectively collapses the first two categories into the final one, and those in the other two categories only become part of those categories by following Jesus through the spirit of the new covenant. Paul's gospel therefore amounts to a single path of salvation via transfer from Boccaccini's third category to one of his other two. Boccaccini's objection that by "under the power of sin" Paul does not mean "that all people are sinners ... but that both Jews and gentiles alike are affected by evil ... as proved by the fact that everybody sins" (111) ultimately makes a distinction without a difference. If everyone

words, "Messiah is the *telos* of the Torah" (Rom 10:4), and spirit-filled gentiles are participating in the redemption of Israel for which Messiah came.[49]

If gentiles have received the spirit promised as part of Israel's restoration and are newly adopted heirs of Abraham, they are by definition part of Israel and therefore Israelites. Similarly, there is no need to posit a hybrid category of "Gentile-Jews" to reflect this ethnic transformation,[50] since gentile believers become Israelites but not Jews, who are a subset of the superordinate category of Israel. For this reason Paul can say, "be blameless also to Jews and to Greeks and to the *ekklēsia* of God" (1 Cor 10:32), since the *ekklēsia* of God is identical with neither but includes persons from both.[51] Indeed, although the binary distinction between Jew and Greek remains for those outside, in Messiah, there is no longer Jew or Greek, only the Israel of God.[52]

In this light, Paul was no more of a supersessionist than Philo, the Dead Sea sectarians, Ezra, Nehemiah, the editors of the Mishnah, or any number of other early Jews who believed that disobedient, unfaithful Jews or Israelites would be cut off and not included in the eschatologically restored people of Israel. In the same way these other Jewish sectarians regard Jews who do not follow their specific interpretation of Torah as apostate but still potentially redeemable if they convert to the sect's way of life, Paul sees Jews who are not yet following Jesus as still being Israelites by nature, though disobedient and in danger of being cut off. So long as time remains, these others can still be saved and participate in

---

    is under the power of sin and therefore sins, everyone has become a sinner, and the Torah could not protect from this but only reveal its truth, which is why justification is necessary for all.

[49] Paula Fredriksen, "Circumcision Is Nothing" (2022), 81.

[50] As Garroway, *Paul's Gentile-Jews*.

[51] *Pace* Garroway, *Paul's Gentile-Jews*, 182–83 n. 49. This explains why "there are indications that Paul's thought tends toward the identification of the Church as a third entity ... though significantly, he speaks in these passages not of Ἰσραήλ, but of Ἰουδαῖοι" (J. Ross Wagner, *Heralds of the Good News* [2003], 279 n. 193). The latter distinction is exactly the point – for Paul, former gentiles are Israelites but not Jews.

[52] J. Louis Martyn's suggestion that Paul's nuanced treatment of "Israel" in Romans "clarifies and supplements his use of the word 'Israel'" (*Galatians* [1997], 32–34, 567 n. 13 [quote 32]) with reference to his *ekklēsias*, such as in Gal 6:16, strikes me as likely correct (cf. J. Louis Martyn, "Romans as One of the Earliest Interpretations of Galatians" [1997], 43–45). Martyn's explanation seems even more likely if, as Douglas Campbell, *Framing Paul* (2014), 37–189, 412–14, has argued, Romans was written shortly after Galatians, perhaps after Paul received more accurate reports of his opponents' arguments.

YHWH's promises to Israel. Such a perspective is better labeled "remnant" or "sectarian" ideology than supersessionism.[53]

Paul was also not anomalous in his judgment that those not born to Jewish or Israelite parents could be integrated into the people of Israel – provision for such incorporation is evident even in the Dead Sea Scrolls.[54] Even his insistence that the "spirit of sanctity" promised as part of Israel's reconciliation and restoration was being received by those in his community was not unique – as discussed above, remarkably similar claims also appear in the Scrolls (e.g., 1QS 3:7, CD 7:4).[55] Even the idea that Israel had been assimilated among the nations and required re-creation through ethnic transformation was not beyond the pale of Jewish interpretation, as later rabbinic tradition includes the same idea applied to the exodus from Egypt.[56] What made Paul distinct was threefold: (1) his claim that Jesus is Israel's messiah and that the "spirit of sanctity" (1:4) is received through fealty and obedience to Jesus, (2) his insistence that the spirit was being received by uncircumcised gentiles, and (3) that reception of the spirit obviated the need for physical circumcision in order for these transformed individuals to become fully converted into Israelite "children of God."

WHY NOT CIRCUMCISION?

Of course, if this reading is correct, it raises an obvious question: If Paul believed his gentile converts had become ethnic Israelites, why should they not be circumcised, since circumcision is the sign of the covenant with Abraham and the one definitive stipulation for Abraham's heirs? The command to circumcise precedes the reception of the Torah at Sinai, so if these gentiles were to be considered Israelites, one would expect that

---

[53] "See Jason F. Moraff, "Among My Own Nation" (2021), 44. For another approach, arguing that supersessionism "is a marker of both Jewish and Christian thought" and an inevitable component of any theology involving special covenantal status, see Amy-Jill Levine, "Supersessionism" (2022), 10.
[54] See Carmen Palmer, *Converts in the Dead Sea Scrolls* (2018). [55] See pp. 79–80.
[56] In Lev. Rab. 23:2, R. Eleazar reads Lev 18:3 together with Song 2:2 and Deut 4:34, "one nation from the midst of another nation," concluding that Israel had assimilated and become effectively indistinguishable from the Egyptians, with that assimilation "represented by three cases: not circumcising, growing the *blorit*, and wearing *kilayim* or mixed materials" (Beth A. Berkowitz, "A Short History of the People Israel from the Patriarchs to the Messiah" [2012], 119). God therefore needed to reverse Israel's assimilation and essentially recreate his people through the exodus. In contrast, Lev. Rab. 32:5 argues that the Israelites were redeemed because they did *not* assimilate.

they should be circumcised. This seems to have been the argument of Paul's opponents, and the debate reflected in Galatians and Romans concerns that very question.

It bears repeating that the claim that such faithful uncircumcised persons were saved as "righteous gentiles" separate from and distinct from Israel would have engendered little if any controversy, nor would such a status require circumcision.[57] But that is not what the apostle argues. Instead, Paul argues that these uncircumcised gentiles are in fact rightful descendants of Abraham and the patriarchs, heirs to the promises of Israel along with their Torah-observant Jewish siblings in Messiah, vigorously resisting any effort to relegate these gentiles into second-class status or anything other than full membership within the same people of God as Jews. That gentiles who submit to and serve the God of Israel might be saved *as gentiles* was hardly objectionable. But Paul's insistence on the equal status of the physically uncircumcised *as part of Israel* understandably resulted in significant resistance from his contemporaries.

Why then does Paul so steadfastly resist the circumcision of these newly recreated Israelites? As observed in Chapter 6, Paul's primary stated rationale is that such persons *have already been circumcised* by God through receiving the spirit, so requiring them to be circumcised by human hands is to invalidate the work of the spirit as the divine agent of Israel's restoration.[58] Requiring physical circumcision would imply that what is truly efficacious for creating Israelites is the work of human hands rather than the work of God. Moreover, if those who are already circumcised still need the spirit for their circumcision and participation in the covenant to be valid (cf. Rom 2:25–29), requiring those who have already received the spirit to validate their reception of the spirit by being physically circumcised is an absurdity. Instead, their foreskin has now been reckoned as circumcision (Rom 2:26), validated by the approval of God himself.[59]

---

[57] See Paula Fredriksen, "Judaism, the Circumcision of Gentiles, and Apocalyptic Hope" (1991), 544–54.

[58] See Normand Bonneau, "Logic of Paul's Argument on the Curse of the Law in Galatians 3:10–14" (1997), 68–70. Garroway, "Circumcision of Christ," 189 n. 21, argues that for Paul the circumcision of the heart is also *reckoned* as "an intangible circumcision of the foreskin of the penis as well" (cf. *Paul's Gentile-Jews*, 115–34).

[59] "The cross puts an end to the need for circumcisions *wrought by men* precisely because it realizes circumcisions *wrought by Christ*" (Garroway, *Paul's Gentile-Jews*, 62, emphasis his).

To become heirs of Abraham, gentiles need divine intervention akin to Abraham's own election, which is precisely what Paul argues has happened through the spirit. By receiving the spirit of Messiah, these gentile individuals have become parts of Messiah's (circumcised) body. These former gentiles have therefore been transformed into actual descendants of Abraham through something more like a DNA transplant, whereas fleshly circumcision amounts to little more than cosmetic surgery, "creating the appearance of kinship, without effecting any underlying genealogical change."[60] Requiring spirit-filled gentiles to go through the rite of circumcision to become full members of Israel therefore not only denies the legitimacy what they have already received by the spirit but also attempts to incorporate them through a process inadequate for the task. Circumcision had never brought about Israel's justification, so why would it do so for gentiles? And inasmuch as the new covenant is contingent on justification, what matters is the circumcision of the heart by the spirit.

Essentially, Paul presses the question: is membership in new covenant Israel defined by the circumcision of the heart by the spirit or by circumcision performed by human hands? Or, more simply: is covenant membership determined by the spirit or the foreskin? If the former, then why should physically uncircumcised people who have already received the spirit be circumcised? If the latter, then the spirit is declared inadequate and ineffectual, the new covenant has not in fact been inaugurated, and Israel remains in need of redemption. Consequently, as Normand Bonneau explains, "to continue maintaining the Jew-Gentile distinction (Gentiles in Christ are still sinners), is tantamount to saying that Christ has not been raised, that the Age to Come has not been inaugurated, that the power of sin still reigns."[61] On the other hand, if both Jews and uncircumcised non-Jews are receiving the spirit in the same way, the implication is that "in Messiah, there is neither Jew nor Greek" (Gal 3:28).[62]

---

[60] Matthew Thiessen, *Paul and the Gentile Problem* (2016), 121, cf. 15, 117. Remarkably, although Thiessen persuasively argues that Paul understands his gentile converts as undergoing an ethnic transformation such that "reception of Christ's *pneuma* materially relates gentiles to Abraham," he stops short of the idea that these gentiles thereby become *Israelites*, despite the fact that Paul argues that Abraham has only one heir (Rom 9:7–13; Gal 3:16–19; 4:22–26).

[61] Bonneau, "Logic of Paul's Argument," 69; cf. Christopher Zoccali, "What's the Problem with the Law?" (2015), 399–400.

[62] It should be noted, however, that this absence of distinction only applies *in Messiah*. For those *outside* Messiah, the distinction between "Jew" (naturally born into Israel) and "Greek" remains.

Paul also points out that circumcision was not an original component of the covenant with Abraham, nor was it the means of Abraham's justification. Instead, the command to circumcise was added after the promise was made, after "fidelity was reckoned to Abraham as justness" (Rom 4:9–12; Gen 15:6). In light of the Genesis narrative to which Paul refers here, the same principle established in Gal 3:19 applies: circumcision was added due to the episode of infidelity that occurs between the promise in Gen 15 and the revised covenant in Gen 17, namely Abraham's infidelity (lack of trust that God could provide an heir otherwise) and injustice toward Hagar.[63] The consequence of Abraham's misdeed is poetically fitting as is typical in Genesis; circumcision involves the very instrument of wrongdoing in the preceding episode. As such, just as the written Torah itself serves as a perpetual reminder of Israel's infidelity "until the seed would come,"[64] circumcision serves as both a perpetual reminder of Abraham's infidelity and the "seal of the justness of the fidelity which he had when uncircumcised" (Rom 4:11) – that is, the fidelity that he demonstrated when he first trusted God, before the infidelity and injustice recounted in Gen 16. Those who have the spirit and obey are in the faithful state Abraham was in Gen 15 and have no need of fleshly circumcision – which was always the sign and physical manifestation of the pneumatic circumcision rather than the thing itself – for Abraham to be their father.[65]

It is nevertheless critical to emphasize that Paul has no objection to circumcision per se, only to circumcision as a rite of entrance into Israel for gentiles already having received the spirit. He resists not circumcision in principle but argues that it does not bring about justification, nor can it transform gentile believers, who can be ethnically transformed into faithful Israelites and heirs of Abraham only through the work of the spirit. There is no indication that Paul discouraged Jewish followers of Jesus to stop circumcising their boys on the eighth day, and I suspect he encouraged rather than discouraged the continuation of this practice "for the sake of conscience" (Rom 13:5; 1 Cor 10:28–29) and as a part of each

---

[63] It is noteworthy in this context that Hagar (הגר) puns on the Hebrew word for "the stranger," while Abraham has just been told that he and his seed will also be "a stranger" (Gen 15:13).

[64] Gal 3:19; cf. Deut 31:20–21; Jub 1:6–25.

[65] The parallelism in Gen 17:10–11 allows exactly this sort of distinction between circumcision (v. 10) and *fleshly* circumcision in much the same way the heavenly Torah can be distinguished from the written revelation through Moses (see the discussion on pp. 95–97).

person remaining "in the state in which he was called" (1 Cor 7:20).[66] One also wonders whether he would have objected to the children of non-Jewish Jesus-followers being circumcised on the eighth day, a question not addressed in his letters. Nevertheless, Paul does not limit his arguments about the inadequacy of fleshly circumcision in the absence of spiritual transformation to those circumcisions performed after the eighth day of a child's life.[67] Instead, he plainly states that regardless of the timing of the circumcision, for those in Messiah, "neither circumcision nor foreskin matters, only fidelity working through love" (Gal 5:6) and "circumcision is nothing and foreskin is nothing, but what matters is keeping the commands of God" (1 Cor 7:19).[68]

STRENGTHS OF THIS READING

This paradigm for understanding Paul's gospel and his perspective on Israel, the gentiles, and the Torah provides an elegant and coherent solution to many of the most troublesome puzzles that have characterized Pauline studies for generations, consistently explaining statements or grammatical features inexplicable in other models. Key sections and chapters often regarded as inscrutable or inconsistent with the rest of the Pauline letters have been shown to be not just coherent with Paul's statements elsewhere but foundational to understanding those statements more fully. Moreover, this reading does so without special pleading or attempting to explain away inconvenient chunks of Paul's letters by appealing to interpolation or scribal error or by assigning especially troublesome parts to the voice of an interlocutor that cannot be reliably isolated or identified.

---

[66] Cf. Thiessen, *Paul and the Gentile Problem*, 165–67.
[67] Contra Thiessen, *Paul and the Gentile Problem*, 67–72; Thiessen, *Contesting Conversion* (2011); cf. Rafael Rodríguez, *If You Call Yourself a Jew* (2014), 56–61. Note that if all circumcisions occurring after the eighth day are invalid and result in that person being cut off from Israel, all of Israel would be illegitimate after the wilderness generation, since "all the people who were born in the wilderness along the way as they came out of Egypt had not been circumcised" (Josh 5:5) and therefore needed to be circumcised as adults upon entry to the land under Joshua (5:2–8). The result of this view would therefore be that Israel has been in the same situation as the nations – cut off and outside the covenant – since the wilderness generation.
[68] Recall that being circumcised in accordance with Torah is not a command that a person keeps on his own behalf and is therefore not included in what matters according to Paul. See the discussion on pp. 172–73, particularly n. 98.

Rather than suggesting that Paul abandoned Judaism and adopted another framework, this paradigm begins by treating Paul's letters as early Jewish literature, putting them in conversation with other Jewish texts from the Second Temple period. In the process, this model applies a thoroughgoing eschatological approach, demonstrating that nearly everything Paul says fits closely within an eschatological framework shared by many of his Jewish predecessors and contemporaries. Paul was not wholly unique, nor was he a modern man among ancient Jews. He was an apocalyptic restorationist more similar to his apocalypticist contemporaries at Qumran than his later readers from fourth-century Hippo, sixteenth-century Germany, or twenty-first century universities.

Not only does this paradigm present Paul in dialogue with other early Jewish literature, it pays especially close attention to oft-ignored distinctions regularly maintained throughout this literature, most notably the distinction between "Jews" and "Israelites," which takes special significance in eschatological contexts both in the Pauline corpus and elsewhere. Moreover, this reading has shed significant light on Paul's use of scripture. Contrary to the common claim that Paul's scriptural allusions, echoes, or citations show little regard for the context from which they are chosen, this reading has shown Paul to have remarkably consistent citational practices, working with the grain of his sources through a specific restorationist lens refracted through a network of key restorationist texts that inform his reading of everything else. In particular, this reading takes seriously Paul's repeated application to gentiles of prophecies about the scattering and restoration of the northern kingdom of Israel – such as the "not my people" (Hos 2:25 [2:23 ET]) and "fullness of the nations" (Gen 48:19) prophecies about northern Israel – a pattern that begs explanation in any other model.

The end result is a picture of an apostle who looks simultaneously more foreign, more coherent, and significantly more Jewish than in other modern reconstructions. Rather than proclaiming a universal gospel of "faith" over and against legalistic "Judaism," Paul proclaims the restoration of Israel through the transformative work of the divine spirit (*pneuma*), a gift from God made possible by the obedient fidelity of Israel's crucified Messiah – a gift surprisingly extended to gentiles as a necessary means of Israel's full restoration. This "spirit of sanctity" (Rom 1:4) fulfills the prophetic promises that Israel would be transformed into an obedient people, doing the works that please God in full. Far from preaching "grace" over and against "works," Paul argues that God has provided the grace necessary to do the works that please God, putting the one who "walks by the spirit" (Gal 5:16; cf. Rom 8:4) in position to receive eternal life when God "will repay each person according to his works" (Rom 2:6), with the spirit transforming its recipients into divine "children of God" (Rom 8:19) above even the angels (1 Cor 6:3).

This reading does not require Paul to have abandoned his foundational priors for an entirely different system of religion. It does not require Paul to have become a man of the future unlike his contemporaries. It does not require Paul to have abandoned the fundamental distinctives of Judaism. Instead, it only requires that Paul, having concluded that the new covenant is being fulfilled through Israel's Messiah Jesus, find scriptural justification for why uncircumcised gentiles were receiving the sacred spirit promised to Israel as part of that new covenant redemption. This is an extremely small shift with massive implications for practice and group formation.[69]

If one wishes to be contentious or improve on the paradigm proposed here, superior explanations will need to be introduced in the following areas at a minimum:

(1) Paul's use of "Israel" and *Ioudaios*. Since it is unlikely that Paul would have idiosyncratically treated "Israel" and "Jews" as synonymous when his predecessors and contemporaries did not, one must explain (a) why Paul is diferent in this respect and (b) why, despite preferring *Ioudaios* when referring to contemporary Jews elsewhere in the letters, he shifts to "Israel" in Rom 9–11 while otherwise limiting "Israel" to biblical, self-referential, or eschatological senses and avoiding the Israel/gentile dichotomy.

(2) Israel's plight under the curse of Torah. Early Jewish literature consistently treats Israel and the subcategory of Jews as "under sin" or in the "age of wrath" awaiting restoration due to having broken covenant. If Paul did not agree, why does he so consistently use language that maps onto that framework as observed in other early Jewish restorationist contexts? Why does he present his

---

[69] Notably, Acts presents "Paul as Torah-observant and faithful to his ancestral customs in every way and as one whose reputation is that he is a teacher of apostasy from Moses whose person and message is viewed as a destabilizing threat to the Jewish ancestral way of life." (Joshua W. Jipp, "The Paul of Acts" [2019], 67). Despite remaining "within Judaism," Paul is "nothing but clear in his unrelenting association between the hope and history of Israel as centering upon God's resurrection and heavenly enthronement of Israel's Davidic Messiah" (68) and that "foundational commitment to Jesus as the risen Messiah results in a totalizing and hegemonic appropriation of Israel's ancestral heritage, customs, and Scriptures" in the context of his Jewish restorationist framework (77–78).

gospel in "new covenant" terms if he believes renewal of the covenant is unnecessary?
(3) Gentile incorporation into Israel. If Paul does not understand his uncircumcised converts as transformed into Israelites, one must explain why he refers to them as descendants not only of Abraham but of "our fathers" in the wilderness (1 Cor 10:1) – a reference that situates the gentiles under not only Abraham but also Israel/Jacob. Moreover, if Paul is not claiming that these gentiles are full Israelites, why do his opponents argue that they must be circumcised, a rite that would be unnecessary unless they were entering the assembly of Israel? And why does Paul consistently apply prophetic declarations about the northern kingdom – about both Israel's disobedience and subsequent gentilization and Israel's redemption and restoration – to gentiles? What other explanation accounts for the idea that gentiles are receiving the spirit promised to Israel and are being "grafted in" to the same entity in which Jews are naturally born?

THE PAYOFF: THE TASK DISCHARGED

In addition to its other strengths, the paradigm put forward in this book makes sense of Paul's argument in the context of early Judaism and the early Jesus-movement while also providing a reasonable explanation for the emergence of the later supersessionist perspective on Israel. In full Jewish sectarian fashion, Paul sees the *ekklēsia* in complete continuity with Israel – in fact as the righteous remainder of Israel being restored as promised (cf. Rom 9:27–29; 11:6). The entire discussion is framed by the prophetic promises of the restoration of all Israel; Paul is at pains to explain how the ingathering of the gentiles relates to these promises. Thus, when Paul asks, "Has God rejected his people?" (Rom 11:1), he is not addressing the fate of the Jews alone but the whole of Israel. He then demonstrates how the incorporation of gentiles into the eschatological *ekklēsia* of new covenant Israel does not invalidate but fulfills God's promise to redeem *all* Israel.

But once the social context had changed and gentiles significantly outnumbered Jews, Paul's arguments were read in ways scarcely conceivable to the apostle, who was shaped by Jewish restoration eschatology and wrote at a time when the *ekklēsia* was still dominated by Jewish leadership (including Paul himself). That said, the patristic perspective did not emerge from thin air but is instead a natural development of

The Payoff

Paul's equation of the *ekklēsia* with eschatological Israel and assertions that faithful, pneumatically transformed gentiles are in fact Israelites.[70] When Paul wrote Romans, an *ekklēsia* led by and primarily composed of Jews was still grappling with the question of gentile inclusion. But within a generation, that problem had long been resolved, and the *ekklēsia* was increasingly composed of gentiles. As the context of early Christianity changed, the nuance and subtlety of Paul's argument about the gentiles' role in Israel's restoration was replaced by the blunt replacement theology or "third race" notion of the later period. Thus, Paul's argument about gentile incorporation into Israel as a part of Israel's restoration was eventually misconstrued as an argument that the gentile church had replaced the Jews as the "true Israel," and his discussion of the promised restoration of Israel in light of gentile incorporation – a discussion rooted in Jewish eschatological concerns – was misinterpreted as a discourse on the fate of the Jews in light of their rejection of the gospel. Ultimately, Rom 9–11 has been misunderstood for so long because interpreters have approached it from the wrong end, asking inverted, anachronistic questions, reading backwards from the perspective of the present situation in the gentile-dominated church rather than forwards from the perspective of early Judaism.

This study therefore provides an elegant solution for Schweitzer's "great and still undischarged task which confronts those engaged in the historical study of primitive Christianity" – the problem of defining the position of Paul and how Paul's gospel relates to the earliest Jesus-movement and later Christianity.[71] It also provides a plausible explanation for the substance of Paul's disagreements with his contemporaries – something that post–New Perspective scholarship has struggled to provide. Sanders, for example, offers only the famous tautology, "this is what Paul finds wrong in Judaism: it is not Christianity."[72] Ultimately, Sanders argues that Paul abandoned covenantal nomism in favor of participationist eschatology, much to the dismay and disappointment of many who recognized Paul on nearly every page of Sanders' sections on Judaism and covenantal nomism.

---

[70] *Pace* Fredriksen, "Circumcision Is Nothing," 83, the equation of Israel with the "mixed body of Jews and gentiles saved through Christ" was *not* the result of the loss of the first generation's imminent eschatology. On the contrary, when "Ephesians collapses the distinction between Israel and the nations" (83), it does not oppose but instead accurately represents Paul's own theology.

[71] Schweitzer, *Paul and His Interpreters*, v.

[72] E. P. Sanders, *Paul and Palestinian Judaism* (1977), 552.

My thesis provides a more robust solution: Paul did not abandon covenantal nomism for another "pattern of religion," nor is his participationist eschatology at odds with a covenantal perspective or Judaism itself. The debate in which Paul was engaged concerned neither legalism nor different patterns of religion nor did he preach inclusiveness over and against Jewish ethnocentrism. Paul was not driven by an ethic of inclusion but rather by a particular understanding of Israel's restoration; he in no way rejected Israel's special status but remained a participant in a long-standing debate about the proper boundaries of Israel and what constitutes Israelite identity. Contrary to Sanders' conclusion that Paul "polemicizes ... against the prior fundamentals of Judaism: the election, the covenant and the law,"[73] Paul continues to preach God's special election of Israel, the lasting value of Israel's covenant, the restoration and ultimate salvation of Israel, and the need for total obedience.

One must also remember that Paul lived in a context in which the very existence of Samaritans meant that there were more claimants to the heritage of Israel than Jews alone, and the primary concern even in Jewish theology was *Israelite* identity and heritage. Paul is another participant in that larger framework of "Israelism," though his extension of Israelite status to physically uncircumcised men represents a departure from a more distinctly Judah-specific form of Israelism – his prior way of life before preaching Israel's restoration through Jesus (Gal 1:13).[74] Once one recognizes this larger category of "Israel" over which various parties contended, including Jews and Samaritans and eventually Christians, it is evident that Paul never departed from this larger theological matrix, nor did he abandon the theological framework he held before his encounter with Jesus. Consequently, if Paul's perspective must be labeled, I suggest he be understood as operating "within Israelism," specifically a restorationist form of Israelism based on the conviction that the new covenant with both Israel and Judah had been inaugurated by the death and resurrection of Israel's messiah, a Jew named Jesus.[75]

In this respect, Sanders' famous dictum requires amendment since there is no indication that Paul found anything wrong with Judaism at all. His

---

[73] Sanders, *PPJ*, 552.

[74] Paul was not even unique among his Jewish contemporaries in deemphasizing physical circumcision. Philo complains of Jews who recognize the allegorical truths of Torah but neglect the literal, even seeing circumcision as unnecessary (*Migr.* 89–92; *QE* 2.2).

[75] This explains why Paul can speak of his "former way of life in Judaism" (Gal 1:13–14) while still regarding himself as an Israelite preaching Israel's restoration.

The Payoff

quarrel was not with *Judaism* but with *other Jews*, some of whom were also followers of Jesus. Paul's arguments consistently presume the validity of the core elements of Judaism, including Israel's special covenant status, the authority of the Torah and the Prophets, and the foundational paradigm of restoration eschatology. Paul in no way critiques the traditional discourse of *Judaism* but rather participates within that discourse, debating the present position on the eschatological timetable and the implications of that position.

Specifically, Paul believed that the age of wrath, in which Israel remained subject to the curses of Torah, had ended with the resurrection of Israel's messiah, which had initiated the promised redemption and resurrection of all Israel by the transforming spirit (*pneuma*), a process surprisingly involving the incorporation of physically foreskinned but spiritually transformed gentiles, fulfilling YHWH's promise to restore "not my people." His various interlocutors, while agreed on the fundamentals of covenant and Israel's need for restoration, disagreed with one or more of these details. It is therefore more accurate to conclude that *Paul finds nothing at all wrong in Judaism; instead, he regards the death and resurrection of Jesus and the consequent spiritual transformation of both Jews and gentiles as the fulfillment of the prophetic promises of Israel's restoration.*

Bibliography

Aageson, James W. "Paul's Use of Scripture: A Comparative Study of Biblical Interpretation in Early Palestinian Judaism and the New Testament with Special Reference to Romans 9–11." PhD diss., University of Oxford, 1984.
———. "Typology, Correspondence, and the Application of Scripture in Romans 9–11." *Journal for the Study of the New Testament* 31 (1987): 51–72.
Abasciano, Brian J. "Diamonds in the Rough: A Reply to Christopher Stanley concerning the Reader Competency of Paul's Original Audiences." *Novum Testamentum* 49.2 (2007): 153–83.
———. *Paul's Use of the Old Testament in Romans 9:1–9: An Intertextual and Theological Exegesis.* London: T&T Clark, 2005.
Abegg, Martin G. "Exile and the Dead Sea Scrolls." Pages 111–25 in *Exile: Old Testament, Jewish, and Christian Conceptions.* Edited by James M. Scott. JSJSup 56. Leiden: Brill, 1997.
Achtemeier, Paul J. *Romans.* IBC. Atlanta: John Knox, 1985.
Ackerman, James S. "The Rabbinic Interpretation of Psalm 82 and the Gospel of John: John 10:34." *The Harvard Theological Review* 59.2 (1966): 186–91.
Ackroyd, Peter R. *Exile and Restoration: A Study of Hebrew Thought of the Sixth Century B.C.* Louisville: Westminster John Knox, 1968.
Aernie, Jeffrey W. *Is Paul Also among the Prophets? An Examination of the Relationship between Paul and the Old Testament Prophetic Tradition in 2 Corinthians.* LNTS 467. London: T&T Clark, 2012.
Akzin, Benjamin. "Who Is a Jew – A Hard Case." *Israel Law Review* 5.2 (1970): 259–63.
Albertz, Rainer. *Israel in Exile: The History and Literature of the Sixth Century B.C.E.* StBibLit 3. Atlanta: SBL Press, 2003.
Aletti, Jean-Noël. ""La dispositio rhétorique dans les épîtres pauliniennes." *New Testament Studies* 38.3 (1992): 385–401.
———. "La présence d'un modèle rhétorique en Romains: Son rôle et son importance." *Biblica* 71 (1990): 1–24.

"Romains 11: Le développement de l'argumentation et ses enjeux exégético-théologiques." Pages 197–223 in *The Letter to the Romans*. Edited by Udo Schnelle. BETL 226. Leuven: Peeters, 2009.
Alexander, Philip S. "Rabbinic Judaism and the New Testament." *Zeitschrift für die neutestamentliche Wissenschaft* 74.3–4 (1983): 237–46.
Allison, Dale C. *Constructing Jesus: Memory, Imagination, and History*. Grand Rapids: Baker Academic, 2010.
——— *The End of the Ages Has Come: An Early Interpretation of the Passion and Resurrection of Jesus*. Eugene: Wipf & Stock, 2013.
——— "The End of the Ages Has Come: An Early Interpretation of the Passion and Resurrection of Jesus." PhD diss., Duke University, 1982.
——— *The Jesus Tradition in Q*. Harrisburg, PA: Trinity Press International, 1997.
——— "Matt. 23:39 = Luke 13:35b as a Conditional Prophecy." *Journal for the Study of the New Testament* 18 (1983): 75–84.
——— "A Plea for Thoroughgoing Eschatology." *Journal of Biblical Literature* 113.4 (1994): 651–68.
Andersen, Francis I. *Habakkuk: A New Translation with Introduction and Commentary*. AB 25. New Haven: Yale University Press, 2001.
Anderson, R. Dean. *Ancient Rhetorical Theory and Paul*. Kampen: Pharos, 1996.
Ashton, John. "The Identity and Function of 'The Ἰουδαῖοι' in the Fourth Gospel." *Novum Testamentum* 27.1 (1985): 40–75.
Atkinson, Kenneth R. *I Cried to the Lord: A Study of the Psalms of Solomon's Historical Background and Social Setting*. JSJSup 84. Leiden: Brill, 2004.
——— "Solomon, Psalms of." Pages 1238–41 in *Eerdmans Dictionary of Early Judaism*. Edited by John J. Collins. Grand Rapids: Eerdmans, 2010.
Atzmon, Gil et al. "Abraham's Children in the Genome Era: Major Jewish Diaspora Populations Comprise Distinct Genetic Clusters with Shared Middle Eastern Ancestry." *American Journal of Human Genetics* 86.6 (2010): 850–59.
Aune, David E. "Charismatic Exegesis in Early Judaism and Early Christianity." Pages 12–50 in *The Pseudepigrapha and Early Biblical Interpretation*. Edited by James H. Charlesworth and Craig A. Evans. JSOTSup 14. Sheffield: JSOT Press, 1993.
Aune, David E., and Eric Clark Stewart. "From the Idealized Past to the Imaginary Future: Eschatological Restoration in Jewish Apocalyptic Literature." Pages 147–77 in *Restoration: Old Testament, Jewish and Christian Perspectives*. Edited by James M. Scott. JSJSup 72. Leiden: Brill, 2001.
Aus, Roger D. "Paul's Travel Plans to Spain and the 'Full Number of the Gentiles' of Rom. XI 25." *Novum Testamentum* 21.3 (1979): 232–62.
Averbeck, Richard E. "Christian Interpretations of Isaiah 53." Pages 33–60 in *The Gospel according to Isaiah 53: Encountering the Suffering Servant in Jewish and Christian Theology*. Edited by Darrell L. Bock and Mitch Glaser. Grand Rapids: Kregel Academic, 2012.
Bachmann, Michael. "Verus Israel: Ein Vorschlag zu einer 'mengentheoretischen' Neubeschreibung der betreffenden paulinischen Terminologie." *New Testament Studies* 48.4 (2002): 500–12.

Badenas, Robert. *Christ: the End of the Law: Romans 10.4 in Pauline Perspective*. JSNTSup 10. Sheffield: JSOT Press, 1987.
Bader, Chris. "When Prophecy Passes Unnoticed: New Perspectives on Failed Prophecy." *Journal for the Scientific Study of Religion* 38.1 (1999): 119–31.
Baer, David. "'It's All about Us!': Nationalistic Exegesis in the Greek Isaiah (Chapters 1–12)." Pages 29–47 in *"As Those Who Are Taught": The Interpretation of Isaiah from the LXX to the SBL*. Edited by Claire Mathews McGinnis and Patricia K. Tull. SBLSym 27. Atlanta: SBL Press, 2006.
Baker, Cynthia M. "A 'Jew' by Any Other Name." *Journal of Ancient Judaism* 2 (2011): 153–80.
Baker, Murray. "Paul and the Salvation of Israel: Paul's Ministry, the Motif of Jealousy, and Israel's Yes." *Catholic Biblical Quarterly* 67.3 (2005): 469–84.
Bamberger, Bernard J. *Proselytism in the Talmudic period*. Cincinnati, OH: Hebrew Union College Press, 1968.
Bandstra, Andrew J. *The Law and the Elements of the World: An Exegetical Study in Aspects of Paul's Teaching*. Kampen: Kok, 1964.
Barclay, John M. G. "By the Grace of God I Am What I Am: Grace and Agency in Philo and Paul." Pages 140–57 in *Divine and Human Agency in Paul and His Cultural Environment*. Edited by John M. G. Barclay and Simon Gathercole. Library of Biblical Studies 335. London: T&T Clark, 2006.
——— "Grace and the Transformation of Agency in Christ." Pages 372–89 in *Redefining First-Century Jewish and Christian identities*. South Bend, IN: University of Notre Dame Press, 2008.
——— "'I Will Have Mercy on Whom I Have Mercy': The Golden Calf and Divine Mercy in Romans 9–11 and Second Temple Judaism." *Early Christianity* 1.1 (2010): 82–106.
——— *Jews in the Mediterranean Diaspora: From Alexander to Trajan (323 BCE–117 CE)*. Berkeley: University of California Press, 1996.
——— *Obeying the Truth: A Study of Paul's Ethics in Galatians*. Edinburgh: T&T Clark, 1988.
——— "Paul and Philo on Circumcision: Romans 2.25–9 in Social and Cultural Context." *New Testament Studies* 44 (1998): 536–56.
——— "Paul, Judaism, and the Jewish People." Pages 188–201 in *The Blackwell Companion to Paul*. Edited by Stephen Westerholm. Blackwell Companions to Religion. Malden: Wiley-Blackwell, 2011.
——— *Paul and the Gift*. Grand Rapids: Eerdmans, 2015.
——— "Ἰουδαῖος: Ethnicity and Translation." Pages 46–58 in *Ethnicity, Race, Religion: Identities and Ideologies in Early Jewish and Christian Texts, and in Modern Biblical Interpretation*. Edited by Katherine M. Hockey and David G. Horrell. London: T&T Clark, 2018.
Barmash, Pamela. "At the Nexus of History and Memory: The Ten Lost Tribes." *Association for Jewish Studies Review* 29.2 (2005): 207–36.
Barrett, C. K. *The Epistle to the Romans*. Translated by Edwyn C. Hoskyns. BNTC 6. Oxford: Oxford University Press, 1991.
——— "Romans 9:30–10:21: Fall and Responsibility of Israel." Pages 132–53 in *Essays on Paul*. Philadelphia: Westminster, 1982.

Barth, Karl. *A Shorter Commentary on Romans*. Translated by David H Van Daalen. Aldershot: Ashgate, 2007.
Barth, Markus. *Ephesians*. AB 34A. Garden City: Doubleday, 1974.
———. *The People of God*. JSNTSup 5. Sheffield: JSOT Press, 1983.
Barton, Stephen C. "Sanctification and Oneness in 1 Corinthians with Implications for the Case of 'Mixed Marriages' (1 Corinthians 7.12–16)." *New Testament Studies* 63.1 (2017): 38–55.
Barzilai, Gad. "Who Is a Jew? Categories, Boundaries, Communities and Citizenship Law in Israel." Pages 27–42 in *Boundaries of Jewish Identity*. Edited by Susan A. Glenn and Naomi B. Sokoloff. Seattle: University of Washington Press, 2010.
Bassler, Jouette M. "Divine Impartiality in Paul's Letter to the Romans." *Novum Testamentum* 26.1 (1984): 43–58.
———. *Divine Impartiality: Paul and a Theological Axiom*. SBLDS 59. Chico, CA: Scholars Press, 1982.
Basta, Pasquale. *Gezerah Shawah: Storia, forme e metodi dell'analogia biblica*. Roma: Pontificio istituto biblico, 2006.
Bates, Matthew W. "Beyond 'Stichwort': A Narrative Approach to Isa 52,7 in Romans 10,15 and 11Q Melchizedek (11Q13)." *Revue biblique* 116.3 (2009): 387–414.
———. *Salvation by Allegiance Alone: Rethinking Faith, Works, and the Gospel of Jesus the King*. Grand Rapids: Baker Academic, 2017.
Battle, John A. Jr. "Paul's Use of the Old Testament in Romans 9:25–26." *Grace Theological Journal* 2.1 (1981): 115–29.
Bauckham, Richard J. *Gospel Women: Studies of the Named Women in the Gospels*. London: Bloomsbury, 2002.
———. "The List of the Tribes in Revelation 7 Again." *Journal for the Study of the New Testament* 42 (1991): 99–115.
———. "The Restoration of Israel in Luke-Acts." Pages 435–87 in *Restoration: Old Testament, Jewish and Christian Perspectives*. Edited by James M. Scott. JSJSup 72. Leiden: Brill, 2001.
———. "Tobit as a Parable for the Exiles of Northern Israel." Pages 140–64 in *Studies in the Book of Tobit: An Multidisciplinary Approach*. Edited by Mark R. J. Bredin. LSTS 55. London: T&T Clark, 2006.
Baur, Ferdinand Christian. *The Church History of the First Three Centuries*. Translated by Allan Menzies. 2 vols. London: Williams and Norgate, 1878.
Baxter, A. G., and John A. Zeisler. "Paul and Arboriculture: Romans 11.17–24." *Journal for the Study of the New Testament* 24 (1985): 25–32.
Baynes, Leslie. *The Heavenly Book Motif in Judeo-Christian Apocalypses, 200 B.C.E.–200 C.E.* JSJSup 152. Leiden: Brill, 2012.
Beale, G. K. *The Book of Revelation*. NIGTC. Grand Rapids: Eerdmans, 1999.
Beale, G. K., and D. A. Carson, eds. *Commentary on the New Testament Use of the Old Testament*. Grand Rapids: Baker, 2007.
Beattie, D. R. G., and Philip R. Davies. "What Does Hebrew Mean?" *Journal of Semitic Studies* 56.1 (2011): 71–83.
Beek, M. A. Review of *Achtzehngebet und Vaterunser und der Reim*, by Karl Georg Kuhn. *Vox Theologica* 21 (1950): 21–22.

Beker, J. Christiaan. "The Faithfulness of God and the Priority of Israel in Paul's Letter to the Romans." *Harvard Theological Review* 79.1–3 (1986): 10–16.

———. *Paul the Apostle: The Triumph of God in Life and Thought*. Philadelphia: Fortress, 1980.

Bekken, Per Jarle. *The Word Is Near You: A Study of Deuteronomy 30:12–14 in Paul's Letter to the Romans in a Jewish Context*. BZNW 144. Berlin: de Gruyter, 2007.

Bell, Richard H. *The Irrevocable Call of God: An Inquiry into Paul's Theology of Israel*. WUNT 184. Tübingen: Mohr Siebeck, 2005.

———. *No One Seeks for God: An Exegetical and Theological Study of Romans 1.18–3.20*. Tübingen: Mohr Siebeck, 1998.

———. *Provoked to Jealousy: The Origin and Purpose of the Jealousy Motif in Romans 9–11*. WUNT 63. Tübingen: Mohr, 1994.

Beller, Steven. *Antisemitism: A Very Short Introduction*. Oxford: Oxford University Press, 2007.

Belleville, Linda. *Reflections of Glory: Paul's Polemical use of the Moses-Doxa Tradition in 2 Corinthians 3.1–18*. London: Bloomsbury, 2015.

Benoit, Pierre. "Conclusion par mode de synthèse." Pages 217–36 in *Die Israelfrage nach Römer 9–11*. Edited by Lorenzo de Lorenzi. Colloquium Paulinum 4. Rome: Abtei von St Paul vor den Mauern, 1977.

Bergmeier, Roland. "Das Gesetz im Römerbrief." Pages 31–102 in *Das Gesetz im Römerbrief und andere Studien zum Neuen Testament*. WUNT 121. Tübingen: Mohr Siebeck, 2000.

Bergsma, John S. *The Jubilee from Leviticus to Qumran: A History of Interpretation*. VTSup 115. Leiden: Brill, 2007.

———. "The Persian Period as Penitential Era: The 'Exegetical Logic' of Daniel 9:1–27." Pages 50–64 in *Exile and Restoration Revisited: Essays on the Babylonian and Persian Period in Memory of Peter R. Ackroyd*. Edited by Gary N. Knoppers, Lester L. Grabbe, and Dierdre N. Fulton. LSTS 73. London: T&T Clark, 2009.

Berkley, Timothy W. *From a Broken Covenant to Circumcision of the Heart: Pauline Intertextual Exegesis in Romans 2:17–29*. SBLDS 175. Atlanta: Society of Biblical Literature, 2000.

Berkowitz, Beth A. "A Short History of the People Israel from the Patriarchs to the Messiah." Pages 112–39 in *Defining Jewish Difference: From Antiquity to the Present*. Cambridge: Cambridge University Press, 2012.

Bernasconi, Rocco. "Tannaitic 'Israel' and the Kutim." Pages 365–92 in *Entre lignes de partage et territoires de passage: les identités religieuses dans les mondes grec et romain. "Paganismes," "judaïsmes," "christianismes."* Edited by Nicole Belayche and Simon C. Mimouni. Collection de la Revue des Études Juives 47. Leuven: Peeters, 2008.

Berrin [Tzoref], Shani L. "The Use of Secondary Biblical Sources in Pesher Nahum." *Dead Sea Discoveries* 11 (2004): 1–11.

Berzon, Todd S. "Ethnicity and Early Christianity: New Approaches to Religious Kinship and Community." *Currents in Biblical Research* 16.2 (2018): 191–227.

Betz, Hans Dieter. *Galatians: A Commentary*. Hermeneia. Philadelphia: Fortress, 1979.

Bird, Michael F. *Jesus and the Origins of the Gentile Mission.* LNTS 331. London: T&T Clark, 2007.

———. *The Saving Righteousness of God: Studies on Paul, Justification and the New Perspective.* Milton Keynes: Paternoster, 2007.

Bird, Michael F., and Preston M. Sprinkle. "Jewish Interpretation of Paul in the Last Thirty Years." *Currents in Biblical Research* 6.3 (2008): 355–76.

Blenkinsopp, Joseph. *Ezra-Nehemiah: A Commentary.* OTL. Louisville: Westminster John Knox, 1988.

———. "Second Isaiah – Prophet of Universalism." *Journal for the Study of the Old Testament* 41 (1988): 83–103.

Block, Daniel I. *The Gods of the Nations: A Study in Ancient Near Eastern National Theology.* Eugene: Wipf & Stock, 2013.

Blumhofer, Christopher Mark. *The Gospel of John and the Future of Israel.* Vol. 177. SNTSMS. Cambridge: Cambridge University Press, 2020.

Boas, Evert van Emde, Albert Rijksbaron, Luuk Huitink, and Mathieu de Bakker. *The Cambridge Grammar of Classical Greek.* Cambridge: Cambridge University Press, 2019.

Boccaccini, Gabriele. *Paul's Three Paths to Salvation.* Grand Rapids: Eerdmans, 2020.

Bockmuehl, Markus N. *Revelation and Mystery in Ancient Judaism and Pauline Christianity.* Tübingen: Mohr, 1990.

Boer, Martinus C. de. *Galatians: A Commentary.* NTL. Louisville, KY: Westminster John Knox, 2011.

Böhm, Martina. *Samarien und die Samaritai bei Lukas: eine Studie zum religionshistorischen und traditionsgeschichtlichen Hintergrund der lukanischen Samarientexte und zu deren topographischer Verhaftung.* WUNT 111. Tübingen: Mohr Siebeck, 1999.

———. "Wer gehörte in hellenistisch-römischer Zeit zu 'Israel'? Historische Voraussetzungen für eine veränderte Perspektiv auf neutestamentliche Texte." Pages 181–202 in *Die Samaritaner und die Bibel: Historische und literarische Wechselwirkungen zwischen biblischen und samaritanischen Traditionen = The Samaritans and the Bible: Historical and Literary Interactions Between Biblical and Samaritan Traditions.* Edited by Jörg Frey, Ursula Schattner-Rieser, and Konrad Schmid. SJ 70. Berlin: de Gruyter, 2012.

Bonneau, Normand. "The Logic of Paul's Argument on the Curse of the Law in Galatians 3:10–14." *Novum Testamentum* 39.1 (1997): 60–80.

Bons, Eberhard, and Patrick Pouchelle, eds. *The Psalms of Solomon: Language, History, Theology.* EJL 40. Atlanta: SBL Press, 2015.

Borgen, Peder. "'There Shall Come Forth a Man': Reflections on Messianic Ideas in Philo." Pages 341–61 in *The Messiah: Developments in Earliest Judaism and Christianity.* Edited by James H. Charlesworth. Princeton Symposium on Judaism and Christian Origins. Minneapolis: Fortress, 1992.

Boring, M. Eugene. *Mark: A Commentary.* Louisville: Westminster John Knox, 2006.

Bornkamm, Günther, ed. *Das Ende des Gesetzes: Paulusstudien.* BEvT. Munich: Kaiser, 1952.

Bourke, Myles M. *A Study of the Metaphor of the Olive Tree in Romans XI.* Studies in Sacred Theology. Washington, DC: Catholic University of America Press, 1947.

Bowman, John. "Samaritan Studies." *Bulletin of the John Rylands University Library of Manchester* 40 (1958): 298–327.

Boyarin, Daniel. "The IOUDAIOI in John and the Prehistory of Judaism." Pages 216–39 in *Pauline Conversations in Context: Essays in Honor of Calvin J. Roetzel.* Edited by Janice Capel Anderson, Philip Sellew, and Claudia Setzer. JSNTSup 221. London: Sheffield Academic, 2002.

A Radical Jew: Paul and the Politics of Identity. Berkeley: University of California Press, 1994.

Boyarin, Daniel, and Jonathan Boyarin. "Diaspora: Generation and the Ground of Jewish Identity." *Critical Inquiry* 19 (1993): 693–725.

Bratsiotis, Panagiotis. "Eine exegetische Notiz zu Röm. IX 3 und X 1." *Novum Testamentum* 5.4 (1962): 299–300.

Brenk, Frederick E. "*Hierosolyma*: The Greek Name of Jerusalem." *Glotta* 87.1–4 (2011): 1–22.

Brettler, Marc Zvi. "Judaism in the Hebrew Bible? The Transition from Ancient Israelite Religion to Judaism." *Catholic Biblical Quarterly* 61.3 (1999): 429–47.

"Predestination in Deuteronomy 30:1–10." Pages 171–88 in *Those Elusive Deuteronomists: The Phenomenon of Pan-Deuteronomism.* Edited by Linda S. Schearing and Steven L. McKenzie. Sheffield: Sheffield Academic, 1999.

Brichto, Herbert Chanan. "The Worship of the Golden Calf: A Literary Analysis of a Fable on Idolatry." *Hebrew Union College Annual* 54 (1983): 1–44.

Brodbeck, David Lee. *Defining Deutschtum: Political Ideology, German Identity, and Music-Critical Discourse in Liberal Vienna.* New York: Oxford University Press, 2014.

Brondos, David. "The Cross and the Curse: Galatians 3.13 and Paul's Doctrine of Redemption." *Journal for the Study of the New Testament* 81 (2001): 3–32.

Brown, Jeannine K., and Kazuhiko Yamazaki-Ransom. "The Parable of the Good Samaritan and the Narrative Portrayal of Samaritans in Luke-Acts." *Journal of Theological Interpretation* 15.2 (2021): 233–46.

Brown, Raymond E. "The Pater Noster as an Eschatological Prayer." Pages 275–320 in *New Testament Essays.* New York: Doubleday, 1968.

The Semitic Background of the Term "Mystery" in the New Testament. Philadelphia: Fortress, 1968.

Brownlee, William H. "The Servant of the Lord in the Qumran Scrolls I." *Bulletin of the American Schools of Oriental Research* 132 (1953): 8–15.

Bruce, F. F. *Commentary on the Book of Acts.* NICNT. Grand Rapids: Eerdmans, 1964.

Bryan, Steven M. *Jesus and Israel's Traditions of Judgement and Restoration.* SNTSMS 117. Cambridge: Cambridge University Press, 2002.

"The Reception of Jeremiah's Prediction of a Seventy-Year Exile." *Journal of Biblical Literature* 137.1 (2018): 107–26.

Bryant, Robert A. *The Risen Crucified Christ in Galatians.* SBLDS 185. Atlanta: Society of Biblical Literature, 2001.

Buell, Denise Kimber. *Why This New Race? Ethnic Reasoning in Early Christianity*. New York: Columbia University Press, 2005.
Bultmann, Rudolf Karl. *Theology of the New Testament*. Translated by Kendrick Grobel. 2nd ed. New York: Charles Scribner's Sons, 1951.
Burford, Alison. *Land and Labor in the Greek World*. Baltimore: Johns Hopkins University Press, 1993.
Burnett, David A. "A Neglected Deuteronomic Scriptural Matrix for the Nature of the Resurrection Body in 1 Cor 15:39–42." Pages 187–211 in *Scripture, Texts, and Tracings in 1 Corinthians*. Edited by B. J. Oropeza, and Linda L. Belleville. Scripture and Paul. Lanham, MD: Lexington/Fortress Academic, 2019.
———. "'So Shall Your Seed Be': Paul's Use of Genesis 15:5 in Romans 4:18 in Light of Early Jewish Deification Traditions." *Journal for the Study of Paul and His Letters* 5.2 (2015): 211–36.
Byrne, Brendan. "Interpreting Romans Theologically in a Post-'New Perspective' Perspective." *Harvard Theological Review* 94.3 (2001): 227–41.
———. "Living out the Righteousness of God: The Contribution of Rom 6:1–8:13 to an Understanding of Paul's Ethical Presuppositions." *Catholic Biblical Quarterly* 43.4 (1981): 557–81.
Cadwallader, Alan H. "Paul Speaks Like a Girl: When Phoebe Reads Romans." Pages 69–94 in *Sexuality, Ideology, and the Bible: Antipodean Engagements*. Edited by Robert J. Myles and Caroline Blyth. The Bible in the Modern World 70. Sheffield: Sheffield Phoenix, 2015.
Caird, George B. "Expository Problems: Predestination – Romans ix.–xi." *Expository Times* 68.11 (1957): 324–27.
Cairns, Francis. "ΕΡΟΣ in Pindar's First Olympian Ode." *Hermes* 105 (1977): 129–32.
Callan, Terrance. "Paul and the Golden Calf." *Proceedings: Eastern Great Lakes and Midwest Biblical Societies* 10 (1990): 1–17.
———. "Pauline Midrash: The Exegetical Background of Gal 3:19b." *Journal of Biblical Literature* 99.4 (1980): 549–67.
Calvin, John. *Calvin's Commentaries on the New Testament*. Edited by David W. Torrance and Thomas F. Torrance. Grand Rapids: Eerdmans, 1961.
Campbell, Douglas A. *The Deliverance of God: A Rereading of Justification in Paul*. Grand Rapids: Eerdmans, 2009.
———. *Framing Paul: An Epistolary Biography*. Grand Rapids: Eerdmans, 2014.
———. *The Quest for Paul's Gospel: A Suggested Strategy*. London: T&T Clark, 2005.
———. "Romans 1:17 – A Crux Interpretum for the πίστις Χριστοῦ Debate." *Journal of Biblical Literature* 113.2 (1994): 265–85.
Campbell, Jonathan G. "Essene-Qumran Origins in the Exile: A Scriptural Basis?" *Journal of Jewish Studies* 46.1–2 (1995): 143–56.
Campbell, William S. "Christ the End of the Law: Romans 10.4." Pages 73–81 in *Studia Biblica 1978: III. Papers on Paul and Other New Testament Authors. Sixth International Congress on Biblical Studies*. Edited by E. A. Livingstone. JSNTSup 3. Sheffield: JSOT Press, 1978.

"Divergent Images of Paul and His Mission." Pages 187–211 in *Reading Israel in Romans*. Edited by Cristina Greenholm and Daniel Patte. Harrisburg, PA: Trinity Press International, 2000.

Paul and the Creation of Christian Identity. London: T&T Clark, 2006.

"Perceptions of Compatibility between Christianity and Judaism in Pauline Interpretation." *Biblical Interpretation Series* 13.3 (2005): 298–316.

Carlson, Stephen C. "Luke 2:2 and the Census." *Luke 2:2 and the Census* (2004): http://hypotyposeis.org/weblog/2004/12/luke-22-and-the-census.html.

Carras, George P. "Romans 2,1–29: A Dialogue on Jewish Ideals." *Biblica* 73.2 (1992): 183–207.

Carroll, Robert P. "Ancient Israelite Prophecy and Dissonance Theory." *Numen* 24.2 (1977): 135–51.

"Deportation and Diasporic Discourses in the Prophetic Literature." Pages 63–88 in *Exile: Old Testament, Jewish, and Christian Conceptions*. Edited by James M. Scott. JSJSup 56. Leiden: Brill, 1997.

"Exile! What Exile? Deportation and the Discourses of Diaspora." Pages 62–79 in *Leading Captivity Captive: "The Exile" as History and Ideology*. Edited by Lester Grabbe. Sheffield: Sheffield Academic, 1998.

Casey, Maurice. "Some Anti-Semitic Assumptions in the 'Theological Dictionary of the New Testament.'" *Novum Testamentum* 41.3 (1999): 280–91.

"Where Wright Is Wrong: A Critical Review of NT Wright's *Jesus and the Victory of God*." *Journal for the Study of the New Testament* 69 (1998): 95–103.

Cassuto, Umberto. "The Prophet Hosea and the Books of the Pentateuch." Pages 79–100 in *Biblical and Oriental Studies: Bible*. Jerusalem: Magnes, 1973.

Celarc, Matiaž. "Christ as the Goal of the Law (Rom 10,4): Christ as the Converging Point in the History of Salvation." *Bogoslovni vestnik/ Theological Quarterly* 79 (2019): 441–56.

Chae, Young S. *Jesus as the Eschatological Davidic Shepherd: Studies in the Old Testament, Second Temple Judaism, and in the Gospel of Matthew*. Tübingen: Mohr Siebeck, 2006.

Chalmers, Matthew. "Review of Judah and Samaria in Postmonarchic Times: Essays on Their Histories and Literatures, by Gary N. Knoppers." *Journal for the Study of Judaism* 53.1 (2021): 144–47.

"Representations of Samaritans in Late Antique Jewish and Christian Texts." PhD diss., University of Pennsylvania, 2019.

"Rethinking Luke 10: The Parable of the Good Samaritan Israelite." *Journal of Biblical Literature* 139.3 (2020): 543–66.

"Samaritans, Biblical Studies, and Ancient Judaism: Recent Trends." *Currents in Biblical Research* 21.1 (2021): 28–64.

Chapple, Allan. "Getting *Romans* to the Right Romans: Phoebe and the Delivery of Paul's Letter." *Tyndale Bulletin* 62.2 (2011): 195–214.

Charles, Ronald. ed. "The New Creation Motif in Romans 8:18–27 in Light of the Book of *Jubilees*." Pages 59–74 in *Paul and Matthew among Jews and Gentiles: Essays in Honour of Terence L. Donaldson*. Edited by Ronald Charles. LNTS. London: Bloomsbury, 2020.

Paul and Matthew among Jews and Gentiles: Essays in Honour of Terence L. Donaldson. LNTS 628. London: Bloomsbury, 2020.

Paul and the Politics of Diaspora. Minneapolis: Fortress, 2014.

Chilton, Bruce D. "Messianic Redemption: Soteriology in the Targum Jonathan to the Former and Latter Prophets." Pages 265–84 in *This World and the World to Come: Soteriology in Early Judaism*. Edited by Daniel M. Gurtner. LSTS 74. London: T&T Clark, 2011.

"Romans 9–11 as Scriptural Interpretation and Dialogue with Judaism." *Ex Auditu* 4 (1988): 27–37.

Christensen, Duane L. *Deuteronomy 21:10–34:12*. WBC 6B. Waco: Word, 2002.

Christiansen, Ellen Juhl. *The Covenant in Judaism and Paul: A Study of Ritual Boundaries as Identity Markers*. Leiden: Brill, 1995.

Clements, Ronald E. "'A Remnant Chosen by Grace' (Romans 11:5): The Old Testament Background and Origin of the Remnant Concept." Pages 106–21 in *Pauline Studies: Essays Presented to F.F. Bruce on his 70th Birthday*. Edited by Donald A. Hagner and Murray J. Harris. Grand Rapids: Eerdmans, 1980.

Coggins, Richard J. *Samaritans and Jews: The Origins of Samaritanism Reconsidered*. WUNT 111. Atlanta: John Knox, 1975.

"The Samaritans and Acts." *New Testament Studies* 28.3 (1982): 423–34.

Cohen, Jeremy. "The Mystery of Israel's Salvation: Romans 11:25–26 in Patristic and Medieval Exegesis." *Harvard Theological Review* 98.3 (2005): 247–81.

Cohen, Robin. *Global Diasporas: An Introduction*. 2nd ed. London: Routledge, 2008.

Cohen, Shaye J. D. *The Beginnings of Jewishness: Boundaries, Varieties, Uncertainties*. Berkeley: University of California Press, 1999.

"Crossing the Boundary and Becoming a Jew." *Harvard Theological Review* 82 (1989): 13–33.

From the Maccabees to the Mishnah. Philadelphia: Westminster, 1987.

Review of *Contesting Conversion: Genealogy, Circumcision, and Identity in Ancient Judaism and Christianity*, by Matthew Thiessen. *Catholic Biblical Quarterly* 75.2 (2013): 379–81.

"'Those Who Say They are Jews and Are Not': How Do You Know a Jew in Antiquity When You See One." Pages 1–45 in *Diasporas in Antiquity*. Edited by Shaye J. D. Cohen and Ernst S. Frerichs. BJS. Atlanta: Scholars Press, 1993.

Cohn-Sherbok, Dan. "Paul and Rabbinic Exegesis." *Scottish Journal of Theology* 35.2 (1982): 117–32.

Colautti, Federico M. *Passover in the Works of Josephus*. JSJSup 75. Leiden: Brill, 2002.

Collins, Adela Yarbro. "Insiders and Outsiders in the Book of Revelation." Pages 187–218 in *"To See Ourselves as Others See Us": Christians, Jews, "Others" in Late Antiquity*. Edited by Jacob Neusner and Ernest S. Frerichs. Chico, CA: Scholars Press, 1975.

"Vilification and Self-Definition in the Book of Revelation." *Harvard Theological Review* 79.1/3 (1986): 308–20.

Collins, Adela Yarbro, and John J. Collins. *King and Messiah as Son of God: Divine, Human, and Angelic Messianic Figures in Biblical and Related Literature*. Grand Rapids: Eerdmans, 2008.

Collins, John J. *Between Athens and Jerusalem: Jewish Identity in the Hellenistic Diaspora*. 2nd ed. Grand Rapids: Eerdmans, 2000.

———. "The Construction of Israel in the Sectarian Rule Books." Pages 25–42 in *Judaism in Late Antiquity: Theory of Israel (Pt. 5 Vol. 1)*. Edited by Alan J Avery-Peck, Jacob Neusner, and Bruce D. Chilton. Leiden: Brill, 2001.

Concannon, Cavan W. *"When You Were Gentiles": Specters of Ethnicity in Roman Corinth and Paul's Corinthian Correspondence*. New Haven: Yale University Press, 2014.

Conzelmann, Hans. *1 Corinthians: A Commentary on the First Epistle to the Corinthians*. Translated by James W. Leitch. Hermeneia. Minneapolis: Fortress, 1975.

Cowan, J. Andrew. "The Curse of the Law, the Covenant, and Anthropology in Galatians 3:10–14: An Examination of Paul's Use of Deuteronomy 27:26." *Journal of Biblical Literature* 139.1 (2020): 211–29.

Coxhead, Steven R. "Deuteronomy 30:11–14 as a Prophecy of the New Covenant in Christ." *The Westminster Theological Journal* 68.2 (2006): 305–20.

Crabbe, Kylie. "Being Found Fighting against God: Luke's Gamaliel and Josephus on Human Responses to Divine Providence." *Zeitschrift für die neutestamentliche Wissenschaft* 106.1 (2015): 21–39.

Cranfield, Charles E. B. *A Critical and Exegetical Commentary on the Epistle to the Romans*. 2 vols. ICC. Edinburgh: T&T Clark, 1979.

———. "Giving a Dog a Bad Name: A Note on H. Räisänen's Paul and the Law." *Journal for the Study of the New Testament* 38 (1990): 77–85.

Crawford, Matthew R. "'Confessing God from a Good Conscience': 1 Peter 3:21 and Early Christian Baptismal Theology." *The Journal of Theological Studies* 67.1 (2016): 23–37.

Cronin, Sonya S. *Raymond Brown, "The Jews," and the Gospel of John: From Apologia to Apology*. LNTS 504. London: T&T Clark, 2015.

Crook, Zeba A. *Reconceptualising Conversion: Patronage, Loyalty, and Conversion in the Religions of the Ancient Mediterranean*. BZNW 130. Berlin: de Gruyter, 2004.

Cross, Frank Moore. "Samaria and Jerusalem in the Era of Restoration." Pages 173–202 in *From Epic to Canon: History and Literature in Ancient Israel*. Baltimore: Johns Hopkins University Press, 2000.

Crossley, James G. "What a Difference a Translation Makes! An Ideological Analysis of the *Ioudaios* Debate." *Marginalia Review of Books* (2014): http://marginalia.lareviewofbooks.org/difference-translation-makes-ideological-analysis-ioudaios-debate-james-crossley.

Crown, Alan D. "Another Look at Samaritan Origins." Pages 133–55 in *New Samaritan Studies of the Société d'Études Samaritaines III–IV: Essays in Honour of G.D. Sixdenier*. Edited by Alan D. Crown and Lucy Davey. Studies in Judaica 5. Sydney: Mandelbaum, 1995.

———. "Redating the Schism between the Judaeans and the Samaritans." *Jewish Quarterly Review* 82.1–2 (1991): 17–50.

Dahl, Nils A. "Contradictions in Scripture." Pages 159–77 in *Studies in Paul: Theology for the Early Christian Mission*. Eugene: Wipf & Stock, 2002.

"The Future of Israel." Pages 137–58 in *Studies in Paul: Theology for the Early Christian Mission*. Eugene: Wipf & Stock, 2002.
Studies in Paul: Theology for the Early Christian Mission. Eugene: Wipf & Stock, 2002.
Dahl, Nils A., and Samuel Sandmel. "Review of *Paul and Palestinian Judaism: Comparison of Patterns of Religion*, by E. P. Sanders." *Recherches de science religieuse* 4 (1978): 153–58.
Danker, Frederick W., Walter Bauer, W. F. Arndt, and F. W. Gingrich. *A Greek-English Lexicon on the New Testament and Other Early Christian Literature*. 3rd rev. ed. Chicago: University of Chicago Press, 2000.
Das, A. Andrew. "The Gentile-Encoded Audience of Romans: The Church Outside the Synagogue." Pages 29–46 in *Reading Paul's Letter to the Romans*. Edited by Jerry L. Sumney. RBS 73. Atlanta: Society of Biblical Literature, 2012.
Paul and the Jews. Library of Pauline Studies. Peabody, MA: Hendrickson, 2003.
Paul and the Stories of Israel: Grand Thematic Narratives in Galatians. Minneapolis: Fortress, 2016.
Solving the Romans Debate. Minneapolis: Fortress, 2007.
Daube, David. "Jesus and the Samaritan Woman: The Meaning of συγχράομαι." *Journal of Biblical Literature* 69.2 (1950): 137–47.
Dautzenberg, Gerhard. "Alter und neuer Bund nach 2 Kor 3." Pages 229–49 in *"Nun steht aber diese Sache im Evangelium." Zur Frage nach den Anfängen des christlichen Antijudaismus*. Edited by Rainer Kampling. Paderborn: Schöningh, 1999.
Davies, Glenn N. *Faith and Obedience in Romans: A Study in Romans 1–4*. JSNTSup 39. Sheffield: Sheffield Academic, 1990.
Davies, Philip R. *The Damascus Covenant: An Interpretation of the "Damascus Document"*. LHBOTS 25. London: Continuum, 1983.
"Exile? What Exile? Whose Exile?" Pages 128–38 in *Leading Captivity Captive: "The Exile" as History and Ideology*. Edited by Lester Grabbe. Sheffield: Sheffield Academic, 1998.
"'Old' and 'New' Israel in the Bible and the Qumran Scrolls: Identity and Difference." Pages 33–42 in *Defining Identities: We, You, and the Other in the Dead Sea Scrolls*. Edited by Florentino García-Martínez and Mladen Popović. Leiden: Brill, 2007.
Davies, W. D. *Jewish and Pauline Studies*. Philadelphia: Fortress, 1984.
Paul and Rabbinic Judaism: Some Rabbinic Elements in Pauline Theology. 2nd ed. London: SPCK, 1955.
"Paul and the Gentiles: A Suggestion Concerning Romans 11:13–24." Pages 153–63 in *Jewish and Pauline Studies*. Philadelphia: Fortress, 1984.
"Paul and the New Exodus." Pages 443–63 in *The Quest for Context and Meaning: Studies in Biblical Intertextuality in Honor of James A. Sanders*. Edited by Craig A. Evans and Shemaryahu Talmon. Leiden: Brill, 1997.
"Paul and the People of Israel." *New Testament Studies* 24.1 (1977): 4–39.
"Reflections on Territory in Judaism." Pages 339–44 in *"Sha'arei Talmon": Studies in Bible, Qumran, and the Ancient Near East Presented to*

Shemaryahu Talmon. Edited by M. Fishbane, Emanuel Tov, and W. W. Fields. Winona Lake: Eisenbrauns, 1992.

Torah in the Messianic Age And/or the Age to Come. JBLMS 7. Philadelphia: Scholars Press, 1952.

Davis, Kipp. "The Apostle Paul in the Prophetic Matrix of Jeremiah: A Response to Lutz Doering." Pages 566–69 in *Jeremiah's Scriptures: Production, Reception, Interaction, and Transformation*. Edited by Hindy Najman and Konrad Schmid. JSJSup 173. Leiden: Brill, 2016.

The Cave 4 Apocryphon of Jeremiah and the Qumran Jeremianic Traditions: Prophetic Persona and the Construction of Community Identity. STDJ 111. Leiden: Brill, 2014.

Dawson, Lorne L. "When Prophecy Fails and Faith Persists: A Theoretical Overview." *Nova Religio: The Journal of Alternative and Emergent Religions* 3.1 (1999): 60–82.

Deeley, Mary Katharine. "Ezekiel's Shepherd and John's Jesus: A Case Study in the Appropriation of Biblical Texts." Pages 252–64 in *Early Christian Interpretation of the Scriptures of Israel: Investigations and Proposals*. Edited by Craig A. Evans and James A. Sanders. JSNTSup 148. Sheffield: Sheffield Academic, 1997.

Dein, Simon. "What Really Happens When Prophecy Fails: The Case of Lubavitch." *Sociology of Religion* 62.3 (2001): 383–401.

Denis, A. M. "L'Apôtre Paul, prophète 'messianique' des Gentiles: Étude thématique de I Thess. II,1–6." *Ephemerides Theologicae Lovanienses* 33 (1957): 245–318.

Dennis, John A. *Jesus' Death and the Gathering of True Israel: The Johannine Appropriation of Restoration Theology in the Light of John 11.47–52*. WUNT 217. Tübingen: Mohr Siebeck, 2006.

Denniston, J. D. *The Greek Particles*. 2nd ed. Oxford: Oxford University Press, 1954.

Derrett, J. Duncan M. "'You Abominate False Gods; but Do You Rob Shrines?' (Rom 2.22b)." *New Testament Studies* 40.4 (1994): 558–71.

deSilva, David A. *Honor, Patronage, Kinship & Purity: Unlocking New Testament Culture*. Downers Grove, IL: InterVarsity, 2000.

Di Lella, Alexander A. "Tobit 4,19 and Romans 9,18: An Intertextual Study." *Biblia* 90.2 (2009): 260–63.

Dibley, Genevive. "The Making and Unmaking of Jews in Second Century BCE Narratives and the Implication for Interpreting Paul." Pages 3–23 in *Israel and the Nations: Paul's Gospel in the Context of Jewish Expectation*. Edited by František Ábel. Minneapolis: Fortress Academic, 2021.

Dimant, Devorah. "Qumran Sectarian Literature." Pages 483–550 in *Jewish Writings of the Second Temple Period*. Edited by Michael E Stone. CRINT 2. Philadelphia: Fortress, 1984.

Dodd, C. H. *According to the Scriptures: The Sub-Structure of New Testament Theology*. London: Collins, 1965.

The Epistle of Paul to the Romans. Moffatt New Testament Commentary. New York: Harper & Brothers, 1932.

Doering, Lutz. "The Commissioning of Paul: Light from the Prophet Jeremiah on the Self-Understanding of the Apostle?" Pages 544–65 in *Jeremiah's Scriptures: Production, Reception, Interaction, and Transformation*. Edited by Hindy Najman and Konrad Schmid. JSJSup 173. Leiden: Brill, 2016.
Donaldson, Terence L. "Jewish Christianity, Israel's Stumbling and the *Sonderweg* Reading of Paul." *Journal for the Study of the New Testament* 29.1 (2006): 27–54.
Paul and the Gentiles: Remapping the Apostle's Convictional World. Minneapolis: Fortress, 1997.
"Proselytes or 'Righteous Gentiles'? The Status of Gentiles in Eschatological Pilgrimage Patterns of Thought." *Journal for the Study of the Pseudepigrapha* 7 (1990): 3–27.
"'Riches for the Gentiles' (Rom 11:12): Israel's Rejection and Paul's Gentile Mission." *JBL* 112.1 (1993): 81–98.
"The 'Curse of the Law' and the Inclusion of the Gentiles: Galatians 3.13–14." *New Testament Studies* 32.1 (1986): 94–112.
Draper, Jonathan A. "'If Those to Whom the W/word of God Came Were Called Gods' – Logos, Wisdom and Prophecy, and John 10:22–30." *HTS Teologiese Studies/Theological Studies* 71.1 (2015): 1–8.
Dreyfus, Francois. "Le Passé et le présent d'Israël (Rom 9,1–5; 11,1–24)." Pages 131–51 in *Die Israelfrage nach Römer 9–11*. Edited by Lorenzo de Lorenzi. Colloquium Paulinum 4. Rome: Abtei von St Paul vor den Mauern, 1977.
Driver, Samuel Rolles. *A Critical and Exegetical Commentary on Deuteronomy*. 3rd ed. ICC. Edinburgh: T&T Clark, 1902.
Duling, Dennis C. "The Promises to David and Their Entrance into Christianity – Nailing Down a Likely Hypothesis." *New Testament Studies* 20.1 (1973): 55–77.
Dumbrell, William J. "Paul's Use of Exodus 34 in 2 Corinthians 3." Pages 179–94 in *God Who Is Rich in Mercy: Essays presented to Dr D. B. Knox*. Edited by Peter T. O'Brien and David G. Peterson. Grand Rapids: Baker, 1986.
Dunn, James D. G. *The Epistle to the Galatians*. Black's New Testament Commentaries. Peabody, MA: Hendrickson, 1993.
Jesus, Paul, and the Law: Studies in Mark and Galatians. Louisville: Westminster John Knox, 1990.
Romans. 2 vols. WBC 38A–B. Nashville: Nelson, 1988.
"'The Letter Kills, but the Spirit Gives Life' (2 Cor. 3:6)." *Pneuma: Journal for the Society of Pentecostal Studies* 35 (2013): 163–79.
"The New Perspective on Paul." *Bulletin of the John Rylands University Library of Manchester* 65 (1983): 95–122.
The New Perspective on Paul. Rev. ed. Grand Rapids: Eerdmans, 2007.
The Partings of the Ways Between Christianity and Judaism and Their Significance for the Character of Christianity. Philadelphia: Trinity Press International, 1991.
"In Search of Common Ground." Pages 309–34 in *Paul and the Mosaic Law: The Third Durham-Tübingen Research Symposium on Earliest Christianity and Judaism (Durham, September, 1994)*. Edited by James D. G. Dunn. WUNT 89. Tübingen: Mohr, 1996.

The Theology of Paul the Apostle. Grand Rapids: Eerdmans, 2006.

Easter, Matthew C. "The Pistis Christou Debate: Main Arguments and Responses in Summary." *Currents in Biblical Research* 9.1 (2010): 33–47.

Eastman, Susan Grove. "The Evil Eye and the Curse of the Law: Galatians 3.1 Revisited." *Journal for the Study of the New Testament* 24.1 (2001): 69–87.

——— "Israel and Divine Mercy in Galatians and Romans." Pages 147–70 in *Between Gospel and Election: Explorations in the Interpretation of Romans 9–11.* Edited by Florian Wilk, J. Ross Wagner, and Frank Schleritt. WUNT 257. Tübingen: Mohr Siebeck, 2010.

——— "Israel and the Mercy of God: A Re-reading of Galatians 6.16 and Romans 9–11." *New Testament Studies* 56.3 (2010): 367–95.

Eckstein, Hans-Joachim. "'Nahe ist dir das Wort': Exegetische Erwägungen zu Röm 10 8." *Zeitschrift für die neutestamentliche Wissenschaft* 79.3–4 (1988): 204–20.

Ehrensperger, Kathy. *That We May Be Mutually Encouraged: Feminism and the New Perspective in Pauline Studies.* New York: T&T Clark, 2004.

Ehrman, Bart D. *The Orthodox Corruption of Scripture: The Effect of Early Christological Controversies on the Text of the New Testament.* Oxford: Oxford University Press, 1993.

Eisenbaum, Pamela. "Paul, Polemics, and the Problem of Essentialism." *Biblical Interpretation Series* 13.3 (2005): 224–38.

——— *Paul Was Not a Christian: The Real Message of a Misunderstood Apostle.* New York: HarperOne, 2009.

Elitsur, Yehudah. "Samaritans in Tannaitic Texts." Pages 393–414 in *Israel and the Bible: Studies in Geography, History, and Biblical Thought.* Edited by Amos Frisch and Yoel Elitsur. Ramat Gan: Bar Ilan University Press, 2000.

Elliot, John H. "Jesus the Israelite Was Neither a 'Jew' Nor a 'Christian': On Correcting Misleading Nomenclature." *Journal for the Study of the Historical Jesus* 5.2 (2007): 119–54.

Elliott, Neil. *The Rhetoric of Romans: Argumentative Constraint and Strategy and Paul's Dialogue with Judaism.* JSNTSup 45. Minneapolis: Fortress, 2006.

Ellis, E. Earle. *Paul's Use of the Old Testament.* Eugene: Wipf & Stock, 2003.

Ellison, H. L. *The Mystery of Israel: An Exposition of Romans 9–11.* Grand Rapids: Eerdmans, 1966.

Elmar, Fabian Firman, and Maria Ananta. "Creature Symbols to Foreshadow Harry's Confrontation with his Past in J. K. Rowling's Harry Potter and the Prisoner of Askaban." *Journal of Language and Literature* 17.2 (2017): 178–92.

Endres, John C. "Eschatological Impulses in Jubilees." Pages 323–37 in *Enoch and the Mosaic Torah: The Evidence of Jubilees.* Edited by Gabriele Boccaccini and Giovanni Ibba. Grand Rapids: Eerdmans, 2009.

Engberg-Pedersen, Troels. "Gift-Giving and Friendship: Seneca and Paul in Romans 1–8 on the Logic of God's Χάρις and Its Human Response." *Harvard Theological Review* 101.1 (2008): 15–44.

Enns, Peter. "Expansions of Scripture." Pages 73–98 in *Justification and Variegated Nomism: Volume I—The Complexities of Second Temple*

Judaism. Edited by D. A. Carson, Peter T. O'Brien, and Mark A. Seifrid. WUNT 140. Grand Rapids: Baker Academic, 2001.

Eskola, Timo. *A Narrative Theology of the New Testament: Exploring the Metanarrative of Exile and Restoration*. WUNT 350. Tübingen: Mohr Siebeck, 2015.

——— "Paul, Predestination and 'Covenantal Nomism' – Re-assessing Paul and Palestinian Judaism." *Journal for the Study of Judaism* 28 (1997): 390–412.

Esler, Philip F. "Ancient Oleiculture and Ethnic Differentiation: The Meaning of the Olive-Tree Image in Romans 11." *Journal for the Study of the New Testament* 26.1 (2003): 103–24.

——— *Conflict and Identity in Romans: The Social Setting of Paul's Letter*. Minneapolis: Fortress, 2003.

Evans, Craig A. "Jesus & the Continuing Exile of Israel." Pages 77–100 in *Jesus & the Restoration of Israel*. Edited by Carey C. Newman. Downers Grove, IL: InterVarsity, 1999.

——— "Predictions of the Destruction of the Herodian Temple in the Pseudepigrapha, Qumran Scrolls, and Related Texts." *Journal for the Study of the Pseudepigrapha* 5.10 (1992): 89–147.

——— "The Twelve Thrones of Israel: Scripture and Politics in Luke 22:24–30." Pages 154–70 in *Luke and Scripture: The Function of Sacred Tradition in Luke-Acts*. Edited by Craig A. Evans and James A. Sanders. Eugene: Wipf & Stock, 2001.

Eyl, Jennifer. "'I Myself Am an Israelite': Paul, Authenticity and Authority." *Journal for the Study of the New Testament* 40.2 (2017): 148–68.

——— "Semantic Voids, New Testament Translation, and Anachronism: The Case of Paul's Use of *Ekklēsia*." *Method & Theory in the Study of Religion* 26.4–5 (2014): 315–39.

Fee, Gordon D. *The First Epistle to the Corinthians*. NICNT. Grand Rapids: Eerdmans, 1987.

Feldman, Louis H. *Jew and Gentile in the Ancient World: Attitudes and Interactions from Alexander to Justinian*. Princeton: Princeton University Press, 1996.

——— "Restoration in Josephus." Pages 223–61 in *Restoration: Old Testament, Jewish and Christian Perspectives*. Edited by James M. Scott. JSJSup 72. Leiden: Brill, 2001.

Feldmeier, Reinhard. "Vater und Töpfer? Zur Identität Gottes im Römerbrief." Pages 377–90 in *Between Gospel and Election: Explorations in the Interpretation of Romans 9–11*. Edited by Florian Wilk, J. Ross Wagner, and Frank Schleritt. WUNT 257. Tübingen: Mohr Siebeck, 2010.

Ferda, Tucker S. "John the Baptist, Isaiah 40, and the Ingathering of the Exiles." *Journal for the Study of the Historical Jesus* 10.2 (2012): 154–88.

Festinger, Leon. *A Theory of Cognitive Dissonance*. Palo Alto: Stanford University Press, 1962.

Festinger, Leon, Henry W. Riecken, and Stanley Schachter. *When Prophecy Fails: A Social and Psychological Study of a Modern Group That Predicted the Destruction of the World*. Minneapolis: University of Minnesota Press, 1956.

Fisch, Yael. "The Origins of Oral Torah: A New Pauline Perspective." *Journal for the Study of Judaism* 51.1 (2020): 43–66.
Fischer, Georg. *Das Trostbüchlein: Text, Komposition und Theologie von Jer 30–31*. Stuttgart: Katholisches Bibelwerk, 1993.
Fitzmyer, Joseph A. *The Acts of the Apostles: A New Translation with Introduction and Commentary*. AB 31. New York: Doubleday, 1998.
———. *Romans*. AB 44. New York: Doubleday, 1993.
———. *Tobit*. CEJL. Berlin: de Gruyter, 2003.
Flanagan, James W. "The Deuteronomic Meaning of the Phrase 'kol yiśrā'ēl.'.=" *Studies in Religion* 6.2 (1976): 159–68.
Floyd, Michael H. "Was Prophetic Hope Born of Disappointment? The Case of Zechariah." Pages 268–96 in *Utopia and Dystopia in Prophetic Literature*. Edited by Ehud Ben Zvi. Publications of the Finnish Exegetical Society. Göttingen: Vandenhoeck & Ruprecht, 2006.
Flückiger, Felix. "Die Werke des Gesetzes bei den Heiden (nach Röm 2, 14ff): Probevorlesung vor der Theologischen Fakultät der Universität Basel am 28. November 1951." *Theologische Zeitschrift* 8 (1952): 17–42.
Forkman, Göran. *The Limits of the Religious Community: Expulsion from the Religious Community Within the Qumran Sect, Within Rabbinic Judaism, and Within Primitive Christianity*. ConBNT 5. Lund: Gleerup, 1972.
Forsdyke, Sara. *Exile, Ostracism, and Democracy: The Politics of Expulsion in Ancient Greece*. Princeton: Princeton University Press, 2005.
Foster, Robert B. *Renaming Abraham's Children: Election, Ethnicity, and the Interpretation of Scripture in Romans 9*. WUNT 421. Tübingen: Mohr Siebeck, 2016.
Hornblower, Simon, and Antony Spawforth, eds. *Oxford Classical Dictionary*. Oxford: Oxford University Press, 1996.
Frankfurter, David. "Jews or Not? Reconstructing the Other in Rev 2:9 and 3:9." *Harvard Theological Review* 94.4 (2001): 403–25.
Fredriksen, Paula. *Augustine on Romans: Propositions from the Epistle to the Romans and Unfinished Commentary on the Epistle to the Romans*. Texts and Translations 23. Chico, CA: Scholars Press, 1982.
———. "'Circumcision Is Nothing': A Non-Reformation Reading of the Letters of Paul." Pages 79–105 in *Protestant Bible Scholarship: Anti-Semitism, Philo-Semitism and Anti-Judaism*. Edited by Arjen F. Bakker et al. JSJSup. Leiden: Brill, 2022.
———. "Compassion Is to Purity as Fish Is to Bicycle and Other Reflections on Constructions of 'Judaism' in Current Work on the Historical Jesus." Pages 55–67 in *Apocalypticism, Anti-Semitism and the Historical Jesus: Subtexts in Criticism*. Edited by John S. Kloppenborg and John W. Marshall. JSNTSup 275. London: T&T Clark, 2005.
———. "God Is Jewish, but Gentiles Don't Have to Be: Ethnicity and Eschatology in Paul's Gospel." Pages 3–19 in *The Message of Paul the Apostle within Second Temple Judaism*. Edited by František Ábel. Lanham, MD: Lexington/Fortress Academic, 2019.
———. "How Jewish Is God?: Divine Ethnicity in Paul's Theology." *Journal of Biblical Literature* 137.1 (2018): 193–212.

"Judaism, the Circumcision of Gentiles, and Apocalyptic Hope: Another Look at Galatians 1 and 2." *Journal of Theological Studies* 42.2 (1991): 532–64.
"Judaizing the Nations: The Ritual Demands of Paul's Gospel." *New Testament Studies* 56 (2010): 232–52.
Paul: The Pagans' Apostle. New Haven: Yale University Press, 2017.
"Paul, Pagans and Eschatological Ethnicities: A Response to Denys McDonald." *Journal for the Study of the New Testament* 45.1 (2022): 51–65.
"Philo, Herod, Paul, and the Many Gods of Ancient Jewish 'Monotheism.'" *Harvard Theological Review* 115.1 (2022): 23–45.
"The Question of Worship: Gods, Pagans, and the Redemption of Israel." Pages 175–201 in *Paul within Judaism: Restoring the First-century Context to the Apostle*. Edited by Mark Nanos and Magnus Zetterholm (Minneapolis: Fortress, 2015).
"What Does It Mean to See Paul 'within Judaism'?" *Journal of Biblical Literature* 141.2 (2022): 359–80.
"Why Should a 'Law-Free' Mission Mean a 'Law-Free' Apostle?" *Journal of Biblical Literature* 134.3 (2015): 637–50.
Frey, Jörg. "The Notion of the Spirit in the Dead Sea Scrolls and in Texts of the Early Jesus Movement." Pages 83–102 in *The Religious Worldviews Reflected in the Dead Sea Scrolls: Proceedings of the Fourteenth International Symposium of the Orion Center for the Study of the Dead Sea Scrolls and Associated Literature, 28–30 May, 2013*. Edited by Ruth A. Clements, Menahem Kister, and Michael Segal. STDJ 127. Leiden: Brill, 2019.
Freyne, Sean. "Behind the Names: Samaritans, Ioudaioi, Galileans." Pages 389–401 in *Text and Artifact in the Religions of Mediterranean Antiquity: Essays in Honour of Peter Richardson(9)*. Edited by Stephen G. Wilson and Michel Desjardins. SCJ 9. Waterloo, ON: Wilfrid Laurier University Press, 2000.
"Studying the Jewish Diaspora in Antiquity." Pages 1–5 in *Jews in the Hellenistic and Roman Cities*. Edited by John R. Bartlett. London: Routledge, 2002.
Frid, Bo. "How Does Romans 2.1 Connect to 1.18–32?" *Svensk exegetisk årsbok* 71 (2006): 109–30.
Friedman, Meir, ed. *Seder Eliyahu Rabbah ve-Seder Eliyahu Zuta (Tana de-ve Eliyahu)*. Jerusalem: Wahrmann, 1969.
Fuller, Michael E. *The Restoration of Israel: Israel's Re-gathering and the Fate of the Nations in Early Jewish Literature and Luke-Acts*. BZNW 138. Berlin: de Gruyter, 2006.
Fung, William Chi-Chau. "Israel's Salvation: The Meaning of 'All Israel' in Romans 11:26." PhD diss., Southern Baptist Theological Seminary, 2004.
Gaca, Kathy L. "Paul's Uncommon Declaration in Romans 1:18–32 and Its Problematic Legacy for Pagan and Christian Relations." *Harvard Theological Review* 92.2 (1999): 165–98.
Gadenz, Pablo T. *Called from the Jews and from the Gentiles: Pauline Ecclesiology in Romans 9–11*. WUNT 267. Tübingen: Mohr Siebeck, 2009.

Gafni, Isaiah. *Land, Center and Diaspora: Jewish Constructs in Late Antiquity.* JSPSup 21. Sheffield: Sheffield Academic, 1997.

Gager, John G. "Jews, Gentiles, and Synagogues in the Book of Acts." *Harvard Theological Review* 79.1 (1986): 91–99.

———. *The Origins of Anti-Semitism: Attitudes toward Judaism In Pagan and Christian Antiquity.* New York: Oxford University Press, 1983.

———. *Reinventing Paul.* London: Oxford University Press, 2000.

García Martínez, Florentino. "Nuevos textos no biblicos procedentes de Qumrán." *Estudios Bíblicos* 49 (1991): 116–23.

———. "The Heavenly Tablets in the Book of Jubilees." Pages 243–60 in *Studies in the Book of Jubilees.* Edited by Matthias Albani, Jörg Frey, and Armin Lange. TSAJ 65. Tübingen: Mohr Siebeck, 1997.

Garlington, Don B. "ΊΕΡΟΣΥΛΕΙΝ and the Idolatry of Israel (Romans 2.22)." *New Testament Studies* 36.1 (1990): 142–51.

———. *Faith, Obedience, and Perseverance: Aspects of Paul's Letter to the Romans.* Eugene: Wipf & Stock, 2009.

———. *"The Obedience of Faith": A Pauline Phrase in Historical Context.* WUNT 38. Tübingen: Mohr Siebeck, 1990.

Garnet, Paul. "Qumran Light on Pauline Soteriology." Pages 19–32 in *Pauline Studies: Essays Presented to F.F. Bruce on his 70th Birthday.* Edited by Donald A. Hagner and Murray J. Harris. Grand Rapids: Eerdmans, 1980.

Garroway, Joshua D. "The Circumcision of Christ: Romans 15.7–13." *Journal for the Study of the New Testament* 34.4 (2012): 303–22.

———. "Ioudaios." Pages 524–26 in *The Jewish Annotated New Testament: New Revised Standard Version Bible Translation.* Edited by Amy-Jill Levine and Marc Zvi Brettler. Oxford: Oxford University Press, 2017.

———. *Paul's Gentile-Jews: Neither Jew nor Gentile, but Both.* New York: Palgrave Macmillan, 2012.

———. "Paul's Gentile Interlocutor in Romans 3." Pages 85–100 in *The So-called Jew in Paul's Letter to the Romans.* Edited by Rafael Rodríguez and Matthew Thiessen. Minneapolis: Fortress, 2016.

———. "Paul: Within Judaism, Without Law." Pages 49–66 in *Law and Lawlessness in Early Judaism and Early Christianity.* Edited by David Lincicum, Ruth Sheridan, and Charles M. Stang. WUNT 420. Tübingen: Mohr Siebeck, 2019.

Gaston, Lloyd. *Paul and the Torah.* Vancouver: University of British Columbia, 1987.

Gathercole, Simon J. "A Conversion of Augustine: From Natural Law to Restored Nature in Romans 2:13–16." Pages 147–72 in *Engaging Augustine on Romans: Self, Context, and Theology in Interpretation.* Edited by Daniel Patte and Eugene TeSelle. Romans through History and Cultures. London: Black, 2002.

———. "A Law unto Themselves: The Gentiles in Romans 2.14–15 Revisited." *Journal for the Study of the New Testament* 24.3 (2002): 27–49.

———. "Torah, Life, and Salvation: Leviticus 18:5 in Early Judaism and the New Testament." Pages 126–45 in *From Prophecy to Testament: The Use of the*

Old Testament in the New. Edited by Craig A. Evans. Peabody, MA: Hendrickson, 2004.
Where Is Boasting?: Early Jewish Soteriology and Paul's Response in Romans 1–5. Grand Rapids: Eerdmans, 2002.
Gaventa, Beverly Roberts. "On the Calling-Into-Being of Israel: Romans 9:6–29." Pages 255–70 in *Between Gospel and Election: Explorations in the Interpretation of Romans 9–11*. Edited by Florian Wilk, J. Ross Wagner, and Frank Schleritt. WUNT 257. Tübingen: Mohr Siebeck, 2010.
"Rescue Mission." *Christian Century* 127.10 (2010): 36–37.
Gerber, Christine. "Blicke auf Paulus: Die New Perspective on Paul in der jüngeren Diskussion." *Verkündigung und Forschung* 55.1 (2010): 45–60.
Getty, Mary Ann. "An Apocalyptic Perspective on Rom 10:4." *Horizons in Biblical Theology* 4.1 (1982): 79–131.
"Paul and the Salvation of Israel: A Perspective on Romans 9–11." *Catholic Biblical Quarterly* 50.3 (1988): 456–69.
Geyser, Albert S. "Israel in the Fourth Gospel." *Neotestamentica* 20 (1986): 13–20.
"The Twelve Tribes in Revelation: Judean and Judeo-Christian Apocalypticism." *New Testament Studies* 28.3 (1982): 388–99.
Gheorghita, Radu. *The Role of the Septuagint in Hebrews: An Investigation of Its Influence with Special Consideration to the Use of Hab 2:3–4 in Heb 10:37–38*. WUNT 160. Tübingen: Mohr Siebeck, 2003.
Gibson, Jack J. *Peter between Jerusalem and Antioch: Peter, James and the Gentiles*. Tübingen: Mohr Siebeck, 2013.
Gibson, Jeffrey B. "Matthew 6:9–13//Luke 11:2–4: An Eschatological Prayer?" *Biblical Theological Bulletin* 31.3 (2001): 96–105.
Gilliard, Frank D. "The Problem of the Antisemitic Comma between 1 Thessalonians 2.14 and 15." *New Testament Studies* 35.4 (1989): 481–502.
Gillighan, Yonder Moynihan. "Jewish Laws on Illicit Marriage, the Defilement of Offspring, and the Holiness of the Temple: A New Halakic Interpretation of 1 Corinthians 7:14." *Journal of Biblical Literature* 121.4 (2002): 711–44.
Ginsberg, Harold Louis. "The Oldest Interpretation of the Suffering Servant." *Vetus Testamentum* 3.4 (1953): 400–404.
Gladd, Benjamin L. *Revealing the Mysterion: The Use of Mystery in Daniel and Second Temple Judaism with Its Bearing on First Corinthians*. Berlin: de Gruyter, 2008.
Glancy, Jennifer A. "Israel vs. Israel in Romans 11:25–32." *Union Seminary Quarterly Review* 45 (1991): 191–203.
Godet, Frédéric Louis. *Commentary on St. Paul's Epistle to the Romans*. New York: Funk & Wagnalls, 1883.
Goldingay, John E. *Daniel*. WBC 30. Waco: Word, 1989.
Goldstein, David. *Classical Greek Syntax: Wackernagel's Law in Herodotus*. BSIELL. Leiden: Brill, 2016.
Goldstein, Jonathan A. "How the Authors of 1 and 2 Maccabees Treated the 'Messianic' Promises." Pages 69–96 in *Judaisms and Their Messiahs at the Turn of the Christian Era*. Edited by Jacob Neusner, William Scott Green, and Ernest S. Frerichs. Cambridge: Cambridge University Press, 1988.

Gombis, Timothy G. "The 'Transgressor' and the 'Curse of the Law': The Logic of Paul's Argument in Galatians 2–3." *New Testament Studies* 53.1 (2007): 81–93.

Goodblatt, David. *Elements of Ancient Jewish Nationalism*. Cambridge: Cambridge University Press, 2006.

———. "From Judeans to Israel: Names of Jewish States in Antiquity." *Journal for the Study of Judaism* 29.1 (1998): 1–36.

———. "'The Israelites who Reside in Judah' (Judith 4:1): On the Conflicted Identities of the Hasmonean State." Pages 74–89 in *Jewish Identities in Antiquity: Studies in Memory of Menahem Stern*. Edited by Lee I. Levine and Daniel R. Schwartz. TSAJ 130. Tübingen: Mohr Siebeck, 2009.

———. "Varieties of Identity in Late Second Temple Judah (200 B.C.E.–135 C.E.)." Pages 11–27 in *Jewish Identity and Politics between the Maccabees and Bar Kokhba: Groups, Normativity, and Rituals*. Edited by Benedikt Eckhardt. Leiden: Brill, 2011.

Goodman, Martin D. *Mission and Conversion: Proselytizing in the Religious History of the Roman Empire*. Oxford: Oxford University Press, 1994.

———. "The Persecution of Paul by Diaspora Jews." Pages 379–87 in *The Beginnings of Christianity: A Collection of Articles*. Edited by Jack Pastor and Menachem Mor. Jerusalem: Yad Ben-Zvi, 2005.

Goodrich, John K. "Sold under Sin: Echoes of Exile in Romans 7.14–25." *New Testament Studies* 59.4 (2013): 476–95.

———. "Until the Fullness of the Gentiles Comes In: A Critical Review of Recent Scholarship on the Salvation of "All Israel" (Romans 11: 26)." *Journal for the Study of Paul and His Letters* 6.1 (2016): 5–32.

Gordon, Benjamin D. "On the Sanctity of Mixtures and Branches: Two Halakic Sayings in Romans 11:16–24." *Journal of Biblical Literature* 135.2 (2016): 355–68.

———. "Sacred Land Endowments and Field Consecrations in Early Judaism." PhD diss., Duke University, 2013.

Gorman, Michael J. *Inhabiting the Cruciform God: Kenosis, Justification, and Theosis in Paul's Narrative Soteriology*. Grand Rapids: Eerdmans, 2009.

———. *The Death of the Messiah and the Birth of the New Covenant: A (Not So) New Model of the Atonement*. Eugene: Wipf & Stock, 2014.

Grabbe, Lester L. "Israel's Historical Reality after the Exile." Pages 9–32 in *The Crisis of Israelite Religion: Transformation of Religious Tradition in Exilic and Post-exilic Times*. Edited by Bob Becking and Marjo Christina Annette Korpel. Leiden: Brill, 1999.

———. "'Mind the Gaps': Ezra, Nehemiah, and the Judaean Restoration." Pages 83–104 in *Restoration: Old Testament, Jewish and Christian Perspectives*. Edited by James M. Scott. JSJSup 72. Leiden: Brill, 2001.

———. *The Roman Period*. Minneapolis: Fortress, 1992.

———. "'They Shall Come Rejoicing to Zion' – or Did They? The Settlement of Yehud in the Early Persian Period." Pages 116–27 in *Exile and Restoration Revisited: Essays on the Babylonian and Persian Period in Memory of Peter R. Ackroyd*. Edited by Gary N. Knoppers, Lester L. Grabbe, and Dierdre N. Fulton. LSTS 73. London: T&T Clark, 2009.

"Triumph of the Pious or Failure of the Xenophobes? The Ezra-Nehemiah Reforms and Their *Nachgeschichte*." Pages 50–65 in *Jewish Local Patriotism and Self-Identification in the Graeco-Roman Period*. Edited by Siân Jones, and Sarah Pearce. LSTS. Sheffield: Sheffield Academic, 1998.

Grasso, Kevin. "A Linguistic Analysis of πίστις χριστοῦ: The Case for the Third View." *Journal for the Study of the New Testament* 43.1 (2020): 108–44.

Greenwood, David C. "On the Jewish Hope for a Restored Northern Kingdom." *Zeitschrift für die alttestamentliche Wissenschaft* 88.3 (1976): 376–85.

Gregory, Bradley C. "The Postexilic Exile in Third Isaiah: Isaiah 61:1–3 in Light of Second Temple Hermeneutics." *Journal of Biblical Literature* 126.3 (2007): 475–96.

Grieb, A. Katherine. "Paul's Theological Preoccupation in Romans 9–11." Pages 391–400 in *Between Gospel and Election: Explorations in the Interpretation of Romans 9–11*. Edited by Florian Wilk, J. Ross Wagner, and Frank Schleritt. WUNT 257. Tübingen: Mohr Siebeck, 2010.

Grindheim, Sigurd. *Christology in the Synoptic Gospels: God or God's Servant*. London: T&T Clark, 2012.

"The Law Kills but the Gospel Gives Life: The Letter-Spirit Dualism in 2 Corinthians 3.5–18." *Journal for the Study of the New Testament* 84 (2001): 97–115.

Grol, Harm van. "'Indeed, Servants We Are': Ezra 9, Nehemiah 9, and 2 Chronicles 12 Compared." Pages 209–27 in *The Crisis of Israelite Religion: Transformation of Religious Tradition in Exilic and Post-exilic Times*. Edited by Bob Becking and Marjo Christina Annette Korpel. Leiden: Brill, 1999.

Gruen, Erich S. "Diaspora and Homeland." Pages 18–46 in *Diasporas and Exiles: Varieties of Jewish Identity*. Edited by Howard Wettstein. Berkeley: University of California Press, 2002.

Grünwaldt, Klaus. *Das Heiligkeitsgesetz Leviticus 17–26: Ursprüngliche Gestalt, Tradition und Theologie*. BZAW 271. Berlin: de Gruyter, 2014.

Grushcow, Lisa. *Writing the Wayward Wife: Rabbinic Interpretations of Sotah*. AJEC 62. Leiden: Brill, 2006.

Guerra, Anthony J. *Romans and the Apologetic Tradition: The Purpose, Genre and Audience of Paul's Letter*. SNTSMS 81. Cambridge: Cambridge University Press, 1995.

"Romans: Paul's Purpose and Audience with Special Attention to Romans 9–11." *Revue biblique* 97.2 (1990): 219–37.

Gundry Volf, Judith M. *Paul and Perseverance: Staying in and Falling Away*. Louisville, KY: Westminster John Knox, 1990.

Gupta, Nijay K. *Paul and the Language of Faith*. Grand Rapids: Eerdmans, 2020.

Haacker, Klaus. "Das Thema von Römer 9–11 als Problem der Auslegungsgeschicte." Pages 55–72 in *Between Gospel and Election: Explorations in the Interpretation of Romans 9–11*. Edited by Florian Wilk, J. Ross Wagner, and Frank Schleritt. WUNT 257. Tübingen: Mohr Siebeck, 2010.

Der Brief des Paulus an die Römer. Theologischer Kommentar zum Neuen Testament. Leipzig: Evangelische Verlagsanstalt, 1999.

Hacham, Noah. "Exile and Self-Identity in the Qumran Sect and in Hellenistic Judaism." Pages 3–21 in *New Perspectives on Old Texts: Proceedings of the Tenth International Symposium of the Orion Center for the Dead Sea Scrolls and Associated Literature, January 2005*. Edited by Esther G. Chazon, Betsy Halpern-Amaru, and Ruth A. Clements. STDJ 88. Leiden: Brill, 2010.

Hafemann, Scott J. "Paul and the Exile of Israel in Galatians 3–4." Pages 329–71 in *Exile: Old Testament, Jewish, and Christian Conceptions*. Edited by James M. Scott. JSJSup 56. Leiden: Brill, 1997.

——— *Paul, Moses, and the History of Israel: The Letter/Spirit Contrast and the Argument from Scripture in 2 Corinthians 3*. Paternoster Biblical Monographs. Eugene: Wipf & Stock, 2005.

——— *Paul: Servant of the New Covenant; Pauline Polarities in Eschatological Perspective*. WUNT 435. Tübingen: Mohr Siebeck, 2020.

——— "The Salvation of Israel in Romans 11:25–32: A Response to Krister Stendahl." *Ex Auditu* 4 (1988): 38–58.

——— "The Spirit of the New Covenant, the Law, and the Temple of God's Presence: Five Theses on Qumran Self-Understanding and the Contours of Paul's Thought." Pages 172–89 in *Evangelium, Schriftauslegung, Kirche: Festschrift für Peter Stuhlmacher zum 65. Geburtstag*. Edited by Jostein Ådna, Scott J. Hafemann, and Otfried Hofius. Göttingen: Vandenhoeck & Ruprecht, 1997.

Hahn, Ferdinand. "Zum Verständnis von Römer 11.26a: 'und so wird ganz Israel gerettet werden.'" Pages 221–36 in *Paul and Paulinism: Essays in Honour of C. K. Barrett*. Edited by Morna D. Hooker and S. G. Wilson. London: SPCK, 1982.

Hahn, Scott W. "'All Israel Will Be Saved': The Restoration of the Twelve Tribes in Romans 9–11." *Letter & Spirit* 10 (2015): 63–104.

——— "Covenant, Oath, and the Aqedah: Διαθήκη in Galatians 3:15–18." *Catholic Biblical Quarterly* 67.1 (2005): 79–100.

Halpern-Amaru, Betsy. "Exile and Return in Jubilees." Pages 127–44 in *Exile: Old Testament, Jewish, and Christian Conceptions*. Edited by James M. Scott. JSJSup 56. Leiden: Brill, 1997.

——— "Land Theology in Philo and Josephus." Pages 65–93 in *The Land of Israel: Jewish Perspectives*. Edited by Lawrence A. Hoffmann. Notre Dame: University of Notre Dame Press, 1986.

Hammond Bammel, Caroline P., ed. *Der Römerbriefkommentar des Origenes: Kritische Ausgabe der Übersetzung Rufins Buch 7–10*. VL. Freiburg: Herder, 1998.

Hanneken, Todd R. "The Status and Interpretation of Jubilees in 4Q390." Pages 407–28 in *A Teacher for All Generations: Essays in Honor of James C. VanderKam*. Edited by Eric F. Mason, Samuel I. Thomas, Alison Schofield, and Eugene Ulrich. JSJSup 2. Leiden: Brill, 2012.

Hanson, Anthony T. *Studies in Paul's Technique and Theology*. Grand Rapids: Eerdmans, 1974.

——— "Vessels of Wrath or Instruments of Wrath? Romans ix. 22–3." *Journal of Theological Studies* 32 (1981): 433–43.

Harmon, Matthew S. "Review of Jesus, the Tribulation, and the End of the Exile: Restoration Eschatology and the Origin of the Atonement, by Brant Pitre." *Review of Biblical Literature* (2007): 1–6.

Harrington, Daniel J. "Baruch, Book of." *Eerdmans Dictionary of Early Judaism*. Edited by John J. Collins. Grand Rapids: Eerdmans, 2010, 425–26.

The Gospel of Matthew. SP 1. Collegeville, MN: Liturgical Press, 1991.

Harrison, A. R. W. *The Law of Athens: Procedure, Volume 2*. 2nd ed. London: Duckworth, 1998.

Harrison, James R. "Paul, Eschatology and the Augustan Age of Grace." *Tyndale Bulletin* 50 (1999): 79–92.

Paul's Language of Grace in Its Graeco-Roman Context. WUNT 172. Tübingen: Mohr Siebeck, 2003.

Hartman, Louis Francis, and Alexander A. Di Lella. *The Book of Daniel*. AB 23. Garden City: Doubleday, 1978.

Harvey, Graham. *The True Israel: Uses of the Names Jew, Hebrew, and Israel in Ancient Jewish and Early Christian Literature*. AGJU 35. Leiden: Brill, 1996.

Hauptman, Judith. *Rereading the Mishnah: A New Approach to Ancient Jewish Texts*. TSAJ 109. Tübingen: Mohr Siebeck, 2005.

Havemann, J. C. T. "Cultivated Olive – Wild Olive: The Olive Tree Metaphor in Romans 11:16-24." *Neotestamentica* 31.1 (1997): 87–106.

Hawthorne, Gerald F., and Ralph P. Martin. *Philippians*. WBC 43. Waco: Word, 2004.

Hayes, Christine E. *What's Divine about Divine Law? Early Perspectives*. Princeton: Princeton University Press, 2017.

Hays, Richard B. "Adam, Israel, Christ: The Question of Covenant in the Theology of Romans." Pages 68–86 in *Pauline Theology III: Romans*. Edited by David M. Hay and E. Elizabeth Johnson. Minneapolis: Fortress, 1995.

The Conversion of the Imagination: Paul as Interpreter of Israel's Scripture. Grand Rapids: Eerdmans, 2005.

Echoes of Scripture in the Letters of Paul. New Haven: Yale University Press, 1989.

The Faith of Jesus Christ: The Narrative Substructure of Galatians 3:1–4:11. Rev. ed. Grand Rapids: Eerdmans, 2002.

"Hope for What We Do Not Yet See: The Salvation of All Israel in Romans 11.25-27." Pages 545–72 in *One God, One People, One Future*. Edited by John Anthony Dunne and Eric Lewellen. Minneapolis: Fortress, 2018.

"Justification." Pages 1129–33 in *The Anchor Yale Bible Dictionary*. Vol. 3. Edited by David Noel Freedman. New Haven: Yale University Press, 1992.

"'The Righteous One' as Eschatological Deliverer: A Case Study in Paul's Apocalyptic Hermeneutics." Pages 191–215 in *Apocalyptic and the New Testament: Essays in Honor of J. Louis Martyn*. Edited by Joel Marcus and Marion L. Soards. JSNTSup 24. London: Bloomsbury, 1989.

Head, Peter M. "Named Letter-Carriers among the Oxyrhynchus Papyri." *Journal for the Study of the New Testament* 31.3 (2009): 279–99.

Heath, Jane. "Moses' End and the Succession: Deuteronomy 31 and 2 Corinthians 3." *New Testament Studies* 60.1 (2014): 37–60.

"The Righteous Gentile Interjects (James 2:18–19 and Romans 2:14–15)." *Novum Testamentum* 55.3 (2013): 272–95.

Heil, John Paul. "Christ, the Termination of the Law (Romans 9:30–10:8)." *Catholic Biblical Quarterly* 63 (2001): 484–98.

Heiser, Michael S. "Deuteronomy 32:8 and the Sons of God." *Bibliotheca Sacra* 158 (2001): 52–74.

——— "The Divine Council in Late Canonical and Non-Canonical Second Temple Jewish Literature." PhD diss., University of Wisconsin-Madison, 2004.

Heliso, Desta. *Pistis and the Righteous One: A Study of Romans 1:17 Against the Background of Scripture and Second Temple Jewish Literature.* WUNT 235. Tübingen: Mohr Siebeck, 2007.

Heller, Jan. "Himmel- und Höllenfahrt nach Römer 10,6–7." *Evangelische Theologie* 32 (1972): 478–86.

Hengel, Martin, and Anna Maria Schwemer. *Paul between Damascus and Antioch: The Unknown Years.* Louisville, KY: Westminster, 1997.

Herman, Gabriel. *Ritualised Friendship and the Greek City.* Cambridge: Cambridge University Press, 2002.

Heschel, Abraham J. *The Prophets.* Perennial Classics. San Francisco: HarperCollins, 2001.

Hess, Jonathan M. *Germans, Jews, and the Claims of Modernity.* New Haven: Yale University Press, 2002.

——— "Jewish Emancipation and the Politics of Race." Pages 203–12 in *The German Invention of Race*. Edited by Sara Eigen and Mark Larrimore. Albany: State University of New York Press, 2006.

Hickling, C. J. A. "Paul's Use of Exodus in the Corinthian Correspondence." Pages 367–76 in *The Corinthian Correspondence*. Edited by Reimund Bieringer. Leuven: Leuven University Press, 1996.

Hicks-Keeton, Jill. *Arguing with Aseneth: Gentile Access to Israel's Living God in Jewish Antiquity.* Oxford: Oxford University Press, 2018.

Himmelfarb, Martha. "Torah, Testimony, and Heavenly Tablets: The Claim to Authority of the Book of Jubilees." Pages 19–29 in *A Multiform Heritage: Studies on Early Judaism and Christianity in Honor of Robert A. Kraft*. Edited by Benjamin G. Wright. Atlanta: Scholars Press, 1999.

Hjelm, Ingrid. "Changing Paradigms: Judaean and Samarian Histories in Light of Recent Research." Pages 161–79 in *Historie og Konstruktion: Festskrift til Niels Peter Lemche i anledning af 60 års fødselsdagen den 6. September 2005*. Edited by Mogens Müller, Thomas L. Thompson, and Niels Peter Lemche. Copenhagen: Museum Tusculanum, 2005.

——— *Jerusalem's Rise to Sovereignty: Zion and Gerizim in Competition.* JSOTSup 404. London: T&T Clark, 2004.

——— "What Do Samaritans and Jews Have in Common? Recent Trends in Samaritan Studies." *Currents in Biblical Research* 3.1 (2004): 9–59.

Hofius, Otfried. "Das Evangelium und Israel: Erwägungen zu Römer 9–11." *Zeitschrift für Theologie und Kirche* 83.3 (1986): 297–324.

——— "Gesetz und Evangelium nach 2 Korinther 3." Pages 75–120 in *Paulusstudien*. WUNT. Tübingen: Mohr Siebeck, 1989.

Holladay, Carl R. "Paul and His Predecessors in the Diaspora: Some Reflections on Ethnic Identity in the Fragmentary Hellenistic Jewish Authors." Pages 429–60 in *Early Christianity and Classical Culture: Comparative Studies in Honor of Abraham J. Malherbe*. Edited by John T. Fitzgerald, Thomas H. Olbricht, and L. Michael White. NovTSup 110. Leiden: Brill, 2003.

Holladay, William L. *Jeremiah I: A Commentary on the Book of the Prophet Jeremiah, Chapters 1–25*. Hermeneia 24A. Philadelphia: Fortress, 1986.

——. *Jeremiah II: A Commentary on the Book of the Prophet Jeremiah, Chapters 26–52*. Hermeneia 24B. Philadelphia: Fortress, 1989.

Hooker, Morna D. "Christ: The 'End' of the Law." Pages 126–46 in *Neotestamentica et Philonica: Studies in Honor of Peder Borgen*. Edited by David E Aune, Torrey Seland, and Jarl Henning Ulrichsen. NovTSup 106. Leiden: Brill, 2005.

——. "Paul and 'Covenantal Nomism.'" Pages 47–56 in *Paul and Paulinism: Essays in Honour of C. K. Barrett*. Edited by Morna D. Hooker, and S. G. Wilson. London: SPCK, 1982.

——. *The Signs of a Prophet: The Prophetic Actions of Jesus*. Harrisburg, PA: Trinity Press International, 1997.

Horrell, David G. *Ethnicity and Inclusion: Religion, Race, and Whiteness in Constructions of Jewish and Christian Identities*. Grand Rapids: Eerdmans, 2020.

——. "Judaean Ethnicity and Christ-Following Voluntarism? A Reply to Steve Mason and Philip Esler." *New Testament Studies* 65.1 (2019): 1–20.

——. "Religion, Ethnicity, and Way of Life: Exploring Categories of Identity." *The Catholic Biblical Quarterly* 83.1 (2021): 38–55.

Horst, Pieter W. Van Der. "Anti-Samaritan Propaganda in Early Judaism." Pages 25–44 in *Persuasion and Dissuasion in Early Christianity, Ancient Judaism, and Hellenism*. Leuven: Peeters, 2003.

——. "'Only Then Will All Israel Be Saved': A Short Note on the Meaning of καὶ οὕτως in Romans 11:26." *Journal of Biblical Literature* 119 (2000): 521–25.

Hossfeld, Frank-Lothar, and Erich Zenger. *Psalms 3: A Commentary on Psalms 101–150*. Translated by Linda M Maloney. Hermeneia. Minneapolis: Fortress, 2011.

Howard, George E. "Christ the End of the Law: The Meaning of Romans 10:4ff." *Journal of Biblical Literature* 88.3 (1969): 331–37.

Hubbard, M. V. *New Creation in Paul's Letters and Thought*. SNTSMS 119. Cambridge: Cambridge University Press, 2002.

Hübner, Hans. *Gottes Ich und Israel: Zum Schriftgebrauch des Paulus in Römer 9–11*. Göttingen: Vandenhoeck & Ruprecht, 1984.

Balz, Horst Robert, and Gerhard Schneider, eds. *Exegetical Dictionary of the New Testament*. 3 vols. Grand Rapids: Eerdmans, 1990.

Hughes, Julie. *Scriptural Allusions and Exegesis in the Hodayot*. STDJ 59. Leiden; Boston: Brill, 2006.

Hultgren, Arland J. *Paul's Gospel and Mission: The Outlook from His Letter to the Romans*. Philadelphia: Fortress, 1985.

"The Scriptural Foundations for Paul's Mission to the Gentiles." Pages 21–44 in *Paul and His Theology*. Edited by Stanley E. Porter. Leiden: Brill, 2006.

Hultgren, Stephen J. *From the Damascus Covenant to the Covenant of the Community: Literary, Historical, and Theological Studies in the Dead Sea Scrolls*. STDJ 66. Leiden: Brill, 2007.

Hultin, Jeremy F. "Who Rebuked Cephas? A New Interpretation of Gal 2:14–17." SBL Annual Meeting (2013): 1–16.

Humphrey, Edith M. "Why Bring the Word Down? The Rhetoric of Demonstration and Disclosure in Romans 9:30–10:21." Pages 129–48 in *Romans and the People of God: Essays in Honor of Gordon D. Fee on the Occasion of His 65th Birthday*. Edited by Sven K. Söderlund, and N. T. Wright. Grand Rapids: Eerdmans, 1999.

Huxley, Aldous. *The Perennial Philosophy*. London: Chatto & Windus, 1947.

Hvalvik, Reidar. "A 'Sonderweg' for Israel: A Critical Examination of a Current Interpretation of Romans 11.25–27." *Journal for the Study of the New Testament* 38 (1990): 87–107.

Irons, Charles Lee. *The Righteousness of God: A Lexical Examination of the Covenant-faithfulness Interpretation*. WUNT 386. Tübingen: Mohr Siebeck, 2015.

Isaac, Jules. *The Teaching of Contempt: Christian Roots of Anti-Semitism*. Translated by Helen Weaver. New York: Holt, Rinehart, & Winston, 1964.

Ito, Akio. "Romans 2: A Deuteronomistic Reading." *Journal for the Study of the New Testament* 59 (1996): 21–37.

"The Written Torah and the Oral Gospel: Romans 10:5–13 in the Dynamic Tension between Orality and Literacy." *Novum Testamentum* 48.3 (2006): 234–60.

Jacobs, Andrew S. "A Jew's Jew: Paul and the Early Christian Problem of Jewish Origins." *Journal of Religion* 86.2 (2006): 258–86.

Janse, Mark. "The Prosodic Basis of Wackernagel's Law." Pages 19–22 in *Actes du XVe Congrès International des Linguistes 4: Les langues menacées (Québec, Université Laval: 9–14 Août 1992)*. Edited by André Crochetière, Jean-Claude Boulanger, and Conrad Ouellon. Sainte-Foy: Les Presses de l'Université Laval, 1993.

Japhet, Sara. "Exile and Restoration in the Book of Chronicles." Pages 33–44 in *The Crisis of Israelite Religion: Transformation of Religious Tradition in Exilic and Post-Exilic Times*. Edited by Bob Becking, and Marjo C. A. Korpel. Oudtestamentlsche Studiën 42. Leiden: Brill, 1999.

Jaubert, Annie. *La notion d'Alliance dans le judaïsme aux abords de l'ère chrétienne*. Patristica Sorbonensia. Paris: Seuil, 1963.

Jeffay, Nathan. "Israeli Government Rejects Orthodox Converts' Bids to Immigrate as Jews." *Forward* (March 16, 2011). https://forward.com/news/136245/israeli-government-rejects-orthodox-converts-bi/.

Jegher-Bucher, Verena. "Erwählung und Verwerfung im Römerbrief? Eine Untersuchung von Röm 11, 11–15." *Theologische Zeitschrift* 47.4 (1991): 326–36.

Jervell, Jacob. *Luke and the People of God: A New Look at Luke-Acts*. Minneapolis: Augsburg, 1972.

"The Lost Sheep of the House of Israel: The Understanding of the Samaritans in Luke-Acts." Pages 113–32 in *Luke and the People of God: A New Look at Luke-Acts*. Minneapolis: Augsburg, 1972.

Jervis, L. Ann. "Did Paul Think in Terms of Two-Age Dualism?" Pages 75–86 in *Paul and Matthew among Jews and Gentiles: Essays in Honour of Terence L. Donaldson*. Edited by Ronald Charles. LNTS 628. London: Bloomsbury, 2020.

Jewett, Robert. "The Basic Human Dilemma: Weakness or Zealous Violence (Romans 7:7–25 and 10:1–18)." *Ex Auditu* 13 (1997): 96–109.

———. "The Law and the Coexistence of Jews and Gentiles in Romans." *Interpretation* 39.4 (1985): 341–56.

———. *Romans: A Commentary*. Hermeneia 66. Minneapolis: Fortress, 2006.

Jipp, Joshua W. *Christ Is King: Paul's Royal Ideology*. Minneapolis: Fortress, 2015.

———. "The Paul of Acts." *Novum Testamentum* 62.1 (2019): 60–78.

———. "What Are the Implications of the Ethnic Identity of Paul's Interlocutor?" Pages 183–203 in *The So-called Jew in Paul's Letter to the Romans*. Edited by Rafael Rodríguez and Matthew Thiessen. Minneapolis: Fortress, 2016.

Johnson Hodge, Caroline. "Apostle to the Gentiles: Constructions of Paul's Identity." *Biblical Interpretation Series* 13.3 (2005): 270–88.

———. "Olive Trees and Ethnicities: Judeans and Gentiles in Romans 11:17–24." Pages 77–89 in *Christians as a Religious Minority in a Multicultural City: Modes of Interaction and Identity Formation in Early Imperial Rome*. Edited by Jürgen Zangenburg and Michael Labahn. JSNTSup 243. London: Continuum, 2004.

———. "The Question of Identity: Gentiles as Gentiles – but also Not – in Pauline Communities." Pages 153–73 in *Paul within Judaism: Restoring the First-Century Context to the Apostle*. Edited by Mark D. Nanos and Magnus Zetterholm. Minneapolis: Augsburg Fortress, 2015.

———. *If Sons, Then Heirs: A Study of Kinship and Ethnicity in the Letters of Paul*. Oxford: Oxford University Press, 2007.

Johnson, E. Elizabeth. *The Function of Apocalyptic and Wisdom Traditions in Rom 9–11*. Atlanta: Scholars Press, 1989.

Juel, Donald H. *Messianic Exegesis: Christological Interpretation of the Old Testament in Early Christianity*. Philadelphia: Fortress, 1988.

Kaatz, Saul. *Die mündliche Lehre und ihr Dogma*. Leipzig: Kaufmann, 1923.

Kaiser, Walter C. "Leviticus 18:5 and Paul: Do This and You Shall Live (Eternally?)." *Journal of the Evangelical Theological Society* 14.1 (1971): 20–28.

———. *The Uses of the Old Testament in the New*. Eugene: Wipf & Stock, 2001.

Käsemann, Ernst. *A Commentary on Romans*. Translated by Geoffrey W. Bromily. Grand Rapids: Eerdmans, 1980.

Kaylor, R. David. *Paul's Covenant Community: Jew and Gentile in Romans*. Atlanta: Westminster John Knox, 1988.

Keck, Leander E. *Romans*. ANTC. Nashville: Abingdon, 2005.

Keddie, G. Anthony. "Paul's Freedom and Moses' Veil: Moral Freedom and the Mosaic Law in 2 Corinthians 3.1–4.6 in Light of Philo." *Journal for the Study of the New Testament* 37.3 (2015): 267–89.

Keller, Winfrid. *Gottes Treue, Israels Heil: Röm 11, 25–27: Die These vom "Sonderweg" in der Diskussion.* SBB. Stuttgart: Katholisches Bibelwerk, 1998.

Ketterling, Matthew D. "God's Sons and the Logic of the Covenant: Divine Sonship in 'Jubilees' and Romans." PhD diss., University of St. Andrews, 2018.

Khobnya, Svetlana. "'The Root' in Paul's Olive Tree Metaphor (Romans 11:16–24)." *Tyndale Bulletin* 64 (2013): 257–73.

Kim, Dongsu. "Reading Paul's καὶ οὕτως πᾶς Ἰσραὴλ σωθήσεται (Rom. 11:26a) in the Context of Romans." *Calvin Theological Journal* 45 (2010): 317–34.

Kim, Johann D. *God, Israel, and the Gentiles: Rhetoric and Situation in Romans 9–11.* SBLDS 176. Atlanta: Society of Biblical Literature, 2000.

Kim, Seyoon. "The 'Mystery' of Rom 11:25–26 Once More." *New Testament Studies* 43 (1997): 412–29.

——. *The Origin of Paul's Gospel.* Tübingen: Mohr, 1981.

Kincaid, John A. "New Covenant Justification by Cardiac Righteousness: An Augustinian Perspective on Pauline Justification." *Letter & Spirit* 12 (2017): 37–58.

King, Justin. "Rhetorical Chain-Link Construction and the Relationship between Romans 7.1–6 and 7.7–8.39: Additional Evidence for Assessing the Argument of Romans 7–8 and the Identity of the Infamous 'I.'" *Journal for the Study of the New Testament* 39.3 (2017): 258–78.

——. *Speech-in-Character, Diatribe, and Romans 3:1–9.* BIS 163. Leiden: Brill, 2018.

Kingsbury, Edwin C. "He Set Ephraim Before Manasseh." *Hebrew Union College Annual* 38 (1967): 129–36.

Kirk, J. R. Daniel. "Reconsidering Dikaiōma in Romans 5:16." *Journal of Biblical Literature* 126.4 (2007): 787–92.

——. *Unlocking Romans: Resurrection and the Justification of God.* Grand Rapids: Eerdmans, 2008.

——. "Why Does the Deliverer Come ἐκ Σιών (Romans 11.26)?" *Journal for the Study of the New Testament* 33.1 (2010): 81–99.

Klein, Anja. "From the 'Right Spirit' to the 'Spirit of Truth': Observations on Ps 51 and 1QS." Pages 171–91 in *The Dynamics of Language and Exegesis at Qumran.* Edited by Devorah Dimant and Reinhard Gregor Kratz. FAT 35. Tübingen: Mohr Siebeck, 2009.

——. "New Material or Traditions Expanded? A Response to Eibert Tigchelaar." Pages 319–26 in *Jeremiah's Scriptures: Production, Reception, Interaction, and Transformation.* Edited by Hindy Najman and Konrad Schmid. JSJSup 173. Leiden: Brill, 2016.

——. "Prophecy Continued: Reflections on Innerbiblical Exegesis in the Book of Ezekiel." *Vetus Testamentum* 60.4 (2010): 571–82.

——. *Schriftauslegung im Ezechielbuch: Redaktionsgeschichtliche Untersuchungen zu Ez 34–39.* BZAW 391. Berlin: de Gruyter, 2008.

Knibb, Michael A. "The Exile in the Literature of the Intertestamental Period." *Heythrop Journal* 17.3 (1976): 253–72.

——. "A Note on 4Q372 and 4Q390." Pages 164–70 in *The Scriptures and the Scrolls: Studies in Honor of A. S. van der Woude on the Occasion of His*

65th Birthday. Edited by Florentino García Martínez, Anthony Hilhorst, and C. J. Labuschagne. Leiden: Brill, 1992.

Knoppers, Gary N. "Did Jacob Become Judah? The Configuration of Israel's Restoration in Deutero-Isaiah." Pages 39–67 in *Samaria, Samarians, Samaritans: Studies on Bible, History and Linguistics*. Edited by József Zsengellér. SJ 66. Berlin: de Gruyter, 2011.

———. *Jews and Samaritans: The Origins and History of Their Early Relations*. New York: Oxford University Press, 2013.

Koch, Dietrich-Alex. "Der Text von Hab 2.4b in der Septuaginta und im Neuen Testament." *Zeitschrift für die neutestamentliche Wissenschaft* 76 (1985): 68–85.

———. *Die Schrift als Zeuge des Evangeliums: Untersuchungen zur Verwendung und zum Verständnis der Schrift bei Paulus*. BHT 69. Tübingen: Mohr, 1986.

Kok, Michael. "The True Covenant People: Ethnic Reasoning in the Epistle of Barnabas." *Studies in Religion* 40.1 (2010): 81–97.

Kooij, Arie van der. "'The Servant of the Lord': A Particular Group of Jews in Egypt according to the Old Greek of Isaiah: Some Comments on LXX Isa 49:1–6 and Related Passages." Pages 383–96 in *Studies in the Book of Isaiah: FS W. A. M. Beuken*. Edited by Jacques van Ruiten and Marc Vervenne. BETL 132. Leuven: Peeters, 1997.

Korner, Ralph J. *The Origin and Meaning of Ekklēsia in the Early Jesus Movement*. AJEC 98. Leiden: Brill, 2017.

Kozman, Rony. "Ezekiel's Promised Spirit as *adam*'s Revelatory Spirit in the Hodayot." *Dead Sea Discoveries* 26.1 (2019): 30–60.

Kraabel, A. Thomas. "Unity and Diversity among Diaspora Synagogues." Pages 49–60 in *Diaspora Jews and Judaism: Essays in Honor of, and in Dialogue with, A. Thomas Kraabel*. Edited by J. Andrew Overman and Robert S. MacLennan. SFSHJ 41. Atlanta: Scholars Press, 1992.

Kraemer, Ross Shepard. *When Aseneth Met Joseph: A Late Antique Tale of the Biblical Patriarch and His Egyptian Wife, Reconsidered*. New York: Oxford University Press, 1998.

Kraus, Wolfgang. "Hab 2:3–4 in the Hebrew Tradition and in the Septuagint, with its Reception in the New Testament." Pages 97–117 in *Septuagint and Reception*. Edited by Johann Cook. VTSup 127. Leiden: Brill, 2009.

Krentz, Edgar. "The Name of God in Disrepute: Romans 2:17–29 [22–23]." *Currents in Theology and Mission* 17.6 (1990): 429–39.

Kuhn, Karl Georg. "Der Talmud, das Gesetzbuch der Juden: Einfuhrende Bemerkungen." Pages 226–33 in *Zur Geschichte und rechtlichen Stellung der Juden in Stadt und Universität Tübingen: Aus den Jahresbänden der wissenschaftlichen Akademie des NSD-Dozentenbundes/Wissenschaftliche Akademie Tübingen des NSD-Dozentenbundes 1 (1937–1939)*. Edited by Thomas Miller. Tübingen: Mohr Siebeck, 1941.

———. "Die Entstehung des talmudischen Denkens." *Forschungen zur Judenfrage* 1 (1937): 63–80.

———. *Die Judenfrage als weltgeschichtliches Problem*. Schriften des Reichsinstituts für Geschichte des neuen Deutschlands. Hamburg: Hanseatische Verlagsanstalt, 1939.

"Ursprung und Wesen der talmudischen Einstellung zum Nichtjuden." *Forschungen zur Judenfrage* 3 (1938): 199–234.

"Weltjudentum in der Antike." *Forschungen zur Judenfrage* 2 (1937): 9–29, 64.

Kittel, Gerhard, and Gerhard Friedrich, eds. *Theological Dictionary of the New Testament*. Translated by Geoffrey W. Bromiley. 10 vols. Grand Rapids: Eerdmans, 1964.

Laato, Timo. *Paul and Judaism: An Anthropological Approach*. Translated by T. McElwain. SFSHJ 115. Atlanta: Scholars Press, 1995.

Lagrange, Marie-Joseph. *Saint Paul, Épître aux Romains*. Paris: Lecoffre, 1950.

Lalleman, Hetty. "Paul's Self-Understanding in the Light of Jeremiah: A Case Study into the Use of the Old Testament in the New Testament." Pages 96–111 in *A God of Faithfulness: Essays in Honour of J. Gordon McConville on His 60th Birthday*. Edited by Jamie A. Grant, Alison Lo, and Gordon J. Wenham. LHBOTS 538. London: T&T Clark, 2011.

Lambert, David A. "Did Israel Believe That Redemption Awaited Its Repentance? The Case of Jubilees 1." *Catholic Biblical Quarterly* 68.4 (2006): 631–50.

How Repentance Became Biblical: Judaism, Christianity, and the Interpretation of Scripture. New York: Oxford University Press, 2016.

"How the 'Torah of Moses' Became Revelation: An Early, Apocalyptic Theory of Pentateuchal Origins." *Journal for the Study of Judaism* 47.1 (2016): 22–54.

Lane, William L. "Covenant: The Key to Paul's Conflict with Corinth." *Tyndale Bulletin* 33 (1982): 3–29.

The Gospel according to Mark. International Greek New Testament Commentary. Grand Rapids: Eerdmans, 1974.

Lang, T. J. *Mystery and the Making of a Christian Historical Consciousness: From Paul to the Second Century*. BZNW 219. Berlin: de Gruyter, 2015.

Langton, Daniel R. "The Myth of the 'Traditional View of Paul' and the Role of the Apostle in Modern Jewish-Christian Polemics." *Journal for the Study of the New Testament* 28.1 (2005): 69–104.

Lee, Jae Hyun. *Paul's Gospel in Romans: A Discourse Analysis of Rom. 1:16–8:39*. Linguistic Biblical Studies 3. Leiden: Brill, 2010.

Légasse, Simon. *L'épître de Paul aux Romains*. LD 10. Paris: Cerf, 2002.

Levenson, Jon D. *The Death and Resurrection of the Beloved Son: The Transformation of Child Sacrifice in Judaism and Christianity*. New Haven: Yale University Press, 1993.

Resurrection and the Restoration of Israel: The Ultimate Victory of the God of Life. New Haven: Yale University Press, 2006.

Levin, Christoph. *Die Verheissung des neuen Bundes in ihrem theologiegeschichtlichen Zusammenhang ausgelegt*. FRLANT 137. Göttingen: Vandenhoeck & Ruprecht, 1985.

Levine, Amy-Jill. *The Misunderstood Jew: The Church and the Scandal of the Jewish Jesus*. San Francisco: HarperOne, 2006.

"Supersessionism: Admit and Address Rather than Debate or Deny." *Religions* 13.155 (2022): 1–12.

Levison, John R. *Filled with the Spirit*. Grand Rapids: Eerdmans, 2009.

Liddell, Henry George, Robert Scott, and Henry Stuart Jones. *A Greek-English Lexicon*. 9th ed. with revised supplement. Oxford: Oxford University Press, 1996.

Lim, Timothy H. *Holy Scripture in the Qumran Commentaries and Pauline Letters*. Oxford: Oxford University Press, 1997.

Lincicum, David. *Paul and the Early Jewish Encounter with Deuteronomy*. WUNT 284. Tübingen: Mohr Siebeck, 2010.

——— "Paul's Engagement with Deuteronomy: Snapshots and Signposts." *Currents in Biblical Research* 7.1 (2008): 37–67.

Linebaugh, Jonathan A. "Announcing the Human: Rethinking the Relationship between Wisdom of Solomon 13–15 and Romans 1.18–2.11." *New Testament Studies* 57.2 (2011): 214–37.

——— *God, Grace, and Righteousness in Wisdom of Solomon and Paul's Letter to the Romans*. NovTSup 152. Leiden: Brill, 2013.

Linville, James Richard. *Israel in the Book of Kings: The Past as a Project of Social Identity*. JSOTSup 272. Sheffield: Sheffield Academic, 1998.

Litwa, M. David. *We Are Being Transformed: Deification in Paul's Soteriology*. BZNW 187. Berlin: de Gruyter, 2012.

Lohfink, Gerhard. *Jesus and Community: The Social Dimension of Christian Faith*. Philadelphia: Fortress, 1984.

Lohse, Eduard. *Der Brief an die Römer*. KEK. Göttingen: Vandenhoeck & Ruprecht, 2003.

Longenecker, Bruce W. *Eschatology and the Covenant: A Comparison of 4 Ezra and Romans 1–11*. London: Bloomsbury, 2015.

Longenecker, Richard N. *The Epistle to the Romans*. NIGTC. Grand Rapids: Eerdmans, 2016.

——— *Paul, Apostle of Liberty*. 2nd ed. Grand Rapids: Eerdmans, 2015.

Lowe, Malcolm. "Who Were the ΙΟΥΔΑΙΟΙ?" *Novum Testamentum* 18.2 (1976): 101–30.

Lucas, Alec J. "Distinct Portraits and Parallel Development of the Knowledge of God in Romans 1:18–32 and Wisdom of Solomon 13–15." Pages 61–82 in *Christian Body, Christian Self: Concepts of Early Christian Personhood*. Edited by Clare K. Rothschild and Trevor W. Thompson. WUNT 284. Tübingen: Mohr Siebeck, 2011.

——— *Evocations of the Calf?: Romans 1:18–2:11 and the Substructure of Psalm 106 (105)*. BZNW 201. Berlin: de Gruyter, 2014.

——— "Paul and the Calf: Texts, Tendencies, and Traditions." Pages 110–31 in *Golden Calf Traditions in Early Judaism*. Edited by Eric F. Mason. TBN 23. Leiden: Brill, 2018.

——— "Reorienting the Structural Paradigm and Social Significance of Romans 1:18–32." *Journal of Biblical Literature* 131.1 (2012): 121–41.

Lundbom, Jack R. *Jeremiah 1–20: A New Translation with Introduction and Commentary*. Accordance electronic ed. AB 21A. New Haven: Yale University Press, 1974.

Luz, Ulrich. *Das Geschichtsverständnis des Paulus*. BEvT 49. Munich: Kaiser, 1968.

Lyonnet, Stanislas. "Saint Paul et l'exégèse juive de son temps. A propos de Rom 10, 6–8." Pages 494–506 in *Mélanges Bibliques rédigés en l'honneur de André Robert*. Paris: Bloud and Gay, 1957.

MacDowell, Douglas M. *Spartan Law*. Scottish Classical Studies 107. Edinburgh: Scottish Academic, 1986.

Mack, Burton L. "Wisdom and Apocalyptic in Philo." *Studia Philonica Annual* 3 (1991): 21–39.

Madigan, Kevin, and Jon D. Levenson. *Resurrection: The Power of God for Christians and Jews*. New Haven: Yale University Press, 2008.

Magen, Yitzhak. *The Samaritans and the Good Samaritan*. Edited by Noga Carmin. Translated by Edward Levin. Judea and Samaria Publications. Jerusalem: Israel Antiquities Authority, 2008.

Malina, Bruce J., and Richard L. Rohrbaugh. *Social-Science Commentary on the Gospel of John*. Minneapolis: Fortress, 1998.

Manning, Gary T. *Echoes of a Prophet: The Use of Ezekiel in the Gospel of John and in Literature of the Second Temple Period*. LNTS 270. London: T&T Clark, 2004.

Marcus, Joel. "The Circumcision and the Uncircumcision in Rome." *New Testament Studies* 35.1 (1989): 67–81.

———. "'The Twelve Tribes in the Diaspora' (James 1.1)." *New Testament Studies* 60.4 (2014): 433–47.

Marcus, Ralph, trans. *Loeb Classical Library*. LCL 489. Cambridge, MA: Harvard University Press, 1937.

Martens, John W. "Romans 2.14–16: A Stoic Reading." *New Testament Studies* 40.1 (1994): 55–67.

Martyn, J. Louis. *Galatians: A New Translation with Introduction and Commentary*. AB 33A. New York: Doubleday, 1997.

———. "Romans as One of the Earliest Interpretations of Galatians." Pages 37–45 in *Theological Issues in the Letters of Paul*. Nashville: Abingdon, 1997.

———. "The Textual Contradiction between Habakkuk 2:4 and Leviticus 18:5." Pages 183–90 in *Theological Issues in the Letters of Paul*. London: A&C Black, 1997.

Mason, Steve. "Jews, Judaeans, Judaizing, Judaism: Problems of Categorization in Ancient History." *Journal for the Study of Judaism* 38 (2007): 457–512.

Maston, Jason. "Anthropological Crisis and Solution in the Hodayot and 1 Corinthians 15." *New Testament Studies* 62.4 (2016): 533–48.

———. *Divine and Human Agency in Second Temple Judaism and Paul: A Comparative Study*. WUNT 297. Tübingen: Mohr Siebeck, 2018.

Matera, Frank J. *Romans*. Paideia: Commentaries on the New Testament. Grand Rapids: Baker Academic, 2010.

Kittel, Gerhard, and Gerhard Friedrich, eds. *Theologisches Wörterbuch zum Neuen Testament*. 10 vols. Stuttgart: Kohlhammer, 1932.

McCaulley, Esau. *Reading While Black: African American Biblical Interpretation as an Exercise in Hope*. Downers Grove, IL: InterVarsity, 2020.

———. *Sharing in the Son's Inheritance: Davidic Messianism and Paul's Worldwide Interpretation of the Abrahamic Land Promise in Galatians*. LNTS. London: Bloomsbury, 2019.

McClachlan, Bonnie. *Age of Grace: Charis in Early Greek Poetry*. Princeton: Princeton University Press, 1993.
Mcconville, J. Gordon. "Ezra-Nehemiah and the Fulfillment of Prophecy." *Vetus Testamentum* 36.2 (1986): 205–24.
McCready, Wayne O. "The 'Day of Small Things' vs. the Latter Days." Pages 223–36 in *Israel's Apostasy and Restoration: Essays in Honor of Roland K. Harrison*. Edited by Avraham Gileadi. Grand Rapids: Baker Books, 1988.
Mcdonald, Denys N. "'Ex-Pagan Pagans'? Paul, Philo, and Gentile Ethnic Reconfiguration." *Journal for the Study of the New Testament* 45.1 (2022): 23–50.
McGlynn, Moyna. *Divine Judgement and Divine Benevolence in the Book of Wisdom*. WUNT 139. Tübingen: Mohr Siebeck, 2001.
McGrath, Alister E. *Iustitia Dei: A History of the Christian Doctrine of Justification*. 4th ed. Cambridge: Cambridge University Press, 2020.
Mckay, Kenneth L. "Time and Aspect in New Testament Greek." *Novum Testamentum* 34.3 (1992): 209–28.
McKnight, Scot. "Jesus and the Twelve." *Bulletin for Biblical Research* 11.2 (2001): 203–31.
― *A Light among the Gentiles: Jewish Missionary Activity in the Second Temple Period*. Minneapolis: Fortress, 1991.
― *A New Vision for Israel: The Teachings of Jesus in National Context*. Grand Rapids: Eerdmans, 1999.
― *Reading Romans Backwards: A Gospel of Peace in the Midst of Empire*. Waco: Baylor University Press, 2019.
Mcneil, Linda. "Bridal Cloths, Cover-Ups, and Kharis: The Carpet Scene in Aeschylus' Agamemnon." *Greece and Rome* 52.1 (2005): 1–17.
Meier, John P. *A Marginal Jew: Rethinking the Historical Jesus*. 4 vols. New York: Doubleday, 1991.
― "Jesus, the Twelve, and the Restoration of Israel." Pages 365–404 in *Restoration: Old Testament, Jewish and Christian Perspectives*. Edited by James M. Scott. JSJSup 72. Leiden: Brill, 2001.
Melton, J. Gordon. "Spiritualization and Reaffirmation: What Really Happens When Prophecy Fails." *American Studies* 26.2 (1985): 17–29.
Meyer, Ben F. *The Aims of Jesus*. London: SCM, 1979.
Meyer, Lester V. "Remnant." *The Anchor Yale Bible Dictionary*. Vol. 5. Edited by David Noel Freedman. New Haven: Yale University Press, 1992, 670–71.
Meyer, Paul W. "Romans 10:4 and the 'End' of the Law." Pages 59–78 in *The Divine Helmsman: Studies on God's Control of Human Events, Presented to Lou H. Silberman*. Edited by James L. Crenshaw and Samuel Sandmel. New York: Ktav, 1996.
Michel, Otto. *Der Brief an die Römer*, vol. 4. 5th ed. KEK. Göttingen: Vandenhoeck & Ruprecht, 1978.
Middlemas, Jill A. "Trito-Isaiah's Intra- and Internationalization: Identity Markers in the Second Temple Period." Pages 105–25 in *Judah and the Judeans in the Achaemenid Period: Negotiating Identity in an International*

Context. Edited by Oded Lipschits, Gary N. Knoppers, and Manfred Oeming. Winona Lake: Eisenbrauns, 2011.

Mielziner, M. *Introduction to the Talmud*. 4th ed. New York: Bloch, 1969.

Milbank, John. "Can a Gift Be Given? Prolegomena to a Future Trinitarian Metaphysic." Pages 119–61 in *Rethinking Metaphysics*. Edited by L. Gregory Jones. London: Blackwell, 1995.

Milgrom, Jacob. *Leviticus 1–16*. AB 3A. New York: Doubleday, 1991.

———. *Leviticus 17–22*. AB 3B. New York: Doubleday, 2000.

Miller, David M. "Ethnicity Comes of Age: An Overview of Twentieth-Century Terms for Ioudaios." *Currents in Biblical Research* 10 (2012): 293–311.

———. "Ethnicity, Religion and the Meaning of Ioudaios in Ancient 'Judaism.'" *Currents in Biblical Research* 12.2 (2014): 216–65.

Montefiore, C. G. *Judaism and St. Paul*. London: Goschen, 1914.

Montgomery, James Alan. *The Samaritans, the Earliest Jewish Sect: Their History, Theology and Literature*. Philadelphia: The John C. Winston Co., 1907.

Moo, Douglas J. *The Epistle to the Romans*. NICNT. Grand Rapids: Eerdmans, 1996.

———. "Israel and Paul in Romans 7.7–12." *New Testament Studies* 32.1 (1986): 122–35.

Moore, George Foot. "Christian Writers on Judaism." *Harvard Theological Review* 14 (1921): 191–254.

Moraff, Jason F. "'Among My Own Nation': Reading the Way, Paul, and 'The Jews' in Acts Within Judaism." PhD diss., Fuller Theological Seminary, 2021.

Morales, Rodrigo J. [Isaac]. *The Spirit and the Restoration of Israel: New Exodus and New Creation Motifs in Galatians*. WUNT 282. Tübingen: Mohr Siebeck, 2010.

Morgan, Teresa. *Roman Faith and Christian Faith: Pistis and Fides in the Early Roman Empire and Early Churches*. Oxford: Oxford University Press, 2015.

Morris, Leon. *The Epistle to the Romans*. Grand Rapids: Eerdmans, 1988.

Moss, R. Waddy. "A Study of Jeremiah's Use (xviii. 1–17) of the Figure of the Potter." *Expository Times* 2.12 (1891): 274–75.

Moule, C. F. D. *An Idiom Book of New Testament Greek*. New York: Cambridge University Press, 1959.

Mroczek, Eva. *The Literary Imagination in Jewish Antiquity*. New York: Oxford University Press, 2016.

Müller, Christian. *Gottes Gerechtigkeit und Gottes Volk: Eine Untersuchung zu Römer 9–11*. Göttingen: Vandenhoeck & Ruprecht, 1964.

Munck, Johannes. *Christ and Israel: An Interpretation of Romans 9–11*. Translated by Ingeborg Nixon. Philadelphia: Fortress, 1967.

Murphy-O'connor, Jerome. "Lots of God-Fearers? Theosebeis in the Aphrodisias Inscription." *Revue biblique* 99 (1992): 418–24.

Mussner, Franz. "Christus [ist] des Gesetzes Ende zur Gerechtigkeit fur jeden, der glaubt." Pages 31–44 in *Paulus – Apostat oder Apostel?* Edited by Markus Barth et al. Regensburg: Pustet, 1977.

———. "Ganz Israel wird gerettet werden (Röm 11,26): Versuch einer Auslegung." *Kairós* 18 (1976): 241–55.

"Mitteilhaberin an der Wurzel: Zur Ekklesiologie von Röm 11,11–24." Pages 153–59 in *Die Kraft der Wurzel: Judentum – Jesus – Kirche*. Freiburg: Herder, 1987.

Traktat über die Juden. München: Kosel, 1979.

Myles, Robert, and James G. Crossley. "Biblical Scholarship, Jews and Israel: On Bruce Malina, Conspiracy Theories and Ideological Contradictions." *BibleInterpcom* (2012). www.bibleinterp.com/opeds/myl368013.shtml.

Najman, Hindy. "The Law of Nature and the Authority of Mosaic Law." *Studia Philonica Annual* 11 (1999): 55–73.

"A Written Copy of the Law of Nature: An Unthinkable Paradox?" *Studia Philonica Annual* 15 (2003): 54–63.

Nanos, Mark D. "'Broken Branches': A Pauline Metaphor Gone Awry?" Pages 339–75 in *Between Gospel and Election: Explorations in the Interpretation of Romans 9–11*. Edited by Florian Wilk, J. Ross Wagner, and Frank Schleritt. WUNT 257. Tübingen: Mohr Siebeck, 2010.

"'Callused,' Not 'Hardened': Paul's Revelation of Temporary Protection Until All Israel Can Be Healed." Pages 52–73 in *Reading Paul in Context: Explorations in Identity Formation. Essays in Honour of William S. Campbell*. Edited by Kathy Ehrensperger and J. Brian Tucker. London: T&T Clark, 2010.

"Introduction." Pages 1–32 in *Paul within Judaism: Restoring the First-Century Context to the Apostle*. Edited by Mark D. Nanos and Magnus Zetterholm. Minneapolis: Augsburg Fortress, 2015.

"Paul and Judaism: Why Not Paul's Judaism?" Pages 117–60 in *Paul Unbound: Other Perspectives on the Apostle*. Edited by Mark D. Given. Peabody, MA: Hendrickson, 2010.

The Mystery of Romans: The Jewish Context of Paul's Letter. Minneapolis: Augsburg Fortress, 1996.

"The Myth of the 'Law-Free' Paul Standing Between Christians and Jews." *Studies in Christian-Jewish Relations* 4 (2009): 1–21.

Nanos, Mark D., and Magnus Zetterholm, eds. *Paul within Judaism: Restoring the First-Century Context to the Apostle*. Minneapolis: Augsburg Fortress, 2015.

Neubrand, Maria, and Johannes Seidel München. "'Eingepfropft in den edlen Ölbaum' (Röm 11,24): Der Ölbaum ist nicht Israel." *Biblische Notizen* 105 (2000): 61–75.

Neusner, Jacob. "Exile and Return as the History of Judaism." Pages 221–37 in *Exile: Old Testament, Jewish, and Christian Conceptions*. Edited by James M. Scott. JSJSup 56. Leiden: Brill, 1997.

Judaism When Christianity Began: A Survey of Belief and Practice. Louisville: Westminster John Knox, 2002.

"The Premise of Paul's Ethnic Israel." Pages 1–20 in *Children of the Flesh, Children of the Promise: A Rabbi Talks with Paul*. Cleveland: Pilgrim, 1995.

Rabbinic Narrative: A Documentary Perspective, Vol 3: Forms, Types and Distribution of Narratives in Song of Songs Rabbah and Lamentations Rabbah and a Reprise of Fathers According to Rabbi Nathan Text A. BRLJ 16. Leiden: Brill, 2003.

"Was Rabbinic Judaism Really 'Ethnic'? A Theological Comparison between Christianity and the So-Called Particularist Religion of Israel." *Catholic Biblical Quarterly* 57.2 (1995): 281–305.

The Way of Torah: An Introduction to Judaism. 5th ed. Belmont, CA: Wadsworth, 1993.

"What Is 'a Judaism'? Seeing the Dead Sea Library as the Statement of a Coherent Judaic Religious System." Pages 3–21 in *Theory of Israel.* Edited by Alan J. Avery-Peck, Jacob Neusner, and Bruce D. Chilton. HOS 56. Leiden: Brill, 2001.

Newman, Judith H. "Speech and Spirit: Paul and the Maskil as Inspired Interpreters of Scripture." Pages 241–64 in *The Holy Spirit, Inspiration, and the Cultures of Antiquity: Multidisciplinary Perspectives.* Edited by Jörg Frey, John R. Levison, and Andrew Bowden. Ekstasis 5. Berlin: de Gruyter, 2014.

Neyrey, Jerome H. "'I Said: You Are Gods': Psalm 82:6 and John 10." *Journal of Biblical Literature* 108.4 (1989): 647–63.

Niebuhr, Karl-Wilhelm. "'Nicht alle aus Israel sind Israel' (Röm 9,6b). Römer 9–11 als Zeugnis paulinischer Anthropologie." Pages 433–61 in *Between Gospel and Election: Explorations in the Interpretation of Romans 9–11.* Edited by Florian Wilk, J. Ross Wagner, and Frank Schleritt. WUNT 257. Tübingen: Mohr Siebeck, 2010.

Nihan, Christophe. "Ethnicity and Identity in Isaiah 56–66." Pages 67–104 in *Judah and the Judeans in the Achaemenid Period: Negotiating Identity in an International Context.* Edited by Oded Lipschits, Gary N. Knoppers, and Manfred Oeming. Winona Lake: Eisenbrauns, 2011.

Nitzan, Bilhah. "The Concept of the Covenant in Qumran Literature." Pages 85–104 in *Historical Perspectives: From the Hasmoneans to Bar Kokhba in Light of the Dead Sea Scrolls.* Edited by David Goodblatt, Avital Pinnick, and Daniel R. Schwartz. STDJ 37. Leiden: Brill, 2000.

Nodet, Etienne. "Israelites, Samaritans, Temples, Jews." Pages 121–71 in *Samaria, Samarians, Samaritans: Studies on Bible, History and Linguistics.* Edited by József Zsengellér. SJ 66. Berlin: de Gruyter, 2011.

Nolland, John. "Grace as Power." *Novum Testamentum* 28.1 (1986): 26–31.

Novenson, Matthew V. *Christ among the Messiahs: Christ Language in Paul and Messiah Language in Ancient Judaism.* New York: Oxford University Press, 2012.

"*Ioudaios*, Pharisee, Zealot." Pages 167–82 in *T&T Clark Handbook to the Historical Paul.* Edited by Ryan S. Schellenberg and Heidi Wendt. London: Bloomsbury, 2022.

"The Jewish Messiahs, the Pauline Christ, and the Gentile Question." *Journal of Biblical Literature* 128.2 (2009): 357–74.

"The Self-Styled Jew of Romans 2 and the Actual Jews of Romans 9–11." Pages 133–62 in *The So-called Jew in Paul's Letter to the Romans.* Edited by Rafael Rodríguez and Matthew Thiessen. Minneapolis: Fortress, 2016.

"Whither the Paul within Judaism *Schule*?" *Journal of the Jesus Movement in Its Jewish Setting* 5 (2018): 79–88.

Nygren, Anders. *Commentary on Romans*. Translated by Carl C. Rassmussen. Philadelphia: Muhlenberg, 1949.

O'Neill, John C. *Paul's Letter to the Romans*. Baltimore: Penguin, 1975.

Oehler, Markus. "The Punishment of Thirty-Nine Lashes (2 Corinthians 11:24) and the Place of Paul in Judaism." *Journal of Biblical Literature* 140.3 (2021): 623–40.

Oliver, Isaac W. *Luke's Jewish Eschatology: The National Restoration of Israel in Luke-Acts*. Oxford: Oxford University Press, 2021.

―――. "Torah Praxis After 70 CE: Reading Matthew and Luke-Acts as Jewish Texts." PhD diss., University of Michigan, 2012.

Olson, Dennis T. "How Does Deuteronomy Do Theology? Literary Juxtaposition and Paradox in the New Moab Covenant in Deuteronomy 29–32." Pages 201–13 in *A God So Near: Essays on Old Testament Theology in Honor of Patrick D. Miller*. Edited by Brent A. Strawn and Nancy R. Bowen. Winona Lake: Eisenbrauns, 2003.

Olson, Robert C. *The Gospel as the Revelation of God's Righteousness: Paul's Use of Isaiah in Romans 1:1–3:26*. WUNT 428. Tübingen: Mohr Siebeck, 2016.

Ophir, Adi, and Ishay Rosen-Zvi. *Goy: Israel's Multiple Others and the Birth of the Gentile*. Oxford: Oxford University Press, 2018.

Oropeza, B. J. "The Expectation of Grace: Paul on Benefaction and the Corinthians' Ingratitude (2 Corinthians 6:1)." *Bulletin for Biblical Research* 24.2 (2014): 207–26.

―――. *Jews, Gentiles, and the Opponents of Paul: The Pauline Letters*. Apostasy in the New Testament Communities 2. Eugene, OR: Cascade, 2012.

―――. "New Covenant Knowledge in an Earthenware Jar: Intertextual Reconfigurations of Jeremiah in 2 Corinthians 1: 21–22, 3: 2–11, and 4: 7." *Bulletin for Biblical Research* 28.3 (2018): 405–24.

―――. "Paul's Use of Deutero-Isaiah in Romans 2:24 and in the Gospel of Romans." Pages 31–49 in *Scripture, Texts, and Tracings in Romans*. Edited by Linda L. Belleville, and A. Andrew Das. Lanham: Lexington/Fortress Academic, 2021.

Ouoba, Elisée. "Paul's Use of Isaiah 27:9 and 59:20–21 in Romans 11:25–27." PhD diss., Wheaton College, 2010.

Palmer, Carmen. *Converts in the Dead Sea Scrolls: The Gēr and Mutable Ethnicity*. Vol. 126. STDJ. Leiden: Brill, 2018.

Pamment, Margaret. "Is There Convincing Evidence of Samaritan Influence on the Fourth Gospel?" *Zeitschrift für die neutestamentliche Wissenschaft* 73.3–4 (1982): 221–30.

Pao, David W. *Acts and the Isaianic New Exodus*. WUNT 130. Tübingen: Mohr Siebeck, 2000.

Papazarkadas, Nikolaos. *Sacred and Public Land in Ancient Athens*. Oxford: Oxford University Press, 2011.

Park, Young-Ho. *Paul's Ekklesia as a Civic Assembly: Understanding the People of God in their Politico-Social World*. WUNT 393. Tübingen: Mohr Siebeck, 2015.

Pate, C. Marvin. *The Reverse of the Curse: Paul, Wisdom, and the Law*. WUNT 114. Tübingen: Mohr Siebeck, 2000.

Payne, Don J. *Already Sanctified: A Theology of the Christian Life in Light of God's Completed Work*. Grand Rapids: Baker Academic, 2020.

Pearson, Birger A. "1 Thessalonians 2:13–16: A Deutero-Pauline Interpolation." *Harvard Theological Review* 64 (1971): 79–94.

Penna, Romano. *Lettera ai Romani II: Rom 6–11. Scritti delle origini cristiane*. Bologna: Dehoniane, 2006.

Peppard, Michael Luke. *The Son of God in the Roman World: Divine Sonship in Its Social and Political Context*. Oxford: Oxford University Press, 2011.

Piper, John. *The Future of Justification: A Response to N. T. Wright*. Wheaton, IL: Crossway, 2007.

Pitre, Brant. *Jesus, the Tribulation, and the End of the Exile: Restoration Eschatology and the Origin of the Atonement*. JSOTSup 37. Grand Rapids: Baker Academic, 2005.

Pitre, Brant, Michael P. Barber, and John A. Kincaid. *Paul, a New Covenant Jew: Rethinking Pauline Theology*. Grand Rapids: Eerdmans, 2019.

Plag, Christoph. *Israels Wege zum Heil: Eine Untersuchung zu Römer 9 bis 11*. AzTh. Stuttgart: Calwer, 1969.

Popkes, Enno Edzard. "Jes 6,9f. MT als impliziter Reflexionshintergrund der paulinischen Verstockungsvorstellung: Ein Beitrag zur paulinischen Jesaja-Rezeption." Pages 755–69 in *The Letter to the Romans*. Edited by Udo Schnelle. BETL 226. Leuven: Peeters, 2009.

———. "'Und David spricht.': Zur Rezeption von Ps LXX 68,23 f. im Kontext von Röm 11,1–10." Pages 321–37 in *Between Gospel and Election: Explorations in the Interpretation of Romans 9–11*. Edited by Florian Wilk, J. Ross Wagner, and Frank Schleritt. WUNT 257. Tübingen: Mohr Siebeck, 2010.

Porter, Calvin L. "Romans 1.18–32: Its Role in the Developing Argument." *New Testament Studies* 40.2 (1994): 210–28.

Porter, Stanley E. "The Concept of Covenant in Paul." Pages 269–85 in *The Concept of the Covenant in the Second Temple Period*. Edited by Stanley E. Porter and Jacqueline C. R. De Roo. JSJSup 71. Leiden; Boston: Brill, 2003.

———. *Verbal Aspect in the Greek of the New Testament, with Reference to Tense and Mood*. New York: Lang, 1989.

Portier-Young, Anathea E. *Apocalypse against Empire: Theologies of Resistance in Early Judaism*. Grand Rapids: Eerdmans, 2011.

Pransky, Tiffany. "Boundaries of Belonging: Conversion in Israel's Law of Return." MA diss., Central European University, 2012.

Pucci Ben Zeev, Miriam. *Jewish Rights in the Roman World: The Greek and Roman Documents Quoted by Josephus Flavius*. TSAJ 74. Tübingen: Mohr Siebeck, 1998.

Pummer, Reinhard. "Samaritanism in Caesarea Maritima." Pages 181–202 in *Religious Rivalries and the Struggle for Success in Caesarea Maritima*. Edited by Terence L. Donaldson. SCJ. Waterloo, ON: Wilfrid Laurier University Press, 2000.

Rahlfs, Alfred, ed. *Septuaginta*. Stuttgart: Deutsche Bibelgesellschaft, 2006.

Rainey, Brian. *Religion, Ethnicity and Xenophobia in the Bible*. London: Routledge, 2018.

Räisänen, Heikki. *Paul and the Law*. 2nd ed. WUNT 29. Tübingen: Mohr, 1987.
"Paul, God, and Israel: Romans 9–11 in Recent Research." Pages 178–206 in *The Social World of Formative Christianity and Judaism: Essays in Tribute of Howard Clark Kee*. Edited by Jacob Neusner, Ernest S. Frerichs, and Peder Borgen. Philadelphia: Fortress, 1988.
"Römer 9–11: Analyse eines geistigen Ringens." *Aufstieg und Niedergang der römischen Welt* 25.4: 2891–939.
Rajak, Tessa. *Translation and Survival: The Greek Bible of the Ancient Jewish Diaspora*. Oxford: Oxford University Press, 2009.
Ramsay, William M. "The Olive-Tree and the Wild-Olive." *Expositor* 2 (1905): 16–34.
Rappaport, Uriel. "Reflections on the Origins of the Samaritans." Pages 10–19 in *Studies in Geography and History in Honour of Yehoshua Ben-Arieh*. Edited by I. Bartal and E. Reiner. Jerusalem: Magnes, 1999.
Raspe, Lucia. "Manetho on the Exodus: A Reappraisal." *Jewish Studies Quarterly* 5.2 (1998): 124–55.
Rastoin, Marc. "Une bien étrange greffe (Rm 11,17): Correspondances rabbiniques d'une expression Paulinienne." *Revue biblique* 114.1 (2007): 73–79.
Ravens, David. *Luke and the Restoration of Israel*. JSNTSup 119. Sheffield: Sheffield Academic, 1995.
Reed, Annette Yoshiko. "Ioudaios Before and After 'Religion.'" *Marginalia Review of Books* (2014). http://marginalia.lareviewofbooks.org/ioudaios-religion-annette-yoshiko-reed/.
Refoulé, François. "*... Et ainsi tout Israël sera sauvé*": *Romans 11.25-32*. LD 117. Paris: Cerf, 1984.
"Romains, X, 4: Encore une fois." *Revue biblique* 91.3 (1984): 321–50.
Reicke, Bo. *The Disobedient Spirits and Christian Baptism: A Study of 1 Peter 3:19 and Its Context*. Eugene: Wipf & Stock, 2005.
Reinbold, Wolfgang. "Israel und das Evangelium: Zur Exegese von Römer 10,19–21." *Zeitschrift für die neutestamentliche Wissenschaft* 86.1-2 (1995): 122–29.
"Zur Bedeutung des Begriffes 'Israel' in Römer 9–11." Pages 401–16 in *Between Gospel and Election: Explorations in the Interpretation of Romans 9–11*. Edited by Florian Wilk, J. Ross Wagner, and Frank Schleritt. WUNT 257. Tübingen: Mohr Siebeck, 2010.
Renz, Thomas. *The Rhetorical Function of the Book of Ezekiel*. VTSup 76. Leiden: Brill, 1999.
Repschinski, Boris. "Ekklesia als Kultgemeinde oder Volksversammlung? Zur Genese des Begriffs in Apostelgeschichte und Matthäusevangelium." *Zeitschrift für katholische Theologie* 137.3/4 (2015): 346–65.
Rhyne, C. Thomas. "Nomos Dikaiosynēs and the Meaning of Romans 10:4." *Catholic Biblical Quarterly* 48.3 (1986): 486–99.
Richardson, Peter. *Israel in the Apostolic Church*. SNTSMS 10. Cambridge: Cambridge University Press, 1969.
Ridderbos, Herman N. *Aan de Romeinen*. Kampen: Kok, 1959.
Paul: An Outline of His Theology. Translated by J. R. De Witt. Grand Rapids: Eerdmans, 1975.

Robinson, J. Armitage. "ΠΩΡΩΣΙΣ and ΠΗΡΩΣΙΣ." *Journal of Theological Studies* 3.9 (1901): 81–96.
Rodrigues, Lancy. "Rom 11:16–24 in the Context of Rom 9–11: A Study of the Allegory of the Olive Tree and Paul's View on the Future Salvation of the Jews." PhD diss., Katholieke Universiteit Leuven, 2003.
Rodríguez, Rafael. *If You Call Yourself a Jew: Reappraising Paul's Letter to the Romans*. Eugene: Cascade, 2014.
——— "Romans 5–8 in Light of Paul's Dialogue with a Gentile." Pages 101–31 in *The So-called Jew in Paul's Letter to the Romans*. Edited by Rafael Rodríguez and Matthew Thiessen. Minneapolis: Fortress, 2016.
Rodríguez, Rafael, and Matthew Thiessen, eds. *The So-called Jew in Paul's Letter to the Romans*. Minneapolis: Fortress, 2016.
Rose, Christian. *Die Wolke der Zeugen: Eine exegetisch-traditionsgeschichtliche Untersuchung zu Hebräer 10,32–12,3*. WUNT 60. Tübingen: Mohr Siebeck, 1994.
Rosen-Zvi, Ishay, and Adi Ophir. "Paul and the Invention of the Gentiles." *Jewish Quarterly Review* 105.1 (2015): 1–41.
Rudman, D. "The Significance of the Phrase 'Fishers of Men' in the Synoptic Gospels." *Irish Biblical Studies* 26.3 (2005): 106–18.
Runesson, Anders. "The Question of Terminology: The Architecture of Contemporary Discussions on Paul." Pages 53–78 in *Paul within Judaism: Restoring the First-century Context to the Apostle*. Edited by Mark D. Nanos and Magnus Zetterholm. Minneapolis: Augsburg Fortress, 2015.
Russell, Walt. "The Apostle Paul's Redemptive-Historical Argumentation in Galatians 5:13–26." *Westminster Theological Journal* 57 (1995): 333–57.
Sailhamer, John H. *The Pentateuch as Narrative: A Biblical-Theological Commentary*. Grand Rapids: Zondervan, 2017.
Samkutty, Vanmelitharayil John. *The Samaritan Mission in Acts*. LNTS 328. London: T&T Clark, 2006.
Sanday, William, and Arthur C. Headlam. *A Critical and Exegetical Commentary on the Epistle to the Romans*. Edinburgh: T&T Clark, 1902.
Sanders, E. P. *Jesus and Judaism*. Minneapolis: Augsburg Fortress, 1985.
——— *Judaism: Practice and Belief 63 BCE–66 CE*. London: SCM, 1992.
——— "Patterns of Religion in Paul and Rabbinic Judaism." *Harvard Theological Review* 66 (1973): 455–78.
——— *Paul and Palestinian Judaism: A Comparison of Patterns of Religion*. Philadelphia: Fortress, 1977.
——— *Paul, the Law, and the Jewish People*. Minneapolis: Fortress, 1983.
——— *Paul: A Very Short Introduction*. Oxford: Oxford University Press, 2001.
——— "Paul's Attitude Toward the Jewish People." *Union Seminary Quarterly Review* 33.3 (1978): 175–87.
Sandler, Adam. "The Chanukah Song." *Saturday Night Live*. Studio City, CA: NBC, 1994.
Sanger, Dieter. "Rettung der Heiden und Erwählung Israels: Einige Vorlaufige Erwagungen zu Romer 11,25–27." *Kerygma and Dogma* 32 (1986): 99–119.
Satlow, Michael L. "Defining Judaism: Accounting for 'Religions' in the Study of Religion." *Journal of the American Academy of Religion* 74.4 (2006): 837–60.

"A History of the Jews or Judaism? On Seth Schwartz's Imperialism and Jewish Society, 200 BCE to 640 CE." *Jewish Quarterly Review* 95.1 (2005): 151–62.

How the Bible Became Holy. New Haven: Yale University Press, 2014.

"Jew or Judaean?" Pages 165–75 in *"The One Who Sows Bountifully": Essays in Honor of Stanley K. Stowers*. Edited by Caroline Johnson Hodge, Saul M. Olyan, Daniel Ullucci, and Emma Wasserman. BJS 356. Providence, RI: Brown Judaic Studies, 2014.

Saulnier, Christiane. "Lois romaines sur les Juifs selon Flavius Josèphe." *Revue biblique* 88.2 (1981): 161–98.

Scafuro, Adele C. "Atimia." Page 923 in *The Encyclopedia of Ancient History*, Edited by Roger S. Bagnall et al. London: Blackwell, 2013.

Schaller, Berndt. "ΕΞΕΙ ΕΚ ΣΙΩΝ Ο ΡΥΟΜΑΝΟΣ: Zur Textgestalt von Jes 59:20f. in Röm 11:26f." Pages 201–6 in *De Septuaginta: Studies in Honour of John William Wevers on his Sixty-Fifth Birthday*. Edited by Albert Pietersma and Claude Cox. Mississauga, ON: Benben, 1984.

Schechter, Solomon. *Aspects of Rabbinic Theology*. New York: Schocken, 1961.

Scheck, Thomas P., ed. *Origen: Commentary on the Epistle to the Romans, Books 6–10*. The Fathers of the Church. Washington, DC: Catholic University of America Press, 2002.

Schenker, Adrian. *Das Neue am neuen Bund und das Alte am alten: Jer 31 in der hebräischen und griechischen Bibel, von der Textgeschichte zu Theologie, Synagoge und Kirche*. Göttingen: Vandenhoeck & Ruprecht, 2006.

Schiffman, Lawrence H. "The Concept of Restoration in the Dead Sea Scrolls." Pages 203–22 in *Restoration: Old Testament, Jewish and Christian Perspectives*. Edited by James M. Scott. JSJSup 72. Leiden: Brill, 2001.

"The Samaritans in Tannaitic Halakhah." *Jewish Quarterly Review* 75.4 (1985): 323–50.

"The Temple Scroll and the Halakhic Pseudepigrapha of the Second Temple Period." Pages 121–31 in *Pseudepigraphic Perspectives: The Apocrypha and Pseudepigrapha in Light of the Dead Sea Scrolls*. Edited by Esther G. Chazon and Michael Stone. Leiden: Brill, 1999.

Schleritt, Frank. "Das Gesetz der Gerechtigkeit: Zur Auslegung von Römer 9,30–33." Pages 111–20 in *Between Gospel and Election: Explorations in the Interpretation of Romans 9–11*. Edited by Florian Wilk, J. Ross Wagner, and Frank Schleritt. WUNT 257. Tübingen: Mohr Siebeck, 2010.

Schlier, Heinrich. *Der Brief an die Galater*. MeyerK. Göttingen: Vandenhoeck & Ruprecht, 1989.

Der Römerbrief: Kommentar. HThK 6. Freiburg: Herder, 1977.

Schmalz, Mathew N. "When Festinger Fails: Prophecy and the Watch Tower." *Religion* 24.4 (2011): 293–308.

Schmeller, Thomas. *Paulus und die "Diatribe": Eine vergleichende Stilinterpretation*. NTAbh. Münster: Aschendorff, 1987.

Schmid, Konrad, and Odil Hannes Steck. "Restoration Expectations in the Prophetic Tradition of the Old Testament." Pages 41–81 in *Restoration: Old Testament, Jewish and Christian Perspectives*. Edited by James M. Scott. JSJSup 72. Leiden: Brill, 2001.

Schnittjer, Gary Edward. *Old Testament Use of Old Testament: A Book-By-Book Guide*. Grand Rapids: Zondervan Academic, 2020.
Schorch, Stefan. "The Construction of Samari(t)an Identity from the Inside and from the Outside." Pages 135–49 in *Between Cooperation and Hostility: Multiple Identities in Ancient Judaism and the Interaction with Foreign Powers*. Edited by Rainer Albertz, and Jakob Wöhrle. JAJSup 11. Göttingen: Vandenhoeck & Ruprecht, 2013.
Schreiner, Thomas R. "Israel's Failure to Attain Righteousness in Romans 9:30–10:3." *Trinity Journal* 12.2 (1991): 209–20.
———. "Paul's View of the Law in Romans 10:4–5." *Westminster Theological Journal* 55 (1993): 113–35.
———. *Romans*. BECNT. Grand Rapids: Baker Academic, 1998.
Friedrich, Gerhard, ed. *Theological Dictionary of the New Testament*. Translated by Geoffrey W. Bromiley. Grand Rapids: Eerdmans, 1964.
Schuller, Eileen M. "4Q372 1: A Text about Joseph." *Revue de Qumran* 14 (1991): 349–76.
Schwartz, Daniel R. "The End of the ΓΗ (Acts 1:8): Beginning or End of the Christian Vision?" *Journal of Biblical Literature* 105.4 (1986): 669–76.
———. "Judeans, Jews, and Their Neighbors." Pages 13–32 in *Between Cooperation and Hostility: Multiple Identities in Ancient Judaism and the Interaction with Foreign Powers*. Edited by Thomas Römer and Jakob Wöhrle. JAJSup 11. Göttingen: Vandenhoeck & Ruprecht, 2013.
———. "'Judaean' or 'Jew'." Pages 3–27 in *Jewish Identity in the Greco-Roman World: Jüdische Identität in der griechish-römischen Welt*. Edited by Jörg Frey and Stephanie Gripentrog. Leiden: Brill, 2007.
Schwartz, Seth. "How Many Judaisms Were There? A Critique of Neusner and Smith on Definition and Mason and Boyarin on Categorization." *Journal of Ancient Judaism* 2.2 (2011): 208–38.
Schweitzer, Albert. *The Mysticism of Paul the Apostle*. Translated by William Montgomery. New York: Seabury, 1968.
———. *Paul and His Interpreters: A Critical History*. Translated by W. Montgomery. London: Black, 1912.
———. *The Quest of the Historical Jesus: A Critical Study of Its Progress from Reimarus to Wrede*. Translated by W. Montgomery, J. R. Coates, Susan Cupitt, and John Bowden. Minneapolis: Fortress, 2001.
———. *Von Reimarus zu Wrede: Eine Geschichte der Leben-Jesu-Forschung*. Tübingen: Mohr Siebeck, 1906.
Schwindt, Rainer. "Mehr Wurzel als Stamm und Krone: Zur Bildrede vom Ölbaum in Röm 11,16–24." *Biblica* 88 (2007): 64–91.
Scobie, Charles H. H. "Israel and the Nations: An Essay in Biblical Theology." *Tyndale Bulletin* 43.2 (1992): 283–305.
———. "Johannine Geography." *Studies in Religion* 11.1 (1982): 77–84.
———. "The Origins and Development of Samaritan Christianity." *New Testament Studies* 19.4 (1973): 390–414.
Scott, James M. *Adoption as Sons of God: An Exegetical Investigation into the Background of ΥΙΟΘΕΣΙΑ in the Pauline Corpus*. WUNT 48. Tübingen: Mohr Siebeck, 1992.

"Exile and Restoration." Pages 251–58 in *Dictionary of Jesus and the Gospels*. Edited by Joel B. Green, Jeanine K. Brown, and Nicholas Perrin. 2nd ed. Downers Grove, IL: InterVarsity Press, 2013.

"Exile and the Self-Understanding of Diaspora Jews in the Greco-Roman Period." Pages 173–218 in *Exile: Old Testament, Jewish, and Christian Conceptions*. Edited by James M. Scott. JSJSup 56. Leiden: Brill, 1997.

On Earth As in Heaven: The Restoration of Sacred Time and Sacred Space in the Book of Jubilees. JSJSup 91. Leiden: Brill, 2005.

"'For as Many as Are of Works of the Law Are under a Curse' (Galatians 3.10)." Pages 187–221 in *Paul and the Scriptures of Israel*. Edited by Craig A. Evans and James A. Sanders. JSNTSup 83. Sheffield: Sheffield Academic, 1993.

Paul and the Nations: The Old Testament and Jewish Background of Paul's Mission to the Nations with Special Reference to the Destination of Galatians. WUNT 84. Tübingen: Mohr Siebeck, 1995.

"Paul's Use of Deuteronomic Tradition." *Journal for Biblical Literature* 112.4 (1993): 645–65.

"Philo and the Restoration of Israel." Pages 553–75 in *Society of Biblical Literature 1995 Seminar Papers*. Edited by Eugene H. Lovering Jr. Atlanta: Scholars Press, 1996.

"Restoration of Israel." Pages 796–805 in *Dictionary of Paul and His Letters*. Edited by Gerald F. Hawthorne and Ralph P. Martin. Downers Grove, IL: InterVarsity Press, 1993.

"And Then All Israel Will Be Saved (Rom 11:26)." Pages 489–526 in *Restoration: Old Testament, Jewish and Christian Perspectives*. Edited by James M. Scott. JSJSup 72. Leiden: Brill, 2001.

"The Use of Scripture in 2 Corinthians 6:16c–18 and Paul's Restoration Theology." *Journal for the Study of the New Testament* 56 (1994): 73–79.

Scott, Michael G. *Somehow I Manage*. Scotts Valley, CA: Createspace, 2019

Seaford, Richard. *Reciprocity and Ritual*. Oxford: Clarendon, 1994.

Sechrest, Love L. *A Former Jew: Paul and the Dialectics of Race*. LNTS 410. London: T&T Clark, 2009.

Seewann, Marie-Irma. "'Verstockung', 'Verhärtung' oder 'Nicht-Erkennen': Überlegungen zu Röm 11, 25." *Kirche und Israel* 12 (1997): 165–70.

Segal, Alan F. "Paul's Experience and Romans 9–11." *Princeton Seminary Bulletin* Suppl. Issue 1 (1990): 57–70.

Seifrid, Mark A. "Paul's Approach to the Old Testament in Rom 10:6–8." *Trinity Journal* 6.1 (1985): 3–37.

"Righteousness Language in the Hebrew Scriptures and Early Judaism." Pages 415–42 in *Justification and Variegated Nomism: Volume I – The Complexities of Second Temple Judaism*. Edited by D. A. Carson, Peter T. O'Brien, and Mark A. Seifrid. WUNT 140. Grand Rapids: Baker Academic, 2001.

"Romans." Pages 607–94 in *Commentary on the New Testament Use of the Old Testament*. Edited by Gregory K. Beale and D. A. Carson. Grand Rapids: Baker, 2007.

"Unrighteous by Faith: Apostolic Proclamation in Romans 1: 18–3: 20." Pages 105–45 in *Justification and Variegated Nomism: Volume II: The Paradoxes of Paul*. Edited by D. A. Carson, Peter T. O'Brien, and Mark A. Seifrid. WUNT 181. Tübingen: Mohr Siebeck, 2004.

Shahar, Yuval. "Imperial Religious Unification Policy and Its Decisive Consequences: Diocletian, the Jews and the Samaritans." Pages 109–19 in *Romans, Barbarians, and the Transformation of the Roman World: Cultural Interaction and the Creation of Identity in Late Antiquity*. Edited by Ralph W. Mathisen and Danuta Shanzer. Farnham: Ashgate, 2011.

Sheinfeld, Shayna. "Who Is the Righteous Remnant in Romans 9–11? The Concept of Remnant in the Hebrew Bible, Early Jewish Literature, and Paul's Letter to the Romans." Pages 33–50 in *Paul the Jew: Rereading the Apostle as a Figure of Second Temple Judaism*. Edited by Gabriele Boccaccini and Carlos A. Segovia. Minneapolis: Fortress, 2016.

Shum, Shiu-Lun. *Paul's Use of Isaiah in Romans: A Comparative Study of Paul's Letter to the Romans and the Sibylline and Qumran Sectarian Texts*. WUNT 156. Tübingen: Mohr Siebeck, 2002.

Siegert, Folker. *Argumentation bei Paulus, gezeigt an Röm 9–11*. WUNT 34. Tübingen: Mohr, 1985.

Simon, Marcel. *Verus Israel: A Study of the Relations between Christians and Jews in the Roman Empire AD 135–425*. Translated by H. McKeating. London: The Littman Library of Jewish Civilization, 1986.

Skinner, John. *A Critical and Exegetical Commentary on Genesis*. 2nd ed. ICC 1. London: T&T Clark, 1930.

Slenczka, Notger. "Römer 9–11 und die Frage nach der Identität Israels." Pages 463–78 in *Between Gospel and Election: Explorations in the Interpretation of Romans 9–11*. Edited by Florian Wilk, J. Ross Wagner, and Frank Schleritt. WUNT 257. Tübingen: Mohr Siebeck, 2010.

Sloan, Paul T. "Paul's Jewish Addressee in Rom 2–4: Revisiting Recent Conversations." *Journal of Theological Studies* (forthcoming).

Smith, Barry Douglas. *Jesus' Last Passover Meal*. Lewiston, NY: Mellen, 1993.

Smith, Christopher R. "The Portrayal of the Church as the New Israel in the Names and Order of the Tribes in Revelation 7.5–8." *Journal for the Study of the New Testament* 39 (1990): 111–18.

Smith, D. Moody. "Ο ΔΕ ΔΙΚΑΙΟΣ ΕΚ ΠΙΣΤΕΩΣ ΖΗΣΕΤΑΙ." Pages 13–25 in *Studies in the History and Text of the New Testament in Honor of Kenneth Willis Clark*. Edited by Boyd L. Daniels and M. Jack Suggs. SD 29. Salt Lake City: University of Utah Press, 1967.

Smith, Jonathan Z. "Fences and Neighbors: Some Contours of Early Judaism." Pages 1–18 in *Imagining Religion: From Babylon to Jonestown*. Chicago: University of Chicago Press, 1982.

Smith, Ralph Lee. *Micah–Malachi*. WBC 32. Nashville: Nelson, 1984.

Smyth, Hubert Weir. *Greek Grammar*. Cambridge, MA: Harvard University Press, 1920.

Snodgrass, Klyne R. "Justification by Grace – To the Doers: An Analysis of the Place of Romans 2 in the Theology of Paul." *New Testament Studies* 32.1 (1986): 72–93.

Snyder, Glenn E. "Paul beyond the Jew/Gentile Dichotomy: A Perspective from Benjamin." *Expositions* 9 (2015): 125–37.
Soloveichik, Meir. "Redemption and the Power of Man." *Azure* 16 (2004): 51–77.
Sorkin, David Jan. *The Transformation of German Jewry, 1780–1840*. New York: Oxford University Press, 1987.
Spilsbury, Paul. "Flavius Josephus on the Rise and Fall of the Roman Empire." *Journal of Theological Studies* 54.1 (2003): 1–24.
——— . *The Image of the Jew in Flavius Josephus' Paraphrase of the Bible*. TSAJ 69. Tübingen: Mohr Siebeck, 1998.
Sprinkle, Preston M. *Law and Life: The Interpretation of Leviticus 18:5 in Early Judaism and in Paul*. WUNT 241. Tübingen: Mohr Siebeck, 2008.
Stacey, W. David. "Appendix: The Lord's Supper as Prophetic Drama." Pages 80–95 in *The Signs of a Prophet: The Prophetic Actions of Jesus*. Edited by Morna D. Hooker. Harrisburg, PA: Trinity Press International, 1997.
Stahl, Michael J. *The "God of Israel" in History and Tradition*. VTSup 187. Leiden: Brill, 2021.
Stanley, Christopher D. *Arguing With Scripture: The Rhetoric of Quotations in the Letters of Paul*. London: T&T Clark, 2004.
——— . *Paul and the Language of Scripture: Citation Technique in the Pauline Epistles and Contemporary Literature*. SNTSMS 74. Cambridge: Cambridge University Press, 1992.
——— . "Paul's 'Use' of Scripture: Why the Audience Matters." Pages 125–55 in *As It Is Written: Studying Paul's Use of Scripture*. Edited by Stanley E. Porter and Christopher D. Stanley. SymS 50. Leiden: Brill, 2008.
Staples, Jason A. "Altered Because of Transgressions? The 'Law of Deeds' in Gal 3,19a." *Zeitschrift für die neutestamentliche Wissenschaft* 106.1 (2015): 126–35.
——— . *The Idea of Israel in Second Temple Judaism: A New Theory of People, Exile, and Israelite Identity*. Cambridge: Cambridge University Press, 2021.
——— . "'Lord LORD': Jesus as YHWH in Matthew and Luke." *New Testament Studies* 64.1 (2018): 1–19.
——— . "'Rise, Kill, and Eat': Animals as Nations in Early Jewish Visionary Literature and Acts 10." *Journal for the Study of the New Testament* 42.1 (2019): 3–17.
——— . "Vessels of Wrath and God's Pathos: Potter/Clay Imagery in Rom 9:20–23." *Harvard Theological Review* 115.2 (2022): 197–218.
——— . "What Do the Gentiles Have to Do with 'All Israel'? A Fresh Look at Romans 11:25–27." *Journal of Biblical Literature* 130.2 (2011): 371–90.
Starling, David I. *Not My People: Gentiles as Exiles in Pauline Hermeneutics*. BZNW 184. Berlin: de Gruyter, 2011.
Steck, Odil Hannes. "Das Problem theologischer Strömungen in nachexilischer Zeit." *Evangelische Theologie* 28 (1968): 445–58.
——— . *Israel und das gewaltsame Geschick der Propheten: Untersuchung zur Überlieferung des deuteronomistischen Geschichtsbildes im Alten Testament, Spätjudentum und Urchristentum*. WMANT 23. Neukirchen-Vluyn: Neukirchener, 1967.

Stegman, Thomas D. "Paul's Use of *dikaio-* Terminology: Moving Beyond N. T. Wright's Forensic Interpretation." *Theological Studies* 72 (2011): 496–524.

Stendahl, Krister. "The Apostle Paul and the Introspective Conscience of the West." *Harvard Thelogical Review* 56.3 (1963): 199–215.

Final Account: Paul's Letter to the Romans. Minneapolis: Fortress, 1993.

Paul among Jews and Gentiles. Philadelphia: Fortress, 1976.

"Paulus och Samvetet." *Svensk exegetisk årsbok* 25 (1960): 62–77.

Stenschke, Christoph. "Römer 9–11 als Teil des Römerbriefs." Pages 197–225 in *Between Gospel and Election: Explorations in the Interpretation of Romans 9–11.* Edited by Florian Wilk, J. Ross Wagner, and Frank Schleritt. WUNT 257. Tübingen: Mohr Siebeck, 2010.

Stern, Menahem, ed. *Greek and Latin Authors on Jews and Judaism, Vol 2: From Tacitus to Simplicius.* Jerusalem: Israel Academy of Sciences and Humanities, 1980.

Steudel, Annette. "Die Texte aus Qumran als Horizont für Römer 9–11: Israel-Theologie, Geschichtsbetrachtung, Schriftauslegung." Pages 111–20 in *between Gospel and Election: Explorations in the Interpretation of Romans 9–11.* Edited by Florian Wilk, J. Ross Wagner, and Frank Schleritt. WUNT 257. Tübingen: Mohr Siebeck, 2010.

Stockhausen, Carol K. "2 Corinthians 3 and the Principles of Pauline Exegesis." Pages 143–64 in *Paul and the Scriptures of Israel.* Edited by Craig A. Evans and James A. Sanders. JSNTSup 83. Sheffield: Sheffield Academic, 1993.

Moses' Veil and the Glory of the New Covenant: The Exegetical Substructure of II Cor. 3,1–4,6. Rome: Pontifical Biblical Institute, 1989.

Stowers, Stanley K. "Apostrophe, ΠΡΟΣΩΠΟΠΟIIA and Paul's Rhetorical Education." Pages 351–69 in *Early Christianity and Classical Culture: Comparative Studies in Honor of Abraham J. Malherbe.* Edited by John T. Fitzgerald, Thomas H. Olbricht, and L. Michael White. NovTSup 110. Leiden: Brill, 2003.

"Paul's Dialogue with a Fellow Jew in Romans 3:1–9." *Catholic Biblical Quarterly* 46.4 (1984): 707–22.

A Rereading of Romans: Justice, Jews, Gentiles. New Haven: Yale University Press, 1994.

"Romans 7.7–25 as a Speech-in-Character (προσωποποιία)." Pages 180–202 in *Paul in His Hellenistic Context.* Edited by Troels Engberg-Pedersen. London: T&T Clark, 1994.

Strobel, August. *Untersuchungen zum eschatologischen Verzögerungsproblem: auf Grund spätjüdisch-urchristlichen Geschichte von Habakuk 2,2 ff.* Leiden: Brill, 1961.

Stuhlmacher, Peter. *Paul's Letter to the Romans: A Commentary.* Translated by Scott J. Hafemann. Louisville: Westminster John Knox, 1994.

Stuhlmann, Rainer. *Das eschatologische Mass im Neuen Testament.* FRLANT 132. Göttingen: Vandenhoeck & Ruprecht, 1983.

Suggs, M. Jack. "'The Word Is Near You': Romans 10: 6–10 within the Purpose of the Letter." Pages 289–312 in *Christian History and Interpretation: Studies Presented to John Knox.* Edited by William R. Farmer, C. F. D.

Moule, and Richard R. Niebuhr. Cambridge: Cambridge University Press, 1967.

Talmon, Shemaryahu. "The Community of the Renewed Covenant: Between Judaism and Christianity." Pages 3–24 in *The Community of the Renewed Covenant: The Notre Dame Symposium on the Dead Sea Scrolls*. Edited by Eugene Ulrich, and James C. VanderKam. CJAS 10. Notre Dame: University of Notre Dame Press, 1994.

"The Emergence of Jewish Sectarianism in the Early Second Temple Period." Pages 587–616 in *Ancient Israelite Religion: Essays in Honor of Frank Moore Cross*. Edited by Patrick D. Miller, Paul D. Hanson, and S. Dean McBride. Philadelphia: Fortress, 1987.

"The New Covenanters of Qumran." *Scientific American* 225.5 (1971): 72–83.

"Waiting for the Messiah: The Spiritual Universe of the Qumran Covenanters." Pages 111–37 in *Judaisms and Their Messiahs at the Turn of the Christian Era*. Edited by Jacob Neusner, William Scott Green, and Ernest S. Frerichs. Cambridge: Cambridge University Press, 1987.

Taylor, Ann. "A Prosodic Account of Clitic Position in Ancient Greek." Pages 478–503 in *Approaching Second. Second-Position Clitics and Related Phenomena*. Edited by Aaron L. Halpern and Arnold M. Zwicky. Stanford: CSLI, 1996.

Tekiner, Roselle. "Race and the Issue of National Identity in Israel." *International Journal of Middle East Studies* 23.1 (1991): 39–55.

Theobald, Michael. *Die überströmende Gnade: Studien zu einem paulinischen Motivfeld*. FB 22. Würzburg: Echter, 1982.

Thiel, Nathan. "'Israel' and 'Jew' as Markers of Jewish Identity in Antiquity: The Problems of Insider/Outsider Classification." *Journal for the Study of Judaism* 45.1 (2014): 80–99.

Thielman, Frank. *From Plight to Solution: A Jewish Framework for Understanding Paul's View of the Law in Galatians and Romans*. NovTSup 61. Leiden: Brill, 1989.

Paul and the Law: A Contextual Approach. Downers Grove, IL: InterVarsity, 1994.

"Paul's View of Israel's Misstep in Rom 9.32–3: Its Origin and Meaning." *New Testament Studies* 64.3 (2018): 362–77.

Thiessen, Jacob. *Gott hat Israel nicht verstoßen: Biblisch-exegetische und theologische Perspektiven in der Verhältnisbestimmung von Israel, Judentum und Gemeinde Jesu*. Edition Israelogie. Frankfurt am Main: Lang, 2010.

Thiessen, Matthew. "Aseneth's Eight-Day Transformation as Scriptural Justification for Conversion." *Journal for the Study of Judaism* 45.2 (2014): 229–49.

Contesting Conversion: Genealogy, Circumcision, and Identity in Ancient Judaism and Christianity. New York: Oxford University Press, 2011.

"The Form and Function of the Song of Moses (Deuteronomy 32:1–43)." *Journal of Biblical Literature* 123.3 (2004): 401–24.

Paul and the Gentile Problem. New York: Oxford University Press, 2016.

"Paul, Essentialism, and the Jewish Law: In Conversation with Christine Hayes." *Journal for the Study of Paul and His Letters* 7.1-2 (2017): 80–85.

———. "Paul's Argument against Gentile Circumcision in Romans 2:17–29." *Novum Testamentum* 56.4 (2014): 373–91.

———. "Paul's So-Called Jew and Lawless Lawkeeping." Pages 59–83 in *The So-called Jew in Paul's Letter to the Romans*. Edited by Rafael Rodríguez and Matthew Thiessen. Minneapolis: Fortress, 2016.

———. "4Q372 1 and the Continuation of Joseph's Exile." *Dead Sea Discoveries* 15 (2008): 380–95.

Thiessen, Matthew, and Paula Fredriksen. "Paul and Israel." Pages 371–88 in *The Oxford Handbook of Pauline Studies*. Edited by Matthew V. Novenson, and R. Barry Matlock. Oxford: Oxford University Press, 2021.

Thomas, Samuel I. *The "Mysteries" of Qumran: Mystery, Secrecy, and Esotericism in the Dead Sea Scrolls*. EJL 25. Leiden: Brill, 2009.

Thornhill, A. Chadwick. *The Chosen People: Election, Paul and Second Temple Judaism*. Grand Rapids: InterVarsity, 2015.

Thorsteinsson, Runar M. *Paul's Interlocutor in Romans 2: Function and Identity in the Context of Ancient Epistolography*. ConBNT 40. Stockholm: Almqvist & Wiksell, 2003.

Thorsteinsson, Runar M., Matthew Thiessen, and Rafael Rodríguez. "Paul's Interlocutor in Romans: The Problem of Identification." Pages 1–37 in *The So-called Jew in Paul's Letter to the Romans*. Edited by Rafael Rodríguez and Matthew Thiessen. Minneapolis: Fortress, 2016.

Thrall, Margaret E. *2 Corinthians: A Critical and Exegetical Commentary*. ICC. Edinburgh: T&T Clark, 1994.

Tiede, David L. "The Exaltation of Jesus and the Restoration of Israel in Acts 1." *Harvard Theological Review* 79.1–3 (1986): 278–86.

Tigay, Jeffrey H. *Deuteronomy*. The JPS Torah Commentary. Philadelphia: Jewish Publication Society, 1996.

Tigchelaar, Eibert J. C. "Historical Origins of the Early Christian Concept of the Holy Spirit: Perspectives from the Dead Sea Scrolls." Pages 167–240 in *The Holy Spirit, Inspiration, and the Cultures of Antiquity: Multidisciplinary Perspectives*. Edited by Jörg Frey, John R. Levison, and Andrew Bowden. Ekstasis 5. Berlin: de Gruyter, 2014.

———. "Jeremiah's Scriptures in the Dead Sea Scrolls and the Growth of a Tradition." Pages 289–306 in *Jeremiah's Scriptures: Production, Reception, Interaction, and Transformation*. Edited by Hindy Najman and Konrad Schmid. JSJSup 173. Leiden: Brill, 2016.

Timmins, Will N. *Romans 7 and Christian Identity*. SNTSMS 170. Cambridge: Cambridge University Press, 2017.

———. "Romans 7 and Speech-In-Character: A Critical Evaluation Of Stowers' Hypothesis." *Zeitschrift für die neutestamentliche Wissenschaft* 107.1 (2016): 94–115.

Tobin, Thomas H. *Paul's Rhetoric in Its Contexts*. Peabody, MA: Hendrickson, 2004.

———. "Philo and the Sibyl: Interpreting Philo's Eschatology." *Studia Philonica Annual* 9 (1997): 84–103.

Todd, S. C. *A Commentary on Lysias, Speeches 1–11*. Oxford: Oxford University Press, 2007.

Tomson, Peter J. "'Die Täter des Gesetzes werden gerechtfertigt werden' (Röm 2,13)—um eine adäquate Perspektive auf den Römerbrief." Pages 183–222 in *Lutherische und neue Paulusperspektive: Beiträge zu einem Schlüsselproblem der gegenwärtigen exegetischen Diskussion*. Edited by Michael Bachmann. WUNT 182. Tübingen: Mohr Siebeck, 2005.

"The Names Israel and Jew in Ancient Judaism and in the New Testament." *Bijdragen: Tijdschrift voor filosophie en theologie* 47 (1986): 120–40, 266.

Trebilco, Paul. "Why Did the Early Christians Call Themselves ἡ ἐκκλησία?" *New Testament Studies* 57.3 (2011): 440–60.

Tyrrell, George. *Christianity at the Cross-roads*. London: Longsmans Green & Co., 1909. Repr., 1963.

Ulrich, Dean R. "How Early Judaism Read Daniel 9:24–27." *Old Testament Essays* 27.3 (2014): 1062–83.

Unnik, Willem Cornelis van. "La conception paulinienne de la Nouvelle Alliance." Pages 174–93 in *Sparsa Collecta: The Collected Essays of W. C. van Unnik: Part One: Evangelia, Paulina, Acta*. Leiden: Brill, 1973.

Unterman, Jeremiah. *From Repentance to Redemption: Jeremiah's Thought in Transition*. JSOTSup 54. London: Continuum, 1987.

Urbach, Ephraim E. "Redemption and Repentance in Talmudic Judaism." Pages 190–206 in *Types of Redemption: Contributions to the Theme of the Study-Conference Held at Jerusalem 14th to 19th July 1968*. Edited by R. J. Zwi Werblowsky, and Jouco Bleeker. Studies in the History of Religion, Supplements to Numen. Leiden: Brill, 1970.

Van Kooten, George H. "'Ἐκκλησία τοῦ θεοῦ: The 'Church of God'and the Civic Assemblies (ἐκκλησίαι) of the Greek Cities in the Roman Empire: A Response to Paul Trebilco and Richard A. Horsley." *New Testament Studies* 58.4 (2012): 522–48.

VanderKam, James C. "Exile in Jewish Apocalyptic Literature." Pages 89–109 in *Exile: Old Testament, Jewish, and Christian Conceptions*. Edited by James M. Scott. JSJSup 56. Leiden: Brill, 1997.

"Recent Scholarship on the Book of Jubilees." *Currents in Biblical Research* 6.3 (2008): 405–31.

The Book of Jubilees: A Translation. CSCO 511. Leuven: Peeters, 1989.

VanLandingham, Chris. *Judgment & Justification in Early Judaism and the Apostle Paul*. Peabody, MA: Hendrickson, 2006.

Villiers, J. L. De. "The Salvation of Israel according to Romans 9–11." *Neotestamentica* 15 (1981): 199–221.

Vischer, Wilhelm. "Das Geheimnis Israels. Eine Erklärung der Kapitel 9–11 des Römerbriefs." *Judaica: Beiträge zum Verständnis des jüdischen Schicksals in Vergangenheit und Gegenwart* 6 (1950): 81–132.

Vleminck, Serge. "La valeur de ἀτιμία dans le droit grec ancien." *Les études classiques* 49 (1981): 251–65.

Vos, J. S. "Antijudaismus/Antisemitismus im Theologischen Wörterbuch zum Neuen Testament." *Nederlands theologisch tijdschrift* 38 (1984): 89–110.

Wackernagel, Jakob. "Über ein Gesetz der indogermanischen Wortstellung." *Indogermanische Forschungen* 1.1 (1892): 333–436.

Wagner, J. Ross. *Heralds of the Good News: Isaiah and Paul in Concert in the Letter to the Romans*. Leiden: Brill, 2003.

———. "'Not from the Jews Only, But Also from the Gentiles': Mercy to the Nations in Romans 9–11." Pages 417–32 in *Between Gospel and Election: Explorations in the Interpretation of Romans 9–11*. Edited by Florian Wilk, J. Ross Wagner, and Frank Schleritt. WUNT 257. Tübingen: Mohr Siebeck, 2010.

———. "'Who Has Believed Our Message?': Paul and Isaiah 'In Concert' in the Letter to the Romans." PhD diss., Duke University, 1999.

Wakefield, Andrew H. *Where to Live: The Hermeneutical Significance of Paul's Citations from Scripture in Galatians 3:1–14*. AcBib 14. Leiden: Brill, 2003.

Wallace, Daniel B. *Greek Grammar beyond the Basics: An Exegetical Syntax of the New Testament with Scripture, Subject, and Greek Word Indexes*. Grand Rapids: Zondervan, 1996.

Ward, Richard F. "Pauline Voice and Presence as Strategic Communication." Pages 95–107 in *Orality and Textuality in Early Christian Literature*. Semeia 65. Atlanta: Scholars Press, 1994.

Wasserman, Emma. *Apocalypse as Holy War: Divine Politics and Polemics in the Letters of Paul*. New Haven: Yale University Press, 2018.

———. "Beyond Apocalyptic Dualism: Ranks of Divinities in 1 Enoch and Daniel." Pages 189–99 in *"The One Who Sows Bountifully": Essays in Honor of Stanley K. Stowers*. Edited by Caroline Johnson Hodge, Saul M. Olyan, Daniel Ullucci, and Emma Wasserman. BJS 356. Providence, RI: Brown Judaic Studies, 2014.

———. "The Death of the Soul in Romans 7: Revisiting Paul's Anthropology in Light of Hellenistic Moral Psychology." *Journal of Biblical Literature* 126.4 (2007): 793–816.

———. *The Death of the Soul in Romans 7: Sin, Death, and the Law in Light of Hellenistic Moral Psychology*. WUNT 256. Tübingen: Mohr Siebeck, 2008.

Waters, Guy Prentiss. *The End of Deuteronomy in the Epistles of Paul*. WUNT 221. Tübingen: Mohr Siebeck, 2006.

Watson, Francis. *Paul and the Hermeneutics of Faith*. London: T&T Clark, 2004.

———. *Paul, Judaism, and the Gentiles: Beyond the New Perspective*. Rev. and exp. ed. Grand Rapids: Eerdmans, 2007.

Watts, John D. W. *Isaiah 1–33*. WBC 24. Grand Rapids: Zondervan, 2005.

Watts, Rikki E. "'For I Am Not Ashamed of the Gospel': Romans 1:16–17 and Habakkuk 2:4." Pages 3–25 in *Romans and the People of God: Essays in Honor of Gordon D. Fee on the Occasion of His 65th Birthday*. Edited by Sven K. Soderlund and N. T. Wright. Grand Rapids: Eerdmans, 1999.

Wehr, Lothar. "'Nahe ist dir das Wort' – die paulinische Schriftinterpretation vor dem Hintergrund frühjüdischer Parallelen am Beispiel von Röm 10,5–10." Pages 192–206 in *Unterwegs mit Paulus: Otto Kuss zum 100. Geburtstag*. Edited by J. Hainz. Regensburg: Pustet, 2006.

Weippert, Helga. "Deine Kinder seien wie die Schößlinge von Ölbäumen rund um deinen Tisch!: Zur Bildsprache in Psalm 128, 3." Pages 163–74 in *Prophetie und Psalmen: Festschrift für Klaus Seybold zum 65. Geburtstag*. Edited by

Hans-Peter Mathys and Beat Weber. AOAT 280. Münster: Ugarit-Verlag, 2001.
Weitzman, Steven. *Song and Story in Biblical Narrative: The History of a Literary Convention in Ancient Israel*. Bloomington: Indiana University Press, 1997.
Wells, Kyle B. *Grace and Agency in Paul and Second Temple Judaism: Interpreting the Transformation of the Heart*. Leiden: Brill, 2014.
"The Vindication of Agents, Divine and Human: Paul's Reading of Deuteronomy 30:1–14 in Romans." Pages 70–97 in *"What Does the Scripture Say": Studies in the Function of Scripture in Early Judaism and Christianity: Volume 2: The Letters and Liturgical Traditions*. Edited by Craig A. Evans and H. Daniel Zacharias. LNTS 470. London: Bloomsbury, 2012.
Wenham, Gordon J. *Genesis 16–50*. WBC 2. Grand Rapids: Zondervan, 1994.
Wenz, Gunther. "Old Perspectives on Paul: Forschungsgeschichtliche Epilegomena zum Paulusjahr." *Kerygma and Dogma* 56.2 (2010): 121–64.
Westerholm, Stephen. *Justification Reconsidered: Rethinking A Pauline Theme*. Grand Rapids: Eerdmans, 2013.
"Law, Grace and the 'Soteriology' of Judaism." Pages 57–74 in *Law in Religious Communities in the Roman Period*. Edited by Peter Richardson and Stephen Westerholm. Waterloo, ON: Wilfrid Laurier University Press, 1991.
"The Righteousness of the Law and the Righteousness of Faith in Romans." *Interpretation* 58.3 (2004): 253–64.
"Torah, Nomos and Law." Pages 44–56 in *Law in Religious Communities in the Roman Period*. Edited by Peter Richardson and Stephen Westerholm. Waterloo, ON: Wilfrid Laurier University Press, 1991.
"Whence 'The Torah' of Second Temple Judaism." Pages 19–43 in *Law in Religious Communities in the Roman Period*. Edited by Peter Richardson and Stephen Westerholm. Waterloo, ON: Wilfrid Laurier University Press, 1991.
White, Ellen. *Yahweh's Council: Its Structure and Membership*. FAT 65. Tübingen: Mohr Siebeck, 2014.
Whitlark, Jason. "Enabling χάρις: Transformation of the Convention of Reciprocity by Philo and in Ephesians." *Perspectives in Religious Studies* 30.3 (2003): 325–58.
Wilckens, Ulrich. *Der Brief an der Römer*. EKKNT VI/1. Neukirchen-Vluyn: Neukirchener, 1980.
Wilcox, Max. "The Promise of the 'Seed' in the New Testament and the Targumim." *Journal for the Study of the New Testament* 2.5 (1979): 2–20.
Wilk, Florian. *Die Bedeutung des Jesajabuches für Paulus*. FRLANT 179. Göttingen: Vandenhoeck & Ruprecht, 1998.
"Paulus als Nutzer, Interpret und Leser des Jesajabuches." Pages 93–116 in *Die Bibel im Dialog der Schriften: Konzepte intertextueller Bibellektüre*. Edited by Stefan Alkier and Richard B. Hays. NET 10. Tübingen: Franke, 2005.
Williams, Jarvis J. *Galatians*. NCCS. Eugene: Wipf & Stock, 2020.
Willitts, Joel. "Context Matters: Paul's Use of Leviticus 18:5 in Galatians 3:12." *Tyndale Bulletin* 54.2 (2003): 105–22.

Matthew's Messianic Shepherd-King: In Search of "the Lost Sheep of the House of Israel." BZNW. Berlin: de Gruyter, 2007.
"Matthew's Messianic Shepherd-King: In Search of 'the Lost Sheep of the House of Israel'." HTS Theological Studies/Teologiese Studies 63.1 (2008): 365–82.
Wills, Lawrence M. "Jew, Judean, Judaism in the Ancient Period: An Alternative Argument." Journal of Ancient Judaism 7.2 (2016): 169–93.
Windisch, Hans. "Das Problem des paulinischen imperativs." Zeitschrift für die neutestamentliche Wissenschaft und die Kunde der älteren Kirche 23 (1924): 265–81.
Windsor, Lionel J. "The Named Jew and the Name of God: The Argument of Romans 2:17–29 in Light of Roman Attitudes to Jewish Teachers." Novum Testamentum 63.2 (2021): 229–48.
Paul and the Vocation of Israel: How Paul's Jewish Identity Informs His Apostolic Ministry, with Special Reference to Romans. BZNW 205. Berlin: de Gruyter, 2014.
Winkle, Ross E. "Another Look at the List of Tribes in Revelation 7." Andrews University Seminary Studies 27.1 (1989): 53–67.
Winston, David. "Philo's Ethical Theory." Aufstieg und Niedergang der römischen Welt 21.1:372–416.
Wisdom, Jeffrey. Blessing for the Nations and the Curse of the Law: Paul's Citation of Genesis and Deuteronomy in Gal 3.8–10. WUNT 133. Tübingen: Mohr Siebeck, 2001.
Witherington III, Ben, and Darlene Hyatt. Paul's Letter to the Romans: A Socio-Rhetorical Commentary. Grand Rapids: Eerdmans, 2004.
Wold, Benjamin G. "Revelation's Plague Septets: New Exodus and Exile." Pages 279–98 in Echoes from the Caves: Qumran and the New Testament. Edited by Florentino García Martínez. STDJ 85. Leiden: Brill, 2009.
Wolff, Christian. Jeremia im Frühjudentum und Urchristentum. TU 118. Berlin: Akademie, 1976.
Wolff, Hans Walter. Hosea: A Commentary on the Book of the Prophet Hosea. Translated by Gary Stansell. Hermeneia. Philadelphia: Fortress, 1974.
Wolosky, Shira. "Well-Spotted: Plots and Reversals." Pages 51–74 in The Riddles of Harry Potter: Secret Passages and Interpretive Quests. New York: Palgrave Macmillan, 2010.
Wolter, Michael. "Ein exegetischer und theologischer Blick auf Röm 11.25–32." New Testament Studies 64.2 (2018): 123–42.
Wood, Thomas Richard. "The Regathering of the People of God: An Investigation into the New Testament's Appropriation of the Old Testament Prophecies Concerning the Regathering of Israel." PhD diss., Trinity Evangelical Divinity School, 2006.
Wright, Benjamin G. III. "Jubilees, Sirach and Sapiential Tradition." Pages 116–30 in Enoch and the Mosaic Mosaic Torah: The Evidence of the Book of Jubilees. Edited by Gabriele Boccaccini and Giovanni Ibba. Grand Rapids: Eerdmans, 2009.
Wright, N. T. The Climax of the Covenant. Minneapolis: Fortress, 1993.
"In Grateful Dialogue: A Response." Pages 244–77 in Jesus & the Restoration of Israel: A Critical Assessment of N.T. Wright's Jesus and the Victory

of God. Edited by Carey C. Newman. Downers Grove, IL: InterVarsity, 1999.
Jesus and the Victory of God. Christian Origins and the Question of God. Minneapolis: Fortress, 1996.
"The Law in Romans 2." Pages 131–50 in *Paul and the Mosaic Law.* Edited by J. D. G. Dunn. WUNT 89. Tübingen: Mohr, 1996.
"The Letter to the Romans: Introduction, Commentary, and Reflection." Pages 393–770 in *The New Interpreter's Bible.* Vol. 10. Nashville: Abingdon, 2002.
"The Lord's Prayer as a Paradigm of Christian Prayer." Pages 132–54 in *Into God's Presence: Prayer in the New Testament.* Edited by Richard N. Longenecker. McMaster New Testament Studies. Grand Rapids: Eerdmans, 2001.
"The Messiah and the People of God: A Study in Pauline Theology with Particular Reference to the Argument of the Epistle to the Romans." DPhil diss., University of Oxford, 1980.
The New Testament and the People of God. Minneapolis: Fortress, 1992.
"Paul and Empire." Pages 285–97 in *The Blackwell Companion to Paul.* Edited by Stephen Westerholm. London: Blackwell, 2011.
Paul and His Recent Interpreters: Some Contemporary Debates. Minneapolis: Fortress, 2015.
Paul and the Faithfulness of God. Minneapolis: Fortress, 2013.
"Paul in Current Anglophone Scholarship." *Expository Times* 123.8 (2012): 367–81.
"Romans 9–11 and the 'New Perspective.'" Pages 37–54 in *Between Gospel and Election: Explorations in the Interpretation of Romans 9–11.* Edited by Florian Wilk, J. Ross Wagner, and Frank Schleritt. WUNT 257. Tübingen: Mohr Siebeck, 2010.
Wu, Jackson [Brad Vaughn]. "Why Is God Justified in Romans?: Vindicating Paul's Use of Psalm 51 in Romans 3:4." *Neotestamentica* 51.2 (2017): 291–314.
Wuellner, Wilhelm H. *The Meaning of "Fishers of Men".* Philadelphia: Westminster, 1967.
Young, Stephen L. "Romans 1.1–5 and Paul's Christological Use of Hab. 2.4 in Rom. 1.17: An Underutilized Consideration in the Debate." *Journal for the Study of the New Testament* 34.3 (2012): 277–85.
Zahn, Molly M. "New Voices, Ancient Words: The Temple Scroll's Reuse of the Bible." Pages 435–58 in *Temple and Worship in Biblical Israel.* Edited by John Day. New York: T&T Clark, 2006.
Zahn, Molly M., and Bernard M. Levinson. "Revelation Regained: The Hermeneutics of כי and אם in the Temple Scroll." *Dead Sea Discoveries* 9.3 (2002): 295–346.
Zahn, Theodor. *Der Brief des Paulus an die Römer.* Kommentar zum Neuen Testament 6. Leipzig: Deichert, 1910.
Zangenberg, Jürgen. *Frühes Christentum in Samarien: topographische und traditionsgeschichtliche Studien zu den Samarientexten im Johannesevangelium.* TANZ. Tübingen: Francke, 1998.

Zeigan, Holger. "Die Wurzel des Ölbaums (Röm 11,1): Eine alternative Perspektive." *Protokolle zur Bibel* 15 (2006): 119–32.
Zeitlin, Solomon. "The Names Hebrew, Jew and Israel: A Historical Study." *Jewish Quarterly Review* 43.4 (1953): 365–79.
Zeller, Dieter. *Der Brief an die Römer*. RNT. Regensburg: Pustet, 1985.
— *Juden und Heiden in der Mission des Paulus: Studien zum Römerbrief*. FB 8. Frankfurt am Main: Echter, 1973.
Zetterholm, Karin Hedner. "The Question of Assumptions: Torah Observance in the First Century." Pages 79–104 in *Paul within Judaism: Restoring the First-Century Context to the Apostle*. Edited by Mark D. Nanos and Magnus Zetterholm. Minneapolis: Augsburg Fortress, 2015.
Zetterholm, Magnus. *Approaches to Paul: A Student's Guide to Recent Scholarship*. Minneapolis: Fortress, 2009.
— "Paul within Judaism: The State of the Questions." Pages 31–52 in *Paul within Judaism: Restoring the First-Century Context to the Apostle*. Edited by Mark D. Nanos and Magnus Zetterholm. Minneapolis: Augsburg Fortress, 2015.
Ziesler, John A. *Paul's Letter to the Romans*. Philadelphia: Trinity Press International, 1989.
Zimmerli, Walther. *Ezekiel II: A Commentary on the Book of the Prophet Ezekiel, Chapters 25–48*. Hermeneia 26B. Philadelphia: Fortress, 1979.
Zoccali, Christopher. "'And So All Israel Will Be Saved': Competing Interpretations of Romans 11.26 in Pauline Scholarship." *Journal for the Study of the New Testament* 30.3 (2008): 289–318.
— "What's the Problem with the Law? Jews, Gentiles, and Covenant Identity in Galatians 3:10–12." *Neotestamentica* 49.2 (2015): 377–415.
— *Whom God Has Called: The Relationship of Church and Israel in Pauline Interpretation, 1920 to the Present*. Eugene: Pickwick, 2010.

Primary Sources Index

Bible
Genesis
1:20–25 123
2:2–3 37
2:17 99
2–3 329
3:22–24 99
4:12–15 99
10 314
15 340
15:6 340
15:13 340
16 340
16:4 309
17 164, 340
17:4 308, 310, 317
17:10–11 340
17:14 256
22 219
22:18 310
25:21–23 308
26:4 310
27:28 309
27:42–45 219
28:3 310
30:30 309
32:12 309
33:3 219
35:11 310
36:7 309
37:18–35 219
41:45–32 314
45:7 207
48:4 310
48:14–20 219
48:16 309
48:19 307–10, 312, 318, 342
49:6 209
49:10 311
Exodus
1:9 309
2:24 118
4:16 94
4:21 210
7:3 210
7:22 210
12:19 164
12:38 35
12:48 164
15:7 309
19:5–6 92
19:17–20:18 92
19:21 93, 309
20:2 92
20:5–6 137
20:19 92, 257
23:2 309
32:1–10 93
32:8 168
32:9 93
32:10 191
32:30–32 188
32:35 188
33:3 93
33:5 93
33:19 191
33–34 229
34:6–7 137, 198

Bible (cont.)
    34:9 93
    34:10 94
    34:28 94
    34:29–35 78, 94, 95
    34:33–35 91
  Leviticus
    7:20–21 292
    7:25 292
    7:27 292
    17:4 292
    17:9 292
    17:14 292
    18:3 337
    18:5 88, 225, 226, 243–47, 252, 253, 254, 258–64
    18:21 228
    18:24 228
    18:29 292
    19:18 114
    19:19 296
    19:8 292
    20:10–20 258
    20:17–18 292
    20:5 292
    22:3 292
    23:29 292
    26:18 228
    26:28 228
    26:40–42 228, 229
    27:32 263
  Numbers
    4:20 93
    5:12 168
    5:19 168
    5:29 168
    9:13 292
    11:29 97
    15:18–20 288
    15:30–31 292
    16:5 170
    18:22 93
    19:13 292
    19:20 292
    21:9 124
    24:13 232
    35:27 99
  Deuteronomy
    4:15–20 124, 128
    4:16–18 123
    4:19 326
    4:25–31 80
    4:27–28 76, 292
    4:29 228, 230
    4:29–31 83, 90, 96
    4:34 337
    5:28–29 93
    6:4 144, 270
    6:5 114
    6:6 80
    7:16 98, 99
    8:17 238
    8:20 98
    9:4 128, 190, 238
    9:6 190, 238
    9:8 190, 191
    9:12 168
    9:16 168
    9:18–19 188, 190
    9:20–29 190
    9:24 128
    9:25–29 188
    9:27 128, 145
    10:16 82, 145
    10:21 122
    18:15 246
    18:15–22 243, 335
    18:19 186
    19:14 328
    23 32
    23:2 [1 ET] 334
    23:4 [3 ET] 32, 209, 312
    23:9 [8 ET] 32, 312
    23:3–8 [4–9 ET] 35
    26:12–14 159
    27:15–26 257
    27:26 255
    28:58–59 255
    28:64 255, 328
    28–29 98, 121, 171
    29:2–4 [3–5 ET] 93
    29:3 [4 ET] 85, 241, 274
    29:18 [19 ET] 160
    29:21 [22 ET] 98
    29:22 [23 ET] 241
    29:22–28 [23–29 ET] 98
    29:26–27 [27–28 ET] 284
    29:27 [28 ET] 60, 275
    29:28 [29 ET] 118, 168, 169, 275, 285, 302
    29–30 80, 90, 168, 170
    29–32 78, 87, 102, 171
    30 88, 121, 171, 226, 242
    30:1 85

30:1–5 90
30:1–10 238, 240, 242
30:1–14 86, 239, 240, 243, 256, 264, 285
30:3–4 65, 83
30:3–5 109
30:4–7 92
30:6 82, 83, 86, 89, 146, 170, 176, 241, 320, 333
30:9–14 239
30:10 89, 125, 163, 176, 240
30:11 88, 239, 241
30:11–14 168, 226, 238–43, 266
30:12 239, 242
30:12–14 118, 222, 236, 238, 241, 242, 243, 244
30:13 240
30:14 241, 242
30:15 88, 218
30:15–20 88, 258
30:16 89, 114, 125, 163, 176
30:17–20 59
30:18–19 98
30:19 88, 97, 125
31:16 85
31:16–22 85
31:16–27 241
31:20–21 88, 340
31:26 86, 134
31:27 91
31:29 91
31:30 334
32 53, 279
32:8 328
32:8–9 326
32:21 49, 206, 278–81, 282, 283
32:23 280
32:26–43 328
32:36 280
32:39 59, 280
32:43 162, 280, 281
34:7 246
34:10 246, 264
Joshua 209
5:5 341
5:5–8 341
6:25 292
7 159
7:22–26 292
Judges
4:7 309
19 130

1 Samuel
12:20–23 271
12:22 275
2 Samuel
7:14 83
18:29 309
23:24–39 35
1 Kings
8:14 334
9:7 292
11:12 205
14:10 292
14:14 292
19 282
21:21 292
2 Kings
9:8 292
10:32 292
16:6 47
17 124, 280
17:13–23 44
17:15 76, 99, 124, 127, 128, 131
17:24 50
17:24–41 48
18:4 124
18:10 124
1 Chronicles
4:18 47
16:32 309
16:35 205
2 Chronicles
22:7 292
29:37 124
30:2 124
30:6–9 229
30:8 124
36:20 292
Ezra
1:5 56
4:1–2 48, 57
4:3 48
4:10 48
6:14 56, 57
6:16–20 57
6:17 56
6:22 57
8:35 57
9:4 57
9:8 56
9:9 57
9:13–14 57, 229

Bible (cont.)
  Nehemiah
    1:3 57
    1:9 229
    9:29 262
    13:4–31 58
    13:17–18 57
    13:18 229
    13:23–20 57
    13:23–29 57, 229
  Esther
    4:17 188
  Job
    9:12 192
    9:19 192
    33:10 192
    33:13 192
  Psalms (MT refs)
    2:2 328
    2:7–8 329
    3:3 122
    14:7 319, 320
    16:10 250
    16:11 250
    18:13 275
    18:43 256
    18:50 [49 ET] 162
    2:7–10 192
    21:5 [21:4 ET] 264
    37:9 292
    37:22 292
    37:28 292
    37:34 292
    37:38 292
    50:2 319
    51 80, 81, 86
    51:4 86
    51:10–11 83
    53:7 319, 320
    62:12 138, 143
    68:11 63
    75:2 118
    81:13 263
    82:1–2 328, 329
    82:5 330
    82:6–7 263
    82:7–8 329
    82:8 329
    83:4 328
    89:12 309
    94:14 271
    95:11 309
    97:7 309
    101:6–8 292
    106:20 93, 121, 122, 129, 146
    107:2–3 65
    107:26 241
    110:1 329
    110:2 319
    116:1 162
    119:11 241
    128:3 295
    128:5 319
    134:3 319
    135:21 319
    20:2 319
    23:1 309
    31:12 192, 210
    37:31 241
  Proverbs
    2:21–22 292
    3:7 302
    22:28 328
  Ecclesiastes
    4:6 309
  Song of Songs
    2:2 337
  Isaiah
    1:8–9 207
    1:9 207, 216
    2:3 319
    5:1–2 295
    5:20–21 126
    8 217
    8:1–22 217
    8:5 192
    8:13 216, 217
    8:13–14 216
    8:14 216, 217
    9:2 [9:1 LXX] 60
    9:19–29 204
    10:5 192, 204
    10:5–19 328
    10:12 210
    10:13 209
    10:22 189
    10:22–23 206, 216
    10:5–11:16 328
    11:10 162, 244
    11:12 65
    11:13 281
    13:5 195
    25:6–9 65
    27:11 292

27:13 65
28:1–22 217
28:16 216, 217
28–29 217
29:10 85, 274
29:16 193
30:10 212
40:2 122
40:9 63
40:10–11 64
42:6 26, 105, 162
43:5 65
43:6 83
43:25–26 176
45:9 193, 207
45:25 176
48:11 328
48:18–19 292
49:1–6 109
49:5 109
49:6 110, 162, 319
49:22 306
49:24–50:2 100
50:8 176
51:4 162
51:5 212
51:7 241
52:5 160, 161, 163
52:7 63
52:13–53:12 54
53:3 209
53:8 54
53:11 176
54:7 65
58:13–14 235
59:20 131, 303, 319, 320
59:21 110
60:3 162
60:4 65, 306
60:5 310
60:9 306
60:21 78
61:1 63, 293
62:2 122
64:8 192
65:2 269, 271
66:20 306, 324
Jeremiah (MT refs)
1:5 26, 74
1:10 74
2:5 124
2:11–13 122, 129

2:21 295
3 282
3:8 76, 108, 281, 286
3:11–12 108, 281, 317
3:12 60
3:14 108
4:4 82
5:20–29 93
6:2 292
6:14–21 57
7 150
7:8 158
7:9–11 159
7:25 93
8:16 309
9 150
9:15 27
9:23–24 [22–23 ET] 298
9:24–25 [25–26 ET] 137, 169
11 132
11:1–14 93
11:16–17 290, 311
12:14–15 275, 284
16:14–18 65, 108
16:18 122
18:1–11 192, 193, 197, 210
18:6 198
19 210
22:28 203, 205, 210, 275, 283, 284, 311
23:3 65
23:7–8 65
25:1 45, 54
25:11–12 45, 54
29:10–14 109, 232
29:14 65
29–31 80, 83
30:3 108
31 68, 78, 81, 90, 281
31:7–8 299
31:8 65
31:9 83
31:10 65
31:15 108
31:27 107
31:28 74
31:31 81, 108
31:31–34 75–78, 80, 81, 83, 111, 232
31:32 76
31:33 77, 80, 82, 146, 147, 241
31:34 265
31–32 74, 79
32:12 47

Bible (cont.)
   32:37 65
   32:39 79
   34:9 47
   38:19 47
   40:11–12 47
   40:15 47
   41:3 47
   41:21 328
   44:1 47
   44:7–12 292
   47:2 309
   48:38 205
   50:25 192, 195, 200
   51:7 292
   51:20 204
   52:28 47
   52:30 47
Lamentations
   5:7 135
Ezekiel
   5:6 128, 163
   8:10 124
   9:7 262
   11:17 65, 109, 205
   11:19 78
   12:15 27
   12:19 309
   14:9 262
   19:7 309
   20:1–31 93
   20:9–44 328
   20:11–21 170
   20:21–27 262
   20:34 109
   20:35 263
   20:37–44 263
   20:38 270
   20:39 262
   28:25 205, 324
   30:12 309
   34:10–23 64
   34:13 205, 324
   34:23 64
   36 68, 80, 81, 263
   36:16–27 161
   36:20–23 27, 161
   36:22 190, 328
   36:22–28 161
   36:23 64
   36:24 205, 324
   36:26 78, 83, 146
   36:27 78, 83, 263
   36:32 190
   37 59, 100, 312, 319
   37:1–14 59, 263, 316
   37:2 285
   37:3 100
   37:5 285
   37:11 99, 285, 312, 316, 330
   37:1–4 99
   37:14 101, 109, 312
   37:15–24 100, 109, 311
   37:16 311
   37:19 312
   37:24 64, 263
   38:8 205, 324
   39:7 64
   39:25 64
   39:27 205, 324
Daniel
   4:35 192
   7:13 237, 269
   7:14 256
   8:19 55, 62
   9 228
   9:24–27 229
   9:25–26 54
   10:10–21 329
   10:13 327
   10:20 327
   11:22 54
   11:36 55, 62
   12:1–3 329
   12:6–7 235
Hosea
   1:9 76, 127, 189, 202, 204, 205, 282
   1:9–2:1 [1:10 ET] 206, 209, 220, 281, 342
   1–3 208
   2:1 [1:10 ET; 2:1] 347
   2:1 [1:10 ET] 202, 279, 324
   2:17 [15 ET] 186
   2:25 [23 ET] 77, 100, 202, 204, 207, 208, 216, 279, 281, 282, 324, 342, 347
   4:6–7 127
   4:17 308
   5:3 308
   5:5 308
   5:7 205
   5:11 308
   6:1 96
   6:2 99
   6:5 99, 119
   6:10 308
   7:1 308

7:8 205, 308
8:1–4 292
8:8 27, 59, 98, 99, 192, 203, 205, 210,
    283, 286, 311, 330
8:11 308
9:15 275
10:1–15 292
10:10 122
13:1 99, 330
13:1–6 59
13:14 330
13:15 192
14:7 290
Joel
  3:1–4 (2:28–32 ET) 149
  3:5 [2:32 ET] 63, 147
  4:16 [3:16 ET] 319
Amos
  1:2 319
  3:2 117
  5:26–27 80
  9:14 209
Micah
  4:2 319
  6:8 137, 333
Nahum
  2:1 [1:15 ET] 63, 292
  2:2 [2:1 ET] 292
Habakkuk
  1:13 249
  2:2 250
  2:3–4 248, 249, 250
  2:4 149, 248, 249, 251, 252, 253, 254,
      257, 258–64
Zephaniah
  1:4–6 292
Zechariah
  1:8–11 328
  1:15 328
  2:6 LXX [MT 2:10] 65
  4:3 290
  4:11–14 290
  9:7 237, 269
  10:9 204
  12:7 69
Malachi
  1:6–14 159
  2:2 124, 159
  2:7 124, 159
  2:8–9 159
  2:10–12 159
  2:10–16 159
  2:17 126, 159

3:8–10 159
3:8–12 159
3:13–23 [ET 3:13–4:3] 159
3:18–21 [ET 3:18–4:3] 292
3:23–24 [ET 4:5–6] 229
Matthew
  3:8–10 186, 269, 292
  3:12 65
  3:24–26 247
  4:19 65
  5:17–20 18
  6:5–6 170
  6:9–13 64
  7:19 292
  8:11–12 65
  10:1–4 63
  10:5 323
  10:6 64
  12:30 65
  12:39–41 241
  13:24–30 65
  13:41–42 65
  13:43 92
  15:24 64
  16:4 241
  17:2 92
  17:26 332
  18:17 167
  19:16–17 243
  19:27–30 64
  21:13 159
  22:9–10 65
  23 138
  23:13 315
  23:37–39 234
  24:31 65
  25:32 65
  25:32–46 138
  28:19 314
Mark
  1:4 227
  1:4–8 234
  1:17 65
  1:19 196
  3:13–19 63
  4:8 195
  4:29 65
  5:42 246
  8:31 246
  9:9–10 246
  9:31 246
  9:47 315
  10:34 246

Bible (cont.)
 11:17 159
 12:23–25 246
 13:2 268
 13:10 314
 13:27 65
Luke
 1:6 125
 3:7–9 186, 269, 292
 3:17 65
 4:21 145
 5:10 65
 6:12–16 63
 6:40 196
 7:19 250
 8:3 184
 9:52 64
 10:33 64
 11:2–4 64
 11:23 65
 11:29–32 241
 12:8 265
 12:47–48 138
 13:29 65
 14:21–23 65
 15:24 99
 17:16 64
 17:18 287
 19:46 159
 22:20 75
 22:28–30 64
 24:10 184
 24:46 246
 24:47 314
John
 1:31 67
 4:1–42 64
 4:9 42
 5:45 86
 6:39–40 246
 6:44 246
 6:54 246
 8:48 64
 10:11–14 64
 10:14–16 311
 10:34–35 263
 11:23–24 246
 11:51–52 311
 12:24 195
 15:2 195
 15:4–10 292
 15:5 291
 20:9 246
Acts
 1:6 67, 268
 2:5 314
 2:17–21 149
 2:22 66
 2:24 246, 250, 261
 2:32 246
 2:27 250
 2:38–39 149
 3:12 66
 3:14–15 249
 3:19–20 234
 3:22–26 246
 3:23 186
 4:2 246
 4:27 67
 5:31 242, 250
 5:35 66
 7:37 246
 7:51–53 249
 8:1 276
 9:15 67, 200
 9:18 283
 9:20 25
 10:35 314
 11:18 244
 13:5 25
 13:14 25
 13:16 66
 13:23 67
 13:33–34 246
 13:43 25
 13:44–48 276
 13:46–47 26
 14:1 25
 15:9 86
 15:14 205
 17:1 25
 17:3 246
 17:17 25
 17:10 25
 17:10–12 276
 17:31 246, 250
 18:4 25
 18:4–7 276
 18:19 25
 19:8 25
 19:8–10 276
 21:28 66
 22:14 249
 23:6 106

24:14 265
26:6–7 106
26:17 205
28:20 67
28:23–29 276
Romans
1:1–2 111
1:2 247, 251
1:2–5 112
1:2–5 242
1:4 82, 106, 247, 251, 252, 337, 342
1:5 26, 27, 96, 111, 251, 259, 333
1:5–6 21
1:7 21
10:9–10 141
1:11–12 26
1:11–15 26
1:15 302
1:16 6, 27, 112, 142, 222, 305
1:16–17 112, 252
1:17 251
1:18 114, 123, 130, 131, 332
1:18–2:11 159, 286
1:18–2:29 107, 112, 113, 116
1:18–32 112, 114–32, 143, 148, 262, 320
1:19 117, 119
1:20 119, 148
1:21 44, 117, 124, 125, 148
1:23 121, 124, 146, 191
1:24 127, 131
1:24–27 130
1:25 117, 125
1:26 127, 131
1:28 117, 127, 131, 148, 290
1:32 114, 117, 125, 126, 159
1–2 147, 171, 219, 282
2:1 115, 132, 142, 152, 153
2:1–10 139
2:1–16 116, 143
2:2 137, 139, 142
2:2–11 12, 90
2:4 121, 140, 168, 196, 197, 203, 289
2:5 127, 132, 140, 145, 168, 190
2:6 138, 179
2:6–11 3, 121
2:6–16 141
2:7 132, 142, 174
2:9–10 27, 112, 130, 142, 143, 282
2:10 132, 142
2:11 159, 166, 282, 299
2:12 120, 127, 143
2:12–13 112, 299

2:12–14 120
2:13 90, 142, 143, 146, 173
2:14 113, 120, 130, 142, 148, 149, 163, 173, 215, 262, 290
2:14–15 9, 146, 168, 171, 172, 173, 215, 311
2:14–16 146, 147, 150, 153, 177, 217
2:14–29 112
2:15 85, 126, 148, 177, 215, 332
2:16 107, 132, 143, 150, 170
2:17 22, 23, 24, 150, 152, 167
2:17–20 157
2:17–25 150, 161
2:17–29 152, 161, 162
2:18–20 150, 154, 321
2:19 162
2:21–23 154–62
2:21–25 142
2:21–27 150
2:22 156
2:22–25 90
2:23 158
2:24 158, 160, 161
2:25 163, 167, 170, 173, 176
2:25–29 90, 113, 163, 172, 338
2:26 125, 126, 163, 171, 172, 173, 176, 297, 338
2:26–27 146, 172, 257
2:27 164, 171, 172, 290
2:27–29 85, 225
2:28 165
2:28–29 12, 165–73, 257, 284, 311
2:29 18, 82, 85, 176
3:1–9 282
3:2 166
3:3 166, 187
3:3–5 142
3:5 86, 139
3:9 8, 12, 24, 114, 127, 139, 142, 166, 180, 256, 286
3:10 258
3:12 140, 203, 289
3:19–20 87, 127
3:19–31 103
3:20 85, 112, 142, 144, 150, 174, 176, 177
3:21 90, 242, 246, 251
3:21–26 251
3:22 12, 166, 246
3:22–23 127
3:23 191
3:24 291

Bible (cont.)
   3:26 272
   3:27 96, 165
   3:28 112, 174
   3:29 38
   3:30 257
   3:31 18, 90, 103, 222, 254
   3–8 180–81
   4:1 70
   4:5–10 127
   4:9–12 340
   4:10–11 165, 310
   4:11 340
   4:15 87, 103, 127, 257
   4:16–18 207
   4:17 248, 310
   4:18 302
   5 277
   5:5 82
   5:6 237
   5:8–10 132
   5:12 191, 302
   5:12–14 119, 165
   5:14 90, 120, 143, 149, 168, 169, 257
   5:15 246, 302
   5:15–21 246, 251
   5:16 125, 149, 171
   5:18 125, 246, 302
   5:19 302
   5:21 302
   6:2 90
   6:2–7 243
   6:3–4 103
   6:4 285, 302
   6:6–8 179
   6:7 244, 262
   6:11 302
   6:14 166
   6:14–15 103
   6:23 291
   7:1 22, 188, 262
   7:4 103, 285
   7:6 85, 103, 165, 225
   7:7 87
   7:7–13 100, 257
   7:8–9 89
   7:10 87, 88, 218, 258
   7:12 87
   7:13 88
   7:14 89, 91
   7:14–25 100
   7:23 100
   7:24 181
   8:1 291
   8:3 89, 102, 159, 287
   8:4 18, 89, 125, 146, 171, 177, 343
   8:4–17 149
   8:6–8 89
   8:9 89
   8:10–11 285
   8:11 82, 252
   8:12 188
   8:14–23 286
   8:15 287, 294
   8:18 272
   8:19 287, 332, 343
   8:23 287, 294
   8:26 332
   8:34 244
   9:1–4 142
   9:1–4 272
   9:3 70, 123, 191
   9:3–4 188
   9:4 111, 123, 188, 286, 294
   9:4–5 12, 188, 191
   9:5 226
   9:6 13, 14, 70, 167, 183, 187, 188, 193, 218, 299, 301
   9:7 309
   9:7–13 219, 339
   9:8 189, 287
   9:9 309
   9:9–12 190
   9:10–13 308
   9:13 309
   9:14 191
   9:14–23 191–201
   9:15–16 191
   9:17 309
   9:17–18 191
   9:18 210, 272, 275
   9:19 192
   9:20 192, 302, 309
   9:20–23 211
   9:21 288
   9:21–26 321
   9:22 127, 193, 194, 195, 199, 210
   9:23 199, 311
   9:23–24 127, 193
   9:24 25, 70, 183, 311, 324
   9:24–26 12, 201–9, 238, 286, 297
   9:25 285, 309

9:25–26 207, 208, 282
9:25–29 204, 301
9:26 9, 100, 208, 287, 311
9:27 13, 189, 298, 299
9:27–28 207, 309, 344
9:29 207, 344
9:30 149, 215, 268, 301
9:30–10:21 222
9:30–31 70
9:30–33 212–19, 222, 272, 298
9:31 13, 245, 273
9:31–33 193
9:32 166, 218, 243
9:33 25, 269, 309
9–11 5, 6, 13, 39, 69, 70, 71, 111, 171, 182, 183, 185, 186, 187, 222, 268, 281, 282, 285, 309, 343
10 29, 320
10:1 69, 188, 221, 252
10:1–4 218, 269
10:1–13 224, 251, 252, 269
10:2 221
10:3 223, 236, 238, 243, 245, 247, 252, 264, 267, 268
10:3–4 221
10:3–9 236
10:4 103, 171, 224, 247, 252, 261, 336
10:5 8, 218, 222, 225, 243–47, 252, 309
10:5–9 245, 253
10:6 128, 223, 298, 302
10:6–7 236
10:6–8 171, 218, 224, 244, 252
10:6–13 222, 244
10:7 156, 240, 242, 309
10:8 265
10:9 221, 226, 244, 251
10:9–13 238, 265, 266
10:11 309
10:12 70, 166, 183
10:13 141, 147, 188
10:15 291, 309
10:16 270
10:19 13, 206, 278, 279, 309
10:20 309
10:21 13, 269, 271
11:1 6, 70, 271, 275, 284, 286, 344
11:2 13, 271, 286, 309
11:3 309
11:5 298, 300, 302
11:6 344

11:7 13, 272, 273, 275, 282, 283, 302, 311
11:8 85, 274
11:8–10 273, 274, 309
11:9 25, 222
11:10 273
11:11 277, 278, 279, 282, 285
11:11–12 22
11:11–15 275, 277, 282, 284, 288
11:11–36 147, 273
11:12 278, 282, 312, 313
11:13 1, 8, 21, 24, 26, 74
11:13–14 22, 26
11:14 189, 211, 279, 283, 285, 301
11:15 101, 275, 278, 280, 283, 286, 312, 318, 319, 325
11:16 193, 288, 289, 293, 294, 295
11:16–24 289–301, 313
11:17–25 167, 189, 220, 311
11:19–23 8
11:22 137, 140, 203, 291, 295
11:23 196, 301
11:25 12, 13, 188, 309, 311, 318
11:25–26 278, 284, 285, 298, 303, 320, 328
11:25–27 111, 301–22
11:26 1, 6, 12, 13, 111, 131, 173, 187, 188, 189, 269, 291, 299, 301
11:27 85, 110, 292
11:28 142
11:28–29 297
11:28–32 320
11:30–32 127, 213
11:31 302
11:33–36 322
11:34–35 309
1–2 147, 171, 219, 282
12:1 188, 324
12:2 101
12:5 291, 302
13:1 117, 166
13:5 172, 332, 340
13:8 90
13:9–10 332
13:10 312
14:1–2 159
14:3 275
14:1 275
14:10–12 138
14:17 166
15:1 22
15:7 275

Bible (cont.)
    15:7–9 23
    15:8–12 162
    15:10 280
    15:12 244, 291
    15:14 84
    15:15 26, 302
    15:16 1, 24, 82, 324
    15:18 111, 259
    15:2 119
    15:20 302
    15:20–22 26
    15:24 26, 302
    15:27 295
    15:29 312
    16:4 310
    16:26 111, 259, 314
1 Corinthians
    1:1 188
    1:10 188, 196
    1:11–13 25
    1:22–24 69
    2:7 330
    2:7–9 328
    2:8 330, 331
    3:13 138
    3:16 96, 330
    4:5 170
    5 266
    5:5 321
    5:6 288
    5:7 193
    5:9–11 27
    5:15 321
    6:3 258, 330, 343
    6:5 22
    6:9 138
    6:11 82
    6:17–19 330
    7:1 27
    7:7–8 171
    7:14 298
    7:19 172, 341
    7:20 341
    7:25–40 171
    8:5–6 327
    8:11–12 159
    8:13 334
    9:19–20 25
    9:20 25, 69
    9:20–22 26
    10:1 9, 318, 331, 344
    10:1–2 331
    10:1–22 122, 128, 188
    10:4 218
    10:7–10 115, 128, 156
    10:11 87
    10:11–12 115
    10:18 70
    10:20–21 327
    10:26 312
    10:28 22
    10:28–29 172, 340
    10:32 69, 336
    11:8 166
    11:22 22
    11:23–25 75
    11:24 69
    11:26 302
    12:2 9, 331
    12:13 69
    14:33 166
    15:23 330
    15:23–28 329
    15:25 302, 329
    15:45 82
    15:50–58 328, 331
    15:51 22
    15:55–56 330
2 Corinthians
    1:14 302
    1:16 69
    1:22 66
    1–4 74
    2:5 302
    2:9 84
    2:17 166
    3 73, 78–85, 91–97, 123, 225, 257
    3:3 78, 89
    3:3–6 74, 84
    3:4–18 103
    3:6 74, 78, 85, 89, 92, 103, 165
    3:7 8, 69, 87, 91–92
    3:8 92
    3:9 91
    3:10 97
    3:13 69, 91, 95
    3:14 75, 91, 95, 96, 273
    3:14–15 85, 95
    3:16–18 97
    4:7 200
    4:13 262

5:10–11 138
5:17 82, 286, 318
6:2 101, 272, 333
10:8 74
11:22 69
11:24 25, 306
13:10 74
13:11 196
Galatians
　1:15 74
　1:4 101, 243, 255, 265, 333
　1:10 170
　1:13 346
　1:13–16 283
　1:16 24, 26, 27
　1:22 69
　2:7 25
　2:7–9 24
　2:8–9 1, 74
　2:9 24, 26, 324
　2:13 69
　2:14 8, 69, 164
　2:15 69, 71, 142, 205
　2:16 174, 265
　2:19 103
　3:2 264
　3:6–14 260
　3:7–8 308, 317
　3:10 8, 85, 255, 258, 264
　3:10–12 262
　3:10–13 10, 102
　3:11 149, 256
　3:11–12 252, 259
　3:1–12 253
　3:12 245, 246, 252, 257, 259, 260, 261, 262
　3:13 261
　3:13–14 149, 264, 346
　3:14 101, 149, 262, 264, 282, 325
　3:16 244, 291
　3:16–19 339
　3:19 96, 177, 257, 311, 340
　3:19–4:7 94, 330
　3:19–4:31 256
　3:21 248, 258
　3:21–25 96
　3:21–29 264
　3:22 258
　3:23–29 96
　3:25 265
　3:26 332
3:28 1, 4, 69, 339
3:29 9, 331
4:1–5 96
4:1–9 329
4:3 255
4:4 237, 312
4:5 286, 294
4:6 332
4:8 120
4:17 11
4:22–26 339
5:1–6 8
5:1–6 264
5:2 22
5:2–4 10
5:3 7, 163, 264
5:4 178
5:6 178, 341
5:6–7 84
5:9 288
5:13–6:2 171
5:13–26 177
5:14 149, 164, 178
5:16 149, 343
5:18 178
5:21 138
5:22 264
5:22–25 84
5:23 177
6:1 196, 275
6:7 138
6:7–8 3, 177, 259
6:15 82, 286
6:16 14, 70, 173, 336
Ephesians
　1:5 294
　1:8–11 328
　1:20–30 331
　2:12 39, 69
　3:1–12 328
　4:17–19 120, 128
　6:12 329
Philippians
　2:8–9 251
　2:9 266
　2:12–13 178
　2:13 264
　2:14–16 138
　2:15 92
　3:2–3 167
　3:3 331

Bible (cont.)
   3:3–11 90
   3:5 69, 70
   3:6 3, 90
   3:18 22
Colossians
   1:26–27 328
   3:11 39, 69
1 Thessalonians
   2:14 69
   2:14–16 268
   3:10 196
   4:8–9 84
   4:9 265
   4:14 246
   4:15 22
   4:16 246
   4:17 237, 269
1 Timothy
   1:4 286
Philemon
   17 275
Hebrews
   3:13 302
   3:16–19 144
   7:15 246
   9:1 125
   9:10 125
   9:16–17 73
   10:35–39 249
   10:37–38 250
   13:21 196
James
   1:1 66
   1:22–24 143
   2:13 137
   2:24 178
   5:6 249
1 Peter
   1:1 66
   2:6–10 207
   2:9–12 13
   3:18 249
   4:18 249
   5:10 196
2 Peter
   3:8 231
   3:11–12 234
   3:15–16 28
1 John
   2:1 249
   2:29 249
   3:7 249

Revelation
   2:9 169
   3:9 169
   5:9–10 13
   6:1–8 327
   7:1–12 66
   7:9 314
   12:3–9 327
   18:6 122
   20:13–14 327

Deuterocanonical and Pseudepigraphal Works
Assumption of Moses 1:18 233
Baruch
   3:16–4:4 118
   3:29–30 241
   3–4 243
2 Baruch 60
   41–51 243
   78:6–7 233
1 Enoch 327
   37–71 248
   38:1–6 248
   39:6 248
   46:3 248
   48:2 248
   53:1–6 248
   62:5 248
   81:1–2 96
   89 55
   91:38 108
   93:2 96
   103:2 96
   106:9 96
4 Ezra
   4:37–38 233
   4:38–42 237
   7:97 92
Joseph and Aseneth 314
Jubilees
   1:5–6 84, 86, 87
   1:5–26 82, 188, 229, 340
   1:15–16 83
   1:22–25 83, 237
   2:17–20 37
   3:10 95
   3:31 95
   5:13 95
   6:17 95
   15:12–13 10
   15:25–26 10
Judith 14:10 9

Letter of Jeremiah 40–41 119
1 Maccabees 47, 61, 154
   1:15 167
   12:21 17
2 Maccabees
   1:42 160
   4:32–34 159
   6:14–15 140
Psalms of Solomon
   2:3 158
   2:11–13 158
   2:18 140
   3:7 275
   8:7–13 158
   8:23 158
   9 141
   9:1–2 141
   9:2 87
   9:4–7 141
   13:5 275
   13:10 275
   14:1–10 243
   17
      26–29 186
Sibylline Oracles
   3 234
   3.70 144
   3.207–208 118
   3.300–462 118
   3.669–670 118
   5 234
Sirach 55, 60, 97
   17:17 327
   27:4 192
   33:21 121
Testament of Asher 6:2 126
Testament of Dan
   6:4 233
Testament of Judah
   19:2 233
   23:5 233
   24:1–3 83
Testament of Levi
   14:4–15:1 157
Testament of Moses
   8:1–3 167
Testament of Naphtali
   2:2 195
   3:3 122
   3:4 119, 123
   4:1 123
   4:5 123
   8:3 205

Testament of Simeon
   3:4 233
   4:2 233
   6:2–7 233
Tobit 60, 323
   4:19 191
   14:5–7 55
Wisdom of Solomon
   6:10 119
   10:15 191
   10:3–11:14 190
   11:9–10 140
   11:21 192
   12:10 140
   12:12 140, 192
   12:20–21 197
   13:1 117
   13:1–14:29 114
   13–15 114, 115, 127, 130
   14:23–27 156, 157
   14:30–31 115
   15:1–4 116, 118, 127
   15:7–8 192
   15:2 119
   15:7–13 114

Dead Sea Scrolls
   11QMelchizedek
      2:9–13 329
   1QH^a
      4:38 80
      12:11 80, 266
      20:14–15 79
   1QpHab
      2:3–4 79
      5:2–6 300
      5:7 79
      7:7 79
   1QS
      3:7 79, 266, 337
      3:7–4:26 82
      4:21–25 82, 232
      5:5 82, 265
      5:7–10 265
      8:4–7 231
      8:13–15 231
      11 193
   4Q171
      2:19 300
      4:10 300
   4Q215a 79
   4Q372 1
      10–15 49, 280

Dead Sea Scrolls (cont.)
  1S 99
    20–22 280
    20–22; 49
  4Q372 3 8 169
  4Q390
    2 i 4–10 157
  4Q390 1 2–10 55
  4QMMT^C
    12–14 49, 79
  4QpNah
    3–4 ii 2 212
  CD (Damascus Document)
    1:4–5 299
    1:5 46, 56, 62, 79, 101, 131
    1:5–12 49, 230
    1:7 299
    1:7–8 232
    1:8–2:1 299
    1:13–5:1 230
    2:7 79
    2:11–13 299
    2:16–17 79
    3:12–17 170
    3:12–4:6 230
    4:2 232
    4:9 79
    4:11 55
    4:15–19 157
    6:2–7:21 230
    6:5 232
    6:10 79
    6:14 79, 231
    6:15–16 157
    6:19 79, 232, 266
    7:4 79, 266, 337
    7:20–21 232
    8:16 232
    8:21 79
    12:23 79
    15:5 300
    15:7/15:07 79
    16:2 79
    19:33 266
    19:33–34 79
    20:12 79, 266
    20:23 79
  Temple Scroll
    en toto, 97

War Scroll
  1:1–3 49, 231
  1:3 263
  5:1 232
  5:1–2 49
  18:1–3 327

Josephus
  Against Apion
    1.309–19 158
    2.168–69 118
    2.20 158
    2.224 118
    2.250–254 118
  Jewish Antiquities
    9.253 205
    11.132–133 50, 313
    11.133 51
    11.173 51
    11.212 205
    11.84–115 48
    13.196 205
    13.254–258 42
    14.228–240 16
    14.234 16
    17.53 73
    17.78 73
    18.286 38
    18.81–84 155
    20.24 143
    4.312–14 132

Philo of Alexandria
  Abraham
    4–6 96
  Agriculture
    6 294
  Alleg. Interp. (Leg.)
    1.47 96
    2.34 293
    2.95 195
    3.241 158
    3.30 195
    3.88–94 307
  Cherubim
    15–17 170
  Confusion
    163 158
    190 233

Primary Sources Index

Contempl. Life
  10–11 118
Creation (Opif.)
  167 195
  4 96
  45 118
  78 195
Decalogue
  121–137 158
  133 158
  52–56 118, 120
  66–81 118, 120
Drunkenness (Ebr.) 42–45 118
Good Person (Prob.) 45–47 93
Heir 179 293
Migration 89–93 233, 346
Moses
  2.11 96
  2.14 96
  2.49–51 93
  2.51–52 96
  2.62 195
Posterity
  89 328
QE
  2.2 346
Rewards (Praem.)
  84 267
  93–97 233
  115 233
  126–161 121
  152 121, 267, 293
  161 213
  162 120, 128
  163 233
  163–165 121
  164–172 233
  166 140
  172 186, 267, 293
  44 293
Sacrifices
  54–57 191
Special Laws (Spec.)
  1.13–19 327
  1.15–21 118
  2.13 158
  3.83 158
  3.97–99 118

Virtues
  156–57, 179, 186, 293
Worse (Det.) 107–08 186

Early Christian Literature
  2 Clement 8:2 211
  1 Clement 29:2–30:1 13
  Acts of Peter and Paul 19:3 38
  Athanasius
    Against the Pagans 129
    On the Incarnation
      11–12:6 128
  Clement of Alexandria
    Exhortation to the Greeks 8 128
  Epistle of Barnabas
    4:7 13
    13 308
    14:5 13
    15:4 231
  Eusebius
    Eclogae propheticae, PG 22.1172 311
  John Chrysostom
    Homilies on Romans
      16:10 213
      3, 5 129
  Justin Martyr
    Dialogue with Trypho
      11.5 13
      25.6–26.1 13
  Origen
    Commentary on Romans
      2.11.4–2.13.7 151
      4.304 271, 303
      8.10 294
  Tatian
    Oration against the Greeks 4.2 128

Greek and Roman Authors 139
  Aristotle
    Generation of Animals
      743a15 210
    Meteorology
      383a25 210
      386a24 210
    Politics 5 1303b 37
  Cicero
    Pro Flacco 28.67 34
  Columella
    De re rustica, 5.9.16–17 293

Greek and Roman Authors (cont.)
  Dio Cassius
    Roman History 37.17.1 15, 34, 154
  Epictetus
    Discourses
      2.12.4–5 139
      2.4.4–6 203
      3.24.33 203
  Plato
    Republic
      6.514a–520a 97
    Symposium
      199d–201c 139
    Timaeus 24d 195
  Pliny
    Natural History 17.241 290
  Plutarch
    Life of Numa
      8.8 115
    Life of Publicola 13.2.4 210
  Pseudo-Aristotle
    Problemata 12.10.1–2 210
  Quintilian
    Institutio Oratoria
      3.7.21 34
      7.7.2 254
  Seneca the Elder
    Controversiae 2.4.14 294
  Tacitus
    Histories
      5.4.1 34
      5.7.2 34
      13.1 34
  Theophrastus
    De causis plantarum
      1.6.10 293, 295
      5.1.3–4 296
    Historia plantarum
      2.1.4 296
  Varro
    Res rustica
      1.40.5 296
      1.41.6 296

Rabbinic Literature
  Avot de Rabbi Natan
    43:1 94
  Babylonian Talmud
    Avodah Zarah
      5a 263
  Bava Batra
    75b 248
  Niddah
    46b 288
  Pesaḥim
    87a–b 208
  Sanhedrin
    92b 100
    97a 231, 237
    97b 235
    97b–98a 235
    98a 237, 269
    98b 245
    99a 237
    110b 60
    111a 186
  Shabbat
    118b 235
  Sukkah
    52a 264
  Yevamot
    63a 295
  Exodus Rabbah
    32:3–7 94
    43:1 94
  Genesis Rabbah 98 60
  Jerusalem Talmud
    Ta'anit 64a 235
    Kil'ayim 27b 295
  Leviticus Rabbah
    11:3 93, 263
    23:2 337
    32:5 337
  Maimonides, Mishneh Torah
    Laws of Repentance 7:5 234
  Mekhilta of Rabbi Ishmael
    9 93
  Mishnah
    Kil'ayim 1:7 296
    Avot 1:17 143
    Pesaḥim 4:8 293
    Sanhedrin
      10:1 6, 19, 186
      10:3 60
    Terumot
      3:1–2 288
      5:1–9 288
    Terumot 5:1–9 288
    Ṭevul Yom
      3:4 288

Yadayim 4:4 209, 312
Nachmanides
   Miqraot Gedolot 5:355 241
Numbers Rabbah 16:24 120
Pesiqta Rabbati
   14:10 93, 263
   20:2 94
Qohelet Rabbah
   8:1.3 263
Qohelet Rabbah 8:1.3 93

Seder Eliyahu Rabbah 10 285
Sifre Deuteronomy
   320 93, 263
   331 280
Song of Songs Rabbah
   1:2 13 92
Tosefta
   Sanhedrin 13:12 60
   Ṭevul Yom
      2:7 288

Author Index

Abasciano, Brian J., 28, 162, 185
Abegg, Martin G., 49
Achtemeier, Paul J., 277
Ackroyd, Peter R., 53
Aernie, Jeffrey W., 74
Albertz, Rainer, 45
Aletti, Jean-Noël, 112, 172, 187, 275, 278, 301
Allison, Dale C., 63, 65, 105, 229, 233, 234
Andersen, Francis I., 250
Ashton, John, 35
Atzmon, Gil, 36
Aune, David E., 107
Averbeck, Richard E., 45

Bachmann, Michael, 14, 39
Baker, Cynthia M., 34, 35
Baker, Murray, 278
Barber, Michael P., 73, 75, 89, 175
Barclay, John M. G., 2, 5, 9, 17, 39, 77, 102, 118, 121, 123, 127, 170, 172, 175, 176, 188, 191, 224
Barmash, Pamela, 56
Barrett, C. K., 184, 214, 218, 222, 227, 236, 238, 302
Barth, Karl, 277
Barth, Markus, 3, 244
Bassler, Jouette M., 123, 129, 130, 133, 137, 138, 140, 142
Bates, Matthew W., 30, 204, 221
Battle, John A., 193, 194, 204, 207, 208
Bauckham, Richard J., 66, 67
Baur, F. C., 5
Baxter, A. G., 290, 293

Baynes, Leslie, 95
Beale, G. K., 45
Beattie, D. R. G., 71
Beker, J. Christiaan, 175, 177, 184, 253, 316
Bekken, Per Jarle, 213, 214, 222, 236, 241, 243, 267
Bell, Richard H., 119, 189, 275, 277, 279, 280, 281, 306
Beller, Steven, 5
Belleville, Linda, 94
Bergmeier, Roland, 149, 179
Bergsma, John S., 55, 228
Bernasconi, Rocco, 43
Berzon, Todd S., 17
Betz, Hans Dieter, 309
Bird, Michael F., 2, 7, 30, 63
Blenkinsopp, Joseph, 56
Blumhofer, Christopher, 229
Boccaccini, Gabriele, 178, 267, 335
Böhm, Martina, 37, 42, 43, 58
Boring, M. Eugene, 65
Boyarin, Daniel, 4, 34, 61
Boyarin, Jonathan, 61
Brettler, Marc Zvi, 85
Brichto, Herbert Chanan, 94
Brondos, David, 86
Brown, Jeannine K., 64
Brown, Raymond E., 64
Brownlee, William H., 54
Bryan, Steven M., 61, 63
Buell, Denise Kimber, 3, 12, 16
Burnett, David A., 101, 124, 287, 326, 329, 331
Byrne, Brendan, 181

Author Index

Cadwallader, Alan H., 27
Callan, Terrance, 94, 122, 128
Campbell, Douglas A., 30, 104, 105, 113, 116, 131, 136, 143, 150, 155, 179, 251, 336
Campbell, Jonathan G., 55
Campbell, William S., 7, 14, 204, 207, 222, 244
Carlson, Stephen C., 51
Carroll, Robert P., 45, 46, 47
Casey, Maurice, 40, 41, 53
Chalmers, Matthew, 43, 64
Chapple, Allan, 27
Charles, Ronald, 54, 131, 144
Chilton, David, 47
Christensen, Duane L., 32
Christiansen, Ellen Juhl, 73
Coggins, Richard J., 42, 65
Cohen, Jeremy, 271, 303
Cohen, Robin, 47
Cohen, Shaye J. D., 9, 10, 16, 18, 19, 34, 35, 40, 42, 47
Collins, Adela Yarbro, 29
Collins, John J., 29, 55
Concannon, Cavan W., 9
Conzelmann, Hans, 69
Cowan, J. Andrew, 97, 101
Coxhead, Steven R., 239, 240, 241, 242
Crabbe, Kylie, 199
Cranfield, C. E. B., 14, 22, 27, 117, 179, 183, 193, 200, 202, 205, 208, 212, 222, 226, 244, 267, 273, 275, 277, 290, 302, 314
Cronin, Sonya S., 36
Crook, Zeba A., 175
Cross, Frank Moore, 42
Crossley, James G., 36
Crown, Alan David, 43

Dahl, Nils A., 104, 202, 208, 245, 253, 278
Das, A. Andrew, 21, 23, 24, 25, 26, 80, 208
Davies, Glenn N., 222
Davies, Philip R., 45, 54
Davies, W. D., 3, 7, 89, 207, 231, 291, 294
Davis, Kipp, 75, 81
Dennis, John A., 63
deSilva, David A., 175
Dibley, Genevive, 10
Dimant, Devorah, 231, 232
Dodd, C. H., 182, 202, 226, 253, 276, 294
Doering, Lutz, 73, 74, 110, 111
Donaldson, Terence L., 2, 7, 9, 10, 14, 86, 106, 184, 255, 256, 259, 261, 262, 276, 278, 305, 306, 319, 334

Dumbrell, William J., 95, 97
Dunn, James D. G., 4, 14, 22, 69, 71, 79, 101, 111, 117, 122, 125, 148, 155, 165, 183, 188, 193, 197, 200, 203, 205, 206, 210, 211, 212, 213, 214, 216, 217, 222, 224, 226, 242, 243, 244, 259, 267, 275, 288, 302, 305, 307, 315

Eastman, Susan Grove, 15, 70, 86, 184
Ehrensperger, Kathy, 5, 7
Ehrman, Bart D., 75
Eisenbaum, Pamela, 7, 8, 9
Elliot, John H., 34, 40, 71
Elliott, Neil, 140
Ellis, E. Earle, 88, 147, 308
Engberg-Pederson, Troels, 175
Enns, Peter, 19, 292, 298
Eskola, Timo, 45, 47, 53, 66
Esler, Philip F., 34, 290, 293, 294, 295
Evans, Craig A., 63, 65, 269
Eyl, Jennifer, 32, 39

Feldman, Louis H., 10, 55
Ferda, Tucker S., 63
Fisch, Yael, 225, 267
Fitzmyer, Joseph A., 85, 124, 130, 183, 192, 196, 203, 212, 213, 217, 222, 226, 275, 284, 302, 307, 315
Forsdyke, Sara, 99
Foster, Robert B., 22, 23, 28, 202, 207, 208, 219
Frankfurter, David, 151, 152
Fredriksen, Paula, 8, 9, 10, 13, 16, 18, 21, 25, 30, 35, 37, 38, 39, 68, 89, 115, 135, 147, 153, 173, 305, 312, 318, 327, 334, 336, 338, 345
Frey, Jörg, 76
Freyne, Sean, 16
Fuller, Michael E., 55, 63

Gaca, Kathy L., 118, 127, 129
Gadenz, Pablo T., 15, 61, 71, 72, 86, 102, 147, 193, 202, 203, 205, 206, 217, 271, 272, 273, 274, 275, 276, 278, 279, 281, 283, 284, 288, 291, 298, 299, 303, 305, 307, 312, 319, 320, 335
Gager, John G., 8, 9, 223, 267, 304
García Martínez, Florentino, 49, 95
Garlington, Don B., 111, 131, 333
Garroway, Joshua D., 9, 11, 17, 40, 103, 116, 139, 142, 151, 172, 294, 297, 298, 301, 314, 320, 323, 332, 335, 336, 338

Gaston, Lloyd, 8, 105, 189, 223, 267, 304
Gathercole, Simon J., 134, 143, 147, 148, 149, 168, 179, 243
Gaventa, Beverly, 132, 184, 189, 194, 199, 201
Gerber, Christine, 2
Getty, Mary Ann, 224, 315, 320
Gibson, Jeffrey B., 64
Goldingay, John E., 54
Goldstein, Jonathan A., 46, 47
Gombis, Timothy G., 86
Goodblatt, David, 41, 48
Goodman, Martin D., 10, 25
Goodrich, John K., 45, 100, 120, 205, 213, 218, 285, 296, 305, 312, 318, 325
Gordon, Benjamin D., 288, 293, 294, 295, 298
Gorman, Michael J., 82, 181
Grabbe, Lester L., 42, 56, 58
Greenwood, David, 46
Grieb, A. Katherine, 184
Grindheim, Sigurd, 92, 96
Grol, Harm van, 57
Gruen, Erich S., 53, 54, 233
Guerra, Anthony J., 22, 23
Gupta, Nijay K., 30

Haacker, Klaus, 5, 301
Hacham, Noah, 49
Hafemann, Scott J., 72, 73, 75, 77, 79, 85, 91, 93, 94, 95, 102, 103, 106, 187, 236
Hahn, Ferdinand, 313
Hahn, Scott W., 70, 74, 188, 271, 272, 282, 306
Halpern-Amaru, Betsy, 55, 186, 233
Hanson, Anthony T., 195, 200, 251, 291, 309
Harrington, Daniel J., 63, 65
Harrison, James R., 101, 175
Harvey, Graham, 39, 69
Hauptman, Judith, 60
Hawthorne, Gerald F., 70
Hayes, Christine E., 318
Hays, Richard B., 30, 54, 73, 78, 94, 125, 160, 162, 192, 198, 202, 208, 210, 226, 238, 242, 244, 248, 249, 250, 251, 252, 253, 264, 271, 277, 280, 302, 309, 319
Head, Peter M., 27
Heath, Jane, 85, 92, 94
Heiser, Michael S., 326
Heliso, Desta, 251
Hengel, Martin, 74
Heschel, Abraham J., 77, 137, 198, 199, 321

Hess, Jonathan M., 5
Hicks-Keeton, Jill, 314
Himmelfarb, Martha, 95
Hjelm, Ingrid, 43, 44, 45
Hofius, Otfried, 79
Holladay, Carl R., 39, 65, 76
Hooker, Morna D., 65, 73, 222
Horrell, David G., 15
Horst, Pieter W. van der, 43
Hubbard, M. V., 84
Hübner, Hans, 15
Hughes, Julie, 80
Hultgren, Arland J., 33
Hultgren, Stephen J., 79, 80, 94, 232
Humphrey, Edith M., 222
Huxley, Aldous, 28
Hyatt, Darlene, 165, 183

Irons, Charles Lee, 30, 102
Isaac, Benjamin, 47
Ito, Akio, 147, 179, 225

Jacobs, Andrew S., 70
Jaubert, Annie, 81
Jeffay, Nathan, 15
Jervell, Jacob, 65, 67
Jervis, L. Ann, 101
Jewett, Robert, 13, 22, 40, 69, 71, 85, 88, 112, 121, 131, 137, 142, 144, 155, 164, 170, 172, 192, 193, 194, 200, 203, 208, 210, 212, 217, 222, 224, 227, 233, 236, 238, 244, 266, 267, 274, 275, 277, 278, 283, 284, 288, 293, 302, 303, 306, 307, 309, 312, 315
Jipp, Joshua W., 29, 123, 129, 141, 227, 244, 247, 248, 251, 258, 343
Johnson Hodge, Caroline, 6, 8, 12, 17, 74, 105, 286, 291, 294, 334, 335

Kaatz, Saul, 38
Käsemann, Ernst, 112, 132, 147, 171, 172, 200, 213, 223, 267, 276, 278, 284, 290, 302, 315
Keck, Leander E., 182, 184, 222
Keddie, G. Anthony, 93
Khobnya, Svetlana, 291
Kim, Dongsu, 290, 298
Kim, Johann D., 187
Kim, Seyoon, 242, 278, 303, 305, 306
Kincaid, John A., 73, 75, 89, 175
King, Justin, 87, 142, 143, 150

Author Index

Kirk, J. R. Daniel, 112, 171, 242, 244, 246, 247, 251, 252, 265, 320
Klein, Anja, 79, 80, 81, 82
Knibb, Michael, 48, 55
Knoppers, Gary, 34, 42, 44, 45
Koch, Dietrich-Alex, 74
Korner, Ralph J., 32
Kozman, Rony, 82, 87
Kraabel, A. Thomas, 47
Kraemer, Ross Shepard, 314
Kuhn, K. G., 38, 40, 41, 71

Laato, Antti, 115
Lagrange, Marie-Joseph, 171, 275, 276
Lalleman, Hetty, 74
Lambert, David A., 59, 61, 77, 83, 86, 95, 97, 229, 230, 233, 237, 238, 266, 291
Lane, William L., 63, 74, 78
Lang, T. J., 107, 302, 304
Langton, Daniel R., 4
Levenson, Jon D., 47, 97, 98, 100, 101, 219
Levin, Christoph, 81
Levine, Amy-Jill, 36, 337
Levison, John R., 149
Lincicum, David, 53, 86
Linebaugh, Jonathan A., 114, 115, 116, 117, 120, 123, 129, 134, 136, 188, 191
Linville, James Richard, 38
Litwa, M. David, 331
Lohfink, Gerhard, 63
Longenecker, Bruce W., 4
Longenecker, Richard N., 45
Lowe, Malcolm, 16
Lucas, Alec J., 94, 117, 122, 123, 128, 129, 132, 134, 145, 190
Luz, Ulrich, 40, 71

Madigan, Kevin, 101
Magen, Yitzhak, 43
Malina, Bruce, 36
Marcus, Joel, 66, 163, 311
Martin, Ralph P., 70
Martyn, J. Louis, 248, 249, 253, 254, 257, 336
Mason, Steve, 34
Maston, Jason, 82, 87
McCaulley, Esau, 207, 314
McConville, J. Gordon, 57, 58, 229
McCready, Wayne O., 57
McDonald, Denys N., 9
McGrath, Alister E., 31
McKnight, Scot, 10, 63, 64, 332

Meier, John P., 63, 64, 65
Meyer, Ben F., 63
Michel, Otto, 40, 71, 88, 147, 193, 195, 200
Middlemas, Jill A., 324
Miller, David M., 16, 34
Montgomery, James Alan, 42
Moo, Douglas J., 13, 15, 39, 71, 155, 183, 188, 189, 192, 194, 200, 202, 203, 213, 217, 223, 226, 238, 239, 252, 267, 273, 275, 276, 283, 289, 302, 303, 307, 319
Moore, George Foot, 3
Moraff, Jason F., 337
Morales, Rodrigo J., 80, 84
Morgan, Teresa, 30
Mroczek, Eva, 95
Munck, Johannes, 188, 195, 201, 208, 268, 307
Murphy-O'Connor, Jerome, 9
Mussner, Franz, 223, 267, 289, 301, 303
Myles, Robert, 36

Najman, Hindy, 95
Nanos, Mark D., 4, 5, 6, 7, 8, 9, 14, 25, 89, 273, 294, 295, 301
Neusner, Jacob, 5, 16, 61, 112, 143, 304, 307
Newman, Judith H., 80
Neyrey, Jerome H., 94
Nitzan, Bilhah, 79
Nodet, Etienne, 57
Novenson, Matthew V., 2, 29, 39, 145, 153, 162, 165, 166, 183, 213, 227, 245, 256, 333

O'Neill, John C., 6
Oehler, Markus, 25
Oliver, Isaac W., 32, 64, 67
Olson, Robert C., 69, 241
Ophir, Adi, 33, 43
Oropeza, B. J., 74, 79, 159, 160, 161, 175, 298

Palmer, Carmen, 17
Park, Young-Ho, 32
Payne, Don J., 32
Pitre, Brant, 45, 53, 56, 57, 60, 63, 64, 65, 73, 75, 89, 175, 228
Plag, Christoph, 6
Porter, Calvin L., 113
Porter, Stanley E., 136, 272
Portier-Young, Anathea, 54
Pucci Ben Zeev, Miriam, 16

Rainey, Brian, 115, 126, 136, 160
Räisänen, Heikki, 7, 148, 267, 315
Rajak, Tessa, 61
Rappaport, Uriel, 42
Ravens, David, 7, 65, 67
Reed, Annette Yoshiko, 35
Repschinski, Boris, 32
Richardson, Peter, 7
Rodrigues, Lancy, 290
Rodríguez, Rafael, 8, 21, 22, 24, 105, 116, 129, 141, 151, 154, 164, 169, 172, 316, 341
Rosen-Zvi, Ishay, 33, 43
Runesson, Anders, 6, 43, 65

Sanders, E. P., 1, 3, 4, 6, 7, 10, 19, 25, 30, 59, 63, 65, 72, 73, 84, 104, 105, 107, 112, 113, 116, 132, 137, 145, 172, 174, 179, 184, 186, 221, 222, 223, 224, 233, 256, 267, 276, 278, 298, 300, 304, 305, 345, 346
Sandler, Adam, 35
Satlow, Michael L., 3, 34, 43, 62
Saulnier, Christiane, 16
Schechter, Solomon, 3
Schiffman, Lawrence H., 43, 55, 97
Schmalz, Matthew N., 46
Schnittjer, Gary Edward, 81
Schorch, Stefan, 42
Schreiner, Thomas R., 48, 155, 213, 214, 222, 223
Schwartz, Barry, 34
Schwartz, Daniel R., 40
Schwartz, Seth, 3, 16, 34
Schweitzer, Albert, 1, 5, 63, 67, 84, 105, 323, 345
Schwemer, Anna Maria, 74
Scott, James M., 33, 53, 62, 83, 86, 255, 286, 294, 302, 303, 306, 307, 313, 314, 319
Segal, Alan F., 189
Seifrid, Mark A., 30, 217, 222, 226, 251, 308
Shahar, Yuval, 34, 43
Simon, Marcel, 3, 13
Sloan, Paul T., 86, 158, 165, 247
Smith, Barry Douglas, 57
Smith, Christopher D., 66
Smith, Jonathan Z., 17
Snodgrass, Klyne R., 89, 113
Snyder, Glenn E., 70
Soloveichik, Meir, 221, 234–36
Sorkin, David Jan, 5
Spilsbury, Paul, 51

Sprinkle, Preston, 2, 7, 88, 243, 245, 262, 263
Stahl, Michael J., 44, 46
Stanley, Christopher D., 27, 72, 75, 226, 309
Staples, Jason A., *passim*
Starling, David I., 5, 9, 72, 78, 106, 127, 162, 187, 200, 201, 202, 203, 206, 236, 281, 332
Steck, Odil Hannes, 53
Stendahl, Krister, 3, 6, 74, 104, 174, 182, 304
Stern, Menahem, 16
Stockhausen, Carol K., 74, 78, 80, 85, 161, 217
Stowers, Stanley K., 8, 21, 22, 23, 114, 115, 116, 123, 136, 139, 223, 244, 246, 251, 278
Stuhlmacher, Peter, 143, 184, 273, 276, 315
Stuhlmann, Rainer, 305, 307, 309, 315

Talmon, Shemaryahu, 42, 81, 186, 230, 233
Thiel, Nathan, 47
Thielman, Frank, 72, 86, 104, 106, 119, 125, 150, 216, 218, 231, 239, 268
Thiessen, Jacob, 201
Thiessen, Matthew, 7, 8, 9, 10, 13, 17, 18, 21, 23, 33, 35, 49, 115, 116, 123, 128, 129, 141, 151, 154, 155, 156, 160, 162, 163, 164, 165, 167, 171, 173, 198, 200, 245, 279, 283, 290, 314, 339, 341
Thorsteinsson, Runar M., 8, 21, 23, 25, 26, 116, 122, 129, 130, 132, 133, 134, 135, 137, 140, 141, 151
Tigay, Jeffrey H., 32
Tigchelaar, Eibert J. C., 81, 82
Timmins, Will N., 87, 88
Tobin, Thomas H., 130, 203, 212, 233, 273, 280, 314
Tomson, Peter J., 39, 40, 71, 143
Trebilco, Paul, 32
Tyrrell, George, 5

Ulrich, Dean R., 55
Urbach, Ephraim E., 235, 320

Van Kooten, George H., 32
VanderKam, James, 55, 77
Vos, J. S., 41

Wagner, J. Ross, 22, 27, 28, 63, 72, 73, 188, 191, 193, 198, 199, 202, 205, 206, 212, 216, 219, 270, 272, 273, 274, 279, 291, 303, 309, 318

Author Index

Ward, Richard F., 27
Wasserman, Emma, 122, 181, 326, 327, 329
Waters, Guy Prentiss, 53, 72, 86, 102, 171, 270, 273, 274, 279, 280
Watson, Francis, 7, 13, 94, 118, 123, 127, 155, 179, 203, 226, 281
Wells, Kyle B., 68, 72, 73, 77, 78, 85, 102, 145, 163, 168, 169, 176, 177, 181, 236, 238, 240, 241
Westerholm, Stephen, 45, 102, 104, 174, 178, 213, 223
White, Ellen, 326
Wilckens, Ulrich, 40
Wilk, Florian, 75, 110, 273, 314
Willitts, Joel, 63, 64, 255, 262
Wills, Lawrence M., 34, 35
Windsor, Lionel J., 24, 151, 162, 325
Winston, David, 96
Wisdom, Jeffrey, 61, 86
Witherington III, Ben, 165, 183

Wolff, Christian, 74
Wood, Thomas Richard, 61, 97, 102
Wright, N. T., 2, 4, 14, 30, 38, 45, 54, 56, 60, 63, 64, 65, 74, 94, 97, 102, 104, 110, 113, 114, 132, 145, 147, 172, 179, 189, 193, 203, 222, 224, 255, 277, 291, 314
Wu, Jackson, 87

Yamazaki-Ransom, Kazuhiko, 64
Young, Stephen L., 27, 112, 247, 251

Zahn, Molly M., 97
Zahn, Theodor, 26
Zeisler, John A., 290, 293
Zeitlin, Solomon, 38
Zetterholm, Karin Hedner, 2, 18
Zetterholm, Magnus, 2, 4, 7, 8
Zimmerli, Walther, 79
Zoccali, Christopher, 2, 13, 14, 257, 259, 262, 284, 302, 303, 312, 339

Subject Index

Abraham, 165, 180, 260, 267, 293, 340
  children of, 8, 11, 17, 186, 189, 269, 292, 308, 318, 338, 344
  promise to/blessing of, 8, 12, 101, 149, 191, 219, 244, 253, 256, 260, 264, 282, 308, 310, 311, 317, 318, 331, 333, 335, 337, 340
  seed of, 9, 11, 189, 244, 271, 274, 287, 325, 334, 335, 336, 337–41
Adam, 87, 99, 119, 326
  glory of, 82, 93
  and Israel, 117, 119, 120, 123, 125, 126, 147, 168, 263, 275
  and messiah, 82, 245
  transgression of. *See* transgression (παράβασις): of Adam
adoption, 17, 83, 208, 286, 294, 298, 316
age of wrath, 52–58, 61, 62, 67, 79, 90, 101–6, 131, 132, 181, 230, 231, 236, 264, 272, 299, 343, 347
allegiance. *See* fidelity/faith (πίστις)
Ammonites, 208, 209
anachronism, 4, 14, 15, 34, 35, 57, 151, 183–85, 224, 333, 345
angels, 23, 37, 65, 93, 96, 249, 257, 258, 305, 326, 327, 328, 329, 330, 343
anthropology, Pauline, 104
anti-Judaism, anti-Semitism, 5, 13, 36, 40–41, 47
anti-legalistic Paul, 2, 3, 216, 223, 226, 253, 258
apocalyptic school of interpretation, 59, 101, 104
apocalyptic/Apocalypticism, 19, 59, 107, 108, 235, 237, 309, 342, 344

Aqiva, Rabbi, 60
Assyria, 44, 48, 49, 53, 56, 57, 58, 60, 98, 204, 206, 207, 209, 216, 280, 287
  intermingling nations, 44, 48, 209, 280, 287
astralization. *See* divinization
atonement, 168, 231, 232, 255

Babylon, 45, 48, 53, 58
Benjamin, 48–49, 51, 56, 58, 70, 231, 271

children of God, 37, 138, 189, 287, 326, 329, 332, 337, 343
Christ. *Ecce* messiah
  as honorific title, 29, 227
circumcision, 162–74, 337–41
  on the eighth day, 10, 153, 164, 167, 172, 340, 341
  of the heart, 80, 82, 83, 84, 85, 86, 89, 107, 112, 149, 153, 162, 163, 165, 168, 170, 173, 182, 228, 239, 265, 311, 325, 331, 338, 339, 340
  as mark of covenant membership, 9–11, 164, 168, 256, 337, 340
  as rite of gentile conversion, 8, 9–11, 23, 151, 164, 167, 169, 177, 337, 339, 340
citizenship, 16, 32, 287
cosmic/celestial framework, 93, 320, 326–31
covenant
  broken, 10, 79, 85–91, 94, 131, 132, 143, 161, 163, 167, 168, 207, 210, 227, 238, 255–57, 318, 343. *See also* infidelity: of Israel
covenantal nomism, 72, 73, 297, 345

Israel's failure to keep. *See* infidelity:of Israel; Israel:under under covenantal curse
new/renewed. *See* new covenant presupposed in Jewish theology, 72–73
cross, 66, 264, 268, 338

David, 35, 83
  Davidic messiah, 29, 44, 64, 83, 109, 237, 245, 256, 263, 264, 343
Dead Sea Scrolls sect. *See* Yaḥad
death
  consequence of sin, 91, 93, 94, 117, 119, 120, 125, 126, 143, 179, 181, 190, 258, 282, 329
  as curse of Torah, 59, 61, 91, 93, 97–101, 103, 117, 120, 125, 129, 181, 190, 218, 246, 258, 261, 280, 282. *See also* Torah:curse of
  ends the jurisdiction of Torah, 181, 243, 265
  exile equated with, 59, 97–101, 102, 324
  of Israel, 75, 91, 93, 102, 280, 330
  of Jesus, 1, 8, 67, 72, 75, 103, 107, 138, 171, 178, 237, 242, 244, 247, 248, 251, 252, 256, 261, 264, 268, 277, 325, 330, 346, 347
  of Moses. *See* Moses:end/death of
  Moses' ministry of. *See* Moses:ministry of death
  participation in Messiah's, 103, 179, 181, 243, 244, 265, 268, 332
diaspora, 15, 27, 42, 47, 48, 53, 56, 61, 66, 123, 141, 310
diatribe, 22
dietary laws, 334
divinization, 82, 93, 258, 330, 331, 343

ekklēsia, 12, 14, 25, 32, 71, 72, 75, 110, 111, 173, 266, 306, 310, 319, 325, 334, 335, 336, 344, 345
election, 6, 7, 12, 14, 32, 65, 66, 77, 117, 143, 172, 248, 272, 286, 292, 295, 297, 298, 307, 319, 320, 321, 339, 346
Eliezer, Rabbi, 60, 208, 235
Elijah, 229, 272, 273, 282
Ephraim, 43–45, 96, 100, 107–12, 205, 217, 219, 281, 282, 305, 307–22
Esau, 189, 201, 219, 308
eschaton, 10, 14, 54, 59, 67, 68, 86, 102, 144, 230, 231, 232, 333

ethnic transformation, 9, 18, 38, 149, 153, 201–9, 210, 286, 295, 298, 314, 315–22, 324, 325, 332, 333–41
ethnicity, 8, 15–19, 34, 151, 153, 224
ethnocentrism, 4, 5, 6, 20, 110, 165, 174, 216, 223, 224, 243, 244, 267, 346
exile
  of both Israel and Judah, 45, 49, 55, 141
  as corrective discipline, 77, 86, 87, 228
  as covenantal curse, 47, 54, 59, 61, 77, 160, 219, 228, 255
  equated with death. *See* death:exile equated with
  involving gentilization, 44, 98, 205, 208, 219, 220, 324, 328, 337
  myth of exile and return, 53, 59, 60, 65
  of northern Israel, 45, 49, 53, 55, 56, 58, 60, 99, 108, 141, 206, 207, 209
  as ongoing, 45–63, 102, 219, 230
exodus, 35, 57, 76, 77, 94, 108, 186, 190, 337
  new/second exodus, 57, 65, 89, 263, 331
exogamy. *See* intermarriage

fictive kinship, 17. *See also* adoption
fidelity/faith (πίστις), 29, 225, 248, 260, 265, 340, 341
  era/age/domain of, 243, 246, 252, 262, 265
  of God, 6, 84, 86, 90, 91, 101, 111, 182, 187, 189, 210, 211, 268, 271, 280, 292, 297, 317, 320, 321, 325
  of Israel, 60, 77, 228, 274, 283, 317, 333
  justification by. *See* justification:by fidelity/faith
  of/in nations/gentiles, 10, 11, 21, 67, 121, 147, 212, 276, 280, 289, 306, 338, 340
  of Messiah, 91, 96, 111, 225, 246–47, 248, 249, 250, 251, 252, 254, 257, 258, 261–62, 264, 265, 326, 342
  and obedience, 21, 30, 68, 89, 111, 175, 178, 238, 259, 295, 297, 321, 329, 333, 340, 342
  participation in messiah's, 96, 225, 228, 243, 247, 258, 261, 265
  relationship to Torah, 6, 90, 96, 212, 252–65
  and the spirit, 90, 102, 149, 180, 242, 257–64, 277, 340
foreskin, 11, 25, 26, 83, 163, 165, 167, 169, 172, 173, 178, 257, 265, 316, 338, 339, 341, 347

Galilee/Galilean, 35, 61
Gamaliel, Rabban, 209
genealogical descent, 16, 17, 69, 286, 339
gentile problem, 7, 127, 128, 325, 333
gentiles, 2
   eschatological pilgrimage of, 208, 256, 304–7, 310, 314
   ethnic transformation of. See ethnic transformation
   former gentiles, 8–12, 43, 71, 316, 331, 335, 339
   fullness of the nations, 271, 278, 301–17
   idolatry/immorality of, 115, 121, 130, 156
   incorporation into Israel, 9, 11, 17, 67, 78, 107, 108, 110, 111, 147, 173, 180, 182, 186, 187, 201–12, 215, 219, 220, 256, 270, 274, 277, 287, 289, 290, 292, 294, 295, 296, 298, 301–17, 324, 325, 328, 334, 335, 337, 339, 344, 345, 347
   Israelites intermarried among, 102, 201–9, 282–87, 337
   as 'not my people', 127, 201–9, 215, 220, 281, 282–87, 311, 316, 319, 324, 342, 347
God of Israel, 6, 8, 9, 38, 44, 58, 136, 137, 326, 327, 331, 334, 335, 338
gods (lesser deities), 8, 16, 18, 37, 76, 88, 96, 122, 155, 255, 263, 326–31, 334
golden calf, 93, 121, 122, 123, 124, 128, 187, 188, 190, 191, 263
grace (χάρις), 2, 3, 4, 5, 74, 84, 94, 103, 121, 198, 227, 231, 267, 280, 283, 329, 333, 342
   age/domain of, 46, 59, 77, 101, 102, 103, 231, 243, 246, 272, 333
   as empowerment, 121, 174–79, 298, 342
   as reciprocal, 174–79

Hagar, 340
heavenly tablets, 95. See also Torah: heavenly/spiritual
Hebrew, 51
   Hebrew of Hebrews, 70
   Paul's knowledge of, 70, 216, 240, 245, 281, 308, 309
Hezekiah, 124, 229, 237
hybridity, 11, 205, 206, 209, 288, 316, 328, 336, 345

idolatry, 115, 120–32, 133, 156, 159, 262
   of Israel, 44, 115, 120–32, 135, 156, 159, 262
Idumaeans, 35, 42

impiety (ἀσέβεια), 112, 114–32, 133, 135, 136, 139, 142, 157, 270, 303, 320
   of gentiles. See gentiles:idolatry/immorality of
   of Israel, 44, 114–32, 133, 135, 157, 303, 319, 320
infidelity
   of Israel, 8, 59, 85–91, 93, 98, 112, 114–32, 154–62, 185, 189, 199, 210, 212, 214, 215, 219, 228, 229, 257, 262, 269, 271, 273, 277, 280, 284, 289, 292, 295, 297, 301, 321, 324, 334. See also Israel:under covenantal curse
   results in removal from covenant, 8, 98, 121, 185, 205, 220, 255, 258, 267, 272, 283, 289, 292, 295, 298, 301, 311, 312, 334, 336
injustice, 76, 77, 82, 86, 87, 90, 102, 112, 114, 115, 126, 127, 130, 131, 133, 135, 136, 141, 142, 176, 177, 180, 191, 233, 237, 251, 340
insider/outsider paradigm, 39–41, 71
intermarriage, 17, 51, 57, 229, 287, 295, 314, 317
Ioudaios, 3, 15, 34–36, 39–41, 42, 48, 50, 51, 52, 58, 60, 66, 68–72, 165, 166, 183, 205, 213, 298, 313, 334, 343
Isaac, 189, 219, 310, 311
Ishmael, 189, 201, 219
Israel
   and Adam. 92, 93, 95, 97, 331. See Adam:and Israel–angelic exaltation of. See also divinization
   all Israel, 6, 13, 14, 18, 20, 46, 54, 55, 56, 62, 63, 70, 95, 100, 107, 108, 111, 173, 182, 187, 188, 232, 269, 271, 278, 293, 299, 300, 301–22, 344
   attempts to restore, 61, 66, 244
   death of. See death:of Israel
   divided kingdoms of, 43–45, 51, 52, 109, 281
   ethnic/empirical Israel, 13, 14, 15–19, 37, 62, 324, 332, 335, 337
   gentilized/assimilated among the nations, 20, 129, 147, 156, 167, 201–9, 219, 220, 282–87, 315, 317, 324, 328, 337, 344
   house of, 55, 64, 75, 99, 100, 108, 124, 161, 169, 190, 198, 206, 263, 285, 290, 311, 312, 316, 319
   including non-Jews, 20, 60, 62, 274, 280, 312, 323, 324, 331, 334, 335

light to the nations, 109, 117, 162, 201, 321, 325
northern tribes/kingdom of, 46, 47, 48, 49, 51, 60, 63, 64, 99, 107–12, 124, 202, 203, 204, 207, 216, 217, 273, 280, 281, 282, 310, 312, 315, 317, 318, 332, 342, 344
  ongoing exile of. *See* exile:as ongoing
  as past, biblical entity, 9, 12, 44, 58, 59, 67, 69, 125, 128, 203, 204, 210, 211, 213, 215, 217, 269, 272, 273, 274
  as presently incomplete, 47, 60, 64, 66, 184, 272, 313
  resurrection of. *See* resurrection:Israel's restoration as
  true Israel, 3, 13, 14, 300, 303, 345
  as twelve tribes, 49, 51, 56, 59, 60, 64, 66, 67, 72, 106, 186, 204, 232, 312, 313
  under covenantal curse, 8, 24, 47, 59, 61, 75–78, 79, 94, 112, 117, 120, 121, 122, 124, 127, 128, 129, 131, 132, 139, 142, 143, 144, 145, 146, 147, 157, 178, 180, 190, 207, 215, 241, 252, 255–57, 262, 263, 280, 282, 284, 318, 335, 343. *See also* infidelity:of Israel
  unfaithful cut off from, 19, 49, 61, 153, 154, 166–74, 186, 270, 290, 291–301, 334, 336
  wrongly glossed as 'Jews', 14, 39, 40, 41, 45, 53, 183, 194, 212, 284, 345

Jacob, 109, 110, 216, 219, 291, 303, 307, 310, 313, 315, 319, 320, 326, 344
Jehoiachin, 203, 204
Jeremiah (prophet), 26, 74
Jerusalem, 24, 45, 56, 57, 59, 69, 124, 127, 157, 158, 159, 199, 218, 234, 248, 255, 256, 268–69, 287, 295, 305, 307
  leaders of, 158, 218, 268–69
  fidelity of, 125
Jesus
  as a Jew, 66, 106, 237, 278, 304, 307, 309, 313, 342, 346
  as Messiah, 2, 8, 10, 20, 21, 29, 174, 212, 221, 224, 226, 234, 236, 246, 247, 248, 250, 251, 256, 265, 266, 267, 268, 269, 329, 337, 343
  as successor of Moses, 92, 186, 246, 264, 335
Jew/Jews
  as alleged term of disparagement, 40
  conflated with Israel, 70, 72, 183, 213, 215, 267, 312, 325
  equal footing with gentiles, 11, 12, 71, 111, 123, 128, 129, 130, 134, 140, 142, 147, 150, 152, 164, 168, 169, 207, 211, 225, 282, 298, 304, 334, 335, 338, 345
  included among Paul's audiences, 23–24, 131, 132, 136, 143, 152, 306
  including tribes of Judah, Levi, Benjamin, 48–49, 51, 56, 71, 231
  as meaning Judahite, 47, 48, 49, 55, 56, 58, 62, 67, 68–72, 108, 110, 282, 323, 324, 325, 336, 346
  naturally born into Israel, 142, 333, 339, 344
  not equivalent to Israel, 39–63, 67, 68–72, 110, 173, 213, 274, 323, 334, 336, 342, 346
  paired with Greeks/gentiles, 1, 8, 12, 24, 25, 27, 69, 111, 127, 130, 133, 135, 139, 140, 141, 143, 168, 190, 193, 201, 224, 265, 266, 267, 269, 277, 282, 305, 311, 319, 339, 347
  primacy within Israel, 69
  so-called Jew, 23–24, 150–54, 162, 167, 169, 183
  as a subset of Israel, 20, 26, 27, 35, 41–63, 68–72, 75, 77, 83, 92, 96, 100, 108, 109, 110, 111, 118, 122, 158, 159, 173, 183, 187, 201, 207, 209, 217, 230, 231, 281, 282, 290, 297, 298, 311, 312–17, 318, 323, 324, 325, 334, 336, 342, 344, 346
Jewish law. *See* Torah
Jewish Revolt (66–73 CE), 56
Jewishness, 16, 18, 29, 34, 153, 154, 167, 172
Joseph, 48–49, 158, 219, 281, 311, 312, 314
  messiah of, 264
  tribes of, 48–49, 207, 281, 312, 314
Joshua (biblical), 92, 188, 246
Joshua, Rabbi, 209, 235
Jubilees, 10, 55, 83, 86, 87, 95, 144, 196, 229, 237, 238, 292
  dating of, 118
Judah, 36, 38, 42, 48, 51, 53, 55, 69
  house of, 55, 75, 108, 290, 311
  as including Levi and Benjamin, 48–49, 56, 231
  southern kingdom of, 43–45, 51
Judah ha-Nasi, 60
judaize, 152, 160
judgment, 159, 329, 330
  based on works, 3, 112, 113, 143, 146, 150, 153, 170, 176, 177, 178, 179, 250, 321

Subject Index

judgment (cont.)
  impartial, 112, 129, 134, 136–44, 145, 147, 150, 152, 163, 168, 169, 172, 198, 215, 228, 282, 321
  just (δίκαιος), 2, 30, 31, 49, 59, 77, 85, 102, 139, 143, 176, 177, 178, 180, 186, 215, 217, 223, 236, 237, 244, 251, 292, 333, 335, 338, 344
  just one, the, 247–58, 260–62, 266
  just requirement (δικαίωμα), 18, 30, 31, 89, 109, 125, 126, 129, 144, 157, 163, 167, 171, 172, 174, 176, 181, 257, 262, 297. See also love command
justice, 30, 66
justification
  as ethical transformation, 20, 59, 77–78, 80, 89, 90, 91–97, 102, 146, 149, 161, 171, 172, 175–81, 182, 204, 237, 241, 244, 252, 257, 264, 266, 269, 316, 319, 332, 333, 340
  by fidelity/faith, 2, 3, 91, 111, 113, 138, 149, 174, 212, 214, 215, 221, 222, 225, 227, 243, 247, 248, 250, 252, 256, 260, 261, 264, 269, 311, 340
  of God, 86, 87, 141, 158, 191, 194
  Israel's restoration requires, 77–78, 90, 91, 102, 176, 228, 264, 267, 269, 319, 332, 333, 336, 339
  paradox of justification, 176, 256
  via spirit. See spirit:agent of justification
justness
  from fidelity, 247–58
justness (δικαιοσύνη), 30, 31, 115, 214
  from fidelity, 91, 222, 225, 243
  of God, 86, 221, 223, 242, 246, 248, 251, 252, 267, 268, 284
  of Messiah, 252

kingdom, 92, 234, 237, 268, 315
  of David, 44
  of God, 63, 64, 65, 66, 67, 92, 138, 234, 315, 329, 330

land of Israel, 46, 48, 49, 50, 51, 55, 56, 57, 58, 60, 61, 70, 78, 85, 88, 98, 99, 109, 128, 160, 188, 190, 207, 229, 230, 232, 238, 239, 280, 292, 341
Law. See Torah
Law-free gospel, 2, 89, 116, 184, 254
legalism, 2, 3, 4, 5, 90, 113, 174, 216, 223, 224, 226, 244, 258, 267, 346

Levi, 58, 156, 157, 231, 235, 237, 269
life
  eternal, 61, 93, 101, 132, 170, 177, 179, 231, 243, 244, 264, 343
  granted by spirit, 78, 90, 92, 97, 100, 101, 109, 112, 125, 165, 170, 177, 208, 269, 285, 286, 319
  meaning of. See truth, absolute
  messiah's power to give, 243, 245, 246, 261, 264, 269
  promise of, 61, 92, 98, 100, 101, 103, 109, 112, 132, 168, 181, 218, 243–47, 256–64
  and Torah, 92, 97, 98, 103, 112, 118, 125, 181, 218, 225, 243–47, 256–64, 265
love command, 31, 88, 89, 114, 129, 146, 164, 176, 241, 320, 332
Lutheran reading of Paul, 2, 3, 4, 216, 223, 224, 244

Marcion, 136, 254
Melchizedek, 329
mercy, 23, 55, 94, 99, 115, 123, 127, 129, 136, 137, 141, 146, 168, 177, 190–212, 213, 220, 233, 257, 281, 296, 311, 317–22, 333
  vessels of, 193–212
messiah
  cross of. See cross
  death of. See death:of Jesus
  in Messiah, 1, 23, 147, 149, 164, 177, 178, 224, 253, 261, 262, 265, 291, 325, 332, 336, 338, 339, 341
  obedience of. See obedience:of Messiah
  power to grant life. See life:messiah's power to give
  successor of Moses. See Jesus:as successor of Moses
  telos of Torah. See Torah:end (τέλος) of Torah
mixtures, 35, 205, 206, 209, 288, 289, 316, 328, 337
Moabites, 209
moral transformation, Behold justification: as ethical transformation
Moses, 81, 83, 88, 97, 120, 132, 187, 188, 191, 198, 224, 225, 229, 242, 272
  end/death of, 91–92, 246
  mediator of Torah, 91, 92, 94–97, 231, 242, 340
  metonymy for written Torah, 92, 95, 96

Subject Index

ministry of death, 8, 87, 88, 91–97, 239, 284
Song of, 49, 86, 279, 280, 281, 326
veiling of, 91, 93, 94, 96
mystery, 107, 110, 180, 198, 202, 285, 301–12, 315, 328, 330

Naphtali, 55, 60, 122, 323
natural law theology, 126, 147, 148, 335
Nazi scholarship, 40–41
new covenant
central to Pauline theology, 72–75, 78–85, 346
includes promise of the spirit, 74, 78–85. See also spirit:included in new covenant
involves justification, 75–85, 90
promised to Israel and Judah, 55, 64, 75, 100, 107, 124, 161, 190, 206, 263, 285, 311, 312, 316, 319, 346
new creation, 82, 84, 144, 147, 286, 318
new heart/new spirit, 78, 80, 81, 90, 102, 112, 146, 161, 162, 177, 263, 324
new perspective on Paul, 4, 5, 7, 20, 110, 165, 216, 223, 224, 243, 244, 346

obedience
consequence of the new covenant, 81, 90, 103, 107, 111, 114, 126, 147, 148, 170, 227, 228, 232, 238, 241, 242, 259, 261, 262, 333, 335, 337
of fidelity, 21, 111, 333
Israel's, 46, 77, 78, 89, 144, 227, 228, 232, 255, 346
of Messiah, 111, 246–47, 251, 254, 259, 261, 329. See also fidelity/faith (πίστις): of Messiah
of the nations, 21, 126, 251, 259, 311, 329, 333
salvation contingent on, 3, 14, 154, 166, 170, 172, 233, 236, 243, 259, 298, 321, 333, 341, 346
old perspective. See Lutheran reading of Paul
olive tree, 289–301, 313, 315

Passover, 57, 164
Paul within Judaism, 7, 8
Paul, the apostle
an apocalyptic, restorationist Jew, 18, 19, 20, 29, 70, 98, 101–6, 107, 174, 184, 208, 313, 333, 342, 344

as apostle of gentiles, 1, 22, 24, 26, 29, 74, 275, 323
Benjaminite, 70–71, 271
covenantal theology of, 72–75, See new covenant:central to Pauline theology
preaching to Jews, 23–24, 25, 131, 132, 136, 143, 152, 306
Peter, 24, 25, 71, 149, 186, 234, 249, 276
Pharisees, 18, 106, 230
Plato, 97, 139, 170, 195, 259
plight, 104, 105
of humanity, 104, 146
of Israel, 52–58, 77, 89, 143, 145, 256, 277, 279, 343
pneuma. See spirit
proselyte/proselytism, 10, 17, 23, 24, 34, 51, 116, 132, 136, 143, 151, 152, 186, 208, 267, 297, 298
puma, divine. See pneuma
purity/purification, 57, 59, 83, 86, 133, 289

radical new perspective on Paul. See Paul within Judaism
religion, 2, 4, 15, 16, 34, 103, 151, 153, 155, 343, 346
remnant, 45, 61, 64, 103, 206, 216, 229, 271, 272, 274, 275, 281, 283, 284, 292, 298, 299–301, 314, 337
repentance, 121, 140, 168, 196, 197, 211, 227, 228, 300
divinely initiated, 140, 227, 228, 232, 233, 235, 236–43, 278, 280, 320
insufficient after broken covenant, 57, 132, 168, 221, 224
restoration contingent on, 57, 227–34, 236, 237
restoration eschatology, 19, 47, 53, 58–67, 71, 72, 76, 80, 82, 84, 85–91, 100, 101–6, 110, 112, 114, 128, 131–32, 139, 143, 144, 145–46, 147, 150, 174, 179–81, 184, 185, 214, 230, 234, 254, 255, 256, 268, 279, 284, 333, 342, 343, 344, 346
restoration of Israel, 20, 54, 56, 59, 61, 63, 65, 106, 182, 206, 234, 269, 311, 331, 334, 342, 345
divinely initiated. See repentance:divinely initiated
for the sake of YHWH's name, 160, 161, 162, 190, 198, 328
involves all twelve tribes, 20, 59, 60, 67, 186, 232, 312

resurrection, 100, 275, 285, 286, 312, 318, 319, 324, 325, 335
  Israel's restoration as, 100, 109, 275, 283, 285, 286, 312, 318, 319, 324, 325, 330, 335
  of Jesus, 72, 107, 242, 248, 250, 268, 329, 347
  as proof Jesus is Messiah, 243, 246, 251, 252, 254, 266, 329
return from exile
  from Babylon, 50, 51, 313
  as resurrection. See resurrection:Israel's restoration as
righteousness. See justness (δικαιοσύνη)
Romans, audience of, 20–28

Sabbath, 10, 37, 58, 229, 235
sacrilege, 154–62
Sadducees, 18, 105
salvation, 218, 220, 223, 224, 227, 265, 266, 277, 281, 282, 298, 303, 321, 335
  contingent on obedience. See obedience: salvation contingent on
  of gentiles, 275, 277, 315, 333
  interdependence of Israel and gentiles, 187, 189, 201–9, 219–20, 224, 275, 276, 277, 279, 282, 285, 302, 303, 307, 313, 314, 315–22, 325, 334
  of Israel, 186, 188, 189, 191, 221, 269, 299, 301–22, 346
  not by faith alone, 178, 180, 233, 298
Samaritans, 26, 48, 49, 50, 62, 64, 68, 255, 280, 283, 287, 323, 346
  intermarriage with non-Israelites, 48, 51, 287
  Israelite status, 41–43, 48, 50, 51, 62, 280, 346
  Jewish polemic against, 43, 48, 50, 51, 287
  not Jews, 42, 48, 50, 280, 287, 323
sanctification, 31, 32, 82, 288, 289, 290, 294, 296, 297
sanctity, 4, 31, 32, 82, 157, 161, 229, 231, 232, 247, 252, 288, 289, 293, 295, 337, 342
sectarianism, 19, 61, 90, 154, 230, 255, 266, 268, 336, 337, 344
seed, 88, 96, 107, 189, 190, 207, 208, 216, 229, 244, 255, 257, 271, 274, 287, 296, 311, 325, 331, 334, 340
  of David, 245
  of Ephraim, 307–22

sin. See transgression (παράβασις)
  forgiveness of, 76, 136, 178, 250, 335
  freedom from, 89, 179, 180, 181, 227, 236, 243, 262, 265. See also justification:as ethical transformation
  Israel under. See Israel:under covenantal curse
  of Adam, 120, 329
  of gentiles, 8, 24, 117, 120, 129, 132, 139, 142, 143, 145, 190, 282, 335
  Torah given to reveal, 85–91, 145, 181, 257, 258
Song of Moses. See Moses:Song of
sons of God. See children of God
Spartans, 17
spirit, 17, 18, 32, 93, 287, 329, 339
  agent of justification, 89, 90, 92, 175, 181, 265, 332, 333, 342, 347
  contrasted with letter, 74, 78, 85, 88, 91, 92, 93, 95, 96, 163, 165, 225
  included in new covenant, 74, 78–85, 89, 91, 92, 102, 168, 170, 173, 174, 254, 266. See also new heart/new spirit
  promised to Israel, 110, 149, 150, 171, 173, 187, 208, 264, 282, 287, 324, 336
  received by gentiles, 84, 85, 90, 110, 149, 150, 171, 187, 208, 281, 282, 324, 333
  source of resurrection/life. See life: granted by spirit
supersessionism, 298, 336, 337, 344
synagogues, 62, 113, 276, 306, 310
  Paul preaching in, 25, 306

Targumim, 240
temple, 9, 48, 53, 55, 56, 57, 58, 59, 101, 124, 131, 155, 157, 159, 160, 195, 218, 229, 231, 255, 262, 268
  Second Temple as inadequate, 46, 55, 56, 57, 58, 131, 255
ten tribes. See Israel:northern tribes/ kingdom of
Torah, 33
  curse of, 47, 59, 61, 77, 79, 97–101, 121, 132, 143, 170, 246, 252, 256, 260, 261, 267, 284, 318, 343, 347. See also death:as curse of Torah
  end (τέλος) of Torah, 8, 103, 171, 214, 218, 222, 223, 245–47, 252, 261, 264–65, 336

fulfillment of, 18, 23, 89, 101, 103, 112, 125, 143, 146, 148, 149, 163, 164, 168, 171, 172, 173, 177, 178, 180, 181, 231, 244, 247, 252, 254, 262, 264, 269, 283, 297, 331, 332, 333, 335
given because of sin, 90, 96, 257, 340
heavenly/spiritual, 89, 95–97, 225, 340
just requirements of. *See* just requirement (δικαίωμα)
letter/written Torah, 11, 74, 78, 85, 86, 88–97, 103, 163, 164, 165, 177, 225, 257, 265, 332, 340
Paul's affirmation of, 88, 89, 254, 257, 260, 261
witness for YHWH against Israel, 85–91, 128, 134, 274
witness of the messiah, 242, 251, 261, 335
written on the heart, 80, 96, 97, 126, 146, 147, 149, 162, 170, 172, 177, 256, 266, 311, 319, 332
transgression (παράβασις), 87, 117, 120, 125, 126, 143, 164, 167, 168, 196, 227, 257, 275, 292, 318, 320

of Adam, 87, 117, 119, 120, 123, 125, 168, 275, 329
as distinct from general sin, 117, 120, 125, 126, 143, 168, 169, 275
truth, absolute. *See* life:meaning of

uncircumcision. *See* foreskin

Wisdom of Solomon, 114
works
  judgment based on. *See* judgment:based on works
  of Torah, 8, 85, 87, 90, 112, 113, 174, 176, 177, 252, 255, 256, 257, 258, 264
works-righteousness, 2, 3, 149, 216, 223, 224. *See also* legalism

Yaḥad, 17, 19, 49, 79, 81, 87, 230–33, 236, 255, 266, 299, 336
Yoḥanan, Rabbi, 60, 208, 237

Zion, 207, 212, 216, 217, 268, 269, 303, 305, 306, 319, 320

Printed by Integrated Books International,
United States of America